D0578675

ENCYCLOPEDIA
OF THE
AMERICAN WEST

PRODUCED BY THE PHILIP LIEF GROUP, INC.

Senior Writer and General Editor:	Robert M. Utley
Writers:	Dale L. Walker, Jace Weaver, George R. Robinson, Shelley Rossell, Arnie Bernstein
Project Editors:	Claudia HCQ Sorsby, Jeannine Ciliotta
Editors:	Stephen Francoeur, Sona Vogel, Barbara Sullivan
Assistant Editors:	Naomi Starr, Jennifer Hirshlag
Copy Editors:	Joyce Nolan, Jack Roberts, Trumbull Rogers, Bruce Stevenson, Beth Wilson
Editorial Assistant:	Linda Barth
Additional Research:	Darren J. Talham
Production Manager:	Nina Neimark
Production Editor:	Kelli Daley
Designer:	Bernard Schleifer
Cartographer:	Arlene Goldberg
Composition:	NK Graphics

ENCYCLOPEDIA
OF THE
AMERICAN WEST

Robert M. Utley,
General Editor

WINGS BOOKS
New York

This 1997 edition is published by Wings Books, a division of Random House Value Publishing, Inc.,
201 East 50th Street, New York, New York 10022, by arrangement with
The Philip Lief Group, Inc.
130 Wall Street
Princeton, NJ 08540

Wings Books and colophon are trademarks of Random House Value Publishing, Inc.

Random House
New York • Toronto • London • Sydney • Auckland
http://www.randomhouse.com

Printed and bound in the United States of America

Library of Congress Cataloging-in-Publication Data
Encyclopedia of the American West / Robert M. Utley, general editor.
p.   cm.
Includes bibliographical references (p. 491)
ISBN 0-517-14988-5 (HC)
1. West (U.S.)—History—Encyclopedias.   2. West (U.S.)—
Biography—Encyclopedias.   I. Utley, Robert Marshall, 1929–
F591.E485   1996b
978'.003—dc20   96-14687
CIP

8   7   6   5   4   3   2   1

Contents

Introduction

For many, the American West conjures up images of a wild, almost mythic place and time. During the nineteenth century, story after story was played out in the vast spaces of North America, from the Mississippi River to the Pacific Ocean. Many groups of Native Americans, each with its own rich cultural heritage (from the Acomas to the Zunis), encountered waves of settlers and immigrants coming to the the new land, bringing ideas and traditions of their own. It was a difficult, challenging time, in which Native Americans, explorers, settlers of all colors and creeds, miners, trappers, outlaws, and many others took part.

The *Encyclopedia of the American West* takes a new look at this fascinating era. Designed in straightforward, A-Z format, this one-volume reference will provide readers with a striking portrait of the varied and diverse groups of people who made up the West. Entries on Native American tribes, such as the Sioux and the Apaches, provide insight into their history and traditions, and record their perspective on the white settlers. Individuals, such as Sequoyah, the Cherokee chief who was the first to create a written language for his people, and the legendary chief Sitting Bull are featured. Other entries describe the immigrants from Europe and Asia—who brought so many of their traditions to the New World—as well as the dangers and rewards they encountered. Unique to this volume is a special emphasis on the contributions of particular religious and ethnic groups in the history of the west: from Mormons, Jews, Jesuits, Franciscans, and Quakers, to Italians, Swedes, Spaniards, Irish, and many others.

Visitors and settlers in the West were repeatedly stunned by the grandeur of the land: flat, endless prairie lands, rich and fertile; barren, blistering deserts; towering mesas and plateaus of unimaginable color; deep canyons cut by cool, fast-flowing water; forests of trees godlike in size; massive walls of snow-capped mountains with hidden veins of silver and gold; and rivers teaming with trout and salmon. The history of the west is inextricably tied to its geography, as successive waves of settlers, miners, trappers, and entrepreneurs tried to exploit the seemingly inexhaustible resources of the land.

The successes and failures of these men and women, from the lone prospector to the railroad magnate, are described fully in the *Encyclopedia of the American West*. To paint a rich and detailed portrait of the land, entries are provided on mountain ranges, rivers, national parks, and each western state.

The conflicts that wracked the west, that brought violence into the everyday lives of those caught in the crossfire, are also here rendered. Gangs, such as the Wild Bunch and the Daltons, brought reckless gun battles into the lives of common folk in small towns. The bloody clash between the Union and the Confederacy during the Civil War found its way out west, too. The unimaginable suffering of Native Americans as they were pushed from their lands onto reservations is here, too, captured in all its tragedy.

With this compelling and evocative encyclopedia, readers, regardless of whether they live in the West or not, can see the countless stories of the frontier brought to life and hear clearly, even now, the echoes from those bygone events in their lives today. To this day, Americans continue to struggle with the legacies of the settlement of the West.

For example, the search for water and the battles over its uses in the West still resonate in today's struggles over water rights (such as the fight between farmers in the San Joaquin Valley in California and the residents of Los Angeles, or the fights repeated in every state out west between electric companies wanting to build dams and environmentalists who want to see rivers run free and wildlife preserved). Large mining companies still compete with small-time prospectors. Even the re-introduction of the wolf to Yellowstone National Park in Wyoming has stirred up ancient fears from pioneer days about the threat that such animals present to livestock and humans.

Although it has been over a century since historian Frederick Jackson Turner claimed that America's frontier was closed, the memories and the legacies of the era of Western expansion live on. This book records, and sometimes celebrates, that ever-present past.

ENCYCLOPEDIA
OF THE
AMERICAN WEST

A

Abilene, Kansas

Abilene was the first of the great cattle towns that sprang up after the Civil War as a transit point for shipping Texas cattle eastward. Until 1867 the village contained only a few log houses. But with the Kansas Pacific Railroad crossing at nearby Mud Creek and the Chisholm Trail connecting Abilene to Texas, the town was ripe for the cattle trade, and Kansas legislators realized its economic benefit. Because the hardy Texas longhorns carried a tick that caused the fatal Texas fever in other livestock, the state's legislators drew a quarantine line, allowing the cattle only on the western half of Kansas. Unfortunately, Abilene lay east of the line but Joseph Conroy, a wealthy livestock dealer who had purchased property around Abilene, fought and won approval to establish Abilene as a cattle shipping point. Over the next five years, nearly 3 million head of cattle were driven up the Chisholm Trail to Abilene, where they were fattened up and shipped east. The accompanying influx of cowboys and other transients brought quick wealth and wilder times, and saloons and brothels soon dotted the town. The famous James Butler "Wild Bill" Hickok worked as a law enforcement officer in Abilene. Later he was gunned down in Deadwood in Dakota Territory. But Abilene citizens and real estate dealers, who were tired of the corruption, joined the enraged farmers, who had lost acres of crops to the free-ranging cattle, to rally against the Abilene cattle market. These political battles caused the town to become more dependent on agriculture, and Texas ranchers began to look to Ellsworth, Kansas, as a place to conduct their profitable business.

Ácoma Indians

The Ácomas, a tribe of Pueblos of the Keresan-language family, reside on and around Ácoma Mesa, a 357-foot-high plateau about 60 miles west of Albuquerque, New Mexico.

Though the Ácomas' reservation encompasses the towns of Acomita and McCartys, where most of the people live year-round, its emotional heart is the "Sky City" of Ácoma (sometimes called Old Ácoma), a traditional-style pueblo thought by many to be the oldest continuously inhabited site in the United States. Although the Keresan-speaking Pueblos entered the region later than some of their relatives, the Ácomas are one of the few Pueblo tribes who were not forced to relocate as a result of interaction with the Spaniards.

The first European contact with Ácomas was recorded by Fray Marcos de Niza in 1539. They were also visited briefly by Francísco de Coronado's expedition in 1540. It was, however, the arrival of Juan de Oñate in the area in 1598 that had the most lasting impact on the Ácomas and other Pueblos. At the time of these early encounters, the Ácomas, believed to number 5,000 to 10,000, ranged over approximately 5 million acres of territory.

Oñate came with 129 colonists who ultimately

LIBRARY OF CONGRESS

Ácoma pueblo, in western New Mexico, dates from approximately 1000 C.E.

settled in Santa Fe. He sought to turn the Pueblos into a subject people, forcibly converting them to Catholicism and using them as involuntary labor. The Ácomas also were taught to grow peaches, peppers, and wheat, and to raise sheep. The last of these skills became an important component of the Acoma economy into the twentieth century.

Along with other Pueblos, Ácomas took part in the Pueblo revolt of 1680, which drove the Spaniards from the region. Enchanted Mesa, an important site for the Ácomas, was fortified in 1694 by the Keresan-speaking Pueblos, who experienced hostility from other Pueblos following the return of the Spaniards because of their supposed allegiance to the foreigners.

Throughout the nineteenth century, the Ácomas raised sheep. This practice, however, gradually gave way around the turn of the century to cattle ranching. Since the 1890s, the tribe has been unrelenting in its efforts to recover the lands that were taken from them. By 1900, their population had dwindled to an estimated 500; it since has recovered to around 4,000.

Adams-Onís Treaty

1819

This far-reaching treaty, negotiated by Secretary of State John Quincy Adams and Luis de Onís, Spanish minister in Washington, resulted in Spain's ceding the Floridas to the United States and in the establishment of the western boundary of the Louisiana Purchase.

Spain relinquished the Floridas (both the eastern and the western portions) because, with its colonial empire collapsing, it could neither promise to settlers protection from the Indians in the territory—a crisis solved temporarily by Andrew Jackson's Indian campaign in Florida in 1814—nor prevent the escape into Florida of American slaves. Moreover, as Adams pointed out, West Florida, on the Gulf of Mexico, was properly U.S. territory under the provisions of the Louisiana Purchase.

In exchange for the Floridas, and for all Spanish rights in the Oregon Territory, the United States agreed to nullify all damage claims by Americans against Spain and to assume payment of those claims up to the amount of $5 million.

Among the future ramifications of the Adams-Onís Treaty, none was to be more significant than the Texas question. Although Adams sought to include Texas among territories ceded to the United States in marking the southwestern boundary, he failed to win the support of the Monroe administration for this plan. The boundary was therefore established at the Sabine River, setting the stage for American-Mexican confrontations, revolution, and

SMITHSONIAN INSTITUTION

This isolated mesa top location helped to protect the Ácomas from their enemies.

ultimate Texan independence in the coming three decades.

Adobe

Adobe is a Spanish word (from the Arabic *at-tub*, the brick) meaning sun-dried bricks composed of a mix of clay and straw, the buildings made from those bricks, and the clay soil used in the making of these bricks. Moist adobe clay is very plastic and can easily be molded into almost any shape. Once it has dried, however, it is virtually indestructible. Indians recognized this characteristic at a very early date and used the muddy soil to make bowls, mugs, pitchers, and other vessels. They also used it in the construction of compact, multi-story, apartment-like dwellings. The glint of the sun reflecting from those buildings later fueled the Spanish conquistadores' gold-hungry dreams of the Seven Cities of Cíbola.

LIBRARY OF CONGRESS

Pueblo in New Mexico built of adobe bricks.

Use of adobe came to the Southwest from Mexico when the Pueblo people brought Mesoamerican culture with them. Later, the Spanish used the material to construct their own dwellings. Because adobe buildings are cheap, easy to build, and very energy efficient, from early days they were found as far north as Wyoming and Montana.

Because it was inexpensive, "adobe" was once synonymous with "inferior." For example, Mexican currency was once termed "dobe dollars." Today, however, it is identified with the Santa Fe style, and adobe houses can be found throughout the United States.

African-Americans in the West

The experience of black Americans in the West provides one of many examples of the complex dialectic of race in this nation's history. African-American history in the West is as fraught with contradiction and irony as any element in the story of the American West, an uneasy blend of triumph and tragedy side by side.

There were blacks in the West as early as there were whites. Black Estevan, one of the survivors of the ill-fated Cabeza de Vaca expedition, earned a reputation as a linguist and medicine man among the southwestern tribes during the early sixteenth cen-

LIBRARY OF CONGRESS

An African-American cowboy, one of the many ethnically diverse men who went to work on the cattle ranches of the West.

tury. The Coronado expedition included several black priests.

The tradition that these inclusions (perhaps unwittingly) established was continued in the eighteenth century and later. A list of the fur traders and trappers of the period features African-Americans in virtually every role. Jean Baptiste Point-du-Sable established a trading post at what is now Chicago. Jim Beckwourth was one of the most famous mountain men. The Lewis and Clark expedition included York, Clark's "manservant," who distinguished himself by his athletic feats, courage, and hunting ability. Jacob Dodson, a free black who was an integral part of John C. Frémont's second and third expeditions, became an experienced Indian fighter. Two of the Astorians, the trappers John Jacob Astor sent to Oregon to establish his foothold there, were black.

However, as it did every other aspect of African-American life, slavery affected all of the relationships between blacks and others on the frontier. Every frontier was a military one while the relations between settlers and Native Americans remained primarily hostile, and it was with great reluctance that white settlers allowed slaves to participate in

NATIONAL ARCHIVES

African-American soldiers of Company B, 25th U.S. Infantry, outside their barracks at Fort Randall, Dakota Territory.

the defense of settlements—who would knowingly give a slave weapons?

In one case, in South Carolina during the Creek War of 1715, slaves were enlisted in the state militia. That was rare, and as their numbers grew, blacks were not allowed to repeat that experience. More typically, Spanish authorities in the Carolinas actively encouraged slaves to run away from their masters, and some tribes—notably the Creeks—gave shelter to runaways. In later years, these runaways acted as agents for Spain and France among the Creeks. Runaway slaves and freedmen often fought alongside both the Spanish and the Seminoles in Florida. Black Seminoles, the sons and daughters of runaway slaves, were at the heart of the 1835 Seminole War, which was as much a fight for black liberation as for Indian freedom.

Free blacks on the frontier during the same period may have enjoyed less discrimination than they would after emancipation. Communities were less settled, many formerly French-controlled regions still offered a fair degree of racial tolerance, and the freedmen were an integral part of the defense of the community. The black mountain men and fur traders were experienced fighters who knew the conditions of the regions they frequented and often functioned as interpreters or guides.

In other areas, a free African-American might be the only skilled craftsman. In one Virginia community, near Staunton, the blacksmith and the farrier were both freedmen. Other freedmen of the antebellum period chose to follow the westward expansion; Texas under the Mexican Republic was particularly attractive because of its comparative racial tolerance.

The California gold rush affected African-Americans as much as it did everyone else who heard of the discovery at Sutter's Mill. Until that time, California's black population had been a small one, composed mainly of deserting sailors. This latter group swelled the ranks of the Forty-niners; both blacks and whites jumped ship at the chance of striking it rich. In addition, many southern prospectors brought their slaves with them, and many freedmen and runaways sought work as miners or in the businesses that sprang up around the goldfields. By the 1850 census, there were nearly 1,000 blacks in California, concentrated primarily in Sacramento and San Francisco. (In Colorado blacks were barred from filing mining claims, which forced runaway slave Barney Ford to find a

A racially mixed group of cowboys.

different line of work in Denver during the 1860s; he ended up as a successful restaurateur and hotel owner.)

California was a free state. Nevertheless, black Californians were denied the right to vote and to an education, and were consistently discriminated against in the court system, where they were prohibited from testifying against whites. The response to these injustices, the California Colored Convention, may rightly be called one of the first black civil rights organizations in the West, if not the entire United States. The group collected thousands of signatures on petitions opposing the discriminatory court system, but the Democratic state legislature chose to ignore them.

It is one of the nastier ironies of American history that Oklahoma had a sizable black population before it had a white one, because each of the Five Civilized Tribes, who had been forcibly removed from slaveholding states in the 1830s and packed off to Oklahoma, included slave owners. These Native Americans were split by the coming of the Civil War, with the Chickasaws, Choctaws, and some of the Seminoles siding with the Confederacy and some of the Cherokees and Creeks with the Union. Nevertheless, the Confederacy negotiated treaties with all five. Needless to say, the black members of the tribes were unanimous in their support of the Union. However, military action in the territories resulted in suffering for all.

Black troops fought in the Civil War, particularly in the western theater. Black and Indian regiments fought in Kansas and in the Indian Territory in campaigns marked by a high level of brutality; Confed-

erate guerrillas disdained to take black prisoners. From these units came the men who would become the legends of the black West: seasoned Indian fighters like Charley Tyler and Britton Johnson, and the black units of the regular army, the Buffalo Soldiers.

Many frontier army posts were garrisoned almost entirely with black troops (under white officers). They fought against hostile Native Americans and Mexican border raiders alike. The campaigns against the Apache chiefs Victorio and Nana were conducted primarily by black troops. In the 20 years of the fiercest Indian wars (1870–1890), 14 African-Americans won the Congressional Medal of Honor.

At the same time, black cowboys were becoming a common sight along the cattle trails. Ranch cooks frequently were African-Americans, and many blacks were skilled horse breakers as well; black rodeo and Wild West Show stars like Bill Pickett were numerous. Black lawmen could be found, too; one of "Hanging Judge" Isaac Parker's most effective deputies was Bass Reeves, who served as a federal marshal for 35 years.

As the Homestead Act attracted would-be farmers to the West, many former slaves swelled their numbers. Perhaps the most famous of these were the exodusters, who migrated to Kansas in the late 1870s; others pushed on to Oklahoma and Colorado.

Within the still independent Indian nations, in Oklahoma and the Indian Territory, blacks probably enjoyed greater social, economic, and political equality than elsewhere in the United States, perhaps in some part because of their hostility to the encroaching whites. When political struggles broke out between full-blood and mixed-blood Native

Americans, the blacks tended to side with the full-bloods. Not surprisingly, when Oklahoma was admitted to the Union in 1907, racial discrimination against both blacks and Indians became the law and practice once more. In fact, one of the last outbursts of Native American armed resistance to white oppression, the Crazy Snake rebellion in March 1909—an attempt to regain Indian independence in the state—drew most of its support from black Creeks and Seminoles.

Although Jim Crow laws, with their enforced segregation, were for the most part a southern phenomenon, de facto segregation existed throughout the West in the post-Reconstruction era. The National Association for the Advancement of Colored People (NAACP) found the West a fertile region for organizing; it had six chapters in the region by 1914, after only five years of existence. One of the organization's first legal victories occurred in Oklahoma, when the U.S. Supreme Court ruled in 1915 that the state's "grandfather clause" was racially discriminatory and therefore unconstitutional.

Alamo, Battle of the

1836

In 1803, the Louisiana Purchase placed the southwestern border of the United States contiguous to that of Spanish-ruled Texas. After Mexico had gained independence from Spain in 1821, its government encouraged the emigration to Texas of U.S. citizens willing to renounce their citizenship. By 1836, some 30,000 Americans had settled in what was then the northern Mexican state of Coahuila y Texas.

In 1834, General Antonio López de Santa Anna took control of the Mexican government, abolished the 1824 constitution, and declared martial law. In January 1836 he gathered an army at Saltillo, 200 miles south of the Rio Grande, and marched north to extinguish the growing rebellion among the Texans.

At this time, just a month before the Texas declaration of independence from Mexico, the Alamo mission in San Antonio had been converted into a fortress. It was built in the form of a large rectangle with a smaller one attached to the eastern side. The

church and a powder magazine occupied the southeastern corner of the three-acre bastion, the whole of which was protected by earthen walls that averaged 12 feet high. Wooden parapets to support gun batteries had been constructed, and irrigation ditches around the outside perimeter of the improvised fortress added to the difficulty of access. Adobe and wood barracks for officers and men were located around three walls of the large rectangle, and a makeshift hospital, a cattle pen, and a horse corral along the walls of the smaller one, adjacent to the church.

The Alamo had been founded in 1718 as the Misión de San Antonio de Valero (named for the Marquis of Valero, Spanish viceroy in Mexico). The original mission of adobe huts and church had been moved several times to various sites along the San Antonio River. Its chief function was to convert the Xarames, Pampoa, Payaya, and Sana tribes of the area. The mission received its popular name about 1801 when Spanish troops from the pueblo of San José y Santiago del Alamo del Parras were stationed there (alamo is Spanish for a type of tree).

There is some evidence that if Sam Houston, commander in chief of the Texas Army, had had his way, the Alamo would never have been defended. Adamantly opposed to fighting behind fortifications, he sought a battle in the open, on familiar terrain, where cavalry and mobile infantry could extend the Mexican lines and distance them from their supplies. Houston may have ordered the removal of the Alamo's guns (one 18-pounder and perhaps 20 smaller, twelve-, eight-, six-, and four-pound cannon), the destruction of the Alamo walls, and evacuation of the site.

Houston is believed to have sent these orders with his old friend Colonel James Bowie, a 40-year-old, Kentucky-born rowdy who had married into a prominent San Antonio family. Bowie was ill—perhaps with tuberculosis—and if he had such orders, seems not to have taken them seriously. At the Alamo, where he found the garrison eager to fight, he assisted in shoring up the gun emplacements and injured himself while helping hoist a cannon onto the ramparts. He was ill and in bed during the siege, so command of the garrison fell to William Barret Travis, aged 27, a South Carolina–born lawyer by training and a soldier by choice.

On February 16, when Santa Anna, with about 2,000 men, 21 cannon, 1,800 pack mules, and some 250 wagons and carts of ammunition and supplies, crossed the Rio Grande, Travis's Alamo command consisted of about 150 men. Included in the number were a dozen Tennessee Mounted Volunteers led by the legendary marksman, backwoods orator, and three-time congressman, David Crockett. Travis had 17 serviceable medium-to-small cannon plus the 18-pounder located on the southwest corner of the fort. Ammunition included standard balls and backup loads of loose horseshoe scrap, nails, and stones. The artillery was commanded by a Tennessee blacksmith, Captain Almeron Dickinson.

Santa Anna, with two brigades of infantry and one of cavalry, plus artillery units and *zapadores* (sappers)—a force numbering perhaps 4,000 (estimates vary)—began the siege of the Alamo on February 24, hammering the walls with the light field artillery and heavy siege guns he had brought from Saltillo.

Hoping for reinforcements, Travis sent a courier to Colonel James Fannin in Goliad, about 90 miles away. Fannin set out on February 26 with over 300 men, but his supply train broke down, and various other mishaps caused him to abandon the march and return to Goliad. Travis's only reinforcements came on March 1, when 32 volunteers from Gonzales arrived, raising the Alamo force to about 183 fighting men.

On the second day of the siege, Travis sent through the Mexican lines his famous "To the People of Texas and all Americans in the world" message, an appeal that, although issued too late to assist him, would soon be heard around the world. It contained the news that the Alamo was besieged by Santa Anna's forces and ended with the pronouncement "I shall never surrender or retreat . . . I call on you, in the name of liberty, of patriotism, and of everything dear to American character, to come to our aid with all dispatch." The last three words—*"Victory or Death!"*—were underlined three times.

On March 5, the tenth day, Travis told his defenders there would be no relief or reinforcements and that the options were to surrender, to try to escape through the Mexican lines, or to stand and fight. Crockett said he didn't like being "hemmed up" and preferred to "march out and die in the open air." Only one man elected to escape, however; he made his way over the wall to safety that night.

At 5 o'clock on the morning of March 6, 1836, Santa Anna began his assault, sending four columns of some 500 men each against the four walls of the Alamo. The trail-toughened Mexican infantry moved forward with scaling ladders, axes, pikes, picks, and muskets with bayonets. Behind them, bugles blared a degüello—a dirge signifying death to all the enemy—and as they closed on the Alamo walls, they shouted, *"Viva Santa Anna!"*

The battle quickly became a melee. On the north wall, Travis, sword in hand, shouted encouragement to his cannoneers; Crockett and his Tennesseans on the south wall fought off the attackers on their scaling ladders in desperate hand-to-hand clubbing, hacking, and bayoneting; the Mexican columns on the east and west veered off and joined a battering ram force on the north side. The dense clot of men at the foot of that wall came under withering fire from above. There were two great assaults, a momentary lull, then the furious fighting resumed as Santa Anna ordered up his reserves and struck the north wall again. There Travis, firing his shotgun into the massed infantry below, was struck in the head by a musket ball and tumbled, dead, down the cannon ramp. Meantime, on the south wall a six-pound cannon in a lunette that jutted out from the wall, and the great 18-pounder on the southwest corner, did great damage to the attackers.

But the end was near: on the northeastern wall, a Mexican officer and his men made their way through a breach and into the Alamo's plaza. On the west side, the thinning ranks of defenders could not prevent the enemy from spilling over the parapets. Santa Anna's force poured in unchecked, and the

DENVER PUBLIC LIBRARY

An 1879 drawing showing President-General Antonio Lopez de Santa Anna and his troops storming the Alamo.

fighting became a savage hand-to-hand, backs-to-the-wall combat. Near the front of the church and hospital, Crockett and his Tennesseans were caught in the open and all killed; on the roof of the church, James Butler Bonham, a boyhood friend of Travis's, and some artillerymen tried to fire their cannon on the plaza below and inflicted some severe if momentary damage before being picked off by Mexican musket fire.

Santa Anna's troops, following the order that there would be no quarter and no prisoners, entered each room of the hospital and barracks, killing all inside. Forty defenders were killed in the hospital. From his cot in a barracks room on the south wall, Bowie is said to have used the two pistols given him by Crockett, then rose to defend himself with his famous knife before being bayoneted to death. One of his sisters-in-law, who was present, later said the Mexican soldiers "tossed his body on their bayonets until their uniforms were dyed with his blood." In the powder magazine on the north side of the church, the Irish-born ordnance chief, Robert Evans, tried to light a trail of gunpowder to blow up the magazine and the church. He was killed before he could do so.

The Alamo fell at 6:30 A.M.; the battle had lasted 90 minutes.

Five defenders survived long enough to be brought before Santa Anna. He was furious at seeing them and ordered them shot. Now all the defenders were dead.

Ten Mexican women (among them two of Bowie's sisters-in-law, who had witnessed his death) and children survived. The others inside who lived to tell the story were Susanna Dickinson, wife of the artillery commander; her 15-month-old daughter, Angelina; and Travis's slave, a man known only as Joe.

The bodies of the defenders were placed between layers of wood and set afire; trenches were dug for the Mexican dead. Santa Anna's casualties are believed to have been at least 600, and of that number at least 200 were dead.

The Alamo victory proved costly for Santa Anna. "Remember the Alamo!" became the rallying cry as the Mexicans were driven from Texas the following April 21 when, at San Jacinto, Sam Houston and 800 men met and defeated Santa Anna's 3,000-man army, capturing the general and forcing him to sign a peace treaty that recognized Texas's independence.

The only U.S. flag to survive the Alamo, from a Louisiana company.

Alaska

Following its disastrous defeat in the Crimean War (1854–1856), Russia, desperate to pay off its war debts, authorized its minister in Washington, Edouard de Stoeckl, to sound out U.S. interest in purchasing Russian America—Alaska. (England, which had defeated Russia in the Crimean War and which Russia feared might seize Alaska, was not interested in acquiring that vast terra incognita.)

Stoeckl's initial talks in Washington were interrupted by the Civil War, but in 1867 he was instructed to renew efforts to sell the territory to the Americans. The discussions began in March 1867 between Stoeckl and Secretary of State William H. Seward, one of the nation's greatest expansionists. Seward was anxious to get the Russian territory and, without authorization, offered Stoeckl $5.5 million. When Stoeckl contacted St. Petersburg, saying he would ask for a higher price, Seward, with the president's support, presented the issue at a cabinet meeting, requesting authorization to spend up to $7 million to purchase the territory. On March 23, Seward met with Stoeckl again, and the main points of the sale were agreed upon: the United States would pay $7.2 million for Russian America. After a tough congressional battle, the purchase was ratified and the American flag was raised on October 18, 1867, over Sitka, capital of Russian America for 68 years.

Seward, in later years, considered the acquisition of Alaska as his greatest accomplishment. He estimated it would take a generation before the American people would understand its importance.

Actually, it would take 30 years before the American people, or their representatives in Washington, would pay much attention to the vast possession to the north (which was called in newspaper editorials and among his colleagues in Washington "Seward's Folly" and "Seward's Icebox").

The United States had purchased 586,400 square miles of new territory, a piece of land twice the size of Texas (indeed, one-fifth the size of the entire United States) bounded by the Arctic and Pacific oceans, the Canadian Yukon to the east and Russian Siberia, 55 miles across the Bering Strait, to the West. The new acquisition, it was soon learned, contained over 15,000 square miles of waterways, the highest mountain in North America (subsequently named Mount McKinley), and seemingly boundless resources of minerals, furs, fish, and timber.

At the time it was acquired, Alaska had about 30,000 indigenous Indians and fewer than 1,000 other inhabitants, mostly Russian and American trappers concentrated around Sitka, the town on Baranov Island (founded in 1799) that remained the capital of the territory until 1900. Some attention was paid to Alaska in 1880 when gold was discovered in the Alaskan Panhandle by Joseph Juneau. Other gold strikes in the region—in the Yukon Territory in 1896 and at the sites of Nome (1898) and Fairbanks (1902)—brought attention to the territory by the end of the century.

In 1884 the territory became a civil district with a governor, and the former goldrush town of Juneau became the capital in 1900. It was not until 1906 that Alaska sent a territorial delegate to Congress. Alaska became the forty-ninth state in 1959.

Residents of Deering, Alaska, congregate around the local shops in 1903.

The lavishly decorated house of a Chilkat chief in Alaska.

Aleuts

There has been considerable confusion concerning the origin and identity of the Aleuts. The origin of the word is unknown but probably derives from their word *aliat,* meaning "island." Logically, the Unangan-speaking inhabitants of the Aleutian archipelago call themselves Aleut, but so do their traditional enemies, the Sugpiaq of the Kodiak archipelago and Prince William Sound, as well as some Yup'ik Eskimos. Anthropologists and linguists, however, generally consider the Unangans to be Aleut.

The Aleuts lived by hunting, primarily seals but also caribou, walruses, and whales. As was true of

An Aleutian seal hunt.

the bison on the Plains, these animals provided almost everything necessary for daily life. Every part of the animal was used for food or for shelter, clothing, tools—even sleds and boats.

The Aleuts were the first in the New World to encounter Russians, beginning with Vitus Bering in 1741. They were often killed by Russian hunters, and in the eighteenth and nineteenth centuries were forced to work for the Russian-American Company. Many were deported and resettled on the Pribilof Islands, on the Kurile Islands north of Japan, in California, and at Russian outposts throughout Alaska. These factors, plus disease (including frequent outbreaks of smallpox), reduced the Aleut population of 25,000 at the time of Russian contact to around 2,000 by the time the United States acquired Alaska in 1867. The Russian Orthodox Church remains an important force in Aleut culture.

The name Alaska derives from an Aleut term meaning "Great Land," their term for the mainland.

American Fur Company

This company, which in its 56-year history became the most powerful of all North American fur enterprises, was founded in April 1808 by John Jacob Astor, a German-born entrepreneur who had come to America in 1793.

The American Fur Company, the parent enterprise under which Astor launched such subsidiaries as the Pacific Fur Company and the South West Company (covering the Great Lakes region), had by 1822 become a formidable force in the fur trade. That year Astor opened a Western Department in St. Louis for the Missouri River trade, and in 1827 he acquired the Columbia Fur Company, combining it with the AFC to form what was called the Upper Missouri Outfit. In 1828 he established a trading post, Fort Union, at the confluence of the Yellowstone and Missouri rivers.

In the 1830s, Astor, who had previously concentrated on the Upper Missouri and Pacific Northwest trade, moved into the Rocky Mountains. There his chief rival was the Rocky Mountain Fur Company, created in 1826. By 1834, Astor had absorbed the remnants of Rocky Mountain Fur, but with the trade in decline, sold his fur interests that year and retired to manage real estate and other interests in New

York City. In 1864, the American Fur Company was sold to the Northwest Fur Company.

The key to the AFC's success was Astor's enormous wealth and political influence. Despite losing Astoria, his base of operations at the mouth of the Columbia River in Oregon Territory during the War of 1812, he manipulated federal laws to abolish government-owned factories and to exclude any but U.S. citizens from engaging in fur trade management and ownership. At its peak of operation, the AFC controlled three-quarters of the American fur trade.

Anasazi Culture

Anasazi is a Navajo name given to the cliff-dwelling culture of the Southwest. The name is generally translated as "ancient people," but it may also mean "enemy ancestors."

The Anasazis flourished in the Four Corners area from about 600 until 1300. Their culture, architecture, and pottery styles strongly reflect Mesoamerican influence. They began as wandering bands of hunters but for unknown reasons developed a more sedentary lifestyle as corn farmers. At first they lived in pit houses dug out of the earth and covered with a superstructure of wood and mud; over the centuries their dwellings evolved into more traditional pueblo styles.

Anasazi culture reached its zenith beginning around 900. During this period, great cliff dwellings up to five stories tall were constructed at Chaco Canyon, Canyon de Chelly, Mesa Verde, and Tsegi Canyon, as well as elsewhere. The reasons for this shift are unknown. It has generally been assumed that the Anasazis moved into these high, inaccessible sites to seek protection from enemies. Others, however, have suggested that it may have had a religious purpose—perhaps the people sought to live closer to the sky.

Around 1200 the Anasazi began to abandon their cliff dwellings throughout Colorado, Arizona, and New Mexico. As with much about the Anasazis, the reasons for this action are mysterious. Drought, soil erosion leading to crop failure, disease, warfare, and religious decree have all been suggested. Perhaps it was some combination of many of these factors. At any rate, by 1300 the Anasazis had left the cliff dwellings completely. It also is unknown

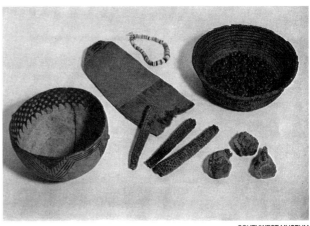

SOUTHWEST MUSEUM

Remains of the Anasazis from about 700 c.e. Shown, clockwise from left, are a pottery bowl based on a basketry design, a yucca fiber sandal, a bead bracelet, a basket of beans, and squash and corn.

whether the Navajo, who were moving into the area around this time, had anything to do with the abandonment. Shortly after the Anasazi cities were evacuated, however, they were occupied by Navajos.

For many years it was thought that the Anasazis disappeared completely. More recent evidence suggests otherwise. Archaeology reveals no great cultural shift in the area. Also, during this period surrounding towns experienced significant population increases and new villages sprang up. It now appears that following their departure from their cliff dwellings the Anasazis joined related communities. They thus became the ancestors of modern-day Pueblo Indians.

Anti-Chinese Riots in the West

During this series of violent uprisings, Chinese immigrants were attacked by workers who feared losing their jobs to the foreign-born laborers.

Chinese workers (also known as "coolies") were often hired because of their willingness to work long hours for low wages. Consequently, they became a prized source of cheap human labor for employers. Because the Chinese were of a different racial and cultural background, they were subject to many prejudices and misunderstandings on the part of whites.

Resentment grew toward the Chinese among white workers, who feared these foreigners were taking their jobs. Employers considered the Chinese "docile" and easily bossed, a situation largely due to language difficulties. The Chinese workers would not complain about poor job conditions, which enabled bosses to exploit white workers as well. During the late 1860s, anti-coolie associations were organized in California and led random attacks on Chinese workers. There were also suspicious fires at factories employing Chinese workers.

By the 1870s this violence had escalated. Although the Chinese were only 8 percent of California's population during the 1870s, they constituted about one-quarter of the work force. Bolstered by Denis Kearney's Workingmen's Party, anti-Chinese riots spread throughout the West, reaching their height in the mid-1880s.

In 1871, two Chinese groups battled in Los Angeles. This infighting led to street violence, resulting in the death of a prominent white Los Angeles resident. An angry mob stormed a building housing many Chinese and lynched eight residents. Chinese homes were looted by rioters. When the riot finally ended, 19 Chinese workers had been killed.

In September 1885, the Union Pacific Railroad decided to replace white workers in Rock Springs, Wyoming, coal mines with cheaper Chinese laborers. Anti-Chinese violence broke out. Almost 30 of the foreign-born workers were killed in the ensuing riot, and 15 were injured. Wyoming's governor called on President Grover Cleveland to send in federal troops to restore order to the area.

Other riots erupted throughout the West while laborers continued to blame the Chinese for deteriorating work environments and low pay. Vigilante mobs forced Chinese residents to leave towns in California and Washington. President Cleveland sent more troops west in 1886, this time to Seattle, Washington, where anti-Chinese riots had boiled over and some 400 Chinese residents were driven from their homes by enraged whites. Fearing for their lives, Chinese workers and their families scattered, some fleeing to the large Chinese community in San Francisco. All the racial violence eventually led to the passage of the Chinese Exclusion Act.

LIBRARY OF CONGRESS

Anti-Chinese riot.

Anza, Juan Bautista de

1735–1788

The son and grandson of soldiers serving in northern New Spain, Juan Bautista de Anza, whose father was killed by the Apaches in 1739, was born in Fronteras, Sonora, Mexico. He volunteered for military service at age 17. During the first 20 years of his military career, he established himself as an indefatigable Apache fighter in the Gila River area of modern-day Arizona, rising to captain and commander of the presidio at Tubac.

In January 1774, Anza, commanding a force of 34 men, set out to blaze a trail from Sonora to Alta California. The expedition established the presidio of San Gabriel, north of modern Los Angeles, and pushed on to Monterey, arriving there in April.

MUSEUM OF NEW MEXICO

Juan Bautista de Anza.

Upon returning to Sonora, Anza was promoted to lieutenant colonel; the viceroy in Mexico City later sent him back to California with a party of 240 colonizers and soldiers. After a six-month march, Anza and his force reached the great bay named for St. Francis of Assisi, and in March 1776, founded the presidio of San Francisco.

After a brief period as commander of the Sonoran garrison, Anza was named governor of New Mexico and arrived in Santa Fe in December 1778. His prowess as an Indian fighter was quickly tested, for the isolated provincial capital lay in the epicenter of raids by Apaches, Utes, Navajos, and Comanches. Together with his efforts to reduce the number of missions and consolidate those remaining to make them easier to defend, Anza's focus in 1779 was to strengthen Santa Fe's defenses and to campaign against the Comanches and their chief, Cuerno Verde ("Green Horn," from the single green-painted buffalo horn the Comanche leader wore as part of his headdress). In a dispatch to his superiors in Mexico City, Anza characterized Cuerno Verde as the "scourge of the kingdom." He set out in August 1779 for the Upper Rio Grande to deal with the redoubtable chief and his band.

With a force that eventually swelled to 600 men, made up of soldiers, settlers, and 160 Pueblo and Ute volunteers, Anza trailed the Comanches to a camp in a valley east of the Continental Divide in Col-

orado, near the Sierra de Almagre (later named Pike's Peak). He defeated them decisively and deployed his forces to await the return of Cuerno Verde and his band from a raid on Taos. The Taos presidio, thanks to Anza's work, had been well fortified, so its garrison successfully repelled the Comanche attack. On September 3, 1779, Anza's huge force and Cuerno Verde's 50-odd Comanches clashed in battle. Anza later described the famous chief riding forward, "his spirit proud and superior to all his followers," and said with finality: "I determined to have his life, and his pride and arrogance precipitated him to this end." The battle resulted in the death of Cuerno Verde, his son, four other chiefs, and ten other Comanches. One man in Anza's force was wounded.

By 1786, through Anza's efforts, the Spanish had established peace with the Comanches, Utes, Navajos, and Hopis. In 1788, Anza returned to Sonora, where he served briefly as commander of the presidio of Tucson. He died on December 19, 1788, and was buried at Arizpe, in the church of Nuestra Señora de la Asunción.

Apache Indians

The Apaches are an Athapaskan tribe of Indians residing mainly in New Mexico and Arizona. The name, derived from the Zuni word for "enemy," was originally applied by that tribe to the Navajos (to whom the Apache are closely related). The principal divisions of the Apaches are the Chiricahua, Mescalero, Mimbreño (eastern Chiricahua), Lipan, and Jicarilla.

Before 1000, the Apaches lived on the Plains, where some continued to live as late as 1700. The introduction of firearms and the arrival of the horse, however, allowed the Comanches and Utes to push them into the Southwest. They probably began arriving in the area around 1400. Thereafter, they defended a large territory against all arrivals.

Pressure from the Apaches helped weaken the Spanish and contributed to the success of the Pueblo revolt of 1680. From 1685 until 1786, the tribe waged constant war against the Spanish, inhibiting their occupation of the region. The Spanish responded with a variety of stratagems—mostly un-

Apache women gathering firewood on the reservation.

An Apache warrior.

successful—to control the Indians, including a bounty for scalps of Apache dead.

After the Spaniards, the Apaches fought the Mexicans. When the United States annexed the region following the Mexican War, it regarded the tribe as a conquered people. The Apaches considered themselves joint victors in a common war with Mexico. The tribe now fought both Mexicans and Americans.

When the U.S. Army occupied New Mexico in 1862, General James Carleton was determined to keep Union supply lines, which ran through Apache territory, open. He planned to do so by eliminating the Apaches. The Apache leader, Mangas Coloradas, and his son-in-law, Cochise, fought back. Mangas was captured and murdered. A number of Apaches were defeated and sent to a Reservation at Bosque Redondo.

Following the war's end and Carleton's departure, the United States sought to confine all the Apaches to reservations. The Apaches' fame rests largely on their resistance to this policy. From 1866 until 1886 a series of Apache leaders (Cochise, Victorio, Juh, Nana, Geronimo) and their followers fought the federal forces to a virtual standstill. It took 5,000 troops to force the surrender of Geronimo and his band of just 36, in 1886, to end the Apache Wars.

Geronimo and his followers were imprisoned at Fort Marion, Florida. Later they were moved to Fort Sill, Indian Territory. Geronimo died at Fort Sill in 1909.

Army scouts on the reservation shared by Kiowas and Comanches seek a site for a military post.

A stone-headed Apache war club.

Arapaho Indians

The Arapahos are an Algonquian tribe of Indians, traditionally closely associated with the Cheyennes.

Arapaho tradition says that they were originally a farming people from around the Red River Valley in northern Minnesota. Probably sometime between 1675 and 1700, forced out by the Chippewas and Sioux, they moved onto the Plains and became mounted buffalo hunters. Shortly thereafter, they

split. The Gros Ventre (or Atsina) moved northwest into Canada. The Arapahos moved southwest, and formed a close alliance with the Cheyennes. After continual warfare with the Sioux, Crows, and other tribes, they migrated southwest, splitting again. The Northern Arapahos settled near the North Platte River in Wyoming. The Southern Arapahos continued toward the Arkansas River in southern Colorado.

Although the tribe generally attempted to live in peace with whites, conflict inevitably arose, and the Arapahos took part in some of the best-known engagements of the Indian wars. Whites had first encountered the tribe when it was living in the area of the Black Hills, but settlement did not encroach upon them until after 1840. The California gold rush in 1849 brought increasing numbers of Euroamericans across their territory. In 1851, the Arapahos joined with other tribes in agreeing to allow roads and military outposts on their lands.

An Arapaho Indian.

In 1864, seeking to clear the Plains of Indians, Colorado officials opened military operations against the Cheyennes and the Arapahos. Scattered fights took place. On November 29, 1864, a force of volunteers commanded by Colonel John M. Chivington attacked a peaceful camp of Cheyennes and Arapahos on Sand Creek, killing 28 men and 105 women and children. Arapaho chief Left Hand was among the wounded. In January 1865, Cheyennes, Arapahos, and Sioux launched raids along a wide front to avenge the Sand Creek Massacre.

More actions followed. Arapahos took part in the Fetterman Massacre in 1866. They were present at Washita in 1868, when Custer attacked Black Kettle's camp, coming to the aid of their Cheyenne allies. Some participated in the Battle of Adobe Walls with Quanah Parker's Comanches in 1874. They also took part in Custer's defeat at the Little Big Horn.

Eventually, the Southern Arapahos were confined to a reservation with the Southern Cheyennes in western Indian Territory. The Northern Arapahos moved to Wyoming's Wind River Reservation in Wyoming in 1876. Both bands were particularly active in the Ghost Dance movement of 1889–1890.

Arikara Indians

The Arikaras are an Indian tribe of the Upper Missouri River region. When first encountered by the Lewis and Clark expedition in 1804, the Arikaras lived in earth-covered lodges on the border of present-day North and South Dakota. In contrast to neighboring nomadic tribes, the Arikaras, a branch of the Pawnees and similar in cultural patterns to the Mandans, were farmers and buffalo hunters, semisettled "village Indians" known to mountain men as "Rickarees" or "Rees."

Originally hostile toward white explorers and traders, the Arikaras posed a significant obstacle to upriver travel on the Missouri River, a circumstance that resulted in the most significant of all Indian-trapper encounters in the early history of the American West.

In the summer of 1823, William H. Ashley and

F. J. HAYNES PHOTO

Wyoming Arapahos meeting with President Chester A. Arthur in 1883.

NEW YORK PUBLIC LIBRARY

An Arikara Indian.

his recruited party of 70 beaver trappers (including many soon to become celebrated mountain men: Jedediah Smith, Jim Bridger, Hugh Glass, Tom Fitzpatrick, Jim Clyman, and William Sublette) made their way from St. Louis to the Upper Missouri. On June 2, some 600 Arikaras attacked the party. They killed 15 of the trappers and wounded 12 others before forcing the Americans to retreat downstream. Ashley managed to get a message to Fort Atkinson, Nebraska, about the incident. The result was the assembling in June 1823 of a 200-man punitive expedition of the Sixth Infantry led by Fort Atkinson's commander, Colonel Henry Leavenworth, a veteran of the War of 1812. His rather grandly named Missouri Legion, joined in their march upriver by some 700 Sioux allies and numerous trapper volunteers from the Missouri Fur Company, arrived at the Arikara village in August with a force of over 1,000 men. On August 14, after some preliminary skirmishing in which Leavenworth's field cannon were used effectively against the crudely barricaded lodges, the commander, in a decision later criticized by trappers and army authorities alike, allowed the Arikaras to abandon their village unpursued. The result of Leavenworth's perceived timidity was the damaging of white prestige among all the Upper Missouri tribes and the closing, for a time at least, of the river to the fur trade.

But the days of the Arikaras as an impediment to the river traffic were numbered. The tribe had already been decimated by disease epidemics in the 1770s, and in 1837 were again struck down by smallpox. The plague killed most of the Mandans and half of the neighboring Arikaras and Hidatsas (also known as the Minatarees), leaving an Arikara population of about 1,000.

For centuries, Arikara, Mandan, and Hidatsa (see Gros Ventres) villages had all been important intertribal trading centers. By the 1850s, the Arikaras had a more stable and friendly relationship with whites, many serving as scouts for the army in its Indian campaigns through the next quarter-century. (The most famous of the Arikara scouts was Bloody Knife, who in 1872 became a leader of the Arikaras attached to newly established Fort Abraham Lincoln in Dakota Territory. He became Lieutenant Colonel George Armstrong Custer's favorite scout and was killed while serving with Major Marcus Reno's detachment in the Battle of the Little Big Horn on June 25, 1876.)

In 1900, about 400 Arikaras were living with Mandans and Hidatsas at Fort Berthold on the Missouri River. They eventually merged with those tribes, losing their cultural identity.

Arizona

The forty-eighth state in the Union, Arizona is known as "the Grand Canyon State." Arizona is marked by deserts and mountains. It is known to have been inhabited over 10,000 years ago by forebears of the Pueblo, Navajo, and Apache tribes. It is believed that the area was first irrigated for farming about 2,000 years ago.

From the mid-1500s through the late 1700s, Spanish explorers and missionaries traveled through this region. In 1736 silver was found near the northern Arizona Altar Valley region. The mines were exhausted within five years. This area was then known as Arizonac ("small spring"), which became the basis for the territory's name, Arizona.

By 1752, white settlers had established settlements in Arizona. Continued skirmishes with native dwellers led to the establishment of Fort Tucson in 1776. This protective stockade was noted for its thick adobe walls.

Arizona became part of Mexico in 1821, when that country achieved independence from Spain. In 1848, the region was ceded to the United States in the Treaty of Guadalupe Hidalgo, which ended the Mexican War. During the Civil War, Confederate troops occupied the land, claiming it as a Southern territory. Union forces were sent to defeat the Confederates, and Arizona was officially declared a United States territory in 1863.

As white settlers continued moving into the region, Navajo and Apache tribes fought the intrusion onto their lands. Despite numerous attacks, army troops ultimately defeated the Indian forces. In 1886, the Apache warrior Geronimo finally surrendered, effectively bringing a close to the uprisings.

Arizona, with its rich veins of copper and other minerals, quickly became a site for widespread mining. As irrigation techniques improved, the parched lands became fertile, and many ranchers chose to raise their stock in Arizona.

The move to make Arizona a state began in the 1890s. Although political squabbles held up the

Artist Richard H. Kern painted these Arizona sandstone formations to look like man-made fortifications.

process for years, Arizona officially became the forty-eighth state on February 14, 1912.

Arizona's landscape is divided into two main sections: the Colorado Plateau and the Basin and Range Region. The Colorado Plateau, in northern Arizona, encompasses about two-fifths of the state. The area is filled with many of the world's natural wonders, including the Grand Canyon, the Colorado River, Monument Valley, the Petrified Forest, and the Painted Desert. The Basin and Range Region, in the southern portion of the state, is known for its mountains and is more fertile, producing the majority of Arizona's

Sprawling Fort Thomas, in the Arizona desert.

crops, which include cotton, lettuce, melons, and oranges. Cattle ranching is Arizona's largest agricultural industry.

Arizona's numerous desert areas are filled with cacti. The mountainous regions support evergreens that include Ponderosa pines, blue spruce, and white fir. Animal life is abundant and extremely varied. Bears, bobcats, and mountain lions can be found in the Arizona forests; the deserts are home to rattlesnakes, Gila monsters, scorpions, and tarantulas. Doves, quail, and roadrunners are among Arizona's native birds.

Arkansas

The twenty-fifth state in the Union, Arkansas is known as "The Land of Opportunity." Arkansas takes its name from two sources: an Indian word meaning "downstream people," and the French word "Arkansas," their name for the Indian village Arkansea.

Arkansas is believed to have been settled origi-

nally by various Indian tribes, including the Caddos, Osages, Cherokees, Tulas, Chickasaws, Chickasawbas, and Quapaws. The first whites came to the area in the 1500s, when the Spanish explorer Hernando de Soto led his party into the Ozark Mountain region. A little over a century later, the French explorers Jacques Marquette and Louis Jolliet entered the Arkansas region after traveling down the Mississippi River to the Arkansas River. French colonists began arriving in 1717, hoping to develop trapping and trading. These endeavors were unsuccessful, however.

After several skirmishes over the territory, Spain acquired Arkansas as part of the Louisiana Territory in 1763. In 1800, the area was turned over to the French and was obtained by the United States as part of the Louisiana Purchase in 1803. Congress declared Arkansas a U.S. territory in 1819, and a state on June 15, 1836.

As the Civil War loomed in 1860, Arkansas was divided over whether to join the Confederacy or remain in the Union. In May 1861, the state voted to unite with the Southern states, though many Arkansas residents remained loyal to the Union. In 1864, following Little Rock's fall to Northern

LIBRARY OF CONGRESS

Arkansas pioneers as depicted in Harper's Weekly, *April 4, 1874.*

troops, Arkansas had two governments: one loyal to the Union, the other to the Confederacy. During the Reconstruction, Arkansas was governed by troops from the United States Army, until it was readmitted to the Union in 1868.

Much political turmoil ensued, and there were several violent outbreaks until President Grant intervened. Rapid growth followed in the 1880s, after rich bauxite mines opened near the state capital of Little Rock. The coming of the railroad and farming and industrial development were important to the state's economic expansion.

Arkansas has many lush areas for farming: cotton, soybeans, and rice are the leading crops. The state also has an abundance of forests—ranging from pines to hardwoods—that covers about 50 percent of the land. The woods are home to a wide variety of animal species including deer, bobcats, muskrats, raccoons, and squirrels. Wild turkeys, geese, and ducks provided settlers with plenty of game for hunting.

The Arkansas landscape is diverse, from the Ozark Mountains to the rich valleys that surround the Arkansas River. Arkansas is also known for its natural springs, including the famed Hot Springs.

Ash Hollow Massacre

See Grattan Massacre

Ashley, William Henry

1778–1838

A Virginian who moved to Missouri about 1802, William Henry Ashley pursued careers in business, land speculation, the military, and politics before entering the fur business. He served on the frontier in the War of 1812 and by the early 1820s was lieutenant governor of the newly created state of Missouri and brigadier general of the state militia.

Although Ashley was not a "mountain man" or a frontiersman, he became the most significant figure in the opening of the Rocky Mountain fur trade. With the famous newspaper notice of 1822 seeking "enterprising young men" for a fur-hunting expedition up the Missouri River he launched a brief but important career. In partnership with Andrew Henry, he established a post at the mouth of the Yellowstone River as a base for trapping the headwaters of the Missouri. His preference was to handle the supply and marketing aspects of the venture in St. Louis while Henry led the field parties, but in both 1822 and 1823 Ashley had to take the field as well. Both expeditions encountered Indian hostility, and the 1823 group suffered a disastrous defeat by Arikara Indians.

Previous initiatives had relied heavily on Indians to trap beaver and exchange skins for white manufactures. Ashley used white men, both free trappers and his own employees, to hunt beaver. Although this angered some Indian tribes, chiefly the militant Blackfeet, it gave new vitality to the fur business and fixed its pattern for two decades. Blocked by Arikaras and Blackfeet on the Missouri, Ashley sent his trappers to the Rocky Mountains and thus tapped a rich new hunting ground. The fur business thus became dependent on land rather than water transportation.

Twice more, between 1824 and 1826, Ashley himself took the field. On these journeys to the Rockies and beyond, he established a new system: the rendezvous and the annual supply caravan. Now trapping parties wintered in the fur country, conducted spring and fall hunts, and assembled at a designated rendezvous each summer to dispose of the year's catch, receive the next year's supplies, and rest and relax. In the spring, trains of pack mules brought the supplies from St. Louis, traveling the overland route up the Platte and across South Pass—a route that would become the Oregon Trail. After the rendezvous, the supply train returned laden with bales of beaver skins.

Having made a fortune at the rendezvous of 1826, near Great Salt Lake, Ashley sold out to three of his associates: Jedediah Smith, David E. Jackson, and William Sublette. He had quickly perceived that the true profits of the fur business lay in supply and marketing rather than in trapping. He continued to supply the field parties from his St. Louis base while devoting himself to politics. Ashley ran unsuccessfully for governor of Missouri but was elected to the U.S. House of Representatives in 1831. Effectively championing western interests, he served until 1837. He died of pneumonia at the age of 60.

Assiniboin Indians

The Assiniboins are a Northern Plains tribe believed to have originated in the sixteenth century as a branch of the Yankton Dakotas (Sioux) with whom they share a dialect, and who allied the Crees and the Ojibwas (Chippewas) of the Great Lakes region. In the seventeenth and eighteenth centuries, the Assiniboins, called Hohe by the Dakotas (who became their tribal enemies, along with the Crows, Blackfeet, and Atsinas), were located around Winnipeg, Manitoba, and in Saskatchewan. By 1850 the Assiniboins were found mostly along the Missouri River north and west of the mouth of the Yellowstone; by the end of the nineteenth century they numbered about 20,000.

In their winter camp at Fort Mandan on the upper Missouri in 1804–1805, Lewis and Clark met with an Assiniboin chief and several tribesmen. The explorers thought the Assiniboins a surly lot who mocked the Mandans for their friendliness to the whites. But the Assiniboins, nomadic buffalo hunters and skilled traders among the other Plains tribes, themselves compiled a record of accord with whites while suffering greatly because of it. They were ravaged by small-

LIBRARY OF CONGRESS

The skin lodge of an Assiniboin chief.

pox around Fort Union, the fur-trading post a few miles above the mouth of the Yellowstone, in the epidemic of 1837. So many died and were buried at the fort that when the cemetery was dug up in the early 1950s, the Assiniboin bones were taken away by the truckload, to be mixed with gravel to pave roads.

By 1843 the Assiniboin population had been

LIBRARY OF CONGRESS

The Assiniboins attacking the Blackfeet at Fort McKenzie. This drawing, as well as the one above, was made by Karl Bodmer, one of few artists to actually witness an Indian battle.

Wi-Jun-Jon, an Assiniboin chief, going to Washington and returning home, as depicted by George Catlin.

reduced to about 4,000. With the Atsina (the Gros Ventre of the Prairies) and Dakota tribes, the Assiniboins live today at Fort Peck and Fort Belknap in Montana.

Astor, John Jacob

1763–1848

Astor, a financier and fur trade entrepreneur who founded the American Fur Company in 1808, dominated the fur business for decades. In 1821 he successfully lobbied Congress to abolish government trading posts, effectively opening up the fur trading business in the Plains and Rockies to private companies.

Astor was born on July 17, 1763, in Waldorf, Germany. In 1779 he went to London, where his brother was established as a manufacturer of flutes and other musical instruments. Astor worked with his brother for four years to gain mercantile experience and establish trade connections. He then traveled to America early in 1784 with a cargo of flutes which

he sold in New York City. He used the profits from the sale to invest in furs; later that same year he returned to London and sold his furs at a profit. Intrigued by the fur business, he decided to return to America for good, and was back before the end of 1784.

After spending several years in New York City, Astor traveled to the Northwest when the British evacuated the area in 1796. The absence of the British meant that furs could be transported more easily to New York City and also enabled the Canadians to trade directly at American ports. In 1808, Astor founded the American Fur Company to challenge the British-Canadian trade along the northern border. Two years later, he founded the Pacific Fur Company, but this venture failed during the War of 1812. After gaining control of the South West Company in 1817, he came to dominate the fur trade in the Northwest.

Astor sold the American Fur Company in 1834 and spent his later years in New York City, where he was also successful in real estate. He died in New York City on March 29, 1848, at the age of 84. At the time of his death, Astor was considered the wealthiest man in the country, with an estate reportedly worth $20 million. However, contemporary historians estimate that his net worth was closer to $8–$10 million.

Athapaskan Indians

One of the major Indian linguistic families in North America, the Athapaskans consist of three divisions. The Northern Athapaskans are tribes in Canada and Alaska, including the Chippewyans, Dogribs, and Koyukons. The Pacific Athapaskans are located along the Northwest Coast of the United States and include the Tolowas and Tlatskanais. The Southern Athapaskans are the Navajos and Apaches in the Southwest and the Kiowa-Apaches of Oklahoma. Athapaskans consider themselves one people separated by history. The presence of Athapaskans in the southern United States is somewhat of a mystery. Unlike their northern relatives, who are hunters, the southern Athapaskans are primarily farmers and stock raisers.

Sometime between 1000 and 1400, the Navajos

LIBRARY OF CONGRESS

Northwest Coast Athapaskan braves wrestle for the hand of a Nootka princess.

and Apaches migrated into the Southwest. Somewhere along the trail from the north, they split into different tribes. The Apache-speaking Kiowa Apache were so named because they were first encountered living under the protection of the Kiowa.

The languages are tonal in character, with the same syllable carrying a different meaning depending upon the tone.

Stephen Austin, educated in Connecticut and Kentucky, was studying law in New Orleans at the time of his father's death and undertook to see his work through. He reached San Antonio in July 1821, and with typical industry and energy, persuaded the newly independent government of Mexico to ratify the Austin grant. With a party of early settlers, he traveled to the lower reaches of the Colorado and Brazos rivers and found what he described as "the most beautiful situation for a town or settlement."

Austin, Moses 1761–1821
and Austin, Stephen Fuller 1793–1836

The Austins were Texas colonizers. Moses Austin was a successful lead-mining entrepreneur in Wythe County, Virginia, where his son Stephen was born. In 1798, the elder Austin took his family to southeastern Missouri, where he petitioned for and received a land grant from the Spanish government of the Northern Louisiana Territory. Austin established a lead mine and a smelter in the town of Potosi. In 1820, having suffered financial ruin in the depression of 1819, he devised a plan to establish an American colony in Texas. Austin traveled to San Antonio de Béxar from New Orleans and petitioned the Spanish governor for a new land grant for that purpose. He received a grant of 200,000 acres to settle 300 families but died, in June 1821, before he could develop his colony.

TEXAS STATE LIBRARY

Stephen Fuller Austin.

The "situation," along the Brazos, was 15 miles from the Gulf of Mexico and 175 miles from San Antonio. There Austin determined to build his town, San Felipe de Austin.

He soon expanded his plan for the American colony and petitioned the governor of the northern Mexican province of Coahuila y Texas for an enormous territory of about 18,000 square miles, estimating he could recruit 1,500 families to settle on the land and develop it. Toward the end of 1821, Austin was in New Orleans to raise capital for his Texas colony; with part of the money gained from selling interests in it, he bought a sloop, the *Lively*, and stocked it with tools and equipment. The vessel ran aground on Galveston Island and was a total loss. The indefatigable Austin immediately returned to his colony. When he arrived in January 1822, he found several settlers had preceded him and built cabins on the land.

Until 1830, Austin managed his domain without significant interference from Mexico City. He was first of all loyal to Mexico, and in addition established a sound legal and court system for the colony, had the land grant carefully surveyed, encouraged trade agreements with the United States, supervised the building of schools and of mills for processing cotton and lumber, and organized local militia to fight marauding Indians—the Karankawas in particular.

In 1830, when Austin's colonies around San Felipe had a population of about 4,000 (about one-quarter the number of Americans in Texas), the Mexican government passed laws attempting to slow Anglo immigration to Texas. In 1833, Texans at the San Felipe Convention drew up a constitution for a proposed independent state government of Texas; Austin was asked to take it to Mexico City, to President Antonio López de Santa Anna. For his efforts Austin was imprisoned briefly in the Mexican capital. In August 1835 he returned to Texas and found the Americans there on the verge of revolution.

In October 1835, Austin served as commander of the Texas Army in San Antonio, then was selected as a commissioner to travel to Washington to seek U.S. recognition of the Republic of Texas. He returned in June 1836, and after defeat by Sam Houston for election as first president of Texas, retired to his cabin on the Brazos, alone (he never married), ill, impoverished, and adrift. Houston saved him from bitterness and humiliation by appointing him as the Republic's secretary of state, an office he held until his death on December 27, 1836. Houston, in announcing Austin's death, said, "The father of Texas is no more."

B

Baca, Elfego

1865–1945

Sheriff, lawyer, and politician, Elfego Baca was one of the most colorful Mexican-American folk heroes of the nineteenth century, and the survivor of one of the West's more storied gun battles. Born in Socorro, New Mexico, he was educated in Topeka, Kansas, until age 15, when his father brought him back to Socorro. The elder Baca was then town marshal at nearby Belen, New Mexico. He was jailed after killing two cowboys, but his son helped him escape.

At 19, Baca, serving as a self-appointed special deputy at Frisco, New Mexico, got into a fight with hands from the Texas-based John B. Slaughter ranch who apparently had been using local Mexicans and their herds for target practice. The next day, Baca found himself cornered in a small shack by an army of vengeance-seeking cowboys, some 80 in number. Miraculously, after a 36-hour siege in which some 4,000 shots were fired, Baca, having killed four and wounded eight of his pursuers, was allowed to surrender to a friendly deputy sheriff. He was twice tried and acquitted in Albuquerque on murder charges stemming from the incident.

An instant folk hero among the Mexican-American population of the region, Baca was ensured of a long and fruitful political career. He was admitted to the bar in 1894 after reading law with a local judge, and won elections for deputy sheriff, country clerk, mayor, district attorney, sheriff, and Socorro County

superintendent of schools. He continued to work as a lawyer and private detective almost until his death in 1945.

Bannock Indians

The Bannocks are a Uzo-Aztecan tribe of Indians related to the Shoshone and living in southeastern Idaho.

During the eighteenth century, the Bannocks migrated from eastern Oregon into Idaho, settling along the Snake and Salmon rivers. They also ranged into western Wyoming. Those living along the Salmon River were encountered by Lewis and Clark in 1805 and probably were referred to by them as the Broken Moccasin tribe.

In 1868, by the Treaty of Fort Bridger, the Bannocks agreed to accept a reservation on the upper Snake River. They were careful, however, to reserve exclusive rights to an area known as Camas Prairie, a significant site where the lilylike camas plant, an important part of the Bannock diet, grew.

Food was scarce on the new reservation, and the Bannocks turned to buffalo hunting with the blessing of their Indian agent. Chronic shortages still occurred, however, and the camas root became even more important to the tribe. In the spring of 1878, the people moved to Camas Prairie, where they found white settlers who had been encroaching on the area for several years. The Bannock chief, Buffalo Horn, ordered the outsiders off the Indians' land. In the ensuing confusion, some of the whites were shot. Though some of the Indians involved returned immediately to the reservation, others fled. Pursued by Army units under General Oliver Howard and Colonel Nelson Miles, they were eventually rounded up by September 1878.

Barbed Wire

Fencing material made out of twisted wire with spaced, coiled barbs played a decisive role in the transition of the West from open plains to enclosed pastures and irrevocably altered the society and economy of the region. Before the invention of cheap man-made material, fences were constructed from whatever natural materials were at hand: stone barriers where stone was plentiful, wooden barricades where forests predominated. In the East, fencing was used to protect crops from grazing animals. In the West, however, there were prairies with few rocks or trees, and the cattle required large open ranges for feeding. The unwritten law of the open range allowed free access to vast areas that provided water and grass. Agricultural interests, on the other hand, demanded enclosed areas for maximum crop yield. Farmers, who were not in the business of raising crops to feed grazing cows, squared off against the cattlemen, insisting that the latter be responsible for the very expensive proposition of confining their stock. Inventive farmers began to use the Osage orange tree, a hardy natural hedging material, that could thrive in various soils.

After the Civil War, demand for meat increased, and by 1870 the buffalo had been hunted to near extinction. Beef was the answer, and the clash between farmers and cowmen escalated into open warfare. A number of inventors had recognized the need for cheap and easily manufactured fencing material, but it was not until 1873 that a DeKalb, Illinois, farmer, Joseph Farwell Glidden, found a solution. Patent number 157,124, issued November 24, 1874, was for a machine that could produce wired barbs entwined by double-strand wires. Glidden began manufacture the same year. Patent refinements led to production of a great variety of wires—single cable, double cable, round, and half-round—across a range of gauges. Barbed-wire production skyrocketed, and between 1875 and 1885 annual production increased from under 300 tons to 100,000 tons. So widespread was the use of barbed wire that by 1890 the open range in the West was nearly all fenced pastureland. Cattle was no longer king; ranchers could isolate their stock and control breeding, and the long drives were supplanted by the railroad that moved the cattle safely and quickly to market, with less weight loss. Homesteaders benefited from this sectioning off of the Great Plains, and as a result, agriculture, settlements, and commerce combined to forge an economy more powerful than either cattlemen or farmers would ever have dreamed.

NEBRASKA STATE HISTORICAL SOCIETY

Wire cutting on a Nebraska ranch, a common practice during the range wars.

Bartlett, John Russell

1805–1886

Although his work to determine the boundary between the United States and Mexico following the Treaty of Guadalupe Hidalgo (1848) was largely a failure, John Russell Bartlett wrote a detailed personal narrative of his work that is regarded as a classic of southwestern history.

He was born in Providence, Rhode Island, and spent his youth in Ontario. In 1836 he moved to New York City and opened a bookstore, which he ran until 1850. Bartlett's study of American Indian ethnology resulted in his cofounding (in 1842) the American Ethnological Society and the publication of his first books, *Progress in Ethnology* (1847) and *Dictionary of Americanisms* (1848).

In June 1850, Bartlett, probably through his Whig political connections, was appointed commissioner of the U.S.–Mexico Boundary Survey; in November he arrived in El Paso with a large entourage of civilians and an 85-man military escort to begin his assigned work. Bartlett's predecessors—Ambrose Sevier, John B. Weller, and John C. Frémont—had left unresolved most of the decisions on the critical portion of the boundary from the Rio Grande westward. The new commissioner and his Mexican counterpart, General Pedro García Condé, quickly came to grips with two serious flaws in the map used by the Guadalupe–Hidalgo Treaty negotiators: a latitude error placing El Paso del Norte (modern Juárez, Mexico, across the Rio Grande from El Paso, Texas) 34 miles too far north and a longitude error placing the Rio Grande 100 miles too far east. These lapses complicated the status of the Santa Rita copper mines and the settlement of Mesilla and its fertile farming valley, both in New Mexico Territory, and a proposed transcontinental railroad route.

The Bartlett-Condé Compromise, worked out toward the end of 1850, in effect gave latitude to the Mexican government, and longitude to the Americans; Bartlett sacrificed Mesilla and the railroad route to protect the copper mines. The compromise was the subject of strong criticism among Bartlett's surveying party and among expansionist Democrats at odds with Whig President Millard Fillmore.

As disputes deepened—the Bartlett-Condé "line" was repudiated in Washington and a new surveyor, Captain William H. Emory, arrived to take over the work from El Paso west—Bartlett set out for San Diego to recommence the boundary work from west to east. After recovering from cholera and making a leisurely trip through northern Sonora and from San Diego to San Francisco and back, he resumed command of the boundary commission in May 1852. He and his party traveled east along the Gila River to the Rio Grande, with side trips to Tucson and Chihuahua, reaching El Paso in August.

By now, however, Bartlett's leadership and his long absences from commission work had been roundly criticized along the border and in Washington. In January 1853 he left the Southwest to return to his native Providence. The boundary work continued until 1853, when James Gadsden's mission to Mexico resulted in the Gadsden Purchase, which ended the Rio Grande–westward boundary dispute and gave the United States its coveted railroad right-of-way and the Mesilla Valley. Bartlett published his invaluable history in 1854 and the following year was elected Rhode Island's secretary of state, an office he held until 1872. Among his many published works is a 10-volume history of Rhode Island through 1792.

A Bartlett sketch of California Indians gambling inside an earth-covered council house.

Basin and Range Province

See Great Basin

Bass, Sam

1851–1878

Sam Bass was a notorious outlaw whose bank and train robberies terrorized citizens in Texas, Nebraska, and the Dakota Territory. Betrayed by a member of his own gang, Bass was fatally shot by the Texas Rangers, and died on his twenty-seventh birthday.

Bass was born on July 21, 1851, in Indiana, and reared by an uncle. At age 18 he went to Denton, Texas, where he worked as a farmhand for Sheriff W. F. Eagan. In 1874, Bass purchased a racehorse and, with it, success. He quit his job and began life as a gambler. In 1875, after winning some ponies at Fort Sill, Indian Territory, Bass took them and a number of others and fled to San Antonio, Texas. It was his first known robbery.

Later he befriended Joel Collins, and they began a freight line operation out of Deadwood, Dakota Territory. They soon sold it to buy a saloon and casino, and finally a mine. Eventually broke, Bass decided to make his money as a robber. He led several desperadoes in seven successful Stagecoach robberies before leaving the Black Hills. On September 18, 1877, Bass and outlaws James Berry, Jack Davis, Bill Heffridge, and Tom Nixon seized more than $60,000 during a

MERCALDO ARCHIVES, UNIVERSITY OF TEXAS

Sam Bass.

train robbery at Big Spring, Nebraska. Within a few weeks, Heffridge, Berry, and Joel Collins were shot, but Bass escaped to Texas and organized another gang.

In the spring of 1878, Bass and his bandits staged four train holdups around Dallas. His former employer, Sheriff Eagan, joined the manhunt for the gang. That summer, Bass planned a bank robbery in Round Rock, Texas. But Jim Murphy, a gang member who later shot himself, betrayed him to the Texas Rangers in exchange for leniency. Ranger George Harrel shot Bass during a bloody clash in the streets of Round Rock, and he died two days later.

Beadle, Erastus

See Dime Novels

Bean, Roy

CA. 1827–1903

Bean's life is so inextricably mixed with folklore and myth that even his most assiduous biographer, C. L. Sonnichsen, had to be content to deal briskly with the few historical facts and devote the balance of his book to Bean tales, of which there is an endless supply.

Roy Bean was born in Mason County, Kentucky, between 1825 and 1830 and spent the first 30 years of his life—if one takes his word and that of the sparse other evidence—in and out of trouble with the law. In 1848, with his brother Sam, he is believed to have trafficked in trade goods on the Santa Fe Trail. He then made his way to Mexico, where he killed a man and fled to California. In San Diego, where another brother, Joshua, operated a saloon, Bean fought a duel in 1852. He was jailed but escaped and went to San Gabriel, north of Los Angeles. Joshua Bean, who either preceded or followed his brother, opened a saloon in San Gabriel and ran it successfully until he was murdered, for reasons not known, in the mid-1850s. Roy took over the saloon and did well with it until, by his own account, he was nearly lynched for courting a

Judge Roy Bean.

until 1902, administering justice and serving liquor, often simultaneously, at the Jersey Lilly.

Among the countless tales, many of them well documented, of Bean's antic administration of justice are these: He once fined a lawyer for using profane language in his court when the lawyer announced he intended to use habeas corpus in defending his client. He assessed a fine of $20 on a saloon patron who said the picture of Lillie Langtry "looked like a range heifer." He sentenced rustlers and horse thieves to be hanged "pronto," and often ended his verdict by ordering that the culprit's neck "be tied to a limb in some open place where his cronies will be sure to see him." He granted quick divorces to couples whose marriages (which he had performed) did not "take hold." And once, after inspecting the corpse of a railroader who had fallen from a bridge, fined the victim the $40 he had in his pocket "for carrying a concealed weapon" and confiscated the pistol "for use by the court."

Bean died in his room in the Jersey Lilly on March 16, 1903.

Spanish girl from a prominent local family. The girl's other suitor and his friends actually strung him up, Bean said, but the rope was too long; and as he clung to life, his toes touching the ground, the young woman he had fought over cut him down. (He did, contemporaries said, have a scar around his neck, and could not turn his head independently of his upper body.)

In New Mexico Territory, and later in San Antonio, Bean served with volunteer Confederate irregulars during the Civil War. He remained in San Antonio for 16 years after the war, married, and worked in the saloon trade. In 1882, Bean left his wife and children, and in a wagon loaded with whiskey and other trade goods, traveled to the junction of the Pecos and Rio Grande, where he opened a tent saloon. In July of that year he moved his operation to Eagle's Nest Springs on the Rio Grande; he named the place Langtry and the saloon the Jersey Lilly, after the English beauty and actress Lillie Langtry, with whom he became infatuated after seeing her photograph. He liked to say she was an "acquaintance," he subscribed to theatrical magazines to follow her career and clip pictures of her, and he steadfastly defended her honor. Sadly, he was never to meet her.

In August 1882, Bean was appointed justice of the peace and, except for one term, served in that capacity (which he called the "Law West of the Pecos")

Bear Flag Republic

1846

The United States had a long history of coveting Alta (Upper, as opposed to Baja, Lower) California before the Mexican War delivered it into American hands. President Andrew Jackson had proposed buying it, and James Polk made its acquisition one of the principal aims of his presidency. In 1846, the great Mexican province lay virtually ungoverned and undefended: only four presidios were strung along its coast, each ill-equipped, ill-armed, and undermanned; the entire population of the province was under 4,000, including about 800 Anglos.

Before the news of the outbreak of the war with Mexico reached the Pacific, an American rebellion was beginning in the northern part of Alta California, centered around the Sacramento Valley, where the Swiss-born entrepreneur John Augustus Sutter had built a fort and, deeply in debt, was encouraging American immigration by offering parcels of the 50,000 acres he held under a Mexican land grant.

In December 1845, Captain John C. Frémont, leading an expedition, rode into Sutter's Fort, then continued south to Monterey, where he informed Mexican officials he was exploring a route to the Oregon Territory. Frémont was permitted to winter in California but was warned to stay inland, away from the settled coastal areas. He defied the order, and Colonel José Castro, commander of Mexican forces in the northern part of the province, gathered his cavalry and forced an infuriated Frémont and his men to abandon their California mission and proceed into Oregon. During the march north, Frémont and his party, which included the American consul in California, Thomas O. Larkin, were discovered on May 9, 1846, at Klamath Lake by a U.S. Marine Corps lieutenant, Archibald Gillespie. An agent and courier for President Polk, Gillespie had confidential dispatches from Washington for Larkin and Frémont that resulted in Frémont's return to Sutter's Fort. (Although the United States did not declare war against Mexico until May 13, Zachary Taylor had massed his forces on the Rio Grande in late March and had fought two battles against the Mexicans by the time Gillespie met the Frémont party. It seems clear that the messages from Polk had to do with the impending war.)

Frémont and his men arrived at Sutter's Fort on June 9. The next day the first overt move toward establishing the short-lived Bear Flag Republic was made. A group of Sacramento Valley settlers, led by Ezekiel Merritt, a trapper described by H. H. Bancroft as "a coarse-grained, loud-mouthed, unprincipled, whiskey-drinking, quarrelsome fellow," ambushed a Mexican officer and nine men who were leading 170 horses to Castro at Santa Clara. Merritt and his raiders left the Mexicans with one horse each, and took the remaining herd back to Sutter's Fort.

Four days later, with Frémont's sanction, Merritt took men and headed south to seize Sonoma and the north San Francisco Bay area. On June 14, the raiders captured the local military commander, Colonel Mariano G. Vallejo (who was, ironically, strongly pro-American and a supporter of U.S. annexation of California) and his family, informed them they were prisoners of war, and removed them to Sutter's Fort. There, Frémont, still smarting over his humiliating expulsion earlier that year, ordered the family jailed.

Meantime, with Sonoma as its capital, the Republic of California was created in a proclamation drafted by William B. Ide, a Vermont-born carpenter and farmer who declared the new government would overthrow the Mexican "military despotism." A newcomer to California, William Todd (a cousin of Mary Todd Lincoln), made the declaration official by presenting the crude flag he had fashioned, depicting a grizzly bear, a red star, and the words "California Republic" on a white field. Thereafter the revolutionaries were known as Bear Flaggers.

Ide and his men, including Americans who came to join them after the proclamation was distributed as far south as Monterey, prepared to defend Sonoma against an expected attack by Castro's army, heading north from San Francisco.

A small skirmish occurred on June 24 at Olompali, a rancho near present-day Novato, in which a Mexican force suffered one killed and several wounded, and the Americans escaped unscathed. A day later, Frémont's command of 90 men arrived in Sonoma to help defend it and captured the nearby settlement of San Rafael. On July 1, having sailed down the coast in an American merchant ship, Frémont and his men entered San Francisco, spiked an ancient Spanish cannon at San Joaquin (at the south entrance to San Francisco Bay), and occupied the presidio. On Independence Day, at a huge banquet and celebration, Frémont announced the creation of the California Battalion of Volunteers, which he would command with Gillespie as his adjutant.

As this military unit was being formally organized, however, events in the south were to end the need for Frémont's battalion and, indeed, for the Bear Flag Republic. On July 2, 1846, Commodore John D. Sloat of the U.S. Navy, who had dispatched two ships ahead of him, sailed into Monterey Bay on his flagship, *Savannah*, and on July 7 occupied Monterey, raising the American flag over California. On July 9, when the news of the American occupation of California was carried to Sonoma by Lieutenant Joseph W. Revere, grandson of Paul Revere, the Bear Flag was lowered from its mast in the public plaza and the Bear Flag Republic came to an end 30 days after its creation.

Beaver

A member of the rodent family found chiefly in North America, the beaver was highly prized by Western trappers and furriers for its pelt.

Reports by scouts and explorers of abundant beaver led to a boom in the fur-trapping business.

Adult beavers are three to four feet long, and can weigh anywhere from 30 to 70 pounds. They have thick brown fur, a humped back, and a long, flat tail that measures about a foot long and six inches thick. This unique appendage serves as a rudder when beavers are swimming and helps the beaver balance when standing on its hind legs. Young beavers, called "kits" or "pups," are born in litters of two to four. The average life span of a beaver is 12 years.

Beavers were trapped for fur and meat. Both white trappers and Indians used the pelts for clothing. A Western trapper named Jim Baird wrote, "beaver is the most precious product this territory produces." From the mid-1600s through the late 1800s, beaver pelts were a valuable commodity for traders. In one 24-year period, the Hudson's Bay Company shipped over 3 million of them to London for use by coat and hat manufacturers. On the frontier, beaver pelts were as good as money. Traders bartered them for ammunition and knives, cooking utensils, tobacco, and blankets. Twelve beaver pelts was the going rate in trade for one rifle.

People writing about the new western frontier were fascinated by the beaver, which was portrayed as an industrious creature living in a harmonious social order. Beavers were also depicted as fierce warriors. Enraged beavers would, the stories claimed, bite off the tails of any other beaver that dared to intrude on their territory. This, wrote one individual, was "the greatest disgrace to which a beaver can be exposed."

Because of the high demand for beaver pelts, the creatures were in danger of extinction by the late 1800s. Government officials in both the United States and Canada passed measures protecting wild beavers in North America.

Becknell, William

1788–1865

Called the "father of the Santa Fe Trail," William Becknell was born in Amherst County, Virginia, and moved to Franklin, Missouri, as a young man. He served in the War of 1812.

After the overthrow of Spanish power in New Mexico in 1821, Becknell and four others went West in hopes of trading goods. After a relatively swift journey (only five months), he sold his goods in Taos and Santa Fe at a huge profit. Encouraged by the financial success and speed of his first endeavor, Becknell advertised the following spring for 70 men to join him on another expedition. With 30 volunteers, he left Missouri on August 4, 1822, with $5,000 in merchandise. They arrived in Santa Fe on November 16, having taken a new route that departed from the Arkansas River near present-day Dodge City and crossed to the Cimarron. Their new route, dubbed the Santa Fe Trail, quickly became the accepted trade route for the prairie.

Becknell led at least one more party to New Mexico, then an 1824 trapping expedition to western Colorado and eastern Utah. He commanded a militia company in the Black Hawk War and, in late 1835, led a group to Texas to take part in the War of Independence against Mexico. He settled near Clarksville, Texas, and remained there until his death in 1865.

Beckwourth, James P.

1798–1866

James Pierson Beckwourth was born at Fredericksburg, Virginia, to a mulatto mother and white father. The family later moved to St. Charles, Missouri, where he was apprenticed to a blacksmith.

In 1824, Beckwourth joined William H. Ashley and

THE STATE HISTORICAL SOCIETY OF COLORADO

Jim Beckwourth.

highly questionable; as one historian has observed, "Beckwourth was probably the biggest liar west of the Mississippi." Beckwourth finally settled in Colorado but later returned to live among the Crows. When he died, he was buried as a Crow, on a tree platform.

Bell, Philip Alexander

1809–1889

Although he is all but forgotten today, Philip Alexander Bell wrote one of the most important early chapters in African-American journalism. Little is known about his early life, but in 1831 he burst on the scene as secretary of a group of "colored citizens" of New York opposed to the Colonization Society and its program of repatriating black Americans to Africa. He was active in numerous other black and interracial organizations and a member of the American Anti-Slavery Society. Bell was an advocate of black self-help programs, and also a staunch antisegregationist.

In 1837 he began publishing a newspaper, the *Weekly Advocate*, with Samuel Cornish as its editor. The second African-American newspaper to be published, it lasted only three months, when it became the *Colored American*. Bell edited the paper under that name until 1839.

His activities for the next several years are unknown, but he re-emerged in San Francisco in 1857. In 1862 he became co-editor of the *Pacific Appeal*, a weekly black newspaper of considerable repute. Finally, in 1865, Bell started another newspaper, *The Elevator*. Both his West Coast journalistic ventures were of high quality, but the readership was undoubtedly too small to sustain them. Bell later became doorkeeper of the California state senate. He is believed to have died in dire poverty.

Bent, Charles

1799–1847

Charles Bent was a highly successful Virginia-born fur trader and businessman who operated

Andrew Henry on a fur-trapping expedition in the Rocky Mountains. He became an experienced trapper, going out with Ashley and others on several occasions in the mid-1820s. During those expeditions, he skirmished with the Blackfeet and other Indians.

In 1828, Beckwourth decided to join the Crow Indians, who welcomed him warmly. He married a succession of Crow women and claimed to have acquitted himself admirably as a member of war parties during his six years with the Crow nation. In the summer of 1835, he joined another expedition, this time to California. Beckwourth fought in the Seminole War under Zachary Taylor. Subsequently, he returned to the West, where he participated in the 1845 California insurrection and the Cheyenne War of 1864.

Beckwourth met an ex-newspaperman, T. D. Bonner, who helped him write an autobiography, which was published in 1856. The reliability of that book is chiefly in Colorado and New Mexico. After the Mexican War he was appointed the first American governor of the New Mexico Territory. The eldest of four brothers, he sought adventure and profit in the fur trade. After a likely stint with John Jacob Astor's American Fur Company he joined the Missouri Fur Company in 1822, becoming a partner in 1825. Severe competition led to the failure of the company, and Bent left Missouri to trade along the Santa Fe Trail with his 20-year-old brother, William, in 1829. The brothers and Ceran St. Vrain organized Bent, St. Vrain and Company in 1831; it soon became the largest trading company in the Southwest, with markets in Taos and Santa Fe.

In 1833, to consolidate Indian trade routes on the Arkansas River, the trio built Bent's Fort north of the juncture of the Purgatoire and Arkansas Rivers in Colorado. From this mountain site the company controlled trade in blankets, buffalo robes, sheep, horses, mules, and the vital Indian fur trade. William was left to run Bent's Fort, and in 1837 the construction of Fort St. Vrain on the South Platte River further extended the company's control.

Charles left for the Mexican province of New Mexico and settled in Taos in 1835. His interest was in land speculation. He married the Mexican governor's daughter, and after the conquest of New Mexico in the Mexican War of 1846, Charles, through his

wealth, prominence, and American heritage, became the first American governor of the province. However, his overbearing manner and harsh tongue had earned him enemies, and in a revolt by Mexican and Taos Indians Charles was killed and scalped.

Bent's Fort

Built in 1833 by the hugely successful fur-trading firm of Bent, St. Vrain and Company 12 miles upstream from the junction of the Purgatoire and Arkansas Rivers in Colorado, Bent's Fort commanded the trading routes north and south along the Platte River and east and west along the Santa Fe Trail. Charles Bent, his brother William, and Ceran St. Vrain were the principals in the trading company. William oversaw the construction, which has led to some confusion about the fort's name—it was commonly known as Bent's Fort, frequently also as Fort William, and later as Bent's Old Fort. From this

Charles Bent.

Exterior and interior views of Bent's Fort.

strategic mountain trading post—the best-known and largest of the period—furs, livestock, and other commodities flowed overland between Indians and whites. Before and during the Mexican War the fort served as supply depot for military maneuvers.

William became the sole owner of the company after St. Vrain's retirement in 1849. Charles had sought other interests in the Mexican province of New Mexico; he settled in Taos in 1835, became the first appointed American governor of the province in 1846, and was killed in an Indian rebellion in January 1847. William thought he could profitably sell the fort to the United States, but the government offered what he believed was an insultingly low price. Angered, he blew up the fort in 1849. In 1853 William built Bent's New Fort 38 miles downstream from the junction of the Purgatoire and Arkansas Rivers, and in 1859 he leased the new fort to the government. William Bent died in 1869.

CHICAGO HISTORICAL SOCIETY

Thomas Hart Benton.

Benton, Thomas Hart

1782–1858

Thomas Hart Benton, born near Hillsborough, North Carolina, was a political writer, U.S. senator, leader of the Democratic Party during the Jackson era, and steadfast proponent of agrarian causes and westward expansion. The oldest of eight children, he redeemed the debt-ridden family estate after his father's death in 1791. After a series of youthful misadventures, several of a violent nature, Benton became a lawyer in 1806 and a Tennessee state legislator in 1809. He served in the War of 1812, but his temper got him into a brawl with General Andrew Jackson, whom Benton shot. Benton then moved to Missouri, where he killed a man in a duel. He served as editor (1818–1826) of the *Missouri Enquirer* and advocated a larger economic role for the West and for the United States through trade with the Far East.

In 1820 Benton was elected as one of the first U.S. senators from Missouri; he gained recognition as an unflappable spokesman for rapid westward settlement and commercial and agrarian development. He championed claims to Spanish and French land grants, and pursued development of the Rocky Mountain fur trade, and the construction of a na-

tional road, canal, and rail system linking East with West. As chairman of the Committee on Indian Affairs he was responsible for removing the Creek Indians from their land in Georgia so that whites could settle on it. In 1825 Benton and Andrew Jackson made up their differences; Benton became a leader of the Democratic Party and supported Jackson's dissolution of the Second Bank of the United States.

Although Benton was a slave owner and pro-Southern, he came to the conclusion that slavery should not be extended to the western territories for several reasons: the geography of the West was unsuited to that institution; slavery would not lead to full and proper national growth; and its spread would prove perilous for maintaining the Union. As the sectional controversy between slave and nonslave interests increased, Benton became unpopular; he lost his Senate seat in 1850, won a seat in the House of Representatives for the 1853–55 term, and lost his bid for the governorship in 1856. He rejected the newly founded Republican Party and even spoke against the Republican presidential nominee, his son-in-law John C. Frémont.

The ex-politician and advocate of Manifest Destiny was not embittered by the turn of events; he devoted the last years of his life to legal and political writings. His *Thirty Years' View* was a two-volume historical account of the U.S. government from 1820 to 1850; *Examination* refuted the Supreme Court ruling on the 1857 Dred Scott decision; and his 16-

volume *Abridgement of the Debates of Congress* encompassed the years 1789 to 1856.

Bierce, Ambrose

1842–CA. 1914

Ambrose Bierce was a journalist and short story writer, notorious in the West for his sarcasm and quick wit. Born in Ohio, Bierce served as a Union Army officer during the Civil War. He later trekked to San Francisco, where his contributions to the *Overland Monthly* and other local papers launched his career. As editor of the *News-Letter*, Bierce's satirical column of verse and commentary gained statewide attention. Although he spent many years in London and Washington, D.C., Bierce maintained a feisty presence in western publications. His "Prattle" column in the San Francisco *Examiner* was read avidly throughout the West Coast. Bierce eventually retired and traveled to Mexico. Although

a mystery surrounds his death, many believe he was killed during the siege of Ojinaga during the revolutionary turmoil of 1914.

The *Devil's Dictionary* (1906) includes numerous cynical definitions from his columns. His short stories are often compared to those of Poe for their elements of horror and of the supernatural. His best-known collection is *Can Such Things Be?* (1893). Bierce also published a 12-volume series, *Collected Works* (1909–1912).

Bierstadt, Albert

1830–1902

Landscape painter, recognized for his immense, romantic canvases of the Rocky Mountain and Hudson River regions. German by birth, Bierstadt was raised in Massachusetts but returned to Europe to study art at the famed Dusseldorf Academy. There he learned the expansive painting style of the Euro-

Ambrose Gwinnet Bierce.

Albert Bierstadt pours himself a drink in a double exposure taken by his brother.

Native Americans look on as Albert Bierstadt sketches in the Sierra Nevada.

pean Romantics. In 1858, he accompanied Frederick Landers on a survey party and laid eyes on the American West for the first time. The young artist was overwhelmed, and set out on his own to sketch the vast terrain. Bierstadt's immense canvases achieved greatest popularity during the 1860s and 1870s.

With the Civil War at an end, artists took in the vastness of the country in its entirety. Typical of the Rocky Mountain School, Bierstadt's canvases were enormous in size to reflect such images as the majestic, jutting peaks of the Rocky Mountains, tall pines, and the vastness of the Grand Canyon. His *Last of the Buffalo* (1888) warned of the vanishing of wildlife and of the Indians who depended on them.

Bierstadt's first Rocky Mountain pictures met with immediate success in 1860 at the National Academy of Design in New York City. The demand for his paintings in England soon made them the highest priced works of any American artist. But by the early 1880s, French Impressionism had gained public favor and relegated Bierstadt's panoramic views to a position of diminished prominence on the American art scene. Sales of his works declined, and he died in New York in 1902, almost forgotten by art critics and collectors. However, a peak in the Rocky Mountains was eventually named in his honor.

Two of his large canvases, *Discovery of the Hudson* and *Settlement of California,* hang in the Capitol in Washington, D.C.

Billy the Kid

1859–1881

Born Henry McCarty, probably in New York City, he moved west with his widowed mother and ended up in New Mexico in 1873. When his mother remarried, he took his stepfather's name, Antrim. Later he adopted the alias of William H. Bonney. Usually he was known as Billy or the Kid.

The Kid's life of crime began in Silver City, New

Billy the Kid.

Mexico, when he was 15. After a brush with the law over a petty theft, he fled to Arizona. There, in a saloon fight on August 17, 1877, he shot and killed "Windy" Cahill, an older and bigger man who had bullied him.

The Kid fled to southeastern New Mexico, where became embroiled in the Lincoln County War, a conflict between rival mercantile firms. Now 17, he signed on with the Tunstall–McSween "Regulators." In a series of gunfights with the Murphy–Dolan forces, he showed himself to be fearless and a crack shot. On April 1, 1878, he participated with five others in the ambush slaying in Lincoln of Sheriff William Brady. In the final battle in the McSween House in Lincoln, on July 19, he led the breakout in which some of the defenders escaped.

In 1879–1880, based at old Fort Sumner in eastern New Mexico, Billy and a handful of comrades rustled cattle from stockmen in the nearby Texas Panhandle. He intended to go straight but never quite got around to it. In December 1880, following a shootout at Stinking Springs, Sheriff Pat Garrett took him into custody. Convicted of the murder of Sheriff Brady and sentenced to be hanged, the Kid was held under guard in Lincoln. On April 28, 1881, he overpowered and killed his guard, fatally shot another deputy, and escaped. Newsmen now named him Billy the Kid.

Sheriff Garrett and his deputies tracked Billy to old Fort Sumner. There, on the night of July 14, 1881, Garrett accidentally confronted the fugitive in the darkened bedroom of one of the old military houses. Garrett fired twice, killing Billy instantly. The Kid was 21.

Fed by dime novels and later by motion pictures, a mighty legend took shape. Contrary to legend, however, Billy did not kill 21 men; he killed four on his own and participated in the killing of several more. He rustled cattle on a minor scale, but he never robbed a bank or store or stagecoach, or engaged in any other serious criminal activity. He was not the captain of an outlaw gang, nor was he a homicidal maniac. Instead, he was an intelligent, cheerful, and well-liked youth with a deadly temper. Despite the reality, Billy the Kid has become a legend cherished by people all over the world.

DENVER PUBLIC LIBRARY

A notice advertising a reward for the capture of Billy the Kid.

Black Bart

See Boles, Charles E.

Black Elk

1863–1950

A distant cousin of Crazy Horse, Black Elk was an Oglala Sioux holy man. He was born near the Little Powder River in Wyoming, and as a teenager, he fought in the battle on the Little Big Horn River in which George Armstrong Custer and his command were annihilated.

Following Crazy Horse's death at Fort Robinson, Nebraska, in 1877, Black Elk was taken by his family into Canada. After Sitting Bull's surrender at Fort Buford, Dakota Territory, in 1881, he and his family were placed on a South Dakota reservation. In 1886 Black Elk joined William F. "Buffalo Bill" Cody's Wild West show (as had Sitting Bull, a year earlier) and traveled with it in the United States and Europe. He returned from a European tour in time to witness the tragedy at Wounded Knee, on the Pine Ridge Reservation in South Dakota, in December 1890.

Black Elk was a lifelong mystic and visionary. His powers as a healer and his preaching on harmony with the changing world were celebrated not only among the Oglalas but also among former white adversaries. In 1930 he was visited on the Pine Ridge Reservation by the poet John G. Neihardt, who interviewed him extensively, translated his memoirs, and published them as *Black Elk Speaks* in 1932. The book was praised by Carl Jung, among others, as an important contribution to world philosophy.

In 1947, at the age of 84, Black Elk, by then one of the few surviving Sioux to have firsthand knowledge of the religion and teachings of his tribe, agreed to have the Sioux ceremonies and thought recorded for posterity. Joseph E. Brown, an anthropologist, translated and wrote Black Elk's testimony on these subjects; the book was published in 1953 as *The Sacred Pipe*. Black Elk died on August 17, 1950.

Black Hawk War

SPRING 1831–AUGUST 3, 1832

Led by Sauk war chief Black Hawk, one of the most implacable opponents of the white westward expansion, a group of approximately 300 Sauk (see Iowa) and Fox warriors, with women and children, crossed the Mississippi River into Illinois in the spring of 1831. Their intent was to take up residence in Saukenuk, their traditional summer camp (present day Rock Island, Illinois). Confronted by a U.S. Army force of 1,500 men, the Indians withdrew across the river into Iowa.

Black Hawk returned the following spring, crossing the Mississippi on April 5, 1832, with a band

GILCREASE INSTITUTE

Black Hawk, right, and his son, painted in 1833.

now estimated at 2,000 warriors, women, and children. A force of federal troops and state militia of equal strength, led by General Samuel Whiteside and Colonel Zachary Taylor, set out in pursuit a month later. A series of skirmishes ensued as Black Hawk's band slipped into Wisconsin. Other tribes, inspired by these successes, began to attack isolated settlements.

On June 15, President Andrew Jackson placed General Winfield Scott in command of the U.S. forces. Black Hawk proceeded west, planning to cross the Mississippi into Minnesota. His band, depleted by starvation and engagements with whites, had shrunk to about 500. On August 3, the federal troops, led by General Henry Atkinson, attacked near the confluence of the Mississippi and the Bad Axe. The resulting battle crushed Black Hawk's band and effectively ended his "war."

Besides Taylor and Scott, other future leaders who served in the action war included Jefferson Davis and Abraham Lincoln.

Black Hills

The Black Hills are a detached range of mountains whose peaks rise, on average, 4,000 feet above

Black Kettle

CA. 1810–1868

Black Kettle's age, parentage, and early life are disputed. By 1860, however, he was the leading peace chief of the Southern Cheyennes. He was highly influential even though ridiculed by the war faction for his consistent willingness to accommodate the whites.

The Southern Cheyennes ranged the buffalo plains of Nebraska and Kansas. The Santa Fe, Smoky Hill, and Oregon Trails cut across their homeland, and after the Civil War, railroads also began to encroach. In dealing with the Cheyennes, the federal government alternated diplomatic initiatives with military campaigns. Black Kettle invariably favored the treaty over the warpath, and he opposed the chiefs who believed war to be the only solution to the rising white threat. His mark headed the list of chiefs who signed the Fort Wise Treaty of 1861, by which the Cheyennes yielded all their lands in exchange for a small reservation south of the Arkansas River. The war chiefs, however, refused to sign, and the Indian War of 1864 resulted.

Black Kettle sought to end the war by negotiating with government officials. At a conference at Camp Weld, near Denver, he was told to take his people to

the prairie; they cover an area of 6,000 square miles in southwest South Dakota and northeastern Wyoming. Although the area was once the home of the Arapahos, Kiowas, and other tribes, it is most closely associated with the Lakota Sioux.

Driven west by constant warfare with the Ojibwa, the Sioux, led by Standing Bull, probably reached the Black Hills (which they called *Paha Sapa*) around 1775. Certainly by the time Lewis and Clark entered the region in 1803, the Sioux were firmly entrenched. The dark, wet, wooded hills stood in stark contrast to the dry grasslands below. Many Lakotas came to see Paha Sapa as sacred.

The Fort Laramie Treaty of April 29, 1868, included the Black Hills in the approximately 35,000 square miles set aside as part of the Great Sioux Reservation, despite rumors of gold in the mountains that began circulating as early as the 1850s. The treaty promised that the Reservation would be a permanent homeland for the Lakotas, but less than five years later white miners were encroaching on the Black Hills, prospecting for gold.

As demand for gold increased, however, the Army was ordered to make a reconnaissance of the area. In 1874, Lieutenant Colonel George Armstrong Custer entered the Black Hills. His main mission was to scout a location for a fort, but he also took prospectors with him to look for gold. Upon returning, Custer said that gold had been found; he was reported as stating that the Hills were teeming with gold "from the grass roots down." Within a year, 11,000 prospectors had invaded. By 1876, 25,000 whites were in the area.

The U.S. government offered first to lease and then to buy the Black Hills from the Lakotas. Although many were adamantly opposed to any transaction, the tribe named a price of $70 million. When the federal commissioners offered only $6 million, negotiations broke down. The stage was set for the Battle of the Little Bighorn.

In the aftermath of the battle, in 1877 the Lakotas were forced to cede the Black Hills. Since then the Lakotas have been unceasing in their efforts to recover Paha Sapa. In 1980, the U.S. Supreme Court affirmed a judgment awarding the Indians over $100 million in damages. The Lakotas, however, refused the award, demanding instead the return of the area.

STATE HISTORICAL SOCIETY OF COLORADO

Black Kettle.

Fort Lyon and surrender. At Fort Lyon, however, the military authorities instructed him to remain in camp on Sand Creek. In truth, Black Kettle's initiative interfered with plans to punish the Indians for summer raids on the travel routes to Denver, and to force them to vacate the lands supposedly yielded at Fort Wise. Black Kettle thought he was at peace, but at dawn on November 29, 1864, Colonel John M. Chivington and a cavalry force attacked the village and perpetrated the infamous Sand Creek Massacre, which took the lives of more than 100 people, most of them women and children.

In one of his many attempts to reach a peaceful settlement with the whites, Black Kettle dictated this letter.

In retaliation for Sand Creek, the Cheyenne war groups joined with the SIOUX to ravage the Plains settlements and travel routes, then withdrew far to the north. Black Kettle and the peace elements remained in the south. In October 1867, with chiefs of the Kiowas and Comanches, he again met with government emissaries and signed the Medicine Lodge Treaty. Like the Fort Wise Treaty, this document bound the Cheyennes to relinquish the Central Plains and settle on reservations to the south, in the Indian Territory.

Although Black Kettle took his own people south, other Cheyenne bands remained in their traditional areas. War erupted again in 1868. Black Kettle tried to stay out of it, but he could not control his young men. A raiding party left a trail in the snow that led to his village on the Washita River. At dawn on November 27, 1868, a military column under Lieutenant Colonel George Armstrong Custer launched a surprise attack. In the first charge, Black Kettle and his wife, seeking to escape, were cut down and fell dead in the icy waters of the river.

Blackfeet Indians

The Blackfeet are a group of Algonquian Native American tribes of the Northern Plains and Canada. They are often confused with the Lakota Sioux tribe that is also named Blackfeet.

The group is composed of the Piegan (or Pikuni), Blood (or Kainah), and the Blackfeet proper (or Siksika). These are separate tribes with a common language but their own organizations. In addition, the Gros Ventre of the Prairie (or Atsina), a division of the Arapahos, and the Sarsi, an Athapaskan-speaking tribe, are closely associated with the Blackfeet and are often erroneously referred to as Blackfeet. The Blackfeet may have migrated from the Northeast. When first encountered by whites in the eighteenth century, they were one of the most powerful groups of Native Americans on the Plains, holding a vast territory east of the Rockies in the United States and Canada. They were at continual war with their neighbors, including the Shoshones, Crees, Arapahos, and Crows.

After the Blackfeet became active in the fur trade, they came into more conflict with other tribes, in-

Bear Bull, Blackfoot medicine man.

Nomadic Canadian Blackfeet Indians lived in buffalo-hide lodges in temporary villages.

United States or Canada. During the campaigns to push all northern tribes onto reservations, U.S. cavalry attacked a peaceful Piegan village on the Marias River in Montana in January 1870. Of the 173 Indi-

cluding the Flatheads. Sometimes the Blackfeet raided the territory of other tribes in order to secure their own borders and to take buffalo. They also allowed both the British to establish trading companies and the United States to set up outposts in their domain. They seem to have reached the height of their power around 1830, with an estimated population of between 10,000 and 18,000 in their territory. But the 1836 smallpox epidemic wiped out half their people, and some villages lost as many as three-quarters of their population.

Although in some ways the fur trade helped the Blackfeet to secure their territory against other Native Americans, it did nothing to affect the demand for land by white settlers. In 1855, in a treaty with the United States that also permitted the building of U.S. roads and forts, Blackfeet territory was defined. The Blackfeet, in exchange, were to receive $20,000 per year for ten years, plus schools, missions, health care, various goods, and protection of their territorial integrity. Most of these promises were not kept.

The Blackfeet were aggressive in the defense of their own lands against other tribes, as well as the

A peace meeting between the Blackfeet and the Nez Perce and Flathead tribes in 1855, painted by Gustavus Sohon.

ans killed, 140 were women and children, 18 were old men, and only 15 were warriors.

Bodmer, Karl

1809–1893

A Swiss draftsman, painter, and etcher whose detailed work provides valuable documentary about Native Americans and landscapes of the American West, Karl Bodmer was selected by Prince Maximilian of Wied, a small German principality, to tour and document scenes of North America in 1832. The prince wanted Bodmer's drawings in order to increase European knowledge of the Native American inhabitants, who had received very little attention. Bodmer studied the paintings of George Catlin and Samuel Seymour to prepare for the two-year assignment. Maximilian and Bodmer set out from St. Louis, Missouri, aboard the American Fur Company steamer, the *Yellowstone,* and traveled up the Missouri River. Bodmer sketched Indians at every opportunity, often taking an entire day to create a single watercolor portrait. He worked meticulously, sketching the jewelry and costumes in great detail. In 1834 Bodmer returned to Europe and worked his sketches into colored engravings for the atlas of Maximilian's work, *Travels.* Bodmer resided in France until his death in 1893. The 427 original watercolors created during the expedition were discovered at Neuweid castle after World War II and are displayed at the Joslyn Art Museum in Omaha, Nebraska.

Boles, Charles E.

CA. 1830–CA. 1917

Little is known of Boles (who also used the name Charles E. Bolton), a California stagecoach robber known as Black Bart, other than his exploits against Wells Fargo during the period 1875–1883. He appears to have been a New Yorker who had come

LIBRARY OF CONGRESS

Karl Bodmer's portrait of Pehriska-Ruhpa, a Moennitarri warrior, in a Dog Dance costume.

LIBRARY OF CONGRESS

Charles E. Boles.

West as a young man, perhaps as a Forty-niner, and had served in the Civil War. In all, he robbed 28 stagecoaches of their strongboxes (he never robbed passengers) in northern California. He wore a linen duster and a flour-sack mask, and carried an unloaded shotgun. Twice he left good-natured verses behind, signed "Black Bart, the Po-8."

After a botched robbery in which he was slightly wounded, Boles was tracked down by a Wells Fargo detective. In November 1883 he pleaded guilty and was sentenced to six years in San Quentin penitentiary. After serving four years, he disappeared. A New York newspaper carried his obituary in 1917.

Bonanza Farms

Bonanza farms were expansive farms that flourished in the 1880s in the wheat fields of the north central prairies and plains. The bonanza farms thrived on the components of industrial capitalism—the application of machinery to mass production, absentee ownership, professional management, specialization, and cheap labor. These sprawling enterprises not only imitated the railroads' corporate design, but were also often formed on former railroad land.

After the Panic of 1873, the Northern Pacific Railroad went bankrupt. Bondholders could turn in their greatly depreciated bonds to obtain portions of its 50 million acres of land in Minnesota and North Dakota. The value for the land at the time was a mere $.37 to $1.65 per acre. Many investors, including the president of the Northern Pacific, George W. Cass, recognized the tremendous opportunity for acquiring huge tracts of land cheaply and had the necessary capital. Those who could purchase over 3,000 acres held title to what would be termed a "bonanza."

Cass and Benjamin Cheney, a director of the Northern Pacific, bought almost 13,500 acres near Casselton, North Dakota, paying about $.40 to $.60 per acre. Almost 90 such great land tracts were bought. They ranged between 15,000 and 50,000 acres. New developments in machinery and milling processes, together with the flat and fertile prairie land, high demand for wheat, and readily available labor force fueled these bonanza farm enterprises.

Most owners, such as the Amenia and Sharon Land Company of Sharon, Connecticut, hired managers and ruled the huge bonanza farms in absentia. Under the managers, the farms were divided and overseen using a professional management system of superintendents, each of whom oversaw several foremen. The mass labor force was often migrant, since fewer hands were needed during seeding and threshing seasons than during plowing and haying seasons. The enormous scale of the farms attracted national attention, and drew an inrush of settlers to the region. The hired men came from nearby homesteads, cities, and lumber camps and usually worked a 13-hour day for wages of $16 to $25 a month with room and board.

Many bonanza owners had assumed that such an operation would be temporary, yet some farms lasted for several years. Rising land taxes and the increasing value of the land, however, caused the dissolution of many bonanza farms with an almost guaranteed profit to the owners.

Bonney, William H.

See Billy the Kid

Boomers

In the eighteenth and nineteenth centuries, the term "boomers" was applied to migrants who moved illegally into land that had not been settled by non–Native Americans and that usually was owned by the federal government. The first example of such a squatter colony goes back to the 1760s, when settlers moved into areas as far-flung as the Old Northwest and West Florida in defiance of the Proclamation of 1763. A more spectacular example dates to 1875–1876, when some 15,000 miners invaded the Black Hills in search of gold.

The term achieved its greatest currency in Oklahoma, where boomers, led by ex-soldier David Payne, invaded lands owned by the Five Civilized Tribes. In spite of numerous arrests and forced removals by the U.S. Army, the boomers kept returning. Payne would continue to battle with U.S. authorities until his death in 1884. The movement he led undoubtedly hastened the opening of the Indian and Oklahoma Territories to white settlers.

Boone, Daniel

1734–1820

Born the son of Quakers living in Reading, Pennsylvania, Boone learned the rudiments of reading and writing, helped the family by farming and blacksmithing, and showed a keen talent for hunting and trapping. The family moved to North Carolina in 1750, and Daniel accompanied the Braddock Expedition to Fort Duquesne in 1755. He married Rebecca Bryan in 1756 but did not settle down to traditional domesticity. Although not the first explorer or discoverer of Kentucky, as legend has it, Boone entered Kentucky in 1767, and again in 1769, when he began a hunt that lasted two years, and traded with the

"Boonesborough" was founded by Boone in 1775.

Daniel Boone.

Shawnee Indians. In 1773, while he was leading several families to settle in Kentucky, his party was attacked by Cherokees; his son James was captured, tortured, and murdered.

Richard Henderson of the Transylvania Company hired Boone in March 1775 to blaze Boone's Trace, or the Wilderness Road, from Cumberland Gap, Virginia, to the Kentucky River; by September he had brought his wife and daughter to the fort and settlement of Boonesborough on the Kentucky River. As a captain in the county militia, he staved off Indian attacks on Boonesborough, but in 1778 he was captured by the Shawnees. He cooperated with them—their chief, Blackfish, adopted Boone as his son, calling him "Big Turtle." After five months Boone escaped and raced to warn the Boonesborough residents of an imminent attack by a joint force of British soldiers and Shawnees. Instrumental in the successful defense against a ten-day siege, Boone was promoted to major. The preservation of the fort proved vital to continued westward migration and settlement.

During the Revolutionary War, Boone served in Fayette County as lieutenant colonel of the militia, legislator, county lieutenant, and deputy surveyor. In 1781 he was captured in Charlottesville, Virginia, by the British under Colonel Banastre Tarleton and released after several days. In 1782 he saw action at

Bryan's Station and the Battle of Blue Licks. After the war Boone moved farther west, seeking less settled areas. He served as a legislator in present-day West Virginia; in 1799 he and his family joined his son Daniel Morgan Boone in Missouri, where he continued to hunt and trap and served as a magistrate.

Boone's continued failure to establish land claims and his indomitable wanderlust kept him moving about. He sold a land grant from the U.S. Congress in 1815 to pay off debts. He died in 1820 but was not forgotten; in 1823 Lord Byron immortalized the backwoods pioneer in buckskin in his poem *Don Juan:*

> Of all men, saving Sylla the man-slayer
> Who passes for in life and death most lucky,
> Of the great names which in our faces stare,
> The General Boon, back-woodsman of
>   Kentucky,
> Was happiest amongst mortals anywhere;
> For killing nothing but a bear or buck, he
> Enjoy'd the lonely, vigorous, harmless days
> Of his old age in wilds of deepest maze.
>
> (Canto VIII, stanza 61)

Boudinot, Elias

1803–1839

Boudinot, a noted Cherokee writer and political figure, was the editor of the first Indian newspaper. He was born Buck Watie (or Gallegina) but changed his name to Elias Boudinot in honor of his mentor of the same name, a former president of the Continental Congress and the president of the American Bible Society.

Educated at the Foreign Mission School in Cornwall, Connecticut, Boudinot early on became a proponent of Christianity and Indian assimilation. He is sometimes credited with being the first Native-American novelist, as the author of *Poor Sarah, or Religion Exemplified in the Life and Death of an Indian Woman*, probably written in 1823. The work, however, little more than a proselytizing pamphlet, is generally considered to have been copied from non-Indian sources. Later, Boudinot helped Samuel Worcester translate the Bible into Cherokee.

From 1824 to 1835 he served as the editor of the

LIBRARY OF CONGRESS

Elias Boudinot.

Cherokee Phoenix. Published in both English and Cherokee, it was the first Indian newspaper in the country. By the early 1830s, Boudinot, along with his cousin John Ridge and other influential Cherokees, became convinced that removal to the West was inevitable. He became a leading figure of the so-called Treaty Party, which advocated negotiation with the United States concerning removal. In 1835, he was a key figure in the negotiation of the Treaty of New Echota, which led to the infamous Trail of Tears. Upon moving to Indian Territory, Boudinot was considered a traitor by those who opposed removal. In 1839, he was ambushed and executed by members of the Cherokee Nation loyal to Principal Chief John Ross.

Bow and Arrow

Along with the tomahawk, the stereotypical weapon of the native peoples in the minds of whites was the bow and arrow. It was the typical weapon used in hunting and warfare before the introduction of firearms, although native tribes also employed spears, war clubs, and blowguns, among other weapons.

It is unknown when the bow and arrow came into

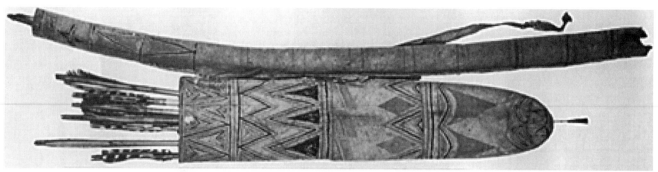

This Apache bow was a deadly weapon in the hands of a skilled warrior.

use among the native peoples of the Americas, but there is scant evidence for them before 500 C.E. By the time of Columbus's arrival in 1492, however, they were in almost universal use.

Depending upon the region, arrowheads were made of a variety of materials, including stone, bone, ivory, copper, and wood. The shaft could be of reed, wood, cane, ivory, or bone. Shafts might be in one piece or a composite of two pieces, sometimes of different material.

A wide variety of bows were used, differing in size, shape, and material. The Sioux bow, made of ash, was strung with two buffalo sinews. The northern Athapaskans produced long, straight bows of birch or willow. The Nez Perce bow, made from the horn of the mountain sheep, was reputedly the most prized bow on the Plains. Other tribes used hickory, oak, or other hardwoods. In the Arctic, whalebone and driftwood were often utilized.

Arrows were kept in a quiver and bows in a bow case. Sometimes these were attached to each other. Cases, quivers, arrows, and bows were often highly decorated.

A good warrior could nock and fire 20 arrows in the time it took to fire a single-shot firearm and re-load once. An arrow shot by an expert bowsman was effective up to 100 yards, and thus more accurate than early guns. In addition, muskets were much more awkward to fire from horseback.

Gradually, as firearms improved and more and more of them were acquired from whites, use of the bow and arrow gave way. Guns provided by white traders allowed the Ojibwas to push the Sioux westward and the Comanches to defeat the Apaches. In the end, the gun would have as major an impact on Native American culture and history as had the horse and metal implements.

Bowie, James

1796–1836

Known as Jim, Bowie was a Kentucky-born frontiersman, settler, and adventurer-turned-soldier who fought for Texas in the Texas Revolution of 1835–1836 and died in the defense of the Alamo. He moved to Louisiana when he was nineteen. There, with his brother Rezin, he allegedly traded in slaves with the pirate Jean Laffite. He served in the Louisiana legislature and was popular in New Orleans so-

James Bowie.

ciety. The Bowie knife, the "Arkansas Toothpick," a curved-tip fighting weapon with a blade of up to eighteen inches, is named for him, although Rezin probably was its designer. Jim moved to Texas in 1828 after reportedly using a Bowie knife to kill a man in a duel. Shortly thereafter, he became a Mexican citizen, married the daughter of the Mexican vice governor in 1831, and acquired vast tracts of land. However, his interest in the revolution against Mexico led Bowie to fight in the Battle of Nacogdoches (1832) and, in 1835, at Mission Concepción, and the Grass Fight. He was commissioned a colonel and joined his small force to that of Colonel William Barret Travis in the defense of an abandoned San Antonio mission known as the Alamo. Bowie contracted typhoid pneumonia and lay on his cot during the thirteen-day siege. He was killed when the superior force of Mexican troops under Santa Anna overran the mission. The massacre of the entire garrison forged the rallying cry "Remember the Alamo!" that soon led Texans under Sam Houston to victory over Santa Anna at the Battle of San Jacinto and to the declaration of Texan independence.

Bozeman Trail

The Bozeman Trail was a short-lived route through the Powder River country of the Sioux to the Montana gold fields in the 1860s. John Bozeman

and John Jacobs established the trail in 1863, cutting 400 miles off the normal route by way of the Great Salt Lake. The Bozeman Trail turned from the Oregon Trail on the North Platte River in Wyoming, crossed the Powder River, then swung around the Bighorn Mountains to Virginia City, Montana.

The U.S. Army established three forts along the trail in 1866 to protect travelers from Indian attacks. They were Forts Reno, Phil Kearny, and C.F. Smith. Angered by the military invasions, Cheyennes and Arapahos joined Red Cloud's Sioux for what would later be called the Red Cloud War of 1866–68. Throughout 1866, warriors harassed military columns and construction parties and closed the trail to emigrants. On December 21, 1866, near Fort Phil Kearny, a force of seven or eight hundred Indians ambushed and annihilated a command of eighty soldiers under Captain William J. Fetterman. In August 1867, massed warriors attacked details near Fort Phil Kearney and Fort C.F. Smith, but in the Wagon Box and Hayfield Fights were driven off by soldiers with newly arrived breech-loading rifles.

The Fetterman Massacre prompted military leaders to call for all-out war, but in Washington peace sentiment prevailed. A peace commission was sent to negotiate treaties with all the tribes of the Great Plains. The Fort Laramie Treaty of 1868, ending the Red Cloud War, provided for the abandonment of the three hated forts. It established the Great Sioux Reservation for those Indians who wished to give up the old free life, but reserved the Powder River country as "unceded Indian territory," to be occupied by the Indians so long as the buffalo endured. Although Red Cloud and many followers settled on the reservation, Sitting Bull, Crazy Horse, and other "nontreaties" remained in the unceded territory until forced out following the Custer debacle at the Little Bighorn.

Brand, Max

See Faust, Frederick Schiller

Branding

Branding, a type of mark ranchers burned and/or cut into livestock to identify ownership, made it easier for cowboys to keep track of animals during cattle drives. Many ranches were named after the brands used on the livestock.

Branding is an ancient system, dating back some 4,000 years. It is believed that the first brands used in the West were those of Hernán Cortés, who in the sixteenth century began marking his cattle with a series of three Latin crosses, using irons similar to fireplace pokers.

As cattle ranching grew into big business during

COLORADO HISTORICAL SOCIETY

Three sisters team up to brand a calf on their father's Colorado ranch. Branding was typically done by men, but Fritz Becker trained his daughters in all aspects of cattle ranching in the hopes that they would run his ranch after he died, which they did.

the nineteenth century, branding became a much more sophisticated operation. The average range cow was marked with a variety of brands from burning irons to sharp knives. Three basic brand types were used to code the herd: Letters and/or numbers, geometric symbols, and pictorial symbols. One cowboy recalled many cowhands who were highly skilled at reading the various combinations of brand codes, even though they could not read or write English. It was said that a good cowpuncher could understand the U.S. Constitution if it were properly branded on the side of a cow. Brands were generally read from left to right, or from head to tail.

The brand was usually applied when the animal was a calf. The calf was roped and held down, then the skin of its flank was stretched smooth. A hot branding iron was applied, burning through the animal's hair into its skin. This painful procedure was described by one cowboy as equivalent to a man sitting "in his bare skin on a red-hot stove for one minute." Sometimes creosote dip was applied to the wound to keep off flies. A good afternoon of branding usually ended with more than 300 animals marked. The left rear flank generally was the accepted area for branding, though the jaw and the side of the animal also could be branded. When cattle changed ownership, cowhands marked out or "vented" the old brand with a slash before putting on the new identification.

To keep track of the herd during cattle drives, various cuts were developed to help cowboys identify the animals for inventory. A jingle bob was a cut on the cow's ear that left the lower portion hanging down. A double over-bit was two triangles cut into the ear. The dewlap was an incision that left a piece of skin hanging three to four inches off an animal's brisket region. The wattle was a cut made into the loose skin of the animal's throat. The resulting flap was tucked inside the wound, leaving an identifying lump under the skin once the cut had healed.

Because of the many brands used and the perennial problem of cattle rustling, in 1848 the Texas legislature declared that all brands must be recorded with local officials. Brand books were kept at the county clerk's office, and ranchers had to study these marks before choosing a unique style of their own.

LIBRARY OF CONGRESS

Cattle brands used by some well-known ranches.

Brannan, Samuel

1819–1889

Pioneer Samuel Brannan, called "the first Forty-niner," came to California in 1846, having sailed around Cape Horn on the *Brooklyn*. He led a party of 238 Mormon settlers to Yerba Buena (as San Francisco was then called). In his first few months there, he established a flour mill, set up a printing press, and published California's first newspaper, the *California Star*.

In 1848, after the discovery of gold on the American River, Brannan cornered the mining supply and equipment market and set up a trading post at Sutter's Fort. During the first year of the California gold rush, he used his position as an elder of the church to divert money from Mormon miners' tithes to his own investments in merchandise and real estate. When Brigham Young sent agents from Salt Lake City to recover "the Lord's money," Brannan announced he would turn over the funds only "when I receive a receipt from the Lord." He was excommunicated from the church.

Brannan was so successful in his investments that he became California's first millionaire. At the peak of his career, in the gold rush years, he is said to have owned at least 20 percent of San Francisco and a similar percentage of Sacramento. In order to protect his vast holdings, he founded San Francisco's Vigilance Committee in 1849.

In 1851, Brannan led a filibustering expedition to the Hawaiian Islands. The failure of this strange mission ruined him financially, and his heavy drinking further contributed to his downfall. He died in poverty at Escondido, near San Diego, on May 14, 1889.

Bridger, James

1804–1881

Born in Richmond, Virginia, Bridger was apprenticed to a blacksmith in St. Louis. There he signed on with William H. Ashley's 1822 expedition to the upper Missouri to collect furs. He then trapped for Andrew Henry and participated in his first battle with the Blackfeet. In 1823 he accompanied Henry in the relief of Ashley after his defeat by the Arikaras.

KANSAS STATE HISTORICAL SOCIETY

James Bridger.

In 1823 Bridger was one of two men left to care for the legendary Hugh Glass after he was mauled by a grizzly bear. Sure that Glass would die, the two abandoned him and rejoined their company. However, Glass recovered and managed to get back to Henry's trading post. Later he found Bridger but, because of his youth, did not take revenge. In 1824 Bridger was one of an Ashley party, led by John H. Weber, that carried American trapping operations west of the Continental Divide. Bridger may have been the first white man to see the Great Salt Lake, although he thought it part of the Pacific.

For the next two decades, Bridger worked the beaver streams of the Rocky Mountains. He developed into one of the ablest of Mountain Men and trapper leaders. After Ashley, Bridger served his successors, Jedediah Smith, William Henry Jackson, and Milton Sublette; then the Rocky Mountain Fur Company; briefly joined a partnership with Thomas Fitzpatrick and Milton Sublette; and finally trapped for the American Fur Company.

No mountain man surpassed Bridger in wilderness skills, nor in the difficult art of survival in a country teeming with hostile Blackfeet warriors. In one of his many battles with native tribes he was struck by two arrows; he carried the head of one embedded in his back until the missionary Dr. Marcus Whitman removed it three years later.

Bridger married a Flathead woman, by whom he had three children. Subsequent wives, after her death, were a Ute and a Shoshone. The latter bore him two more children. Bridger acquired a national reputation as a teller of tall tales about the West—many of which turned out to be true.

With the decline of the fur trade, Bridger built a trading post to supply emigrants traveling on the Oregon Trail. Erected in 1843 on Black's Fork of the Green River in present southwestern Wyoming, Fort Bridger became an important way station for travelers to California and Oregon. Years of friction with Mormon authorities in Salt Lake City led to his ouster from the fort in 1853.

During the 1850s and 1860s, Bridger became a popular guide for emigrant trains and military exploring expeditions. He was chief guide for General Albert Sidney Johnston's army, which marched on Utah in the Mormon War of 1857–1858. In 1866 he served as a guide for Colonel Henry B. Carrington when the army built forts on the Bozeman Trail to the Montana goldfields. Bridger spent his last years on a farm near Kansas City, Missouri, where he died at the age of 77.

Brown, Clara

1803–1883

With tremendous resourcefulness, Aunt Clara Brown bought her own freedom from slavery and took many relatives and other blacks to begin a new life in Colorado after the Civil War.

Born in Virginia in 1803, Brown was sold with her mother to a slave owner who traveled west. Several years and owners later, she purchased her own freedom. In 1859 she convinced a group of gold prospectors in St. Louis, Missouri, to hire her as a cook and

Clara Brown.

three years later she joined a wagon train across the Plains into Colorado.

Central City, Colorado, became home to 59-year-old Brown, who threw all her energy into earning enough money to free her family from slavery. In addition to operating her own laundry business and working as a nurse, Brown devoted time to the community. She helped start the first Sunday School in West Denver and Central City, and opened her home for services while the church was being constructed. Through the years she invested in mining claims when she could, and by 1866 she had earned an incredible $10,000.

After the Civil War, Brown searched desperately for her family. She found 34 relatives, bringing them to Leavenworth, Kansas, by steamboat and then across the Plains to Denver in a wagon she'd bought herself. "Aunt Clara" sponsored many other black wagon trains in her lifetime, and was finally reunited with her daughter shortly before she died in 1883. The Colorado Pioneers Association of Central City buried her with honors.

Brown, John

1800–1859

Abolitionist and leader of armed resistance to proslavery forces in "Bleeding Kansas" during the turbulent 1850s, John Brown led raids throughout Kansas and Missouri to block the movement of slavery westward. After trying to incite a major slave uprising with a raid on the United States arsenal at Harpers Ferry, Virginia, Brown was convicted of treason and executed in 1859. He is a controversial figure: a martyr to some and a murderer to others.

Brown's crusade against slavery took place late in his life. He had tried and failed at over 15 businesses, moving around New England and the Midwest with his family of twenty children from two marriages. At age 49 he finally settled in North Elba, New York, where wealthy abolitionist Gerrit Smith had established a farming community for free blacks.

In 1855, five of Brown's sons joined the Kansas free soil movement to prevent slavery from spreading into the western territories. But living near the

John Brown.

border at Osawatomie made them targets for violence from Missouri pro-slavery groups. The strong-willed Brown left his wife and younger children to bring guns and ammunition to the troubled region and on May 24, 1856, he and his small band attacked two pro-slavery families and took five lives in what became called the Potawatomi Creek Massacre. For months Brown led guerrilla-style attacks in Kansas, convinced that a conspiracy existed to oust the free-soilers and that he was God's tool for revenge.

In 1857 free-staters gained control of the Kansas legislature and Brown headed south to plan a large-scale slave revolt. The raid at Harpers Ferry (in Virginia, although today this area is in West Virginia) failed when the slave uprising he expected never occurred. He was hanged on December 2, 1859. John Brown had lived in Kansas less than two years, but remains one of the most controversial figures in Kansas history.

Bryan, William Jennings

1860–1925

Few figures in public life better embodied the complexities of American politics than William Jennings Bryan, "the Great Commoner." On the one hand, he was an ardent supporter of Free Silver (the position for which he is best remembered), an unflagging opponent of American imperialism and the urban party machines of his era, and an advocate of government ownership of railroads. On the other, he was a strong advocate of fundamentalist Christianity, the chief attorney for the prosecution in the Dayton, Tennessee, trial of John Scopes for teaching evolution, and a firm believer in agrarian values.

Bryan was the son of a well-to-do farmer and politician, born in Salem, Illinois, and educated at Whipple Academy and Illinois College. After two years at Union College of Law in Chicago, he practiced law without distinction in Jacksonville, Illinois, from 1883 to 1887. At the urging of friends, he moved to Lincoln, Nebraska, and began to pursue a career in politics.

In 1890, Bryan won election to the first of two terms in the U.S. House of Representatives. In that time, he established himself as one of the leaders of the Free Silver movement, an opponent of protective tariffs, and a key spokesman for western regional interests, "the boy orator of the Platte." After an unsuccessful Senate campaign (when state legislators still chose U.S. senators), he spent a year and a half editing the Omaha *World-Herald*, using it to advance his political career, and building up the Free Silver forces within the Democratic party. He hoped for the presidential nomination in 1896.

Only 36, Bryan went to the 1896 Democratic Convention fully expecting to be the party's nominee, and after his brilliant, rousing, and oft-quoted "Cross of Gold" speech at that gathering, his nomination was inevitable. He spoke for westerners who had been battered by the recent depression, by what they perceived as the unfair monetary policies of eastern mercantile interests. In the campaign that followed, a watershed political race that helped redefine American politics, he was tireless. He traveled over 18,000 miles through 27 states. He easily carried the West and the traditionally Democratic South, but his virtually single-issue campaign had little appeal for voters in the industrial states of the East and Midwest.

Bryan would repeat his performance in two more presidential elections, losing to McKinley again four years later and to Taft in 1908. In 1912, he helped throw the Democratic convention to Woodrow Wilson and was named secretary of state for his efforts. He worked for better relations with Latin America, and resigned in protest over Wilson's rebuke to the Germans after the *Lusitania* sinking in 1915. For the last decade of his life, he devoted himself to antimilitarism, prohibition, and fundamentalist Christianity, once more catching the national spotlight (with disastrous results) in the famous Scopes trial.

Buffalo

"Buffalo" is a common name for the American bison, the short-horned shaggy bovine that was crucial to the lives of the native peoples of North America. A full-grown bull can stand six and a half feet high at the shoulders and weigh 2,000 pounds.

At the time the Europeans arrived, it is estimated that there were as many as 60 million buffalo in North America. They ranged over most of the continent from the Allegheny Mountains to the Rockies and from northern Mexico to western Canada. The eastern bison was a woodland creature and seldom lived in large herds. It was extinct east of the Mississippi by the end of the eighteenth century.

Though these eastern animals were known and hunted by native peoples, it is the buffalo of the western Plains that is most closely associated with

Native Americans. In the early nineteenth century the buffalo population is estimated to have been between 15 and 50 million. They roamed in herds that could number in the hundreds of thousands, covering the land as far as the eye could see. One traveler claimed that one could walk on the backs of a herd from horizon to horizon and never touch the ground. Another estimated that he rode through one herd for 100 miles. It was said that the earth shook and that there was a sound like thunder when these great herds moved.

The buffalo provided almost everything necessary for the Plains tribes who hunted them. The meat provided food. The hides were tanned and made into clothing, shelter, and leather goods. The bones, hooves, and horns were cut or carved into household tools and other implements. The sinew became bindings. The brains, fat, and liver were used to tan the hides. The dung was used as fuel.

Although whites began hunting as soon as they arrived in the West, the wholesale slaughter of the buffalo did not begin until after the Civil War. The expansion of the railroads, the introduction of the repeating rifle, and increased settlement made buffalo hunting simple and easy; between 1866 and 1887, millions upon millions of the animals were exterminated. Much of the friction between the Plains tribes and the settlers is attributable to the destruction of the buffalo. Professional hunters would kill entire herds, cutting out only the tongue (prized as a delicacy in the East) and sometimes skinning the corpses, leaving the rest to rot.

The destruction of the buffalo was also approved of as a means of prosecuting the Indian Wars. Killing off the buffalo deprived the tribes of food and disrupted their economy. It was thought that once the buffalo were gone, it would be a simple matter to turn the native tribes into settled farmers.

The northern herds were wiped out by 1884, and the last band of the southern herds was killed in 1887. The last wild buffalo was killed in Oklahoma in October 1890. In the mid-twentieth century, a small number were released into the tall grass prairie in hopes of generating a wild herd once more.

WALTERS ART GALLERY

Indians chase a herd of buffalo over a cliff in a painting by Jacob Miller.

Buffalo Bill

See Cody, William

Buffalo Soldiers

"Buffalo Soldiers" was the name given to the black soldiers of the U.S. regular army who fought Indians and policed the western frontier in the decades following the Civil War. "Buffalo" derived from the men's hair, which the Indians thought resembled the woolly fur of the buffalo. The name originated with the 10th Cavalry, and eventually a buffalo became the central ornament of the regimental crest. In time, however, all the "blacks in blue" adopted the label and bore it with pride.

The Army Act of July 28, 1866, authorized a regular army that included two cavalry and four infantry regiments composed of black enlisted men and white officers: the 9th and 10th Cavalry and the 38th through 41st Infantry. When the army was reduced in 1869, the four infantry regiments were consolidated into the 24th and 25th. These were the outfits that came to be known in the West as the buffalo soldiers.

Not all the recruits were former slaves. Most, in fact, were free blacks of Northern parentage, and many had served with distinction in U.S. Colored Troops units during the Civil War. In sharp contrast to the white units, the black regiments consistently had the lowest desertion and the highest reenlistment rates in the army. A regular if modest income, shelter, clothing, and an enviable status for the times made military service very attractive to blacks confronted with racism and limited economic opportunity. As the years passed, the four black regiments grew heavy with veterans and developed conspicuous unit pride and esprit de corps. Eighteen soldiers won the Medal of Honor for feats of heroism in the Indian Wars.

Despite their proven worth, the black regiments endured racial prejudice. In 1873 an officer's wife, praising a commander for abolishing racially mixed guards, recorded a typical sentiment: "It was outrageous to put white and black in the same little guard room, and colored sergeants over white corporals and privates." Most officers of black units took pride in their men but suffered social condescension and even ostracism from the rest of the officer corps. Worse yet, the black regiments were discriminated against in both quantity and quality of supplies, equipment, and horses. For twenty-five years they remained without relief in the most difficult and dangerous sectors of the frontier.

Nevertheless, they wrote a record of distinction.

MONTANA HISTORICAL SOCIETY

10th Cavalry soldiers in Montana.

LIBRARY OF CONGRESS

An unidentified buffalo soldier photographed in South Dakota at the end of the Indian wars.

Their most arduous and significant service occurred in the deserts and mountains of West Texas, New Mexico, and Arizona. In particular, the warfare with the Apache chief Victorio in 1879–1880 was difficult. In New Mexico, 9th cavalrymen under Major Albert P. Morrow scoured a tangle of rugged peaks and canyons, struggled through rain and mud and heat and dust, lived on salt pork and mule meat, endured thirst, walked when their horses broke down, and fought when they could find the enemy. In Texas, 10th cavalrymen under Colonel Benjamin H. Grierson endured similar hardships in an effort to head off Victorio when he took refuge in Mexico. Twice, Grierson seized critical water holes and forced the Apaches back into Mexico, where Mexican troops finally attacked and killed Victorio.

A memorable triumph occurred at the very close of the Indian Wars, in the Ghost Dance campaign in South Dakota in 1890. After the tragedy at Wounded Knee, the famous 7th Cavalry, once led by Custer, allowed itself to be drawn into a trap at Drexel Mission. As the Sioux closed in and threatened to overwhelm the 7th, Major Guy V. Henry's squadron of the 9th rode to the rescue.

Typically, infantry duty was less glamorous than cavalry duty. Foot soldiers garrisoned the fort, guarded the supply depot, and escorted the wagon trains. The infantry also built roads, bridges, and telegraph lines. The 24th and 25th Infantry saw some action, but the 9th and 10th Cavalry took the battle honors.

Although they were less exciting, in the long run the constructive achievements were of more lasting value than chasing Apaches. The black troops left many monuments to their service in more than a quarter-century on the frontiers of the Southwest and the Great Plains.

Buffalo Soldiers earned their reputation in the Indian Wars but served creditably in the Spanish-American War and well into the twentieth century. Their history ended in 1950, when President Harry S. Truman abolished black units and integrated the armed services.

Buntline, Ned

See Judson, Edward Z. C.

Bureau of Indian Affairs

The Bureau of Indian Affairs is the government agency charged with administering all federal responsibilities toward Indian tribes except medical care, which was transferred to the U.S. Public Health Service in 1954.

When Congress established the War Department in 1789, it assigned Indian affairs to the secretary of war but provided no staff for the function. Not all relations with native peoples were hostile, and the increasing number of treaties created federal obligations that had to be administered. In 1806, with congressional authorization of government trading houses to conduct trade, the office of superintendent of Indian trade was placed in the War Department, and this official gradually took over Indian affairs from the secretary. In 1822, however, Congress abolished the trading houses, throwing the burden back on the secretary of war. Secretary of War John C. Calhoun set up an Indian Bureau within the department and placed Thomas L. McKenney, former superintendent of Indian trade, in charge. It was not until 1832 that Congress authorized the post of commissioner of Indian affairs as a presidential appointment within the War Department. In 1849 the bureau was transferred to the newly created Department of the Interior, where it remains today.

The principal task of the bureau was to manage the reservations. As the result of treaty, conquest, or the growing scarcity of game and other resources on which the native people depended for food, one tribe after another was forced to settle on a reservation. By the 1880s, the bureau had 2,000 to 3,000 employees and governed the affairs of 260,000 Native Americans assigned to 138 reservations, mostly in the West.

On the reservations the Indian agents and their staffs pursued a twofold program: They sought to control the native tribes and keep them away from the corridors of westward expansion and the white settlements growing up all over the West. The agents also sought to "civilize" the tribes, to transform them into Christian farmers embracing the values of nineteenth-century white Americans. The goal, as one bureau head phrased it with unconscious irony, was "to make the Indian feel at home in America." Employing an elaborate system of rewards and penalties, agents, schoolteachers, farming instructors, missionaries, native police, and sometimes soldiers labored to attain these two objectives.

A vital feature of the civilization policy, embodied in law by the Dawes Act of 1887, was allotment of reservation lands in individual parcels to heads of families. Administration of the allotment program was a major responsibility of the Indian Bureau. Allotment, proponents argued, would make every man a farmer supporting his own family. This would free people from dependence on government handouts, break down tribal allegiance, and promote "progress." The effect was less happy: Reservation lands, most of them unsuitable for farming, were endlessly subdivided as they passed from one generation to the next.

Bureau personnel were among the least qualified of any federal agency. Patronage politics controlled appointments, from the commissioner down to the lowest clerk or blacksmith. Service to a political party rather than knowledge or experience was the basis for selection. To make the situation even worse, the agency was a dumping ground for party hacks who could not be placed elsewhere. Each time the White House changed parties, so did virtually every post in the Indian Bureau.

In addition to ignorance and inefficiency, Indian Bureau personnel labored under constant and often well-founded accusations of fraud and corruption. The millions of dollars in supplies, rations, and other merchandise issued each year in fulfillment of treaty obligations offered abundant opportunities for graft. Not all agents were crooked, but enough were to give the Indian Bureau a reputation for corruption that lasted into the twentieth century.

The native tribes suffered severely from misguided policies applied by personnel who were incompetent, dishonest, or both. Most of the Indian Wars grew out of intolerable conditions on the reservations. The native peoples bolted, the army pursued, and at war's end the people returned to their reservation homes. Military officers complained of having to risk their lives in a war that had been caused by their own government's bungling. For 30 years they campaigned to have the Indian Bureau transferred back to the War Department, a source of contention that further hampered its effectiveness. Several times Congress came close to voting the measure, but the opposition of humanitarian groups and, for congressmen, the prospect of lost patronage raised powerful obstacles.

With the election of Franklin D. Roosevelt in 1932, the Indian Bureau entered a new phase. Crusading reformer John Collier became commissioner of Indian Affairs and won a major reversal of the old policies. The "Indian New Deal" and the Indian Reorganization Act of 1934 set the bureau on a course of reviving tribal traditions and encouraging self-determination. Much of Collier's work, however, was undone by the disastrous "termination" program of the Eisenhower years, which aimed at ending all government responsibility for Native Americans and setting them adrift in the larger society. After termination was discarded, the Red Power movement of the 1970s further weakened the Indian Bureau. Throughout the twentieth century, the agency has continued to be rocked by controversy.

Butterfield, John

1801–1869

John Butterfield was born and raised in Berne, near Albany, New York, and after a public school education began his career as a stagecoach driver in Albany at the age of 19. After settling in Utica, New York (1822), he became manager of the mail stage line between Albany and Buffalo. Intent on expanding his interests, he acquired a controlling share in several stagecoach lines in central New York and invested in steamers on Lake Ontario and the St. Lawrence River. In Utica he organized the first horse-drawn street railway system and the first local steam railroad.

Butterfield and Wasson and Company, organized

Butterfield Station workers transfer goods and stagecoach passengers to a more practical "celerity wagon" built for the harsh country.

in 1849 as an express mail business, was Butterfield's first venture; consolidation the following year with Livingston & Fargo and Wells & Company led to the formation of the American Express Company. This firm was awarded a $600,000 congressional contract in 1857 to operate the first transcontinental stage line. In 1858, to fulfill a personal contract awarded him to carry mail between San Francisco and the Missouri River, Butterfield founded the Overland Mail Company. He served as president until 1860, when a conflict with the other directors of the company resulted in his leaving.

Butterfield was involved in the founding of the New York, Albany and Buffalo Telegraph Company in association with Henry Wells and Crawford Livingston; built the Butterfield House and Garder block in Utica; and in 1856 served as mayor of Utica, where he died on November 14, 1869.

C

Cabeza de Vaca, Álvar Núñez

CA. 1490–1557

Born Álvar Núñez de Vera in Jerez de la Frontera, near Seville, Spain, he adopted the name Cabeza de Vaca (Cow's Head) from the thirteenth-century exploit of an ancestor, leader of a Christian army against the Moors, who used a cow's skull to mark a mountain pass.

Cabeza de Vaca was a *hidalgo* (landed aristocrat) and a veteran soldier by 1528, when, as a member of the ill-fated 260-man expedition of Pánfilo de Narváez, he landed on the west coast of Florida. He and three other men—captains Andrés Dorantes and Alonso del Castillo, and Dorantes's slave, a black man named Esteban—were the only survivors of the Narváez expedition. They made their way to Malhado (Bad Luck) Island—possibly Galveston Island—on the Gulf coast of Texas; Cabeza de Vaca lived as a medicine man and trader among the Charucco Indians on the Texas mainland until September 1532, when he and his companions began their trek westward.

Their three-year, 6,000-mile odyssey from the east coast of Texas across the trackless deserts of the Southwest—modern-day Texas, New Mexico, Arizona, and northern Mexico from Chihuahua to Sinaloa—to Culiacán on the Gulf of California, is among the epic journeys of world history. The native tribes they encountered welcomed the bearded, half-naked, sun-baked white men as healers, and

sometimes gods; taught them to eat the fruit of the prickly pear cactus; provided meat by bringing down deer and buffalo; and followed them, often in huge retinues, as they continued westward and south-

Álvar Núñez Cabeza de Vaca.

59

westward. On other occasions, Cabeza de Vaca and his companions were virtual slaves of some tribes, and feared for their safety.

In northwestern Mexico, the travelers finally encountered time signs of other Spaniards: they found wandering, starving Indians and deserted and burned-out villages, the work of Spanish slave hunters. In the spring of 1536 the wanderers, accompanied by several hundred Pimas who had earlier befriended them, encountered a Spanish soldier, a lieutenant in the service of the chief slave hunter and acting governor of the region, Núñez de Guzmán.

Cabeza de Vaca's journey ended in April 1536, when he and his companions reached Culiacán and reported to the Spanish viceroy there. They were welcomed as heroes in Mexico City the following July—nearly eight years after they had landed on the Florida coast. Castillo and Dorantes traveled to Spain with Cabeza de Vaca, then returned to Mexico, where they lived out their lives as wealthy men. The slave Esteban, who served as a guide and interpreter for Fray Marcos de Niza's explorations in search of the Seven Cities of Cíbola, was captured by Zuni Indians in 1539 near the present-day border between New Mexico and Arizona, and put to death as a spy.

In Spain, Cabeza de Vaca wrote an account of his travels as part of the viceroy's report to the crown, then expanded his own narration into a book titled *Los náufragios* (The Shipwrecked), which was published in 1542. By then, he was in Brazil and Paraguay as captain-general of the Río de la Plata provinces. After a year there, he was deposed and imprisoned by Spanish authorities. He returned to Spain, then, after a brief exile in North Africa, retired. Cabeza de Vaca, described by Samuel Eliot Morison as "a tall man with a bright red beard," and considered by Morison and other historians as among the more enlightened, humane, capable, and honest sixteenth-century conquistadores, died in Seville on September 15, 1557.

Calamity, Jane

See Martha Canary

California

Stretching between the Pacific Ocean and the Cascade and Sierra Nevada mountain ranges, California is the most economically productive and populous U.S. state today. Since gold was discovered in 1848, it has attracted millions in search of a better life. California's remarkable landscape includes the highest point in the continental United States, Mount Whitney (14,491 feet), and the lowest point in the Western Hemisphere, Death Valley (282 feet below sea level). Almost half of its forests lie in 22 national parks.

Indians had lived in California for thousands of years before Europeans came. Although minor English and Russian claims along the rocky California coast existed as early as 1579, the first settlement was established in 1769 by Captain Gaspar de Portola, the Spanish governor of Baja California. Father Junipero Serra accompanied the expedition and

California is shown as an offshore island in this 1650 map.

founded a mission near San Diego. Over the next fifty years, Franciscans founded 21 missions. These controlled great landholdings and used Indian labor.

After Mexico gained independence from Spain in 1821, vast private land holdings called *ranchos* were created as the government sold the mission lands. California was ceded to the United States under the Treaty of Guadalupe Hidalgo after the Mexican War (1846–1848). Only days before the treaty was signed, however, gold was discovered at Sutter's mill near Sacramento. The news soon brought tens of thousands of Forty-niners to stake claims.

California became the 31st state in the Union under the Compromise of 1850, and Sacramento became the permanent capital in 1854. California was a free state, although violence against Indians, Mexicans, Chinese, and blacks was common. The Civil War had little direct effect on California, although its position as a free (nonslavery) state was crucial. Gold production dwindled by the early 1850s and citrus and grain farms flourished.

The first transcontinental railroad was completed in 1869. The 30,000 Chinese laborers who had been brought over to help build the western section, the Central Pacific, remained in California and were often willing to work for lower wages than the white settlers. These Chinese faced violent discrimination during the depressed economy of the 1870s, and in 1882 the federal government banned further Chinese immigration.

The Southern Pacific, successor to the Central Pacific, quickly turned into a powerful political machine and ruled state government for decades. Only

with the election of Governor Hiram W. Johnson in 1911 was the state freed from the company's iron grip. Johnson successfully pushed Progressive reforms, such as the workmen's compensation, to make the government more responsive to popular needs.

California Gold Rush

1848–1852

Although it had some small-scale forerunners in Georgia and the Carolinas, the chance discovery

LIBRARY OF CONGRESS

A driftwood Yurok Indian house in California's gold rush country, sketched by Forty-niner J. Goldsborough Bruff.

AMON CARTER MUSEUM, FORT WORTH, TEXAS

A romantic painting of California as a golden paradise depicts harvest time near San Jose.

Miners at work.

Simple, sturdy machinery was practical for year-round use at Nome Beach.

of gold a hundred miles northeast of San Francisco marked the opening of the first great American gold rush. Others would follow—gold in the Fraser River country of British Columbia in 1858, at Pike's Peak in Colorado in 1859, in Idaho, Montana, the Black Hills, the Klondike in Canada's Yukon Territory in 1896, and in Nome, Alaska, in 1900—but none had the impact on Western history, in truth as well as myth, as what followed the spotting of a gold particle in a millrace on the American River on January 24, 1848, on the heels of the war with Mexico.

It is a curious fact of history that the Spaniards, who tirelessly searched for gold in the new world, ruled Alta California up to the moment of the strike at Sutter's Mill and yet never seem to have searched for gold in their westernmost American territory. Neither, for that matter, did the man who discovered it, a 38-year-old former New Jersey carpenter named James Wilson Marshall.

In 1848, Marshall was in partnership with the German-born Swiss immigrant John Augustus Sut-

ter, a man whose Mexican land grants had enabled him to build an agricultural empire in the Sacramento Valley of northern California and to establish Sutter's Fort (near the present-day capital city of Sacramento) as capital of what he called New Helvetia. Marshall, that auspicious January 24, was building a sawmill on the south fork of the American River, 50 miles north of Sutter's Fort, when he stumbled upon one of the richest placer gold deposits of history nine days before the signing of the Treaty of Guadalupe Hidalgo, which ended the war with Mexico and ceded California to the United States.

(Gold is chemically inert and retains its form and composition even after eons of erosion and weathering. Most gold, unlike silver, for example, comes from placer deposits rather than veins in rocks. Placer gold, eroded and weathered from rocks and abraded into dust, flakes, and nuggets, is washed free and ends up, mixed with sand and gravel, in streambeds. The placer miner of 1848–1852 had to remove the gold through various methods of washing the debris that contained it—by gold pan, rockers, and sluices.)

The first public notice of the strike on the American River appeared in a San Francisco newspaper on March 18, 1848, under the heading "GOLD MINE FOUND." The news became known in New York by summer when a soldier serving in California reported it in the *New York Herald*. Within a few

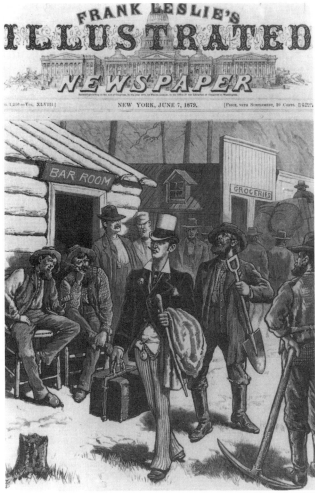

This 1879 illustration mocks the fastidious appearance of a moneyed easterner trying to jump on the gold rush bandwagon. Established miners considered such newcomers unsuited for the rough life of a prospector.

of the grand "adventure" of crossing the plains, deserts, and mountains to the goldfields. In fact, the journey was not only difficult but exceedingly dangerous. In 1849, the most frenetic year of the California gold rush, an estimated 90,000 aspiring Forty-niners departed from various points on the map for California. Only about half this number actually reached the Sacramento Valley.

The greatest number of Forty-niners were farmers and tradesmen (fewer than 2 percent of those on the Overland Trail in 1849–1850 were women); some came as far away as China, Latin America, and Europe; many were opportunists, seeing California as a way to escape the law or home responsibilities or simply as a way to a new life and a second chance. A popular mining camp song portrayed those who came west to escape:

Oh, what was your name in the States?
Was it Thompson or Johnson or Bates?
Did you flee for your life or murder your wife?
Say, what was your name in the States?

One thing that saved the lives of overland travelers was the companies formed for mutual assistance and protection—particularly against Indians, the single most frightening prospect of the journey to easterners. Many of the companies and individual travelers outfitted along the Missouri River and started west via the Overland Trail out of Independence, Missouri, or Council Bluffs, Iowa. They followed the Platte and Sweetwater rivers to South Pass, journeyed around the southern Salt Lake to the Humbolt River (which the Forty-niners called the "Humbug" since it was usually dry), then through the desert to the foothills of the Sierra and across the Sierra's treacherous mountain ridges, streams and ravines to the Sacramento Valley.

Others followed the Santa Fe Trail out of Independence. Some took this route by traveling over the Kansas prairies, following the Arkansas River to Bent's Fort in southern Colorado, and taking the Raton Pass south into New Mexico and Santa Fe. Others opted for the Cimarron Cutoff, drier and more dangerous, but time-saving, across Glorieta Pass and into Santa Fe. There, after rest and recuperation, most of the Santa Fe Trail goldseekers headed south, following the Gila River and crossing Arizona and perhaps joining other expeditions coming west from Texas and New Orleans to cross the deserts of Ari-

weeks, the western foothills of the Sierra Nevada were swarming with prospectors; by the end of the year President James K. Polk had acknowledged reports from the goldfields in his farewell address to Congress; by January 1849, shipping companies were frantically signing up passengers for the long and difficult voyage from East Coast ports to Cape Horn, or via the Panama or Nicaraguan routes to the Pacific.

Popular guidebooks appeared in the East, most often written by entrepreneurs whose knowledge of the journey was limited to outdated maps, newspaper accounts, and wishful thinking. These painted an imaginative and for the most part fraudulent picture zona and southern California to the coast, and then picking up a steamer to San Francisco.

In all cases, the journey west was costly in time (100 days from the Missouri to the Sacramento via the Overland Trail was considered an excellent average) and trouble. As many as 1,500 people died along the trail in 1849 from cholera; hundreds of others died of tick and Rocky Mountain spotted fever, scurvy, drowning, raids by Mexican bandits and Indians, sunstroke, cold, thirst, and hunger. For those coming long distances from the east, the exuberant "Ho for California!" and "California or Bust!" signs on overloaded mule and ox wagons hid the miseries of the overland routes to the New Eldorado: mud, rain, hail, snow, storms, clouds of mosquitos and sand fleas, scant grass for the grazing of the oxen, horses and mules, the incessant search for water and game. The Overland Trail travelers had the added daily worry of reaching the eastern foothills of the Sierras before autumn, when snow would block the passes to the west.

The sea routes to California required a considerable (for 1849) cash outlay—$300 minimum, $450 for a Pacific Mail steamer out of New York—to book the passage. The main routes were around Cape Horn or overland via Panama's Chagres River to Panama City and the Pacific. The latter required transportation by canoe or other shallow-water vessel for the three-day, 40-mile trip from the Chagres to the Pacific. Then the traveler had to wangle and jostle for a berth on a California-bound steamer. These routes took an average of six months from an eastern seaboard port to San Francisco.

At the time of James Marshall's discovery on the American River, the whole of the sleepy frontier outpost of Alta California had a population of about 14,000. Most of the permanent residents were of Spanish-Mexican origin and scattered about small settlements from San Diego to San Francisco. By the end of 1849 the population had swollen to 100,000; that of Sacramento, at Sutter's Fort, was now 12,000. Placer gold claims were being worked from the Trinity River on the north as far as the Tuolummne on the south—a 400-mile stretch of gold-bearing streams that included the Feather, Yuba, American, Stanislaus, and Merced, and a field that ran to the western edge of the Sierra.

In 1848–1849, with gold selling at $15 to $16 an ounce, a miner working hard at the back-breaking toil of panning or shoveling sand and gravel into a rocker or cradle, or the "Long Tom"—a lengthy sluice which greatly increased the amount of gravel that could be washed—might earn $16 a day, although a half-ounce of gold per day was considered a bare subsistence wage. It is estimated that one in a hundred earned more than these meager wages, even during the 1849–1850 peak period. By 1852, at the end of the boom, miners were lucky to earn $5 a day at their claims.

The California gold strike gave the post-Mexican War national economy a needed boost and produced even more significant and lasting benefits: it helped California bypass territorial status and move swiftly from a conquered Mexican province in 1848 to the 31st state of the Union in 1850, and it provided the new state with the pioneering population that transformed it into a prosperous land.

John A. Sutter died in 1880 in Washington, D.C., where he had gone to ask the government for $125,000 in reimbursements for the aid he had given California-bound emigrants and for the losses he had incurred on his property. He correctly pointed out that what was discovered on his property had led to the enrichment of the United States. He made 16 petitions to Congress, all of which failed. (An estimated $500 million in gold was mined in California between 1848 and 1857.)

James Marshall died penniless in 1885 and was buried in Coloma. A statue of him stands there today, his finger pointing toward the place he found the gold.

California Trail

This emigrant route, branching off the older Oregon Trail at Fort Hall in present-day Idaho, was blazed by a party of trappers led by Joseph R. Walker, a 33-year-old Tennesseean who had come to Missouri in 1818. Walker also had surveyed the Santa Fe Trail and had served as a frontier lawman; he became the very paradigm of the American mountain man.

In 1832, Captain Benjamin L. E. Bonneville, on leave from the army, led an expedition of 110 trappers from Fort Osage, Missouri, to the Rocky Mountains with the intent of pushing west to open new beaver-trapping grounds. After the Green River,

HENRY E. HUNTINGTON LIBRARY, SAN MARINO

Vultures circle above abandoned cattle carcasses in the desert along the California Trail.

Wyoming, Rendezvous in 1833, a detachment of 40 men, led by Walker, Bonneville's second-in-command, departed on August 20 to find a new northern route to California. (In 1826–1827, the great fur trader–explorer Jedediah Smith had reached California in the first expedition to enter the Spanish province from the southwest. Peter Skene Ogden of the Hudson's Bay Company also crossed the Mojave Desert to California in 1829.)

Walker and his party of veteran trappers traveled from Green River to the Great Salt Lake, then struck due west to the Humboldt River. (In the swamps of the Humboldt Sink in western Nevada, the expedition had its only serious encounter with native tribes. In a small battle they killed some Diggers, members of a tribe that subsisted on roots, insects, fish, and small game.) Walker then led his men along the Humboldt across present-day Nevada to the formidable Sierra Nevada. It took three weeks to cross these mountains, and on November 13, 1833, Walker and his party became the first Europeans to see the Yosemite Valley. From there they followed the Merced River to the San Joaquin and pushed on to the eastern shore of San Francisco Bay, then south to Monterey, capital of Spanish Alta California.

Walker's expedition pioneered the California Trail, a route that, despite its arduousness, was soon to become a major path to the land of plenty. In 1841 the first homesteaders made their way overland from Missouri to California, attracted by glowing tales of a "perfect paradise" and a "land of perpetual spring" brought back by men in Walker's and other expeditions. In that year, a party that had taken the Oregon Trail along the Platte River arrived at Soda Springs, on the Bear River in Idaho. There the group split in two, with half heading for Oregon, half for California. The latter contingent, made up of 32 men, one woman, and her child, was led by Captain John Bartleson and a New Yorker, John Bidwell. Having no guide nor dependable map, the party followed the Walker route to the Humboldt River. They skirted the Great Salt Lake where, tormented with thirst, they left their wagons and used pack animals—which, over the months to come, they eventually ate—to make their way to the Humboldt. There they turned southwest and followed the California Trail into the Sierra Nevada. Thirty-three of the homesteaders reached the Yosemite Valley in November 1841, California's first cross-country settlers.

The California Trail was traveled in the 1840s by such explorers as James Clyman and John C. Frémont and was used extensively during the gold rush. One of the most celebrated episodes in western U.S. history, the tragedy of the ill-fated Donner party of 1846–1847, occurred when a party left the California Trail at Fort Bridger, Wyoming, and had to winter in the Sierras. Only 47 of the Donner party's 87 members survived.

Californios

Californios were native-born Californians of Spanish-Mexican stock, the early colonists of the state; it was a term used widely between the 1830s and 1850s. The Californios established the great *ranchos* of the state, dividing the state's arable land into cattle-raising enterprises. It is generally believed that this system was designed to give Mexico more control over the territory than had the previous mission system. However, when the Californios granted trade concessions to Anglo traders, they sowed the seeds of the American acquisition of California. For example, John Sutter, on whose property gold would be found, controlled 50,000 acres on the Sacramento River. As the California gold rush brought more Americans to the state, the Rancho System began to break down, with the Californios ceding too much control to outsiders like Sutter.

During the Mexican War, John C. Frémont believed that the Californios could be won over to the American cause and, in fact, the ties between them and the Mexican government were minimal. However, hostilities between Yankees—both Frémont's forces and raiders from Sutter's Fort—and the Californio general José Maria Castro, gradually led to more open confrontations. With Frémont's blessing, an American group declared its independence as the short-lived California Republic (the so-called Bear Flag Republic). The Bear Flaggers were absorbed into the U.S. forces led by Commodore Robert Stockton, who declared the entire territory a U.S. possession.

Californios under Captain José Maria Flores then seized several U.S. installations, including Los Angeles. They defeated General Stephen Watts

Californio Juan Bandini and his daughter, Margarita. Despite his stern appearance, Bandini was a lover of life famed for his fiestas.

These elegant young women from the Vallejo ranch led a life of leisure as did many early California ranchers and their families.

Kearny's command at San Pascual. However, the much greater U.S. forces eventually prevailed, the Californio rebels dispersed, and Flores fled to Mexico.

Camp Grant Massacre

1871

This raid on a peaceful camp of Apaches in Arizona's Arivaipa Canyon resulted in the slaughter of over 100 Indians, mostly women and children. With a growing population of non-Indian settlers, including miners, ranchers, and cattlemen, competition for land and resources intensified, as did conflict with Apaches native to the area. To avoid fighting, the Arivaipa band of Western Apaches sought asylum near Camp Grant. A short time after asylum was granted, an unknown Apache attacked a baggage train 50 miles from Camp Grant, killing a man and kidnapping a woman. The Tucson *Citizen* attributed a half dozen other raids to the Apaches, and the group at Camp Grant quickly became the suspects. On April 30, 1871, the Tucson Committee of Public Safety, along with 48 Mexicans and 94 Papago Indians, descended on the Apache camp. The expedition was led by Jesus Maria Elias, and when it was over, more than one hundred Apache men, women, and children were dead. Twenty-seven Apache children were sold into slavery or given to Papago families.

The Camp Grant Massacre was unique in its excesses, and touched off a national scandal. Intense protest in the East forced a trial of the perpetrators, although a verdict of acquittal was returned. President Grant described the attack as "purely murder."

Campbell, Robert

1804–1879

A Scot born in Ireland, Robert Campbell emigrated to America about 1823 and sought a cure for his tuberculosis by journeying west to St. Louis. In 1825 he joined a party of 60 trappers under Jedediah S. Smith in the expedition sponsored by William H. Ashley. He rose to become a brigade leader for Ashley and a noted trapper on the Upper Missouri River and in the Rocky Mountains.

In 1827–1828, Campbell trapped in Flathead, Blackfeet, and Crow country and tramped the northern Plains and Rockies in search of beaver. In 1828, en route to the Green River Rendezvous, he and his party of trappers were attacked by a Blackfeet band. One man was killed before the trappers were rescued.

In 1829, Campbell returned to St. Louis and set up a business that sold supplies to trappers. After visiting Ireland in 1830–1831, he joined William Sublette in a trading and trapping venture in the Rockies. There he took part in the Battle of Pierre's Hole, in present Idaho, with the Gros Ventre Indians in July 1832, and is credited with saving Sublette's life. Afterward he and Sublette entered into a trading partnership, each earning a fortune in the business; they built Fort William on the Missouri River and briefly challenged the hegemony of the American Fur Company, which had a post located nearby at Fort Union.

In 1841 Campbell married and retired to the merchant trade in St. Louis. He helped form a regiment in the Mexican War in 1846 but did not see active service. He died in St. Louis on October 16, 1879. Of his 13 children, three sons survived him. Among the legendary figures of the fur trade era, Campbell was known for his gentle character, integrity, and loyalty to his friends.

Canary, Martha Jane

1852–1903

Martha Jane Canary (a.k.a. "Calamity Jane") was a frontier heroine, sharpshooter, and cowgirl, whose name has a prominent place among frontier figures. Because both she and others often fabricated stories of her supposed exploits, the legendary and actual deeds of her life are difficult to distinguish.

Calamity was born Martha Jane Canary near Princeton, Missouri, in 1852, the eldest of six

Martha "Calamity Jane" Canary.

children. At age 13, she headed west with her parents to the gold rush town of Virginia City, Montana. Fiercely independent, "Marthy" wore men's trousers, hunted, and learned to swear, gamble, and swallow whiskey among the roughest men. After her parents died, Calamity wandered around the West, seeking adventure. She tried to earn a living by cooking and taking in washing but soon donned buckskin pants, men's shirts, and a wide-brimmed hat and went off in search of more exciting jobs.

In 1875 she accompanied the Newton-Jenney geological expedition to the Black Hills and there joined General George Cook's force; but when the men saw her swimming and discovered that their comrade was a woman, they forced her out. Calamity worked several jobs around Montana, Wyoming, and Kansas, claiming to have been a bullwhacker, teamster, construction worker, and Pony Express rider—even, she bragged, an army scout for General Custer. Had not a bout of pneumonia forced her to rest, she asserted, she too would have died in his famous last Battle of Little Bighorn. It is said she single-handedly saved the Cheyenne-to-Deadwood stagecoach after its driver had been fatally shot . . . but this may be a tall tale as well.

How she got her name remains speculation. One possibility is that since females were sometimes referred to as "Janes," one who constantly showed up at such events as shootings might have gained a reputation as a "calamity Jane." Others believe Canary received her nickname during Deadwood's smallpox epidemic of 1878, when she cared selflessly for the sick.

The name "Burke" on her tombstone stems from her brief union with Clinton Burke from El Paso, Texas. She lived with various soldiers, miners, and ranchers, whom she referred to as her husbands. Calamity also claimed to have legally married James Butler "Wild Bill" Hickok near Deadwood Gulch in Dakota Territory, but no evidence has been found to support this.

The fame of this rough frontierswoman spread largely from Ned Wheeler's sensational "Calamity Jane" stories. Yet the New York writer's depiction of Canary derived from his imagination. The real Calamity was far different from the heroine portrayed in the popular Dime Novels. She drank heavily and was often jailed until she sobered up. For a short time she traveled with a performing company throughout the Midwest. But she became nervous and frustrated, telling tales in front of groups of strangers and soon quit. Calamity may have begun to believe the tales of her exploits and peddled a short autobiographical pamphlet full of wild adventures. When she died in 1903, the town gave her a proper burial. At her request, her grave lies next to that of Wild Bill's in Mount Moriah Cemetery in Deadwood, South Dakota.

Carleton, James Henry

1814–1873

A Maine native, James Henry Carleton was appointed to the regular army in 1841. As a dragoon officer he participated in many frontier marches and Indian campaigns during the 1840s and 1850s, serving in nearly every part of the West. He also distinguished himself in Mexican War combat.

Carleton's most significant service was during the Civil War. In California he raised the California Column of 1,800 volunteers to march to the relief of New Mexico, threatened with Confederate invasion by a Texan force under General Henry H. Sibley. The

James Henry Carleton.

column reached the Rio Grande in the summer of 1862, after the Confederates had been expelled from New Mexico.

Appointed brigadier general, Carleton assumed command of the Department of New Mexico and passed the remaining war years overseeing campaigns against native tribes. Working largely through his senior subordinate, Colonel Christopher "Kit" Carson, Carleton launched offensives first against the Mescalero Apaches, then against the Navajos. His method was to wage ruthless and unrelenting war until an enemy surrendered, then exile them to a remote reservation he established on the Pecos River in eastern New Mexico called Bosque Redondo. Carson's operations in 1862–1863 ended with the confinement of the Mescaleros at Bosque Redondo. In 1863–1864, closely supervised and pressed by Carleton, Carson conducted a roundup of the Navajos. In a series of cruel "Long Marches,"

some 8,000 Navajos were relocated at Bosque Redondo. Here, far from their homeland, they suffered and died of disease and malnutrition. Autocratic and domineering, Carleton refused to admit any flaws in his plan and quarreled incessantly with civil officials. Not until after his transfer did the government admit failure and allow the Navajos to return to their homes.

Returned to the regular army in 1866 as a lieutenant colonel, Carleton died of pneumonia in San Antonio, Texas, in 1873.

Carson, Christopher Houston "Kit"

1809–1868

One recent biography of Carson is subtitled *A Pattern for Heroes,* an apt description of a man who was born in the decade of the Lewis and Clark expedition and who died in the decade of the Civil War. A frontiersman, scout, and soldier, his life bracketed the years of the real "Old West," and his eventful life epitomized it.

Carson was born near Richmond, Kentucky, and moved with his family to Howard County, Missouri, about 1812. After an apprenticeship to a saddlemaker, he ran away from home in August 1826 and joined a trade caravan heading for New Mexico. From Santa Fe, Carson made his way to Taos, center of the fur trade in the Southwest, and over the next five years worked as a trapper, teamster, cook, and Spanish-English interpreter (although illiterate, he was a quick learner) as far south as El Paso, Texas, and Chihuahua, Mexico, and as far west as California.

By 1831, when he returned to Taos, Carson had fought Apaches in the Southwest and Klamath Indians in California, traveled over thousands of miles of virgin western America, learned to trap and hunt and live among, and earn the trust of, the toughest of frontiersmen—and he had just passed his twenty-first birthday.

During the next decade, Carson trapped throughout the Rocky Mountains with such mountain man legends as Thomas "Broken Hand" Fitzpatrick, Jim Bridger, and Joe Meek. For a time he worked for the

Christopher Houston "Kit" Carson.

Hudson's Bay Company along the Mary's (later Humboldt) River. He often fought against the Sioux and Blackfeet, implacable enemies of the white trapper-intruders, and even against the Comanches after moving down into their tribal lands from the Arkansas River. Carson was with Bridger at the Rendezvous on the Green River in 1835. During that trade fair an incident occurred that would later be celebrated in dime novels as well as serious chronicles of the fur trade.

A big, boisterous bully of a Frenchman named Shunar (probably Chouinard) ran afoul of the American trappers and apparently singled out Carson for abuse, since both men were vying for the attentions of an Arapaho girl in the camp. The two fought a horseback duel. The Frenchman got off a rifle shot that grazed Carson's skull and singed his hair; Carson shot the Frenchman in the forearm with his pistol, dismounted, and went for another gun. Shunar begged for his life and Carson, somewhat reluctantly,

granted it. (He later married the Arapaho girl and after her death took a Cheyenne wife.)

In 1838 Carson joined a trading expedition into Navajo country, and after his return worked as a hunter out of Bent's Fort on the Arkansas. In 1842 in Missouri, where he had gone to visit relatives, he met John C. Frémont, then preparing the first of his four western expeditions, and was hired as a guide. As his biographers like to point out, it was Carson who found the paths through the Rockies to Oregon and California for the great "Pathfinder." But to Frémont's credit, when he wrote his memoirs in 1887, Carson was given credit not only for his work as guide and hunter, but also for his vast knowledge of Indian lore, his "frank speech and address," his "prompt, self-sacrificing, and true" character, his loyalty and courage.

After Frémont's first expedition, Carson returned to Taos and in February 1843 married 15-year-old Josefa Jaramillo, sister-in-law of Charles Bent (who with Ceran St. Vrain had opened Bent's Fort in 1833). In subsequent Frémont expeditions, Carson explored the Great Salt Lake, the Oregon Trail to Fort Vancouver, and routes across the Sierras to Sutter's Fort, ranging from Oregon Territory south to the Mojave Desert. He was with Frémont during the formation of the short-lived Bear Flag Republic, and served in his California Battalion.

At the outset of the Mexican War, Carson was dispatched to Washington with messages for President Polk. In Socorro, New Mexico, however, he met General Stephen Watts Kearny and returned with him to California. En route to San Diego, he fought at San Pascual in December 1846 and in the engagement on the San Gabriel River the following January.

After the war, Carson joined Lucien Maxwell in farming operations at Rayado, New Mexico, and occasionally served as guide and scout into Apache country. He joined trapping expeditions around the Southwest, and in 1853 made a sheep drive with Maxwell to California. During this relatively calm period Carson dictated his life story to a friend. The manuscript was used as the basis for an 1858 "biography." When portions of it were read to him, Carson opined that the author had "laid it on a leetle too thick."

He served as Indian agent in northern New Mexico (in particular to the Utes, a people he loved) until the outbreak of the Civil War, when he resigned to become a colonel of the First New Mexico Volunteer Infantry. Carson served at the Battle of Valverde (1862) and in the long "scorched earth" campaign against the Navajos (1863–1864). In November 1864 he led a military expedition of 335 men and 75 scouts against 3,000 Kiowas, Comanches, and Arapahos on the Canadian River. The indecisive battle at the old Bent trading post called Adobe Walls resulted in Indian casualties of about 60 versus 2 men lost in Carson's force.

After visits to Washington, New York, and Boston, Carson returned to New Mexico in April 1868, suffering from chest and neck pains and a chronic bronchial condition. He lived to see the birth of Josefita, his and Josefa's seventh child, and the death of his beloved wife ten days later. Carson survived Josefa by exactly one month, dying of an aneurysm on May 23, 1868, at Fort Lyon, Colorado, where he had gone for treatment. In January 1869, Carson and Josefa were reburied, side by side, in Taos.

Carson was unprepossessing in appearance. General William Tecumseh Sherman described the then celebrated frontiersman as "a small, stoop-shouldered man, with reddish hair, freckled face, soft blue eyes, and nothing to indicate extraordinary courage or daring."

Cassidy, Butch

See Parker, Robert Leroy

Cather, Willa

1873–1947

Willa Cather was a Pulitzer Prize–winning novelist and short story writer whose work portrayed pioneer life in the Nebraska prairies and southwestern deserts. Although she spent only her youth among the rugged pioneers of Webster County, Nebraska, almost all of Cather's fiction examines themes of courage in pioneer life.

Willa Cather was born on December 7, 1873, in Virginia; as a young child she moved with her family to a ranch near the frontier village of Red Cloud, Nebraska. Until high school she was taught at home. Later she attended the University of Nebraska, where she wrote for the *Nebraska State Journal*. Upon graduation in 1895, she moved to Pittsburgh and supported herself as a journalist and high school teacher, writing as much as she could. The success of her first collection of stories, *The Troll Garden* (1905), earned her a position with the popular *McClure's Magazine*.

In 1912 Cather met Sarah Orne Jewett, a New England writer, who convinced her to quit journalism and write novels full-time. Short visits to her brother in the Southwest and to Red Cloud made the West the focus of all her later fiction. *O Pioneers!* (1913), which centers on a young woman's struggles on the Nebraska frontier, was praised by critics. Her next major successes, *My Antonia* (1918), *Death Comes for the Archbishop* (1927), and *A Lost Lady* (1933), also focus on frontier life in Nebraska. Cather was awarded the Pulitzer Prize in 1922 for *One of Ours* and elected to the American Academy of Arts and Letters in 1938. She died in New York City on April 24, 1947.

Catlin, George

1796–1872

George Catlin was a painter and writer whose work is an invaluable eyewitness account of Indian and frontier life in North and South America. Catlin's first sight of an Indian delegation so astounded him that he dedicated his life to spreading the message of the value of their vanishing culture. Hundreds of his detailed paintings were exhibited throughout the United States and Europe in his lifetime.

Catlin, a native of Wilkes-Barre, Pennsylvania, first established himself in law, opening a practice in 1820. Although he had no formal training in art, his passion for sketching and painting soon earned him a reputation as an artist. By 1823 Catlin had abandoned the legal profession and settled in Philadelphia as a portrait painter.

When Catlin spotted a group of Indian chieftains walking through Philadelphia, he was so strongly af-

George Catlin portrays himself surrounded by Mandan tribesmen watching in wonder as he paints the image of Chief Mah-to-toh-pa.

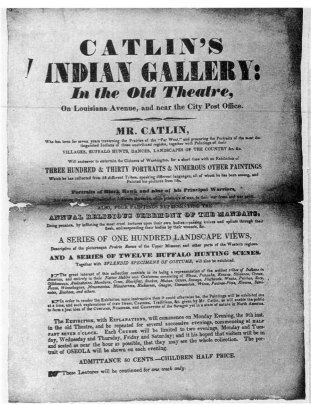

A poster announcing an exhibition of Indian paintings and landscapes by George Catlin.

fected that he embarked upon a study of some eastern reservation tribes. In 1832, after petitioning his friend William Clark, explorer and at the time Superintendent of Indian affairs for the Missouri Territory, Catlin gained approval to board the American Fur Company steamer *Yellowstone* for its maiden voyage up the Missouri River.

For the next several years Catlin traveled throughout the West, painting among the Indians during the summer and returning east to earn money during the winter. He was the first white man to visit southwestern Minnesota's ancient quarry where for centuries Indian tribes had mined a soft red stone to make their tobacco pipes; the mineral was later called Catlinite in honor of the artist.

Catlin offered to sell his impressive collection of over 500 detailed oil portraits and scenes, painted from 1829 to 1838, to the U.S. Congress. When he was turned down, the artist created a traveling Indian Gallery. With several Indians, he toured the eastern United States and Europe. The gallery was famous as far away as London and Paris and would inspire artist Paul Kane's later depictions of the Plains Indians.

Catlin published details of his early travels in the two-volume *Notes to the Manners, Customs, and Condition of the North American Indians* (1841), which contains more than 300 engravings. Other publications include *Eight Years Travel and Residence in Europe* (1848) and *Last Rambles Amongst the Indians of the Rocky Mountains and the Andes* (1868). Some critics argue that Catlin's work must be read with skepticism, that Catlin viewed the Indians as noble savages whose minds were blank slates waiting to be impressed with the ways of white civilization.

Over 600 of Catlin's early paintings are on exhibit at the National Portrait Gallery and the Smithsonian Institution in Washington, D.C. The American Museum of Natural History in New York City holds most of the works from his traveling Indian Gallery.

Other important collections are found at the Joslyn Art Museum in Omaha, Nebraska, and at the Thomas Gilcrease Institute of American History and Art in Tulsa, Oklahoma.

Catron, Thomas Benton

1840–1921

One of New Mexico's most prominent political figures of the late nineteenth and early twentieth centuries, Thomas Benton Catron was born on October 6, 1840, and reared on a farm near Lexington, Missouri. After graduating from the University of Missouri at Columbia (July 1860), the aspiring lawyer enlisted with the Confederacy and fought in several battles in the Civil War.

Catron moved to Santa Fe, New Mexico, in July 1866, gained admission to the bar the following year, and entered a law practice with his longtime friend and sometime rival Stephen B. Elkins. He began making political inroads in Sante Fe and in 1872 was appointed U.S. attorney for the Territory of New Mexico. There was no Republican party in New Mexico when Catron arrived there, but he was present when it was formed in 1867, and in time he became its acknowledged leader. He was not above using his political influence to advance his business interests. Catron's cronies, the leading Republicans in New Mexico, became known as the "Sante Fe Ring" and were suspected of questionable maneuvers relating to ownership of Spanish and Mexican land grants.

In 1906 Catron was elected mayor of Santa Fe, and in 1912, when New Mexico gained statehood, he became one of the first two senators from that state. He died in Santa Fe on May 15, 1921.

Cattle Industry

Although the great era of the western cattle industry was in the years between the end of the Civil War and about 1885—the time of unfenced land— the business of raising range cattle and taking them to market for sale was operating in Texas in the eigh-

NEW YORK PUBLIC LIBRARY

A day's work in the slaughterhouse.

teenth century, when huge herds of Spanish cattle were driven to New Orleans for shipment to eastern and northern seaboard markets.

In Texas the cattle introduced into the New World by the Spanish, the longhorn, a lean and self-sufficient animal of Spanish origin, became the prime animal of the early cattle business. In the wild, the longhorn was scrawny and its meat stringy, but as it bred with other stock and was fattened in good pasturage, it became salable. Selling

LIBRARY OF CONGRESS

Samuel Maverick, a Texas cattleman, left his mark on the world by refusing to brand his cattle, giving a new name to rebels everywhere.

cattle for meat began to take precedence over the sale of hides, once the most lucrative part of cattle raising.

During the Mexican War, Texas cattlemen sold their stock to the army, though they still made occasional drives to Galveston and New Orleans; during the Civil War, with Texas (and its estimated 3 million head of cattle) a part of the Confederacy, the Union blockade of Southern ports put an end to this enterprise. By the end of the Civil War, when a steer

LIBRARY OF CONGRESS

Railroad stock cars revolutionized the cattle industry.

was worth only about $6–$7 in Texas but six times that amount in the North and East, the real western cattle industry began. Its center was in the area from San Antonio south to Laredo and east to the Gulf Coast of Texas, a region of good grazing land and ample water. Other profitable cattle raising occurred along the Oregon Trail, in Montana and Wyoming, the Upper Rio Grande in Colorado, and New Mexico Territory.

Although many large cattle spreads grew from modest beginnings, capital was needed to take a herd to market: wages for cowboys and the costs of wagons, horses, and the necessary equipment of the trail. Moreover, in addition to the hazards of the trail—weather, streams and rivers to be forded, Indian attacks—good grazing land and ample water were needed to bring the animals to market fat and healthy (and therefore able to fetch top dollar).

Texas, with its good grass and water, had the most significant trails north to the railheads in Kansas (from which the animals were shipped, most often, to Chicago, where the Union Stockyards, opened in 1865, had become the center of the western meat-packing industry) and the home of most of the West's most prominent cattle barons: Richard King, Charles Goodnight, Oliver Loving, Abel Borden, "Shanghai" Pierce, and John Chisum.

Although barbed wire and other fencing were introduced in the 1870s, the free-range cattle industry continued through the 1880s and peaked with 6 million head driven to market on the various trails. In the last two decades of the nineteenth century various breeds of cattle—Angus, Hereford, and shorthorn among them—had superseded the Texas longhorn. In the same period, fencing and farming began taking over the once open grazing lands. The cattle kingdom effectively ended with the widespread use of barbed wire and the spread of the railroad throughout the West.

Cattle Rustling

The stockman of the West had much to contend with in raising and delivering beef to market. First were the vagaries of nature, not just the perpetual need for good grazing and water for the animals, but flooding rains or parching droughts, blizzards, hail

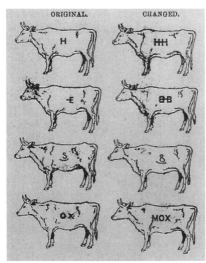

ORIGINAL.   CHANGED.

UNIVERSITY OF WYOMING, LARAMIE

Cattle thieves typically changed existing brands before reselling the cattle. This 1892 magazine article shows examples of tampered brands.

and dust storms, and plagues of locusts, flies, and mosquitoes. Of human problems—and there were many, from hiring dependable cowboys to dealing with sheep grazers and native tribes—nothing surpassed in importance the war between cattleman and cattle rustler.

Cattle rustling in America may have begun in 1611 when the first beef cattle were landed in Jamestown, Virginia; it was certainly known in the early nineteenth-century Southeast and Southwest, when herds of 10,000 to 15,000 cattle were not uncommon. But the apogee of rustling occurred in post–Civil War Texas, in the era of the great cattle kings and their drives to railheads in Kansas and other states. As early as 1868, Texas cattlemen formed protective organizations and hired stock detectives to combat the growing problem of cattle theft. Similar measures were taken in Colorado, Wyoming, and Montana as the cattle industry moved north, and territorial legislatures, alarmed at the growing menace, passed stringent laws in an effort to curb rustling and the harsh frontier justice—the lynch rope—that accompanied it.

Common practices of rustlers were to steal mavericks (motherless, unbranded calves) and cut strays from a herd, then to brand or rebrand them with a running iron, a branding iron used to draw a brand freehand or alter an existing brand. Although mas-

sive rustling operations died out with the end of the open range, vestiges of this dishonorable practice are still occasionally reported in cattle operations today.

Cattle Towns

In the two decades following the Civil War, when stockmen, particularly in Texas, needed to move cattle to northern buyers, they drove their herds up existing trails, often old Indian paths across the prairies, or blazed new ones—the Chisholm Trail and Western Trail out of San Antonio, for example—to reach the railheads. There the cattle were allowed to graze and fatten before being transported by rail to markets.

Since Kansas was the principal western railroad terminus in this period, special boomtowns sprang up to receive the cattle. These were places where the railroad had arrived and sidings were in place, where the farmers had not yet invaded and therefore good temporary grazing land was available, and where stockyards had been built to hold the cattle until sale and shipping. The places in Kansas fitting the cowmen's bill of particulars included Abilene, Newton (which had the briefest—one year—and among the most raucous lives of the Kansas cowtowns), Ellsworth, Wichita, Dodge City, and Caldwell.

LIBRARY OF CONGRESS

Trail hands quenching their thirst in a cattle town saloon.

There were other cattle trails and other cattle towns in California, New Mexico, Wyoming, the Dakotas, and Nebraska, among other places, but the Texas trails to Kansas led to the most prominent and typical of the cowtowns of the Old West. The first of them, Abilene, set the pattern for those that followed. It had been surveyed and given its name in 1860, the year before Kansas was admitted to the union, but until 1867 it was, in the words of Illinois promoter and entrepreneur Joseph G. McCoy, "a small, dead place consisting of about a dozen log huts." McCoy, knowing the Kansas Pacific Railroad would soon reach the town, bought 250 acres of land at Abilene and used it to build a stockyard adjacent to the railroad siding. He also financed, with the help of others, construction of a livery stable, a barn, and a hotel called the Drover's Cottage. By the end of the year, 35,000 head of cattle and their bosses, drovers, and cowboys had made Abilene a cow town. The glory days lasted five years.

The criminal element that seeped into every such town—whether mining or cattle—came early to Abilene, where there was little law and virtually no order. During cattle season, it was said that "hell is now in session." In 1870, after the town had been incorporated, its mayor hired a marshal, a former New York policeman named Thomas James Smith, called "Bear River Tom." Smith performed well, enforcing the town's new no-guns ordinances. Five months after becoming marshal, he rode onto the prairie in search of a farmer wanted for murder. He found his man in his remote dugout but was attacked by the killer's companion. Bear River Tom Smith was beheaded with an ax.

The following spring, with the herds on the way from Texas, Abilene's city fathers hired gambler-gunman James Butler "Wild Bill" Hickok to tame the town for $150 a month. All went well until October 1871, when Hickok killed two men—one a policeman friend who innocently walked into the fracas—in a minor street disturbance. Hickok was discharged.

Something was happening to Abilene, as it would to all the Kansas cattle towns that succeeded it. The towns made money from the stockmen and cowboys and those who followed them, but paid a heavy price. Part of that price was the attraction of speculators, outlaws, prostitutes (Wichita in its boom days had an estimated 300 "calico queens"), gamblers, and con artists. Another part was the conflicts between cattlemen, accustomed to free grazing and expecting perquisites from the towns they were enriching, and area farmers who fenced their land against the invading cattle and called for quarantines against the diseases the Texas cattle often carried.

By 1872 Abilene's citizens, now changed by the influx of farmers into the region, no longer wanted the raucous cattle trade and issued a manifesto to Texas newspapers asking stockmen to take their cattle elsewhere. For a while, the stockmen were happy to take their business to a place where they would be appreciated. Sixty miles southwest of Abilene, the town of Ellsworth, founded in 1867, wanted the cattle trade and even opened a trail from Fort Cobb in Indian Territory to draw stockmen from that point as well as from Texas. By 1872 Ellsworth was a bustling cattle town and already in a trade war with Wichita. Ellsworth boasted that its stockyards were the biggest in the state, called attention to its new and sumptuous Grand Central Hotel, and even hired Texas cattle baron Abel "Shanghai" Pierce to influence fellow Texans to drive their herds to Ellsworth. Wichita won the battle as the railroads drew the cattle business westward in their wake, but the boom there lasted only until 1876.

Dodge City, founded in 1872 near Fort Dodge and the Santa Fe Trail, became the next cattle town of choice and was to have the longest (and loudest) life of any of them. Dodge had a history as a buffalo-hide trading center before the first Texas cattle arrived in 1876, and in its eight years as the prime terminus of the Texas drives, it gained the reputation of being the wildest town of all, despite the presence of such renowned lawmen as Wyatt Earp and William B. "Bat" Masterson. Dodge, with its motto "Cowboy Capital of the World" and advertising "drinks two for a quarter and no grangers," perhaps more than any other town of its era symbolized the noisy, lawless, dangerous underside of cow town life. When Dodge City went tame, and despite the momentary rise of Caldwell, 50 miles south of Wichita, on the Chisholm Trail, the cow town era was over.

In 1884, the entire state of Kansas was quarantined against Texas cattle, a death blow that had been signaled far earlier. In 1874 farmers had arrived in central Kansas in such great numbers that they were able to form cooperatives that pressed for grazing and quarantine laws, and to influence businessmen and local and state politicians to combat the lawlessness the herds brought in their wake. Some years before Dodge and Caldwell played their roles as the last of the cow towns, Kansas was changing to a predominantly agricultural economy. Ultimately, two elements ended the era of the cattle town: the ever expanding railroads, whose presence gave rise to the towns to begin with, moved lines into Texas, ending the need for the cattle drive; and the grangers, nemesis of the cowmen, who had won all the battles.

Central Pacific Railroad

The west-to-east half of the first transcontinental railroad, the Central Pacific was founded on June 28, 1861, and incorporated under California law. It was the inspiration of engineer and pioneer railroader Theodore D. Judah, who died in 1863, before construction began. The future of the line therefore fell to a group of Sacramento merchants—Leland Stanford, Collis P. Huntington, Mark Hopkins, and Charles Crocker—who became known in railroad history as "the Big Four."

After a period of debate over the originating city—

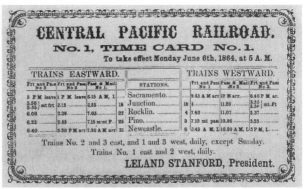

SOUTHERN PACIFIC TRANSPORTATION COMPANY

Central Pacific timetable, published in 1864.

San Francisco and Sacramento were the prime contenders—the California legislature, in 1863–1864, authorized the sale of bonds in support of the railroad. With a federal government loan of $48,000 per mile of track, construction began in 1864. By July of that year tracks had been completed to Newcastle, 31 miles east of Sacramento. When Irish workers went on strike in 1865, Crocker hired Chinese laborers at $30 a month; by the end of the year, he had 7,000 Chinese and 2,500 whites working on the tracks.

In 1867, the first Central Pacific locomotive crossed the Sierra Nevada summit, and the railroad had won the necessary legislation to push east "until they shall meet and connect with the Union Pacific Railroad." The great race between the two lines was at its peak in 1868; 10 miles of track were laid in a day. Congress decreed that the two lines should meet at Promontory Summit, just west of Ogden, Utah; and there on May 10, 1869, the final spikes were driven connecting the eastern seaboard with the Pacific. The Central Pacific had constructed 690 miles of track over some of the most formidable terrain in America.

The railroad found itself in serious financial straits in 1895 when millions of dollars in government subsidy bonds came due. Huntington's controversial re-funding bill placed his Southern Pacific Railroad behind in paying the reduced debts. The Central Pacific, merged into the Southern Pacific, was acquired by Edward Harriman in 1900.

CALIFORNIA STATE RAILROAD MUSEUM

The winter of 1866–1867 dumped 14 blizzards on Central Pacific Railroad workers, shown here shoveling snow from the tracks in the High Sierra.

Chapultepec, Battle of

See Mexican War

Charbonneau, Jean Baptiste

1805–1866

John Baptiste Charbonneau was mountain man, trapper, guide, and miner, born on the Upper Missouri River during the Lewis and Clark expedition. He was the son of the Shoshone guide Sacagawea and her husband, the expedition's interpreter, Touissant Charbonneau. William Clark, who nicknamed Jean Baptiste "Pomp" or "Pompey," persuaded his parents to leave the boy in his care, to be educated in St. Louis.

In 1823, young Charbonneau accompanied the western traveler Prince Paul of Württemberg to Europe and remained for six years, becoming a capable linguist. He returned to the Missouri River country in 1829, worked as a trapper in Idaho and Utah, and traveled with such mountain man legends as Jim Bridger, Jim Beckwourth, and Joe Meek. He became a guide from Santa Fe to San Diego in 1846 during the war with Mexico and served for a time as the *alcalde* (mayor) of Mission San Luis Rey, California.

Charbonneau spent many years in the goldfields of the American River country around Sacramento. He died, probably of pneumonia, in Oregon.

Cherokee Bill

See Goldsby, Crawford

Cherokees

See Five Civilized Tribes

Cheyenne Indians

The Cheyennes, an Algonquian tribe of Plains Indians, figured prominently in some of the best-known clashes with whites on the western frontier. They did much to inhibit white settlement, and reportedly no tribe lost so many of its number in the process.

Like the Arapahos, with whom the tribe was closely associated, the Cheyennes were forced out of Minnesota sometime between 1675 and 1700 by conflict with the Chippewas (or Ojibwas) and Sioux. They gradually changed from a sedentary farming lifestyle to one of horse-mounted buffalo hunting. By the time Lewis and Clark encountered them in 1804, they were living in the vicinity of the Black Hills.

In 1832, about half the tribe moved to the south, along the Arkansas River in Colorado. These became known as the Southern Cheyennes. Those

SMITHSONIAN INSTITUTION, BUREAU OF AMERICAN ETHOLOGY

Cheyenne chief Little Wolf.

SMITHSONIAN INSTITUTION

*Cheyenne leader Two Moons led his
people to a reservation in 1876.*

who remained in their homeland became known as the Northern Cheyennes. (The split was made official with the Fort Laramie Treaty of 1851.)

Beginning in 1840, increasing numbers of whites began to infringe upon the territory of the Southern Cheyennes. The process accelerated as a result of the California Gold Rush in 1849. In the 1850s and 1860s, the Cheyennes retaliated by sporadic raids on white travel routes, and made a few forays into Mexico. They also engaged in border warfare with surrounding tribes, principally the Utes.

In February 1861, by the Treaty of Fort Wise, the Cheyenne peace chiefs, in an action repudiated by the war chiefs, ceded most of their land to the United States in exchange for a small reservation south of the Arkansas River. Much of the time, though, they continued to range over their old territory. They managed to remain at peace, despite ever greater numbers of white settlers in the area. They kept the promise, given at Fort Laramie, to refrain from warfare.

In 1864 the Sioux, angered by punitive expeditions against them, staged a series of raids for which the Cheyennes and their Arapaho allies received the blame. Scattered fighting ensued. On November 29, 1864, troops under the command of Colonel John M. Chivington attacked the peaceful camp of Cheyenne chief Black Kettle on Sand Creek; 28 men and 105 women and children were killed. In 1865, the Cheyennes and their allies launched raids to avenge

the Sand Creek Massacre. In December 1866, they participated in the Fetterman fight. In 1867, by the Medicine Lodge Treaty, the Southern Cheyennes agreed to move to a reservation in the Indian Territory (in Oklahoma). There, on the Washita River in 1868, Custer's 7th Cavalry attacked Black Kettle once again, this time killing the peace chief. Later the tribe participated in the general Indian uprising of 1874–1875.

Northern Cheyennes took part in the Battle of the Little Bighorn. As a result, they were removed to join their southern relatives in the Indian Territory. In September 1878, fed up with conditions on the reservation, a group left and headed north. The resulting chase, trumpeted as a major Indian war by a press and public that made waiting for the word from the West a national pastime, ended in disaster. Even so, the Cheyennes were allowed to remain in the north, part with the Sioux at Pine Ridge Agency and the rest near Fort Keogh on their former Montana ranges.

Chickasaw

See Five Civilized Tribes

Chief Joseph

CA. 1840–1904

Known as Heimot Tooyalaket to his people, Joseph was the son of Wellamotkin, known as Old Joseph among whites. Hence the son was called Young Joseph. He was educated at a Presbyterian mission school near modern-day Lewiston, Idaho.

When Wellamotkin died in 1871, Young Joseph became chief of his band of Nez Perce, located in the Wallowa Valley in northeastern Oregon. Whites had been settling in this area for many years, and an 1863 treaty, executed by some Nez Perce bands, established a reservation for the tribe in Idaho. On his deathbed, however, his father reminded Joseph that he had never consented to any treaty: "This country holds your father's body. Never sell the bones of your father and mother."

SMITHSONIAN INSTITUTION

Chief Joseph.

Joseph protested encroachment by settlers, and in 1873 President Ulysses S. Grant set aside the Wallowa Valley as a reservation for Joseph's Nez Perces. Continued pressure, however, led to a reversal of the order in 1875. A special commission was appointed to meet with the Nez Perces in November 1876. Despite Joseph's firm refusal to negotiate any relinquishment of their territory, the commission ordered the Wallowa Nez Perces to move to the Idaho reservation. If they failed to do so voluntarily, they would be removed by force.

Joseph came under extreme pressure from his people on both sides of the issue—those who wanted to accept the government's demand and those who wished to fight. At first, he agreed to move to the reservation. But tempers flared, and after a raiding party killed four whites, Joseph knew that a peaceful move was not possible. He united with other bands of the tribe in White Bird Canyon. When General O. O. Howard dispatched elements of the 1st Cavalry to retrieve them, the Nez Perces defeated the federal force. But, realizing that they could not remain at the canyon, they eventually determined to flee to Canada.

Much controversy surrounds the events of the next few months. To some, Joseph was a masterful tactician who planned and executed one of the most successful long retreats in military history. Others contend that the successes of the Nez Perce were the result of overconfidence and blunders on the part of the U.S. Army, and that Joseph, at any rate, was a "camp chief" in charge of the infirm, women, and

COLLECTION OF DR. C. M. DRURY

Chief Joseph's tribe stands proudly in this photograph, despite their recent defeat.

children. The truth probably lies somewhere in between. For eastern newspapers and a public grown weary of the Indian Wars, however, Joseph became a symbol of heroic resistance, and the flight of the Nez Perce became a cause célèbre. Engaging in constant rearguard action and generally fighting the army only on ground they selected, the Indians traveled 1,300 miles and came within 50 miles of the Canadian border. On September 30, 1877, they were surprised by troops under General Nelson Miles and eventually forced to yield.

Joseph's speech upon surrender ("I will fight no more forever") confirmed his legendary status in the popular imagination. His people were ultimately sent to a reservation in Washington. When he died of a massive heart attack in 1904, the surgeon who attended him reported the cause of death as "a broken heart."

Chinese Settlers in the West

The first Chinese who landed in San Francisco in 1848 came mainly from Kwangtung Province in southern China. They were welcomed initially as a cheap labor supply. They came for economic opportunity unavailable in China, and after they had saved enough, intended to return to China and their families. The Chinese were separated from both Americans and more traditional immigrants by their desired temporary status, isolationism, unique cultural heritage and language, and the obvious ethnic differences. The lure of the 1849 gold rush was not restricted to white men, but whites did not welcome competition when it came to gold prospecting. The phrase reflecting this sentiment was "Not a Chinaman's Chance." The Foreign Miner's Law of 1850, enacted to restrict Mexican prospectors on American soil, was applied to the Chinese, many of whom were forced to return to San Francisco. In the 1850s fear of economic competition from Chinese exploded into race riots; nevertheless, through the 1870s Chinese continued to come in droves to try their luck in the American West.

The construction of the transcontinental railroad from 1860 to 1869 fueled the continual need for cheap labor. The work on the railroad moved many Chinese out of California, and when that source of employment ceased, they gravitated to the few

DENVER PUBLIC LIBRARY

A Chinese family photographed during a wedding reception in their new hometown of Idaho City, Idaho.

LIBRARY OF CONGRESS

Chinese immigrants at work.

LIBRARY OF CONGRESS

Caricatures of Chinese settlers in San Francisco.

DENVER PUBLIC LIBRARY, WESTERN HISTORY DEPARTMENT

Anti-Chinese sentiment in California.

large cities that had Chinatowns and found employment at low wages. The most frequent occupations for Chinese were working in laundries or restaurants.

Frequently, associations of Chinese merchants arranged to pay passage to the United States in return for years of indentured servitude. Under these conditions Chinese laborers made enough to live but not to prosper, thereby ending hopes of returning to their families. In response to popular xenophobia, Chinese immigration was legally restricted by a series of measures culminating in the Exclusion Act Of 1882 that suspended further immigration for ten years, was extended another decade by the Geary Act of 1892, and was made permanent in 1902. Chinese women were even more severely restricted

from entering the United States; by 1882 they represented only 5 percent of the 100,000 Chinese living in the West. For Chinese men the prospect of bringing their family from China or starting one in the United States was curtailed. It was not until 1943 (the quota for that year was 105), with the spread of communism in China and China's joining the Allies in World War II, that restrictions were relaxed, and it was not until 1965 that restrictions were entirely removed.

A black chapter in the history of the American West was the treatment given Chinese by Americans either in an official capacity through legislation or by private and mob acts of hostility. In San Francisco a "cubic air" ordinance required a minimum of 500 cubic feet of air space for each person dwelling in a lodging house, an attempt to break up the overcrowding in Chinatown; the "queue" ordinance required that jailed Chinese have their hair cut short, an insult to their cultural values; and an ordinance directed against the extensive Chinese laundry commerce required a fee for the use of horse-drawn delivery vehicles and an even higher fee for not using them. In 1871 in Los Angeles, a mob killed 19 Chinese; in 1880, Denver's Chinatown was burned to the ground; in 1885, 28 Chinese coal miners were killed in Wyoming. Many Chinese who could returned to China. By 1920 the Chinese population in the United States was only 61,000.

Chinook Indians

The Chinooks, a Penutian tribe that lived around the mouth of the Columbia River in southwestern Washington and northeastern Oregon, so dominated the area that their name became a broad term covering several tribes (including the Wasco and Wishram) who lived in the region. They were first encountered by the Lewis and Clark expedition.

Because the Chinooks were prolific traders, their name was applied around 1800 to so-called Chinook jargon, a trading language composed of a mixture of English, French, and Chinook words. When first studied in 1841, it was said to be limited to 300 words. By 1894, this number had grown to about 1,000, approximately half of which were derived from English. The language was widely employed throughout the Northwest and into Canada and Alaska. It was still in limited use as late as 1920. Besides commerce, the jargon was used to negotiate a number of treaties with Northwest Coast tribes in the 1850s. As a result of the limited vocabulary and simple grammar of the jargon, the interpretation of these treaties became the source of important litigation in the twentieth century.

The tribe's name was also appropriated to designate the warm, wet wind that blows in from the Oregon coast and the warm dry wind that descends the eastern slope of the Rockies.

Indian Sugar Camp *by Seth Eastman depicts Chippewa women making maple sugar.*

An engraving depicting a battle on Lake Superior between the Chippawas and the Foxes.

Chippewa Indians

An Algonquian tribe (also known as Ojibway or Ojibwa), the Chippewas were located primarily around the Great Lakes in the United States and Canada and on the northern Plains. They should not be confused with the Chipewyans, an Athapaskan-speaking tribe in eastern Canada.

The Chippewas are closely related to the Ottawas and the Potawatomis. Their legend maintains that all three were once a single people living on the Atlantic coast, from which they migrated. They engaged in prolonged and continual warfare with the Fox, Cheyennes, Arapahos, and Sioux. They were active participants in the fur trade. With the advantage of firearms, which they had acquired from white traders, the Chippewas gradually drove these other tribes from the area. By 1700, they had expanded their territory as far west as the eastern prairies. They also expanded eastward, taking over lands claimed by the Iroquois. Rarely in conflict with whites, they raided other Indians as far west as the Rockies.

After the arrival of the horse on the northern Plains, some Chippewas adopted Plains Indian ways. Others remained faithful to the older way. During the autumn the latter dispersed into bands to hunt. They gathered again in the summer to fish. Some grew corn and gathered wild rice.

The Chippewas often joined the French to fight against the English. After the French and Indian War, they remained largely peaceful. They, did, however, join in Pontiac's war in 1763–1764, and they also participated in Tecumseh's uprising in the early nineteenth century. Those living in the United States made a peace treaty in 1815 and agreed to live on reservations. However, the tribe remained at war with the Sioux. In 1846, the U.S. government placed the Winnebagos in Minnesota to act as a buffer between the Chippewas and their enemies.

In the 1830s, when the world fur market suddenly collapsed, the economy of the tribe was threatened. Beginning in 1837, white expansion forced the Chippewas to cede vast tracts of land in exchange for fixed annual payments. In 1854, the tribe was one of the first to have allotment forced upon it. By 1884, their numbers had dwindled to less than half that at first white contact. In 1889, all unallotted Chippewa lands were assigned.

Today the Chippewas live in the United States and Canada. In the United States, they live mainly in Minnesota, but significant numbers also live in Wisconsin, Michigan, North Dakota, and Montana.

Chiricahua

See Apaches

Chisholm Trail

Jesse Chisholm (1805–1868), son of Scots-Cherokee parents, came from Tennessee to Fort Gibson in present-day Oklahoma as a young man and began trading with the Osage, Wichita, Kiowa, and Comanche tribes along the Little Arkansas River. His knowledge of these tribes (it was said he knew 14 Plains dialects) led to his employment as an interpreter at various treaty councils and as a guide through Indian country.

Chisholm's travels with wagons of trade goods between his post on the Canadian River in Indian territory, and Wichita, Kansas, was the genesis of the trail later named for him. He died of cholera in his camp at Left Hand Spring, near present-day Geary, Oklahoma, in March 1868. A stone marker near where he died carries his epitaph: "No one left his home cold or hungry."

Today a name as familiar in western history as the Little Bighorn or the Alamo, the old trade road that became known as the Chisholm Trail was orig-

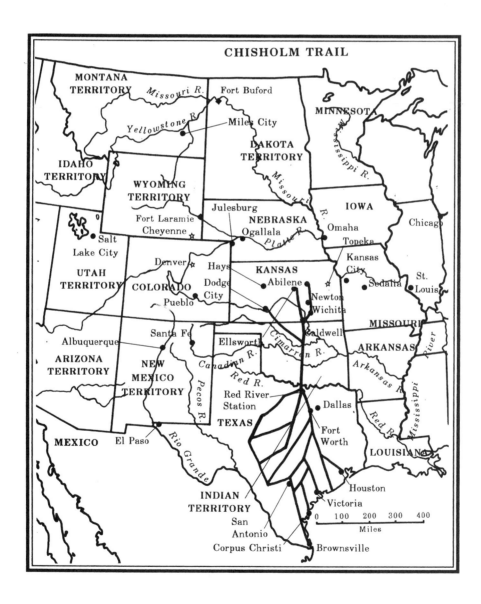

Jesse Chisholm.

Chisum, John Simpson

1824–1884

John Simpson Chisum was a cattle rancher born in Tennessee. Despite the similarity of their names, he was not related to Jesse Chisholm. After a brief, apparently successful career as a construction contractor, and eight years as the county clerk of Lamar County, Texas, Chisum entered the cattle business in 1854. During the Civil War, he supplied cattle to the Confederacy. He was also associated with the pioneering cattleman Charles Goodnight.

By 1873, Chisum had a sizable ranch at South Spring on the Pecos River in New Mexico. He was among the first Texans to ranch in this area, and despite problems with rustlers (see Cattle Rustling) and Indians, he expanded his spread to the point where he was running between 60,000 and 100,000 head of cattle.

Chisum is also remembered for his involvement

inally a modest 220 miles long. It was first used by cattlemen in 1867 when Colonel O. O. Wheeler and his partners, taking a herd of longhorns from central Texas to Abilene, Kansas, used the trail to cross Indian Territory. Others followed, and Chisholm's name was soon given to the entire cattle route from San Antonio almost due north across the Red River to Caldwell, Wichita, Abilene, Ellsworth (the northern terminus varied), and other railheads in Kansas.

The greatest use of the Chisholm Trail was between 1867 and 1875; by the latter year cattlemen were using the Western Trail, to the west of the Chisholm, which terminated at Dodge City, Kansas.

It has been estimated that in eight seasons, some two million head of longhorns moved up the Chisholm Trail to Kansas, then on to feedlots in St. Louis and to slaughterhouses in Chicago and points east.

John Simpson Chisum.

in the Lincoln County War, which pitted large ranchers against smallholders and merchants, and involved such mythic figures as Billy the Kid and Sheriff Pat Garrett. His precise role in the conflict is murky—he was a secretive man who did much of his business verbally—but he was a friend of other big ranchers like John Henry Tunstall, and he helped get Garrett elected sheriff in 1880. Chisum certainly was not directly involved in the violence, but it is unlikely he was neutral.

Although his holdings were depleted by rustlers, Indians, and competition from other ranchers, when Chisum died at Eureka Springs, Arkansas, he left his brothers an estate worth half a million dollars. Part of his original ranch is still in operation as the South Spring Dairy Ranch.

Chocktaws

See Five Civilized Tribes

Cíbola, Seven Golden Cities of

See Coronado, Francisco; and Cabeza de Vaca, Álvar Núñez

Civil War in the West

The Civil War in the West had three major themes: Blue against Gray, Blue and Gray against native tribes, and tribe against tribe. Union and Confederate armies battled for possession of Missouri, Kansas, Arkansas, the Indian Territory, Louisiana, Texas, and New Mexico. Units also found themselves diverted to campaigns against Indian tribes. The most intensive operations involved Union armies, but in Texas, Confederate forces attempted to defend the frontiers against aggressive tribes. In the Indian Territory the war divided tribal groups and set off internal strife that reflected the clash of the larger antagonists.

STATE HISTORICAL SOCIETY OF MISSOURI

A heartwrenching portrait by George Caleb Bingham entitled Order No. 11. *In 1863, Union general Thomas Ewing gave all civilians in four Missouri counties not loyal to the Union cause 15 days to leave their homes. This act resulted in violence when Union guerrillas took it upon themselves to loot departing citizens' homes.*

The westward movement did not slow during the war years; in fact, more people than ever made their way west. The administration of President Abraham Lincoln tried to retain the loyalty of westerners and install supportive governments in the states and territories. Western mines helped finance the war, and the discovery of new mines in Idaho, Montana, Colorado, and Arizona lured fortune seekers.

Although most of the western states and territories contained pro-Southern elements, only Arkansas, Louisiana, and Texas joined the Confederacy. Missouri hung in the balance, both sides struggling for its allegiance. For two years, Confederate General Sterling Price sought to win Missouri for the South while Union General Samuel Curtis fended off his attempts. On August 10, 1861, at Wilson's Creek in southwestern Missouri, Price won a decisive victory in a battle that took the life of the Union commander, General Nathaniel Lyon. On March 6–8, 1862, however, Curtis defeated Price at Pea Ridge, Arkansas. Although this battle secured Missouri for the Union, Price did not give up. In the autumn of 1864, he drove on St. Louis and Jefferson City. Failing to win those objectives, Price turned west toward Kansas City and met fierce resistance. After the battles of Westport and Mine Creek, October 23 and 25, 1864, the offensive ended in the virtual destruction of Price's army. Again Curtis played an important part in defeating his rival.

As the armies struggled with each other, bands of guerrillas roamed the western borders of Missouri and Arkansas. Although they were supposedly Confederate, they fought less for a cause than for themselves, and they followed none of the traditional rules of war. Groups battled each other when they were not robbing and terrorizing helpless citizens. The most infamous raider was the Confederate captain William Clarke Quantrill. He led his band of desperadoes in raids and expeditions that kept the border in constant fear and turmoil. The sack of Lawrence, in which some 150 Kansans died in August 1863, was his worst crime. Quantrill ultimately drifted east and died in Kentucky.

Shock waves from Missouri, Arkansas, and Kansas rolled over the Indian Territory and divided the tribes that had lost their original homes under the government's Indian removal policy. The Cherokees, Creeks, and Seminoles each split into factions that lined up with either the Union or the Confederacy. The Choctaws and Chickasaws sided with the South. The South had the advantage, for some tribes owned black slaves and had homelands that bordered the Confederacy, far beyond Union influence. Enlisted by the Arkansas poet Albert Pike, regiments from each of the tribes fought with Confederate armies in Arkansas, Louisiana, and the Indian Territory. The Cherokee Stand Watie was the only Indian to rise to the rank of general and was the last Confederate general to lay down his arms.

Throughout 1862–1864 armies fought over Arkansas and Louisiana. The biggest operation was an offensive mounted in Louisiana by Nathaniel Banks, a Union general who had no military experience. Designed to conquer Louisiana for the Union, the Red River Expedition of 1864 had more than enough men and supplies to crush Confederate General Edmund Kirby-Smith. But in four major battles in April and May 1864, the federal soldiers fought desperately under able subordinates but could not overcome Banks's failings.

For the Confederates, Texas was a conduit for badly needed supplies. Galveston was a major port for cargo vessels running the Union blockade. It fell to a Union amphibious force in October 1862, but was soon retaken by Confederates and held throughout the war. Another important entry point for war supplies was the lower Rio Grande, where foreign shipments were brought from Matamoros, Mexico, to Brownsville, Texas. Banks took Brownsville in November 1864, but the supply line merely shifted upriver.

The Confederacy's most ambitious venture in the West was the invasion of New Mexico, with its ultimate objective the gold mines of Colorado and even of California. General Henry Hopkins Sibley led a brigade of 3,000 Texans from San Antonio to El Paso and then up the Rio Grande into New Mexico. At the Battle of Valverde, on February 16, 1862, he defeated a Union force under Colonel Edward R. S. Canby. After occupying Albuquerque and Santa Fe, Sibley's troops moved at the Union supply depot of Fort Union but were blocked at Glorieta Pass by a federal force rushed south from Colorado under Colonel John P. Slough. With Sibley absent in Santa Fe, the two forces met at Glorieta Pass on March 27 and 28, 1862. Although the Confederates prevailed in the pass, a separate Union force destroyed their supply train in Apache Canyon. That setback forced the Texans to abandon New Mexico.

Many Union units mobilized to fight the Confederacy never saw a Confederate soldier; instead, they fought Indians on the frontier. Most were volunteers recruited in the West. They and their generals often fought more aggressively and competently—though with less humanity toward their foes—than the supposedly professional garrisons they replaced. General James H. Carleton organized a force of 1,800 men in California, and in the spring of 1862 marched across the Arizona desert to head off Sibley's invasion of New Mexico. The California Column arrived too late to fight Confederates and spent the rest of the war fighting Indians—successfully. Carleton's most notable feat, carried out in the field by Colonel Christopher "Kit" Carson, was the conquest of the powerful Navajos, who were rounded up in the winter of 1863–1864 and herded onto a reservation far from their homeland. Another column formed in California was headed by General Patrick E. Connor. He led his men across Nevada to occupy the Salt Lake Valley. There he fought incessantly with Brigham Young and other Mormon leaders, and campaigned against Indians threatening the overland travel routes. Connor won a decisive victory over the Shoshones at the Battle of Bear River, January 29, 1863.

An uprising of Minnesota Sioux in August 1862 set off a chain reaction on the northern Plains that ultimately involved large numbers of troops raised for the Civil War. Minnesota volunteers under General Henry Hastings Sibley suppressed the rebellion in Minnesota. The decisive action occurred at Wood Lake on September 23, 1862. The Minnesota war spilled over into Dakota Territory to the west and soon embroiled the Tetons and other Sioux. In 1863 Sibley campaigned westward while another army under General Alfred Sully pushed north, up the Missouri River. Both fought battles with their quarry: Sibley at Big Mound, Dead Buffalo Lake, and Stony Lake in July; Sully at Whitestone Hill in September. Armies took the field again in 1864, with Sully winning two major victories, at Killdeer Mountain on July 28 and in the Badlands on August 6–9.

In 1864–1865 the entire Great Plains burst into flame. On November 29, 1864, Colorado troops under Colonel John M. Chivington, a stormy Methodist preacher, attacked the Cheyenne encampment of Black Kettle on Sand Creek and perpetrated a shocking massacre. Sand Creek infuriated all the Plains tribes and ignited a general war. In the summer of 1865, General Connor launched three strong columns against the Sioux and Cheyennes of the northern Plains. But the columns wandered blindly across vast distances remote from supply bases, and two nearly collapsed before struggling to safety.

During the final two years of the Civil War, special volunteer regiments campaigned in the West, chiefly on the Upper Missouri and along the overland routes of the Great Plains. These were galvanized Yankees, Confederate captives recruited in the prison camps of the North and sent west to fight Indians. They served with credit and often with distinction.

After the Civil War ended at Appomattox in April 1865, the volunteer units in the West began to disband. By summer's end, most had gone home. The men of the regular army returned to their frontier duties.

Clark, George Rogers

1752–1818

A frontier soldier and the older brother of William Clark, partner with Meriwether Lewis in the 1803–1806 expedition across the western continent, George Rogers Clark was born in Albermarle County, Virginia, and studied surveying as a youth. He took part in Lord Dunmore's War of 1774 against the Shawnees in western Pennsylvania and the Ohio River Valley, and the next year became involved in Kentucky affairs, specifically in petitioning to create Kentucky County out of Virginia territory and to build forts there for the protection of settlers against Indian attacks. (Thomas Jefferson, whose family's farm adjoined that of the Clarks, helped persuade the Virginia Assembly to grant the petition.)

In the summer of 1778, Clark raised an army of 350 men to attack the native tribes in Illinois country who were threatening the Kentucky settlements and to drive the British from the Northwest. With his tiny force he took the Kaskaskia, Illinois, outpost from the British and also captured Cahokia and Vincennes, Indiana. Vincennes, which Clark renamed Fort Patrick Henry (after the governor of Virginia) was subsequently reoccupied by General Henry Hamilton, commander at Detroit, who named it Fort Sackville. In February 1779, Clark and a force of 230 Americans and Frenchmen marched back to Sackville and forced its surrender.

Clark's major objective in the Revolutionary War in the West, to take Detroit from the British, was never accomplished due to lack of adequate supplies and manpower. In mid-1779, he withdrew his meager force to Fort Nelson, near present-day Louisville, Kentucky. Following the war, Clark served as an Indian commissioner and was the focus of a scandal fomented by General James Wilkinson. Clark was stripped of his commission and ruined financially. He retired to Locust Grove, near Louisville, and died there on February 13, 1818.

Clark, William

1770–1838

Son of a distinguished Virginia family and younger brother of the Revolutionary War hero George Rogers Clark, William Clark at age 14 accompanied his family across the Appalachian Mountains to settle in Kentucky. As a young officer of militia, he developed into an accomplished frontiersman and Indian fighter, a robust, 6-foot campaigner conspicuous for his flaming red hair. Commissioned in the infant regular army, he participated in General "Mad Anthony" Wayne's Indian campaign of 1794 and fought at the decisive Battle of Fallen Timbers.

After resigning from the army in 1796, Clark assumed the management of the family's plantation near Louisville, Kentucky. Here in 1803 he received a letter from an old army comrade, Meriwether Lewis, now private secretary to President Thomas Jefferson, inviting him to join in an expedition to explore the American West.

Thus William Clark became the second of the "two captains" who opened the door to Jefferson's newly acquired but largely unknown Louisiana Purchase. The Lewis and Clark Expedition of 1804–1806 ascended the Missouri River to its source, crossed the Rocky Mountains, and descended to the Pacific Ocean, then returned by much the same route. This journey of discovery is one of the great adventure stories of American history. The information the two captains brought back—geographical, ethnological, and scientific—delighted Jefferson and his inner circle, but because of greatly delayed publication did not significantly expand public knowledge or influence public policy. Among the most valuable results was a map drawn by Clark, finally published in 1814, that corrected previous misconceptions of the West's geography.

Clark's enduring fame rests almost entirely on his role in the Lewis and Clark expedition. However, he pursued a distinguished career afterward. Appointed Indian agent for western tribes in 1807, he established himself in St. Louis and lived there for the rest of his life. From 1813 until Missouri became a state in 1821, he served as territorial governor. Clark's most significant influence on the West came after his appointment in 1822 as superintendent of Indian affairs for the trans-Mississippi region, a post he held until his death 16 years later. All the western agents and subagents reported to him, and all traders and trappers heading into the West had to obtain licenses from him. Delegations of chiefs from the upper Mississippi and Missouri rivers and even from the Rocky Mountains came to St. Louis to confer with "Red Head" in his home, which was decorated with Indian artifacts and paintings of Indian leaders. Sometimes he ventured from his base to negotiate treaties, such as that concluded in 1825 at Prairie du Chien, Wisconsin, with Sac And Fox and associated tribes. Both Indians and whites respected Clark as a man who knew the West and its peoples from personal experience and who dealt with the Indians knowingly and compassionately.

INDEPENDENCE NATIONAL
HISTORICAL PARK COLLECTION

William Clark.

Clemens, Samuel Langhorne

1835–1910

Samuel "Mark Twain" Clemens was a humorist, novelist, short-story writer, and lecturer whose honest humanity, ironic humor, vernacular speech, and tall tales captured a worldwide audience and a continued popularity for his simple and direct narrative. Samuel Clemens lived in Hannibal, Missouri, on the Mississippi River from the age of 4 to 18. It was this Mississippi Valley heritage that would inform his novels of boyhood, *The Adventures of Tom Sawyer* (1876) and *The Adventures of Huckleberry Finn* (1884), the latter generally regarded as his finest effort. In 1851 he became a printer's devil for his brother Orion's paper, the *Hannibal Journal,* and then worked as an itinerant printer for a year or so in St. Louis, New York City, and Philadelphia. Continuing a lifelong obsession with the Mississippi and consistent with a constitutional restlessness, Samuel signed on as an apprentice steamboat pilot in 1857, becoming a fully licensed pilot in 1859. However, wanderlust led him to a brief stint in the Confederate militia, and in 1861 he accompanied Orion to Nevada, where his brother was to serve as secretary to the territorial governor. A year later he was a reporter for a paper in Virginia City, writing under the byline Mark Twain, a rivermen's expression for "two fathoms deep" or the depth of 12 feet that is the bare minimum draft for safe riverboat navigation.

Mark Twain's literary success began in 1865 when his story "The Celebrated Jumping Frog of Calaveras County" appeared in the New York periodical, *The Saturday Press.* As a roving newspaper correspondent he traveled to the Sandwich Islands, the Mediterranean, and the Holy Land, and in 1869 he collected these travel letters into *The Innocents Abroad; or, The New Pilgrim's Progress.* In 1870 he married Olivia Langdon and later settled in Redding, Connecticut, as a wealthy and popular author. *Roughing It* (1872), *The Gilded Age* (coauthored with Charles Dudley Warner, 1873), and "Old Times on the Mississippi" (1875), *The Adventures of Tom Sawyer* (1876), *A Tramp Abroad* (1880), *The Prince and the Pauper* (1881), *Life on the Mississippi* (1883), *The Adventures of Huckleberry Finn* (1884), *A Connecticut Yankee in King Arthur's Court* (1889), and *The Tragedy of Pudd'nhead Wilson* (1894) followed.

Samuel Langhorne Clemens.

DRINKING SLUMGULLION

A playful illustration from Roughing It, *the novel in which Mark Twain introduced the world to the "tenderfoot," or novice western traveler.*

However, a publishing house in which he'd invested heavily failed in 1894 and he was forced to appease his creditors by writing for money. The money he earned from these books and a highly successful round-the-world tour as a public lecturer left him debt-free by 1898. His last three books, *The Man that Corrupted Hadleyburg* (1900), *What Is Man?* (1906), and *The Mysterious Stranger* written in 1898, published in 1916, were a marked departure from his humorous writings and emphasized man's inhumanity to man.

Olivia Clemens died in 1904, their daughter Jean in 1909, and in 1910, coincident with the return of Halley's comet, which had last passed by earth during the year of his birth, Mark Twain's mortal star blinked out. An autobiography he had begun to dictate to Jean in 1906 remained unfinished.

Clovis Culture

"Clovis culture" refers to a prehistoric Native-American site near Clovis, New Mexico; it was formerly believed to be the oldest Indian culture in the Americas.

In 1932, a road crew working near Clovis uncovered a deposit of fossilized bones. Subsequent excavations revealed stone implements as well. Among the bones were some from an extinct species of bison, as well as some from a mammoth. It appeared from the evidence that the latter had either become mired in a bog or had been chased there in a coordinated action by hunters. At any rate, the mammoth had been killed by spears or projectiles, and had been eaten.

The distinctive feature of the Clovis culture (also known as the Llano) is the particular spear point associated with it. The so-called Clovis fluted, thin and about three to four inches long, shows definite shaping and a narrow channel from its base toward the point. Clovis fluted points were subsequently discovered in all 48 contiguous states and in Mexico. The points are almost always associated with mammoth bones.

Scientific dating placed the Clovis find at 12,000 years ago. Other early Indian sites were also dated to this point or later. This finding established the so-called Clovis barrier, the presumed earliest date of habitation of the Americas. This theory stood for many years and is still accepted by some. More recent discoveries have established that humans were in the Americas at least 30,000–40,000 years ago. Some disputed evidence places the date even earlier, perhaps as much as 75,000 years or more.

Cochise

CA. 1812–1874

Nothing is known about Cochise's birth or early life, but by the 1850s he had emerged as a prominent and respected chief among the Chokonen people (central Chiricahua Apache), leading by his personal integrity and moral example. Perhaps more than any other Apache, he wished to live in peace with whites, but a series of mistakes and deceptions on the part of U.S. Army officers led him to wage a long and successful guerrilla war.

In 1856, Cochise agreed to allow whites to pass through Chiricahua territory. His people even cut firewood for the stage station at Apache Pass. In 1861, however, Cochise's band was accused of theft by Lieutenant George N. Bascom of the 7th Infantry, who made a bungled attempt to arrest him. Though Cochise escaped, his brother and two nephews were captured and executed. Cochise then joined forces with his father-in-law, Mangas Coloradas, to drive whites from Apache lands. On July 15, 1862, 500 warriors under Mangas and Cochise engaged 300 U.S. soldiers at Apache Pass, but they were defeated.

After Mangas was killed in 1863, Cochise became the principal chief of all the Chiricahuas. In 1871, he was invited to come to Washington to make peace but refused. General George Crook dispatched five companies of cavalry into the Chiricahua Mountains to find Cochise, but he eluded them. He sent word to General Gordon Granger in Santa Fe that he would meet with him to discuss peace. Following negotiations, the Indian leader agreed to settle his people on a reservation at Cañada Alamosa. After only a few months, however, an order came to remove all Apaches to Fort Tularosa, and Cochise again slipped away with his people. President Grant then sent General O. O. Howard to meet with him. Accompanied by a long-time friend of Cochise's, in 1872 Howard's party obtained the chief's agreement to settle on a reservation that included a portion of the Chiricahua Mountains; here he died in 1874.

Cody, William Frederick "Buffalo Bill"

1846–1917

Frontiersman, scout, and showman, Cody was the emblem of the American West for half a century; no personality before or since symbolized it in the popular mind more indelibly than the extraordinary Buffalo Bill.

Cody was born near Le Claire, Iowa; his family moved to Salt Creek Valley, near Leavenworth, Kansas Territory, in 1854. Young Cody's first employment was as a teamster for a freight company. He experimented with mining and trapping in the years up to 1860–1861, when, at age 15, he rode with the Pony Express for the Russell, Majors & Waddell Company.

During the Civil War, Cody joined Kansas freebooters—horse thieves, for the most part—and served with other irregular militia before formally enlisting, in 1864, as a private in the 7th Kansas Volunteers and later serving with the 7th Kansas Volunteer Cavalry. He was discharged in September 1865, and within a few weeks was employed as scout and dispatch bearer for the army in Kiowa and Comanche lands along the Santa Fe Trail.

Cody married Louisa Frederici in 1866, and for a brief time retired from scouting to run a hotel. But he soon returned to the life he loved, scouting for Lieutenant Colonel George Armstrong Custer out of Fort Hays in 1867, and for such other officers as William B. Hazen and Philip H. Sheridan from forts Larned, Hays, and Dodge, rising to chief of scouts for the 5th Cavalry. It appears that Cody received his famous nickname in 1867 while hunting buffalo for Union Pacific construction crews.

Between 1866 and 1872, Cody took part in an estimated 14 Indian fights. Among the most celebrated were skirmishes against the Cheyennes, at Elephant Rock and Spring Creek during the Republican River campaign, commanded by Major Eugene A. Carr of the 5th Cavalry. At Summit Springs, just over the Kansas line in Colorado Territory, on July 11, 1869, Cody and a contingent of Pawnee scouts led Carr's force of 244 men into a camp of Cheyenne Dog Soldiers—the tribal warrior society. The brief battle resulted in the rout of the camp, the capture of over 400 horses, and the killing of 52 Cheyennes. Cody was credited by Carr and others with killing the Dog Soldier leader, Tall Bull.

A short time after the Summit Springs battle, Cody met the dime novelist Edward Z. C. Judson, who wrote under the name Ned Buntline; in 1869, Buntline wrote the first of a long series of sensational stories on Buffalo Bill's adventures.

In 1872, after Indian fights at Birdwood Creek and

A 1910 advertisement for one of Buffalo Bill's many "final" appearances.

Buffalo Bill and some of his Native-American performers.

elsewhere in Nebraska, Cody was awarded the Medal of Honor for his long service in the Indian campaigns. (The medal was rescinded in 1917 because Cody was ruled a civilian and therefore not qualified to receive the nation's highest honor for valor in battle. In 1989, however, the Medal of Honor was restored to Cody, 72 years after his death, following a new ruling by the army.)

The year 1872 marked Cody's debut as a showman. Buntline persuaded him to come to Chicago to appear in a melodrama he had written, *The Scouts of the Prairie*. The play, for all its ridiculous dialogue, costumes, sets, and its stilted action, was a success. Cody continued to make dramatic appearances over the next decade. He returned west between theatrical seasons to guide hunters and the army in Indian campaigns.

Cody served as chief scout at the start of General George Crook's Yellowstone expedition in 1876. On July 17, 1876, 22 days after the Custer battle, Cody had his most famous Indian fight, one that was to be the subject of countless dime novels and dramatic tableaus. It was a "duel" of sorts with the Cheyenne war leader Yellow Hand (more correctly Yellow Hair) at Hat Creek, near present-day Montrose, Nebraska. The two met accidentally, it appears, and they fired at each other simultaneously. Yellow Hand's bullet missed Cody, but Cody's struck the Cheyenne in the

leg, causing his horse to fall. Dismounted, each fired again; this time Cody's bullet killed Yellow Hand. The Cheyenne's scalp, which Cody grandly called "the first scalp for Custer," became one of his prized and most often displayed possessions.

After his retirement from scouting, Cody ranched in the area north of North Platte, Nebraska, while continuing his stage appearances. In 1882, in North Platte and in Council Bluffs, Iowa, he launched his world-famous "Buffalo Bill's Wild West," an extravaganza that came to include a Pony Express race, a runaway stagecoach, a reenactment of the Custer battle, and sharpshooting, roping, and riding exhibitions. Cody's "Wild West" performers included such celebrated figures as Annie "Little Sure Shot" Oakley and, in 1885, the Hunkpapa Sioux chief Sitting Bull. The show was a huge success from the beginning, and Cody, who never missed a performance, took it to Europe in 1887, 1889, and 1906—to the delight of sold-out audiences and an ecstatic press—and to the World's Columbian Exposition at Chicago in 1893.

Late in 1890 Cody returned west to the Standing Rock Indian Agency in North Dakota, to persuade his friend Sitting Bull to surrender to Major General Nelson A. Miles, but was recalled before he could visit the Sioux. (Sitting Bull was killed on December 15, within days of Cody's intended visit.)

The master showman made his last European tour in 1906. In 1908 he merged his "Wild West" with a show owned by Gordon W. "Pawnee Bill" Lillie. After leaving that operation, he performed periodically with the Sells-Floto Circus until the month before his death on January 10, 1917. Cody was laid to rest atop Lookout Mountain, above Denver, despite his wish to be buried on Cedar Mountain, overlooking the Wyoming town he had named for himself. Harry Tammen, owner of the *Denver Post*, paid for his burial. Cody was a tall, robust, handsome, and courtly man of good humor, with an affinity for strong liquor, expert with a tall story and in embroidering, unnecessarily, his eventful life.

Coeur d'Alene

From the French for "awl-heart," Coeur d'Alene was the translation by French trappers of the Indian word *skitswish*. The tribe of that name, related to the Flatheads, had historically lived in northern Idaho in the vicinity of today's Lake Coeur d'Alene, and their reservation is located there.

The Coeur d'Alenes were a nonnomadic hunting tribe first encountered, at least by Americans, during the Lewis and Clark expedition. Their name was adopted for a lake, river, city, and mountain range in northern Idaho. The city, 33 miles east of Spokane, Washington, and seat of Kootenai County, thrives today with a population of over 25,000.

A silver strike in the Coeur d'Alene country in 1884 revealed that the area was one of the richest silver-lead regions in the world. The stampede began when a prospector named Noah Kellogg stumbled on veins of silver-bearing ore. (Legend has it that one of Kellogg's mules ran off and was found standing on an outcropping of galena, a mixture of silver and lead.) Within a month of the strike, the town of Wardner had sprung up south of the Coeur d'Alene River. The site would yield some $300 million in ore over the next 60 years. In 1892, the Coeur d'Alene district was the scene of a historic labor strike in which miners objected to the establishment of a $.50-a-day wage. In response to the walkout, mine owners shipped in workers from as far away as Michigan, including immigrants ignorant of their role as strikebreakers. The strikers responded by blowing up a mill, killing one man and injuring 20 others. The strike ended after Idaho governor Frank Steunenberg sent in the National Guard to stop the violence, aided by 20 companies of U.S. Infantry

LIBRARY OF CONGRESS

The Sacred Heart mission settlement in Idaho, built by Father Point, assisted by Coeur d'Alene Indians.

troops authorized by President Benjamin Harrison. One outgrowth of the strike was the creation of the powerful Western Federation of Miners labor union.

Colorado

The topography of Colorado, the 38th state to join the Union, is dominated by the Great Plains, the Rocky Mountains, and the Colorado Plateau. The Great Plains, a flat stretch of land, occupies over one-third of the state. The Rocky Mountains, rising to the west of the Plains, cover approximately another third. Mount Elbert, with an elevation of 14,433 feet, is the highest peak in the entire Rocky Mountain system. The western third of Colorado is covered by the Colorado Plateau, a region of valleys, mesas, and deep canyons. Six major rivers rise in Colorado: the Colorado, Arkansas, North and South Platte, Republican, and the Rio Grande.

Evidence shows that Colorado was occupied by nomadic hunters over 10,000 years ago. More recent Indian tribes to inhabit the area include the Utes of the mountain valleys, the Arapahos and Cheyennes, who occupied the eastern prairies, the Comanches, Kiowas, and Apaches in the south, and the Sioux in the north.

DENVER PUBLIC LIBRARY

Miners playing cards in Cripple Creek, Colorado, in the 1890s. They are warmed by a cast-iron stove, a rare luxury in mining towns at this time.

The earliest European explorers were Spanish. At some point between 1164 and 1680, the Spanish soldier Juan de Archoleta wandered with a small expedition from New Mexico, where the Spanish had established settlements, into southeastern Colorado and thus became the first European to visit Colorado. On the whole, Spain never successfully established a lasting foothold in Colorado. The Spanish did, though, continue to explore the region somewhat, most notably in the 1776 expedition of Fathers Francisco Dominguez and Silvestre Escalante. With a small party numbering less than ten, the two priests set out from Sante Fe, heading northwest up into Colorado, where they then crossed westward into Utah, then south in Arizona, and finally east back to Sante Fe.

The United States acquired the central and eastern section of Colorado in 1803 with the Louisiana Purchase, and American-sponsored exploration quickly followed. In 1806, Lieutenant Zebulon Pike led a team to the Colorado Rockies, Royal Gorge, and the Sangre de Cristo Mountains. In 1820, Major Stephen Long headed an expedition of nineteen men to Colorado with the goal of finding the sources of the Arkansas, Platte, and Red Rivers. Although they never discovered the river sources, they succeeded in scaling Pike's Peak, which Pike's own team had failed to do when they discovered the mountain fourteen years earlier.

In the early 1850s, farmers from New Mexico ventured north and became the first permanent white settlers in Colorado. However, it was the discovery of gold in 1858 near present-day Denver that sparked a rush of settlers. It is estimated that the Pikes' Peak gold rush brought 50,000 men to the region by the spring of 1859. The settlers ignored Indian claims to the territory and established the unrecognized Territory of Jefferson. In 1861, Congress officially formed the Colorado Territory, setting boundaries that exist today. President Ulysses S. Grant issued the official proclamation of statehood for Colorado, the Centennial State, on August 1, 1876.

Colorado grew rapidly after entering the Union: The mining industry flourished, and eventually miners pushed into areas reserved for the Ute Indians. The miners were looking for an excuse to remove the Utes from their land, and the Meeker Massacre in 1879 provided one. After a party of Utes, resisting government civilization programs,

This railroad poster romanticized the natural beauty of Colorado to attract wealthy tourists.

Colorado River

A major river in the Southwest, the Colorado drains seven states and a portion of Mexico. The source of the river is Grand Lake in the western slopes of the Colorado Rockies. From there it falls southwest about 1,400 miles through several spectacular canyons, including the Grand Canyon. At Gore Canyon, the Colorado drops 360 feet within five miles. The river then winds through the desert and flows into the Gulf of California.

The land along the Colorado has been occupied for thousands of years. Pueblo dwellings are found along its basin, and evidence exists of water management and irrigation in the region long before the arrival of the Spanish in 1540. By the time the Spaniards arrived, most tribes had abandoned the area. The first Spanish explorers of the Colorado River, both of

The Colorado River.

killed Agent Nathan Meeker and other agency personnel, their lands were taken, and they were forced to re-settle in Utah. In the following years, the Cripple Creek mines opened in Colorado; they were the site of the famous labor strikes of 1894 and 1904. Today mining plays a smaller role in Colorado's economy, with manufacturing accounting for over half the value of goods produced. Tourism produces more revenue than mining, drawing an estimated 8 million people annually to restored mining towns, resorts such as Aspen, and the Rocky Mountain National Park. Colorado's capital, and largest city, is Denver.

John Russell Bartlett, commissioner of the Mexican Boundary Survey, sketched this view of Fort Yuma, at the Colorado River.

whom were part of the Coronado expedition, were Hernando de Alarcon in 1540, and Garcia Lopez De Cárdenas two years later. The river was named for the reddish color of its water by the Spanish priest and explorer Francisco Hermengildo Garcés. Fur trappers were the first Americans to explore the Colorado.

The main cities on the Colorado include Yuma, Arizona, and Grand Junction, Colorado. The seasonal fluctuation in the flow of the Colorado has been controlled by the construction of several dams, including the Hoover Dam, completed in 1936. Several national parks are located along or near the river, notably Rocky Mountain National Park, Canyonlands National Park, and Grand Canyon National Park.

ENGRAVED BY HW SMITH

Samuel Colt.

Colt Revolver

See Colt, Samuel

Colt, Samuel

1814–1862

Samuel Colt was an inventor and manufacturer. Born in Hartford, Connecticut, this avatar of Yankee ingenuity began his career inauspiciously, going to sea at age 16. While on a voyage to Singapore, he whittled a wooden model for a revolver-type handgun and, within a year, constructed two working models and patented them. Unfortunately, his first actual pistol, which was marketed from 1836 to 1842, was poorly made and did not sell particularly well.

Colt had financial troubles throughout this period and finally was forced to shut down his Patent Arms Company, then located in Paterson, N.J. Five years later, he would achieve the success he sought. The 1847 model revolver, which was actually manufactured by Whitney Armory because Colt no longer had a factory at his disposal, was a vastly improved weapon. The improvements were introduced by Captain Samuel H. Walker of the Texas Rangers, who had been taken with Colt's original idea of a re-

volving chamber dispensing bullets, allowing a man on horseback to fire a number of shots before reloading. Called the Walker Colt, the 1847 gun was a great success. Colt received a contract from the government for 1,100 of the revolvers for use in the Mexican War, and he was now able to start his own plant again, this time in his native Hartford.

With the gold rush speeding westward movement, there was a new, ready market for high-quality handguns, and Colt's sales soared. During the 1850s, the use of Colt-manufactured handguns became so prevalent that his name became a synonym for handgun. In the Civil War, Colt revolvers were widely used as well. The classic Colts of the period were the Model 1851 Navy, a .36 caliber, and the Model 1860 Army, a .44 caliber.

The biggest breakthrough made by the Colt organization after the acceptance of the revolver itself was the move in 1873 from percussion cap–fired ammunition made of loose powder and ball in a paper or linen cartridge to a newly invented metal cartridge. This cartridge contained its own primer and powder, with the bullet at the open end of a hollow copper or brass tube. The pistol that fired this ammunition is perhaps the most famous of Colt's many models. It was called the Peacemaker, and was frequently eulogized as "the gun that won the West," which is perhaps only a mild exaggeration.

An 1860 Colt .44 and accessories.

Colt himself remained in charge of his company until his death in 1862. In addition to his important innovations in firearms, he developed a submarine battery which was used in harbor defense, and a submarine telegraph cable.

Colter, John

CA. 1774–1813

As a member of Manuel Lisa's fur trapping party in 1807, Colter was sent to northwestern Wyoming. Although he did not enter what is now Yellowstone National Park, he was the first non-native to discover nearby hot springs and other thermal phenomena of the northern Rockies.

Colter spent the first five years of his life near Staunton, Virginia, then moved with his family to Maysville, Kentucky. It was there, on October 15, 1803, that he was recruited by Captain Meriwether Lewis. Although enlisted as a private, he soon gained the confidence of Lewis and Clark and was given many important and dangerous assignments. In acknowledgment of his expert hunting skills, a tributary of the Clearwater River was christened "Colter's Creek."

Colter was honorably discharged from the expedition on the return journey so that he could join two trappers in a venture up the Missouri River. The trapping partnership did not last, however, and in the spring of 1807 Colter set out alone down the Missouri River toward St. Louis. At the mouth of the Platte he met a trapping party led by Manuel Lisa, who convinced Colter to join him. It was while on a trading mission to the Crow and other Indian tribes that Colter traveled alone through western Wyoming in 1807. Coming upon hot springs in the area, he became the first white man to discover and describe the thermal phenomena of the northern Rockies. He is also believed to be the first white explorer of the Teton Range.

Colter returned to St. Louis in May 1809 and shortly thereafter signed on with Andrew Henry's trapping expedition up the Missouri River. He was sent with John Potts, another member of the Lewis and Clark expedition, to trap in Blackfeet territory. Near the Three Forks of the Missouri, the men came in conflict with the Blackfeet: Potts was killed, and Colter made a narrow escape. Undaunted, he returned to the area the following year, serving as a guide for about 30 of Lisa's men. The group was constructing a post between the Madison and Jefferson rivers when the Blackfeet descended on them, killing five men. Colter barely escaped for the second time and returned to St. Louis in May 1810.

Colter then married and settled on a farm near Charette, Franklin County, Missouri. William Clark sought his counsel on a map of the Northwest, which was published in the 1814 Biddle edition of the Lewis and Clark journals. The path he took when he first explored the region appears as a dotted line on the map, marked "Colter's Route." Colter lived the rest of his life in Charette as a farmer, and died of jaundice in November 1813.

Columbia River

The Columbia River, the most powerful river in the United States, rises in Columbia Lake in British Columbia, Canada, and enters the United States in northeastern Washington. The river forms part of the border between Oregon and Washington and empties into the Pacific Ocean; it is 1,214 miles long. The Columbia drains an area of 258,000 square miles in Canada and four northwestern U.S. states. The Willamette, Snake, and Kootenay rivers are its main tributaries.

In 1792, Robert Gray became the first known European to sail into the Columbia, which was named for his ship. He traded with the Chinook Indians. Settlers later arrived and traded with numerous local tribes, such as the Spokane, Coeur D'Alenes, Sanpoils, and Okanogan, until the Indians were forced onto the Colville Reservation west of the river. The Lewis and Clark Expedition explored the Columbia in 1805, and by the 1850s even steamboats were braving its rapids.

Hydroelectric development has proceeded rapidly since the 1930s, and there are now 11 mainstream dams. The Columbia and its tributaries make up one-third of all U.S. hydroelectric potential. Commercial fishing industries have pulled salmon and other fish from its fast-flowing waters since the 1860s.

Comanche Indians

This Indian tribe became known as perhaps the fiercest warriors of the Plains. Beginning in the late 1600s, the Comanches migrated south from Wyoming to Nebraska, where they probably acquired horses and became nomadic buffalo hunters. They continued to move south, and by 1719 they were in present-day Kansas. In turn, they pushed the Apaches before them, defeating them by means of newly acquired firearms. Joining with their linguistic cousins, the Utes, they raided deep into Mexico. They became the terror of the Spaniards, the Mexicans, and the Texans. They also continued to raid other Indian tribes.

Though they made their first treaty with the United States in 1835 and tried to live in peace with the whites, they continued to raid other Indian tribes. In the 1830s, some of the Five Civilized Tribes were afraid to take possession of lands assigned to them in Indian Territory because of Comanche raids. The Comanches blamed the U.S. government for introducing the newcomers. They hated the Texans and never understood that Texas had become part of the United States; they continued to make a distinction between Americans and Texans.

In the decades before the Civil War, white settlers continued to enter Comanche territory. In 1853, the Comanches, in alliance with other tribes, made a

PANHANDLE PLAINS HISTORICAL MUSEUM

Comanche Chief Quanah Parker, whose mother was a captured white woman, donned this stunning war bonnet for battle.

This painting of a Comanche encampment in Texas shows women readying buffalo hides to be stitched together to make tipis.

Comanche Chief Otter Belt.

concerted attempt to turn back the invaders. They were defeated by an alliance of whites and other settled Indian tribes. By the Medicine Lodge Treaties in 1867, the Comanches were settled on a reservation in the southwestern part of Indian Territory. While a

majority of the tribe went to live on these lands, a small minority continued to roam their old territory and staged raids until 1874.

In 1873–1874, a prophet named Isatai arose among the Comanches. He promised that the buffalo would return if the Indians destroyed the white invaders. Believing in his promised supernatural protection, the Comanches made plans to attack a camp of buffalo hunters at Adobe Walls in the Texas Panhandle. Though some of the Comanches were not pleased with the decision, the attack went forward under the direction of Quanah Parker. The attack failed, but it led to a general uprising known as the Red River War in 1874–1875. By the end of the nineteenth century, the Comanches had settled down on the reservation. They farmed and raised cattle, but to a great extent supported themselves by leasing grazing land to whites.

Compromise of 1850

The Compromise of 1850 was legislation enacted by the U.S. Congress that aimed at ending sectional disputes regarding new territories acquired after the Mexican War.

In the years following the Mexican War, sectional antagonism revived. The Wilmot Proviso, which prohibited slavery in the new territories, was one of the most hotly debated issues facing the Union. With the exception of the Iowa state legislature, Northern states supported the provision, while Southern states were united in their opposition. The South, led by John C. Calhoun, threatened to secede rather than agree to the proviso, and a convention was called to discuss their options. One suggestion favored extending the 36° 30′ line set in the Missouri Compromise to the Pacific Coast and allowing slavery below it. Another favored popular sovereignty in the new territory. Other issues fueling the sectional conflict were the disputes over Texas boundary claims, Northern discontent with the existence of slavery and the slave trade in Washington, D.C., and Southern concerns over the lack of enforcement of the fugitive slave laws. Furthermore, when California sought admission to the Union as a free state, the existing balance between slave and free states was threatened. The Congress that convened in December 1849 faced an impending national crisis.

In January 1850 Henry Clay introduced a bill aimed at satisfying all Northern and Southern concerns. Congress debated the bill intensely for months, and a version closely resembling Clay's was passed in September 1850. The compromise admitted California to the Union as a free state. Slave trading was abolished in Washington, D.C., but slavery itself was left intact. The Texas boundary dispute was settled, with the federal government paying Texas $10 million to cover debts contracted by the state. In addition, the territories of Utah and New Mexico were granted popular sovereignty, and much tougher fugitive slave laws were passed.

Comstock, Henry T. P.

1820–1870

Comstock, a prospector, is best known for his association with the famous Comstock Lode, discovered in Nevada in 1859. Although he was not responsible for the discovery of the giant silver deposits, Comstock often referred to the lode as "my mine" and "Comstock's lode." Ultimately the mine

became known to miners and geologists all over the world as the Comstock Lode.

Comstock sold one claim from the Comstock Lode for $10,000 and another for two mules. After thriving in Virginia City, Nevada, for a short period, he sold his interest in the mine and opened general merchandise stores in Silver City and Carson City. When these stores failed, he lost his small fortune and roamed north to Montana, where he hoped to strike it rich again as a prospector. He committed suicide on September 27, 1870, by shooting himself in the head.

Comstock Lode

The Comstock Lode, a rich silver deposit in the Washoe Valley of Nevada, was most productive between 1859 and 1880, a period in which it produced an impressive $500 million worth of ore. During their heyday, the Comstock mines gave rise to boomtowns such as Virginia City and created individual fortunes for men such as George Hearst and John Percival Jones. By the early 1880s, annual production from the Comstock Lode had dropped dramatically, and mining continued only on a limited basis.

The Comstock Lode was discovered in the spring

Henry T. P. Comstock.

Miners took frequent water breaks in the intense heat of the Comstock Mines.

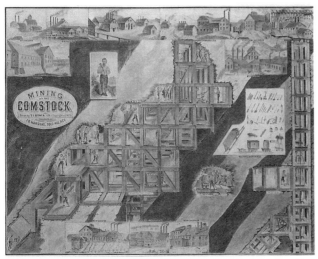

UNIVERSITY OF CALIFORNIA

Mining operations created an intricate network of tunnels in the earth, depicted here in 1876 in "Mining on the Creek," made at Gold Hill, Nevada.

of 1859 by two Irishmen, Peter O'Riely and Pat McLaughlin, who were digging on a new claim at the head of Six Mile Canyon. They were encouraged to find gold at this location but were annoyed at the presence of a blue-black clay that got in their way. That afternoon, Henry Thomas Paige Comstock came riding into the area and, guessing that something good had been found, managed to convince O'Riely and McLaughlin that they were on land that belonged to him. To settle the issue, he invited the two into partnership. What they had really discovered was not a placer mine, but a silver vein traceable for two and a half miles. Thus Comstock did not actually discover the Comstock Lode but, through his unjustified claims and persistent self-promotion, caused the silver lode to carry his name.

Operations at the site grew quickly, and the Comstock Lode became internationally famous. Most of those who rushed to the Washoe region were leaving placer camps in California that had started to decay. Although some new recruits from the East were attracted to the area, the lode remained mostly in the hands of Californians. Because few had the capital or experience for the lode mining of silver, many turned to claims speculation. There were 17,000 claims, but half of the production and 80 percent of the dividends came from two mines: the Crown Point and Belcher, and the Consolidated Virginia and California.

Sometimes reaching a depth of 3,000 feet, the Comstock mines required much more equipment and capital than had been necessary in California. As a result, the technological advances in mining veins on a large scale made necessary by the Comstock Lode were significant in the later development of quartz mines in California and vein mines in Utah and Nevada. One of the most important innovations at Comstock was the "square set" pattern of underground timbers, developed by Philip Deidesheimer, a German engineer. This technique, which solved the problem of how to keep underground chambers from caving in, was studied and applied by engineers throughout the world.

Many of the skilled and resourceful miners from the Comstock Lode brought their expertise to other mines throughout the Far West and became a significant presence in the 1870s and 1880s. In addition, manufacturers in San Francisco produced and shipped equipment whose design was greatly influenced by the demands of the Comstock. Not only did the Comstock mines lead the West in production and technological advancement, but the miners' unions took a lead in the mining labor movement in the West. The presence of a much larger work force, together with the increased danger of working in a larger mine, made an effective labor organization necessary.

Conestoga Wagon

The greatest and most familiar of the covered wagons, the Conestoga wagon had a considerable history before its appearance as the settlers' conveyance of choice west of the Mississippi. A variation of the Conestoga wagon (the name is derived from the Conestoga River Valley around Lancaster County, Pennsylvania, where the wagons were manufactured) was used early in the eighteenth century to haul goods from Lancaster to Philadelphia, and Conestogas were used during the French and Indian War as supply wagons.

Originally a Pennsylvania Dutch design, a typical Conestoga of the mid-nineteenth century took four workmen about two months to build. It was a huge vehicle, 26 feet long and 12 feet high and weighing, empty, over 3,000 pounds. Its deep bed was about 16 feet long, 4 feet wide, and 4 feet deep. It was bowed slightly in the middle, it ends arching upward, boatlike, so that on rough terrain its cargo would shift toward the center and not toward the end gates. Flooring and sideboards were inch-thick poplar; the frame, of oak.

From the Conestoga's sideboards, 6 to 16 curved wooden bows held the white canvas or homespun cloth cover, the front and back of which was puckered with a drawstring, the sides lashed to the sideboards. The boat shape of the wagon caused the cover to extend farther fore and aft than the wagon bed itself.

The running gear or frame-wheel assembly was extremely sturdy: heavy iron braces, hickory axles, and wheel hubs of sweetgum, a wood almost impossible to split. The back wheels were larger than the front: three feet, six inches, in front and four feet, eight inches, in back, with four-inch rims being the common size. The wheels were shod with half-inch iron, usually two curved pieces welded by the blacksmith, fitted around the wooden rim of the wagon wheel, and shrunk with a cold-water bath to snug them against the rim. The wheels were slightly dished outward to give balance to the heavy wagon, and were held on the axle by huge linchpins. They were braked by a cross beam underneath the rear of the wagon bed, with a block of hickory wood on each end serving as a shoe. A brake lever on the left side of the wagon pressed the hickory blocks against the iron "tires" on the rear wheels. The wagons were brightly and patriotically painted with a blue body and red running gear, topped by the snowy-white canvas cover.

Conestogas were usually pulled by three teams—six horses in three pairs: lead, swing, and wheel. Favored animals (some of them called Conestoga horses) were bays and chestnuts, weighing 1,800 pounds or more, that could haul a loaded wagon 12–18 miles a day. (The frame of bells on the collars of the horses gave rise to the expression "I'll be there with bells on." The bells were not used in Indian country.) Oxen also were used to pull Conestogas (an ox-drawn wagon train was called a bull train) but were slower; and if mules were used, it took at least 10 to equal the power of 6 big horses.

Conestogas were designed for hauling freight and not for passenger travel, so the teamster generally strode alongside his wagon or rested by riding occasionally on the left wheel horse. Use of these great vehicles of westward expansion declined rapidly after the Civil War as railroads penetrated the West.

Continental Divide

Also called the Great Divide, this is the line separating the areas in America that drain east toward the Atlantic Ocean, and the areas that drain west toward the Pacific. The divide follows the crest of the Rocky Mountains, entering the United States in northwestern Montana, winding through Wyoming and Colorado, and exiting through New Mexico. Thousands of feet high in most places, the divide lies so flat across some regions of Wyoming that it is difficult to detect its crest.

The Continental Divide marked the western boundary of the Louisiana Purchase of 1803 and so became a border of the United States. It was crossed by white men for the first time during the Lewis and Clark Expedition of 1804–1806. For the next 50 years the Great Divide was explored by some mountain men and trappers. In 1858, however, the discovery of gold at Pikes Peak brought a rush of prospectors. Over the next 40 years mining camps and towns sprang up along the divide. Many of these became thriving communities, including Alder Gulch and Virginia City in Montana; Atlantic City in Wyoming; and Cripple Creek, Aspen, and Central City in Colorado. Although many of the settlements became Ghost Towns, some survived as resorts and tourist towns. The Great Divide is a place of spectacular scenery: Glacier, Yellowstone, and Rocky Mountain National Parks are all on the Continental Divide.

Cooper, James Fenimore

1789–1851

A novelist, historian, and social critic, Cooper is best remembered for his fictional tales of Leatherstocking. The value of Cooper's contribution to Western literature is often debated: Some criticize his fiction as unrealistic; others credit him with creating a new genre—the frontier tale.

When Cooper was a year old, his wealthy Quaker parents settled in Cooperstown, New York, founded earlier by his father. Expelled from Yale for misconduct, Cooper was sent away to begin a naval career.

JOHN WELSEY JARVIS,
LIBRARY OF CONGRESS

James Fenimore Cooper.

In 1811, he abandoned this life and married Susan DeLancy. Rumor has it that Cooper once criticized a novel with the claim that he could do better and, when challenged by his wife, did just that. *Precaution* (1820) was the first of his many frontier tales, sea romances, and works of social criticism. He died in Cooperstown in 1851.

Cooper's most influential works were *The Leatherstocking Tales*, the adventures of frontiersman Natty Bumppo (Leatherstocking) and Chingachgook, his Indian companion. The series includes *The Pioneers* (1823), *The Last of the Mohicans* (1826), *The Prairie* (1827), *The Pathfinder* (1840), and *The Deerslayer* (1841).

Coronado, Francisco Vazquez de

CA. 1510–1554

A Spanish explorer of the American Southwest, Coronado failed to find the riches he was seeking, but did discover many important landmarks, among them the Grand Canyon.

Coronado left Spain in 1535, accompanying Antonio de Mendoza, the Spanish viceroy, to Mexico.

Three years later he was appointed governor of Nueva Galicia, a province in northwest Mexico. In 1539 Fray Marcos de Niza traveled north to present-day New Mexico and returned with stories of lavish wealth and treasures in the Seven Golden Cities of Cibola. Inspired by these accounts, Mendoza organized an expedition led by Coronado to explore the region and search for the treasure. The expedition departed in the spring of 1540 from Campostela, Mexico, about 500 miles northwest of Mexico City. Three hundred Spaniards, 800 Indians, and a number of horses, pigs, and cattle advanced up the west coast of Mexico to the area along the Arizona-New Mexico border. In July 1540 a small detachment from the main expedition captured Cibola, one of a cluster of Zuni towns located in northwest New Mexico. Instead of a city of gold, however, the Spaniards found a small settlement consisting of mud huts stacked on top of one another. The Spanish soldiers stormed the village, leaving dozens of dead Zunis, and Cibola became Coronado's base camp for several months.

One of Coronado's lieutenants, Garcia Lopez de Cárdenas, ventured west to the Colorado River and became the first white man to see the Grand Canyon. Two ships led by Hernando de Alarcon sailed up the Gulf of California and through the mouth of the Colorado River. He and his men were the first Spaniards to set eyes on California. In New Mexico, two Indian prisoners told Coronado of their home in a place called Quivara, located in modern Kansas. In the spring of 1541, Coronado and about 30 other men went across the panhandles of Texas and Oklahoma to explore the area. Upon reaching the Arkansas River, they encountered the Indians of Quivara but were once more disappointed to find no treasure, no gold, and no wealth. Coronado returned to Mexico in 1542, forced to report at an official inquiry that the expedition had not been a success.

Coronado was investigated for Indian uprisings that had occurred in his province during his absence; for mistreating Indians; and for not pressing beyond Quivara to search for the fabled gilded cities. With the help of Mendoza he was subsequently cleared of all charges, but he was ultimately stripped of his governorship. He held a seat on the council in Mexico City, however, until his death on September 22, 1554. Although the expedition was a failure in the eyes of Spanish officials who had hoped to discover vast riches, Coronado's travels added significantly to the geographical knowledge of the American Southwest and is therefore considered by historians to be one of the most successful explorations of North America.

Cortinas, Juan Nepomuceno

1824–1892

Cortinas was a Mexican cultural hero and bandit who fought for the rights of his oppressed countrymen. By the mid-nineteenth century, many Mexicans in the Southwest were aware that Anglo law was undermining their power as landowners. Son of a wealthy family, Cortinas felt his own power as a community leader threatened by the Anglocontrolled police, courts, and laws that relegated Mexicans to second-class citizenship. He declared a Mexican Republic near his ranch in the Rio Grande Valley of Texas in 1859, and in its brief existence it served as a refuge for other frustrated Mexicans.

In July 1859 Cortinas witnessed the beating of a Mexican by a marshal from nearby Brownsville. Killing or abusing Mexicans was not unlawful, and when the marshal ignored his request to stop, Cortinas exploded. He injured the marshal and rescued the Mexican, thus beginning his revolt.

Two months later Cortinas and about a hundred men raided Brownsville, virtually the only Anglo community in the region. The rebels occupied the city, released the prisoners from jail, and raised the Mexican flag in this "Republic of the Rio Grande." Others joined him in the struggle against local authorities and Texas Rangers, and his actions moved many Mexicans to try to repossess the land that had been once been theirs.

Cortinas was eventually defeated by the U.S. Army, but escaped across the border to safety. He continued his raids from Mexico as an army general under President Benito Juárez. The U.S. Army sent Colonel Robert E. Lee to Texas with instructions to enter Mexico, if necessary. When Porfirío Díaz gained power, fear of invasion prompted him to imprison Cortinas in 1875. Cortinas was released from prison 15 years later, and when he died in 1892, he was praised as a patriot by his countrymen.

Covered Wagons

See Conestoga Wagon; Wagon Trains

TEXAS STATE ARCHIVES

Juan Nepomuceno Cortinas.

Cowboys

No figure more vividly personifies the Old West than the cowboy—the plainsman who tended cattle during the heyday of the open range. The popular image of the American cowboy is in large part myth, tailored by film and print as a colorful, free-spirited, self-reliant, adventuresome, efficient, and skilled practitioner of an exotic trade. The image is not entirely false, for to a greater or lesser degree the genuine cowboy could have all these qualities. But he was mainly a drudge laborer, leading a life of hard and endless work varied by relentless boredom. He was paid meager wages, provided crude lodging, fed a poor diet, and exposed daily to hardships and danger. Yet the man on horseback has always stirred the imagination of Americans, and the western cowboy is the classic American horseman.

J.H.C. GRABILL, LIBRARY OF CONGRESS

A stern-looking trail boss surveys the range.

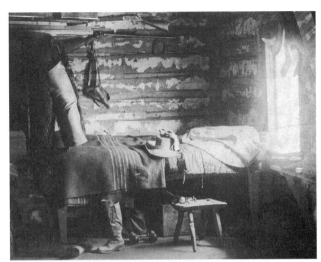

WESTERN HISTORY RESEARCH CENTER, UNIVERSITY OF WYOMING

A cowboy's bunk.

The cowboy flourished in the two decades following the Civil War. These were the peak years of the Open Range, when stockmen grazed their herds on the unfenced sweep of public domain and needed cowhands to perform all the chores of tending cows. The cattle industry took root in Texas when returning Confederate soldiers found great herds of wild longhorns that needed only to be rounded up and transported to the beef markets of the East. The cowmen blazed trails north to the railroads being built west across Kansas and Nebraska. Over the Chisholm Trail and parallel trails they launched the "trail drive," first to the railheads from which the animals could be shipped to slaughter pens in the East, then to the northern Plains, where fresh grasslands invited expansion. To handle the cattle on their home pastures and to drive them to market or to new pastures, the cowboy was essential.

Most cowboys of the open-range period were youthful veterans of the Civil War, mainly Confederates abandoning the wreckage of their prewar lives. They were restless and often rootless, used to hardship, and like many looked to the West for a new beginning. Most were white Southerners, but many (one in seven is an authoritative estimate)

were blacks, and as many were Hispanics. Some were Indians. The blacks were mostly former slaves or freedmen. Neither they nor the Hispanics and Indians found easy acceptance in the cowboy culture. But the life threw men together in mutual dependence, and the able cowboy of color encountered less racism and more opportunity than in many other environments of the time.

The successful cowboy possessed a range of skills developed by practice, experience, and learning from more accomplished comrades. Topping the list was horsemanship—piloting a mount in all the specialized tasks of managing cattle, including bringing a calf to ground, turning a straying steer back into the herd, shepherding a two-mile string of cows across a river, and trying to stop a stampede without getting trampled. Roping was another skill, employed chiefly at branding time. Dropping a loop over a running calf from horseback, toppling it to ground, then dismounting and immobilizing the animal called for strength, dexterity, and proficiency with horse and rope. It also presented bone-smashing dangers.

Among other skills were branding—applying the heated iron to a calf to mark ownership; castration—a crude surgical operation that added weight to an animal but often caused infection that the cowboy had to doctor; and dehorning—shortening the horns to prevent injury to horses, cowboys, and other cattle. The cowboy functioned as a team member in herding—gathering scattered animals in a herd,

Hungry cowboys heading for dinner in Mora County, New Mexico, around 1895.

keeping them together night and day, and guiding them across river-scored plains to a destination that could be hundreds of miles away.

To the specialized skills were added the more mundane jobs of ranch and farm, such as repair of tools and upkeep of corrals, barns, bunkhouses, and windmills. Marksmanship was admired but not as important as the other skills. Contrary to the popular conception of cowboys as quick-draw, deadly gunmen, they rarely used rifles or pistols on humans. Cowboys carried firearms chiefly for protection of themselves and their herds against predators.

The Hispanic cowboys, especially in the Southwest, recalled the Spanish origins of the cattle industry. Nearly all the techniques of stock raising came from Spanish practice. Mexico's vaqueros drifted north and taught the Americans how to be cowboys—how to ride and rope and herd the longhorns that also were Spanish in origin. The vaqueros peppered the cowboy's language with Spanish words and introduced specialized equipment and clothing. "Remuda," "lariat," "chaps," "lasso," "wrangler," and countless other words derived from Spanish terminology. The cowboy's special saddle, with its prominent horn for anchoring a lasso, was a gift of the vaquero. So were *chapaneres,* the floppy leather "chaps" that protected a horseman's legs from the thorny chaparral (another Spanish term) that grew in much of the cattle country.

Aside from the vocabulary, the American cowboys refined some of the vaquero's other offerings. One was headgear. The somewhat ungainly sombrero became the more versatile but equally protective Stetson. A strictly American innovation came from Levi Strauss, whose durable and well-crafted "levis" of blue denim dressed the cowboy, and ultimately most Americans. The cowboy's wardrobe also included the distinctive cowboy boot, with its pointed toe and high heel affording a tighter grip on the stirrup. The boots supported spurs, with the rowel points dulled to guide, not hurt. A large neckerchief soaked up sweat and, drawn over the nose, warded off dust. A long yellow rubber slicker afforded covering in a downpour. Denim jackets and heavy wool capotes (cloaks) were worn in cold weather, although they restricted movement. The costume was serviceable if nondescript, with little of the showy ornamentation of Hollywood depictions.

In addition to $35 to $40 a month in wages, the cowboy received food and shelter. At the ranch he slept in a bunkhouse, where he was assigned a bunk and a patch of wall to hang his hat and coat. The room was hot in summer, cold in winter, poorly lighted, and had no privacy. On the trail or during roundup, the cowboy's shelter consisted of his blanket for covering and his saddle for a pillow. In the open the chuck wagon, presided over by the chuck wrangler, provided two meals a day—usually bacon (that is, salt pork), beans, sourdough biscuits, and coffee. At the ranch the cookhouse furnished somewhat more varied meals, but the food was still basic and repetitious.

For the cowboy, the highlights of the working year were the roundup and the trail drive. On the home spread, the spring roundup gathered all the stock from far-flung ranges to which they had wandered during the winter. At the designated site, area stockmen assembled to segregate their herds, cut out and brand the calves born during the winter, castrate and dehorn as needed. On southern ranges, the trail drive to market began in spring. On a northern range, the drive took place after the fall roundup.

The trail drive was the great adventure of the year, especially the early long drives from Texas to Kansas railheads. A trail herd typically numbered up to 3,000 head, with about ten men as herders. The daily drive began at dawn and lasted until sundown, with the men in constant motion through heat and dust or rain and mud to keep the herd together. River crossings were especially difficult. If watering places were widely separated, cattle could grow restless with thirst. At night, with the cowboys riding the edges in shifts, tension in the herd could rise until nearly any unusual noise would set off a stampede. Thunder and lightning storms were a constant threat to herd control, particularly at night. By the time the drive ended, the men were exhausted from 14-hour days of hard labor.

They were also ready for fun. The stereotype of the wild cowboy at trail's end in some Kansas cattle town is not mythical. Often they spent all their hard-earned wages on a mad carnival of drinking, gambling, whoring, and roughhousing.

For most cowboys, job security was nonexistent. Except for a few hands to take care of the ranch, the roundup and the trail drive accounted for the year's employment. When they were no longer needed, most hands drifted, picking up whatever employment they could, until again called on for the roundup and trail drive.

Cowboys worked with stock before and after the brief period of the open range, but they were not the same men. The devastating winter of 1886–1887, coupled with the introduction of barbed wire, doomed the open range. Fencing turned ranching into a different industry. More and more, the cowboy became a farm laborer. Deprived of a life marked by the trail drive and the unfenced range, he lost many of the defining characteristics by which later Americans typecast him. He still lives, however, in print and film, in a greatly changed reality, and above all in the American imagination.

Crazy Horse

CA. 1840–1877

Born Tashunka-uitko into the Oglala tribe of the Lakota (or Teton) Sioux, horse-mounted nomads who ranged the buffalo country of the northern Great Plains, Crazy Horse received his father's name after outstanding combat exploits marked him as a warrior of great potential. A quiet loner, eccentric in dress and unpredictable in behavior, a mystic and introvert, he yearned only to excel in war, which he did consistently and conspicuously.

Designated one of the four Oglala "shirt wearers" in 1865, Crazy Horse wore that political mantle uncomfortably, rarely attending leadership councils or contributing to their deliberations. In 1870, following an attempt to steal another man's wife, he lost

LIBRARY OF CONGRESS

A contemporary drawing of Crazy Horse leading his braves against George Crook's soldiers at Rosebud Creek in Montana in 1876.

This drawing by Amos Bad Heart Bull, a Sioux, shows that the artist believed that Crazy Horse was murdered by a Camp Robinson guard, although the official story held that the Sioux chief was killed in a struggle.

to enforce the order. On June 25, 1876, combined Lakota and Cheyenne warriors wiped out Lieutenant Colonel George Armstrong Custer and more than 250 soldiers of the 7th Cavalry at the Battle of the Little Bighorn—an Indian triumph in which Crazy Horse played a notable role.

The Little Bighorn, however, contained the seeds of defeat. Army columns crisscrossed the Powder River country throughout the winter and finally drove nearly all the fugitives to surrender. On May 6, 1877, Crazy Horse laid down his arms at Camp Robinson, Nebraska. He did not take well to reservation life or to the loss of his freedom. Throughout the summer he and his people grew more and more resentful. A series of misunderstandings led to his arrest. On September 5, 1877, in a guardhouse scuffle, he received a fatal wound from a soldier's bayonet. His people buried him at an unknown spot on the Plains.

his shirt-wearer rank. Thereafter he devoted himself exclusively to war and ultimately became the greatest Lakota warrior.

In addition to countless war honors in fights with enemy tribes, Crazy Horse gained distinction in warfare with the U.S. Army. In Red Cloud's war over the Bozeman Trail to the Montana goldfields in 1866–1868, Crazy Horse headed the decoy party that lured Captain William J. Fetterman and 80 soldiers to annihilation on December 21, 1866. He also participated in the Wagon Box Fight near Fort Phil Kearny on August 2, 1867.

The Treaty of Fort Laramie of 1868 divided each Lakota tribe into two major factions. One settled on the Great Sioux Reservation and grew dependent on government rations. The other remained in the Powder River country—designated unceded Indian territory in the treaty—and avoided all association with white people. Sitting Bull led these "nontreaties," with Crazy Horse as a firm and influential supporter. Government officials increasingly called these people "hostiles."

Crazy Horse gained new fame in the Sioux War of 1876. This war originated in the government's effort to possess the Black Hills, a part of the Sioux reservation where gold had been discovered. To neutralize the "nontreaties," authorities ordered them to settle on the reservation and sent military columns

Creeks

See Five Civilized Tribes

Cripple Creek, Colorado

Cripple Creek was one of the state's last mining towns and site of the Cripple Creek strikes. Although only 20 miles from Pike's Peak, Cripple

Members of the Cripple Creek Mining Exchange rejoice at a new discovery in this contemporary magazine illustration.

Creek was not discovered as a rich source of gold until 1890. Within two years, more than 5,000 people had come to the town, with an additional 5,000 housed in nearby camps. In 1893 a financial panic hit the western mines particularly hard. Many mines were forced to close, and thousands of miners flocked to the Cripple Creek region, where the mines were still active. Owners, complaining of reduced profits, moved to extend the workday from eight to ten hours without increasing pay. The miners revolted and demanded a return to the eight-hour shift. With the newly formed Western Federation of Miners on their side, the miners settled the dispute in their favor in 1894.

The following nine years were relatively quiet at Cripple Creek. But when 23 men were fired from nearby Standard Mill in 1903, the WFM responded by calling for strikes at all mines supplying ore to the mill. This, the second major strike at Cripple Creek, turned into one of the bloodiest in American labor history. Strikebreakers were imported from mines as far away as Minnesota, and some mines reopened. Isolated fights broke out, and Colorado governor James Peabody called in the state militia. The conflict escalated on June 6, 1904, when Harry Orchard blew up the Independence railroad station, killing 13 nonunion miners and injuring 6 others. In response, martial law was instituted in Cripple Creek, and hundreds of union miners were rounded up and either jailed or driven from their camps. By the end of the summer the mines had reopened with nonunion workers, signaling a defeat for the Western Federation of Miners.

Crocker, Charles

1822–1888

Crocker is best known as one of the "Big Four," a quartet of extraordinarily talented railroad promoters who built the Central Pacific Railroad. Along with Leland Stanford, Mark Hopkins, and Collis P. Huntington, Crocker built a railroad across the Sierra Nevadas that eventually became the western link of the transcontinental railroad.

Given his great eventual success, Crocker had an inauspicious beginning. Born in Troy, New York, he

was the son of an unsuccessful liquor salesman and was at various times a farmhand, a sawmill operator, and the owner of an iron forge. When news of the discovery of gold in California reached Iowa, where he was living in 1849, Crocker, his two younger brothers, and several others headed West. He quickly learned that the fastest way to make a fortune in California did not require a pick or a pan; he went into retailing, and made a fortune selling goods needed by those who were still digging.

Theodore Dehone Judah, the apostle of the trans-Sierra Nevada railway, approached Crocker and his trio of compatriots in 1859 to urge them to undertake its construction. The quartet of transplanted Easterners saw the profit-making potential of his dream and raised $200,000, which Judah and Stanford took East to use to lobby Congress. Huntington secured a federal subsidy, and for the next five years the partners worked the local municipalities, look-

Crocker lent his name to this 1864 ad for a road built to bring supplies to the railroad.

ing for financing. Stanford was elected governor in 1861, advancing their cause considerably.

For Crocker, the role of superintendent of construction was a natural. When day laborers were scarce, he imported Chinese labor. In the face of almost insurmountable obstacles, natural and otherwise, his crews laid track at an astonishing rate. The Central Pacific completed its line a full seven years ahead of the government's deadline.

With that task done, Crocker turned his attention first to the Southern Pacific and then to nonrailroad projects. However, he was restless and unfulfilled. After a long and unhappy stay in New York, he returned to San Francisco, where, for all intents and purposes, he ate himself to death.

Davy Crockett.

Crockett, David

1786–1836

Crockett was the fifth of nine children born to cash-poor homesteaders John and Rebecca Crockett on a hardscrabble farm. The family moved several times and ran an inn on the road between Abingdon, Virginia, and Knoxville, Tennessee, for two decades. With only a rudimentary education given him by his parents, Crockett at age 12 worked as a cattle driver and the next year left home for three years when his father threatened to beat him for not going to school. He worked as a teamster, bonded himself out to a farmer, did odd jobs, and, after returning home, helped pay off some of his father's debts. He then worked for three years as a hired hand, content to live in near poverty. After losing his first love to another, Crockett decided that without education he would get nowhere. He therefore attended school, acquiring more education than he would later let on when presenting himself as a self-made man. His next romance led to an acceptance of his proposal, but his fiancée married another, and Crockett fell into a deep depression for nearly nine months. Finally, he met Mary "Polly" Findlay, fell in love, courted her, and married her the day before his twentieth birthday.

In 1813 Crockett enlisted in the Tennessee Volunteers as a mounted rifleman in the expedition against the Creek Indians led by Andrew Jackson in retribution for the destruction of Fort Mims. He would later exaggerate his role in the campaign as well the time he actually served. In 1814 Crockett signed on for a campaign in Florida against the British and Indians, but missed out on the main fighting. Arriving home, he found Polly ill with malaria; she died within weeks, leaving three children. In later years, he would not give her death date so he would not be accused of playing soldier while his wife was dying. Called back to militia duty, Crockett legally paid a surrogate to complete his enlistment. Ironically, he was elected lieutenant by the militia, his first public office. He married Elizabeth Patton in the summer of 1815, gaining a sizable dowry that would allow him to pursue a political career. At the time, a candidate had to be male and own at least 200 acres of land. Over the next five years the couple had four children. Elizabeth was an effective and frugal farm manager and reared the children while her peripatetic husband went on long hunts. Moving to Giles County, Tennessee, at the end of 1816, the Crocketts increased their holdings through land speculation and ownership of a gun-

Davy Crockett battles a bear in this cartoon from Davy Crockett's Almanac.

powder factory and a distillery. In 1817 Crockett was confirmed a county magistrate without any law background and was elected lieutenant colonel of the county militia.

Crockett decided to run for the state legislature in 1821. His speeches, delivered in rough country vernacular, were unique and effective: he peppered his audiences with outlandish boasts, humorous anecdotes, and scathing denunciations of his enemies, and played up his illiterate, self-made common man image, his own creation. He won the seat but proved an ineffective legislator. The family moved to north-

western Tennessee and Crockett, awarded a .41-caliber Kentucky rifle he named "Old Betsy," began to build a reputation as a redoubtable killer of black bears—105 during the winter of 1825–1826. In 1823, as a result of a practical joke, he was listed as a candidate for the legislature for the Western District, a large, sparsely populated area. Crockett stumped the district and beat three other candidates, with squatters' rights his major campaign plank. He lost his bid for a congressional seat in 1825 but won in 1827. Once in Washington, carousing, boredom, and illness kept him away from many sessions. A fellow Kentucky representative named Thomas Chilton became his friend and wrote many of Crockett's speeches. Unprepared for Congress's tortoiselike procedures, tedious orations, and constant compromises, a disappointed Crockett saw his land bill—granting land to squatters in the Western District—tabled. His constituents gave him a two-to-one victory in the 1829 election, but his growing disagreements with Andrew Jackson over Jackson's plan to relocate southeastern Indian tribes west of the Mississippi led to his defection from the Democratic party.

The next campaign turned nasty, with the usual imputations of Crockett's impropriety, his love for "Arden Spirits" and gambling, and the added charge of fraud because he had missed so many votes that he had not fully earned his salary. He lost his congressional seat in 1831 but won it again in 1833. By this time Crockett's fame had spread to the stage, where the main character of *The Lion of the West* was a boastful Kentucky congressman named Nimrod Wildfire. Crockett, pursuing a more serious public image, asked Chilton to write his "autobiography," *A Narrative of the Life of David Crockett of the State of Tennessee,* including in its epigraph Crockett's motto: "Be always sure you are right, and then go ahead!" The book became an instant best-seller, further enshrining him as a legend so mired in apocrypha that it is very difficult to separate man from myth.

Crockett continued to push for his land bill in the House, without success. He told his constituents that if he was not reelected, "they go to hell, and I would go to Texas." In November 1835 Crockett, ever loyal to the frontier, left his family and took up the cause of the Texas Revolution, believing that the Mexican territory belonged to the United States as a result of the Louisiana Purchase. He hoped he might win a seat in the Texas Constitutional Convention but arrived in San Antonio too late to be elected. The decision to make a last stand at the Alamo mission against the large advancing army of Mexicans under Santa Anna, the resultant 13-day siege, and the massacre of the garrison are legendary. Crockett was one of six or seven survivors taken prisoner and brought before Santa Anna; he protested that he was only an explorer who had sought refuge at the mission. A skeptical Santa Anna ordered his own entourage to draw their sabers and butcher the unarmed men.

Crook, George

1829–1890

An Ohio-born West Point graduate (1852), Crook passed his years as a lieutenant in California and Oregon. He saw much field service and gained a deep understanding of and sympathy for the Native American tribes. His Civil War record was creditable though not outstanding, and he ended the war a major general of volunteers. In the postwar regular army, he was a lieutenant colonel of infantry.

In campaigns against the Paiutes of eastern Oregon in 1867–1869, Crook developed methods of Indian fighting that became his hallmarks in other theaters: unrelenting pursuit of an enemy, reliance on pack mules rather than wagons for supply, and extensive use of Indian auxiliaries. Mules freed him from having to follow roads and allowed him to go wherever the Indians went. Indian scout units gave him the benefit of Indian thought and practice and demoralized his quarry by having their own people tracking them. Crook's success in Oregon led to his transfer to Arizona in 1871, to take command of a military department disheartened by Apache warfare. His brilliant Tonto Basin campaign in the winter of 1872–1873, featuring the techniques used in Oregon, solidified his reputation as a leading Indian fighter and gained him promotion to brigadier general.

Assigned to the northern Plains in 1875, Crook arrived as events escalated toward the Great Sioux War of 1876. In the campaign to force the nontreaty bands of Sitting Bull, Crazy Horse, and other chiefs onto a reservation, Crook commanded one of three columns converging on the Yellowstone River basin.

LIBRARY OF CONGRESS

General Crook hired this group of Apache scouts to help him track down Geronimo.

ARIZONA HISTORICAL SOCIETY

General George Crook with an Apache scout.

He suffered reverses at the battles of Powder River and the Rosebud. A week after the latter, the Sioux and Cheyennes wiped out Custer at the Little Bighorn. Despite successes later in the season, Crook's record in the war of 1876 was the worst of his career. Sent against the Arizona Apaches in 1882, Crook restored his reputation. Using the methods that had worked earlier, he ran down Geronimo and other raiding bands high in the nearly impenetrable recesses of Mexico's Sierra Madre and induced them to return to the San Carlos Reservation. In 1885, Geronimo again broke loose and took refuge in Mexico. Again (in 1886) Crook captured him, only to have Geronimo bolt once more. Discouraged and resentful of orders that would have forced him to break faith with the Indians, Crook asked to be relieved of his command. General Nelson A. Miles brought the uprising to an end.

Promoted to major general in 1888, Crook commanded the Division of the Missouri from headquarters in Chicago. He died there of a heart attack at the age of 61. Reticent, taciturn, plain in appearance and manner, Crook was very different from his ostentatious archrival, Nelson Miles. Although Miles was the preeminent Indian fighter of his time, Crook ranks as the most thoughtful and innovative. Crook combined success in war with sympathy and fair treatment of the Indians in peace. But his unconventional methods never gained favor with the army, and he alone made them work on a large scale.

recorded in 1780, their population was estimated at between 4,000 and 5,000. The 1837 epidemic reduced that number by as much as half. By the turn of the twentieth century, there were only around 1,800 Crows remaining.

More than 38.5 million acres on the upper Yellowstone were recognized as Crow lands by the Fort Laramie Treaty of 1851. The Treaty of 1868 established a Crow reservation in Montana. However,

DENVER PUBLIC LIBRARY

Crow Indian on the Lookout, *a painting by Alfred Jacob Miller.*

Crow Indians

The Crows, the westernmost Siouan tribe of Native Americans, formerly occupied the Bighorn River valley and the area around the headwaters of the Yellowstone in Montana. They are closely related to the Hidatsa, from whom they separated, probably around 1600, forming the Mountain Crow and the River Crow.

Originally sedentary, village-dwelling farmers, the Crows became avid riders after introduction of the horse around 1740. They became buffalo hunters and moved from earth lodges to tepees. Though initially friendly to arriving whites, they were constantly at war with neighboring tribes.

The tribe was decimated by the smallpox epidemics of the early nineteenth century. When first

LIBRARY OF CONGRESS

These Crow warriors were captured in Montana for attacking government troops at the urging of Sitting Bull.

pressure from miners, ranchers, and settlers forced the constant contraction of the reservation boundaries, and by 1905, their total territory had been reduced to a little more than 2 million acres.

Throughout the nineteenth century, the Crows were often considered traitors by other Indian tribes because of their work for the U.S. Army. Crows informed the federal troops of the number of hostile warriors prior to the Fetterman fight. They also served as scouts for General George Custer at the Battle of The Little Bighorn. When approached by representatives of Chief Joseph's Nez Perce during that group's attempted flight to Canada, the Crows refused to provide them with a haven, stating that they were at peace with the United States and were army scouts. When, however, the army did contact the Crows to serve as scouts against the fleeing Nez Perce, a great number of Crows were too busy, and those who did serve did so without much enthusiasm.

Curtis Act

See Dawes Act

Custer, George Armstrong

1839–1876

The flamboyant "boy general" of the Civil War, Custer achieved fame as an Indian fighter on the western frontier and immortality for his dramatic death at the Battle of the Little Bighorn.

Born in New Rumley, Ohio, "Autie" Custer won appointment to West Point, from which he graduated at the bottom of his class in 1861. However, as a staff officer for General George B. McClellan and later for General Alfred Pleasanton, he swiftly demonstrated superior military aptitude and a heedless courage that served him well in combat. Pleasonton judged him fit for high rank, and in June 1863, at the age of 23, Captain Custer became Brigadier General Custer, commanding the Michigan Cavalry Brigade. In the Battle of Gettysburg he led the brigade in a pivotal action against the Confederate cavalry of General J. E. B. Stuart that launched his rapid rise to fame.

For the rest of the war, Custer displayed able leadership. Distinguished by his long yellow hair and gaudy uniform, he became noted for slashing cavalry charges and for a personal fearlessness that earned the devotion of his men. In the spring of 1864 his brigade performed well in the Battle of the Wilderness and in General Philip H. Sheridan's cavalry raid around Richmond. During that operation, at the Battle of Yellow Tavern, one of his Michigan troopers killed the legendary Confederate cavalry chief "Jeb" Stuart. Impressed with Custer's energy and zeal, Sheridan became his lifelong patron. In Sheridan's Shenandoah Valley operations the following autumn and winter, Custer distinguished himself in the battles of Winchester, Fisher's Hill, Cedar Creek, and Waynesboro. This led to his promotion to major general and command of the 3rd Cavalry Division.

In the Appomattox campaign of April 1865, Custer and his division compiled an outstanding combat record. At Dinwiddie Court House, Five Forks, Sayler's Creek, and finally Appomattox Station, the 3rd Division was in the forefront and Custer was conspicuous for his bravery and leader-

George Armstrong Custer in 1865.

On November 27, 1868, General Custer surprised the Cheyenne camp of Chief Black Kettle, who was killed in the charge. Painter Charles Schreyvogel immortalized this significant event in southern plains warfare.

ship. To him came the white towel on a pole that signaled the surrender of General Robert E. Lee's army. War's end found the young general of 25 a hero, idolized by the public and respected by his superiors.

Early in 1864 Custer had married Elizabeth Bacon of Monroe, Michigan. The attractive, vivacious, and intelligent Libbie followed her husband on campaign wherever possible, and in Washington won the hearts of senators, cabinet officers, and even President Abraham Lincoln. At the close of the Civil War, Custer returned to the regular army. As lieutenant colonel of the newly authorized 7th Cavalry, he made a new name for himself on the western frontier. Affecting fringed buckskin instead of velvet and gold lace, he emerged as the personification of the vigorous Indian fighter and master plainsman and hunter. In the frequent absence of the regiment's colonel, Custer commanded the 7th Cavalry, and in popular eyes it was his regiment.

Custer's first experience with Indians, in Kansas in 1867, ended in embarrassing failure. The hostile Cheyennes eluded him, and the regiment collapsed in exhaustion. A court-martial found him guilty of a series of charges and sentenced him to one year's suspension of rank and pay. The humiliation was partly lessened by the sympathy of his mentor, General Sheridan, who recalled him to active duty in 1868 before the end of his suspension. As Sheridan's

striking arm in the winter campaign of 1868–1869 against the southern Plains Indians, Custer restored himself to favor. On November 27, 1868, he surprised and attacked Chief Black Kettle's Cheyenne village on the Washita River in present-day Oklahoma. Washita laid the groundwork for Custer's reputation as an Indian fighter.

After two years of Reconstruction duty in Kentucky (1871–1873), Custer and the 7th Cavalry returned to the frontier, to Dakota Territory. Guarding surveyors for the Northern Pacific Railroad on the Yellowstone River in the summer of 1873, he fought two rousing battles with Sioux warriors and once more gained public notice as an Indian fighter. At Fort Abraham Lincoln, on the Missouri River opposite the Northern Pacific railhead at Bismarck, he and Libbie became widely known for their hospitality.

Easterners looked on Custer as the army's foremost Indian fighter. In fact, he was no more successful than some of his peers. His regiment, moreover, was badly divided. Some of his men worshipped him, others loathed him. He wrote popular magazine articles and a book, *My Life on the Plains* (1874). And always, as in the Civil War, he made good newspaper copy.

In 1874 Custer led the 7th Cavalry in an exploration of the Black Hills. Part of the Great Sioux Reservation, guaranteed the Sioux by the Fort

Laramie Treaty of 1868, the Black Hills had long been coveted by whites who thought they contained gold. The Custer expedition found gold, and the news set off a gold rush. The Black Hills gold rush led to the Great Sioux War of 1876. Custer and the 7th Cavalry rode with one of the armies converging on the Indian country. On June 25, 1876, he attacked the village of Sitting Bull and Crazy Horse on the Little Big Horn River in Montana. In a sequence of moves that will remain controversial, he and five companies were wiped out.

Custer's last stand brought Custer an immortality that fit the dashing persona of his life. Elizabeth Custer devoted the rest of her long life to defending and glorifying her husband. Controversy kept the Little Bighorn alive. The image of "Long Hair," standing on a hilltop, troopers falling around him, shouting Sioux closing in for the kill, remains an icon in American folklore.

Custer's Last Stand

See Custer, George Armstrong

D

Dakota Indians

See Sioux Indians

Dalton Gang

Inheritors of the James and Younger brothers' legacy of Midwestern outlawry, Grattan (1861–

1892), Robert (1867–1892), and Emmett (1871–1937) were three of the 15 children of saloonkeeper Lewis Dalton and Adeline Younger (aunt of the Younger brothers). The family settled in Montgomery County, Kansas, in the Civil War years, not far from Coffeyville, where the brothers' fate would be sealed in 1892. They later moved to a Missouri farm and, when the boys were in their teens, to Indian Territory.

In 1884 an older brother, Frank, became a U.S. deputy marshal in the jurisdiction of Fort Smith,

MERCALDO ARCHIVES

Emmet Dalton.

MERCALDO ARCHIVES

Robert Dalton.

MERCALDO ARCHIVES

Grattan Dalton.

Arkansas, celebrated for its "hanging judge," Isaac Parker. On November 27, 1887, Frank Dalton was killed while attempting to arrest a horse thief. His place was taken by Grattan (Grat), unofficially assisted by Bob and Emmett.

By 1890 the Dalton brothers, with Bob at their head as chief of the Indian police in the Osage Nation, were known to have a profitable sideline as cattle rustlers and horse thieves in Indian Territory. After they were joined by some other professionals, they engaged in full-time work outside the law: cattle and horse theft was followed by train and bank robbery.

In February 1891 the brothers (including William, born in 1863 and a rising figure in California state politics) were accused of robbing a bank in Bakersfield, California. Only Grat was convicted, and he managed to escape imprisonment by a daring dive into the San Joaquin River from a train taking him to Folsom Prison. Grat returned to Indian Territory and rejoined his brothers and other gang members. They robbed a Santa Fe train near Wharton, Oklahoma, in May 1891, another near Redrock, and a third near

Adair, fleeing with their loot to a hideout in caves along the Cimarron River.

In 1892, with the law closing in on them, Bob (who was quoted as saying he intended to "beat anything Jesse James ever did") and Grat formed the fateful plan to rob the two banks in Coffeyville, Kansas, a scheme that split the Dalton gang into disputing factions. Worse, as in the case of the James-Younger raid on Northfield, Minnesota, in 1876, word of the impending robberies leaked out and Coffeyville's lawmen were waiting.

On October 5, 1892, Bob, Grat and Emmett, wearing crude disguises, together with gang members Dick Broadwell and Bill Powers, rode into Coffeyville. They were recognized instantly as they entered the first bank, and a wild gun battle ensued. In 15 minutes all the Dalton gang had been killed except Emmett, who was severely wounded. Four Coffeyville citizens were dead.

Emmett recovered from his wounds and stood trial. He served 14 years of a life sentence in the Kansas State Penitentiary before being pardoned in 1907. He settled in Los Angeles, married, engaged in

Condon & Company, the site of the Dalton Gang's last bank robbery attempt, was left with bullet holes in the windows but its funds intact after angry townspeople caught the gang in the act.

real estate work, and became a movie bit player. He collaborated with a ghost writer on the book *When the Daltons Rode* (published in 1931) and died in Los Angeles on July 13, 1937.

The fourth Dalton brother, William, had had a successful career in California as a state assemblyman before being accused of complicity in the Bakersfield train robbery. He returned to Oklahoma before the Coffeyville raid but disagreed with his brothers over their plans and joined Bill Doolin's gang of outlaws. On September 1, 1893, William killed U.S. Deputy Marshal Lafe Shadley at Ingalls, Oklahoma, and rode with Doolin through the following year before forming his own outlaw gang. He was killed on June 8, 1894, in the town of Elk, near Ardmore, Oklahoma, while resisting arrest.

Danish Settlers in the West

During the 1840s and 1850s, immigrants from Denmark began to settle in Wisconsin and Michigan; most came from the islands off Jutland, Denmark's main peninsula. Beginning in the mid-1850s a large Danish community grew up in Elk Horn, Iowa; Kimballton and Council Bluffs, Iowa, also had large Danish populations. These settlers were mainly disillusioned Danish Mormons who had begun the arduous trip with Joseph Smith and his followers from St. Louis, Missouri, to Salt Lake City, Utah, but who had wearied of the journey and dropped out.

By 1883, over half a million letters had been sent to Denmark by Danish settlers, urging others to make the trip to the American West. In the mid-1880s, Danish communities sprouted in Nebraska, Montana, and North and South Dakota. Unlike their predecessors, these settlers were largely from Jutland. Most of the immigrants became farmers, though there were also Danish ranchers.

To maintain the culture of their homeland, Danish settlers established folk high schools and churches; often their new communities resembled their native towns and villages. Danish immigrants founded two colleges: Dana College at Blair, Nebraska, in 1884; and Grand View College in Des Moines, Iowa, in 1896.

Dawes Act

Dawes Act was the popular name for the General Allotment Act of 1887; it is the best-known of a series of legislative enactments designed to break tribal lands into parcels held by individuals.

Throughout the nineteenth century, the solution most consistently proposed for the "Indian Problem" was allotment of land held communally by tribes. It was generally conceded that the civilization and assimilation of the native population would not occur without the destruction of tribal ties and the introduction of incentives provided by private property. The goal was to turn Native Americans into responsible citizen-farmers following the Jeffersonian agrarian model.

In 1883, Albert K. Smiley, a member of the Board of Indian Commissioners established as part of President Grant's peace policy, invited persons concerned about federal Indian policy to a conference at Lake Mohonk in New York. That meeting established a group of reformers known as the Friends of the Indian, which met yearly. Their legislative agenda consisted of three principal items: allotment, citizenship for Indians, and universal education administered by the government.

Four years after the first Lake Mohonk Conference, and persistent lobbying by the reformers, Congress passed the General Allotment Act. The act was named after its sponsor, Senator Henry L. Dawes, who felt that the legislation was all that was needed to assimilate Indians fully into American society. The avowed goal of U.S. policy was to destroy Indian tribalism by the abolition of their land base.

The principal provision of the act was the allotment of a quarter-section (160 acres) homestead to each head of a household. Eighty acres was to be given to each single person over 18 years of age and every orphan under 18. All other persons under 18 were to be given 40 acres. American citizenship was to be conferred on those allottees who abandoned their tribe and adopted "the habits of civilized life." "Surplus lands" (those not required for allotment) were freed for white settlement. In order to protect Indians from unscrupulous whites, the United States was to hold allotted lands in trust for 25 years, during which time they could not be sold.

Some tribes were exempted from the operation of the act, primarily the Five Civilized Tribes and the

Osage in Oklahoma. The Curtis Act of 1898, sponsored by Charles Curtis (himself a Kansa), applied the principles of the Dawes Act to Indian Territory. In 1906, Congress passed the Osage Allotment Act.

As a result of allotment and subsequent sales, total Indian landholdings declined from approximately 139 million acres in 1887 to around 34 million acres in 1934. More than 80 percent of the value of land belonging to Indians in 1887 was lost.

De Quille, Dan

1829–1898

Born William Wright in Ohio, the journalist and humorist Dan De Quille was already an experienced newspaperman when he went to California in 1857 as a goldseeker. He found his true home in Nevada Territory in 1861; there he joined the Comstock Lode silver boom around Virginia City and began a long association (1861–1893) with the boomtown's paper, the *Territorial Enterprise.*

De Quille's extensive travels in the silver lode country, his knowledge of the Indians, especially the Paiutes, of the region, and his open, good-natured personality and quick wit combined to make him one of the best journalists in the territorial West. He even inspired Mark Twain (see Clemens, Samuel Langhorne), who worked with him for a time on the *Enterprise.*

Among De Quille's claims to fame was his mastery of the hoax—the wholly imaginative, often patently ridiculous story that, because of the author's skill in making it credible, was widely believed and reprinted in major newspapers. Among his most celebrated hoaxes was one that appeared in the *Enterprise* in 1874. It told of the death of one Jonathan Newhouse, who had invented an apparatus he called "solar armor," intended to protect the wearer from the fierce heat of the sun when crossing deserts and alkali plains. De Quille described the intricate device, consisting of a body armor of water-saturated sponges, and Newhouse's test of it by attempting to cross Death Valley on foot. The inventor was found, De Quille wrote, 20 miles into the desert, his corpse frozen, an icicle hanging from his nose. "There he had perished because his armor had worked too well."

De Quille's serious work included accurate and meticulously researched books on the Comstock claims.

He died in West Liberty, Iowa, on March 16, 1898.

De Smet, Pierre-Jean

1801–1873

Belgian-born Pierre-Jean De Smet emigrated to the United States in 1821 and was ordained a Jesuit in 1827. In 1838, after teaching in St. Louis and studying in Europe, he was assigned as a missionary to the Potawatomis in Iowa. In 1840 he was sent to the Flathead tribal region of the Rocky Mountains; he founded St. Mary's Mission in the Bitterroot Valley of Montana, a convent and school in the Willamette region of Oregon, and a mission on Idaho's Pend Oreille Lake.

In his over three decades as missionary in the Pacific Northwest, De Smet, a stocky, charming, energetic, and perpetually cheerful man, journeyed over 100,000 miles on horseback, ministering to remote tribes as far north as Hudson's Bay posts in Canada. He also traveled often (19 times in all) to Europe to assemble companies of priests and nuns for work among his beloved Flatheads, Teton and Yankton Sioux, Blackfeet, Yakimas, and other Indian tribes. "No White man has ever come close to equaling his universal appeal to the Indian," a biographer says.

De Smet served as mediator several times in Indian-white disputes, notably in the Yakima War in Washington in 1858–1859 and during the Fort Laramie Treaty signing between the Sioux and U.S. commissioners in 1868. He published works in six languages on the Indian missions; his own letters and accounts of his travels ran to four volumes when published in 1905.

De Smet died in St. Louis on May 23, 1873.

Deadwood Dick

See Love, Nat

Father De Smet photographed with some of his converts.

Deadwood Gulch

In the Black Hills of Dakota, Deadwood Gulch was the site of several mining towns and furious prospecting activity following the discovery of gold in 1874. Most of the mining towns eventually disappeared when the gold did, but others, like Deadwood and Lead, grew into cities.

In 1875 a prospecting party discovered gold in a gulch so overrun with fallen trees they called it Deadwood Gulch. Camping there over the winter, they called the first settlement Gayville, after a member of their party, William Gay. Lead was established farther up the gulch on July 10, 1876, and Central City, one of the largest towns, was formally organized on January 20, 1877.

Deadwood was perhaps the most infamous town

Deadwood in 1888. Many of its buildings have been preserved as historical landmarks.

in the gulch. Established below Gayville on April 26, 1876, it swiftly became home to nearly 2,000 people, most from other mining towns. One of the wildest towns on the frontier, it buzzed with a mixture of prospectors, miners, outlaws, and gamblers. Its host of legendary characters include Deadwood Dick (a fictitious dime-novel hero), Wild Bill Hickok, who was murdered there in 1876, and Calamity Jane (see Canary, Martha). Tourists still visit Mount Moriah Cemetery in Deadwood, where Calamity Jane and Wild Bill Hickok are buried.

Death Valley

Death Valley, covering an area 140 miles long and 5 to 15 miles wide in southeastern California between the Panamint Range on the west and the Amargosa Range on the east, boasts the lowest elevation in the Western Hemisphere (282 feet below sea level at its lowest point). It was given its ominous name by a party of gold-seekers and settlers who crossed it in 1849. Death Valley became legendary when their tragic tale was recounted by survivor Lewis Manly.

As the hottest region in North America, Death Valley's ground temperatures sometimes exceed 125 degrees F. In 1913 its air temperature reached 134 degrees F., the highest ever recorded in the United States. These harsh conditions exist because moisture from the Pacific Ocean condenses before it crosses the Panamint Range, leaving the valley with an average annual rainfall of 1.5 inches. Furnace Creek and Amargosa River, which carry mountain rains into the valley, are often dry.

Prehistoric lakes left salt flats in the lowest areas, which are devoid of life. Higher in the valley, salt grass, mesquite, cactus, and poppies survive on the thin sand layer. Coyotes, ravens, kangaroo rats, horned toads, bighorn sheep, and wild burros inhabit the surrounding foothills.

Death Valley has been mined for gold, silver, copper, lead, and especially borax. The old mining settlements, now ghost towns, add to the region's attraction for tourists. Death Valley National Monument, established in 1933, covers 2,981 square miles.

Deere, John

1804–1886

Deere was an American inventor and plow manufacturer whose steel plows offered pioneer farmers a more productive means of tilling soil. Deere was born in Rutland, Vermont. At 17 he began a four-year apprenticeship to a blacksmith in Middlebury, Vermont. After mastering the trade, he spent 12 years using his skills. In 1837 he moved to Grand Detour, Illinois, and opened a blacksmith shop with Leonard Andrus. Working with midwestern farmers, Deere quickly learned that the cast-iron plows manufactured in the East would not turn the hard prairie soil.

Within a year he and Andrus had designed three new plows to meet pioneer needs. They constructed the share, or cutting part, from steel cut from an old sawmill blade and shaped over a log. Prairie farmers soon realized the benefit of the new design, and demand grew. By 1846 annual plow sales had reached 1,000. That year, Deere sold his interest in the business to Andrus and moved to Moline, Illinois, where he founded Deere and Company. The company grew rapidly, in 1858 reaching an annual output of over 13,000 plows. Deere and Company was incorporated

LIBRARY OF CONGRESS

John Deere.

10 years later. Deere continued to experiment with new designs and had the first American plow steel rolled in Pittsburgh. He remained president of the company until his death on May 17, 1886.

Denver, Colorado

Capital of Colorado, Denver is located on the South Platte River in the north central part of the state. An economic base for much of the Great Plains and Rocky Mountain areas, Denver is the largest city between the Pacific Coast and St. Louis, Missouri. Known as the Mile High City, Denver sits at an elevation of about one mile above sea level, where the Great Plains and Rocky Mountains meet.

Like most cities in the Colorado Rockies, Denver began as makeshift camp for miners and prospectors. When William Green Russell discovered a small deposit of gold at the mouth of the Cherry Creek and South Platte River in 1858, exaggerated reports quickly spread to California and to the East. The following year, thousands of prospectors rushed to the region of Pike's Peak. Many of the fifty-niners visited Russell's camp, and soon a small settlement was established on the site of present-day Denver.

Denver, named after James W. Denver, the governor of Kansas Territory in 1858, received his support and became the seat of Arapaho County. The city was elected capital of Colorado Territory in 1867, and state capital in 1881.

MATHEWS, PENCIL SKETCHES OF COLORADO

A Denver street, 1866.

Desert

Hot, arid lands are found in the American Southwest in Arizona, New Mexico, Nevada, Utah, and California.

Deserts are generally defined as land with less than 20 inches of rainfall per year. Average daytime summer temperatures can reach 125 degrees F. Despite its seemingly inhospitable climate, the desert supports an abundance of plant and animal life. Varieties of mesquite, paloverde, and cactus are indigenous to desert regions of North America. The saguaro cactus of Arizona is often a source of water for desert animals. Other types of cactus include or-

LIBRARY OF CONGRESS

A depiction of Denver, Colorado, before the 1866 discovery of gold built up the city.

CENTER FOR AMERICAN HISTORY, THE UNIVERSITY OF TEXAS AT AUSTIN

Charles Koppel captured the desolation of the Colorado Desert.

gan-pipe, pitahaya, bisnaga (barrel cactus), cholla, staghorn, pincushion, prickly pear, and hedgehog. Another common desert plant, the creosote bush, was used for medicinal purposes by western settlers despite its nickname "stink bush."

The American desert also teems with animal life. Hummingbirds and doves can often be found nesting in stately saguaro cacti; other desert birds include quail, hawks, and owls. Buzzards, which scavenge the remains of any creature succumbing to the intense heat of the desert, circle slowly above. Coyotes, kit foxes, jackrabbits, bobcats, kangaroo rats, gophers, tortoises, Gila monsters, roadrunners, and rattlesnakes are among other animals native to the desert.

Major desert areas of the American West include the Colorado Desert, Death Valley, the Great Salt Lake Desert, the Mojave Desert, and the Painted Desert.

The desert is part of the West's myth and legend. One writer claimed the heat was so intense on the desert floor that travelers could hear plants crackling as they rode by. In addition to the blazing heat, travelers through the desert had to be wary of the wildlife. Rattlesnakes were a constant hazard, whether slithering along the trail or hidden under bushes and rocks. Many an unwary traveler fell prey to these venomous reptiles. Cougars were a constant threat, as were peccaries, wild pigs with sharp hooves and razor-sharp tusks. Though smaller than cougars, peccaries traveled in packs, which often made them more dangerous to desert travelers.

Desert Land Act

1877

The Desert Land Act of 1877, passed as an amendment to the Homestead Act of 1862, was designed to encourage settlement in the desert areas of the West. Although drafted with good intentions, it was a major instrument of fraud for cattle ranchers looking to acquire large amounts of land from the government at little cost.

The Homestead Act of 1862 was passed to encourage settlement in the West but fell short of its goals. As a result, two amendments were added: the Timber Culture Act of 1873, and the Desert Land

Act of 1877. The former was designed to promote the planting of trees on the prairie and the latter to promote the development of desert land in the West. The law stated that a settler could purchase one section of land, 640 acres, with the proviso that the land would be irrigated within three years. Upon applying for a claim, the settler was required to pay 25 cents per acre. After proof of compliance with the irrigation stipulation, and an additional payment of $1 per acre, the claimant would be granted title to the tract.

Although passed as a measure to aid pioneers, the Desert Land Act was heavily lobbied for by cattle ranchers, who ultimately benefited most. They could take out a claim and satisfy the irrigation requirement with as little as a bucket of water. Cattlemen gained title by hiring cowboys, who would file claims and then sign over their deeds for a small price. Another indication of the failure of the Desert Land Act is that of the nine million acres that were originally claimed, titles were issued for only two million acres.

Dime Novels

These Wild West adventure stories, full of blood and guts, pandered to the sensationalistic streak in eastern readers from 1860 until well into the twentieth century. Although previous mass-market publishing ventures—low-cost, short adventure fiction for a wide readership—had proved profitable, it was Erastus F. Beadle's Dime Library series, launched in June 1860, that realized the potential of the genre. The first 10-cent novel was *Malaeska: The Indian Wife of the White Hunter*, by Mrs. Ann S. Stephens. Beadle, a New York City publisher, developed the series formula and operated it as a serious commercial enterprise. The Dime Library ran to over 300 individual titles that spawned thousands of clones.

Several literary figures, such as Deadwood Dick, Calamity Jane (Canary, Martha), and Hurricane Hal were introduced by Beadle and became successful series focusing on a single melodramatic figure. The standard length of a dime novel was 30,000 to 50,000 words, and hack writers could churn out a new title every three days. Prentiss Ingraham wrote over 600 adventure novels and is reported to have produced an entire novel in a day and a half.

Edward L. Wheeler's Hurricane Nell.

Real-life characters were also lionized by the dime novels. "Buffalo Bill" Cody went from western scout to eastern actor portraying himself in ever more sensational deeds scripted by busy writers in a race to satisfy an insatiable public. So effective was this myth-making medium that Cody came to believe the stories his press agents concocted and recounted them as gospel truth.

Dodge City, Kansas

Dodge City, Kansas, was one of the wildest cattle towns of the Midwest during the heyday of the Texas cattle drives in the 1870s and early 1880s. Fort Dodge, in southwestern Kansas's Cheyenne Indian Territory, was on both the Arkansas River and the Santa Fe Railroad. Some of its soldiers recognized a

great development opportunity in 1872 and joined the few local merchants to form the Dodge City Town Company. With the purchase of 87 acres for $108.75, the partnership began a profitable operation shipping buffalo hides. As that trade dwindled, Dodge City merchants set their eyes on the Texas cattle market.

Because Texas longhorns carried a tick whose bite was fatal to other livestock, the Kansas legislature officially banned longhorns from a large part of the state. This forced Wichita to close its prosperous cattle business, and Dodge City quickly boomed.

Shrewd merchants welcomed the influx of ranchers and cowboys. Robert Wright, one of the original proprietors, did a retail trade of $250,000 annually. To service the thrill-seeking, six-shooter-slinging transients, the town boasted saloons, gambling halls, brothels, and dance halls. Although Dodge City has a legendary reputation for violence, only 15 homicides occurred there between 1877 and 1885.

Farmers protested the all-out invasion of the free-roaming cattle, which ruined their crops. Merchant Robert Wright, the town's elected legislator and chair of the committee handling quarantine matters, was determined to protect the city's cattle interests; in 1883 he helped create the Western Kansas Cattle Growers' Association to combat the agrarian groups. A drought from 1878 to 1881, followed by an influx

Group portrait of legendary gunfighters, taken in Dodge City. Clockwise, from left: W.H. Harris, Luke Short, Bat Masterson, Neal Brown, McNeal, Wyatt Earp, C. Bassett.

of settlers, shifted the city's economy from cattle to one that emphasized agriculture. In 1885 the entire state was quarantined, leaving Dodge City to the farmers.

Doniphan, Alexander

1808–1887

In the midst of the Mexican War, General Stephen Watts Kearney was offered the services of a regiment of Missouri volunteers headed by their chosen colonel, Alexander Doniphan. Doniphan was well known as a popular frontier lawyer. In his new post of military leader, he won many victories.

In 1846, Kearny ordered Doniphan and his troops to take Chihuahua, Mexico. They endured terrible conditions on the march south, including passage through Mexican territory known as Jornada del Muerto (Dead Man's Journey). Despite bitter cold and a serious lack of essential supplies, "Doniphan's Thousands" (also known as "Doniphan's Missourians") valiantly turned back the better-equipped Mexican forces at Brazito on Christmas Day. The march to Chihuahua continued some 300 miles through treacherous desert. Reinforcements joined Doniphan's Missourians, and the band reached the outskirts of Chihuahua on February 27, 1847. Doniphan's force was a hodgepodge of a thousand ill-equipped soldiers, mountain men, and other volunteers. Between their regular troops and the volunteer militia, the Mexicans had more than 4,000 soldiers to repel Doniphan's advance. The next day Doniphan began his attack; four days later, the Americans took Chihuahua. Amazingly, Doniphan lost only six men in the battle, compared with Mexican casualties reported to number 600. Doniphan later joined Zachary Taylor's command, taking troops victoriously through another 600 miles of hostile Mexican territory.

Donner Party

The Donner party was a group of settlers bound for California who met a terrible fate in the Sierra Nevada.

George Donner, a 62-year old farmer from Illinois, and his brother, Jacob, organized the party. In 1846, the 27 men, 17 women, and 43 children of the Donner party set off in 23 wagons. Following the advice of Lansford W. Hastings in his *Emigrant's Guide to Oregon and California*, the leaders chose to leave the regular California Trail at Hastings' Cutoff. Because of disputes among the leaders and Hastings' misinformation, the group lost weeks of precious time crossing the Wasatch Mountains and the Salt Lake Desert. They approached the pass in the Sierra Nevada in late October, already weary and low on supplies. Two men were sent ahead to bring more supplies from California; one returned with food and two Indian guides.

At last they were ready to move on through the pass. Then a blizzard struck, leaving the group snowbound high in the mountains. They hastily constructed cabins roofed with ox hides and wagon canvas. The snow on the pass increased and the food supply became desperately short. After the remaining livestock wandered off in mid-December, the panic-stricken party sent off a small group, the "For-

THE BANCROFT LIBRARY

Bleak illustration of the Donner Party during their futile attempt to make it through the Sierra Pass.

lorn Hope." These eight men, five women, and the two Indian guides set out with six days of scanty rations. A severe storm hit on Christmas night, forcing the group to huddle beneath blankets for days without food. Four died and the others resorted to cannibalism to survive. Two more died, and the Indian guides, who refused to eat flesh, were shot and also eaten. Seven emaciated and exhausted survivors reached an Indian camp on January 10, 1847, 32 days after their journey began.

Meanwhile, the survivors in the mountains were eating hides in snow 13 feet deep. On February 18, a rescue party arrived and led 22 of the group down the mountain. But the cache of food which had been buried for the return trip was discovered by animals. Several days later, this starving group met another relief party headed by James F. Reed, who had earlier been part of the group.

Reed brought 15 emaciated survivors down the mountain. A storm hit and they huddled by a fire, which kept sinking into the water from melting snow. On March 8 the stronger members pressed on. Those huddled around the fire had some fuel but no food. When a third relief party found the group around the fire, three had died and the rest had resorted to cannibalism. Part of this relief party continued on to the cabin settlement, where they found the few survivors eating their only food—the bodies of those already dead. The party returned with the ablest travelers, leaving at the camp a dying George Donner, his wife Tamsen, an elderly Mrs. Graves, and a German named Keseberg. When a party went back in the spring, all except Keseberg were dead.

In 1918, the Pioneer Monument was erected at the site of the mountain camp in remembrance of the ill-fated Donner party, and the site of the tragedy became known as the Donner Pass.

Douglas, Stephen A.

1813–1861

A politician and one of the great apostles of westward expansion prior to the Civil War, Douglas is probably best remembered for his political duels with Abraham Lincoln and his role in the ultimately disastrous compromises on the expansion of slavery.

Stephen A. Douglas.

Douglas was a fervent believer in the Union, but his attempts to preserve it undoubtedly helped to bring on the Civil War.

Douglas was born in Vermont but made his reputation as a representative and senator from Illinois, where he took up residence at the age of 20. He served in the state legislature and on the Illinois Supreme Court before running successfully for Congress in 1842. He served in the House through 1847, then in the Senate until his death from typhoid fever.

In Congress, Douglas was an advocate of Manifest Destiny and a tireless promoter of western interests, pushing for measures that would expedite the growth of the territories: the easing of immigration laws, protection of settlers from Indians, a homestead act, land grants to railroads, the annexation of Texas and Oregon, the Mexican War.

The only thing that stood in the way of the steady growth of the West was the thorny issue of slavery, and it was on that question that Douglas, in his zeal to promote the push westward, made his reputation. It was also on that question that his vision came up painfully short, with disastrous results for the nation.

Douglas was a primary exponent of popular sovereignty, the principle that the inhabitants of the territories should decide the slavery question for themselves. In 1849 he proposed that California be admitted to the Union as a free state, with other territories to apply popular sovereignty. He was instrumental in the passage of the Compromise of 1850, which contained those proposals, drafting the bill and shepherding it through the Senate.

However, it was the controversial Kansas-Nebraska Act (1854) that revealed the shortcomings of the compromise approach to the slavery question. The bill as passed was quite different from the one Douglas had envisioned, repealing the Missouri Compromise's ban on slavery in that state. But he remained a vigorous supporter of the act once it became law, even after the explosion of violence in the two affected territories made it clear that the compromise would not hold.

The slavery question would be at the heart of Douglas's final run for the Senate in 1858, an election in which he was opposed by Abraham Lincoln. The debates between the two men are an eloquent examination of the issue in its day and in all its complexity. Douglas won reelection, but pro-slavery senators managed to wrest from him the chairmanship of the Committee on Territories, which he had previously held.

Douglas was the Democratic candidate for president in 1860, as the result of a devastating split between Southern party members and the rest of the organization. The Southerners, disgusted with Douglas's call for nonintervention on the slavery question in the territories, ran John C. Breckinridge as their candidate. To his credit, Douglas campaigned actively in the South, arguing strenuously against secession. With the Democratic vote split, Lincoln squeaked into the White House. When war broke out not long after, Douglas was one of Lincoln's most vocal supporters and, in fact, was on a tour of the Northwest to urge Democrats to support the Union when he was stricken with his fatal illness.

Dred Scott Decision

MARCH 6, 1857

This U.S. Supreme Court decision held that a black slave had no right to citizenship under the U.S. Constitution. The ruling, a clear victory for slaveholders in the South, effectively legalized slavery in all territories and added fuel to the conflict between North and South.

Dred Scott was a slave whose owner, John Emerson, had taken him from Missouri, a slave state, to Illinois, a free state. Later Emerson took Scott to Louisiana Territory, which was made a free territory under the Missouri Compromise. When Scott was returned to Missouri, he filed a suit against Emerson's widow, requesting his freedom on the grounds that he had resided in free territory. A Missouri court ruled in favor of Scott, but Mrs. Emerson's lawyers appealed to the Missouri Supreme Court. That court, declaring that Congress had no authority under the Constitution to regulate slavery in the territories, ruled in favor of Emerson in 1852. Scott's lawyers appealed the verdict to the U.S. Supreme Court, which heard the case in the 1856–1857 term.

The court reached a decision on March 6, 1857, by a seven-to-two vote. Although each justice wrote an opinion, that by Chief Justice Roger B. Taney was

LIBRARY OF CONGRESS

Dred Scott.

delivered as the opinion of the court and is most often cited. Taney declared that a Negro, whether slave or free, was not included in the category of "citizen" under the U.S. Constitution and therefore was not entitled to any rights so granted. Taney stated that Negroes had "no rights that a white man was bound to respect," including the right to sue in federal courts. Scott was not a citizen of Missouri and therefore had no right to sue in a Missouri court.

The decision did not end there: it went on to denounce the Missouri Compromise of 1820, which prohibited slavery north of the latitude 36 degrees 30 minutes as unconstitutional. Slaves, it was declared, were property, and their masters were guaranteed property rights under the Fifth Amendment. No act of Congress or of a territorial legislature was entitled to deprive a citizen of property without due process of law. Finally, the justices ruled that regardless of Scott's stay in Illinois, he had returned to Missouri and was subject to Missouri law.

The Dred Scott decision was seen as a major blow to the Republican party, which was formed to prevent the expansion of slavery into the western territories. President Buchanan, inaugurated just two days before the Court's decision, hoped (along with the South) that the ruling would put an end to the slavery issue. Instead the Republican party grew stronger, and the North became more united in its antislavery sentiment. The decision did nothing to calm the country's explosive political climate, which culminated four years later in the outbreak of the Civil War. The Dred Scott decision was also only the second time the Supreme Court ruled an act of Congress unconstitutional (the first was the *Marbury v. Madison* decision 54 years earlier).

Dry Farming

Dry farming is a method of growing crops in areas where water is scarce.

As they moved westward, farmers found that in many regions there was not enough water for their crops, and so new forms of cultivation had to be devised. One of these new techniques was dry farming.

The principle behind dry farming is water storage.

Farmers would plow a series of deep channels in the land to catch and hold rainwater and melting snow. The soil was carefully weeded so that the precious water would go only to the crops. In summer, plowing was repeated to create a dust mulch. The success of dry farming also depended on the type of soil, when the rainy season occurred, and how concentrated the wet weather was. Fields would be rotated for planting each year so that the soil could replenish its nutrients while conserving water naturally stored in the ground.

Dry farming was practiced throughout the West, particularly from Texas, north through Canada, from the Dakotas west to the Rocky Mountains, and in parts of California. Hard wheats, sorghums, and other grains proved to be the best crops for dry farming. Many immigrant farmers adapted dry farming techniques to crops they brought with them from their native lands. Dry farming proved to be a boon to farmers in areas that previously were considered unusable for farming.

Dude Ranch

Dude ranches are "tourist" ranches. They were first established in the 1870s, for eastern and foreign visitors wanting a taste of western life.

As the mystique of cowboy life began to capture people's imaginations, many tourists headed West on vacation to experience this adventurous world for themselves. Locals regarded these visitors with some amusement, referring to them as "dudes." The term "dude" is thought by some to come from the German expression *Dudendop*, which means "lazy fellow." Others suggest that its origin was the Scottish word for clothing, "duds." Dudes were easily spotted by their store-bought, too-clean, western-style outfits, which stood out beside the range-hardened authentic garb of the cowhands.

In the 1870s, some Colorado ranchers realized there was money to be made from these wealthy dudes, and they began taking on paying "guests" who wanted to see real western life. In the 1880s, rich British game hunters began trekking West to practice their sport on the rich variety of wildlife. Howard Eaton of South Dakota began taking in available for vacations, Easterners headed West in record numbers.

Although dude ranches were popular with tourists, hardened cowhands felt it was beneath their dignity to work at these businesses. Many refused to work at dude ranches and poked fun at their colleagues who did. However, as the popularity of dude ranches continued to grow in the 1920s and 1930s, reluctant cowhands were forced to change their minds. In the 1920s, as cattle prices dropped, real range jobs became few and far between, and range workers, trading their pride for a steady paycheck, took to entertaining wide-eyed tourists.

Dude ranches continue to flourish today, and are a major source of tourism in the American Southwest. Ironically, with the decline of cowboy culture, today's dude ranches are now almost the only places left where one can see and participate in Old West range life. Although many tourists enjoy sleeping under the stars, most dude ranches offer a variety of amenities—including air conditioning, television, and swimming pools—that range hands of the 1880s never dreamed of.

This newspaper illustration pokes fun at Duke Alexis's failed attempt to hunt buffalo. The dude ranch exploits of wealthy easterners and Europeans were a constant source of amusement for locals.

these English visitors at his ranch. He soon realized, however, that better game and abundant fishing were to be had in the Big Horn Mountains of Wyoming, and he promptly opened a ranch there exclusively for the tourist trade. This was the official birth of the dude ranch.

At first dude ranches catered only to the wealthy, but over time they began courting trade from all social classes. Most played up to eastern fantasies of what the West was like, and gave their guests staged gunfights, cowboy and Indian battles, and recreations of familiar legends.

Dude ranches enjoyed a boom shortly after the outbreak of World War I. With Europe no longer

Dull Knife

CA. 1810–1883

Also known as Morning Star, Dull Knife was born and died near the Rosebud River in Montana. He seems to have been little known until after the Sand Creek Massacre of 1864. Dull Knife took part in the Cheyenne-Arapaho war in 1864–1865 and became known to whites as a signatory of the Fort Laramie Treaty of 1868.

In 1876, some of Dull Knife's Northern Cheyennes fought against Crook at the Battle of the Rosebud and against Custer at the Little Bighorn, but the Cheyenne chief did not participate in either battle. In November 1876, his village on the Powder River was attacked and destroyed by Colonel Ranald MacKenzie's force. The following spring Dull Knife and his Cheyennes surrendered to army authorities and were packed off to Indian Territory.

After nearly two years, during which the Cheyennes suffered disease, hunger, and despair on the lands assigned to them in Indian Territory, Dull Knife joined forces with the veteran Cheyenne war leader Little Wolf. They gathered over 300 of their people and began the 1,500-mile march north to their homelands. After crossing the Platte, Dull Knife's band split from Little Wolf's and surrendered to authorities at Fort Robinson, Nebraska. In January 1879 these Cheyennes, ordered to return to Indian Territory, attempted to escape from Fort Robinson. Dull Knife lost a third of his followers in the pursuit and from the bitter cold.

Dull Knife escaped and survived the winter. He was eventually permitted to live in the northern lands of his birth. He stayed with Red Cloud's Sioux from 1880 until his death and was buried near the Rosebud.

Duniway, Abigail Scott

1834–1915

Abigail Scott Duniway was a crusader for Women's Suffrage whose lectures and writings were instrumental in gaining voting rights for women in several western states. Her lifelong dream was finally realized in 1912, when Oregon passed a suffrage bill, but she died five years before Congress granted women's suffrage nationwide.

Duniway was born in Tazewell County, Illinois. Almost completely self-taught, she read newspapers avidly and was influenced by women's rights advocate Elizabeth Cady Stanton. In 1852, financial hardship forced her father to move west with his wife and 11 children. Duniway later described this arduous journey in her first book, *Captain Gray's Company; or, Crossing the Plains and Living in Oregon* (1959).

In Oregon Abigail Scott married Benjamin Duniway (1853), and became a schoolteacher and advocate of women's suffrage. In 1857, the state rejected a bill granting women voting and property rights. Opposition from Scott Duniway's brother, Harvey Scott, the powerful editor of the *Oregonian*, was partially responsible.

In 1870, she worked to establish a newspaper. The first issue of the weekly *New Northwest* came off the press (her sons were the typesetters) on May 5, 1871. The *New Northwest* was "not a Women's Rights, but a Human Rights organization," influencing political thought and encouraging women to seek education and enter professions. When the National Women's Suffrage Association convened in Washington, D.C., in 1886, Duniway was recognized as the leading women's advocate in the West.

Although suffrage was again defeated in 1886 and 1888, Duniway's tireless efforts in Oregon helped pass the Sole Trader Bill, which allowed women to keep property without liability for a husband's debts. In 1878 the enactment of the Married Women's Property Act gave wives the right to keep wages and own, manage, sell, or will property (New York and Massachusetts women had enjoyed such liberty since the 1850s).

In 1886 Harvey Scott convinced her to sell the *New Northwest*. For the next 20 years, Scott Duniway struggled with suffrage and grew frustrated by loss of support from prohibitionist women. In 1912, when Oregon finally granted women suffrage, Governor Oswald West asked her to write and sign the equal suffrage proclamation. At age 78, she became the first registered woman voter in her county. After publishing her autobiography, *Path Breaking* (1914), Scott Duniway spent her remaining energy fighting for national women's suffrage. She died five years before an amendment to the Constitution granting women the vote was ratified.

Dust Bowl

Dust Bowl describes the approximately 150,000-square-mile area that includes the Oklahoma and Texas panhandles and adjacent parts of Colorado, New Mexico, and Kansas. The term was coined by an Associated Press correspondent who visited the area in 1935 at the height of the dust storms.

The dust bowl area is a short-grass region with an annual rainfall of less than 20 inches. Early white settlers used the area for livestock grazing, but during World War I, much of the region's natural grass cover was plowed up and the area planted with winter wheat. Crops were abundant, but rainfall was unpredictable. In the early 1930s the region suffered severe drought; the land dried up and seed failed to germinate. Without the root system of the grasses, the soil was picked up and propelled by strong winds, causing massive dust storms whose clouds could be seen from up to a hundred miles away. Drifts of blowing dust piled up and even buried fences, roads, and houses. Farmers had to adapt or die, and more than half the population left the area.

Increased rainfall returned in the 1940s, and with the help of the federal government the region became productive once more. Grass and trees were planted in a soil conservation effort, and improved agricultural methods were introduced. Drought returned in the 1950s, but with new dry farming techniques the area endured. John Steinbeck's novel *The Grapes of Wrath* (1939) describes the hardships and migration of the Dust Bowl farmers.

E

Earp, Wyatt

1848–1929

Earp's name is among those universally recognized in the history of the American West, and he was its most celebrated, if not most capable, lawman.

Wyatt Berry Stapp Earp was born in Monmouth, Illinois. In Wyatt's childhood, the family moved from place to place, including Iowa and San Bernardino, California.

In February 1870, a month after he married Urilla Sutherland in Lamar, Missouri, Earp got his first law

enforcement job when he was appointed constable of Lamar. He left the town in 1871 after his wife died of typhoid fever. He then traveled to Indian Territory, Kansas, Texas, and New Mexico, earning his living as a gambler, teamster, buffalo hunter, section hand on the Union Pacific Railroad, and law officer.

In 1875 Earp served as a policeman in Wichita, Kansas; in 1878 he was assistant city marshal in Dodge City—a period in which he met Luke Short, Bat Masterson, and John "Doc" Holliday. In Dodge City he also met Cecelia "Mattie" Blaylock, who traveled with him to New Mexico and whom he subsequently married.

In December 1879, Earp and Mattie arrived in the mining boomtown of Tombstone, Arizona Territory, and were joined by his brothers Virgil (1843–1906), Morgan (1851–1882), James (1841–1926), and Warren (1855–1900). In 1880, Virgil was appointed town marshal. Wyatt, who had the faro concession at the Oriental Saloon and worked occasionally as a Wells, Fargo stagecoach guard, served periodically as his deputy.

The conflict between the Earps and the Clantons (Newman or "Old Man Clanton," and his sons Ike, Phin, and Billy) and the McLaury brothers (Tom and Frank), known cattle rustlers, boiled over on October 26, 1881, when the factions met in a shootout near the O.K. Corral in Tombstone. The brief and furious gunfight left three dead—the McLaurys and Billy Clanton—and Virgil and Morgan Earp wounded. (In the aftermath of the O.K. Corral fight, Morgan Earp was killed on March 18, 1882, while playing billiards in a Tombstone saloon.)

Wyatt Earp on his horse.

A factor in the hatred between the Earps and the Clantons was Wyatt's involvement with the San Francisco actress Josephine Sarah Marcus, who had come to Tombstone with a troupe performing Gilbert and Sullivan's *H.M.S. Pinafore.* Marcus was the temporary girlfriend of the pro-Clanton sheriff of Cochise County, John Harris "Johnny" Behan. From 1883 on, Wyatt and Josie were inseparable, and after Mattie Earp's death in 1888, they were married.

Gambling and mining ventures took Wyatt and Josie to Colorado, Idaho, Arizona, Alaska, and California over the years that followed the Tombstone sojourn. From 1906 until 1929, the Earps traveled from their Los Angeles home to mining claims in the Mojave Desert and Arizona, and to such other properties as a copper mine and oil wells.

In his Los Angeles years, Earp became friends with such movie actors as William S. Hart and Tom Mix. He felt a special kinship with Mix, who had been a marshal in Colorado and Oklahoma. Earp died on January 13, 1929.

Earp spent only about six of his 80 years as a lawman. In his youth he was over six feet tall, blond, and blue-eyed. His moustache was always carefully trimmed, and even as an old man he never left his house without coat and tie. He was a modest man who avoided publicity and remained silent on such celebrated events as the O.K. Corral fight.

Bat Masterson, a long-time friend, wrote in 1907 that Earp was "one of the few men I personally knew in the West in the early days whom I regarded as absolutely destitute of physical fear." He added that Earp was a "quiet, unassuming man, not given to brag or bluster, but at all times and under all circumstances a loyal friend and an equally dangerous enemy."

Stuart Lake's *Wyatt Earp, Frontier Marshal* (1931) was the first of the pro-Earp works; over the years numerous anti-Earp books have appeared that insist he was little more than a paid killer, claim jumper, card sharp, pimp, and horse thief. Earp remains a controversial figure.

Education in the West

There was no established school system in the early days of the frontier. Often the Bible was the

Cynthia Pease Mann, left, leads her class of children of all ages in exercises in this Boise, Idaho, children's home.

only book people owned. Many parents passed what little education they had on to their children. Wealthier families were able to hire tutors who would teach the children reading, writing, and arithmetic.

As families continued to settle the frontier lands, teachers were in demand. Education was looked on as a lowly, though necessary vocation; pay was usually poor and teachers were employed only for the months that school was in session. The first teachers in the West were men. Those who knew Greek or Latin were considered immensely learned. Other would-be educators were fast-talking, illiterate con artists who knew little more than their students.

Teachers were commonly referred to as "perfessers" and their students as "scholars." School was usually conducted in a one-room building. The teacher usually did double and triple duty, serving not only as teacher, but also as janitor and building caretaker. Scholars were notorious for misbehavior, and classrooms were often battlefields where little was accomplished. Because teaching was regarded as a lowly profession, settlers were reluctant to pay taxes for local schools. Some one-room schoolhouses were run by local authorities; others were built by concerned community members. Many small towns experienced a teacher shortage.

In the latter half of the century, teaching in the West became the domain of women. Male educators found better money and working conditions in the

ROY ANDREWS COLLECTION, UNIVERSITY OF OREGON LIBRARY

Two young girls share a secret over lunch in this portrait taken at a frontier school in Oregon.

East. Women found teaching a way to independence. Being a teacher was also one of the few careers open to women in the nineteenth century. To lure some of these women West, some communities offered room and board; others advertised the availability of single men for the usually unmarried teachers. Some communities believed teaching and married life were not compatible, and sometimes a new woman schoolteacher would be forced to sign a statement pledging to remain single for at least three years.

Educational opportunities for minorities varied. Communities of freed slaves created school systems comparable to those of whites. Native American children were largely relegated to poorer facilities on reservations. In 1894, the Bureau of Indian Affairs established a system to integrate Native American and white children within public schools. The Native American students faced much prejudice within the system. Often they were discouraged from learning tribal languages and customs.

Universities and colleges were also important educational institutions in the West. In 1834, Jesuits established St. Louis University in St. Louis, Missouri. This was the first Catholic institution for higher learning in the West. In 1845 the Texas Baptist Education Society founded what would later become Baylor University, and in 1853 Methodists opened Williamette University in Salem, Oregon. In 1855 the College of California opened its doors in the city of Oakland. This was the first college in the West to offer classes equivalent to those offered in eastern colleges. By the end of the century, state and private universities were found throughout the West.

El Paso, Texas

El Paso, situated on the western edge of Texas at the bank of the Rio Grande, faces the Mexican city of Ciudad Juarez. The two cities grew together but were separated after the Mexican War. Today they form the largest international metropolitan border area in North America.

The Tanpachoa Indians had lived in the area for centuries before the Europeans arrived. In 1598, Juan de Oñate crossed through the area en route to New Mexico. He named it El Paso del Norte, and claimed this "pass of the north" for himself. Traders, missionaries, and soldiers regularly used this mountain route to travel from Mexico City to Santa Fe. The first permanent settlement was established in 1680 during a revolt against the Spanish. The site was declared U.S. territory in 1848, and Fort Bliss was subsequently established to enforce the Treaty of Guadalupe Hidalgo. A few local settlements appeared, and the village of Franklin became known as El Paso after an 1858 state survey. The arrival of several railroads after 1881 brought a surge in population, as well as groups of transients and wild times. The gentleman-outlaw John Wesley Hardin was gunned down in El Paso in 1896.

Changes in the course of the Rio Grande after 1848 caused a border dispute that remained unsettled until 1963, when 437 acres of land were ceded to Mexico. When El Paso was incorporated in 1873, it had only 23 Anglo and 150 Mexican inhabitants. Today El Paso's population exceeds 500,000.

Emperor Norton

1819–1880

In the history of San Francisco, a town with more than its share of characters, there have been few as renowned for their eccentricity as Joshua A. Norton, the self-proclaimed Emperor of the United States. Norton, who was born in England, had been a successful merchant in his younger days. He arrived in San Francisco at the age of 30 with $40,000, which he managed to multiply several times over until, in the 1850s, he was reputedly worth over a quarter of a million dollars. However, Norton overreached himself in 1854 when he and several friends attempted to corner the rice market. Their failure left them broke, and Norton disappeared for several years.

When he reappeared in 1859, he had a new name, Norton I, a new rank, emperor, a new outfit that included a sword, an old uniform and military cap, and a retinue of two mongrel dogs, Bummer and Lazarus. Norton issued a proclamation to the citizens of San Francisco that he, as emperor, would be responsible for their well-being. In reality, of course, it was the other way around; printers ran off his currency free of charge, and bartenders around town honored it willingly. He fed off the free lunch then offered in most taverns, rode public transit for free, was given merchandise by friendly store owners and even loans by local banks. When his dogs died, their funeral was attended by thousands of citizens, and when Norton himself died in 1880, the royal funeral drew 10,000 San Franciscans.

Empresario System

In the 1820s, new settlers began arriving in Texas, which at that time was part of Mexico. To regulate this population explosion, and at the same time instill a sense of patriotism in the newcomers, the Mexican government set up the empresario system.

Under this system, an immigration agent received a land grant in return for his promise to bring in a certain number of families to settle on the acreage. Stephen F. Austin, whose father, Moses, had guided Americans to the Texas lands, was perhaps the most prosperous of these agents. His initial success in bringing new settlers to Texas gained him three additional empresario contracts. Austin's duties included mediating differences between American settlers and Mexican officials. Austin was paid a fee by the immigrants for the right to live on his holdings, a charge deeply resented by most of the settlers.

Within a few years, the empresario system had brought more than 7,000 Americans to Texas. Most of them settled in the eastern and central parts of the future state, and had little to do with the Mexicans who lived farther south. The large influx of Americans eventually led to trouble. One empresario, an American named Haden Edwards, attempted to establish his own country in 1826. He did not receive wide support, and his rebellion failed miserably. However, the episode forced the Mexican government to reconsider the policy of allowing so many Americans to move into Texas. Immigration was severely cut back, and in 1830 the empresario system was abolished.

Eskimo People

Eskimos are a group of people native to Alaska and the surrounding islands. These Native Americans and their Aleutian neighbors did not face the forced moves, loss of lands, and devastating warfare that other North American Indians endured. Although their land belongs under the jurisdiction of the United States, native Alaskans today enjoy much political autonomy and legal protection.

For centuries, Eskimos lived along the coastal regions of the Bering Sea and the Arctic Ocean. In the late eighteenth century, British fur trading groups advanced inland from the east coast and Russian fur traders moved in from the opposite shore. Although the interaction brought positive changes in such areas as the economy, the encroachment on their lands caused the Eskimos to lose valuable hunting grounds and the game on which they depended for food, clothing, and other necessities.

The Russians came to Alaska in the 1740s but did not establish a settlement until 1784, when competition from other Europeans led to the czar's government to make its claims more tangible. In the nineteenth century, the Russian America Company

Early photograph of Eskimos spearfishing.

ing response to the American presence convinced Washington not to extend its federal Indian policy to Alaska. By 1877, the U.S. Army had withdrawn from the territory. Eskimos and other native groups were never restricted to reservations. Although gold-seeking whites sometimes turned them out, no treaties deprived them of their rights to the land. Further, although Christian missionaries had a notable influence, the Eskimos were not forced to conform to the religion and customs of western civilization.

The Organic Act of 1884 ended military rule in the region and allowed the formation of a civil government. This lasted until 1912, when Alaska became a territory. Although it came too late to save other frontier tribes, the American public's changing attitude toward Native Americans helped pass the Alaska Native Claims Settlement Act of 1971, which continues to protect Eskimo rights to the land.

ruled the region and treated the native peoples cruelly.

In 1867, U.S. Secretary of State William Henry Seward convinced Congress to purchase Alaska for $7.2 million. Although the non–Native-American presence there increased steadily, there was no rush of settlers to the region. The sparse population, the harsh Arctic climate, and the Eskimos' unthreaten-

Exodusters

Although slavery had been abolished, African-Americans still suffered greatly in the post–Civil War South. The rise of the Ku Klux Klan, combined

Eskimo painted in 1832 by John Halkett, a Hudson's Bay Company employee stationed in Canada.

with openly racist local governments, forced many freed slaves to consider relocating to a more hospitable region. A movement to create new settlements exclusively for blacks spread through African-American churches and other assemblies in the South. In 1879, a 70-year-old former slave named Benjamin Singleton—known as "Pap" to his followers—declared himself an instrument of God's will. He united African-Americans in a move to the West, and dreamed of creating a new society on the plains of Kansas. The new towns were to be segregated from existing white communities and were meant to be independent societies run for and by blacks.

Singleton founded two such Kansas communities in 1879, joining the town of Nicodemus, Kansas, which had been established by African-American settlers from Kentucky in 1877. Through letters, handbills, and word of mouth, many blacks heard the call and left the hostile South for a utopian life in Kansas. It is believed that as many as 26,000 people made this exodus between 1879 and 1880; hence the term "exodusters."

Not all whites were happy to see their former slaves go. Black workers were a cheap source of labor in the South, and some bosses resorted to violence in order to keep them from leaving. African-American migrants also faced discrimination on the road to Kansas. Some ferryboat captains, for example, refused to let blacks board their vessels for the trip across the Mississippi River.

F

Family Life in the West

Traditionally, families had stayed together in the same area for generations. With the great exodus to the West, the notion of family was redefined in America. Sons and daughters would marry and head West, in many cases saying goodbye to their parents and relatives for life. Husbands would leave their families to find land on the frontier, only to disappear and never be heard from again.

With the abundance of open land and fresh prospects, the West seemed ideal to families looking for a new start in life. However, the journey West was hard and dangerous. A variety of illnesses, including cholera, swept through many wagon trains. In addition, bad weather, accidents, wild animals, and attacks by outlaws or Indians compounded the settlers' troubles.

Gender roles for men and women on the trail followed traditional stereotypes. For the most part, husbands were in charge of driving covered wagons while wives stayed in back to watch the children. When the wagon train rested, women took care of

NATIONAL ARCHIVES

Major Anson Mills and the officers of the 10th Cavalry, stationed at Fort Grant, Arizona, picnicking with their families near the Gila River.

NEBRASKA HISTORICAL SOCIETY

Homesteaders in the Loup Valley, Nebraska.

This pioneer family posed outside with their organ rather than let their friends back East see their sod house.

Frontier families raised lots of children to work the farms.

household duties, including cooking, repairing torn clothing, and—on those rare occasions when enough water was available—washing. To get their tasks done, mothers often had older children watch the youngest family members. Men and older boys made necessary repairs on wagons, cared for the animals, and hunted for fresh game.

Women often had to make this journey while pregnant. Expecting a baby was no excuse for avoiding the hard work on the trail. Only after childbirth could a woman expect some relief, when her husband and older children would take over her duties. Often newborn infants could not survive life on the trail. When a baby died, there generally was no time or money for a funeral: The child was buried on the side of the road and the family moved on.

Privacy was a rare and cherished commodity, as most wagon trains involved a large number of people. Family time on the trail was limited; activities were usually community affairs rather than household ventures.

Many women kept diaries, and these journals were sent back to family and friends in the East who were considering making the trip themselves. A good diary usually recorded day-to-day activities, and described the best trails, important landmarks, and hazards to be wary of. Many of these diaries became valuable family heirlooms, as well as providing a unique look at life under the harsh circumstances of the frontier.

Once settled in the new land, male and female roles remained fairly traditional. Men were responsible for home building and farm work; women took care of the household, and in some cases educated their children. And although many miles separated western settlers from their relatives in the East, women maintained the connection by regularly sending and receiving letters, photographs, and newspaper clippings.

Fargo, William George

1818–1881

William George Fargo, co-founder of Wells, Fargo and Company and the American Express Company, was born in Pompey, Onondaga County, New York. As a youth Fargo carried the mail; worked as a clerk in Syracuse; and later ran his own store with his brother. He entered the freight business in 1840 when he became an agent for the Auburn and Syracuse Railroad, and shortly thereafter became a messenger for the Livingston, Wells and Pomeroy express business. Wells and Company, Fargo's partnership with Henry Wells and Daniel Dunning (1894), was the first express business to operate west of Buffalo, New York. In 1851 Wells, Fargo and Company was formed to provide transportation and communication service between New York and San Francisco. The company soon expanded its operations to cover the entire West Coast and became the largest and most prosperous of its kind. In the meantime, three competing firms merged into the American Express Company, of which Fargo served as president from 1868 until his death. He also served two terms as mayor of Buffalo (1862–1866) where he died on August 3, 1881.

Farming Techniques in the West

Farming techniques in the West were as varied as the land itself. The method a farmer chose depended on a number of factors, including the area, climate, type of soil, and kinds of crops or livestock to be raised.

The earliest farming was done by Native Americans. In the desert regions of Arizona, wild plants such as cactus fruits, mesquite beans, seeds, berries, and acorns were simply gathered from their natural sources. In arid climates, irrigation systems were developed for the growing of "maize," or corn. The irrigation trenches were dug with bare hands or with crude tools. Seeds were planted in late spring or early summer, and crops harvested in the fall. Hun-

dreds of years after this irrigation system was first used, settlers in the Arizona territories once more employed the long-forgotten canals to bring water to their own farms.

As white exploration of the West grew, so did the variety of crops and techniques used in farming. The land seemed endless, and so did the agricultural possibilities. European immigrants brought their own farming methods which they adapted and honed for the different soils and climates they found in America.

The first challenge to many western farmers was to remove enough trees from the land to make room for crops. Many acres of American forests were cleared for planting. The cut trees were used for fuel, housing, and tool-making. As the westward movement reached treeless regions, many farmers were amazed to find that the seemingly barren soil was just as fertile as the land they had left behind. These new lands also had the advantage of not having endless numbers of trees that had to be uprooted. Of course, the trees had also been easy sources of fuel and lumber, and many farmers soon regretted leaving them behind.

Though farming essentially remained the same as it had been for thousands of years, progress came in the nineteenth-century West with the rise of technology. Tools such as the cotton gin, the wheat

OKLAHOMA HISTORICAL SOCIETY

A farmer and his family display the fruits of their labor: carrots, cabbages, corn, and potatoes.

A horse-powered threshing machine at use on an Idaho farm.

thresher, the McCormick reaper, and the steel plow helped farming became a powerful industry. In the early nineteenth century, the average farm raised enough crops and livestock to feed the family. By the 1890s, farming had become more complicated. Though farmers often grew only one crop, such as wheat or corn, they raised it in abundance. The developing cattle-ranching and sheep-farming industries also contributed to these new technologies, as farmers sought better ways to raise livestock.

New techniques had to be developed for the harsher desert climates. Irrigation remained an age-old and popular farming method. Dry Farming was a method developed in areas previously thought unsuitable for raising crops.

Faust, Frederick Schiller

1892–1944

Born in Seattle, Washington, Faust was orphaned at a young age and raised in the San Joaquin Valley of California. He attended the University of California at Berkeley, where he wrote a great number of poems, stories, and essays that appeared in student publications. These early works demonstrated the amazing range and productivity that characterized his career.

Two of Faust's greatest aspirations—to serve in France during World War I and to win fame as a poet—eluded him. He married in 1917 and that year began selling stories to a variety of pulp magazines in New York City. In two decades of writing, he produced an estimated 30 million words of fiction (the equivalent of over 500 full-length books) under a bewildering number of pen names. Among the names was Max Brand, used principally but not exclusively for his western novels and stories.

Although Faust, through his Max Brand identity, is most often associated with western stories, he wrote fiction in virtually all fields—detective stories, science fiction, action adventure, romance, spy tales, and historical works. He also published four books of poetry (the only work he took seriously). With the demise of the pulps in the 1930s, Faust made the transition to "slick" magazines, selling his work regularly to such periodicals as *Cosmo-*

politan, *Coltier's, Harper's,* and *Saturday Evening Post.*

Among the most successful of the Faust-as-Brand novels were *The Untamed* (1919), *Destry Rides Again* (1930), and the series of stories involving a young physician named James Kildare, a character featured in both movie and television series.

At the peak of his productivity, Faust earned more than $70,000 a year and was among America's wealthiest authors. In 1926 he moved with his family to a villa near Florence, Italy; in 1938 he went to Hollywood and for seven years worked as a screenwriter for MGM, Columbia, and Warner Brothers.

Although he suffered from a weak heart most of his life, drank heavily, and was 52 years old, Faust in 1944 became a war correspondent for *Harper's* magazine, attached to the 5th Army. He was killed in action on May 11, 1944, near the village of Santa Maria Infante, Italy, not far from his Florence home.

Many of his 200 western novels remain in print, giving Faust—and Max Brand—a continuing worldwide audience.

Fetterman, William J.

1833–1866

Fetterman was the U.S. Army officer responsible for one of the worst United States military disasters of the Indian Wars prior to the Battle of the Little Bighorn.

William Fetterman was the son of an army lieutenant. A Civil War hero, he served with the 18th U.S. Infantry Regiment during that conflict; he was also decorated and given the brevet rank of lieutenant colonel. He was known for his bravery, his flamboyant dress and manner, and his arrogance.

In November 1866 he rejoined the 18th Infantry as a captain at Fort Phil Kearny in the Dakota Territory on the Bozeman Trail. Colonel Henry B. Carrington, commander of the regiment, viewed his mission as essentially defensive. Fetterman, however, was impatient. With a firm belief in his own ability and that of his troops, he boasted: "Give me 80 men, and I'll ride roughshod through the whole Sioux nation." In this way, he believed, he would settle "the whole Indian business," once and for all.

The Fetterman Massacre.

Sioux raiding parties regularly harassed work details sent out from the fort. Colonel Carrington sent relief columns to protect them, always with explicit orders not to pursue the attackers over a nearby ridge. When on December 21 Indians attacked an army wood train, Fetterman demanded that he be permitted to lead the relief detail. Carrington agreed. As it happened, Fetterman departed the fort that day with exactly 80 men. Disobeying orders, he allowed himself to be lured over the ridge by a decoy party led by Crazy Horse. Over the ridge, a force of several hundred Sioux were waiting, and within 40 minutes, Fetterman's force had been wiped out. The Sioux nation had ridden roughshod over Captain Fetterman.

Fifty-niners

Fifty-niners were prospectors who rushed to Colorado in 1859 in response to gold found first at Pike's Peak in 1858 and then around Boulder and Denver the following year. Between 50,000 and 100,000 people set out for Colorado from the Missouri frontier, an influx second only to that of 1849. This gold rush continued throughout the Civil War years.

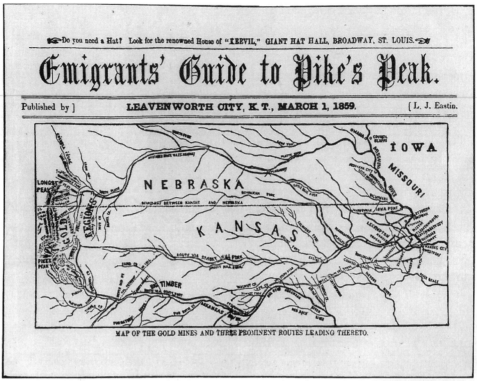

Map of trails leading to Pike's Peak, 1859.

William Green Russell, a miner with experience in Georgia and California, heard stories that gold had been discovered in the Colorado Rockies and organized a party of 20 men to head for the Pike's Peak region. Together with about 50 Cherokees, the party traveled from Georgia to Kansas and on to the north-central Colorado region. The group spread seeds of gold fever through every settlement they passed. Before they had even arrived in Colorado, other companies had been formed to follow them.

Russell and his men set up camp on the east side of Cherry Creek but found little success there. Russell then persuaded a dozen to follow him up the Platte River to the mouth of Dry Creek. Here they made a placer strike that yielded about $10 a day per man—better than they had been doing, but not enough to justify real enthusiasm. But a trader on his way back to the Missouri frontier brought with him a small sample of Russell's gold, as well as exaggerated stories of the magnitude of the discovery. Soon news of a new gold rush exploded across the nation; newspapers carried head-lines proclaiming "The New Eldorado." The rush to Pike's Peak was on, with a new slogan, "Pike's Peak or Bust." By the end of 1858, at least four cities had been established near the fork of the Platte River and Cherry Creek. Of them, only Denver survived.

When the first Fifty-niners arrived in Colorado, many were disappointed and felt misled. However, new finds in 1859 turned things around. Most of the early prospecting had been done along creeks and rivers close to the base of the mountains. More experienced prospectors moved into the higher canyons. In January 1859 John S. Gregory ascended North Clear Creek and discovered gold in a gulch. With the discovery of another rich outcropping four months later, the treasure trove became known as Gregory Gulch. Another prospector, George A. Jackson, made a promising find on Chicago Creek. At the same time, a group of prospectors discovered gold near Boulder Creek, at a site they named Gold Hill. These and other later discoveries sustained the gold rush to Colorado.

Fink, Mike

CA. 1770–1823

Mike Fink was a scout, trapper, and folk hero whose feats and tall tales made him a legend among keelboatmen and frontiersmen in the Mississippi Valley. Historians have had difficulty separating fact from fiction when attempting to document the details of Fink's life.

Legend holds that Fink, born around 1770 close to Pittsburgh, Pennsylvania, started out as a market hunter bringing fresh game to supply the markets of Pittsburgh. He also served as a scout before becoming a boatman. He then captained his own keelboat on the Mississippi. Fink gained notoriety for his expert marksmanship, his fights with Indians, his practical jokes, and his outrageous tales of drinking and fighting. Stories about him spread rapidly, and soon he became a living legend in the Mississippi Valley.

In 1822 Fink joined a fur-trapping expedition to the upper Missouri River led by William H. Ashley. During the hunt, Fink killed a man while attempting to shoot a tin can off his head. It is not known exactly why Fink missed the tin can, for this was a feat he often performed. Whatever the reason, another man on the expedition, possibly a companion of the man killed, shot and killed Fink.

Although the details of Fink's real life and death are sketchy, the mythical Mike Fink is an important part of the Mississippi keelboat era. Books such as J. M. Field's *Mike Fink: The Last of the Boatmen* (1847) and Emerson Bennett's *Mike Fink: A Legend of the Ohio* (1848) were especially important in perpetuating his legend.

Fitzpatrick, Thomas

1799–1854

"Broken Hand," as the Indians called Fitzpatrick because of a hand crippled by a firearms accident, was one of the most resourceful of the mountain men who hunted beaver skins during the heyday of the Rocky Mountain fur trade. An Irish immigrant,

he gravitated to St. Louis and in 1823 participated in William H. Ashley's expedition to the upper Missouri, including the battle with the Arikara Indians and the abortive military campaign to punish these Indians. With Jedediah Smith and a small party of Ashley men, he pushed west to Crow Indian country and ultimately, early in 1824, rediscovered South Pass, the landmark portal of the westward movement, and opened the rich beaver grounds of the upper Green River.

With Ashley's retirement from the fur trade, Fitzpatrick emerged as one of a handful of entrepreneurs who exploited the fur resources of the Rocky Mountains until the collapse of the beaver market in the late 1830s. His range encompassed the upper Snake River drainage area, the Three Forks country at the head of the Missouri River, and the Yellowstone Basin. He led trapping parties for Smith, William Henry Jackson, and Milton Sublette and later was himself a partner in the Rocky Mountain Fur Company. Still later, as the American Fur Company came to dominate the business, he entered the service of that firm. Throughout these years, Fitzpatrick's exploits in overcoming wilderness perils, in repeated combats with Blackfeet Indians, and in encounters with grizzly bears and bison form a continuous saga of high adventure.

With the decline of the fur trade, Fitzpatrick applied his experience to America's westward movement. In 1841 he guided the first emigrant party on the Oregon Trail as far as Fort Hall in present-day Idaho. In 1842 he guided the second Oregon-bound train from Fort Laramie to Fort Hall. In 1843–1844, with Kit Carson, Fitzpatrick served as guide for the second expedition of Lieutenant John C. Frémont, which surveyed and mapped the Pacific Northwest, California, the southwestern deserts, and the Great Basin. In 1844–1845 Fitzpatrick performed a similar service for the military expeditions to the Great Plains of Colonel Stephen Watts Kearny and Lieutenant James W. Abert. With the outbreak of the Mexican War in 1846, Fitzpatrick accompanied General Kearny's Army of the West in the march to New Mexico but then was sent back to Washington as a dispatch bearer.

Appointed U.S. Indian agent to the tribes of the Great Plains in 1846, Fitzpatrick served with distinction. Better than almost anyone else, he knew Indians. In addition, unlike most old mountain men, he was literate and unusually intelligent. His contributions to the formulation of federal policy, including a leading role in negotiating the Fort Laramie Treaty of 1851 and the Fort Atkinson Treaty of 1853, were substantial. In 1854, however, while on an official visit to Washington, D.C., pneumonia cut short his life and his career in the Indian service.

Five Civilized Tribes

Historically, this term has been used to identify the five tribes that incorporated major features of white civilization into their own civilization. These tribes were the Cherokees, Creeks, Choctaws, Chickasaws, and Seminoles. Before they borrowed elements of the encroaching white culture, however, they had their own civilization—not at all inferior, just very different. Five Nations is a better, more accurate description, even though that same term also describes the Five Nations of the Iroquois Confederacy.

OKLAHOMA HISTORICAL SOCIETY

Two Choctaw women, photographed by artist/naturalist Heinrich Mollhausen.

In colonial times, the homeland of the Five Nations extended across what became the southeastern United States after the American Revolution. The Cherokees lived on both sides of the Appalachian Mountains at the border of the Carolinas and Tennessee and spilled off to the south into northwestern Georgia. The Creeks, a confederation of loosely affiliated tribes, were divided into the Lower Creeks in southern Georgia and the Upper Creeks in northern Alabama. The Choctaws spread across the Mississippi River into Louisiana, while the Chickasaws occupied both sides of the Mississippi, in northern Louisiana and western Tennessee. An offshoot tribe of Creeks took the name Seminole and settled in Florida.

The Five Nations made greater efforts than other tribes to develop institutions that would strengthen their ability to deal with European invaders. Originally theocracies, dominated if not ruled by priests or holy men, they substituted civil and military leaders for this priesthood early in the colonial period. In fact, Cherokee and Creek towns were designated either "red" or "white" for war or peace. The reds carried out any activity involving warfare or force of arms; the whites instead were responsible for initiating and maintaining peace. After their theocratic phase, the Five Nations consisted of virtually autonomous villages whose headmen met periodically in weak national councils. The demands of dealing with colonial powers, however, produced leaders in all the nations who worked to strengthen central authority and to present a unified front to the invaders. Feuds broke out as proponents of change clashed with conservatives clinging to old ways.

The society of the Five Nations centered on hunting, gathering, and the cultivation of corn, beans, and squash. During the growing season, the people lived in fixed villages, sometimes fortified; in winter they scattered to hunt. An important feature of their economy was trade with whites, in which deerskins and fur pelts were exchanged for European manufactured goods. As the fur trade diminished in the early years of the nineteenth century, however, the people increasingly relied on subsistence farming and animal husbandry. A minority became successful planters or merchants.

In the decades after the American Revolution, white immigrants were a growing threat to the territory and culture of the Five Nations. Factions of each tribe tried to resist by borrowing from the culture of the newcomers. Most influential was the Cherokee principal chief John Ross. Under his leadership, in 1827 the Cherokees established a constitutional government patterned after the U.S. model. Already Sequoyah had invented a Cherokee alphabet, and with Ross's patronage a native newspaper, the *Cherokee Phoenix*, began publication at New Echota, Georgia. His efforts led to U.S. Supreme Court decisions that affirmed Cherokee sovereignty and denied the authority of the state of Georgia to extinguish Native American title to lands within its boundaries.

All the tribes boasted strong leaders like Ross, which is one explanation for the constant factionalism. Many tribal leaders took non-Indian names, reflecting the assimilation of European traders, mainly Scots, into Indian life. The Creek chieftain Alexander McGillivray negotiated a treaty with President George Washington but died at an early age in 1791. Successive generations of Creek McIntoshes carried on McGillivray's leadership role. The Colbert family dynasty dominated Chickasaw affairs for many years. But this tribe also took pride in their Indian names, as exemplified by their last war chief, Tishomingo. Other tribal leaders who maintained their Indian identity were the Choctaw Pushmataha and the great Seminole chieftain Osceola.

Ross and leaders in the other tribes tried to present a united front to reverse the growing strength of the Indian Removal policy of the U.S. government. This measure, first advocated by President Thomas Jefferson and embraced in the 1830s by President Andrew Jackson, aimed at removing all Indians from the East and resettling them west of the Mississippi. Jackson not only refused to use federal power to enforce the Supreme Court decisions protecting Cherokee rights, he vigorously pressed the removal program and allowed, even encouraged, settlers from the state of Georgia to overrun Cherokee lands.

Following congressional passage of the Indian Removal Act in May 1830, federal officials moved swiftly to conclude removal treaties with each of the tribes. They met similar conflicting responses in all the tribes. One faction would want to fight stubbornly against removal, while another would offer to bargain away tribal lands and freedom and agree to move West. The Seminoles, relatively secure in their Florida swamps, fought for three wars before they finally gave in. All tribes, however, eventually ceded their lands and migrated to the Indian Territory (modern-day Oklahoma). The Cherokee Trail of

Tears, a time of intense suffering, sickness, and death, is the best known of the tribal ordeals, but everyone affected by this brutal policy experienced their own trails of tears en route to their new homes.

The population of the Five Nations fluctuated greatly throughout their history, and even official estimates vary. Warfare, European diseases, and intoxicants exacted a fearful toll on the tribal populations in the eighteenth century, but those populations recovered with the decline in warfare. By the time of Indian Removal, the Cherokees and Creeks each numbered around 20,000 people, the Choctaws 15,000, and the Chickasaws 5,000. The Seminole population ranged between 2,000 and 4,000.

In the newly established Indian Territory, the Five Nations set out to overcome the bitter legacy of factionalism and to build new lives and new constitutional governments. Each of the tribes constituted a "nation," with national boundaries, a constitution, and political institutions rooted in American democracy but also reflecting Indian traditions. In a fertile land, the people took up individual homesteads and farmed in much the same way as did white yeoman farmers. Some were even drawn into the cotton plantation economy of the antebellum South. They developed effective public school systems and embraced Christianity. They were led by a gifted elite, of whom John Ross continued to be an outstanding exemplar.

Unfortunately, factionalism continued to be a disruptive element running through this record of apparent success. Those who had opposed the removal

LIBRARY OF CONGRESS

Written in both English and Cherokee, the Cherokee Advocate *was an attempt to bridge the gap between white and Cherokee culture.*

treaties and those who had favored them sought to overcome differences made all but irreconcilable by violence, bloodshed, and even assassination. As the leading opponent of removal among the Cherokees, John Ross played a key role in the feuds of his nation, and his quarrels with the John Ridge family and others who had promoted removal disrupted the first decades in the West.

The Civil War reopened all the old wounds, as each nation fought over which side to favor. The old proremoval faction tended to side with the South, the antiremoval with the North. The proximity of the Indian Territory to Confederate Arkansas and Texas denied the nations any choice of remaining neutral. Despite Ross's opposition, the Cherokees joined the Confederacy. The Choctaws and Chickasaws also backed the South, while the Creeks and the Seminoles broke into bitterly quarreling divisions. At war's end the federal government punished the Five Nations, even those that supported the Union, by taking much of their lands, which supposedly had been guaranteed by the removal treaties.

Thanks to their continuing policy of assimilation and emulating elements of white society, the people of the Five Nations came close to fitting the image of the ideal Indian conceived by the reform groups that dominated U.S. Indian policy in the decades following the Civil War. But land boomers wanted the Indian lands, and they portrayed tribal ownership of land as inherently savage and brutal (uncivilized). They joined with the reformers to support a policy of allotment of tribal land into individual parcels, giving back any land that was "left over" to the United States. The "severalty" program thus became a guise for opening "surplus" lands to white settlement and ultimately for extinguishing tribal sovereignty. With the aid of several laws and government negotiating commissions, the alliance of land boomer and reformer prevailed: The great land rushes of the 1890s were largely at the expense of the land holdings of the Five Nations. Finally in 1906, tribal sovereignty was extinguished altogether. The following year, the state of Oklahoma was created and entered the American Union. The citizens of the Five Nations became citizens of the state of Oklahoma.

Today the people of the Five Nations retain vestiges of their heritage and identity but are hardly distinguishable from their white neighbors. At the same time, their tribal governments have been reinstituted, along with their historic capitals, and tribal pride and identity are being restored. The few remnants of the tribes that escaped Indian Removal and succeeded in remaining in their traditional homes still live in the Southeast. The North Carolina Cherokees and the Seminoles in Florida display perhaps the most visible evidence of the original Indian spirit and character.

Flathead Indians

The Flatheads (or Salishes) are an Algonquian tribe of Native Americans, now part of the Confederated Salish and Kootenai tribes, residing on a reservation in western Montana.

Originally one of the most powerful tribes in the West, the Flatheads occupied lands along Flathead Lake, in the Flathead Valley of Montana, and ranged over a large area of the Pacific Northwest. They made annual expeditions east to hunt buffalo. Their name is a misnomer, probably given to them by white explorers who thought they were members of a different tribe. In fact, the Salish were one of the few tribes in the region who did not practice head-flattening—purposefully altering the cranial shape of a newborn infant's head in the cradle. Another theory maintains that the epithet was bestowed by neighboring tribes who looked upon their own heads as pointed rather than flat.

The Flatheads were courageous in battle and generally accommodating to whites. Having heard about Christianity, they sent messengers to St. Louis to request a priest. Pierre-Jean De Smet answered the call and established a successful mission among them in the Bitterroot Valley in the 1840s. In 1855 the church was moved to Mission Valley, the site of modern-day St. Ignatius.

In that same year, the United States concluded the Hellgate Treaty with the Salishes, Kalispels, Kootenais, and Pend d'Oreilles. The Bitterroot Salishes were given land in the Bitterroot Valley. In 1891, however, against the wishes of Chief Charlo, they were forced to relinquish this territory and move to the present-day Flathead Reservation.

In 1885 Louis Riel staged a rebellion of Métis (persons of mixed Indian and French descent) in Canada. After the revolt's collapse, many Métis fled into Montana, some of them settling among the Flatheads, with whom they had had trading relations for more than a hundred years. In 1887 Pierre Busha, a Métis leader, appealed to the Confederated Tribes for permission to settle 60 families on the Flathead Reservation. The request was refused, however, because of the impending resettlement of Charlo's band.

One of the most distinguished Flatheads was D'Arcy McNickle, born of mixed parentage after the Riel Rebellion. He worked with the Bureau of Indian Affairs and was one of the founders of the National Congress of American Indians. He was also a noted novelist, historian, and anthropologist, and the author of many books on his fellow Native Americans.

During the nineteenth century, cattle ranching, combined with farming, was an important source of livelihood on the reservation.

Flipper, Henry Ossian

1856–1940

Henry Ossian Flipper was a soldier in the U.S. Army from 1878 to 1881, and the first African-American to graduate from West Point.

Flipper was born to slave parents near Thomasville, Georgia, on March 21, 1856. In 1873 he accepted a nomination to West Point, where he was determined not to be hounded out of school as his African-American predecessors had been. When he graduated, he turned down an invitation from Liberia to command its army and chose instead to go west as the only African-American officer in the U.S. military. While serving in the 10th Cavalry in Indian Territory, he devised an elaborate drainage ditch to prevent mosquitoes from breeding and transmitting malaria. Today, Flipper's Ditch is a national historic landmark.

Flipper was later transferred to Fort Davis, Texas, where he served under the command of Lieutenant Colonel William Rufus Shafter, a racist who hated the idea of working with an African-American officer. When Shafter could not transfer Flipper from his unit, he joined with two other officers to frame the black soldier for embezzling Army funds. Flipper faced a court-martial, and although the judges found him not guilty of embezzlement, he was found guilty of conduct unbecoming an officer and received a dishonorable discharge on December 8, 1881.

Henry O. Flipper.

Although Flipper enjoyed a successful civilian career, he remained haunted by his unjust court-martial and filed nine appeals with military review boards to clear his name. Each time he was denied. On April 26, 1940, he died of a heart attack, but 36 years after his death, the military did overturn his court-martial and granted him an honorable discharge on December 13, 1976.

Folsom Culture

Folsom refers to a prehistoric Native American culture, named after the site where its remains were first uncovered.

In 1925 a cowboy searching for lost cattle near Folsom, New Mexico, discovered some projectile points or spearheads. Excavation the following year uncovered the remains of the extinct big-horned bison. Between 1926 and 1928, skeletal remains of 23 animals were found at the site. The bones were grouped together and showed evidence that the animals had been killed and butchered by humans. These discoveries at Folsom, coupled with a similar find at Fort Collins, Colorado, represented the first real evidence of early human habitation in the Americas.

Folsom spearheads were carved with elaborate fluting, the exact purpose of which is a subject of some conjecture. The fluting may have been incorporated for purely aesthetic reasons. More likely, however, the grooves made the point lighter so that the spear to which it was attached could be thrown more easily. Another theory suggests that the fluting may have facilitated the flow of blood from the wounds inflicted, thus increasing the chances of making a kill in the hunt.

In the decade following the New Mexico discovery, Folsom spear points were found at other sites in the Southwest. Other tools, including hammers, scrapers, choppers, and knives, were also unearthed. The remains of a workshop gave clues as to how Folsom spearheads were manufactured. A Folsom site near Lubbock, Texas, yielded some charred bones. These bones made radiocarbon dating possible for the first time. The test results indicated that the bones were 9,883 years old (plus or minus 350 years). Today it is believed that the Folsom culture flourished between 9,000 and 11,000 years ago.

Though these excavations brought to light much information about Folsom hunting methods and butchering techniques, very little was still known about the daily life of the Folsom culture. Then, in 1966, a graduate student from the University of New Mexico uncovered a site outside of Albuquerque. Known as the Rio Rancho site, it is the most important Folsom site yet discovered. Remains of at least two lodges were discovered. These homes were circular and about 15 feet in diameter. They consisted of a frame of small poles covered with bison hides. Cooking hearths were found outside the lodges, and a variety of implements was unearthed. Further study is being continued on this and other Folsom sites.

It is believed that the Folsom culture is related to the Clovis Culture, discovered in New Mexico in 1932. The Clovis culture predates the Folsom by approximately 2,000 years.

Forsyth, George Alexander

1837–1915

Forsyth was a soldier best known for his involvement in the battle of Beecher's Island. During the Civil War he achieved the rank of brevet brigadier general and was involved in close to 90 engagements. From 1881 to 1883 he participated in campaigns against the Apaches in New Mexico.

In the summer of 1868, under the direction of Major General Philip Sheridan, Forsyth led a detachment of 50 civilian scouts to search out Indian camps. On September 17 he and his men engaged about 750 Cheyenne and Sioux warriors near the Arikaree fork of the Republican River. Forsyth's men took refuge on an island in the river bed, and by the end of the night 22 were dead and the remaining were surrounded. The besieged men were encircled for eight days, until couriers who slipped out at night were able to summon reinforcements. The island and battle took their name from Lieutenant Frederick Beecher, killed in the fighting.

Fort Atkinson

Fort Atkinson was established on the banks of the Missouri River, near present-day Omaha, Nebraska, in 1819 by Colonel Henry Atkinson. The fort was the first west of the Missouri and one of the earliest built west of the Mississippi. The plan to establish Fort Atkinson and others on the frontier came in the wake of the War of 1812. Secretary of War John C. Calhoun sent expeditions west with the goal of offsetting the influence of the British in North America, impressing the Indians with military might, and creating a string of military strongholds on the frontier. During Fort Atkinson's brief existence (eight years), the fort served as a base for traders and explorers and as a center for management of Indian tribes. Soldiers stationed at the fort spent much of their time farming and raising livestock.

Soldiers from the fort set out in 1823 under the command of Colonel Henry Leavenworth to punish the Arikara Indians who had attacked William Ashley and his team of trappers. An expedition led by Colonel Atkinson two years later proved more successful when treaties were negotiated with twelve tribes, some of whom had been involved in the attack on Ashley.

Fort Atkinson, which was off the main travel routes (particularly the Santa Fe Trail) and far from sizable communities, was replaced in 1827 by Fort Leavenworth, Kansas.

Fort Benton

Fort Benton was first established as Fort Lewis by the American Fur Company in 1846. Fort Lewis was first built on the mouth of the Marias River in Montana, then rebuilt four years later by Alexander Culbertson. At that time it was renamed Fort Benton in honor of Senator Thomas Hart Benton of Missouri. The fort, strategically located at the head of steamboat navigation on the Missouri, was 250 feet square and housed a pair of bastions at diagonal corners. It was eventually purchased by the U.S. government, and troops were first stationed there on October 11, 1869. The military found that the adobe structures within the fort were not adequate for housing soldiers, and lodging had to be rented in town. The Army utilized the post primarily for transporting freight to and from Fort Ellis and Fort Shaw. When the Army abandoned Fort Benton on October 31, 1869, the troops who had occupied it were moved to Fort Shaw. Turned over to the Department of the Interior on January 5, 1883, Fort Benton's ruins are now part of a five-acre park overlooking the Missouri River.

Fort Bliss

Fort Bliss is located in El Paso, Texas. The first post, built by Major Benjamin Beall in November 1848 during the Mexican War, lasted until 1851, at which time it was abandoned. Renewed conflict with Apache Indians near El Paso prompted the reestablishment of Fort Bliss, and in 1854 it was of-

ficially given its name, honoring Mexican War veteran William Wallace Smith Bliss.

In 1861, the fort was surrendered to Confederate forces. It served as their headquarters in the Civil War, until the Union army recaptured it in August 1862. Six years later Fort Bliss was relocated once more when water from the Rio Grande began to undermine its foundation. The Fort Bliss located on the current site was occupied in October 1893, and Captain William H. McLaughlin was its first commander. Since then, the fort has been in constant use by the U.S. Army.

Fort Bowie

Fort Bowie was established in 1862 by the California Volunteers under General James Henry Carleton. Strategically located in Apache Pass on the Mesilla-Tuscon road and the Butterfield Trail, it was the site of the Bascom Affair. Here in 1861 Lieutenant George Bascom attempted to hold Apache leader Cochise hostage on charges of abducting a child. Cochise promptly cut a hole in a tent and escaped, but Lt. Bascom ordered the other Apache hostages hanged. The fort was built by Carleton after the battle of Apache pass to protect his supply line to California.

Defeated Apaches gathered around a porch at Fort Bowie, Arizona.

Fort Bowie was rebuilt nearby in 1868, and became an important post in the U.S. Army's campaign against the Chiricahua Apache Indians, when it served as a base of operations for General George Crook and General Nelson A. Miles who were responsible for tracking down the elusive Apache chieftain Geronimo. Once they had been forced to surrender, Geronimo's band was sent to the fort before being shipped to Fort Marion, Florida.

Fort Hall

Fort Hall, the first permanent U.S. post west of the Great Divide, was established in 1834 by fur-trader Nathaniel Wyeth who used the fort as his own trading post when the Rocky Mountain Fur Company defaulted on his contract. Located at the juncture of the Snake and Blackfoot rivers in Idaho, the fort was an 80-square-foot stockade built of cottonwood tree trunks. Wyeth's ventures failed, and in 1836 he sold Fort Hall to the Hudson's Bay Company, which subsequently abandoned it in the winter of 1855–1856. In 1841, Fort Hall served as a resting point for the Bidwell-Patterson Party, the first group of emigrants to make the rugged journey to the Columbia and Willamette valleys in Oregon. Located along the Oregon Trail, Fort Hall was an important outpost for emigrants making the arduous journey to Oregon and California. During 1859 and 1860, U.S. troops occupied the fort while aiding and protecting emigrant trains.

Fort Laramie

In 1834 Fort William, later known as Fort Laramie, was built at the confluence of the Laramie and North Platte rivers by the fur traders William Sublette and Robert Campbell. Situated on the Oregon Trail at the foot of the Rocky Mountains in present-day Wyoming, Fort Laramie was a vital fur-trading post while pelts were plentiful. In 1841, when the fur trade began to decline, a second Fort Laramie (named Fort John) was built. As westward pioneer migration began accelerating between 1841 and 1849, the U.S. government finally bought Fort Laramie in 1849 to protect travelers venturing west on the Oregon Trail. The fort then became a military outpost and was in continuous operation until it was abandoned in 1890. Today it is a national historic site.

Fort Laramie Treaties

Two treaties were signed at Fort Laramie, Wyoming, between the U.S. government and Indians of the northern Plains. The first, in 1851, drew boundaries around tribal ranges, as defined by the tribes. The second treaty, in 1868, established the Great Sioux Reservation and set up the policy of forming the Indians into peaceful farmers.

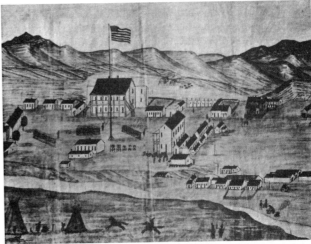

Fort Laramie as sketched by C. Moellman, a bugler in the 11th Ohio Cavalry.

Fort Hall, as drawn by J. Goldsborough Bruff in 1849.

UNIVERSITY OF WYOMING LIBRARY

Treaty commisioners cluster around a young Sioux woman during the 1868 talks.

In 1851 U.S. Indian Agent Thomas Fitzpatrick met with Indian representatives within his jurisdiction from the Sioux, Cheyenne, Crow, Blackfeet, Arapaho, Assiniboin, Gros Ventre, Mandan, and Arikara tribes. Also known as Fitzpatrick's Treaty or the Treaty of Horse Creek, this first. Laramie treaty defined tribal areas for the Indians. The tribal signatories agreed to live peacefully among themselves and with the white immigrant wagon trains, to not interfere with the building of roads and military posts in their tribal ranges, and to make restitution for any future hostile actions. This first treaty was part of a concerted federal campaign to protect travelers on the Oregon Trail

The U.S. government agreed to distribute an annuity of $50,000 between the signatory tribes for fifty years, but the U.S. Senate, before ratifying the treaty, unilaterally adjusted this period of payment to fifteen years and increased the amount to $70,000. Neither side could possibly abide by the provisions of the treaty. The discovery of gold in California in 1849 greatly increased traffic over the roads through the Indian country and led to hostilities on both sides.

The second peace commission meeting at Fort Laramie in 1868 was aimed at ending the Red Cloud War for the Bozeman Trail. This treaty provided for the abandonment of the military posts on the trail, the establishment of a Great Sioux Reservation in western Dakota on which all tribes were to live, and an "unceded Indian country" west of the reservation where Indians could remain so long as the buffalo survived. On the reservation the Indians would be issued rations and taught to support themselves by farming.

Fort Leavenworth

Fort Leavenworth, established in 1827, is the oldest permanent military post west of the Missouri River. Colonel Henry Leavenworth selected the site on the banks of the Missouri River in Kansas to protect travelers along the Santa Fe Trail, which cut through land declared Indian Territory. The fort served as a base for expeditions into the western region under Colonel Henry Dodge in 1835 and Colonel Stephen Watts Kearny in 1839 and 1845. Its strategic position at the head of the Santa Fe, Smoky Hill, and Oregon Trails made Fort Leavenworth a key military site during both the Mexican War and Civil War. In 1846, on the outbreak of the Mexican War, Colonel Kearny, the post commander, marched 1,700 troops from the fort and successfully captured Santa Fe, New Mexico, and Los Angeles, California. Eight years later, Leavenworth served as temporary capital of the newly formed Kansas Territory. During the Civil War, its location made Fort Leavenworth a key supply site. It was also there that Colonel Benjamin H. Grierson organized the famous 10th Cavalry in 1867. This regiment of about 700 black soldiers served actively on the frontier.

In 1881, the fort began a school for infantry and cavalry officers. It later became the General Service and Staff School and finally the Command and General Staff College, which operates today. Over 100 structures at the fort date back to the nineteenth and early twentieth centuries. The oldest of these, a barracks called the Rookery dating back to 1832, is still in use.

Fort Riley

Fort Riley was established by Captain Charles S. Lovell on May 17, 1853, in northeastern Kansas to protect travelers along the Santa Fe and Oregon

Soldiers stationed at Fort Riley spar during off hours. Note the skeleton in the audience.

Fort Ross, founded in 1812, was originally a Russian colony.

Trails. Located at a strategic point where the Smoky Hill and Republican rivers converge to form the Kansas River, Fort Riley was first called Camp Center, because it was believed to be near the geographical center of the United States. Later it was renamed to honor Major General Bennett Riley.

In 1855, a major cholera epidemic killed about 100 soldiers and workers, and 100 more deserted. Even so, construction continued and the settlement soon grew into an important cavalry post. In 1866, the famous 7th Cavalry was organized there, with Lt. Col. George A. Custer second in command. Fort Riley became the headquarters of the U.S. cavalry after the Plains Indians were subdued by the military. It presently houses the 1st Infantry Division (MECH), 3rd ROTC Region, and an NCO Academy.

Fort Ross

Fort Ross was founded by I. A. Kuskov of the Russian-American Company in 1812 as the fort for a Russian settlement just north of San Francisco near the mouth of the Russian River. Kuskov believed the location to be the perfect place to establish a post for his party of 135 Russians and Aleuts. The name "Ross" derives from a Russian term for Russia.

Kuskov had already established several small shelters on the California coast from the Bodega Bay northward. The Russian-American Company's interest lay primarily in supplying Russia with sea otter and fur seal pelts. But it was also hoped that the site would become an agricultural and manufacturing center, so that they could increase the food supply to northern settlements in Alaska, and also increase Russian presence in the territory.

However, over the next two decades the number of sea otters and fur seals diminished greatly and the Russian attempts to develop agriculture and raise livestock were largely unproductive. Conflicts with settlers and Mexican officials staking claims around the area hampered the company's efforts to push settlement further inland to more fertile ground. These mounting failures finally convinced the Russians to abandon Fort Ross in 1841. The property was then sold to John A. Sutter of Sutter's Fort for $30,000. After changing owners several more times, Fort Ross was presented to the state of California in 1906. After much restoration, it now stands as a state historical monument.

Fort Smith

Fort Smith, now a city in Arkansas, began as a military post in 1817. The fort was founded in response to conflict between the Osage Indians, the original inhabitants of the area, and the Cherokees, who were pushed into the area after being forced to leave their homeland. Named after General Thomas A. Smith, the fort was located at the confluence of the Arkansas and Poteau rivers. It was only occupied for seven years, during which time a settlement grew adjacent to it. In 1838, settlers at Fort Smith expressed fear of renewed tribal violence, and a second fort was built on the site of the original.

Fort Smith was incorporated as a town in 1842, and three years later the second nearby fort was converted into a supply depot. The town flourished into a city, prospered as a trading post and supply base, and served as shipping center on the Arkansas River. In 1858, Fort Smith was a key stop on John Butterfield's Overland Stage Line.

The fort was turned over to the Federal Court for the Western District of Arkansas in 1871. Judge Isaac Parker presided over the court from 1875 to 1896, and also had jurisdiction over the adjacent Indian Territory. Judge Parker dedicated himself to bringing peace and justice to an area notorious for lawlessness, and gained a reputation for strongly supporting Indian rights. The incorruptible judge earned the nickname "Hanging Judge" after he meted out 79 sentences of executions during his tenure.

The city of Fort Smith developed into an industrial center, particularly after the discovery of a natural gas field and the Arkansas-Oklahoma coalfield nearby.

Fort Snelling

Built in 1819, Fort Snelling is located at the junction of the Mississippi and Minnesota Rivers in Minnesota. Originally named Fort St. Anthony, Fort Snelling marked the first white settlement of the present-day Minneapolis–St. Paul region.

The land on which the fort sits was purchased from the Sioux in 1806 by Zebulon M. Pike. Reportedly, the Sioux were not paid until the fort was built 13 years later. Colonel Henry Leavenworth oversaw construction of the original post on the south side of the Minnesota River, but spring flooding forced relocation to the right bank. In September 1820, Colonel Josiah Snelling selected a third and final location for the fort. It was not officially designated Fort Snelling until January 7, 1825.

The fort never fired its cannons in open warfare, and it served primarily as a military center and a base for western exploration. In 1857, Fort Snelling and its surrounding reservation, were sold to

Franklin Steele, who envisioned the development of "The City of Fort Snelling." With the financial panic of 1857, and a declining real-estate market, Steele's plans failed to materialize. The U.S. Army returned to Fort Snelling after the Civil War, and in 1866 designated it as the headquarters and supply base for the Military Department of Dakota, which reached from the Mississippi River to the Rocky Mountains. In subsequent years, soldiers from Fort Snelling fought in many Indian campaigns, and in the Spanish-American War. The fort was decommissioned in 1946, and in 1960 it became Minnesota's first National Historic Landmark.

Fort Union

Fort Union, established alongside the Santa Fe Trail in New Mexico, became the largest U.S. Army post in the nineteenth-century southwestern fron-

MUSEUM OF NEW MEXICO

Fire trucks at Fort Union.

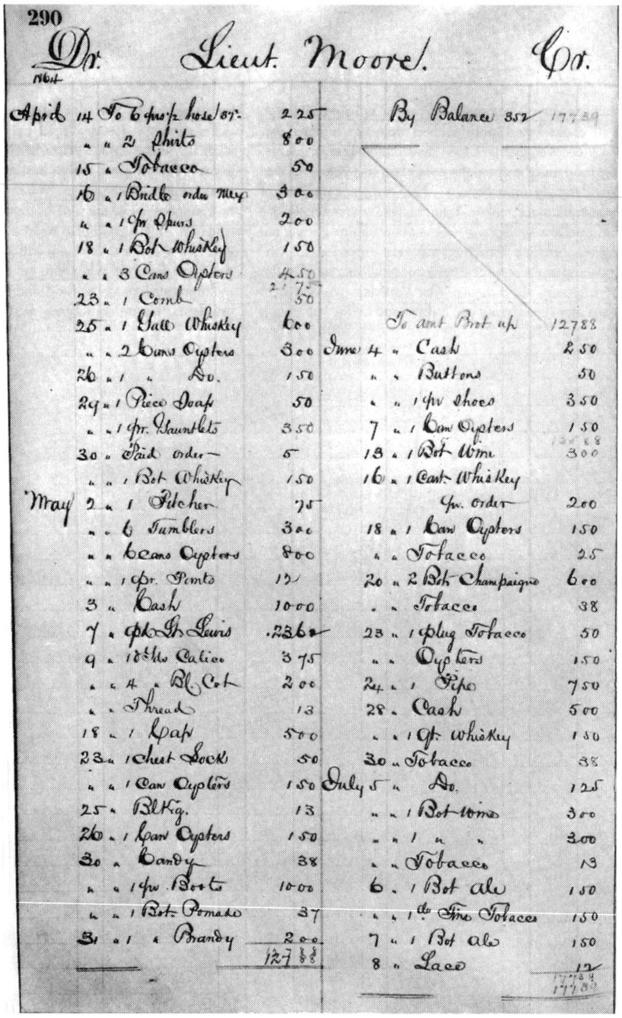
290

Dr. Lieut. Moore. Cr.

1864

April 14	To 6 prs. hose/st.	2 25		By Balance 352	177 39
" "	2 Shirts	8 00			
15 "	Tobacco	50			
16 "	1 Bridle order Mey	3 00			
" "	1 pr Spurs	2 00			
18 "	1 Bot. Whiskey	1 50			
" "	3 Cans Oysters	4 50			
23 "	1 Comb	50		To amt Brot up	127 88
25 "	1 Gall. Whiskey	6 00	June 4 "	Cash	2 50
" "	2 Cans Oysters	3 00	" "	Buttons	50
26 "	1 " Do.	1 50	" "	1 pr Shoes	3 50
29 "	1 Piece Soap	50	7 "	1 Can Oysters	1 50
" "	1 pr. Gauntlets	3 50	13 "	1 Bot. Wine	3 00
30 "	Paid order —	5	16 "	1 Cask Whiskey pr. order	2 00
" "	1 Bot. Whiskey	1 50	18 "	1 Can Oysters	1 50
May 2 "	1 Pitcher	75	" "	Tobacco	25
" "	6 Tumblers	3 00	20 "	2 Bot. Champaigne	6 00
" "	6 cans Oysters	8 00	" "	Tobacco	38
" "	1 pr. Pants	12	23 "	1 plug Tobacco	50
3 "	Cash	10 00	" "	Oysters	1 50
7 "	pd. G. Lewis	236	24 "	1 Pipe	7 50
9 "	10 yds Calico	3 75	28 "	Cash	5 00
" "	4 " Bl. Cot.	2 00	" "	1 qt. Whiskey	1 50
" "	Thread	13	30 "	Tobacco	38
18 "	1 Cap	5 00	July 5 "	Do.	1 25
23 "	1 chest Lock	50	" "	1 Bot. Wine	3 00
" "	1 Can Oysters	1 50	" "	1 " "	3 00
25 "	Bl. Kg.	13	" "	Tobacco	13
26 "	1 Can Oysters	1 50	6 "	1 Bot ale	1 50
30 "	Candy	38	" "	1 do. Fine Tobacco	1 50
" "	1 pr Boots	10 00	7 "	1 Bot ale	1 50
" "	1 Bot. Pomade	37	8 "	Lace	12
31 "	1 " Brandy	2 00			
		127 88			177 39

LIBRARY OF CONGRESS

This document records a Fort Union lieutenant's purchases over a few months. Lieutenant Moore was no stranger to the better things in life, as can be seen in his many orders for luxury items such as oysters and champagne.

tier. Lieutenant Colonel Edwin Vose Sumner established the post on July 26, 1851, near the strategic fork of the Mountain and Cimarron branches of the Santa Fe Trail. Within a few years, Fort Union was the main U.S. Army's southwestern depot, sending supplies from the east to distant frontier posts. The threat of Confederate invasion of New Mexico during the Civil War launched construction of a star fort across from Fort Union on the opposite bank of Coyote Creek. In 1863, Brigadier General James H. Carleton ordered construction of a third post which was completed six years later. Fort Union then acted as the main supply depot for the Department of New Mexico. But when the Santa Fe Railroad arrived in 1879, the fort's days as a supplier were numbered. Its arsenal was discontinued within three years, and the fort was abandoned in 1891. The site of Fort Union and its ruins are now a national monument.

Fort Union Trading Post

Fort Union Trading Post was established in 1829 in present-day North Dakota by fur trader Kenneth McKenzie. McKenzie built the post for the American Fur Company on the Missouri River near the mouth of the Yellowstone. As manager of Fort Union, McKenzie was successful in bringing in trade from the Blackfeet. Under McKenzie, Fort Union quickly grew to become the most important trading post on the Missouri River. After a decline in demand for beaver pelts, the post began to rely on the trade of buffalo hides, and was quite successful through 1837. When two smallpox epidemics decimated the Indian population in the region, trading slowed considerably, and the fort was sold to the North West Fur Company. The new owners were unsuccessful in revitalizing Fort Union, and it was abandoned in 1867. Today, the fort, now a national historic site, has been restored on its original site, and it houses many artifacts from its early trading years.

Fort Vancouver

Fort Vancouver, near the Washington-Oregon border, was first erected as a trading post by the Hudson's Bay Company in 1825. Fort Vancouver was located on what is now the present-day town of Vancouver, near the Columbia and Willamette rivers, opposite Portland, Oregon. Named for the English navigator and explorer, Captain George Vancouver, the trading post was directed by Dr. John M. McLoughlin, head of the Hudson's Bay Company in the area, and enjoyed a flurry of activity as a key British trading center.

The United States made it a military post on May 15, 1848, and after the construction of barracks, it was designated Fort Vancouver on July 13, 1853. Six years later, the Vancouver arsenal was established. The name of the post was changed to Vancouver Barracks on April 5, 1879. The U.S. military occupied the post until 1947.

Forty-niners

See California Gold Rush

Franciscans

The Franciscans are Roman Catholic missionaries whose order was originally founded by Saint Francis of Assisi around 1210. During early Spanish exploration of the West, this centuries-old religious sect worked to convert Native Americans to Christianity.

As the Spanish continued their exploration throughout the American Southwest during the 1500s, Roman Catholic missionaries began to accompany the explorers. These clerics established centers, called missions, to serve as schools and as religious centers to promote the converting of Native Americans to Christianity.

The Franciscans were not met with open arms, and many became martyrs to their cause. Some were killed by Indian tribes; others succumbed to the arduous rigors of desert travel. However, the Spanish quest for gold in the California and Arizona regions continued to bring in more explorers, and with them, new Franciscans. A few scant missions were established among the Hopis, but all of these had fallen by 1680.

Jesuits were the next influential Christians in the area, which was now known as New Spain. However, in 1767 other church officials became envious of the Jesuit strongholds in Portuguese, French, and Spanish territories. Through a combination of political maneuverings and papal edicts, the Jesuits were banned from all Spanish holdings, and once more the Franciscans emerged as a presence in the Southwest. San Xavier del Bac, an abandoned Franciscan

MISSION SAN LUIS REY

The palatial San Luis Rey de Francia mission, located north of San Diego, was the biggest of all the Franciscan settlements.

mission originally constructed in 1700 near what is now Tucson, Arizona, was completely rebuilt. The renovation was supervised by Francisco Tomas Garces, a Spanish priest known as the White Dove of the Desert. His vision transformed the simple mission into a major religious center.

The Franciscans continued to make progress in the Southwest, settling the lands that would eventually become California. They established a new center in what is now San Diego. The purpose of this mission was twofold: As well as being a spiritual hub for converting and "civilizing" the indigenous populations, it was also a stronghold for establishing and reinforcing Spanish conquest.

As the Spanish continued exploring California, Arizona, New Mexico, and Utah, the Franciscans continued to set up missions along the way. Initially their intent was to convert and educate, but they also tried to reorder the lives of the people they encountered, among them the Yuma and the Hopi. At the same time, Spanish cattle began intruding onto the crop lands of the Yumas. Enraged by the Spanish encroachments on their ancient homelands, the Yumas rebelled. Violent skirmishes resulted, and many Franciscans—including Francisco Tomas Garces—were killed in the uprisings. Garces never saw the completed San Xavier del Bac.

Despite the turmoil to the east, the Franciscan presence remained strong in northern California. Over the next few years, with forceful help sometimes supplied by accompanying Spanish armies, the Franciscans established a chain of missions northward up the California coast and succeeded in baptizing nearly 54,000 native people in the San Francisco region. Baptized Indians were called "neophytes" by the missionaries. The neophytes were used as a source of cheap labor in building up Spanish holdings. The Franciscans often continued to carry on their work, often against the will of the native populations. While missions were considered houses of worship, and thus communal in nature, it was the Franciscans who decreed exactly how life should be lived. This continually led to discontentment and resentment among their would-be followers.

Eventually the Franciscan movement began spreading east toward New Mexico, and in the early 1800s, as Spanish influence in the western regions diminished, the power of the Spanish Franciscans also began to weaken. By 1848, Mexican bishops had taken control over most of the Franciscan missions.

Free Soil Party

The Free Soil Party was founded in 1848 with the aim of establishing "free" or non-slave states in the Union.

In the 1840s, a national debate raged over the question of whether to continue or to abolish slavery in the United States. An amendment known as the Wilmot Proviso was drafted by congressional Northern Democrats who cared little for the pro-slavery positions of their Southern counterparts. The amendment, which would have prohibited slavery in territories obtained from Mexico, was passed by the House of Representatives in 1846. However, Southern Democratic strongholds

in the Senate defeated the measure. The political rift between Northern and Southern Democrats widened.

Two years later the Free Soil Party was formed in Buffalo, New York. It consisted of two major groups: disaffected Democrats known as the Barnburners, and members of the former Liberty Party, a political faction opposed to the admission of new slave states to the Union. The Free Soilers ran under the motto "Free Soil, Free Speech, Free Labor, and Free Men." Their first presidential candidate was former Chief Executive Martin Van Buren. Though they failed in this bid for the presidency, the Free Soilers managed to get 291,000 votes in the elections of 1848, sending 13 party members to the House of Representatives and one to the Senate.

Though Free Soilers were against new slave states, for many, their position was not based entirely upon noble opposition to slavery; there was simply a different attitude up North toward economic and class divisions. Like many Northerners, some Free Soilers didn't see slavery as immoral. In their view, the problem was that slave labor took away jobs from whites, and this was a situation they didn't want to see being perpetuated in the growing nation. Consequently, Free Soilers were responsible for anti-black measures that prohibited either freed people or runaway slaves from settling in Kansas. This was the beginning of what was to become a violent confrontation.

As more Free Soilers settled in the Kansas territory, their political strength grew. The opposition brought in recruits from Missouri to vote in the 1855 elections, thus assuring pro-slavery factions of victory. A congressional investigation ensued, and showed that over three-fourths of the 6,318 votes cast in the election were illegal. However, the pro-slave forces continued to hold office in the territory capital of Lecompton. Free Soilers, who outnumbered pro-slavers in Kansas, decided to form their own government in Topeka. They were declared treasonous by a pro-slavery judge, and troops from Missouri were sent to arrest the Free Soilers. A terrific battle erupted in Lawrence, the seat of Free Soil activity in Kansas. Free Soil leaders were arrested and the town itself was pillaged in what was known as "The Sack of Lawrence." Battles continued in Kansas for the next few years. Businesses and farms were sometimes burned to the ground in midnight raids.

In 1857 Kansas submitted a constitution to the

U.S. Congress in hopes of becoming a state. Among the provisions in this document was an amendment supporting slavery in Kansas. The amendment was written in such a convoluted manner that slavery would be approved regardless of a yes or no vote. Free Soilers, who still made up the majority of the Kansas population, refused to participate in these constitutional proceedings. Despite President Buchanan's approval of this constitution, statehood for pro-slave Kansas was voted down in the Congress. The Free Soilers continued their battle, both politically and physically. Kansas finally was admitted into the Union in 1861, after the start of the Civil War. The Free Soilers had won. Ultimately the Free Soil party was absorbed by the Republicans.

Frémont, John Charles

1813–1890

John Charles Frémont, called the Pathfinder, was an explorer, soldier, and politician. Born the bastard son of a French adventurer in Savannah, Georgia, Frémont moved with his unmarried parents from his birthplace to Nashville, Tennessee. Within days of their arrival, a pistol duel was fought outside his parents' hotel room between future president Andrew Jackson and the baby Frémont's future father-in-law, Thomas Hart Benton. The Frémonts kept moving—to Virginia, then to Charleston, South Carolina, where the father died, leaving the family in poverty.

Young Frémont attended Charleston College in 1828 and was expelled for "incorrigible negligence." In 1833 he met Joel Poinsett, the noted botanist and statesman, who secured for Frémont a position as a teacher of mathematics on a U.S. warship bound for South America and in 1836 as a surveyor on a route for a projected railroad through the unsettled regions of Ohio, Kentucky, and Tennessee.

In 1838, with Poinsett now secretary of war in the cabinet of President Martin Van Buren, Frémont secured an appointment as a second lieutenant in the army Topographical Engineers and was assigned to accompany explorer Joseph N. Nicollet to the western territories. The expedition set out in the spring of 1839 to explore and map the Dakota and Minnesota territories.

In 1841, in Washington, D.C. to work on the surveys of the Nicollet expedition, Frémont met Senator Thomas Hart Benton of Missouri, a persuasive advocate of the exploration of Oregon and the far West, and fell in love with Benton's daughter, Jessie. Although she was barely 15 and Frémont was 28, the two eloped and were married on October 19, 1841. The senator's anger soon subsided and Frémont was welcomed into the family.

That year Nicollet was preparing a new expedition, this time to find an overland route for Oregon-bound emigrants. When the Frenchman's health failed, Frémont was given command. In June 1842,

LIBRARY OF CONGRESS

In an illustration accompanying Fremont's Memoirs, *his third expedition is startled by an apparition of a starving old Indian woman.*

YALE UNIVERSITY LIBRARY

Frémont's battle with the Klamath Indians was depicted in his Memoirs of My Life.

the party set out from St. Louis, following the Kansas River and traveling northwest to the Platte, and then up the North Platte toward the Rocky Mountains. On August 8, the explorers arrived at South Pass and later established camp in the Wind River Mountains. On the return trip the party explored the North Platte, reached Fort Laramie at the end of August, and St. Louis in October. With the Frémont party were the German topographer Charles Preuss, the hunter Lucian B. Maxwell, and the guide Christopher "Kit" Carson. Fremont's report with Preuss's maps was widely read and stirred public interest in the west.

Frémont's second expedition, which lasted 14 months, followed the first's route to South Pass, then turned south and east toward the Great Salt Lake, arriving there on September 9, 1843, then on to Fort Hall on the Snake River. It followed the Snake to Fort Boise, crossing into Oregon Territory in mid-October.

Frémont now determined to push on to Mexican-controlled Alta California despite Mexico's strained relations with the United States, and led his party into present-day Nevada. At the end of January, 1844, the expedition crossed into California territory. The explorers discovered Lake Tahoe, crossed the Sierras, and marched into the Sacramento Valley, reaching Sutter's Fort in early March. They returned via southern Utah, the South Platte, and Bent's Fort on the Arkansas. Frémont arrived back in Washington in August and spent seven months dictating his account of the expedition to his wife Jessie.

In November 1845, Frémont was back at Sutter's Fort with 62 men, ostensibly for further "scientific" studies but perhaps in reality to be in the vicinity in the event of war with Mexico and a takeover of California. In Monterey, after the Mexican military commander of Alta California, José Castro, ordered him to leave, Frémont moved up the Sacramento to Klamath Lake. There, in May, 1846, he is believed to have received messages from the U.S. War Department instructing him in the event of war with Mexico. Frémont quickly gathered his expedition and marched toward San Francisco, where he encouraged the open rebellion against Mexico by American settlers in the area (then known as the Bear Flag Republic) and where he made the arrangements for the capitulation of California on January 12, 1847.

A year later, after various squabbles with Briga-dier General Stephen Watts Kearny, Frémont was court-martialed on charges of mutiny, disobedience of orders, and conduct prejudicial to order. He was allowed to resign his commission.

Frémont and his beloved Jessie moved to California in 1848 and settled near San Francisco Bay. During the winter of 1849, he led an expedition into New Mexico Territory to locate a railroad route, and in the mountains lost 11 of his 33 men in the winter snows, including veteran mountain man Bill Williams, whom Frémont blamed for misdirecting the exploring party. Frémont then made a fortune in the California Gold Rush and built a lavish estate in Monterey. He served a month in Washington as a California senator but was defeated for reelection. He was nominated as the Republican candidate for the presidency in 1856, but took no active part in the campaign and lost the election to James Buchanan by about a half-million popular votes out of the over three million cast.

In the Civil War, Frémont served as a major general of volunteers in command of the new Department of the West but was removed on charges of awarding government contracts unfairly (he was innocent). Afterward he served briefly with the Army of Virginia, but then returned to California and became deeply involved in mining, railroad promotion and other enterprises, all of which failed. In 1878 he was given the territorial governorship of Arizona at a salary of $2,600 a year, a position historian H. H. Bancroft said was given him "merely that his chronic poverty might be relieved." He resigned the position in 1883 after a largely absentee tenure.

Frémont died in a Manhattan rooming house on July 13, 1890. Jessie Benton Frémont died in 1902.

Frontier

In the context of the history of the American West, Yale University historians Howard Lamar and Leonard Thompson define frontier as a "zone of interaction between two or more previously distinct peoples."

In 1893, University of Wisconsin historian Frederick Jackson Turner, in his celebrated and influential essay "The Significance of the Frontier in American History," said that the true "point of

Westward the Course of the Empire Takes Its Way

view" of the history of America "is not the Atlantic coast, it is the Great West," and spoke of the frontier as "the outer edge of the wave—the meeting point between savagery and civilization," and "the hither edge of free land." Turner wrote that while the Atlantic coast was the first American frontier, it was European in nature and that the frontier became "more and more American" as it moved westward. He marked the end of the frontier at 1890 when the U.S. Census reported the cessation of westward migration.

Modern historians have taken a dim view of the Turner thesis, especially because he paid no attention to such influences in Western history as women, Native Americans, Hispanics, and African-Americans. But as his most recent editor has pointed out, Turner "tried to see American history as something more than dead words on a page," and his thesis remains a seminal statement on the American West.

Frontier Thesis

"The existence of an area of free land, its continuous recession, and the advance of American settlement westward explain American development." So declared the young historian Frederick Jackson

Turner (1861–1932) at a meeting of the American Historical Association in Chicago on July 12, 1893. In the 1890 census, for the first time, the Census Bureau had been unable to trace a distinct frontier line of settlement on the map of the United States. In this development Turner discerned a watershed of American history. The westward-moving frontier, he believed, was the central determinant of the American character. It had directed the course of American history, shaped American political, economic, and social institutions, and given definition and vitality to American democracy. Its disappearance meant great changes in American life.

Incorporated in a published article entitled "The Significance of the Frontier in American History," Turner's ideas spread throughout the historical profession. His own long tenure as a professor at Harvard University ensured their persistence, although in evolving form. His article, often reprinted, became required classroom reading. His thesis, embedded in countless textbooks, took on the aura of gospel. As later generations of scholars would point out, however, Turner presented his thesis less as hypothesis than as actual finding and offered little convincing evidence to back it up. He wrote more in metaphors and imagery than in precise scholarly language. He allowed contradictions, inconsistencies, vagueness, and even questionable method to creep into his presentation. Ignoring other obvious factors, he reduced the vast complexity of history to a single, simple, and appealing proposition.

In the 1930s and 1940s, after Turner's death, critics leveled these and other charges against his doctrine. In particular, economic determinists launched attacks against an explanation that failed to take account of economic factors. Depression and war elevated industrialism, government planning, and internationalism over Turner's stress on agrarianism, individualism, and nationalism. Beginning in the 1950s, Turner disciples, especially Ray Allen Billington, set about testing his hypothesis. Turner himself had qualified much of his original dogmatism. His successors made still more modifications and conceded the importance of other historical forces. Although battered, his thesis still held firm in university classrooms.

By the 1980s, Turner was again under attack. Now scholars pointed to his fixation on white Anglo-Saxon frontiersmen, to the exclusion of other frontiers and other races—Indians, Hispanics, and blacks in particular. Proponents of the New Western History of the 1990s rejected Turner altogether.

He resists complete extinction. As a century of controversy shows, his ideas contain enough truth, or at least enough provocative thought, to endure in historical interpretations. In the late twentieth century, hardly anyone accepts the frontier thesis as originally advanced by Turner. But many believe that, much revised by later research, it still offers insights into the nature of the frontier process and its influence on the development of American character and American institutions.

Froth Flotation

See Mining Methods

Fur Trade

More than 250 years before the Lewis and Clark expedition gave rise to the American fur trapping and trading enterprise in the trans-Mississippi west, explorations (1534–1542) by Jacques Cartier had established such a trade with Indian tribes in the St.

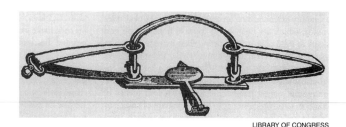

The Newhouse beaver trap.

Lawrence River valley around the future city of Montreal, Canada. In 1603, under orders from Henry IV of France, Samuel de Champlain made a voyage to the Gulf of St. Lawrence for the express purpose of trading in furs. The French would have a monopoly on this trade until 1610, when the English navigator Henry Hudson, searching for the fabled Northwest Passage, discovered the huge inland sea in north-central Canada that was subsequently named for him (Hudson Bay).

Hudson's explorations led to the formation of the Hudson's Bay Company, which was chartered in 1670 for the purpose of establishing a trading monopoly—principally in furs—in the region. By the beginning of the eighteenth century, this trade had centered on pursuit of the beaver *(castor canadensis)*. The silky, rich brown, waterproof fur of this animal—a slightly different species of which was known in Europe—was used in making felt hats, coats, muffs, linings, and other clothing; its scaly tail was prized as a meat substitute in Catholic Europe, and its scrotal secretion, called castoreum, was used in perfume and in medicines as a headache and fever remedy.

Until their expulsion from North America in 1763, the French remained the most successful of all nations in the fur trade, establishing a string of trading posts from Maine west to the Great Lakes and north into the Canadian interior. French *coureurs de bois* (runners of the woods) traded with the Hurons, Ottawas, Miamis, Illinois, and other tribes, established posts and forts, and in general solidified control by New France over the Northeast fur trade. In the eighteenth century, the French *voyageur*, the French-Indian *métis*, moved fur shipments, bound in 100-pound packs, by canoe (some so huge it took a dozen men to paddle them, and four to carry them on portages), pirogue (a hollowed-out cottonwood log, some as long as 70 feet) and keelboat along the waterways from Montreal to the Great Lakes and the Mississippi River.

By the 1730s American involvement in the fur trade centered principally on the upper Ohio River and flourished until the French blocked expansion of it around Lake Erie. The Anglo-French wars, ending in 1763, opened the American trade east of the Mississippi, and for the next 80 years, the fur trade followed westward exploration, expansion, and settlement.

After the Louisiana Purchase in 1803 and the

Lewis and Clark expedition of 1804–1806, which moved through some of the richest trapping country in North America, the center of the fur trade was in the upper Missouri River region. Manuel Lisa, one of the Lewis and Clark suppliers, became a pioneer in the upper Missouri trade in 1807 when he opened a trading post named Fort Raymond in present-day Montana. Two years later, with William Clark, Jean Pierre, Auguste Pierre Chouteau, and others, Lisa founded the Missouri Fur Company in St. Louis.

The American Fur Company, which would be-

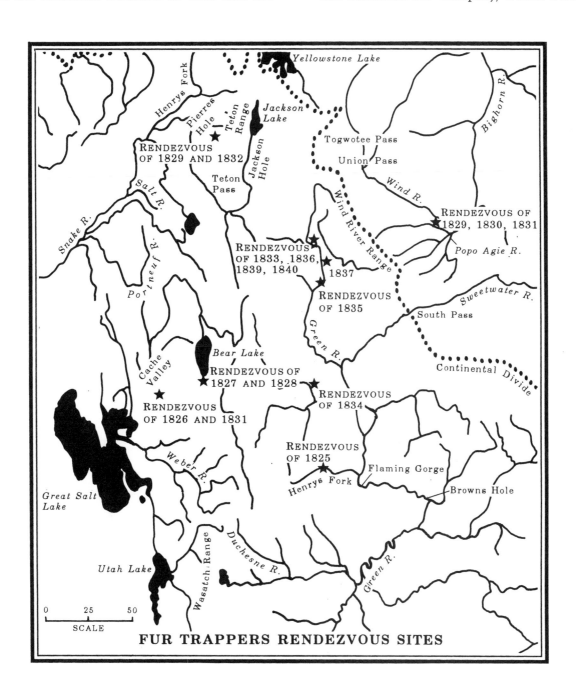

FUR TRAPPERS RENDEZVOUS SITES

come the most powerful of them all, was organized by John Jacob Astor in 1808, and in 1810 Astor's Pacific Fur Company dominated the fur trade in the Pacific Northwest and led to the founding of Astoria, Oregon, which was subsequently taken over by the British in the War of 1812.

Before the era of the free trapper and the brigade rendezvous system, which replaced the old trading posts in the central Rocky Mountains, the American-Canadian fur trade operated in a "factory" system. These "factories," combination trading posts and Indian agencies, were established by the govern-

Scenes from the life of a trapper.

ment with licensed agents (factors) appointed by the government to administer trade of such items as firearms, powder and ball, traps, axes, blankets, food, and tobacco with the Indians in exchange for furs, and to lure Indian tribes from association with the British. The system worked reasonably well—although the factors were prohibited from extending credit to the Indians—until the War of 1812, when British traders left the Northwest and American free enterprise replaced the factory system.

In 1822, entrepreneurs William Henry Ashley and Andrew Henry advertised for "enterprising young men" to join a trapping expedition to the upper Missouri. The result was a gathering of some of the most celebrated figures in the "free trapper" era—Jedediah Smith, James Clyman, Mike Fink, Etienne Provost, Jim "Old Gabe" Bridger, Hugh Glass, Bill Sublette, Jim Beckwourth, Tom "Broken Hand" Fitzpatrick, Joseph R. Walker, and others—that would lead to exploration of the Yellowstone River, the South Pass on the Continental Divide, the Great Salt Lake, and the overland routes to Oregon and California.

Ashley's "brigades" of free trappers, supplied with strings of packhorses, followed a system established by Donald Mackenzie of the North West Company in his work in the Snake River country by holding an annual rendezvous, a sort of trade fair where company-associated and free trappers and Indians could come to trade in their pelts and plews (the mountain man's word for a beaver fur) for powder, lead, tobacco, traps, guns, and whiskey. The first rendezvous was held in midsummer 1825 at Henry's Fork on the Green River in present-day Wyoming. These colorful annual gatherings continued for 15 years, with furs exchanged for money (beaver hides fetched $5 a pound in St. Louis) and the money exchanged for the goods brought by pack train from St. Louis. Hundreds of drunken mountain men, traders, and Indians held horse races, wrestling contests, duels, and buffalo chases before heading back into the mountains for another year of working their trap lines.

South of the Rocky Mountains, the fur trade was given impetus with the opening of the Santa Fe Trail in 1821 and of Bent's Fort on the Arkansas River in 1833. Taos (in New Mexico) became home for trappers working in the southern Rockies, the Great Basin, and as far south as the Gila River. But by the late 1830s the market for beaver fur was in sharp decline (the silk hat was introduced in Europe in this period) and by 1840, the year the last Green River rendezvous was held, the fur trade era—the era of the first true westerners—had all but ended.

The real importance of those three picturesque decades was the journeys and trailblazing of the trappers—the Mountain Men—which opened the American frontier from New Mexico to Canada, from the Mississippi to the Pacific Coast.

G

Gadsden Purchase

DECEMBER 30, 1853

The Gadsden Purchase was a strip of land between Texas and California purchased from the Mexican government in 1853 for $10 million. The purchase, negotiated by diplomat James Gadsden, consisted of more than 29 million acres of land and was obtained largely to provide a southern railroad route between the Mississippi River and the Pacific coast. However, the intervention of the Civil War forced a postponement of the railroad project.

The treaty was negotiated under the Democratic administration of President Franklin Pierce. With the influence of Secretary of War Jefferson Davis, Gadsden was appointed minister to Mexico in 1853 and was dispatched to the country to settle a boundary dispute. The Pierce administration held that the boundary with Mexico had not been surveyed officially, and therefore neither country should take possession of the Mesilla Valley. Secretary of State W. L. Marcy pointed out to Pierce that surveys indicated a route along the Gila River was unsuitable for the construction of a railroad, whereas a route farther south, in Mexican territory, would be ideal.

Gadsden arrived in Mexico and had his first meeting with President Santa Anna on August 17, 1853. Santa Anna had been elected president the previous March, and he found the country in tremendous debt and the people discontented. Fearing a loss of power unless he secured funds immediately, Santa Anna was willing to negotiate. The treaty that resulted, signed on December 30, 1853, gave Mexico $10 million in exchange for the land that became southern Arizona and New Mexico.

Gall

CA. 1840–1894

Gall, also called Pizi, was a celebrated Hunkpapa Sioux war chief and was one of their most aggressive leaders.

Known in his childhood as Matohinshda (Bear-Shedding-His-Hair), Gall distinguished himself by his courage and ingenuity and was thought to be marked for greatness. One story tells of Gall defeating a Cheyenne boy (who would become the noted chief Roman Nose) in a wrestling match. When Gall was orphaned, he was adopted as a brother by Sitting Bull, who became his mentor.

Gall was known for his dour disposition and his quickness to anger at an insult or injustice. He became an implacable foe of whites. He was present with Red Cloud during the latter's war against white encroachment. Sources credit him, along with Crazy Horse and Hump, with developing the decoy tricks employed in the Fetterman fight. By 1876, he was widely acknowledged as Sitting Bull's chief lieutenant.

At the Little Bighorn, the first attack by Major Reno virtually wiped out Gall's family. Surprised, Gall reportedly mounted his horse naked and rallied

Gall, the Sioux war chief.

A gambling saloon.

his warriors, eventually frightening Reno into retreat. He then mounted a frontal attack on Custer, while others struck from the rear.

Gall went to Canada with Sitting Bull, but returned disillusioned in 1881. "Buffalo Bill" Cody tried to persuade him to join his Wild West show, as Sitting Bull had, but the war chief reportedly replied, "I am not an animal to be exhibited before a crowd." He died in Oak Creek, South Dakota, on December 5, 1894.

Gambling in the West

Part of the West's legacy is its gambling lore. Money, entire ranches, and quite often lives could be lost over a single hand of cards.

With the West's lack of cultural resources, gambling quickly became a favorite form of entertainment. Card and dice games were organized in just about any conceivable spot. Bunk houses on ranches usually held a regular card game after a hard day's work. Though many high-minded ranch owners strictly prohibited gambling on their premises, it was difficult to keep bored cowhands from dealing a few hands. Some cowboys hid contraband decks of

cards, greasy, aged and occasionally incomplete but still good for a night's amusement. During cattle drives, even the most puritanical ranch owner usually relented and allowed cowhands to gamble on the interminable trail.

Quick to realize how much money was to be made on games of chance, saloons and brothels did double duty as gambling halls. San Francisco in particular had a number of popular establishments, which featured card and dice games, liquor, music, dancing, and prostitution. One observer commented that San Francisco had more gambling halls than the Mississippi River had catfish.

Other gambling operations followed the building of the Union Pacific Railroad. At the end of the day, railroad workers would set up an area at the end of the tracks for gambling. These portable casinos would last until the camp moved on. The nomadic operations were often referred to as "Hell on Wheels."

While cowboys and railworkers turned to gambling as a diversion from their hard labors, another figure was prominent in Western gambling halls.

Professional gamblers, who made careers out of fleecing suckers in games of chance, began heading West in search of easy prey. Some of these card sharks were known as "pasteboard pirates" or "locusts of lechery." Many had perfected their skills aboard floating riverboat casinos on the Mississippi River. These hustlers considered themselves part of a gentrified trade and usually dressed the part, often sporting fancy black suits, silk top hats, and flashing diamond rings on their fingers and diamond stickpins in their lapels.

Another feature of professional gambling was the "capper," an accomplice employed by a hustler to entice others into card games. The capper would pretend to beat the professional in a few hands. Gullible gamblers, thinking to make some easy money, would join the game and would generally find themselves broke before the end of the night.

With so much cash changing hands between strangers, most of whom were drinking, violence was a common problem in gambling establishments. Fights and shootings often erupted when someone felt cheated in poker. The small Derringer pistol, which could easily be hidden under a belt or beneath a waistcoat, was often the defensive weapon of choice for gamblers who were apt to be caught cheating.

One of the most famous card game shootouts involved gambling lawman Wild Bill Hickock. He was killed over a poker hand in the town of Deadwood (Gulch), Dakota Territory in 1876. When he died, Hickock was holding an ace of spades, an ace of clubs, the eight of spades, the eight of clubs and either the queen or jack of diamonds (accounts differ). This legendary grouping became known to card players as the "Dead Man's Hand."

Gambling wasn't limited to games of chance. One western scribe told of a gambler who was shot and not expected to live the night. Other patrons of the saloon, including the doctor who treated the wounded man, placed bets on exactly when the victim would expire.

With vice running rampant, traveling preachers felt called to bring the word of the Lord into these dens of iniquity. Some saloons reserved time for religious services, with clergy preaching against gambling, drinking, and prostitution. Lacking pulpits, these frontier ministers often stood behind bars or card tables to deliver their sermons. Once the prayers were through, patrons would go right back to the business of poker.

By the end of the nineteenth century, gambling had reached its peak. As the western population grew, town councils began to outlaw drinking and gambling to accommodate more sedate citizens.

Gambling in the West underwent a renaissance shortly after World War II when the Nevada town of Las Vegas became a hub for the burgeoning casino industry. Many of the new establishments built on the famed Las Vegas strip deliberately used Old West motifs. In a throwback to earlier times, the popular tourist area became known as "Glitter Gulch."

Garland, Hamlin

1860–1940

Hamlin Garland was a novelist and story writer whose short stories express the reality of the harsh life on midwestern farms. As a boy, Hannibal Hamlin Garland witnessed his father's many hardships trying to earn a living through farming on the Great Plains. He determined to unmask the romanticized image of rural life and accomplished this with his first collection of published stories, *Main-Travelled Roads* (1891).

Garland was reared on a farm near West Salem, Wisconsin, until financial difficulties forced the family to move first to Osage, Iowa, and then again to a

Hamlin Garland.

farm in Brown County, Dakota Territory. Resolving to abandon the hardscrabble lifestyle of his father, Garland relocated to Illinois in 1882, where he became a schoolteacher; the following year he accepted a position in Boston. An avid reader, Garland was particularly influenced by Herbert Spencer's evolutionary theories and economist Henry George's "single tax" ideas.

In 1891 Garland published *Main-Travelled Roads,* a collection of six stories that portrayed the economic repression, physical hardship, and emotional strain of rural life on the Great Plains. The now classic story "Under the Lion's Paw" tells of a farmer who becomes penalized for his diligent work because of a law that allows the landlord to raise his rent excessively. Other novels of reform followed, including *Jason Edwards: An Average Man* (1892), *Prairie Folks* (1893), and *Crumbling Idols* (1894).

Garland also wrote western romances, which include *The Rose of Dutcher's Coolly* (1895) and *The Captain of the Gray Horse Troop* (1902). His first autobiographical work, *A Son of the Middle Border* (1917), describes his family background and childhood. Garland moved to Los Angeles in 1929 and lived there until his death in 1940.

Garrett, Patrick Floyd Jarvis

1850–1908

Born in Alabama and reared in Louisiana, Pat Garrett moved to Texas in the 1870s to become a cattle drover and a buffalo hunter. In 1878, as the buffalo herds in Texas diminished, he headed West into New Mexico. In the Pecos River town of Fort Sumner, his gangly frame, six and a half feet tall in boots and hat, gained him instant recognition. He married, dabbled in ranching, and tended bar. He was known as a tough, resolute man, quiet and soft-spoken but not to be trifled with. His marksmanship, horsemanship, and cool bravery evoked admiration.

By 1880, in the wake of the Lincoln County War, rustlers were preying on the cattle herds of Pecos Valley stockmen, who persuaded Garrett to stand for sheriff and clean up the county. One of these rustlers was William H. Bonney, later known as

LIBRARY OF CONGRESS

Patrick F.J. Garrett.

Billy the Kid. Garrett had known Billy in Fort Sumner, but they were not close friends.

As the Kid's criminal exploits drew more and more newspaper coverage, he became the man to track down. In December 1880 Garrett and a posse followed him and four comrades to an abandoned house at Stinking Springs, near Fort Sumner. After an exchange of gunfire that took the life of Billy's friend Charles Bowdre, the fugitives surrendered. Tried and convicted of the murder of Sheriff William Brady during the Lincoln County War, Billy was confined in Lincoln to await execution. On April 28, 1881, with Garrett out of town, the Kid killed two deputies and escaped.

Garrett launched another manhunt and once more narrowed the search to Fort Sumner. There, on July 14, 1881, in the darkened bedroom of one of the old military houses, Garrett accidentally came upon the Kid. As the outlaw unaccountably hesitated, the sheriff fired two shots. Billy the Kid died instantly.

Pat Garrett's subsequent career was anticlimactic. Although lionized as the slayer of Billy the Kid, he was also criticized by many who thought he had not given the Kid a fair chance. With the help of a ghostwriter, he published *The Authentic Life of Billy the Kid,* which was a financial failure but which laid the groundwork for the mighty legend of Billy the Kid.

For the rest of his life, Garrett devoted himself to farming and stock raising, without much success. He doted on his wife and growing family. After a ranching venture in Texas, he returned to New Mexico in 1896 to aid the law in solving the notorious murder of Albert J. Fountain and his son in the White Sands. This assignment ended inconclusively, after a shootout in which Garrett participated.

Following a two-year term as collector of customs in El Paso, Garrett returned to the White Sands country near Alamogordo to take up ranching. Again he was caught up in the chronic feuds of area stockmen, which at length led to his murder. Historians still dispute who may have been his killer.

German Settlers in the West

A mass exodus from Germany to America began in the 1840s, and continued through the 1880s. These Germans were the largest group of Europeans to settle in the new land. In 1854, it was estimated that Germans comprised at least 50 percent of all foreign immigrants in the United States. In the mid-1800s American railroad companies sent agents to Germany where they circulated information about the abundance of work and land in the United States. A series of poor harvests in Germany at the same time was also believed to have been a motivating factor for many German immigrants. Others came to America during the Reconstruction era to escape from a series of wars that erupted in Germany during the 1860s.

Since many of these German immigrants were farmers, they naturally headed West in search of land. Others took jobs with the railroads or mining operations. Germans, along with Irish immigrants, made up a considerable part of San Francisco's working class by the end of the nineteenth century. Their presence in the labor force was strong and German workers were active in San Francisco's early union movements. Some Germans were also Mennonite missionaries who brought their beliefs to Native American populations.

Gentrified German farmers often hired workers to clear new farm land. This practice, which was common in their home country, was mocked by long-time Americans. Hardened pioneers knew that

LIBRARY OF CONGRESS

Emigrants Crossing the Plains, *by Albert Bierstadt, was inspired by a wagon train of German settlers he met while traveling through Nebraska.*

an occasional tree stump in the field was a nuisance to be tolerated. However, Germans—along with English settlers—preferred the European custom of hired labor clearing fields of clutter. This became an expensive convenience, and many of these luxury-minded German immigrants ended up losing their land in bankruptcy.

Like other foreign settlers, the Germans tended to establish close-knit communities throughout the western territories. Bonded by their common language, culture, and history, German enclaves sprouted over the years in Ohio, Wisconsin, Nebraska, Kansas, Texas, and Oklahoma. German churches, newspapers, and social organizations were popular with these settlers. Churches often served as the focus of German culture within these communities. German-language newspapers such as *Oklahoma Staats-Zeitung* and *Der Kingfisher Journal* provided farmers with news of the homeland. These tabloids also provided links between German-American communities, as well as quoting the going rate for grain or cattle in the Chicago and Kansas City stock markets. German social clubs were convivial meeting-places; these lively hubs held traditional dances, evenings of German music, and other cultural activities.

One aspect of American culture that some Germans appreciated was the equality of clothing. In the homeland, one could tell social ranking by the way people dressed. On the prairie, clothing was designed to be practical rather than to make a statement. Settlers wrote home to their loved ones, who shuddered in horror at the thought of homogeneous apparel.

Geronimo

CA.1823–1909

More than any other Native American, Apache leader Geronimo symbolized the terror and cruelty of Indian warfare. His surrender in 1886 to the U.S. Army marked the end of centuries of war between Native Americans and whites for possession of the North American continent.

Although the year of Geronimo's birth remains obscure, he was born a Bedonkohe Apache around

Apache leader Geronimo.

the headwaters of the Gila River in the mountains of southwestern New Mexico. In later years he became identified with the Chiricahua Apache. His Apache name was Goyahkla, or "One Who Yawns."

Geronimo's preeminence in war had its origins in generations of hostility between his people and the Hispanic colonizers of what became the American Southwest. More personally, it began with a tragedy that occurred about 1850. In Mexico, he and his comrades returned from a late-night drinking bout to discover that a Mexican force had fallen on their camp. "I found that my aged mother, my young wife, and my three small children were among the slain," he remembered many years later. "I was never again contented in our quiet home. I had vowed vengeance upon the Mexican troops."

In a revenge expedition the following year, Goyahkla acquired his new name. The most plausible explanation is that he fought with such conspicuous ferocity that the Mexican soldiers cried out, "*Cuidado!* Watch out! Geronimo!"—possibly a rough Spanish corruption of the guttural Apache utterance of Goyahkla. Admiring warriors picked up the terrified shout as a battle cry, and thenceforth Goyahkla was Geronimo.

The Apaches conducted raids and waged war. The raids were economic in purpose, to supplement the always scarce and undependable food resources of the desert, and aimed more at plunder than homicide. Warfare, however, undertaken only after intolerable provocation, was aimed at slaying the enemy. Both Mexicans and Americans furnished the provocation and all too frequently came to understand the terrible finality of an encounter with Geronimo and his followers.

In addition to superior fighting skills, Geronimo possessed the mystical gift of "Power." During a religious experience, he heard a voice promise that no gun could ever kill him. Besides arming him with a reckless self-assurance in battle, his special Power seemed to endow him with extrasensory perception. Repeatedly he foresaw dangers or sensed distant happenings, astonishing his companions and enhancing his stature. Although not a chief, and despised by many of his own people, Geronimo compiled a record of intransigence in peace and proficiency in war that made him the terror of two nations. Mexican peasants saw him as a devil sent to punish them for their sins. Americans of New Mexico and Arizona looked on him as the personification of the merciless brutality of the Apaches.

Other Apache leaders enjoyed greater prestige, but it was the squat, thickset Geronimo who emerged in the 1880s as the most prominent war leader. None of the others equaled him in mastery of the fighting style that so confounded the U.S. Army. In cunning, endurance, perseverance, ruthlessness, fighting skill, and command of the harsh conditions of his homeland, he excelled. Of all the Apaches, recalled one of his followers, "Geronimo seemed to be the most intelligent and resourceful as well as the most vigorous and farsighted. In times of danger he was a man to be relied upon."

As U.S. authorities began to concentrate the Apaches on reservations in the 1870s, Geronimo treated this new situation with ambivalence. In succession he lived and drew rations on three reservations. But he also continued to raid in Mexico and often spent months with the Nednhi Apache in Mexico's Sierra Madre.

Geronimo's final years of warfare were associated with the San Carlos Reservation in Arizona. This was the most forbidding, corrupt, and tumultuous reservation in the West—a desolate, malarial, sunblasted bottom of the Gila River. Life here could not be expected to change so fiercely independent a

LIBRARY OF CONGRESS

Geronimo with his family in a pumpkin patch.

spirit as Geronimo's. In the autumn of 1881 he and a band of followers broke for Mexico, leaving a swath of bloody destruction in their wake. From sanctuaries high in the rugged Sierra Madre, they struck across the border in Arizona.

In September 1882 General George Crook assumed command of the U.S. Army in Arizona. A decade earlier, he had achieved success against the Apache. His innovative methods included mobility attained by supplying his men with pack mules rather than wagon trains and a reliance on Indian scout units rather than regular troops. In the spring of 1883, with Mexican permission, he moved into the Sierra Madre. A surprise attack on an Apache camp led to talks in which Geronimo and others, disheartened by Crook's ability to reach their hitherto safe refuge, agreed to return to San Carlos.

Swiftly Geronimo grew dissatisfied. Again in the spring of 1885, he and a band of fighters broke loose and dashed for Mexico. Again Crook set forth to dig them out of their mountain hideaway and return them to the reservation. Employing the same unconventional methods, he once more succeeded in bringing about Geronimo's surrender. Geronimo had second thoughts, however, and fled to the mountains. Ordered to repudiate agreements made with other chiefs, Crook asked to be relieved of his command.

General Nelson A. Miles took his place. Throughout the summer of 1886 he used conventional methods but finally had to fall back on Crook's approach. The key to victory lay in moving all the reservation Chiricahua, Geronimo's people, to exile in Florida. When Geronimo learned of this, he agreed to join them in Florida. The surrender ceremony, in Skeleton Canyon, Arizona, on September 4, 1886, signaled the close of Indian warfare. Confined first in Florida, then in Alabama, Geronimo and the Chiricahua were at last allowed to settle near Fort Sill in present Oklahoma in 1894. They never returned to Arizona. In his late years Geronimo became a celebrity, much in demand for parades and expositions. As he approached his ninetieth year, pneumonia took his life.

SMITHSONIAN INSTITUTION

Rare photograph of a man and a woman participating in the Ghost Dance ceremony.

Ghost Dance

The Ghost Dance was the name of the revitalization movement that swept the Native American tribes of the West in the late 1880s and early 1890s. It represented a search for spiritual solutions to unbearable afflictions. Although a peaceful teaching, among the Sioux of North and South Dakota the Ghost Dance led to violence. After the terrible tragedy at Wounded Knee, the Ghost Dance collapsed or went underground.

The Ghost Dance grew out of the breakdown of the traditional Indian culture. With confinement on a reservation, the old ways vanished. Such activities as war and the hunt had once dominated daily life and shaped the central values and institutions of tribal society. On the reservations, where theIndians depended on the government for rations and other necessities, government officials attempted to substitute the values and institutions of white society to transform all Indians into imitation whites.

Unsurprisingly, the reservation life, and the government's attempt to "civilize" the Indians, tore down the traditional culture without replacing it with something new and vital. The Dawes Act of 1887 added further tension by launching a concerted drive to allot reservation lands to individual families and cede the "surplus" for white settlers. All over the West, Indians closed the decade of the 1880s beset by cultural disintegration and feelings of helplessness and hopelessness. In such conditions, the promise of the Ghost Dance fell on fertile soil.

The Ghost Dance was not a unique phenomenon. Throughout human history, peoples similarly afflicted have sought similar remedies. James Mooney, a perceptive government ethnologist who studied the Ghost Dance shortly after it broke over the West, discerned in it a universal instinct of peoples in crisis: "When the race lies crushed and groaning under an alien yoke, how natural is the dream of a redeemer, an Arthur, who shall return from exile or awake from some long sleep to drive out the usurper and win back for his people what they have lost. The hope becomes a faith and the faith becomes the creed of priests and prophets, until the hero is a god and the dream a religion, looking to some great miracle of nature for its culmination and accomplishment." Such was the vision of the Paiute holy man Wovoka (1856–1932). He originated the Ghost Dance, and at his brush lodge on a reservation in Nevada he received delegates from tribes all over the West who came to learn its precepts. They returned to their homes as apostles of the new doctrine and instructed their people in its beliefs and practices.

Although heavily influenced by Christianity, the Ghost Dance also featured native concepts and ceremonies. The most characteristic were the Ghost Dance and ghost shirt. By dancing the Ghost Dance wearing the distinctive ghost shirt, believers could hasten the end of the old, worn-out world and the advent of a new world. In this blissful realm, Indians would be free of the white burden and reside for eternity among all the generations of Indians who had died. It was a land without white people, full of game and other riches, free of sickness and want. Dancers strove for an emotional peak in which they would "die" and be transported to this paradise, where they could see the prophesied wonders and visit with friends and relatives long dead.

Reflecting the teachings of Christian missionaries, Wovoka came to be known as the Messiah. When pilgrims sat at his feet, he showed them scars on his hands where centuries before the whites had nailed him to a cross. He preached a moral code grounded in Christian ethics. "Do not tell lies," he urged. "Do right always." "Do no harm to anyone." All peoples must live in peace: "You must not fight." Indians were not to remove whites from the new world by violence; that would be accomplished by divine means. When the ground trembled, which Wovoka foretold would occur in the spring of 1891, believers should fix in their hair sacred feathers by which to soar aloft while a new land covered the old. The new land would push the white people before it, back across the ocean where they came from. When the cataclysm subsided, the Indians would lower themselves from the sky into the new world of abundance and delight.

Spread by pilgrims returning home from Nevada, the Ghost Dance took root on nearly every reservation in the West. Some tribes embraced it with fervor, others adopted it tepidly, and a few rejected it altogether. As it radiated east from Nevada, it underwent changes reflecting the perceptions of the various apostles. On each reservation, therefore, the Ghost Dance took forms differing in slight or important ways from the original version preached by Wovoka.

Only among the Sioux of North and South Dakota did Wovoka's message of peace end in bloodshed. The leading apostles, Short Bull and Kicking Bear, did not openly advocate violence. But their rhetoric grew militant, disorder intensified in some places beyond the ability of tribal police to contain it, and much publicity was given to the power of ghost shirts to turn away the bullets of the white man. Government officials as well as nearby white settlers took alarm. On November 20, 1890, troops were sent to occupy the Pine Ridge and Rosebud agencies. The Ghost Dancers fled to a remote tableland and prepared to defend themselves. The stage was set for confrontation.

The standoff could probably have been resolved peacefully except for a determination to remove from the reservations certain leaders regarded as troublemakers. On December 15 an attempt by tribal police to arrest Sitting Bull led to a shootout in which he was killed. A similar resolve to seize Big Foot ended on the bloody field of Wounded Knee, on December 29, 1890, where more than 200 people were cut down by U.S. Army units. For the Sioux and for tribes all over the West, Wounded Knee shattered Wovoka's dream. When his predicted millennium did not materialize in the spring of 1891, many of the faithful lost interest. Others took their beliefs underground. In some tribes, in much altered form, the Ghost Dance persists today.

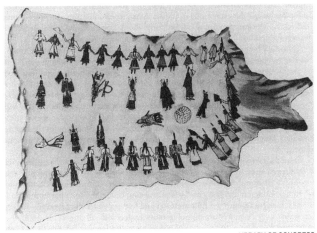

LIBRARY OF CONGRESS

Buckskin painting of the Ghost Dance, created by Yellow Nose, Ute captive of the Cheyennes.

Cattle graze in a field in what remains of Bodie, California.

Ghost Towns

Ghost towns are any abandoned towns in the American West where empty buildings still stand after the inhabitants are gone.

Most ghost towns are former mining hubs; the miners came in, extracted the valuable minerals from the area, then left for new sources of gold and silver. With the influx of miners in an area, small towns would quickly spring up to meet the needs of the new population. While farmers usually found that a general store and a post office in town were sufficient, miners required hotels and banks, and of course, saloons in which to blow off steam and gamble away their earnings. Other vital services usually

Chickens wander freely in the streets of Silver City, Idaho, a once booming mining town.

included a barber shop and the sheriff's office. The fickle nature of mining led to the growth of many such boom towns. They could be built quickly and abandoned just as rapidly when miners went on to new veins.

The 1850s saw many boom towns built and deserted. Though the population was gone, the hotels and saloons remained. These buildings, standing alone in the middle of nowhere, became known as "ghost towns." Many ghost towns were repopulated in the late nineteenth century, as technological advancements provided new opportunities to harvest minerals from old mines. After the mines had been completely emptied of resources, the towns were abandoned once more.

Many towns, in remote mountain or wilderness regions, remained hidden for decades. Buildings decayed, dust settled and it was only the occasional traveler who might stumble onto an abandoned site. The only real inhabitants were generally termites feeding off the wooden buildings. In the mid-twentieth century, the U.S. Forest Service and Bureau of Land Management began demolishing many ghost towns. Other ghost towns were plundered by vandals searching for coins, guns, and other artifacts the original settlers had left behind.

Beginning in the 1930s, a movement slowly arose among the descendants of some of the original Western settlers to restore some ghost towns. Montana was at the forefront of the preservation movement, refurbishing the rickety buildings and turning them into historic sites.

Today there are numerous ghost towns throughout the West. Some are still abandoned and slowly decaying, but others are thriving tourist attractions. Some ghost town entrepreneurs have even constructed new buildings designed to appear decayed. Ghost towns also double as living museums. Western shows are a popular attraction, with tourists snapping photos of "cowboys" holding a "gunfight" in the center of town. One of the most famous "working" ghost towns is Tombstone, Arizona where Wyatt Earp had his famous shoot-out at the O.K. Corral. Other notable Western ghost towns include Virginia City, Nevada and Central City, Colorado. Ghost towns, both populated and abandoned, can be found throughout the West as far north as Alaska, down through California, New Mexico, Arizona, Utah, Idaho, and Nevada, and other states.

Glass, Hugh

DIED CA. 1833

Mountain man Hugh Glass might warrant little mention in the annals of the Old West were it not for his famous crawl in 1823 after being mauled by a grizzly bear. That event, among the most compelling stories of the Old West, has been celebrated in an epic poem by John G. Neihardt (*The Song of Hugh Glass*, 1915) and in such novels as Frederic Manfred's *Lord Grizzly* (1954) and *Wilderness* by Roger Zelazny and Gerald Hausman (1994).

Virtually nothing is known of Glass's early life or, indeed, any phase of his life. He was probably Irish-born, may have been a seaman, and is said to have served as a pirate with Jean Lafitte in the Gulf of Mexico.

Legend has Glass wandering westward from the Gulf Coast of Texas, being captured by Indians and escaping to make his way to St. Louis, where in 1823 he joined William H. Ashley's expedition up the Missouri River. He was apparently wounded at least once in a battle with the Arikaras—his nemesis a decade later—and was one of 13 men who traveled overland to the relief of a fur trading crew at Fort Henry at the mouth of the Yellowstone River.

In August 1823, on the Grand River of present-day South Dakota, Glass, in a trapping party, was mauled by a grizzly bear and left in the care of two young volunteers, Jim Bridger and John S. Fitzgerald. When these men became convinced that he would not survive his wounds, they took his rifle, rejoined their partners, and reported Glass dead.

But he did not die. Subsisting on berries and the carcasses of animals abandoned by wolves and other forest predators, his legs and ribs crushed and his scalp laid open from the bear attack, Glass crawled (some say as far as 300 miles) down the Grand River to the Missouri River, was befriended by Indians, and made his way to Fort Kiowa above the confluence of the White and Missouri rivers.

Legend has it that after he recovered he began a search for the men who abandoned him, trailing them up the Missouri and Yellowstone to the Big Horn, intending a terrible revenge. The story goes that he found Bridger on the Big Horn and spared him for his youth, moved on and confronted Fitzgerald at Fort Atkinson on the Missouri, recovered his rifle, and let Fitzgerald go. (Another version is that Glass discovered Fitzgerald was now in the army and out of reach.)

After his ordeal, Glass traded out of Santa Fe, trapped in Ute country, and worked as a hunter out of Fort Union. In the winter of 1832–33, Glass and fellow trappers Edward Rose and a man named Menard were killed by the Arikaras on the Yellowstone River below the Big Horn.

Glidden, Joseph

1813–1906

Joseph Glidden was credited with inventing the first successful barbed-wire fencing, which changed the course of western agriculture and ranching by bringing an end to open-range cattle grazing.

Joseph Farwell Glidden was born in Charlestown, New Hampshire, in January 18, 1813. At age 29 he headed west and two years later bought a farm in DeKalb County, Illinois. At a county fair in 1873, Glidden was intrigued by the display of Henry Rose, a local farmer who had devised a wooden fence with wire barbs to control a wandering cow. Inspired, Glidden applied Rose's idea to wire and soon patented his invention.

Within two months Glidden's patent was challenged by Jacob Haish, another local farmer who claimed that the invention was his. Nonetheless, Glidden soon received orders from neighbors and formed a partnership with local hardware store owner Isaac Leonard Ellwood. Their business was

MUSEUM OF TEXAS TECHNICAL UNIVERSITY

Joseph Glidden.

NORTHERN ILLINOIS UNIVERSITY ARCHIVES

The original model for Glidden's barbing machine was fashioned from parts of a coffee mill.

eventually bought out by Washburn & Moen, a Massachusetts wire company, for $60,000 and royalties of $.25 per 100 pounds sold. Glidden invested in a Texas ranch, which he gave to his daughter before he returned to Illinois. He died in 1906.

Gold

From the earliest days of their awareness of the New World, European conquerors and settlers had dreamed of a continent rich in gold. The Spanish conquistadors came in search of the legendary Seven Cities of Gold, and the English, having heard stories of Spanish gold discoveries, hoped for more of the same (not realizing how few of those stories had even a grain of truth in them). In fact, the English found their riches in the fur trade, whose profits surpassed any they might have realized from the mining of gold. However, the lucrative fur trade began to wane in the early nineteenth century, having propelled the first great wave of western exploration and expansion to Oregon and along the Santa Fe Trail.

Then on January 24, 1848, gold was found by James Marshall in the millrace at Sutter's Mill in California. The result, the California Gold Rush, changed the course of western expansion dramatically, affecting virtually every aspect of westward movement. Gold fever brought people to the West Coast from every part of the country, as well as from Europe and Asia, causing the population of California to explode from an estimated 20,000 in 1848 to 223,000 in late 1852.

What did the would-be gold miners find when they got to the goldfields out west? Those who thought that gold would be lying in stream beds ready for them to pick up and put in their pockets—a vision not unlike that of the conquistadors—were in for a nasty surprise. Gold mining, especially in the California Gold Rush, was back-breaking work and for many the only fruits of their labors were broken dreams.

Sluicing was the most common method used by the gold hunters. Dr. Thomas Clark describes the following process, as performed with a "Long Tom":

[T]he "Long Tom" . . . consisted of two troughs, the upper one having an iron baffle or seine in the lower half of its bottom, to feed the fine earth into the lower trough so that the gold could be caught behind a series of cleats. The sluice box was a long yard-wide trough of almost indeterminate length with cleats in the

Searching for gold in a riverbed.

bottom to check the flow of gold dust which sank while the greater portion of earth and rock was carried away. Placer mining on a big scale could be carried on only by the use of pumping machinery and the employment of large numbers of men. This required careful channeling of streams, the opening of elaborate sluiceways, and the removal of virtual mountains of earth.

As a result, placer mining quickly became the province of large corporations rather than the hardy forty-niner with a mule.

How much worse it would have been for the lone prospector had the gold in California primarily been located in veins! In sluice mining, the prospector finds gold in stream beds and in loose rock and gravel. Even a man or woman with limited skills, capital, and equipment can separate the gold from the dirt.

For vein mining, one had to have enough capital, crews, and equipment to sink a mine shaft and extract ore. Later gold booms, such as the one that exploded in Colorado, were based around vein mining, but the lonely prospector could still make a little money by speculating in "claims," established with only minimal effort at extraction. The real money came from selling to a large mining corporation.

Gold Rush

See California Gold Rush, Klondike Gold Rush, and Fifty-niners

Goldsby, Crawford

1876–1896

Outlaw Goldsby Crawford, who was also known as "Cherokee Bill," was born in Fort Concho, Texas. His family moved to Fort Gibson, Oklahoma, when he was seven. A product of a complex mixed marriage, part black, part Cherokee, part Mexican, part Anglo, Goldsby probably experienced a considerable amount of racism in his youth. At 14, he killed his brother-in-law, allegedly for beating his sister, an auspicious start to his brief career.

Cherokee Bill Goldsby quickly developed a reputation as a ladies' man and a mankiller, although it is unclear whether there was truth to either. Working the Oklahoma territory, he allegedly killed a railroad agent at Nowata and an unarmed bystander at Lenapah. He was a member of the Bill Cook gang for a while, participating in store holdups and at least one train robbery. He was captured in February 1895 and had the bad luck to come up before Judge Isaac Parker, the "hanging judge" of Fort Smith, Arkansas. Parker sentenced him to hang, but Goldsby attempted to escape on July 26. He killed a prison guard, tried to free fellow prisoners, and set off a mammoth gunfight. The escape failed and Judge Parker, enraged by his actions, sentenced Cherokee Bill to hang the following day. This time, he did.

Goliad, Battle of

Goliad, Texas—once the Spanish mission and presidio of La Bahía—was a largely Mexican area of about 800 people. In the early 1700s, La Bahía was home to Spanish cattle ranches. By the 1830s, Goliad's economy still depended on the cattle industry.

It was believed the best Mexican herdsmen came from this area.

In the 1830s tensions were rising between Mexico and the United States over the fate of Texas. Mexico feared that the large influx of American settlers in the territory would eventually force the ceding of this valuable land to the growing United States. Furthermore, American pioneers were profiting from their Texas investments while Mexicans remained in poverty. As the number of American educational facilities and new homes quickly outgrew their Mexican rivals, conflict appeared imminent. Laws were enacted by Mexico which prohibited American expansion throughout Texas, and troops were sent from the capital in Mexico City to maintain order.

The American settlers refused to obey these new regulations. They began calling themselves Texians, and declared themselves a republic on March 2, 1836.

The Mexican forces retaliated without mercy. They first attacked a Texas force in an old Spanish mission known as the Alamo. There were no survivors, and the slogan "Remember the Alamo!" became a rallying cry for Texan revolutionaries.

The second skirmish erupted in Goliad. Once more, the Mexican leader Santa Anna led his troops in a bloody and victorious charge against American settlers. Santa Anna took the Goliad Texians prisoner. He considered them criminals and ordered the execution of 371 people. This defeat became known as the Battle of Goliad.

Goodnight, Charles

1836–1929

The man who became known as a trailblazer, livestock breeder, and one of the most successful cattlemen of Texas history was born in Macoupin County, Illinois, and brought by his family to Milan County, Texas, in 1846. In his 20s, Goodnight served as a Texas Ranger and scout and saw action in the Pease River fight in 1857 in which Comanche chief Peta Nocona, father of Quanah Parker, was killed. In the Civil War, Goodnight served as a scout and guide for a frontier regiment.

In 1865 he owned a herd of cattle in Palo Pinto County, Texas, and was seeking a better market for his animals when he joined forces with veteran cattleman Oliver Loving, who already had acquired a vast knowledge of trail-driving from taking his herds to markets in Illinois and Colorado. In June 1866, Goodnight and Loving hired 18 men and put together a herd of 2,000 head and pointed them toward New Mexico Territory, where the U.S. Army needed meat and was paying eight cents a pound for it. The 600-mile trail that the two men broke, from Fort Belknap on the Red Fork of the Brazos River to Fort Sumner, New Mexico (and later extended to Pueblo and Denver, Colorado) became familiar in the Old West as the Goodnight-Loving Trail, one of the most heavily trafficked of all southwestern cattle trails.

After Loving's death at the hands of Indians, Goodnight continued using the trail for the next three years, working with New Mexico cattleman John Chisum in 1871 and clearing a profit of $17,000. By 1873, Goodnight was wealthy. Soon after, however, he was nearly ruined by investments in a stock growers' bank in Pueblo. He recovered eventually, assisted by his wife Mary Ann, who presided over the business of their Palo Duro spread.

Goodnight blazed a trail from Alamogordo Creek, New Mexico, to Granada, Colorado, in 1875, but his Colorado ranching effort was never successful and the following year he moved his herd of 1,800 head

DENVER PUBLIC LIBRARY

Charles Goodnight.

to Palo Duro Canyon in the Texas Panhandle. In 1876 he created a new trail to Dodge City, Kansas, and there went into partnership with John G. Adair, Irish-born inheritor of a family fortune who invested $500,000 to allow Goodnight to buy the Palo Duro Canyon section by section (at prices of about 75 cents an acre). Adair's backing also enabled Goodnight to buy 2,000 blooded bulls. In a brief period of time, the Goodnight-Adair ranch, called the JA Ranch, was running 60,000 head of cattle on 600,000 acres of land.

It is said that Goodnight, at the peak of the operation, was selling 30,000 head a year and by 1882 was bringing in a net annual income of $500,000.

Goodnight believed strongly in herd development and improvement. He bred one of the best-blooded herds in the West through the introduction of Hereford bulls and experimented unsuccessfully in breeding buffalo to Polled Angus cattle—to produce an animal he called the "cattalo."

He was a founder of the Panhandle Stockman's Association, created in 1880, which was instrumental in improving breeding methods and ridding the region of rustlers and outlaws. He was never averse to lynching rustlers, but had a reputation as a mild-mannered if stern boss who championed the cowboys' cause. He fired cowboys for raking their horses with spurs and for fighting among themselves, and he instructed his men that if they stopped to talk out on the range they were to dismount and ease the saddle girth on their horses.

In 1888, the JA Ranch was divided between Goodnight and Adair's widow. In 1890, Goodnight sold his portion, a 40,000-acre tract he called the Quitaque. He spent the rest of his life investing in Mexican mining and operating a small ranch at Goodnight, the Panhandle town named for him. He died in Tucson, Arizona, on December 12, 1929.

Goodnight-Loving Trail

This cattle trail from Fort Belknap on the Brazos River of Texas to Fort Sumner, New Mexico Territory, was named for Texas cattlemen Charles Goodnight and Oliver Loving (ca. 1812–1867). Goodnight, who had built up a herd of cattle in Palo Pinto County, Texas, after the Civil War, sought better markets for his beef than he could find in Reconstruction-era Texas. He joined forces with a like-minded Palo Pinto cowman, the Kentuckian Oliver Loving, a veteran trailblazer who had lived in Texas since 1845. In 1866, the partners, with 18 cowboys and 2,000 head, blazed the trail into New Mexico Territory for the market on the Bosque Redondo Navajo Reservation, where U.S. government buyers paid eight cents a pound for the beef. They lost 400 head on the trail, mostly from the lack of water between the Concho and Pecos rivers.

The next year, Goodnight and Loving drove a third herd along the trail to Fort Sumner, this time with tragic consequences. Loving and another man went ahead to reach Fort Sumner and announce the herd's arrival to beef buyers. Along the Pecos, Loving was shot in the arm and side by raiding Comanches and, believing his wounds fatal, sent the other man back to Goodnight with the news. Loving survived a week in the desert. He was finally found by Mexican travelers and taken on to Fort Sumner, where his gangrenous arm was amputated. He died in July 1867, and was buried in Weatherford, Texas.

Until 1870, Goodnight continued to use the trail he and Loving had pioneered. Despite its waterless stretches, the trail was widely used by other cattlemen taking their herds to market in New Mexico and Colorado.

Gould, Jay

1836–1892

Jay Gould was a financier who built an empire in the railroad business. Gould was born on May 27, 1836, in Roxbury, New York. His mother died when he was four years old, and he was raised on a farm in the Catskills by his father and five older sisters. At an early age he decided that farming was not a career that suited him, and at 13 he left home to pursue an education at Hobart College. After working for a few years as a surveyor in New York, Ohio, and Michigan, Gould accumulated about $5,000, and invested it in his first major business operation. In August of 1856 he formed a partnership with Zadock Pratt in the tannery business. This venture lasted only three

Railroad financier Jay Gould.

years, but earned Gould enough money that he was able to establish himself as a prevailing financial force in New York City.

Gould's career as a railroad czar began in 1860 when a former partner, D. M. Wilson, offered Gould $50,000 worth of mortgage bonds in the Rutland & Washington Railroad for ten cents on the dollar. Gould seized the opportunity and proceeded to pour all of his energies into studying railroads. The lessons he learned from the Rutland experience opened his eyes to the railroad industry and helped him become a successful railroad speculator. In 1867, Gould became involved with the Erie Railroad and together with Daniel Drew and Jim Fisk entered into a drawn-out battle to wrest control of the railroad from Commodore Cornelius Vanderbilt. When the dust settled, Gould was in control of the Erie. He resigned as president in 1872, and the following year invested in the Union Pacific Railroad.

In 1874, Gould was elected to the board of the Union Pacific, and began an intense effort to rescue the company from financial disaster. After gaining control of the Union Pacific, Gould seized the Kansas Pacific railroad and merged the two. He then acquired the Missouri Pacific, the St. Louis, Iron Mountain and Pacific, and the Texas and Pacific, creating a railway system that controlled the Southwest and provided the only competition to the Santa Fe. His business interests extended beyond the railroads, because by this time he had also acquired the Western Union Telegraph Company, several newspapers, and Manhattan Elevated, the New York City rapid transit system.

Gould's legacy is that of a man largely condemned as deceitful, treacherous, and destructively monopolistic. Yet one must bear in mind that most of what we know of him, and particularly of the last decade of his life, comes from the press. The New York newspapers especially felt threatened by Gould, and some considered him a mortal foe. Gould died in New York City on December 2, 1892, after a long struggle with tuberculosis. The value of his estate was estimated at $72 million.

Graham-Tewksbury Feud

This seven-year range war in Arizona's remote Pleasant Valley, in the Tonto Basin northeast of Phoenix, involved the families of John D. Tewksbury (a New Englander married to an Indian woman), Ohioan Thomas H. Graham, and Texan Mart Blevins.

The sons of the Graham-Tewksbury clans worked together as cowboys, perhaps were partners in a rustling operation, and were apparently friendly until about 1884, when a quarrel over the registration of a brand split them into bitter factions. The Graham faction was aided by the five sons of neighboring rancher Mart Blevins.

The bloody feud began in 1886, when the Tewksbury family leased some of their grazing land to sheepmen from the Flagstaff area. Since the entire Tonto Basin region was cattle country under common rancher agreement, the cattle interests moved to crush the sheepmen—and the Tewksbury family with them. Despite the efforts of Tom Graham to prevent bloodshed, many sheep were killed and at least one man—a Navajo sheepherder—in February 1887.

Even with the sheepmen out of the Tonto Basin, the feud flared in the summer of 1887 with the disappearance of Mart Blevins, patriarch of the family of Graham partisans. On August 9, Mart's son Hampton and four other men, including cowhands from the Aztec Land and Cattle Company (known as the Hashknife Outfit), rode to the Tewksbury ranch. Blevins spoke to Jim Tewksbury and as he and his partners turned to leave, Tewksbury and some unknown others fired on them from the doorway of the ranch house, killing Hampton Blevins and a man named John Paine, said to be a Hashknife hired gun in the employ of the Graham family. The survivors, all of them wounded, claimed the shooting was unprovoked. Tewksbury said the men were looking for a fight and were drawing their guns as they turned their horses away from him.

On September 2, 1887, Tom Graham led a raid on the Tewksbury ranch. In the fighting, John Tewksbury Jr., and one William Jacobs were killed. Eventually a Yavapai County posse arrived and drove the attackers off the Tewksbury property.

Two days after this battle, in the town of Holbrook, 75 miles from the Tewksbury ranch, Andy Blevins (who had taken the name of Cooper in Texas, where he was wanted for rustling and murder), bragged that he had killed John Tewksbury and Jacobs. The new sheriff of Apache County, Commodore Perry Owens (named for the hero of the Battle of Lake Erie), attempted to serve a warrant on Andy Blevins for horse theft and when Blevins resisted arrest, Owens shot him (Blevins died the next day). In the same shootout, Owens also killed Andy Blevins's brother, Sam Houston Blevins, a friend, Mose Roberts, and wounded another Blevins brother, John.

On September 21, Yavapai County sheriff William Mulvenon and a posse of 25 men set out to arrest both faction leaders. At the Graham ranch, John Graham and Charles Blevins were killed resisting arrest. At the Tewksbury ranch, seven men, including the two remaining Tewksbury brothers, surrendered without a fight and were subsequently indicted for murder. They were tried in June 1888 for the murder of Hampton Blevins, but since no one would testify against them, they were released.

By now, Tom Graham was the only survivor of his family and only one Blevins son had survived. Of the Tewksburys, Jim died of tuberculosis in Prescott at the end of 1888 and Ed led a peaceful life until 1892, when Tom Graham returned to Pleasant Valley on cattle business. That August he was ambushed and killed by two men, later identified as Ed Tewksbury and one John Rhodes. Only Tewks-

bury stood trial for the murder. He was convicted in December 1893. He spent about two years in prison before his second trial resulted in a hung jury. Charges against him were dropped in 1896. Ed Tewksbury became a deputy sheriff in Globe and died in 1904.

The Graham-Tewksbury Feud, which formed the backdrop and plot of Zane Grey's aptly named *To the Last Man* (1922), cost the lives of at least 25 men.

Grand Canyon

The Grand Canyon is a magnificent gorge in northwestern Arizona carved by the Colorado River into rocks 1.7 billion years old. Measured at river

COLLECTION OF MARK KLETT

The Grand Canyon, *by William Bell.*

Grand Canyon from To-Ro-Weap, looking east.

Limestone, sandstone, lava, and other rocks, striated along the canyon's walls, change in color as dawn passes to dusk and provide one of several breathtaking attractions for tourists visiting Grand Canyon National Park. Established in 1919, the park covers an area of 1,904 square miles (1.2 million acres).

Archaeological evidence suggests that an agricultural tribe settled in the Grand Canyon region about 2,500 years ago. The Anasazi, as they called themselves, were ancestors of the modern Hopi Indians and built the cliff dwellings discovered in Mesa Verde in Colorado.

The first nonindigenous person to view the canyon (in 1540) was Spanish explorer Garcia López de Cardenas, an officer of the Coronado expedition. But it was John Wesley Powell, in the late nineteenth century, who realized the canyon's geological significance. In 1869 he traveled through the canyon by boat, making numerous expeditions along the Colorado River and its hundreds of tributaries. The Grand Canyon has been an invaluable resource for later geologists developing stratigraphy, the science of interpreting successive rock layers to determine geologic history.

Extreme differences in climate allow for a great range of wildlife in the region. Spruce, aspen, and fir trees 8,000 feet above sea level rise out of the snow. Ponderosa pine and piñon-juniper woodland dominate to 7,000 feet, then give way to desert grassland, sagebrush, and various cacti. From about 4,000 to 1,200 feet, the lowest point in the park, temperatures soar past 100 degrees F. and rainfall is scarce. But dense vegetation thrives along the banks of the Colorado River and its tributaries.

Wildlife varies from the bighorn sheep, bobcats, rattlesnakes, and lizards of the rocky cliffs to the squirrels, raccoons, otters, and even scorpions of the lush river region. The Grand Canyon is home to a variety of birds and fish, and several species, such as the river's humpback chub, exist only in this specific habitat and face extinction.

In deference to environmental concerns over air and noise pollution, tourist-carrying helicopters and planes have been restricted to certain areas and altitudes. Moreover, the Clean Air Act was passed and is strictly enforced to minimize the pollution that invades the area from as far away as Los Angeles. On a truly clear day, visual range at the Grand Canyon can extend to a distance of 225 miles.

level, the Grand Canyon stretches 277 miles in length from Lees Ferry to Lake Mead, near the borders of Arizona and Nevada. The center of the gorge stands over a mile deep, and its width expands from 0.1 to 18 miles.

The Grand Canyon cuts through the Kaibab Plateau, which is itself sloped to such an extent that the canyon's North Rim, at more than 8,000 feet above sea level, stands over 1,000 feet higher than the South Rim—a significant disparity that explains why the Colorado River drops 2,215 feet over almost 200 rapids as it winds through the canyon. Visitors up to the challenge are challenged with the most heart-stoppingly dangerous white-water-rapid runs in the country. Lava Falls, the largest of its waterfalls, drops 37 feet.

Grand Tetons

The Grand Tetons are a mountain chain of the Rocky Mountains extending south of Yellowstone National Park in northwestern Wyoming and eastern Idaho. The Teton Range is about 40 miles long and 10 to 15 miles wide. The highest peak, Grand Teton, reaches an elevation of 13,776 feet.

Unlike the mountains of volcanic origin in the Rockies, the Tetons are fault-block mountains. Formed about 60 million years ago, the fault block developed when underground stresses sheared the earth's crust along Teton fault. Two segments were displaced: one thrust about 20,000 feet upward west of the fault, and the other depressed, forming the valley known as Jackson Hole, to the east. The process occurred gradually, and later glaciers carved the flat rock into the sharp peaks that exist today.

The Tetons were visited by man as long as 10,500 years ago. Wandering tribes found the area rich in animal and plant life, and evidence of ancient quarrying exists on the Tetons' west slope. In later years, many indigenous tribes, such as the Ute, Blackfeet, Nez Perce, Crow, and Shoshoni, came to the Tetons to hunt buffalo in the summer season, but left for more sheltered territory in the winter. The Shoshoni were the only Indians to live year round in the Tetons, taking refuge from the Blackfeet Indians.

The first white man to explore the Tetons was fur trader John Colter (1807), but it was not until the 1820s, when the Rocky Mountain fur trade was at its height, that the Tetons were fully explored. Then, mountain men such as Kit Carson, Jedediah Smith, and Bill Sublette traversed every canyon of the range, setting beaver traps in the waterways and searching the forests and plains for game. The first comprehensive study of the area was conducted in 1872 by Ferdinand Hayden, whose party included a geologist, zoologists, a photographer, and artist Thomas Moran, whose oil paintings introduced easterners to a part of the West yet unknown. By the end of the nineteenth century, prospectors, lumbermen, and cattle ranchers inhabited the Tetons.

The Teton Range lies in Grand Teton National Park, which encompasses 485 square miles in northwest Wyoming and was established on February 26, 1929. Grand Teton and neighboring Mounts Owen and Morgan rise abruptly from Jackson Hole, providing spectacular scenery for the approximately three million tourists who visit annually. Adding to the natural splendor of the park are glaciers, lakes, rivers, hot springs, and waterfalls.

One intriguing puzzle among plant life in the Tetons is the existence of purple saxifrage, a species identical to the saxifrage native to the Alps. Botanists theorize that ice sheets carried this plant south from the Arctic, and upon receding left it behind to flourish. Animal life in the Tetons is abundant and diverse. Moose, elk, and antelope roam the forests, meadows, and plains, while the many streams and lakes support beaver, otter, swans, and ducks.

Grangers

The Grangers was a movement begun in 1867 to promote populist ideas among American farmers.

As the agriculture industry in America continued to grow, farmers across the country realized that they had many problems in common. These included natural forces such as floods, fires, and locusts, as well as economic concerns having to do with large railroad companies, banks, and grain elevators, among others. In December 1867, Secretary of Agriculture Oliver Hudson Kelley resigned from office to form the National Grange of the Patrons of Husbandry, commonly referred to as the Grangers. Kelley's goal was to bring together farmers everywhere in the United States, to solve these problems through a united political movement.

Membership in the Grangers was small at first, but gradually, as the populist movement spread West, the Grangers developed into a powerful force. In 1871, farmers joined the Grangers in record numbers, and three years later the movement claimed over 1.5 million members. Public Granger meetings ignited attendees with fiery speeches, rallying farmers against big business.

In March of 1874, the Grangers claimed their first major victory. The Iowa legislature passed statutes that regulated the rate railroad companies could charge for freight. Wisconsin passed a similar law and the Grangers became known as a force to be dealt with.

Jay Gould, a railroad baron, feared that this

populist activity would ruin his many business interests. To squelch Granger complaints about his freight rates, Gould traveled through the Midwest vowing he would cut all rail services for farmers.

The Granger movement did not limit itself to farmers' rights. It also helped improve mail delivery in rural areas, and was an early crusader for conservation. The Grangers actively courted women to join the party, demanding that they be given equal rights and the opportunity to vote in elections.

Grant's Peace Policy

1872

This was a plan instituted by President Ulysses S. Grant whereby Christian civilians would replace military personnel in the administration of Indian affairs on reservations.

In 1869, the Quakers recommended to the recently elected President Grant that religious workers were better equipped than the military, morally and spiritually, to manage Indian agencies on behalf of the federal government. Grant agreed, and by 1872, 13 denominations had been given exclusive control over 73 agencies. Among the denominations participating in the program were the Quakers, Catholics, Episcopalians, and Lutherans. The Methodists received the largest allocation. Grant also created the Board of Indian Commissioners, composed of wealthy lay Christians, to exercise joint control, with the Secretary of the Interior, over procurement and disbursement of funds for reservations. The hope was to weed out the corruption that had afflicted Indian administration.

It was believed by all concerned that the Indian nations were dying out, and that there was little hope of the people surviving in the form of permanent Christian congregations. Missions were established and maintained, however, to assimilate those Indians who remained, and to smooth their transition from "tribalism" to "civilization."

Under the policy, denominations were given complete control over the reservations they administered, free from interference by other churches. Representatives of one denomination could enter a reservation run by another only with special permission. Indians were given no choice of Christian association, and their traditional religious practice was outlawed. Assimilation was the driving aim. Reservation schools became little more than mouthpieces of the religious denominations, and attendance at church services was mandatory for students.

The years from the implementation of the Peace Policy in 1872 until the passage of the Dawes Act in 1887 represent the high-water mark in Christian missions to Indians. The missions succeeded in converting many Indians to Christianity. Allotment, however, led, for a variety of reasons, to a decline in Christian fervor among the tribes. Under the Dawes Act "allotted" parcels of land of limited acreage were given to individual tribal members. Each individual who accepted this condition would be given American citizenship. Surpluses of land left over after all the "allotments" had been parceled out would be given to white settlers. Allotted Indian lands were held in trust for 25 years by the federal government to protect them from unscrupulous private land developers. Ironically, as a result of allotment tribal lands diminished from 139 million acres in 1887 to 34 million acres by 1934 and the value of these lands decreased by 80 percent.

The "ecclesiastical serfdom" of the Peace Policy, with its reservation monopolies, came to an end with the implementation of the Indian New Deal, early in the administration of President Franklin Roosevelt decades later. Its effects, however, can be seen on reservations to the present day.

Grattan Massacre

1854

This engagement between the Sioux and the U.S. Army near Fort Laramie in 1854 began as a massacre of Indians but ended with the destruction of an entire Army unit. It is also known as the Battle of the Mormon's Cow.

The incident began when a hungry young Lakota Sioux came upon a lame cow in a river bottom. He killed it, butchered it, and shared it with his friends. Word of the impromptu feast got back to the owner, a Mormon emigrant with a nearby wagon train. Despite the fact that he had probably abandoned the animal

MERCALDO ARCHIVES

Spotted Tail, one of the Lakota who surrendered to the U.S. government for their involvement in the Grattan battle, eventually became a Sioux chief.

because of its weakened condition, he went to Fort Laramie and demanded that the Army force the Indians responsible to make restitution.

Conquering Bear, whom the federal government had named supreme chief of the Lakota, went to the fort and offered to pay $10 in damages. When the owner claimed the cow was worth $25, the chief departed.

A young lieutenant named John Lawrence Grattan was dispatched to Conquering Bear's camp to obtain payment. With him were 30 troops, a civilian interpreter, and two cannons. The interpreter was reportedly drunk. Exhorting his men with talk of conquering or dying, Grattan and his column departed.

At Conquering Bear's camp, Grattan deployed his troops and positioned the cannons. When the chief refused to pay the amount demanded, an argument ensued. Grattan opened fire, killing several Indians and fatally wounding the chief. Recovering from their initial surprise, the Indians responded, killing Grattan and all his men, except one who survived just long enough to get word back to the fort.

To avenge the death of Grattan and his command, 1,300 troops under Colonel William S. Harney left Fort Leavenworth. They found a band of Indians at Ash Hollow and attacked them, killing 86 and capturing the rest. Shortly after Ash Hollow, a young Lakota named Spotted Tail and several others surrendered to be punished for the Grattan battle. Spotted Tail was released a year later.

Great Basin

The Great Basin is a desert region in the American West that stretches into six different states.

The Great Basin is comprised of parts of California, Oregon, Idaho, Wyoming, Utah, and Nevada, and encompasses 200,000 square miles. The land is noted for rocky desert terrain in some spots, and mountainous regions in other areas. Water from streams either evaporates quickly or drains into one of the area's lakes, or "sinks." These sinks are depressions in the ground that hold water, much like a kitchen sink. The largest of the sinks is the Great Salt Lake in Utah.

Native American tribes living in the Great Basin had few natural resources at their disposal. For food they hunted rabbits, and in harder times ate insects, snakes, and lizards. Vegetation was limited, though some edible roots could be found. The Goisuites, Paiutes, Utes, and Bannocks who made their home in this area used bushes and dry grass to build makeshift shelters. Other tribes looked on these people with disdain, and whites traveling through the area dismissed them as "diggers."

Brigham Young chose the Great Basin as the final settlement for his Mormon followers. Though the land was difficult to plow and fresh water was scarce, Young and his aide, Sam Brannan, found an area near the Great Salt Lake that—with a great deal of hard work—was turned into a farming settlement.

Great Northern Railroad

The Great Northern Railway was created by James Jerome Hill to connect St. Paul, Minnesota, with Winnipeg, Manitoba. Hill, along with Norman W.

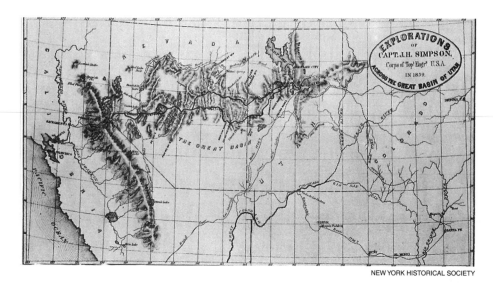

J.H. Simpson's map of the Great Basin region.

Kittson, Donald A. Smith, and George Stephen, bought out the struggling St. Paul and Pacific Railroad from the bankrupt Northern Pacific in 1878. He risked his entire savings in the venture, completing the takeover in 1879. Hill's strategy was to use profits from the railroad to build extensions into the grain-growing areas of the Red River valley between St. Paul and Winnipeg.

In 1889 the railroad was renamed the Great Northern Railway, and construction began on a western extension. The railroad, which reached Puget Sound in 1893, was one of the only two transcontinental railways to avoid bankruptcy in the 1890s depression. The Great Northern became part of the Burlington Northern Railroad when in 1970 it merged with the Burlington, the Northern Pacific, and two other lines.

The Great Northern Railroad makes a stop in St. Paul, Minnesota, before going on to North Dakota.

wild horses, deer, and enormous herds of buffalo. Quail, turkey and tremendous flocks of the now-extinct passenger pigeon were birds native to the area.

The Great Plains were first inhabited by the Plains Indians. Many tribes lived there including the Caddos, Omahas, Osages, Otos, Poncas, Quapaws, Wichitas, Comanches, Kiowas, Arapahos, Crows, Cheyennes and the Plains Apaches. They raised corn and hunted buffalo on these lands for hundreds of years until white settlers began migrating into the region.

As this westward migration grew, pioneers traveled through the Great Plains in greater and greater numbers. Many settled there. The area was excellent for planting wheat and other crops. To western

Great Plains

"Great Plains" was the name given to the high grass regions of the American West.

The Great Plains was an enormous expanse of land west of the Mississippi and east of the Rocky Mountains. Its summers were unbearably hot, its winters bitterly cold. Rainstorms and blizzards could be deadly to those unprepared for nature's onslaught. The abundant animal life included gophers, rabbits, pioneers, this vast new land had seemingly endless possibilities. However, life here was difficult. Without an abundance of wood, houses literally had to be made from the earth. The extremes of climate often forced many would-be inhabitants to either head further West or return to the East. Only the hardiest and those most willing and able to adapt to this beautiful but harsh land remained. "Living in Nebraska is a lot like being hanged," said one farmer of his Great Plains home. "The initial shock is a bit abrupt, but once you hang there for a while you sort of get used to it."

Great Salt Lake

The Great Salt Lake, the largest saltwater lake in the western hemisphere, lies in northwestern Utah between the Great Salt Lake Desert to the west and the mighty peaks of the Wasatch Mountains to the east. The Great Salt Lake is what remains from the glacial Lake Bonneville, which had encompassed approximately 20,000 square miles during the Pleistocene Epoch. Located in the Great Basin, this shallow lake lies approximately 4,200 feet above sea level and is subject to great fluctuations in area, having increased from 1,640 square miles in 1982 to 2,450 square miles in 1986.

The first nonindigenous person known to lay eyes on the Great Salt (in 1823) was James Bridger, a skilled hunter and trapper. Surrounded as it is by the Great Salt Desert, the lake is a welcome sight to anyone traveling in the area. Mountain man Jedediah Smith first beheld the lake in 1826 and described it as a "home in the wilderness." On July 24, 1857, Brigham Young first saw the Great Salt Lake and ended his 1,500-mile journey to settle there.

Although three rivers rush fresh water into it, the Great Salt Lake has no outlet (it was originally supposed that the Buenaventura River connected the Great Salt Lake to the Pacific Ocean, but Jedediah Smith later proved this to be a myth). Therefore, the lake retains all those salts and dissolved minerals that rivers normally carry away to the ocean, making it highly saline. Fifteen kinds of salt, including table salt, are found in and around the Great Salt Lake.

Unfortunately the lake's extreme salinity makes it habitable only for colonial algae and brine shrimp; no other marine life can thrive in its depths. However, blue herons, pelicans, and even a wild buffalo herd inhabit the lake's numerous small islands.

Drawing of the Great Salt Lake, ca. 1853.

LIBRARY OF CONGRESS

The horned toad, native to the Valley of the Great Salt Lake.

LIBRARY OF CONGRESS

Horace Greeley.

Greeley, Horace

1811–1872

Horace Greeley was best known as a political leader and founder and editor of the influential *New York Tribune.* As a politician and newspaperman he was a vigorous advocate of land reform to prevent land monopolization in the Western Territories.

Greeley, a native of New Hampshire, embarked on a career in journalism at age 20, working his way up in positions at several New York newspapers until he was named senior editor of *The New Yorker* in 1834. To further disseminate the issues of Whig Party platforms, in 1841 he founded the daily *New York Tribune* and under his leadership it became a highly regarded political forum. Greeley's editorial columns roared against slavery, promoted abolition, and hailed land reform as the solution to labor's problems. This attention to land reform increased both his readership in the West and western support for free lands. Greeley condemned the rail-

roads' monopolization of western land. He supported limitation of ownership, and freedom for small homesteads from debt foreclosure, and he helped push passage of the Homestead Act of 1862.

Political frustration moved him to join the new Republican Party and later the Liberal Republican Party, which supported his presidential campaign against Ulysses S. Grant in 1872. At a time when Greeley held over 40 percent of the popular vote, the vicious political mud slinging and the death of his wife proved overwhelming and he died before the electoral college met, on November 29, 1872.

Gros Ventre Indians

The Gros Ventres (also known as the Atsinas) were an Algonqian Native American tribe related to the Arapahos and traditionally allied with the Blackfeet. Their name means "big bellies," and considerable confusion has arisen because the Hidatsas were sometimes called the Gros Ventres of the Missouri, and the Crows, because of their relationship to the Hidatsas, were referred to as the Gros Ventres of the Prairies.

The Gros Ventres were originally united as one people with the Arapahos. In the early eighteenth century, however, the tribe divided. The Gros Ventres, whose name for themselves is A'aninin (White

Clay People), moved northwest from Montana into Canada. By the time white fur traders first encountered them around 1750, they were living under the protection of the Blackfeet, toward whom they had once been hostile.

In the late eighteenth and early nineteenth centuries, the Gros Ventres engaged in intermittent warfare with the Canadians. By the first decade of the nineteenth century, conflict with better-armed tribes forced them south to the Missouri River. The next few years found them fighting groups as diverse as the Mexicans in the Cimarron and white trappers in Idaho.

The traditional hunting way of life of the tribe passed with the annihilation of the buffalo. In 1888, they agreed to cede their larger territory for a reservation, and they were settled at Fort Belknap in Montana. In the agreement with the tribe, the federal government stipulated that the reservation could be shared with such other tribes as the President might choose to locate there. As a result, the Assiniboins, a Siouan tribe once the mortal enemy of the Gros Ventre, also share the reservation.

The tribe began its first legal action in 1891 to recover compensation for land taken by an 1855 treaty. Litigation concerning the cessions in 1855 and 1888 continued into the 1980s, almost a century later.

In 1896, over the objections of many tribal members, federal commissioners W. C. Pollock and W. M. Clements negotiated the sale of a 28-square-mile strip of land to mining interests. Threatening that the Gros Ventre and Assiniboin people would starve for two years unless they signed, the commissioners coerced the tribal leaders' agreement. As a result of mining operations, both land and water were contaminated. The land is still being mined today.

The Gros Ventre tribe never numbered more than 3,000 persons; by 1900, it had declined to only 576.

Guadalupe Hidalgo, Treaty of

FEBRUARY 2, 1848

The Treaty of Guadalupe Hidalgo, signed on February 2, 1848, ended the Mexican War (1846–1848). Transferring California and New Mexico to the United States, it established the Rio Grande as the of-

ficial boundary of Texas. The treaty was signed by Nicholas P. Trist for the United States and, together with the Louisiana Purchase, marks one of the most important land acquisitions in U.S. history.

In April 1847, President James Polk appointed Trist as the U.S. peace commissioner for the Mexican War. The draft treaty Polk and his advisers created for Trist to use as a guide demanded, among other things, the cession of Alta and Baja California and New Mexico, the right of passage through the Gulf of Tehuantepec, and the recognition of the Rio Grande as the southwestern border of Texas. In return, they declared that the United States would be willing to pay $15 million and assume up to $3 million in claims against Mexico by U.S. citizens. With this draft in hand, Trist landed in Vera Cruz, Mexico, on May 6, 1847.

In August 1847, President Santa Anna agreed to an armistice. Four men appointed as peace commissioners met on August 27 with Trist, who gave them a copy of the draft treaty. However, the commissioners had intercepted a message from Secretary of State James Buchanan instructing Trist that the cession of Baja California was negotiable. Consequently, the Mexicans steadfastly refused to give it up. Santa Anna rejected the initial peace agreement immediately. While negotiations continued, the armistice ended, and on September 14, 1847, the U.S. Army captured Mexico City. Just as the chaos in the Mexican government seemed to be settling and it looked as though peace talks would resume, Trist received orders from Buchanan to cease diplomatic talks and return to Washington. Trist notified the Mexican government of his recall on November 24, but by December 4 he had decided to disobey his orders. Although outraged by Trist, Polk took no action at this time (though he was later to publicly scorn his emissary for what he felt had been gross insubordination). Meanwhile Trist continued to negotiate. Political leadership in Mexico had been in turmoil, and final negotiations did not begin until January 2, 1848, when Peña y Peña took power as president. The treaty was signed one month later in the Villa de Guadalupe Hidalgo, a shrine to the patron saint of Mexico.

As a result of the terms of the final treaty, the United States took Alta California and New Mexico, and the Mexican government recognized the Rio Grande as the southern border of Texas. In return the United States agreed to pay Mexico $15 million and assume the claims of American citizens against

Mexico. In addition, U.S. citizenship was offered to any Mexican residing in the newly acquired area. Although signed, the treaty still required ratification. After some deliberation Polk sent the document to the Senate, which (reluctantly) ratified it on March 10, 1848. The Mexican boundary was later adjusted by the Gadsden Purchase in 1853. And Nicholas Trist, for all his efforts, was publicly scorned by Polk.

Gunfighters

These were law officers and desperadoes (and some who were a bit of both) known for their skill with firearms.

The gunfighter was both hero and villain in the making of the West. The age of the gunfighter arose during the 1850s, as expansion continued throughout the Western territories. Varying social problems sprang up, and official authorities were few and far between. Wars between whites and Indians, ranchers and farmers, and many others were constantly erupting. Moreover, in something unofficially known as "the Code of the West," criminal justice was often handled on the spot. For any number of offenses, ranging from cattle rustling to bank robbery to cheating at cards, opponents would face off to settle discord. Generally speaking, the better gunfighter was the winner of any disagreement.

Many of these gunfighters became well known as outlaws. They included such infamous names as William Bonney (Billy The Kid), Jesse and Frank James, Cole Younger, and Belle Starr. By some accounts these people were simply cold-blooded killers; others described the outlaw gunfighters as champions of the poor and weak, in the mould of Robin Hood. As banks and railroads often engaged in unfair business practices and imposed high prices on Western settlers, gunfighters who robbed these institutions often became public heroes. For a time, Jesse James capitalized on this notoriety by sending letters to various newspapers, including the *Kansas City Times*. In one note James wrote ". . . Detectives are a brave lot of boys . . . charge houses, break down doors and make the grey hairs stand up on the heads of unarmed victims."

Other gunfighters were noted law officials. They included such well-known names as Bat Masterson,

Wyatt Earp, Wild Bill Hickock, and Doc Holliday. These arbitrators of justice managed to keep the peace when outlaw gunfighters became too unruly. Earp and Holliday were involved in one of the most famous of all the Western incidents, the gunfight at the O.K. Corral, in Tombstone, Arizona.

A whole cultural industry sprang up around the legends of gunfighters. In the 1870s, pulp fiction writers began turning out highly fictionalized accounts of their exploits. These inexpensive stories—popularly referred to as Dime Novels—set down the mythology of gunfighters, building on stories that were popularly told. Many of these quickly written fictions became basis for enduring American legends. With the rise of the film industry of the twentieth century, gunfighters became a popular subject for many Hollywood movie makers as well. Accounts of Jesse James and Wyatt Earp were filmed many times over. Many of these Westerns—both cheaply-made "B" pictures, as well as classics like *Gunfight at the O.K. Corral*—furthered the romantic image of the Western gunfighter in American popular culture.

Gutiérrez-Magee Expedition

1812–1813

During the 1810–11 revolution in Mexico, José Bernardo Maximiliano Gutiérrez de Lara was dispatched by the rebels to Washington to seek U.S. assistance for the insurrection against Spain. When the rebellion ended in failure, Gutiérrez made his way to Natchitoches on the Louisiana-Texas border and there, in September 1811, met Augustus William Magee, a former U.S. Army lieutenant under General James Wilkinson's command in Louisiana.

The two mapped out a plan to invade and conquer Spanish-controlled Texas with Gutiérrez as nominal commander of the expedition and Magee as colonel. Since Louisiana—especially New Orleans—was a hotbed of restless adventurers, the conspirators quickly recruited an "army," a ragtag force of under 100 (some sources say 300) Americans, Louisiana Frenchmen, rebel Mexicans, Texas Indians, and other freebooters.

In August 1812, this band crossed the Sabine River and captured the Texas town of Nacogdoches without resistance. The force now grew to perhaps 800 men and marched south to La Bahía, capturing it and its stores and ammunition. But at La Bahía, the Gutiérrez-Magee army was besieged for four months by a force of 1,400 men under Royalist Governor Manuel María de Salcedo. During one of Salcedo's attacks on the town, Magee died under mysterious circumstances (he may have committed suicide). The siege ended in February 1813 and Salcedo's force was defeated in March at Rosillo, near San Antonio de Béxar.

Béxar soon fell to the invaders but thereafter the expedition began disintegrating. Many of the volunteers deserted after Gutiérrez ordered the execution of Salcedo and 15 other captives. Although new recruits came forward, swelling the ranks to 3,000 men at its peak, Gutiérrez lost control of his army. He was courtmartialed in July 1813 for ordering the executions, and resigned as commander. He was replaced by José Alvarez de Toledo.

Meantime, a strong Royalist army of 2,000 men under General Joaquín de Arredondo crossed the Rio Grande and led Alvarez into a trap on the Medina River, 15 miles from Béxar, on August 18. More than a thousand of Alvarez's force were killed (including 112 who were executed after the fight); Spanish losses were 55 dead and 178 wounded.

Gutiérrez, who had left Béxar for New Orleans before the battle, returned to Mexico after its independence, served as governor of Tamaulipas and in other political and military posts, and died in Santiago, Nuevo Leon, in 1841.

H

Haish, Jacob

1827–1927

Jacob Haish was an inventor and manufacturer, best known for devising and patenting the "s" barbed wire.

Haish (b. Baden, Germany, on March 9, 1827) and his family immigrated to the United States when he was ten years old, ultimately settling in De Kalb County, Illinois. As a young man, after building a successful business as a contractor and lumber dealer in De Kalb, Haish began to experiment with barbed wire. However, when he tried to patent the result in 1873, he discovered that his fellow towns-man Joseph H. Glidden had applied for a similar patent only two months earlier. Although his challenge to Glidden's patent was unsuccessful, Haish persisted with his experiments until he developed the "s" barbed wire, which he patented on August 31, 1875.

Haish's "s" became the best-selling barbed wire in the West. Over the years, Haish continued to manufacture barbed wire and other products, including plain wire, nails, staples, and woven-wire fencing. He died on February 19, 1927, a few weeks before his 100th birthday.

Hardin, John Wesley

1853–1895

Gunman and killer of at least 27, perhaps as many as 40, men, Hardin was born in Bonham, Texas, the son of a Methodist preacher who gave his son the name of Methodism's founder. He grew up in the turmoil of Reconstruction and his first killings, an ex-slave in 1868 and perhaps five others (including two former Union soldiers) by 1871, were an outgrowth of Hardin's Confederate sympathies. Subsequent killings seem to have been rooted in a volatile temper and a love for alcohol and gambling.

By his own account, he killed eight men while working as a cowboy driving a herd up the Chisholm Trail to Abilene, Kansas, in 1871. He was a participant in the Sutton-Taylor Feud (which ran from 1867 to 1877) in central Texas, then again joined a cattle drive to Abilene. In May 1874 he killed, probably in self-defense, deputy sheriff Charles Webb in the town of Comanche, Texas. Now on the run from the law, Hardin fled to Alabama, then to Florida. He was captured by Texas Rangers in Pensacola and returned to Comanche, where he was tried for Webb's murder. In September 1878 he was sentenced to 25 years in prison at Huntsville, Texas.

In prison, between escape attempts, Hardin educated himself in theology, science, literature, and law and was granted a pardon in 1894. The next year he went to El Paso, Texas, to practice law but quickly fell back into his lifelong habits of drinking and gambling. On August 19, standing at the bar of

John Wesley Hardin.

the Seminole warrior Chakaika, who had previously attacked and beaten him in July 1839. In December 1840, Harney's unit hunted Chakaika down and killed him. Harney's character is revealed in two incidents: When his force became lost in the tangled swamps, Harney ordered some local Indian women to show him the way, threatening to hang their children if they refused. Second, in the actual attack on Chakaika, Harney dressed and painted his men as Indians, in defiance of orders.

For his success in Florida, Harney was made a colonel and assigned to the command of General Winfield Scott. As the army's ranking cavalry officer, he clashed with Scott repeatedly. During the Mexican War, Scott had him court-martialed for resuming his command after he had had him relieved. Harney apologized and, after lobbying by his supporters in Washington, was reinstated. His subsequent performance in the Mexican War was nothing less than brilliant, particularly at the Battle of Cerro Gordo in 1847.

After the Grattan Massacre of 1854, Harney, now a brigadier general, was recalled from a European vacation to deal with the Sioux. In the summer of 1855, he led a combined force of 700 infantry, cavalry, and artillery out of Fort Leavenworth. On September 3, he surrounded the Brulé Sioux village of Chief Little Thunder. Harney refused Little Thunder's offer of surrender, attacked the village, and killed more than 100 men, women, and children.

With Harney's force now moving into Sioux hunting grounds on the way to Fort Pierre, the Sioux sent several large delegations, who pleaded for peace. At a large council, both sides reaffirmed the Fort Laramie Treaty of 1851, and the Sioux agreed to surrender those responsible for the Grattan incident.

Harney was next assigned to Utah, where he was sent to deal with the Mormons. His solution to friction between Mormons and others was to hang Brigham Young and other Mormon leaders. However, before he could put that simple strategy into practice, he was reassigned to Oregon. In Oregon, his behavior was the same: He seized San Juan Island, sparking a border dispute with the British and forcing Washington to order his recall.

He served as commander of the Department of the West until 1861. Suspected of being a Southern sympathizer (he had allowed General Sterling Price of the pro-slavery Missouri militia a free hand), he was given no command and was retired in 1863. In

the Acme Saloon, Hardin was shot in the back of the head by El Paso constable John Selman, a man who sought fame by killing the West's most feared gunman.

Harney, William S.

1800–1889

Harney was a U.S. Army general; he began his military career in 1818 as second lieutenant and rose quickly in rank. He served in the Black Hawk War and was involved in the Battle of Bad Axe. He first achieved prominence for his role in the Second Seminole War. In his most noteworthy encounter of that campaign, he led a punitive expedition against

1867, he was asked to serve on a peace commission that tried unsuccessfully to negotiate a new treaty with the Sioux. He then retired to Florida, where he died at the age of 88.

Harney, an imposing 6 foot 3 inches, was often a bully, insubordinate, and a vicious killer. However, he could also be a man of great vision; he proposed the establishment of a tribal police force and government under U.S. supervision as early as 1851.

Harte, Bret

1836–1902

Short-story writer Francis Bret Harte is best remembered for his tales of mining camp life during the California Gold Rush.

Harte was born in Albany, New York, in 1836, the son of a schoolteacher. Plagued by financial difficulties, the family was forced to relocate a number of times. Harte was only nine years old at the time of his father's death, and eight years later he followed his mother when she moved to California. Although not a gold-seeker himself, Harte spent several years working at odd jobs around mining camps. These experiences inspired much of his later fiction.

In 1860, Harte settled in San Francisco and became a typesetter for *The Golden Era*. He wrote when he could and published two collections of poems, *Outcroppings* (1865) and *The Lost Galleon and Other Tales* (1867). His well-received collection of parodies, *Condensed Novels and Other Papers* (1867), contains "Muck-a-Muck," a popular satire of James Fenimore Cooper's *Leatherstocking Tales*. After Harte was appointed editor of the *Overland Monthly*, his first contribution, "The Luck of Roaring Camp," spread his name nationwide. His most popular tales of life in the Forty-niner mining camps were collected as *The Luck of Roaring Camp and Other Stories* (1870).

His popularity earned him a $10,000 contract with the *Atlantic Monthly* in the East, but the contract was not renewed when his contributions proved disappointing. Harte published more mining stories in *Tales of the Argonauts* (1875) and *Ah Sin* (1877), a collaboration with Mark Twain. As his popularity dwindled, Harte took a government position in Europe in 1898. While continuing to write, he

Francis Bret Harte.

never regained the stature he had held during the 1870s. Harte died in London in 1902.

Hastings, Lanford W.

CA. 1818–CA. 1868

Lanford Hastings was an expansionist, a wagon-train leader, and a lawyer. His life and achievements are shrouded in mystery: He gave two different dates for his birth, which apparently took place in Knox City, Ohio. In 1842 he led the first planned overland wagon migration of any size to Oregon. He is credited with surveying the site of Oregon City while there. He went on to California, which he left in the fall of 1843, traveling to New Orleans and Missouri by way of Mexico City. There is no evidence supporting a popular story that he went to Texas to confer with Sam Houston regarding independence for California. In 1845, he wrote and published one of the first guidebooks to the region.

His next project would have far-reaching and disastrous consequences. Trying to divert Oregon-bound wagon trains to California, he took a party east from Oregon as far as Fort Bridger to establish a trail down Weber Canyon and through the Utah-Nevada desert and the Sierra Nevada. Many parties taking this route met with terrible obstacles and often ran out of water. The Donner party was trying to follow the cutoff that bears Hastings' name.

After serving as a captain in the California Battalion in 1846, Hastings practiced law in Arizona. A supporter of the Confederacy, he concocted a wild scheme to seize southern California, Arizona, and New Mexico for the South. After the Civil War he retreated to Brazil, where he hoped to start a colony of former Confederates. He even published a guidebook to the Amazon in 1867. He died shortly thereafter.

Hayden, Ferdinand V.

1829–1887

Ferdinand Hayden was a geologist whose work helped promote the creation of Yellowstone National Park. As head of the U.S. Geographical and Geological Survey of the Territories, Hayden surveyed the land from the Grand Tetons to the southwestern cliff dwellings. His boundless energy earned him the name "Man-Who-Picks-Up-Stones-Running" from the Sioux, who watched him racing around with his tools.

Ferdinand Vandiveer Hayden was born on September 7, 1829, in Westfield, Massachusetts, and raised near Rochester, New York. Bright and ambitious, Hayden taught school at age 16. He graduated from Oberlin College and later Albany Medical School, receiving his M.D. in 1853. A fossil-collecting visit to Dakota's White River Badlands changed the course of his career and made his life's ambition to be a geologist.

Hayden joined several expeditions in Kansas, Nebraska, and the Dakotas. While a member of Captain William F. Raynolds's survey party, which tried unsuccessfully to reach the upper Yellowstone region, Hayden published numerous reports in scientific publications.

Hayden and his team sit down to lunch in a Wyoming meadow.

During the Civil War, Hayden served as a surgeon and in 1865 joined the faculty of the University of Pennsylvania as a professor of geology and mineralogy. For two summers the distinguished professor accompanied various government-sponsored expeditions to the West; by the third summer's expedition, a geological survey of Nebraska, he was traveling as geologist in charge. His energy and excellence in the field led him subsequently to help organize and direct the Geological and Geographical Survey of the Territories, and he resigned from the university in 1872 to undertake this work full-time.

Perhaps best-known among his accomplishments was his work in the Yellowstone region. After gaining the support of Congress, Hayden was awarded $40,000 to head the first scientific expedition into Yellowstone. His entourage of 21 men, including photographer William Henry Jackson and landscape artist Thomas Moran, began the trek in 1871; for months, the team scrambled around Mammoth Hot Springs, Tower Falls, and the Grand Canyon of the Yellowstone, where the river plunges 308 feet over the Lower Falls, taking samples, measurements, and photographs whenever possible. When the expedition disbanded on October 1, 1871, Hayden headed to Washington, D.C., with his report. The photographs in particular moved Congress to create Yellowstone National Park, and President Grant signed the bill on March 1, 1872.

In 1872 Hayden launched the first scientific exploration of the Teton Range, encountered initially on the Raynolds expedition years earlier. Jackson was also there, taking the first photographs of the magnificent range. During later explorations into Colorado, Hayden discovered the cliff dwellings at Mesa Verde and the Mount of the Holy Cross. In 1879 his survey was merged with the U.S. Geological Survey, and it was under these auspices that the eminent scientist continued his work in the Rocky Mountain region until his retirement on New Year's Eve 1886. Hayden died on December 22, 1887.

INTERNATIONAL MUSEUM OF PHOTOGRAPHY

Hayden conducting a survey.

Haywood, William Dudley ("Big Bill")

1869–1928

A labor leader who devoted his career to resisting the capitalist structure, Haywood was a prominent figure in the Western Federation of Miners (WFM) and one of the founding fathers of the Industrial Workers of the World (IWW). Feared by the moneyed class as a militant radical, for the working class Haywood was a hero. His life embodied the struggle against what he saw as a brutal capitalist system.

Haywood, born in Salt Lake City, Utah, on February 4, 1869, was 15 when he took his first job at a mine in Humbolt County, Nevada, where he worked for three years. As a youth he also worked as a cowboy and homesteader in Utah and Idaho. In 1896 he joined the WFM in Silver City, Idaho, and two years later was selected as the local delegate. As he moved up through WFM ranks, he became known as a militant labor unionist.

In 1905, Harry Orchard assassinated former Idaho governor Frank Steunenberg. Haywood and the WFM were suspected of masterminding the assassination, for which Haywood was tried in 1906. The

William Dudley Haywood.

This hospital in Cottage Grove, Oregon, was founded by Doctors Katherine and Henry Schleef.

proceedings gained the attention of the nation, pitting famous defense attorney Clarence Darrow against future senator William Borah. To the public the trial represented the struggle between the rising labor movement and the beleaguered capitalists of the West. Haywood's acquittal was viewed as a victory for radical union forces.

Haywood was among the founding fathers of the IWW at Chicago in 1905. When he left the WFM in 1908, his association with the IWW strengthened. In 1918 federal agents arrested Haywood and several other IWW officials on charges of sedition. The group was charged and convicted, but in 1921, while free on bail, Haywood escaped to Soviet Russia. He died in Moscow on May 18, 1928.

Health and Medicine in the Old West

By modern standards, medical practices in the West were primitive. There was a lack of clean health facilities, qualified doctors, or proper medicine. Still, the fight against illnesses and injuries was effectively fought in a variety of ways.

On the range, cowboys often had to withstand injury through sheer determination. Gunpowder was liberally applied as a cure-all on cuts and other wounds. Cuts that required stitches were generally sewn up with only a stiff drink for anesthetic. As in the Civil War, amputations were done by saw and often resulted in gangrene and/or death.

Pioneers on the trail westward faced a host of diseases. Epidemics were common. Typical diseases that swept through wagon trains and farming lands included cholera, dysentery, malaria, measles, mumps, scarlet fever, smallpox, and typhoid. Other problems faced were snake and other animal bites, poison ivy, injuries resulting from accidents, and toothaches.

Diaries of pioneers heading West routinely chronicle the never-ending battle against illness and accidents, and the variety of remedies used to fight these maladies. Some popular home remedies included quinine for use against malaria, citric acid to fight the constant threat of scurvy, and opium and whiskey as painkillers. Castor oil was routinely used to combat dysentery and diarrhea (also known as "the bloody flux").

Cholera, an illness which causes diarrhea, cramps, and vomiting, took a heavy toll. This highly infectious disease was generally caused by drinking contaminated water, and could kill a victim within a matter of hours. Those who died of cholera were usually buried quickly and their personal effects—such as clothing and bedding—were burned. Though many remedies were tried, including laudanum (an

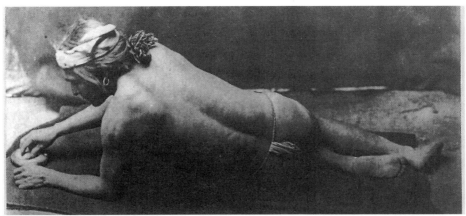

A Zuni medicine man mixes together herbs.

opium-based treatment) and camphor, these cures provided little relief.

Native American tribes were hit hard by the diseases white settlers carried with them to the West. Cholera and smallpox devastated many tribes, as epidemics swept through the lands. However, tribes and settlers in the Black Hills of South Dakota were less affected by the bitter spread of cholera, due in large part to the abundance of fresh drinking water available in the mountainous region.

As the fear of disease and illness spread, a number of bogus medical practitioners began traveling throughout the West. They hawked useless medicines, praised as "cure-alls" for any number of minor aches and major illnesses. Often these spurious remedies were nothing more than water, or alcohol. However, the phony physicians running these medicine shows often raked in a good deal of money from buyers desperate for relief from pain and illness.

Hickok, James Butler ("Wild Bill")

1837–1876

In 1867 "Wild Bill" Hickok—whose exploits were by then the subject of great exaggeration in dime novels—was interviewed by the adventurous Henry M. Stanley (the same Stanley who would, in 1871, "find" Dr. Livingstone in Africa). According to Stan-ley he asked: "I say, Bill, or Mr. Hickok, how many white men have you killed, to your certain knowledge?" Hickok responded: "I would be willing to take my oath on the Bible tomorrow that I have killed over a hundred."

Stanley may have concocted, or at least doctored, Hickok's answer, or Hickok may have said what Stanley claimed, but the story illustrates the difficulty of pinning down facts about the exploits of this

James Butler ("Wild Bill") Hickok.

legendary lawman-gambler, one of the most compelling figures of the Old West whose most careful biographer has been able to trace to him only seven killings.

Hickok was born on a farm in Homer (later Troy Grove), Illinois, and left home in 1856 for the Kansas frontier, where he worked as a teamster, stagecoach driver, and, beginning in 1858 in Monticello, Kansas, as a sometime lawman. In the Civil War years, when his exploits came to public notice, he was mauled by a bear in Raton Pass during a trip over the Santa Fe Trail (he killed the animal). In 1861 he killed his first recorded human victim, one David McCanles, at the Rock Creek stagecoach station in Nebraska in a fight over a mistress the two men shared. Soon after this, a *Harper's Weekly* article about him began the "Wild Bill" legend.

He served as a civilian scout and wagonmaster in the Civil War and participated in the bloody Battle at Pea Ridge, Arkansas, in March 1862. In July 1865 he was again involved in a dispute over a woman, this time resulting in a gun battle in Springfield, Missouri, in which he killed a man named Dave Tutt. After the war, Hickok served as scout for Generals Philip Sheridan and Winfield Scott Hancock, and as a guide for hunting parties. In 1866, while serving as deputy U.S. marshal at Fort Riley, Kansas, he met Lieutenant Colonel George A. Custer and for a time scouted for Custer. Not much later, in 1867, the first dime novel adventures of Hickok appeared.

In 1868 he became sheriff of Ellis County, Kansas, during which tenure he killed two drunken cavalry soldiers and a local troublemaker in saloon confrontations. In 1871 he became city marshal of Abilene, Kansas, during the town's last year as a cattletown and railhead. On October 5, 1871, Hickok killed Texan Phil Coe, who with Ben Thompson had opened the Bull's Head Saloon and decorated the establishment with an obscene sign Abilene city fathers ordered removed. In the gunfight Hickok also accidentally shot and killed his deputy, Mike Williams, and was subsequently dismissed as marshal. (Hickok paid for Williams's funeral, and it is said that after this incident he never fired a shot at another man.)

After Abilene and for the next five years Hickok roamed the West, his reputation as a gunman growing despite his inactivity and failing eyesight. He spent one season, 1873, with Buffalo Bill in a dramatic production called *The Scouts of the Plains*, and in 1876 he married Agnes Lake, a circus owner, in Cheyenne, Wyoming. (In 1870, Hickok is said to have married prostitute Martha Jane Canary, known as "Calamity Jane." There is no evidence of this, nor that the two cohabitated, although she claimed him as one of her 12 husbands.)

At Deadwood, Dakota Territory, on the afternoon of August 2, 1876, Hickok was playing poker at the No. 10 Saloon and had just been dealt a queen and two pairs—aces and eights—when a drifter named Jack McCall, armed with a .45 Colt revolver, walked up behind the former lawman and fired a shot into Hickok's head. The bullet emerged from his right cheekbone and wounded another player at the table, Frank Massie, a Missouri riverboat pilot. McCall, who had lost $110 in poker to Hickok the previous day, was tried and hanged for the murder on March 1, 1877, in Yankton, Dakota Territory.

Hickok was buried at Ingleside, near Deadwood; his body was removed to Deadwood's Mt. Moriah Cemetery in 1879. In 1903, acceding to what was said to be her last wish, "Calamity Jane" Canary was buried next to Hickok.

Hickok was a long-nosed but handsome man with flowing, ringleted blond hair. His admirers said he was mild-mannered and courteous, and, like Wyatt Earp, a staunch and loyal friend and a bitter and deadly enemy.

Hidatsa

See Gros Ventres

Hill, James Jerome

1838–1916

James Hill was a railroad magnate who, in 1879 with three other investors, acquired the bankrupt St. Paul & Pacific Railroad and, from it, built the Great Northern Railway. Under his supervision, construction of the railway was completed to Winnipeg and then westward to Puget Sound.

Hill was born on September 16, 1838, on a small farm near Rockwood, Ontario. As a youth he was an avid student despite limited educational opportuni-

James Hill, left, and his son Louis.

ties. Although he wanted to become a doctor, Hill's formal education ended at his father's death in 1852, and he spent two years as a store clerk in Rockwood and nearby Guelph. At 17 he left Canada and traveled east to New York. After sampling Philadelphia, Baltimore, Charleston, Savannah, and Pittsburgh, he "took a notion to go and see St. Paul," arriving in Minnesota on July 21, 1865. There he worked for a time on Mississippi River steamboats and eventually settled down as a freight agent for the Northwest Packet Company.

In St. Paul Hill became involved in many successful ventures, including general merchandising and dealing in coal. In partnership with Norman W. Kittson, he operated a steamboat service down the Red River to Winnipeg. Hill and Kittson later joined Donald A. Smith and George Stephen and bought out the struggling St. Paul & Pacific Railroad with the aim of completing the route between St. Paul and Winnipeg. Hill risked his entire savings to buy the railroad's bonds from the Dutch holders, and in 1879 the takeover was complete. By 1893 the railroad, now called the Great Northern Railway, had reached Puget Sound and was one of only two transcontinental railways to avoid bankruptcy during the depression of the 1890s.

Hill retired from the railroad in 1912 and within three months had purchased two banks in St. Paul. In his later years he spoke widely about farming and agricultural diversity in the Northwest. He died in Minnesota on May 29, 1916.

Hogan

See Navajo Indians and Indian Dwellings

Hohokam Culture

An early Native American civilization of the American Southwest, the Hohokams are probably the ancestors of the modern Tohono O'odham (Papago) and Pima tribes. Their name derives from *Huhugam O'odham* in the modern Pima language, meaning "the people who vanished."

The Hohokams appeared about 2,000 years ago, occupying an area across southern Arizona into Mexico. They hunted a variety of game, including deer, bighorn sheep, bear, and antelope. They were also farmers; their principal crop was corn, and they cultivated pumpkins as well. They grew these crops

Among the oldest artifacts found in North America, these Hohokam heads are thought to have been made in the first century C.E.

Decorated vessel, typical of early Hohokam artwork. This example was found in southern Arizona.

by means of an elaborate system of shallow irrigation canals which carried water from the Gila and Salt River systems. On major streams in the system, they built dams and redirected the flow into the canals, which were as much as 30 feet wide. By C.E. 900–1000, the canals were often 10 to 16 miles long.

The Hohokams possessed a highly developed culture. They produced beautiful jewelry and pottery. They were among the first to use acid etching techniques to create designs on marine shells. They also borrowed ideas from Mexican civilizations. They built pyramids and ball courts, on which they used rubber balls imported from Central America. They appear to have known astronomy and used it to calculate planting dates. They lived in pit-house villages near their cultivated fields.

At some point (the exact date is unknown), an influx of Indians from the outside occurred. The new arrivals settled peacefully among the Hohokams and became a part of their culture. With their help, Hohokam canals grew even larger. Immense houses of adobe, from one to many stories high, were constructed and surrounded by adobe walls. The remains of one still exist at Casa Grande, near present-day Phoenix. The newcomers also appear to have brought a new variety of corn with them.

Sometime around 1400, the urbanized centers of the Hohokams and their distinctive civilization disintegrated. It is generally assumed that the Hohokams became the Papago and Pima peoples. But some of their supposed descendants told early Euro-

pean explorers that, although they held the abandoned villages sacred, they had no connection with the vanished people. Some Pimas tell legends that relate how their ancestors drove the Hohokams from their cities. Still others, agreeing with the more mainstream scientific view, contend that they are, in fact, descended from the Hohokams.

Holladay, Ben

1819–1887

Ben Holladay was a transportation entrepreneur known for his overland freight and stagecoach lines. Holladay's interest in transportation began with freighting during the Mexican War and soon turned to stagecoaching with the Overland Stage Line. Through transporting mail and passengers, he gradually built an empire—the Holladay Overland Mail

Ben Holladay.

and Express Company, which he ultimately sold (in 1866) to Wells, Fargo and Company.

Holladay was born in Carlisle County, Kentucky, in 1819. When he was 16, his family moved to western Missouri, where Holladay experimented with a variety of occupations, including tavernkeeper, hotel keeper, general store proprietor, druggist, and postmaster. In 1846, during the Mexican War, he moved supplies for Stephen W. Kearney's Army of the West. Recognizing an opportunity, Holladay purchased surplus goods from the government after the war and traveled with 50 wagonloads to Salt Lake City. Within a few days all the merchandise had been sold at a large profit.

Holladay's business boomed, and in 1858 he developed a relationship with freight operators Russell, Majors, and Waddell, assisting them financially with the establishment of the Pony Express two years later. When Russell, Majors, and Waddell went bankrupt in 1863, Holladay acquired control of its stage line operations and established the Overland Stage Line, which operated the eastern section of the trans-Missouri stage mail and connected with Holladay's other stage lines in Salt Lake City. In addition to this lucrative venture, he also acquired many other mail contracts and ran stagecoach lines in Nebraska, Colorado, Idaho, Montana, Oregon, and Washington.

In 1866 Holladay sold his overland stage business to Wells, Fargo and Company, and invested in the Northern Pacific Transportation Company. He retired from business in 1876 and died in Portland, Oregon, in 1887.

Holliday, John Henry ("Doc")

1851–1887

A gambler and gunman, "Doc" Holliday was a loyal friend to Wyatt Earp and few others. Holliday, whose father became a major in the Confederate Army, was born in Griffin, Georgia, in a family of moderate means and raised in the genteel Southern tradition. The Hollidays moved to Valdosta when John was 11. He left home in about 1867, listing his occupation as "student" in 1870 when he returned to visit his parents.

John Henry "Doc" Holliday.

He appears to have graduated from a dental college in either Pennsylvania or Maryland in about 1872 and practiced dentistry briefly in Atlanta and in Griffin. In the early 1870s he developed the chronic cough and symptoms of pulmonary tuberculosis, the disease that claimed his mother. He headed West in 1873, seeking a drier climate.

In Dallas, Texas, he practiced dentistry and there was drawn into the gambling profession. He was a particularly good poker and faro player. In 1875 he was arrested for the first time after being involved in a shooting incident, and thereafter drifted to Jacksboro, Texas (where he is said to have been involved in a gunfight with three soldiers, one of whom died), Dodge City (where he probably met Wyatt Earp for the first time and also "Big Nose" Kate Elder, whom he subsequently married in St. Louis), Fort Griffin, Pueblo, Denver, Cheyenne, and Deadwood, gambling and drinking heavily as his disease advanced.

In 1879 Holliday traveled to Trinidad, then Leadville, Colorado, then south to Las Vegas, New Mexico, where he became a partner in a saloon and where, on July 19, he killed a man named Mike Gordon, who had tried to wreck the establishment. That year he also came under suspicion of robbing a Santa Fe–Las Vegas stagecoach and for a train robbery in the Las Vegas vicinity that October. The following year Holliday killed a bartender, one Charley White, in Las Vegas in an argument and soon after accompanied or followed Wyatt Earp to Tombstone, Arizona Territory. (The friendship between the two has never really been explained, but Earp said that Doc had saved his life in Dodge City by coming to his rescue in a fight with some cowboys.)

In Tombstone, where he was a liability to his friend Earp, who served as a deputy marshal, Holliday seems to have practiced his professions of dentistry and gambling, and perhaps his sideline of stagecoach robbing as well. He was the principal suspect in the March 15, 1881, stage robbery in which drivers Budd Philpot and Peter Roerig were killed and was arrested for the crime after Kate Holliday signed a statement against him. Kate and Doc separated soon after, and the following April Holliday shot and wounded saloon owner Milt Joyce after Joyce openly accused Holliday of the stagecoach killings.

He was free on bail when the famous O.K. Corral gunfight of October 26, 1881, occurred. Armed with a shotgun and sidearm, Doc played a prominent role in the fight, killing Tom McLaury. In March 1882 he assisted the Earps in gunning down Frank Stillwell at a train station in Tucson and Florentino Cruz in Tombstone, both of whom were suspected of having had a hand in the murder of Morgan Earp.

Holliday accompanied the Earps from Tombstone to Colorado and was arrested in Denver on trumped-up charges while authorities were drawing up papers to have him extradited for the Stillwell-Cruz killings. Bat Masterson intervened with the governor of Colorado, probably at Wyatt Earp's request, and Holliday was released. In August 1884, in Leadville, Colorado, Holliday shot bartender Billy Allen, from whom he had borrowed $5, in the arm. He was arrested, tried, and acquitted of the charge. In 1887, Holliday went to Glenwood Springs, Colorado, for treatment of his disease. He died there on November 8 at the age of 36.

From most accounts, Holliday was a quarrelsome and mean drunk and an unrepentant killer whose single close friend was Wyatt Earp. In film versions of the O.K. Corral gunfight he has been depicted, probably correctly, as having no fear and indeed welcoming the chance to die violently rather than from the ravages of his disease.

Homestead Act

1862

Passed by Congress in 1862, the Homestead Act provided a virtually free quarter-section (160 acres)

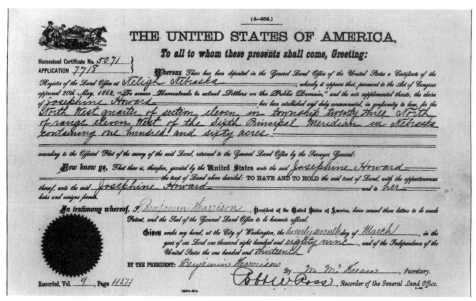

Women, as well as men, took advantage of the Homestead Act. Josephine Howard earned this deed after five years of hard work.

of federal land in the West to any citizen or intended citizen over the age of 21 who agreed to settle the land, beginning January 1 of the following year. For a nominal fee, title would be given after the settler had lived on the land for five years.

The bill was the result of a long struggle dating back to shortly after the American Revolution, over free grants of land. At the conclusion of the War of Independence, the newly formed U.S. government stopped making free grants to settlers and established a high price for western lands. Western pioneers lobbied hard for the return of free land grants or at least a reduction in prices. They also wanted the right of "preemption," under which they could work the land for a time before purchasing it. Their position was supported by the new labor movement and the newly formed Republican party.

By 1854, the last two measures had been granted. Members of Congress from the South, however, were reluctant to support free land grants, fearing that a giveaway would accelerate the development of non-slave states in the West. When a weak homestead bill was passed in 1860, President Buchanan vetoed it.

With the coming of secession and the Civil War, the Republicans had a clear majority in Congress, and the Homestead Act, sponsored by Pennsylvania Republican Galusha A. Grow, was passed and signed into law by President Lincoln. Under its provisions, there was no limit on the amount of land that could be sold to individuals. However, a large area—approximately eight times the size of Kansas—was already committed by grants to railroads and the states, allotment of Indian lands, and the continued sale of public land to speculators.

The underlying theory of the homestead movement was that the availability of nearly free land in the West would drain off a surplus of workers in the eastern urban centers, a surplus that left workers at the mercy of factory owners (hence the labor movement's support). For westerners, the appeal of the legislation was the potential for the creation of an agrarian utopia of free farmers working the land and building the nation.

After the act was signed into law, the availability of homesteads was advertised by the land-grant railroads, the states, and real estate interests. Even more compelling were the letters that immigrants wrote to their families back home. Between 1863 and 1890, nearly one million people filed homestead applications.

Hopi Indians

The Hopis are an Uzo-Aztecan tribe of Native Americans, living on three mesas in northeastern Arizona. The ridges are known as First Mesa, Second Mesa, and Third Mesa. Traditionally they have lived in pueblo-type dwellings and are considered one of the Pueblo tribes.

Historians generally believe that the Hopis traveled across the Bering Strait during the last Ice Age and migrated from the California desert to the area of their present home between A.D. 500–700, though some estimates place their arrival much earlier (ca. C.E. 300). The Hopis sometimes speak of a migration as well, but their account relates a crossing to the "New World" by boat rather than on foot. More often, however, they speak of emerging into this world from under the earth. At any rate, dating of a beam in one home at Oraibi, the principal Hopi village, reveals that it was cut around 1350. Evidence shows the village probably was settled

SMITHSONIAN INSTITUTION

A Hopi man and his unmarried daughter, in traditional "squash blossom" hairdo, pose in Walpi, Arizona.

A young Hopi woman, ca. 1879.

sometime between 900 and 1150, making it one of the oldest continuously inhabited sites in North America.

The Hopis came under Spanish domination along with the other Pueblo peoples. Because of their remoteness from Santa Fe, their villages became a haven for those fleeing the Spaniards throughout the seventeenth century. Firmly opposed to the Spaniards, they successfully kept missionaries out of their territory and went so far as to destroy one Hopi village that favored the foreigners' return.

Between 1858 and 1873, Mormon missionaries made annual trips to the Hopi region. They founded Tuba City near the Hopi village of Moenkopi, naming it in honor of Teuvi, one of their few Hopi converts. When the Navajos returned to the area in 1868, the sedentary, farming Hopis were subjected to raids by their seminomadic neighbors. The return also marked the beginning of land disputes with the Navajos that continue to the present day. In 1882,

the Hopis were given 2.5 million acres by order of President Chester Arthur. Although the land encompassed most of the three mesas, it was still only a small piece of the territory they had previously held. During this period, a split among the Hopis, dividing them into "friendlies" and "hostiles," began to develop.

In 1887, the government opened a school about 30 miles from Oraibi, and Hopi children were forcibly taken away to the new institution. In 1890, federal troops arrived at Oraibi to demand students. Shortly thereafter, surveyors began to plot the Hopi reservation for allotment according to the provi-

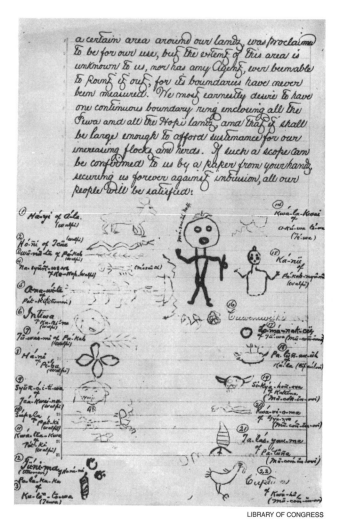

A Hopi petition, drafted in 1894, asking for an official U.S. government survey of grazing lands promised to the Hopis. The tribal leaders signed this document with their totemic symbols, still in use at the time.

sions of the Dawes Act. "Hostiles" pulled up the markers and harassed the soldiers.

The situation continued to deteriorate. Shortly after the turn of the twentieth century, the split became irrevocable. On September 6, 1906, the "friendlies" expelled the "hostiles" from Oraibi. The latter group left to found Hotevilla the same day.

Horse

The first horses on the North American continent lived millions of years ago. They were about the size of dogs, and they eventually died out. In the late 1500s, the Spanish Council of the Indies began to expand colonizing efforts in the New World. In 1598, Spanish explorer Don Juan de Oñate headed into the lands north of Mexico. In 1601 he traveled

COFFRIN'S OLD WEST GALLERY

Veteran bronco buster Lee Warren "gentles" a wild mustang, the favorite type of horse for rangework.

through what is now Oklahoma and Kansas. As he traveled, Oñate left behind horses, animals new to the area. His action changed the course of history in the West.

WESTERN COLLECTION

Most historians believe that the thousands of wild mustangs roaming the Southwest during the 1800s were descended from horses brought to America by sixteenth-century Spanish explorers.

By 1690, the horse had become part of everyday life for native peoples. With horses, they had an invaluable source of transportation. Hunters could pursue buffalo herds. The horse was also good for quick advance and retreat during tribal wars. As horses spread from tribe to tribe, their usefulness increased, as did their place in native mythology. Horses gradually worked their way into many oral tales and fables. Horse trading and stealing became common.

Herds of wild horses began migrating throughout the Southwest and other parts of North America. By the time of the American Revolution, the horse was part of everyday life for both Native Americans and settlers. The move West relied heavily on horses: Pioneers, farmers, hunters, explorers and others simply could not have done what they did without the horse to provide transportation and labor. To the cowhand, a good horse was priceless. An old cowboy saying claimed "a man afoot is no man at all." Indeed, without horses range work would have been impossible. Horses were used for rounding up cattle, for transportation, and for other ranch business. For amusement, ranchhands staged horse races when a day's work was done. Generally, most ranch workers didn't own a horse but used one supplied by the ranch. The lucky few cowboys who had their own mounts generally allowed their animals to be grouped with stock horses on a ranch. This was a good faith gesture on the part of both owner and ranchhand. While horses were always treated with great care, during range rides or emergencies a horse might be ridden until the animal dropped dead from exhaustion.

When the herds of wild horses were rounded up, it was necessary to tame—or "break"—them for domestic use. Generally the wild horse would be put in a corral and blindfolded. The animal would then be mounted and released into the corral. A cowboy would have to hang on, trying to coerce the horse into accepting a rider. This was dangerous work, and a much-admired skill among cowhands. Legends grew and were passed on about cowboys with the unique ability to break wild horses.

Other uses for the horse included delivering mail (and later the Pony Express), pulling wagons and stagecoaches, farming, military functions, and entertainment. Horse trading and horse rustling were also both big businesses in the West.

Houston, Samuel

1793–1863

Soldier, statesman, and son of a career army officer and veteran of the Revolutionary War who died while inspecting frontier posts, Houston was born near Lexington, Virginia, but moved with his mother, five brothers, and three sisters to a Tennessee farm in 1807. As a teenager, Sam began a lifelong association with the Cherokees by living with the tribe along the Tennessee River, learning their language and customs, and earning their confidence and even a Cherokee name—*Co-lon-neh*, the Raven.

Houston joined the 7th Infantry Regiment in 1813 and accompanied Andrew Jackson in the campaign against the Creeks in Alabama, distinguishing himself in the Battle of Horseshoe Bend (March 27, 1814) and earning a lieutenant's commission from Jackson, but suffering wounds from arrow and gunshot in his leg, arm, and shoulder. He resigned from the army after the war and in 1818 completed a law course and bar examination. With the endorsement of Jackson, now his friend and benefactor, Houston won election as district attorney for the Nashville district and later served as the state's adjutant general and major general of militia.

By the time he was 30 he had been elected to Congress, where he served two terms and helped elect

THE INSTITUTE OF TEXAN CULTURES

Samuel Houston.

Jackson, known as "Old Hickory," as president. Jackson showed his appreciation for Houston's devotion by putting his friend's name forward for the Tennessee governorship, an office Houston won. He was a flamboyant character—a tall, muscular, volcano of a man campaigning in Cherokee buckskins and a scarlet sash tied around his swashbuckler's black trousers.

In 1829 Houston married Eliza Allen, daughter of a wealthy Tennessee family, but the marriage dissolved in three months. The despondent Houston resigned as governor and drifted to Arkansas, where he lived among his old friends, the Cherokees. He established a trading post on the Verdigris River near Fort Gibson, lived with a Cherokee woman, and became such a notorious whiskey addict that the Cherokees gave him a new name—"Big Drunk."

As spokesman for the Cherokees, Houston peri-

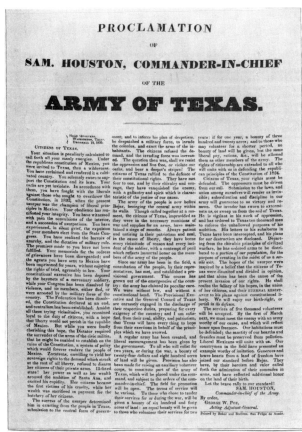

LIBRARY OF CONGRESS

Sam Houston authored this flyer calling for volunteers for his fledgling Texas Army.

odically traveled to Washington on Indian affairs. In 1832 he went to Texas for the first time, perhaps on an unofficial mission for the president, and wrote to Jackson saying he had information "touching on the acquisition of Texas by the United States," a measure, he said, that was "desired by 19/20ths of the population of the province." After several additional trips to the province, he settled in Nacogdoches, reopened his law practice, and quickly became involved in the movement for Texan independence.

In 1835, a Texan revolution against Mexico now a certainty, Houston was selected as commander in chief of the Department of Nacogdoches and made an appeal for volunteers, offering "a good rifle and 100 rounds of ammunition" to the able-bodied men who came forward. In November he was named commander in chief of the Texas Army and in March of the following year signed the Texas declaration of independence at Washington-on-the-Brazos.

With Santa Anna's army approaching the Rio Grande in February 1836, Houston apparently attempted to have the Alamo fortification demolished, its cannon removed, and its garrison and residents escorted to safety. But on March 6 Santa Anna attacked and all 183 of the defenders, including Houston's close friend James Bowie, were killed.

Houston was in Gonzales when news of the Alamo loss reached him and was en route to the Brazos River when he received word of the loss of Fannin's force at Goliad. Houston's tactic for the moment was to fall back to the Colorado, then to the Brazos, to the north, then east, to allow time to build up his small army of ill-trained recruits. These methods were of grave concern to Texas interim president David G. Burnet, who sent a message to the general saying: "Sir, the enemy are laughing you to scorn. You must fight." Even Houston's troops talked about deposing him and finding a commander who would make a stand against the Mexicans. But Houston shrewdly bided his time. He had trusted scouts and knew Santa Anna's movements, knew that the Mexican president-general had fragmented his army, and knew the strengths and weaknesses of his own force.

On April 17 he ordered his column south. His scouts brought word that Santa Anna's force was camped on the San Jacinto River and on April 20 Houston's army, numbering 783 men, arrived at the juncture of Buffalo Bayou and the San Jacinto. After minor skirmishes that day, both armies rested. On April 21, Santa Anna's force, with reinforcements arriving that morning, had swelled to about 1,500 men. Houston ordered the burning of a bridge to prevent additional men arriving. Then, at 4:00 P.M., he led his troops to battle, an improvised fife and drum unit playing "Come to the Bower," the Texans shouting "Remember the Alamo!" and "Remember Goliad!"

The battle was a rout and a slaughter. In less than 20 minutes, 630 of Santa Anna's troops were killed, 208 wounded, and 730 taken prisoner. Houston, who suffered an ankle wound, lost 6 men killed and 25 wounded. Santa Anna, wearing a private's uniform, was taken prisoner together with his army's weapons, supplies, horses, pack train, and $12,000 in silver. After Santa Anna ordered all Mexican forces back across the Rio Grande, Houston was taken to New Orleans to have his painful ankle wound attended to. Meantime, independence had been won at San Jacinto and Houston was elected the first president of the new Republic of Texas. His first duties were to secure U.S. recognition and to see Santa Anna returned safely to Mexico City.

Houston married Margaret Moffette Lea of Alabama in 1840 (they would have eight children in all), served twice as president of Texas, was offered and declined a general's command in the war with Mexico, and, in 1846, returned to Washington as senator from Texas, which was annexed as a state that year. Houston served in the Senate for 14 years. Among his special causes were Indian affairs, abolition of slavery, and preservation of the Union. The latter caused him problems at home, but in 1859 he was elected governor of his state. He continued to oppose secession—"Let me tell you what is coming," he said in one of his impassioned speeches, "Your fathers and husbands, your sons and brothers, will be herded at the point of the bayonet. . . . the North is determined to preserve the Union"—and when Texas voted to secede, he resisted joining the Confederacy and refused to swear an oath of loyalty to it. As a result, the Texas legislature declared the office of governor vacant and Houston retired to his farm in Huntsville.

He died there on July 26, 1863, his family gathered around him, his wife holding his hand, his last words "Texas—Texas!—Margaret!"

Howard, Oliver Otis

1830–1909

An army officer, Howard was a controversial figure during his lifetime. A pious (some would say sanctimonious) Christian, his deeply held beliefs led him to seek justice for black causes, a position quite unprecedented for a white officer, even in the Union Army. His record in Indian affairs was not as clear, and ultimately not without bloodshed.

A New Englander by birth, Howard was a graduate of West Point and served briefly and competently in the Seminole War. It was in the Civil War that he first made his mark, losing an arm at Fair Oaks and winning the Congressional Medal of Honor and a special citation from Congress for his actions at Gettysburg. At the end of the war, President Johnson named him head of the Freedmen's Bureau, and

LIBRARY OF CONGRESS

Oliver Otis Howard.

it was in that position that he served with most distinction, showing himself a staunch supporter of the newly freed slaves and working to protect their rights. He was a tireless advocate for African-Americans, and was the founder and first president of Howard University, the traditionally black college that bears his name.

In 1872 President Grant named Howard a special commissioner for Indian affairs, sending him to the Southwest to try to make peace with the Apaches. Howard first met with the Apache leader Victorio; on the strength of their lengthy and cordial talks, he rode to Cochise's stronghold, accompanied by only two men: his adjutant, Joseph Sladen, and Indian agent Tom Jeffords, who was known and trusted by the Apaches. The result of this courageous act was an 11-day conference between the two men that led to a treaty establishing a reservation for the Chiracahua Apaches and a peace that lasted for four years.

In 1874, Howard was chosen to command the Department of the Columbia. One of his priorities was to settle a dispute with the Nez Perces over the Wallowa Valley in northeastern Oregon, which Old Joseph of the Nez Perces claimed had never been ceded to the government in an 1863 treaty. According to Old Joseph, the Nez Perces who signed the treaty did not represent those tribes living in the valley. Although President Ulysses Grant had issued and executive order on June 16, 1873, allowing the nontreaty Nez Perces to remain in the valley, he later reversed his decision in 1875 after protests from settlers who wanted the disputed land.

Unwilling to move from their land, the Nez Perces faced growing pressure from both the army and from ever-encroaching settlers. When the Nez Perces, now lead by Young Joseph, refused in the summer of 1877 to accept General Howard's solution—that the Nez Perces sell their land to the government and move to the Lapwai reservation in what is now western Idaho—the strong-willed Howard delivered an ultimatum requiring the Nez Perces to go to the reservation within thirty days or face the general's soldiers.

Realizing they were outnumbered, the Nez Perces gave in and started the journey to the reservation. While on their way, several younger Nez Perces attacked and killed some settlers. When the army responded to the killings by sending one hundred cavalrymen to punish the Nez Perces, the Nez Perces successfully drove off their attack on June 17, 1877, in what was later called the Battle of White Bird Canyon. Howard's response to this embarrassing defeat was to accompany four hundred of his troops and to confront the renegade Nez Perces. After clashing with the Nez Perces in early July near the Clearwater River and doing substantial damage to their forces, Howard failed to prevent the remaining Nez Perces from escaping. A council of Nez Perces chiefs then decided to set out on what became a 1,300 mile fighting retreat, led by Chief Joseph, with the goal of finding safety with tribes of Crow in Montana or possibly with Sitting Bull, who had fled to Canada.

Although it was Colonel Nelson Miles who eventually cut short the Nez Perces' flight only forty miles from the Canadian border, Howard finally caught up with Chief Joseph in time to hear the chief's eloquent surrender speech on October 5, 1877.

Howard was also involved in campaigns against the Bannocks and the Paiutes in 1878 and later at the end of the campaign against Geronimo.

Hudson's Bay Company

In 1659, 60 years after Henry Hudson's discovery of the vast (475,000 square mile) inland sea in North America that would bear his name, French trappers Pierre-Esprit Radisson and Medard Chouart found a fur trade bonanza in their journeys from the Mississippi headwaters east to the St. Lawrence River Valley and north to Hudson Bay. But French authorities confiscated the furs and jailed the trappers for trading with the Indians without official sanction.

In 1665, Radisson and Chouart went to England and told Charles II of the riches in fur-bearing animals that lay in the New Wales (as Hudson Bay was then called) region. The Frenchmen entered English service and in 1668 were equipped with two ships, the *Eaglet* and the *Nonesuch*, to return to the bay and trap beaver. Only the *Nonesuch* was able to complete the voyage, returning to England with a modest shipload of furs after a year in New Wales. The *Nonesuch* expedition inspired King Charles in 1670 to create The Governor and Company of Adventurers of England Trading Into Hudson's Bay—the Hudson's Bay Company. The company, formed

Photograph of Jasper's House, a well-used Hudson's Bay Company stop in the Canadian Rockies.

for the purpose of importing into England furs obtained by bartering with Indians, was chartered to Charles's cousin, Prince Rupert, a Royalist general of horse in the English Civil War known as "the Mad Cavalier." He became the company's first governor and had 17 other noblemen as partners. Their instructions were to maintain the right to all trade and traffic "to and from all havens, bays, creeks, rivers, lakes and seas into which they shall find entrance or passage by water or land out of the territories, limits or places aforesaid." In brief, the Hudson's Bay Company was to monopolize the fur trade around all the territory watered by the rivers and streams emptying into Hudson Bay—a territory of about 1.5 million square miles. The Hudson's Bay Company was managed locally by a governor, deputy governor, and seven-member board, all answerable to the stockholders who met periodically in England.

After founding its first settlement in Prince Rupert's Land (which the Hudson Bay territory was then called) on James Bay, the southern extension of the bay, the Hudson's Bay Company's growth was halted by over four decades of conflict between Britain and France that followed. The company suffered a serious setback in 1686 when a French force of 100 men marched the 800 miles north from Montreal to the Hudson's Bay Company outposts. The French seized the strongest of the James Bay posts, Rupert House and Albany Fort, and dominated the

area until 1713. In that year the long series of Anglo-French wars in Europe and North America ended, and the Treaty of Utrecht ceded Newfoundland, Acadia, and the Hudson Bay region to England.

But even with the end of the French wars, the Hudson's Bay Company experienced an agonizingly slow growth. It had only a few trading stations and 120 employees in 1749, and its inactivity caused attempts to be made in London to dissolve the charter. Only after the Treaty of Paris in 1763, under which all of France's North American possessions (except Louisiana) were ceded to England, did the company begin to expand from Fort Garry (Winnipeg today) to the Rocky Mountains and into west-central Canada.

The Hudson's Bay Company's fur trade monopoly got its most serious challenge in 1784 when Simon McTavish, a 29-year-old Scotsman involved in the fur trade above the Great Lakes, organized competing fur traders, many of them former employees of John Jacob Astor, at Montreal expressly to compete with the Hudson's Bay Company. McTavish's North West Fur Company—the "Nor'westers" as they were called—took their coat of arms and motto, "Perseverance," to such trading posts as Fort Chippewayan on the Peace River in British Columbia and Fort William on Lake Superior (which was opened in answer to the creation of the company's Cumberland House in the Canadian heartland of

Saskatchewan), and fought its fur trade war with the Hudson's Bay Company in Alberta and the Lake Athabasca region of Saskatchewan.

An outgrowth of the rivalry between the two companies was the work of two of the greatest explorers in North American history: Alexander Mackenzie, a Scot who had served in Loyalist forces in the American Revolution, and David Thompson, a Welshman who had gone to work for the Hudson's Bay Company in 1784 and transferred his allegiance to the North West Company in 1797.

Thompson charted the Columbia River system to the Pacific, located the sources of the Mississippi, explored the Missouri River, and retired in 1812 after logging over 50,000 miles of canoe and foot travel through the American Northwest. Mackenzie, in 1789, began a journey from the Arctic Sea to British Columbia, the Canadian Rockies, and down the Fraser River to the Pacific.

The Hudson's Bay–North West rivalry ended in 1821 when the two companies merged, the Hudson's Bay Company retaining the name and representing British fur trading interests in North America.

One of the most disastrous episodes in the company's history occurred in 1811 when Thomas Douglas, the Fifth Earl of Selkirk and a major stockholder, was granted 116,000 square miles of territory in the valley of the Red River (in today's Manitoba and Minnesota). Lord Selkirk intended to set up an agricultural colony in his wind-scoured wilderness and succeeded in attracting his first settlers there in 1812. The "governor" of Selkirk's colony, Miles Macdonnell, quickly alienated the local *métis* (descendants of *voyageur* fathers and Indian mothers), and the Nor'westers joined in the conflict on the side of the *métis*. The factions engaged in battle in 1816, and more than 20 white settlers were killed by the *métis* at Fort Douglas in the Selkirk colony. After its merger with the North West Company and the failure of Selkirk's struggling domain (he died in 1820), the Hudson's Bay Company transferred his territory back to its control.

In the period 1821–1870, the company faced increased competition with American fur companies and independent trappers. Its influence dwindled with the decline of the fur trade after 1840. In 1868, the Hudson's Bay Company surrendered its charter and rights to the new Dominion of Canada, which purchased the Hudson's Bay territories for £300,000. The company continued its fur trading and general store enterprises, as it does to this day.

Huntington, Collis P.

1821–1900

Collis Huntington was one of the "Big Four" (entrepreneurial financiers) investors who started the Central Pacific and Southern Pacific Railroads. Huntington served as the eastern agent for the railroads and for many years pursued new routes and lines. When the Pennsylvania Railroad's Thomas Scott began working on an Atlantic–Pacific line, Huntington foiled his efforts by lobbying successfully to prevent him from receiving a federal land grant.

Huntington, who was born in Harwinton, Connecticut in 1821, left school at the age of 14 and went to New York City. Later he spent time in the South, peddling watches and buying up unpaid promissory notes. Eventually he returned to the North and invested in a country store in Oneonta, New York, with his brother. In 1849 Huntington joined the rush to California. But one day in the mines convinced him his fortune lay not in mining, but in supplying the miner. In partnership with Mark Hopkins, a recent acquaintance, he set up a store in Sacramento to provide prospecting and mining supplies.

In 1861 Huntington, Hopkins, Leland Stanford, and Charles Crocker each invested $15,000 to buy

SOUTHERN PACIFIC TRANSPORTATION
COMPANY

Collis P. Huntington.

stock in a company that would become the Central Pacific Railroad, which united with the Union Pacific in 1869 to form the first transcontinental railroad. In 1884 Huntington tried to sell his interest in the railroad but could not find a buyer. Consequently the Central Pacific and Southern Pacific Railroads benefited from his managerial brilliance throughout the 1880s. In 1890 Huntington became its president, retiring nine years later to a mountain lodge in the Adirondacks. He died the following year.

Idaho

A state in the Pacific Northwest, Idaho has been inhabited for at least 14,000 years. By the 1800s, Indian tribes in the region included the Kutenais, Coeur d'Alenes, and Nez Perces in the north, and Northern Shoshonis and Northern Paiutes in the south. Not until the Lewis and Clark expedition of 1805–1806 did white men begin to explore the area, making Idaho the last state to be entered by whites. Fur traders, primarily British, were the next to arrive, and Idaho became a region of border disputes between British and American trappers. In addition to trappers and mountain men, missionaries also traveled to Idaho and, in some cases, converted Indians to the white man's way of life. Some Nez Perces and Coeur d'Alenes turned to farming, and others constructed flour mills and sawmills.

The flow of settlers increased over time, and in 1860 permanent settlement began when Mormons traveled northward from Utah into Idaho, and miners came from the Pacific Coast. By 1862, most of the population of Washington Territory lived in Idaho, and the following year Congress established the Idaho Territory. The territory encompassed parts of the present-day states of Montana and Wyoming, and was the last of the large western territories to be organized.

The establishment of a territorial government in Idaho proved to be a formidable task. The original governor, William Henson Wallace, was soon elected to Congress as the delegate from Idaho. President Abraham Lincoln appointed Caleb Lyon, an ec-

centric art and literary critic from New York, to succeed Wallace. One of Lyon's first acts of legislation was to move the capital of the territory from Lewiston to Boise, enraging residents of Lewiston, who then petitioned a judge to prevent the transfer of the state seal. Lyon evaded a court summons by leaving town on a duck hunting trip, and he subsequently

IDAHO HISTORICAL SOCIETY

An Idaho woman admires her nearly completed log cabin. Neighbors from miles around would pitch in to raise a cabin.

219

abandoned the territory for Washington, D.C. Idaho went without a governor for eight months before territorial secretary Clinton Dewitt Smith arrived. Smith continued the capital debate and successfully transported the seal and archives from Lewiston to Boise. However, after only seven months in office, he drank himself to death. Horace Gilson then took charge temporarily, while back in Washington, D.C., Caleb Lyon was appointed to return to Idaho as governor. Gilson acted as secretary under Lyon, and in 1860 absconded to Hong Kong with the entire territorial treasury of $41,062. Later, Lyon departed with the Nez Perces treasury of $46,418. After David Ballard arrived as governor later that year, Idaho managed to maintain a functioning government. Statehood was granted on July 3, 1890, making Idaho the 43rd state in the Union.

One of the most brutal conflicts between whites and Native Americans took place in southeastern Idaho. California volunteers, who in 1863 had been sent to protect settlers at Franklin, virtually annihilated a band of Shoshonis, leaving over 360 dead, among them at least 90 women and children. The Nez Perce War of 1877 also took place in Idaho. In this encounter hundreds of Nez Perces were driven from their land and exiled to Oklahoma.

Idaho developed quickly in the early 1900s when the booming lumber industry relieved economic dependence on mining. Farming also expanded, and in addition to its famous potatoes, Idaho today produces wheat, corn, barley, and apples. Tourism is also gaining in importance in Idaho as the state is home to some of the nation's last true wilderness areas.

Immigration

See African Americans in the West; Chinese Settlers in the West; Danish Settlers in the West; German Settlers in the West; Irish Settlers in the West; Italian Settlers in the West; Japanese Settlers in the West; Jewish Settlers in the West; Mexicans in the West; Norwegian Settlers in the West; and Swedish Settlers in the West.

Indian Policy, U.S.

The Indian policy of the United States consisted of the overall strategy of dealing with Native Americans who occupied lands within the national boundaries, together with the courses of action adopted to carry it out. Indian policy changed as administrations and conditions changed, but at its heart lay a single controlling issue: how to resolve the conflict over land between westward-moving pioneers and the Native American occupants.

After the United States gained its independence from England, the government conceded that, within the American legal system, the Indians held title to their homelands. But Indian policy centered on how to transfer that title to the United States so that the lands could be settled by whites. Throughout the period of westward expansion, until it was discontinued in 1871, the treaty supposedly was the primary means for resolving land issues and governing the relationship between the United States and its "domestic dependent nations," as Chief Justice John Marshall defined the Indian tribes in 1831. In truth, however, the treaty was merely one nation's attempt to rationalize and legitimize the seizure of another nation's homeland—a seizure that was accomplished by force when diplomacy did not work.

The treaty system between the U.S. government and the Indians contained major flaws. When vital interests were involved, for example, neither Congress nor the executive branch had the same scruples about violating these treaties as they did treaties with foreign nations. Nor could the tribes always carry out their promises. Chiefs almost never represented all the people for whom they spoke, and frequently they did not even understand or know what they had agreed to, either because of bad interpreters or the deceit of government negotiators. Treaties were thus broken not by one side or the other, but usually by both.

One by-product of the treaties was the annuity system—the practice of paying for land with cash dispensed in annual installments over a period of years. It was a system easily abused, especially by politically well-connected traders who sat at disbursing tables collecting real and/or fictional debts incurred during the year by the Indians to whom annuities were to be paid. Aggravating the abuse was the custom of making lump-sum payments to chiefs for distribution to their people, especially when a

An 1876 illustration that played upon anti-Indian fears. The sign refers to Custer's stunning defeat, during which four of his relatives were also killed.

chief formed a corrupt alliance with unscrupulous whites. Cash annuities also helped the trade in liquor, giving white traders the opportunity to siphon off payments and intensify the curse of drunkenness.

Despite being rooted in the self-interest of white citizens, American Indian policy nevertheless included a humanitarian aspect. Since much of the friction with the tribes resulted from the Indians being mistreated by white traders, in 1796 Congress authorized an official trading system. At government trading posts Indians could barter for white manufactured goods at fair prices and meet with honest practices. This factory system, however, could not compete with private traders and also aroused their opposition, so the trading system was abandoned in 1822.

President Thomas Jefferson's answer to the recurring Indian Wars was removal: Remove the tribes from the East to the West, to land not inhabited by whites or included within the boundaries of any

state. Such land was officially designated Indian Country (present-day Oklahoma), and here eastern tribes could live in free and happy isolation from white people. Under Presidents James Monroe and Andrew Jackson, the practice of removal dominated Indian policy. Throughout the 1830s and 1840s, as a result of treaties imposed on the eastern tribes, about 50,000 Native Americans were uprooted and moved west, many suffering great hardship and impoverishment in the process. When it was all over, Native Americans had yielded 100 million acres of eastern homeland in return for 32 million western acres and $68 million in annuity promises.

Indian Country, however, was not a fulfillment of Jefferson's promise. The Permanent Indian Frontier that was to separate Indians and whites (a chain of military posts extending from Minnesota to Louisiana) proved very temporary. The Oregon boundary treaty of 1846 and the Mexican-American War of 1846–1848 extended America's western boundary to the Pacific Ocean, destroyed the Permanent Indian Frontier, and thus doomed the concept of Indian Country. White immigrants moving toward Oregon and California in the 1850s made new policies imperative.

The answer was the reservation. Reservations had existed east of the Mississippi, but not until the 1850s did the idea become basic federal Indian policy. This policy called for concentrating the Indians on small, well-defined tracts of land, protecting them from white contamination, teaching them to become self-sufficient farmers, and conferring on them the blessings of white Christian civilization. The policy met both practical and moral objectives: it cleared the tribes from the travel routes and settled areas of the white people while also advancing what one official called "the great work of regenerating the Indian race." The latter purpose drew on the prevalent white belief that the tribes' salvation lay in the white man's "civilization," in their transformation into imitation white people.

Increasingly in the 1850s and 1860s treaties defined reservations on which the Native Americans agreed to settle. Instead of cash, the treaties typically promised annuities in the form of rations, clothing, schools, farming tools and instructors, and other benefits. They also transferred title to all lands outside the reservations to the United States. The treaty system ended because the House of Representatives came to demand participation in the ratification of treaties, whereas before the process had involved only

EVER OUR INDIAN POLICY.
THE ONLY GOOD INDIAN IS THE DEAD ONE!

JUDGE, JAN. 3, 1891

Satirical illustration of rabid anti-Indian sentiment prevalent in 1891.

the Senate. After 1871, however, "agreements"—treaties in all but name—continued to regulate relations with Native American groups.

Although the reservation policy was the underlying cause of most of the great Indian wars of the 1860s and 1870s, with the U.S. Army battling to force tribes onto reservations or return them to reservations from which they had fled, these decades of warfare also witnessed major peace initiatives. At the close of the Civil War, Indian policy was dominated by advocates of "conquest by kindness." In an effort to clear the travel routes across the Great Plains, the Peace Commission of 1867–1868 negotiated the Fort Laramie

and Medicine Lodge Treaties with the Plains Indians; however these treaties did not end warfare or immediately confine the tribes to the reservations set aside for them.

The principles behind the Peace Commission, however, found expression in the Peace Policy of President Ulysses S. Grant, who took office in March 1869. More than a body of specific measures, Grant's Peace Policy was a slogan that echoed the administration's view of the correct approach to Indian problems. Also called the Quaker Policy, the Peace Policy aimed to elevate the efficiency and honesty of reservation management by appointing

Quakers and other religious representatives as Indian agents. Another Grant measure was to divide the responsibility of the Indian Bureau and the U.S. Army at the reservation boundary: on the reservation all Native Americans were peaceable; off the reservation all were hostile.

The Peace Policy proved no more successful than any other at ending wars or introducing enlightened, just, and humane relations between whites and Indians. It became obvious that religious affiliation was no guarantee of honesty or competence. Often peaceful Indians were off the reservation while hostiles were on it. Not until the Indians could be made dependent on the government through a shrinking land and subsistence base and the operations of the U.S. Army could the reservation policy be enforced.

As the last of the Indian wars ended in the 1880s, the reservation for the first time became virtually a sealed laboratory for policy experiments. The goal of "civilizing" the tribes had always moved policy makers, but not until Native Americans had been entirely deprived of freedom could it be seriously attempted. The end of fighting coincided with the rise of reform groups in the East. Dedicated to justice and fair play, the humanitarians sought to present Native Americans with the greatest gift in their power—their own culture.

For a generation, the agenda of the reformers (and thus of the government) included agricultural self-support, education and Christianity, patriotic allegiance to "Americanism," protection and punishment according to law (Anglo-Saxon law, not tribal law), and title to individual parcels of land. The last, called allotment in severalty, would promote personal self-reliance and self-support in daily life while emphasizing the family at the expense of the tribe. In theory allotment, launched by the Dawes Act of 1887, would unleash the forces that would ultimately destroy the reservations and the Indian Bureau that administered them. Once all Indians owned their own land and became full-fledged American citizens, nothing but skin color would distinguish them from other Americans.

The program did not succeed. It was not well managed, and it rested on ideas that would later be found invalid. It also reflected the prevailing white belief that Native American culture contained nothing worth preserving, another notion rejected by later generations. Instead of substituting a new culture for an old, the civilization program merely broke down the old. The resulting demoralization created fertile soil for the Ghost Dance troubles of 1890.

Despite their obvious flaws and the damage they inflicted on the victims, the reservation policies prevailed well into the twentieth century. Not until the 1930s when the Indian New Deal of Franklin D. Roosevelt's administration appeared were the old assumptions and the old policies discarded.

Indian Territory

See Oklahoma.

Indian Wars

The Indian Wars of the United States resulted from the threat to tribal land and way of life posed by the westward movement of white Americans. Often tribes met the invasion of their homeland with aggression against settlers and travelers, and finally, when hostilities escalated, with full-scale war against organized military forces.

Indian wars marked the entire colonial period and continued between the Appalachian Mountains and the Mississippi River after Americans won independence from England. In the early decades of the nineteenth century, the United States used military force to support diplomacy in bringing about the removal of all eastern Indians to new homes west of the Mississippi River. The federal government sought to end hostilities by dividing Indians and whites with a Permanent Indian Frontier extending from Minnesota to Louisiana. In 1845–1848, however, the acquisition of Texas, Oregon, California, and New Mexico doomed the concept. Beginning with the California Gold Rush in 1848, warfare with Native Americans dogged the westward movement until the frontier vanished in 1890.

In California, miners overran most of the small native groups in the gold fields of the Sierra Nevada. In northern California and southern Oregon, however, stronger tribes fought back, and U.S. Army troops campaigned through the 1850s. The most se-

Cheyenne braves battling the U.S. Army at North Platte River.

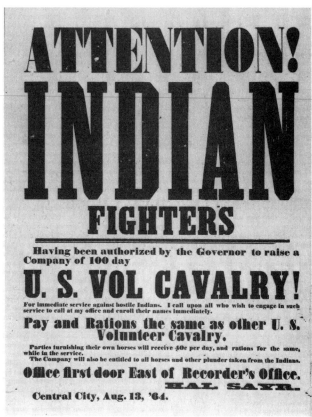

Ads such as this garnered a big response.

rious clash was the Rogue River War of 1855. At the same time, north of the Columbia River, another gold strike set off a rush into Yakima Indian country, and an able chieftain named Kamiakin rebelled. The Yakima and Rogue River wars ended in 1856 with the collapse of Indian resistance. Two years later, however, Kamiakin sought to form a confederation of tribes of the Columbia Basin. Colonel George Wright prosecuted a ruthless offensive and, at the Battles of Four Lakes and Spokane Plains (September 1 and 5, 1858), ended Indian warfare in the Pacific Northwest.

In the 1850s other areas of settlement also suffered hostilities. The most intense were in Texas, where settlers pushed the frontier westward and the U.S. Army tried to protect them from raiding parties of Kiowas, Comanches, and Apaches. A chain of military posts extending from the Red River to the Rio Grande failed to keep off the raiders. In New Mexico old rivalries between Hispanic colonizers and Apaches and Navajos spilled over to the American newcomers. Raids, counterraids, and military offensives troubled the territory. The U.S. Army established a system of forts, but peace was achieved no more than in Texas.

On the Great Plains wars broke out along the Oregon-California Trail, the Santa Fe Trail, and the trails across Texas. Sioux and Cheyennes first slipped into hostilities in 1854–1855. Near Fort Laramie, the Grattan Massacre of August 19, 1854,

caused by the rash actions of a young officer, led to General William S. Harney's campaign of 1855. At the Battle of Bluewater, September 3, 1855, Harney destroyed a Sioux village and killed Chief Little Thunder. To the south, Kiowas, Comanches, and Cheyennes threatened the commerce with Santa Fe and raided deep into Texas. Forts at strategic points along the trails and military columns operating between them brought only occasional relief.

The Civil War years of 1861–1865 were marked by intensified fighting with the volunteer units that replaced the regulars. In Minnesota, years of grievances boiled over in the Sioux uprising of 1862, which took the lives of 400 settlers. General Henry H. Sibley put down the rebellion, but it spread into Dakota Territory, where other Sioux resented gold seekers crossing their homeland to the newly opened mines of western Montana. In 1863 both Sibley and General Alfred Sully campaigned on the up-

A Skirmish, *by Charles Schreyvogel, dramatizes a battle fought against Sioux leader Crazy Horse in 1876.*

per Missouri River. Both fought successful battles with the Sioux. The following summer Sully again invaded the Sioux domain and routed the warriors of Sitting Bull at the Battle of Killdeer Mountain, on July 28, 1864.

In New Mexico the Apache and Navajo wars continued. General James H. Carleton took command and sent troops into the field. In 1863–1864, under Colonel Christopher "Kit" Carson, they rounded up Mescalero Apaches and Navajos and confined them on a bleak Reservation far from their homelands. On the central Plains during the summer of 1864, Indian unrest threatened the trails from the East to Denver, Colorado, and led to the tragic and treacherous attack by Colonel John M. Chivington on Black Kettle's Cheyenne village at Sand Creek, November 29, 1864. Sand Creek set off a general war that spread over all the Plains country in 1865. A three-pronged offensive on the northern Plains, directed by General Patrick E. Connor, failed when columns encountered bad weather and ran out of supplies.

At the close of the Civil War, the volunteers were mustered out and regular troops returned to frontier duty. In Arizona and New Mexico, Apache hostilities persisted. In Texas the usual raids from the north rippled along the frontier of settlement and even into Mexico. And on the Great Plains the fighting continued. Red Cloud's Sioux closed the Bozeman Trail to the Montana mines and besieged the three forts established to protect travelers. On December 21, 1866, warriors wiped out an 80-man

force of soldiers under Captain William J. Fetterman near Fort Phil Kearny, Wyoming.

The Fetterman disaster and other reverses prompted the government to launch a peace movement. Treaties established reservations and enticed many Native Americans with promises of rations and other annuities to give up their freedom and live on government handouts. At Fort Laramie and Medicine Lodge, Plains Indians agreed to live on reservations. Most of the remaining wars were fought to make tribes go to reservations or return to reservations from which they had escaped.

On the southern Plains, a war in 1868–1869 forced the Cheyennes, Kiowas, and Comanches to new reservations in the Indian Territory. The culmination of this conflict was the Battle of the Washita, November 27, 1868, in which Lieutenant Colonel George A. Custer fell on the Cheyenne village of Black Kettle. The chief had escaped Sand Creek but now, with his wife, died in the opening charge. In 1874 these tribes, discontented with reservation life, broke loose and fled west. The Red River War lasted until the spring of 1875 and, with the surrender of the fugitives, ended warfare on the southern Plains and along the Texas frontier.

On the northern Plains, new tensions arose as Railroads moved toward Sioux country and gold was discovered in the Black Hills, part of the Great Sioux Reservation. This resulted in the Great Sioux War of 1876 and the army sought to force Sitting Bull, Crazy Horse, Black Moon, and other chiefs to give up their freedom and go to the reservation. Three columns converged on the Sioux hunting grounds. Riding with one was Custer. On June 25, 1876, he attacked a great village of Sioux and Cheyennes on the Little Big Horn River in Montana. The force under his personal command, 212 men, was wiped out. The disaster so stunned Americans that large armies took the field, and by the spring of 1877 most of the Sioux and Cheyennes had surrendered. Sitting Bull sought refuge in Canada, but gave up in 1881.

In November 1872 a war flared with the Modocs of northeastern California when the government tried to force a band under Captain Jack and other leaders to live on a reservation. The Modocs took refuge in a lava flow called the Stronghold and withstood a military siege for four months. The highlight of this conflict was the assassination by Jack and other Modocs of General Edward R.S. Canby during a peace conference. The Modocs were finally flushed out of their fortress, run down, and the leaders hanged.

In 1877 the government ordered all Nez Perces of Idaho and Oregon to go to their Idaho reservation. Under Chief Joseph and other leaders, about 800 people conducted a desperate fighting retreat across the Bitterroot Mountains to Montana. They outran, outwitted, and outfought their pursuers until they had almost reached safety in Canada. On October 5, however, following a battle and a five-day siege at Bear Paw Mountain, Montana, the Nez Perces surrendered to Colonel Nelson A. Miles.

Other mountain tribes also resisted before giving in. In 1878 the Bannocks and Paiutes of Idaho and eastern Oregon fought and were defeated. In 1879 the Utes of Colorado met a similar fate.

The last holdouts were the Apaches of Arizona and New Mexico. Under Cochise, Apache warriors terrified the Southwest and Mexico from 1861 until General Oliver O. Howard made peace with them in 1872. General George Crook conducted a brilliant campaign against other Apache warriors in the Tonto Basin in 1872–1873. Peace came for a time, but a government attempt to concentrate all the Apaches on the hot and corrupt San Carlos Reservation led to new fighting. Victorio's War in 1879–1880 rolled across much of Arizona, New Mexico, West Texas, and even Mexico, where Mexican troops finally killed the chief and crushed the rebellion.

The most famous Apache leader was Geronimo. His little band of fighters spread terror among settlements on both sides of the Mexican border and defied the armies of two nations. General Crook enlisted other Apache tribesmen and penetrated Geronimo's mountain hideaways in Mexico. Twice Crook forced Geronimo to surrender, but in the end it was General Nelson A. Miles who brought Geronimo in for the last time and ended Apache warfare.

One final bloodletting occurred at Wounded Knee, South Dakota, on December 29, 1890. This was hardly war, however, but a spiritual revival that blew up in unintended and unexpected violence. The end of four centuries of warfare in North America dates not from Wounded Knee but from September 4, 1886, the day Geronimo surrendered to General Miles in Skeleton Canyon, Arizona.

Indiana

The 19th state admitted to the Union, Indiana (which means "land of the Indians") was inhabited by the Delaware, Miami, Piankashaw, Potawatomi, and Shawnee tribes when the first Europeans arrived. French explorers and missionaries found their way to the region in the late 1670s. Jacques Marquette, a Jesuit missionary, was probably the first white man to see Indiana, but it was Robert Cavelier, Sieur de La Salle, who in 1679 was the first to explore the region, crossing into the northwest corner of today's state while seeking a portage from Lake Michigan to the Mississippi.

The French established numerous trading and trapping outposts in Indiana. The most prominent were Fort Miami (1704), near what is Fort Wayne, Indiana, today; Fort Ouiatanon (1717), near present-day Lafayette, Indiana; and Vincennes (1731), the largest of these outposts, which grew into a sizable and prosperous town. However, the French were dispossessed by the British at the end of the French and Indian War in 1763. British restrictions on further white settlements in the region were not binding, so the French settlers remained.

The territory changed hands once more 20 years later when it was ceded to the Americans by the Treaty of Paris, which finalized the ending of the American Revolution. During the Revolution, Vincennes was the site of a successful engagement for the revolutionaries that was commanded by George Rogers Clark. In 1784, Clark and his men established the first American settlement in the region, Clarksville.

The Northwest Territory, which included Indiana, was established by the Ordinance of 1787. Skirmishing between Indians and settlers continued until the Battle of Fallen Timbers (1794), in which General Anthony Wayne decisively defeated the Miamis led by Little Turtle. His officers included a lieutenant, William Henry Harrison, who received a special commendation for valor; Harrison would be appointed secretary of the Northwest Territory three years later and was the first governor of the Indiana Territory when it was created by an Act of Congress in 1800.

Harrison pushed for the expansion of settlement in Indiana, alarming Tecumseh, chief of the Shawnee. Tecumseh tried to organize the territory's Native Americans into a confederacy to resist further white encroachment, a move that, in turn, provoked Harrison into attacking the Indians at Tippecanoe while Tecumseh was away. Although the battle was indecisive, it broke up the confederation (and earned Harrison the nickname that helped elect him to the White House). Indiana was admitted to the Union on December 11, 1816.

Iowa

The 29th state in the Union, Iowa was settled first by members of the Mesquakie, Peoria, Miami, and Sioux tribes. The name derives from the name of a Sioux tribe. As was the case with neighboring states, the first white men to explore Iowa were French. Louis Jolliet and Jacques Marquette visited there in June 1673. From that date until 1762, Iowa was a French territory, but no permanent settlements were established until after they ceded it to the Spanish.

Under Spain, three private land grants were made: to Julien Dubuque in 1796, to Louis H. Tesson in 1700, and to Basil Giard in 1800. With the cooperation and agreement of the Mesquakie Indians, Dubuque, who gave his name to one of the states principal cities, operated a lead mine near that present-day city. After his death in 1810, the Indians took over the mine and ran it until 1832. The territory reverted back to French control in 1800, but was sold to the United States as part of the Louisiana Purchase in 1803.

Although Lewis and Clark and Zebulon Pike all passed through the area, Americans showed little interest in Iowa. In fact, until the major influx of white settlers in the 1820s, the fight for title to Iowa was between competing Native American tribes. The United States established eight forts in what is now Iowa between 1808 and 1862, none of them held for very long. In fact, there were no major battles between white settlers and Indians in Iowa after the United States took control.

The notable exception was the Spirit Lake Massacre in 1857, in which a band of Sioux attacked isolated settlements in the northwest part of the state in retaliation for the murder of their chief's family by white traders. About 50 whites were killed and several women abducted.

The most unusual event in white-Indian relations in Iowa history occurred in 1852, when some Mesquakies who had been removed to Kansas joined with other members of the tribe still residing in Iowa and purchased a tract of about 80 acres of bottomland in eastern Iowa. They were welcomed as a spur to economic growth, and some of the land is still held by tribe members today.

NEW YORK PUBLIC LIBRARY

Mormon settlers crossing the prairies of Iowa.

The Iowa Territory was created by an Act of Congress in 1838, ending two years in which Iowa was part of the Wisconsin Territory. The state was admitted to the Union in December 1846.

Irish Settlers in the West

Although the Irish are most firmly identified with the development of the East Coast's urban areas, particularly Boston and New York, a good number can be found in the West. (Admittedly, nearly 90 percent of Americans of Irish descent lived in the Northeast in 1900.) Perhaps it was a reaction against the agrarian life they had fled in Ireland, but few Irish settlers in the United States chose to take up farming. Even when following the westward expansion, they gravitated toward growing urban centers. San Francisco, for example, has had a sizable Irish-American population since the middle of the nineteenth century.

The great wave of Irish immigration to America occurred between 1815 and 1920, when 5½ million people left Ireland to escape poverty, famine, and political oppression by the British. In the 30 years between 1815 and 1845 alone, a million Irish men and women came to the United States.

As the first of the great immigrant waves, the Irish found America to be a society in formation, fluid and open. At the same time, discrimination against Catholics and the Irish was common and often vicious. In the West, however, they found communities that lacked the established hierarchy and cultural elitism that breeds such attitudes.

The bulk of the great Irish immigration wave of the nineteenth century went no further west than Illinois, but in 1860 over 33,000 Irish lived in California, mostly in San Francisco. Like so many others, the Irish were drawn to the West Coast by the gold rush of 1848–1849, and they stayed. As with other immigrant groups, those who were successful would send for those left in the old country, who would come to join a community of immigrants.

The aspect of Western life in which the Irish were most deeply involved was the construction of the great transcontinental railroad. They were given the most hazardous jobs, low pay, and poor treatment. And as the Irish organized labor unions, they found themselves played off against other ethnic groups, particularly the Chinese in railroad work and African-Americans in the South and East. Irish women found themselves competing with the Chinese for domestic work on the West Coast, and an anti-Chinese labor movement led by an Irishman, Dennis Kearney, grew out of this conflict in San Francisco in the middle of the nineteenth century.

The Irish were among the first American immigrant groups to unionize, and were enthusiastic union supporters. Mother Jones, famous for her organizing work among Western miners, was actually Mary Harris from County Cork. Through their union activities, the Irish were able to transform them-

LIBRARY OF CONGRESS

Irish immigrants at work on the Union Pacific tracks.

High-spirited Ollie Beers works on an irrigation ditch at her family's Colorado farm.

crops; Spanish colonists in missions and presidios built *acequias* (irrigation ditches) for their small farming plots; and in the Southwest desert country, today as for hundreds of years, stream and river water is diverted to flood land to make it easier to plow and plant.

By the mid-nineteenth century, with significant growth in farming in the West, large-scale irrigation became necessary. Ditches were constructed to convey water under so-called riparian rights, by which a landowner was entitled to the use of all the water abutting his land. This practice was expanded, often illegally, by farmers and ranchers who appropriated water from neighboring lands and fought out the ownership in court or, as territorial newspapers of the day attest, in violent confrontations.

The first federal assistance for irrigation occurred in 1888 when Congress authorized John Wesley Powell, the Colorado River explorer, to make an irrigation survey of the West. This work resulted in the ceding of millions of acres of federal land to states and territories under the provision that funds would be made available for irrigation.

Large-scale irrigation of the West developed into the building of reservoirs to store water and make it available when natural waterways were low or dry during drought periods. Huge federally financed reclamation projects followed, reclaiming arid lands through the building of dams to store and divert water—projects such as Hoover Dam on the Colorado River, the Grand Coulee on the Columbia River, and many others.

selves into higher-paid workers. They would come to dominate the construction and building-trades industries and unions, entirely appropriate fields for an urban people such as Irish-Americans became.

Irrigation

Since most of the trans-Mississippi West receives insufficient rainfall to support farming, irrigation has long been used for crop growing throughout the region. Pre-Columbian Pueblo Indians diverted stream water to their corn, bean, squash, and tomato

Italian Settlers in the West

The Italian experience in the West is similar to that of the Irish in one important respect: the ethnic group is primarily identified with the East Coast, and in fact, in the nineteenth century was to be found in much greater concentrations in eastern urban centers than in the West. Unlike the Irish, however, the Italians were doubly disadvantaged: not only were they Catholic (which was a source of discrimination in the aggressively Protestant United States), they also spoke a different language. And because they arrived later in the century, they were subjected to discriminatory immigration laws, with quotas on how many Italians could enter the country.

Italian miners congregate in Bingham Canyon, Utah.

The first Italians to make a mark in the West were Roman Catholic missionaries like Joseph Cataldo in the Plains states and Anthony Ravalli in the Pacific Northwest. Italian explorers added to the map of the West as well, most significantly an aide to LaSalle, who explored the lower Mississippi in the late 1600s. Later, Italians would be attracted to California, particularly San Francisco, by the gold rush. To this day, the city has a significant Italian-American population and Italian-American politicians have enjoyed considerable success there.

Unlike the Irish, Italians of peasant stock were generally content to stick to farming when they arrived in the New World. More than half of the Italians who emigrated to the United States between 1890 and 1910 were farmers by occupation in Italy, and many northern Italians continued as farmers. A list of major wine producers in California is headed by the Gallo family, and DiGiorgio and Maggio are still prominent names in the West Coast produce industry.

As with the Irish, the largest concentration of Italians in the West was found in the cities. San Francisco, Denver, and Seattle all boasted sizable populations. At one time, San Francisco could claim five Italian-language newspapers, and numerous Italian cultural and fraternal groups.

J

Jackson, Helen Hunt

1830–1885

Helen Jackson was a novelist and poet, whose highly acclaimed *A Century of Dishonor* helped stir public outrage at the U.S. government's mistreatment of Native Americans.

Jackson was born Helen Fiske on October 14, 1830, in Amherst, Massachusetts, where she became a lifelong friend of the poet Emily Dickinson. She was orphaned young and in 1852 married Edward Hunt, whose military career forced them to move often. Edward died in a tragic accident in 1863, and their two young sons died shortly thereafter, leaving Helen alone.

After a move to Newport, Rhode Island, she met the writer Thomas Wentworth Higginson and, with his encouragement, began writing. She published several poems, as well as a series of popular short stories (under the pseudonym Saxe Holm). But a recurring illness forced Jackson to relocate to Colorado Springs, where in 1875 she married William Sharpless Jackson.

During a visit to Boston, Jackson attended a lecture by Thomas H. Tibbles and learned of the unjust treatment accorded the Ponca tribe by the U.S. government. Although she had previously shown neither interest nor sympathy for Native Americans, Jackson devoted the rest of her energy to spreading public awareness and changing the U.S. government's Indian policy. Her crusade began with the formation of the Boston Indian Citizenship Associa-

HUNTINGTON LIBRARY, SAN MARINO, CALIFORNIA

Helen Hunt Jackson.

231

tion. Traveling with Tibbles, she gathered information and wrote scathing letters to newspapers and magazines around the country. The culmination of her efforts, *A Century of Dishonor* (1881), described in detail the government's myriad broken treaties and unjust treatment of seven tribes, including the Cheyennes, Nez Perces, Sioux, and Cherokees. It also detailed four outrageous massacres of Indians by the U.S. military. At her own expense, Jackson sent copies to every member of Congress, following them up with personal interviews.

During the first few months of 1881, a President's Commission issued a report favorable to the Indian cause, and a bill was passed to try to reimburse and relocate the Poncas. Encouraged, Jackson wrote about the Mission Indians in California. Nevertheless, Indian dispossession continued, and Jackson resolved to "do for the Indian what Harriet Beecher Stowe had done for Blacks." *Ramona* (1884) achieved immediate popularity, but as a nostalgic romance about an idealized, old-world, Spanish life in California, it seemed to do little to further Jackson's cause. When reviewers failed even to mention Indians, Jackson believed the book a failure. Her health failed, and from her deathbed in California she wrote to President Grover Cleveland, urging the Indian cause. She died on August 12, 1885.

Jackson, William Henry

1843–1942

Survey artist, photographer, and painter (self-taught), Jackson was one of the earliest and most famous photographers of life and landscapes of the American West.

Jackson, who was born in 1843 in Keeseville, New York, completed high school and worked as a photographer for two years before serving in the Civil War. When in 1866 he was hired to assist a wagon train bound for the Montana mines, Jackson took advantage of the opportunity to sketch scenes of the American heartland along the way. A year later he drove horses from California to Omaha, Nebraska, and, having scant funds, set up a photography studio.

In 1870, Jackson was hired as the official photographer for the Hayden Geological Survey of the Ter-

William Henry Jackson at work in the Yosemite Valley

ritories, a position he held for the next eight years. Working in 1871 with survey artists Thomas Moran and William H. Holmes, he took the first photographs of the Yellowstone region and completed several watercolors as well.

Jackson's photographs attracted the attention of

Harper's Weekly, which hired him to produce photographs as well as paintings of the land and people of the West. The Detroit Publishing Company offered him a staff position in 1898, and there he remained until his retirement 26 years later at the age of 81. Jackson settled in Washington, D.C., where he continued to write and paint about his frontier experiences until his death in 1942, at the age of 99.

A large collection of Jackson's work is held at the Thomas Gilcrease Institute of American History and Art in Tulsa, Oklahoma. Illustrations of his watercolors are shown in *Picture Maker of the Old West*, published in 1947 by his son, Clarence S. Jackson.

James, Alexander Frank 1843–1915
and James, Jesse Woodson 1847–1882

The American West's most famous outlaws, these brothers had a long career as robbers and murderers, and captured the popular imagination as modern-day Robin Hoods who were driven to a life of crime. Their father, the Reverend Robert James, set out for California from Missouri, leaving the boys and their mother, when Jesse was three years old.

Missouri in the 1850s reflected the growing sectional conflict that led to the Civil War, and the boys, sympathetic to the Southern cause, played their parts in the coming conflict. The older Frank hooked up with William Clarke Quantrill's band of guerrillas, Quantrill's Raiders, operating on the Kansas-Missouri border, and made friends with another raider, Cole Younger. In 1864 Jesse joined "Bloody Bill" Anderson's Rebel guerrilla band. In raids on anti-slavery towns and Union soldiers, the brothers learned the hit-and-run tactics that would become the trademark of their later banditry. Both bands surrendered at war's end, but Jesse was shot and seriously wounded by Union troops while attempting to surrender.

After Jesse's recovery, the brothers robbed the bank at Liberty, Missouri, on February 13, 1866, killing a bystander. Cole Younger joined the James boys, as did several of his younger brothers over the

S.P. STEVENS

The James gang, with Jesse at the far left.

The James gang visits a town, leaving mayhem in their wake.

next few years. The gang continued to rob banks from Iowa to Alabama to Texas, and, in 1873, added train robbing to their lengthy résumé of holdups of stagecoaches, stores, and individuals.

The gang enjoyed widespread support in the poor rural Ozark Mountains, and writers began presenting them as folk heroes to eastern readers hungry for Western adventure. Public sympathy for the outlaws grew when Pinkerton detectives, in their zeal to capture them, threw a bomb into their mother's house, killing Jesse's 8-year-old half-brother and severing their mother's right arm. On September 7, 1876, in a disastrous attempt to rob the First National Bank of Northfield, Minnesota, Jesse and Frank were the only ones of the eight-man gang to avoid death or capture. Cole, Jim, and Bob Younger were captured and given life sentences. Lying low for three years under aliases in Nashville, Tennessee, the James brothers regrouped with a new gang and then, in October 1879, robbed a train near Glendale, Missouri.

Further murders and robberies resulted in the offering of $5,000 bounty for the capture and conviction of either brother. One of the gang members, Robert Ford, could not pass up such a reward, and on April 3, 1882, he shot Jesse in the head while Jesse stood on a chair straightening a picture on the wall of his home. Within a few months Frank surrendered to the authorities, who were unable to convict him in three separate trials for murder,

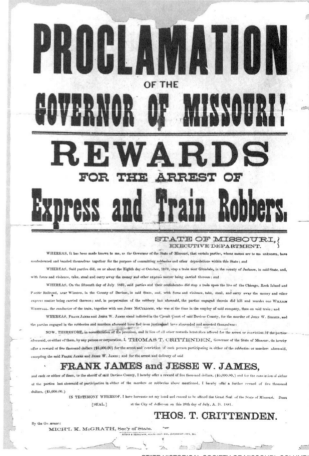

Wanted poster for the James brothers.

robbery, and armed robbery, and the older James brother went free, living a sedate life on his family's farm. In 1915 Frank died in the room in which he was born.

Japanese Settlers in the West

Like the Irish, the Japanese were compelled to emigrate to the United States by a severe agricultural depression, this one occurring in the 1880s as a result of the economic upheavals of the Meiji restoration. Prior to that time, as Japan had been by and large a society closed to the West until Commodore Matthew Perry sailed there in 1853, few Japanese had come to the United States. There had been a colony, which ultimately failed, at Gold Hill in Eldorado County, California, led by a German who had taken Japanese citizenship, J. H. Schnell (a.k.a. Matsudaira Takebe), but until late in the nineteenth century there were fewer than 200 Japanese in the United States.

In the 1880s, with a depression hitting Japanese farmers hard, their government officially sanctioned the recruitment of contract labor. For Hawaiian sugar planters, it could not have come at a better time; Chinese labor was drying up as the Chinese finished their contracts and moved into business for themselves. By 1894, the Japanese made up the bulk of agricultural labor in the Islands.

The Meiji Restoration had an unexpected benefit for Japanese who immigrated to the United States. With a strong central government (unlike China's), the Japanese were able to negotiate forcefully with the United States on immigration treaties. As a result of the 1908 Gentlemen's Agreement, Japanese women were allowed to come to the United States as family members. This proviso prompted a rash of so-called picture brides, women who were married by arrangements between families, and sent to Hawaii or to the mainland to join their heretofore unseen husbands. In return, Japan agreed not to issue passports for workers for the mainland United States.

Conditions in the Hawaiian labor camps were deplorable. The hours were long; the work was backbreaking; the camps were unsanitary and crowded;

and pay was meager (although generous by the standards of Japanese farm labor at home). The Japanese farm workers organized unions, did what they could to beautify the camps, and established schools for their children and social organizations for the growing Japanese community in Hawaii.

In California, the Japanese faced the same racism that had greeted the Chinese 50 years earlier. When the San Francisco Board of Education tried to segregate Japanese and Korean children with Chinese in the "Oriental School" in 1906, strong protests by the Japanese government ultimately led to the negotiation of the 1908 agreement. The culmination of the anti-Japanese campaign came with the Alien Land Act of 1913, which barred aliens ineligible for U.S. citizenship (a category that at that time included the Japanese) from owning land in California or leasing any for more than three years. The anti-Japanese wave continued into the 1920s, which saw the passage of further discriminatory legislation that clearly targeted Japanese immigrants both in California and Washington, D.C.

Anti-Japanese sentiment grew with the declaration of World War II, and in the wake of the Japanese attack on Pearl Harbor in December 1941, thousands of Japanese and Japanese-Americans were taken to internment camps in the West. The camps were located in desolate regions in remote desert areas. Some 35,000 Japanese-Americans served heroically and honorably in the U.S. Armed Forces in World War II, while their families were literally being held prisoner by the U.S. government.

Jesuits

Of all the religious orders of the Catholic Church that engaged in missionary work in the New World, none were more persistent or dedicated, or took greater risks, than the Society of Jesus, or Jesuits. A highly disciplined order founded by St. Ignatius of Loyola in Spain in the 1540s, its members worked with particular distinction in foreign Missions, in education, and in the sciences and humanities. In the seventeenth and early eighteenth centuries, the Jesuits were particularly active in the Southwest in Arizona and New Mexico, and in the French-controlled Northeast and Midwest, converting Native Americans to Catholicism.

Although the Jesuits were preceded in New Spain by the Franciscans, first arriving in Sinaloa in 1591, they were intensely active. Father Eusebio Kino, "the Apostle of Arizona," founded two dozen missions and personally baptized 4,500 Indians over an area thousands of miles wide. In 1701, Kino established the first Jesuit mission in what is now Arizona. However, the Jesuit missions in Arizona did not outlive him by long.

In 1767, the Jesuits were expelled from New Spain by order of Carlos III, the Spanish king, who was consolidating his political power and modernizing his country by attempting to drag the religious orders into line. In the Southwest, his army rounded up the priests at Tutubama, took them on a disease-ridden voyage across the Gulf of California, and then on a death march across Mexico. Many did not survive.

The priests fared only marginally better in French-held provinces. Father Isaac Jogues was captured by Mohawks in 1642 and tortured; when he returned to America four years later, he was tortured and killed by the Iroquois. Before 1776, it is estimated that Native American tribes had killed 84 missionaries of various orders.

The Jesuits, however, also enjoyed considerable success in their missionary work. Marquette began working along the Mississippi River, and others followed. Jesuit missionaries made conversions among the Arkansas, Caddo, Chickasaw, Chippewa, Choctaw, Fox, Illinois, Miami, Natchez, Pawnee, and Winnebago Indians and dozens of others. As in New Spain, however, the power of the conversions probably didn't long survive the departure of the missionaries.

Even after attempts by the Pope to suppress the order, Jesuit missionaries continued to ply their trade in the New World. The most successful and prominent of them, Jean Pierre de Smet, was a popular figure among the Plains Indians and even served as a peace agent in the Indian Wars of the region. The Jesuits continued their work in the Northwest, again with considerable success, with nine missions and stations ministering to some 7,000 Native Americans.

Where their work was successful, the missionaries left behind a legacy effective enough that the next generation of the priesthood among the tribes would be administered by converts themselves. The Jesuits undoubtedly owed much of their success to their policy of accommodating native cultures, requiring minimal adoption of white ways. Rather than "civilizing" them by wrenching them away from their traditional social structures, the Jesuits counseled respect for those aspects of Native American culture that were compatible with Christian belief. The result was that in North and Latin America, the Jesuits are estimated to have baptized as many as two million Native Americans in their missions, an impressive record given the sparseness of their own numbers.

Jewish Settlers in the West

Although the first Jews arrived in the United States in 1654, they did not head for the West in substantial numbers until the California gold rush of 1849. There were, of course, pockets of Jewish immigration prior to that, but their numbers were limited; the first major wave of Jewish arrivals in the New World did not take place until anti-Semitic rioting swept German cities in the late 1830s.

In 1817, Cincinnati received its first permanent Jewish resident, a British watchmaker named Joseph Jonas. For two years, he was the city's only Jew and something of a curiosity. After three of his fellows joined him in 1819, they held the city's first Jewish prayer service. By 1836, the city had its own synagogue.

The growth of the Jewish community in Illinois, particularly around Chicago, was spurred by William Renau, one of the founders of the Jewish fraternal organization B'nai Brith. Renau traveled around the country promoting the idea of Jewish settlement in agricultural communities. After the opening of the Illinois & Michigan Canal and the completion of the Galena & Chicago Railroad, the community grew quickly.

These two cities showed the typical pattern of growth in the Jewish community prior to the next major wave of immigration, again primarily from Germany, in 1848–1849. The German communities of cities like Cincinnati and St. Louis benefited from an influx of German Jews, but the newcomers also tried their hands down the Mississippi in cities like

Levi Strauss.

Natchez, Vicksburg, Shreveport and, most of all, New Orleans. And with the Mexican War over, still more Jewish settlers poured West. Wyatt Earp was appointed town marshal of Dodge City by a Jewish city councilman, Adolph Gluck. Omaha tradesman Julius Meyer was voted an honorary Pawnee chief. Sigmund Schlosinger, a Hungarian Jew, was a scout on the Kansas-Colorado border. Adah Isaacs Menken was a celebrated actress who performed memorably in Virginia City, and Sarah Marcus, another Jewish actress, was Wyatt Earp's common-law wife. In fact, Earp is buried in a Jewish cemetery.

Most of the new Jewish settlers were merchants. Among the names from the pioneer days that are still familiar today are Levi Strauss, of blue jeans fame, Isaac and Joseph Magnin, and Adolph Sutro, all of whom settled in the San Francisco Bay Area. In New Mexico, Jewish merchants grew successful by supplying the traffic on the Sante Fe Trail from the 1850s to the 1880s. Although Jewish businessmen established a solid foothold as shopkeepers and bankers in New Mexico in the second half of the 1800s, they sensed that they would be unwelcome in larger businesses and stayed away from railroads and other big companies.

In spite of rampant anti-Semitism, Jews rose to prominence in western law and politics as well. Henry Lyons was chief justice of the Supreme Court

Jewish children in San Francisco gather for a party, 1898.

of California in 1852, and Edward Salomon was governor of Washington Territory between 1870 and 1872.

With the decline of the mining economy in the early 1880s, many Jews moved from the fading boom towns back to larger cities, with the result that most of the West's urban centers had sizable Jewish communities by the turn of the century.

Johnson County War

1892

Cattle rustling—some of it real, much of it fabricated—lay at the heart of this Wyoming range war. A precipitating factor in the conflict was the lynching of Ella "Cattle Kate" Watson and James Averill on the Sweetwater range on July 20, 1889. The murders were ostensibly punishment for their rustling the cattle of powerful stockman Albert Bothwell, but Watson and Averill's real crime was that they were homesteading on land Bothwell claimed as part of his grazing domain.

The big and influential ranchers, represented by

Saloon keeper Jim Averell was unfortunate enough to settle on Wyoming land desired by the cattle barons. He was lynched in 1889.

the Wyoming Stock Growers Association (WSGA) and its militant faction, the Cheyenne Club, reacted to the perceived failure of juries to convict known rustlers by practicing the classic Old West measure

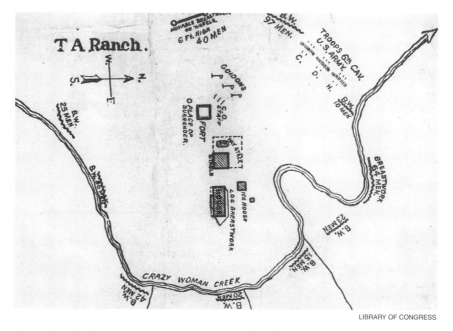

Plan of the final battle in the Johnson County War. The U.S. cavalry, top right, arrived just in time to keep the vigilantes from being defeated.

of forming a group of Vigilantes—"Regulators"—to find and punish the wrongdoers.

In April 1892, 41 vigilantes, made up of Wyoming cattlemen, stock detectives, and 21 hired Texas gunmen, arrived by train in Casper. The leader of the group was Frank M. Canton, former sheriff of Johnson County and at the time a detective for the WSGA. He led his men on horseback north to the town of Buffalo, seat of Johnson County. The plan was to kill Johnson County Sheriff William G. "Red" Angus, elected by the anti-WSGA faction of small and independent ranchers (all of whom were called "rustlers" by the WSGA), then to fan out and kill as many "rustlers" in Johnson and adjoining counties as could be found.

The hired guns advanced to the Powder River and at the KC Ranch found two known rustlers, Nick Ray and Nate Champion, and killed both of them. A third man escaped from the ranch house and rallied Sheriff Angus and others. On April 10, when Canton's band neared the town of Buffalo, they were warned that Angus and his deputies, the townspeople and area ranchers, were armed and ready for them.

Canton led his vigilantes back 14 miles below Buffalo to the TA Ranch, where they were boxed in by some 300 men recruited by Sheriff Angus. The attackers, after exchanging ineffective gunfire with the holed-up vigilantes, hastily threw together a six-foot-high movable breastwork made up of the running gears of two wagons lashed together. This weird device, with upwards of 40 men crouched behind it, was pushed steadily toward the ranch house, the objective being to get close enough to lob dynamite bombs into the house and kill or at least flush out the occupants. On April 13, as the besiegers were making progress toward the house, the battle ended abruptly with the arrival of three troops of U.S. Cavalry from Fort McKinney, led by Col. J. J. Van Horn. Van Horn arranged a ceasefire with Angus and the surrender of the vigilantes.

Only two of the 46 Regulators had been wounded in the siege, one of whom subsequently died. None of the vigilantes or their employers were tried for the killings of Ray and Champion, and after a nominal trial in Cheyenne, all were released. But public opinion turned against the WSGA and its servants, especially after the defection of Asa Shinn Mercer, publisher of the influential and pro-WSGA Cheyenne newspaper, *Northwestern Live Stock Journal.*

After the Johnson County incident, Mercer, who had earlier supported even such an atrocity as the lynchings of Watson and Averill, began printing stories on the illegal activities of the WSGA. He was beaten, sued, and had his newspaper boycotted by the large stock-growing interests in Wyoming. He persisted in his revelations, however, and in 1894 published his book, *Banditti of the Plains*, which, despite its vitriol, remains highly regarded by students of the cattle wars of the West.

Judson, Edward Z. C.

1821–1886

An author (known to thousands of readers as Ned Buntline) who immortalized Western heroes such as "Buffalo Bill" in sensational dime novels, Edward Zane Carroll Judson was born in Harpersfield, New York, on March 20, 1821. Soon afterward the family settled in Philadelphia, Pennsylvania, where Judson's father practiced law. At age 11 the adventurous youth ran away to sea and soon entered government service on a man-of-war. At 13, after he rescued a shipwrecked crew, President Martin Van Buren

LIBRARY OF CONGRESS

Judson's Scouts of the Prairies starred, from left to right, Judson himself, Bill Cody, Italian dancer Giuseppina Murlacchi, and scout Texas Jack Omohundro.

granted him a commission as midshipman in the navy.

A few years later Judson began writing humorous sketches about navy life, signing them "Ned Buntline." His first published story, "The Captain's Pig," appeared in *Knickerbocker Magazine* in 1838 and was highly praised. Eager to capitalize on his newfound popularity, he resigned from the navy in 1842 and began a weekly paper in Kentucky called *Ned Buntline's Own*. The writer continued to live up to his tough reputation as "best shot in the navy," singlehandedly capturing two men wanted for murder.

Later injured in a skirmish, Judson moved to New York City. His affiliation with an anti-immigrant movement led him to organize the political "Know-Nothing" party, which admitted only native-born Americans. In 1849 Judson was arrested for inciting the Astor Place riots against the English actor William Macready; upon conviction, he was fined $250 and sentenced to a year of imprisonment.

After his release, Judson became a prolific writer of sensational stories for weekly papers, but he remained true to his old beliefs, touting "Americanism" as well as temperance in tours out West. His influential meeting with William Frederick "Buffalo Bill" Cody spurred the novel *Buffalo Bill, the King of the Border Men* (1869), after which he hastily scribbled out a play, hiring Cody and Texas Jack Omhundro for the lead roles. The ad hoc collaboration was an instant hit and toured the Midwest.

Judson wrote over 400 adventure-filled tales of the Wild West and the sea. Besides Ned Buntline, Judson published under the pseudonyms Julia Manners, Edward Minturen, and Charles H. Cranston. He died at his Catskill cabin on July 16, 1886.

K

Kansas

The 34th state to enter the Union, Kansas is currently one of the country's leading agricultural states.

The early inhabitants of Kansas were seminomadic tribes. When Francisco Vasquez de Coronado arrived in Kansas in 1541 in search of the gilded city of Quivara, the area was occupied primarily by Osage, Pawnee, and Kansas Indians. The Kansas, the people for whom the state was named, migrated to the Great Plains from the Ohio Valley. The Pawnees, once numbering about 25,000, arrived from the Southwest.

Kansas was originally claimed by France as part of Louisiana. After being ceded to Spain in 1762, and transferred back to France, the area was acquired by the United States in the Louisiana Purchase of 1803. The first American exploration of the region was conducted by Lewis and Clark in 1804. Other notable explorers were Lieutenant Zebulon Pike, who explored the prairie country in 1806, and Major Stephen H. Long, who traversed the state in 1819–1820. Pike and Long reported that the Plains were unfit for human habitation, and Long even labeled the region the "Great American Desert."

As a result of Long's classification of the land, the U.S. government designated the region as a reservation for Indians pushed out of the East. The Kansas and Osages were forced to give up their land for the relocated Shawnees and other tribes. Soon, however, an increasing number of emigrants traveled West over the Oregon and Santa Fe Trails, and pressure mounted to open Kansas for settlement, an act eventually accomplished by the Kansas-Nebraska Act of 1854, which established the two territories. By 1880, nearly all the Native Americans in Kansas had been forced to surrender their land and retreat to the region that became Oklahoma.

The Kansas-Nebraska Act repealed the Missouri Compromise of 1820, thereby establishing Popular Sovereignty and permitting individual territories to decide for themselves on the issue of slavery. Consequently, pro-slavery groups migrated to the newly established territory, while at the same time the Emigrant Aid Company promoted the immigration of anti-slavery settlers from the North. Rivalry between the two groups soon erupted in violence as both scrambled to establish their own territorial governments. The pro-slavery group held elections in 1854 and 1855, and soon thereafter enacted the "Bogus Laws," calling for punishment by death for anyone aiding in the rebellion of slaves or free blacks. The anti-slavery faction responded with raids on slaveholders. Abolitionist farmers were opposed to slavery on economic grounds; they feared competition from slaveholding plantations and free blacks. The violence between the rival factions escalated to such a point that the territory became known as "Bleeding Kansas." After prolonged controversy, an anti-slavery constitution was signed in 1859, and Kansas entered the Union as a free state in 1861. Throughout the Civil War, however, violent attacks continued along the Missouri-Kansas border.

Kansas experienced tremendous population growth in the 1870s and 1880s. Good soil and consistent rainfall, coupled with rapid Railroad ex-

The personal calling card of Susanna Salter, the first woman elected mayor in Kansas (and America).

pansion, attracted thousands, including many immigrants from Germany, Sweden, and Russia. The Exoduster movement, the first major migration of free blacks from the South, peaked in 1879 and brought over 6,000 blacks to Kansas. Farmers prospered, and increased food demand in the early twentieth century brought boom times to the Plains. However, severe drought and high winds struck in the early 1930s, and southwestern Kansas was in the heart of the Dust Bowl. Since then, improved farming techniques and increased irrigation have made Kansas one of the most productive agricultural states in the country. The petroleum and aircraft industries have made Wichita the largest city in Kansas, followed by Kansas City and Topeka, the state's capital.

Kansas Indians

The Kansas (or Konzas) are a Siouan tribe of Indians, now known as the Kaws, who are closely related to the Omahas.

According to tradition among the Kansa, Omaha, Osage, Ponca, and Quapaw tribes, they were all once a single people, living east of the Ohio Valley in Indiana and Kentucky. Their languages and similarities in custom and tribal organization seem to confirm this. The five tribes gradually split apart, and sometime before the mid-seventeenth century the Kansas arrived in what is today northeast Kansas.

With the arrival of whites in the area, the Kansas were badly oppressed and exploited by missionaries, settlers, and developers. Despite the best efforts of their revered chief, Al-le-go-wa-ho, the tribe was removed to Indian Territory in 1873. In 1902, the Kaw Allotment Act was passed under the sponsorship of Charles Curtis, himself a Kansa (see Dawes Act). Later Curtis served as vice-president under Herbert Hoover, the only Native American in history to hold that office.

Kansas-Nebraska Act

MAY 30, 1854

The Kansas-Nebraska Act was signed into law on May 30, 1854. It established the territories of Kansas and Nebraska, repealed the Missouri Compromise, and changed the law covering the expansion of slavery into new territories.

The last of three attempts at compromise between pro- and anti-slavery forces in the nation and Congress, the Kansas-Nebraska Act was Illinois Senator Stephen Douglas's attempt to bring a peaceful resolution to sectional differences. In fact, it had almost the exact opposite effect, leading to bloodshed in the territories and stepping up the secession movement in the South.

Douglas, who was chair of the Senate Committee on Territories, argued that it was imperative that Kansas and Nebraska be organized as territories, in large part because the proposed transcontinental railroad was meant to run through them. Pro-slavery congressmen would not tolerate the admission to the Union of more free states and territories.

Douglas's compromise called for repeal of the restriction on slavery enacted by the Missouri Compromise, which forbade the practice in all Louisiana Purchase territories other than Missouri itself. The new territories of Kansas and Nebraska would address the issue through "popular sovereignty"; that is, the decision would be made by the settlers themselves. However, this plan remained ambiguous, as no one could agree on exactly when this decision would be made. Because the territories were to be admitted at the same time, most interested parties assumed that Kansas would be slave, and Nebraska free.

After three months of bitter debate in both houses of Congress, the bill was passed, thanks in no small part to the support of President Franklin Pierce and the pro-slavery Southern bloc.

The legislation produced several unexpected results. First, it caused a major reshuffling of political party affiliations; out of their opposition to the law, former Whigs, Free Soilers, and anti-slavery Democrats banded together to form the Republican Party. Anti-slavery forces denounced Douglas for selling out to the South for a chance at the presidency, a charge he vehemently denied. Douglas argued that the act was a logical extension of the Compromise of 1850, in which the doctrine of "popular sovereignty" was first enunciated.

There was a more ominous reaction to the bill's passage. Because the principle of "popular sovereignty" was to apply to the two territories, both pro- and anti-slavery forces began to vigorously marshall their supporters in drives to populate the areas with their own sympathizers. The Emigrant Aid Company was formed in Massachusetts by abolitionists, helping to ship eastern opponents of slavery into Kansas. Missouri-based pro-slavery forces did the same. Towns were founded by groups from each side—Lawrence and Topeka by free-soil forces, Atchison and Leavenworth by supporters of slavery.

The initial elections of 1854 and 1855 were won by the pro-slavery forces, aided immeasurably by the presence of armed Missourians at polling places and rampant ballot-box stuffing by their allies. Eventually, Kansas found itself with two state governments, each denying the other's legitimacy. Inevitably, violence followed, the tragedy known as "bleeding Kansas," as both sides killed their opponents indiscriminately, a brutal preview of the larger conflict to come.

Kearny, Stephen Watts

1794–1848

Stephen Watts Kearny was a frontier army officer. The youngest of 15 children of a well-to-do family, he briefly attended Columbia University before accepting a commission as a first lieutenant at the start of the War of 1812. He was wounded and captured in the

LIBRARY OF CONGRESS

Stephen Watts Kearny.

October 1813 Battle of Queenston Heights, above the Niagara River in Canada, but was later exchanged for British prisoners. He was made a captain shortly afterward, and was transferred to the frontier in 1819; he would be stationed in the West almost continuously after that.

Kearny rose in rank steadily, and was made colonel of a regiment of dragoons in 1836; he is often cited as the father of the U.S. Cavalry, into which the dragoons evolved. His command was active in patrolling the trouble spots of the West and in overseeing expeditions through the territory.

In June 1846 he was made a brigadier general and placed in command of the Army of the West in the Mexican War. He took his force of 1,660 men to Santa Fe and served as military governor of New Mexico for about a month. Having organized a civil government, he set out for the West Coast with a force of some 300 dragoons. However, receiving (premature) information that California had surrendered to Frémont and Stockton, he sent back all but 100 of them. On December 6 they attacked a superior force of Mexicans at San Pasqual but were repulsed with numerous casualties; Kearny himself was wounded twice. Aided by a relief force dispatched by Commodore Robert Field Stockton, Kearny and his men were able to reach San Diego. From there the combined American force marched to Los Angeles with only minor opposition. The surrender of California followed shortly. Kearny and Stockton then had an intense squabble over who was to take command, with Frémont, the civil governor, siding with Stockton, who had appointed him. Washington, however, confirmed Kearny's command, and ordered Frémont back east, where he was court-martialed. Kearny continued to Mexico, where he served as civil governor of Vera Cruz. There he contracted a tropical disease that ruined his health. He died in St. Louis a short time later.

King Ranch

A sprawling cattle and oil refining empire, the King Ranch grew from 75,000 acres in Texas in the 1850s to over 12 million acres throughout several counties today. On July 25, 1853, former riverboat captain Richard King purchased Juan Mendila's Spanish land grant of about 75,000 acres of the Santa Gertrudis Creek region in Nueces County, Texas. Besides raising cattle, he bred horses and bought more land whenever possible. When King died in

King Ranch founder Richard King.

1885, his wife took charge, and it was her wisdom and vision that shaped the future of the ranch.

Henrietta Chamberlain King inherited half a million acres of land and a $500,000 debt. When she died in 1925, the estate encompassed over one million acres and was worth almost $5.5 million. Her efforts to restore her husband's enterprise were overwhelmingly successful: She put in a rail line to ship the cattle straight to market, which decreased the number of livestock lost en route. By breeding Brahmin cattle with Shorthorns, Ms. King produced the famous Santa Gertrudis beef cattle, a highly disease-resistant strain able to thrive in harsh climates. During a devastating drought she brought in well-drilling equipment and saved the cattle.

Under her direction, the town of Kingsville was formed. She donated money to build churches and schools in this shipping center and lobbied to keep saloons out. Over time the number of settlers increased, and Ms. King profited as owner and operator of the town's lumber company, weekly newspaper, and cotton gin. Together with her son-in-law, Robert Kleberg, Ms. King developed racehorses, breeding three Kentucky Derby winners. When oil was discovered on the property, she reinvested in land as her husband had done. After her death in 1925, the ranch became incorporated and remained in the family. Over 400 oil-producing wells were developed on the property by 1950, and today the ranch extends to millions of acres in Australia, Venezuela, Brazil, and Morocco.

Kino, Eusebio Francisco

1645–1711

A Jesuit missionary, an explorer, a mathematician, Father Kino was a polymath, a man of incredible energy and learning. He spread Christianity through a sizable part of what is now Arizona, founding over 20 missions, opening up the Gila, Yuma, and Colorado rivers to whites for the first time, performing the first astronomical calculations in the New World, and leaving behind maps of such excellence that they were unchanged for almost a century.

Kino, who would earn the nickname "the Apostle

of Arizona," was born in Italy of Austrian lineage. Trained in astronomy and mathematics in Germany, he entered the priesthood in 1665 and volunteered for missionary work in the Orient. Instead, he was sent west in the service of Spain and eventually arrived in Mexico in 1681.

The roots of the southwestern cattle industry can be traced to the system of rancho-missions that he established in Arizona. At his missions, he introduced European grains and fruits, including grapes. He was a superb church builder as well.

In his relentless push westward, Kino became the first to confirm that California was not an island, as had previously been believed, but could be reached by an overland route. At least 20 cities in the present Southwest were founded as a result of his work. Appropriately for a man who was known to ride an average of 50 miles a day, he died on the trail, at the Mass of Dedication of a new chapel at Magdalena, a mission he had founded.

Kiowa Indians

See Apache Indians

Kiva

A ceremonial chamber of the Pueblo and Hopi Indians of the Southwest, the kiva was used for religious and sometimes for social purposes.

Kivas can be found in the remains of the Anasazi culture; the rooms seem to have been designed for magnificent ceremonies. The chamber doubled as a religious space and as a kind of men's clubhouse. Women were either not permitted entry at all or could enter only on special occasions, provided they possessed the requisite ritual knowledge.

Like their modern-day counterparts, Anasazi kivas were circular and located underground (though Zuni kivas are above ground). They probably evolved from the underground pit houses in which the Anasazi lived before they developed into the more familiar cliff dwellings.

The kiva symbolizes the earth's womb from which the Pueblo people emerged into this world. At death, it is believed, a person's breath returns to this site of original emergence before becoming part of the clouds.

Kivas are holy sites, and strict rules govern their use. They are the domain of specific clans and religious groups. Often outsiders are not permitted inside, and since the late nineteenth century, photographs of the interior of the kiva have been prohibited.

Klondike Gold Rush

"The last grand adventure," as one of its modern chroniclers described it, the gold rush to the Klondike River in Canada's Yukon Territory in 1896–1898 came at a time of great social and economic ferment in the United States. It occurred in the decade of the Panic of 1893, the Pullman Strike, Eugene Debs, Coxey's Army, the Populists, William Jennings Bryan and the Free Silver movement, the Spanish-American War, the Wobblies, unemployment lines, hoboes riding the rails, and the grim exposés of the underbelly of American life by Jacob Riis, Upton Sinclair, Stephen Crane, and Lincoln Steffens.

The Klondike—a mysterious place "up north" that few could find on a map (from Thron-diuck, a

LIBRARY OF CONGRESS

Some Klondike gold miners used oxen to carry their possessions.

Tagish Indian name meaning "Hammer Water")—provided an escape, a real one for the relatively few who got there, a vicarious one for those who followed the grand adventure in the newspapers. This was a time when escaping from the cruel realities of life was a means of surviving them.

The first prospectors in the Upper Yukon River country came down the Porcupine River to the Yukon Basin in 1873. These men and the handful who followed them through the 1880s formed the original group of Sourdoughs, the Yukon pioneer brotherhood. Among them was Robert Henderson, a man who became a sort of James Marshall of the Klondike—the forgotten discoverer. A big, dour sailor from Nova Scotia, Henderson was among the few who had made test pans around the creeks and feeders of the Klondike. On a stream he called Gold Bottom, he made a small eight-cent pan "prospect" (a trace of gold in a pan was called "colors;" a measurable amount, no matter how small, was called a "prospect"), then headed downriver for supplies. At

LIBRARY OF CONGRESS

Prospectors en route to Chilkoot Summit.

the mouth of the Klondike he encountered George Washington Carmack, a man familiar in the Yukon as a "squaw man," and told Carmack about the promising lead.

Born in Port Costa on San Francisco Bay and the son of a Forty-niner, Carmack had come to Alaska about 1887 and had worked for a time as a packer on Chilkoot Pass above the coastal town of Dyea. He spoke both the Chilkoot and Tagish dialects, was married to a Tagish woman, and was called by the mildly contemptuous name "Siwash George." Carmack, his brother-in-law Skookum Jim, and another Indian relative called Tagish Charlie were hunters and salmon fishermen, and although they prospected a bit in the vicinity of the mining camp of Fortymile, Carmack and his kin were mainly drifters and ne'er-do-wells. But it was Carmack, not the stalwart pioneer Robert Henderson, who started the gold rush.

About three weeks after Henderson's prospect, Carmack, Tagish Charlie, and Skookum Jim washed some promising gravel on Gold Bottom, then switched to nearby Rabbit Creek. On August 16, 1896, they hit a quarter-ounce of gold—$4 worth—in their first pan. They renamed Rabbit Creek Bonanza, blazed a spruce tree with a hand-ax, staked out three 500-foot claims, and registered them in Fortymile. In a saloon there, Carmack poured some rough gold dust from a shotgun shell into a "blower," a gold-weighing scale, and announced his discovery to a wide-eyed audience. Within weeks some 700 miners in the Yukon Basin stampeded to the Klondike.

The first evidence of the gold strike in the Yukon Territory came with the docking of the steamship *Portland* in Seattle on July 17, 1897, and the *Excelsior* at San Francisco the next day. Off these vessels trudged several men carrying bags, packs, boxes, and moosehide sacks of Klondike gold. Within a few days newspapers from coast to coast echoed the headline of the Seattle *Post-Intelligencer:* GOLD! GOLD! GOLD! GOLD!

Those who heard the siren song and went north quickly discovered that there were but two reasonable routes to the goldfields. Both of them were cruelly arduous and more terrible in many ways than the overland trails to California in 1849. From the Pacific Coast steamers took prospectors up the Lynn Canal above Juneau to the jumping-off towns of Skagway and Dyea. From these points the miners chose either the Chilkoot or White Pass across the

A group of actresses heading for work in Dawson pose in hiking clothes.

coastal mountains to lakes which served as waterways leading to the Yukon river. The Klondike goldfields and the boomtown of Dawson lay 600 miles to the north. As of 1897 the Northwest Mounted Police, who manned the passes and inspected those who crossed them, required each person entering the Yukon Territory to bring a full year's provisions and equipment—flour, bacon, beans, dried fruit, dehydrated potatoes, canned goods, tenting gear, and clothing. These items, plus essential placer mining tools, amounted to a ton of goods to be freighted to the Klondike.

Those who took the shorter but more backbreaking Chilkoot route carried the required provisions across a pass which had an upward grade of 30 percent on its last four-mile leg. A half-mile from the summit, at a rest stop called the Scales, the miner's provisions were weighed by polite but firm officers of the Northwest Mounted Police. Few could carry more than 50 pounds on the six-hour climb up the 1,500 ice-carved steps to the summit, and many took three months to move their gear across.

Those who could afford to bring or buy pack animals took the Skagway Trail 45 miles across White Pass to Lake Bennett, a narrow, nightmarish path on which 3,000 horses and mules died of maltreatment, starvation, and neglect in 1897–1898, a scene of horror which seared the mind of a young Klondiker from San Francisco named Jack London who would later write of it as "Dead Horse Trail." By far the worst route, an insane 2,400 miles in length, used Edmonton, Canada, as the jumping-off place and went through some of the most forbidding country in North America. Of the 1,500–2,000 seekers who used the Edmonton trail, about a half dozen made it to the goldfields by 1898, and another 100 or fewer by 1899 when the rush was all but over.

By the fall of 1897, some 30,000 goldseekers had reached Dyea and Skagway, most of them completing their portages across the coastal passes at a time when the winter freeze locked the lakes and rivers in ice. Ten thousand people wintered on the shore of Lake Bennett alone, waiting for the spring thaw, assembling or building from local timber the boats that would take them to the Yukon and the goldfields. Many, however, died in tents and lean-tos fighting starvation, scurvy, pneumonia, and frostbite. Temperatures fell to 60° below.

In May 1898, a huge and ungainly flotilla of rafts, scows, barges, dories, and makeshift vessels of every description floated down Lake Bennett over frothing rapids to Lake Leberge, completed a two-week run to the Lewes River, then to the Yukon. Those who survived arrived in Dawson in late June, swelling the town's population to 25,000 and making it the largest city in Canada west of Winnipeg.

In Dawson, where firewood was selling for $25 a cord, coal oil for $25 a gallon, potatoes for $1 each and eggs for $1.50 each, only the saloons along Front Street, the main thoroughfare of ankle-deep mud, were thriving. The newly arrived miners learned that most of the Klondike and its tributaries had been staked long before. Precious few were getting rich; few, in fact, were making "wages"—$10 a day—from their labor.

In 1898, the most frantic year of the gold rush, about 40,000 prospectors, including those early, lucky ones, were at work around Dawson. By 1899, when a railroad had been completed from Skagway to White Horse and steamboats took miners up the Yukon to Dawson, the rush was over. Dawson's population dwindled to 10,000.

While it lasted, however, the Klondike had drawn or produced some fascinating figures in American history: Alexander Pantages, later the motion picture magnate; Tex Rickard, the prizefight promoter; Sid Grauman of the later Chinese Theater; flamboyant figures like Jefferson D. "Soapy" Smith, "Swiftwater" Bill Gates, and "Klondike Mike" Mahoney; authors Jack London, Rex Beach, Joaquin Miller, and Hamlin Garland.

Most accounts give these numbers: About 100,000 people set out for the goldfields, about a third of that number actually got to Dawson, and about half that number actually mined for gold. Perhaps 4,000 prospectors, most of them Yukon veterans, actually found some gold, and a few hundred of those got rich. About one in 100 found more than wages in the paydirt of the Klondike; the others ended up working for somebody else or returning home. The gold rush produced about $22 million in gold through 1900.

L

Lamar, Mirabeau Buonaparte

1798–1859

A noted statesman of French ancestry, Lamar was born near Louisville, Georgia, to plantation-owning parents. At an early age he showed a talent for art and literature and was educated in private schools.

He entered politics in 1828 as secretary to Governor George Troup of Georgia, and in the same year began publication of the Louisville *Enquirer*, a newspaper supporting Troup's administration. In 1832 and 1834 Lamar also ran unsuccessfully for Congress.

In 1835 Lamar traveled to Texas, then a Mexican province, with fellow Georgian James Walker Fannin (who was subsequently executed by Mexican troops at Goliad in March 1836). He joined the Texas army as a private and served under Sam Houston at the Battle of San Jacinto. Ten days after the battle, Lamar was named secretary of war in the cabinet of interim Texas Republic president David G. Burnet.

In the fall of 1836 Houston was elected president and Lamar vice-president of the republic; two years later, Lamar defeated Houston for the presidency. During his administration Lamar sought and gained recognition of Texan independence by European powers, established the capital at Austin, and set aside lands for schools and universities. During his term he first opposed annexation of Texas by the United States, but changed his view on the question after his retirement in 1841. In the Mexican War he fought under General Zachary Taylor at the battle of Monterey. Upon his return home he won election to the Texas state legislature, and later served as U.S. Minister to Nicaragua and Costa Rica.

Lamar died on December 19, 1859, at his plantation in Richmond, Texas.

TEXAS STATE ARCHIVES

Mirabeau Buonaparte Lamar.

Laramie Loafers

The Laramie Loafers was a term used for a group of Sioux Indians who lingered about Fort Laramie in Wyoming Territory, shrewdly arranging exchanges between Indians needing supplies from the fort commissary and whites needing such Indian commodities as quality buffalo and beaver skins. The derogatory label conjures a distorted image of Big Mouth, Little Crow, and other members of this group, who actually played an important role supplying ammunition to the Indians during Red Cloud's war.

Colonel Henry Maynadier, a commander stationed at Fort Laramie, employed the Laramie Loafers to negotiate with Red Cloud and the other chiefs whose tribes were blocking the Bozeman Trail. Being a vital link from the fort to other stations in Montana, the government wanted the trail safe for the expected influx of settlers to the Northwest. Although the increase in settlers meant more profits for the Loafers, they nevertheless used their advantageous position to obtain what small number of rifles and ammunition they could for Red Cloud, who was preparing to defend the Powder River country with his Arapaho and Cheyenne allies. When the tribes won the Fetterman Massacre, or Battle of the One Hundred Slain, Red Cloud refused to sign a peace treaty until the officers agreed to open Fort Laramie as a trading post for the Sioux. The terms were accepted and the treaty signed, but when the Indians arrived in the spring of 1869, the commander refused to allow trade. Trade, he insisted, would be restricted to Fort Randall, which was 300 miles away on the Missouri River where game was scarce. For the Laramie Loafers, this move to an unfamiliar environment among strangers essentially ended their prosperous venture.

Laredo, Texas

Laredo, Texas, stands on the bank of the Rio Grande, across from the Mexican city of Nuevo Laredo. Before European settlement, Apache and Comanche Indians lived in the area. Unlike the majority of Spanish settlements in Texas, Laredo was established without a Mission or a presidio.

Don Jose de Escandon actively pushed for settlement of the Texas area, and in 1755 he permitted Tomas Sanchez de la Barrera y Gallardo and a small group of settlers to establish Laredo. The town soon grew into an important trading depot between the Mexican provinces and Texas.

Santa Anna marched his troops through Laredo en route to the Alamo, and marched them back through Laredo after defeat at San Jacinto. For 283 days in 1839–1840 Laredo was hailed as the capital of the Republic of the Rio Grande, when separatists seceded in revolt against Santa Anna's government. But Santa Anna's military stormed the town, capturing and beheading the Republic's leader, Antonio Zapata, and publicly displaying his head as a warning to others.

The Treaty of Guadalupe Hidalgo established the Rio Grande as the border between Mexico and Texas in 1848. Confederates controlled the town during the Civil War and used it as a cotton shipping center. Although Laredo's population increased during the 1880s and 1890s as settlers arrived on newly extended Texas railways, those who crossed the border into Laredo during the Mexican Revolution of 1910 were faced with great anti-Mexican sentiment.

As of 1990, Laredo had approximately 123,000 inhabitants. Numerous cattle ranches, irrigated farms, and petroleum and natural gas fields lie in the surrounding region, and Laredo's port still bustles with activity.

Lewis and Clark Expedition

1804–1806

The enterprise originated with President Thomas Jefferson, who for nearly 20 years had been curious about the vast and little-known western reaches of the North American continent. His interest reflected both an inquiring scientific mind and a concern for the destiny of the infant United States. When he gained congressional backing for the venture early in 1803, none of the lands to be explored belonged to the United States. France and Spain divided the largest portion, while Great Britain, Spain, Russia, and the United States disputed ownership of the Pacific Northwest. By the time the expedition was organized, however, Jefferson had seized the opportunity suddenly offered by Napoleon to buy

Louisiana, which included the Great Plains and Rocky Mountains as far west as the Continental Divide. In ascending the Missouri River and crossing the mountains to the Pacific, the explorers would be examining the Louisiana Purchase, strengthening American claims to the disputed territory, and, they and the president hoped, discovering the long-sought Northwest Passage between the Atlantic and the Pacific.

To head the expedition Jefferson selected Captain Meriwether Lewis, who had been detailed from the regular army as his private secretary. Lewis chose as co-leader William Clark, a comrade from Indian campaigns who had left the army to manage his family's Kentucky plantation. At Camp Wood River, on the shore of the Mississippi River opposite the mouth of the Missouri, Lewis and Clark passed the winter of 1803–1804 fitting out the expedition. It consisted of the two captains, twenty-seven soldiers, a mixed-blood hunter and interpreter, Clark's black slave York, and a detail of soldiers and boatmen who would return after the first season.

The mission of the expedition had been laid out in detail in written instructions and in conversations between the president and Lewis. The first objective was geographical—to explore the Missouri River and its tributaries, to cross the Rockies by the best pass, and to find the best waterway down to the Pacific Ocean. The geographical purpose reflected both commercial and geopolitical ambitions. The fur re-

sources of the West invited American exploitation and a trade connection with the Orient. The imperial rivalry in the Pacific Northwest and the existence of imperial powers to the north and south of Louisiana led the new nation to establish a presence in the West and gain all possible knowledge about it. Thus the expedition was not only to gather data about the Native American tribes and their relationships with one another, but also to establish friendly diplomatic and commercial bonds with them. Finally, the explorers were to record details on a range of scientific topics: soils, flora, fauna, minerals, topography, climate, and other features of concern to scientists as well as to diplomats and entrepreneurs.

MISSOURI HISTORICAL SOCIETY

Among the many Native American objects that Lewis and Clark obtained on their expedition was this Cree dress. Some of the glass beads decorating the garment had been acquired by the Crees from white fur traders.

ACADEMY OF NATURAL SCIENCES OF PHILADELPHIA

The grizzly bear was one of the species native only to the American West that Lewis and Clark encountered on their expedition.

In a 55-foot keelboat and two pirogues (dugout canoes), Lewis and Clark and their men embarked on their epic adventure on May 14, 1804. Through the summer and autumn they poled and hauled their way up the Missouri River. In October they halted at the villages of the Mandan and Hidatsa (or Minitari) Indians near the mouth of the Knife River in present North Dakota. Erecting a log shelter, Fort Mandan, they spent the winter becoming acquainted with the Indians and questioning them about the land to the west.

Early in April 1805, as the extra men turned back down the Missouri in the keelboat, the Corps of Discovery resumed its journey in the two original pirogues and six more fashioned at Fort Mandan. Three new recruits went along: Toussaint Charbonneau, a mixed-blood fur trader living with the Hidatsas, hired as a guide; one of his two Indian wives, Sacagewea; and her two-month-old infant, Jean Baptiste Charbonneau. Sacagewea was a Shoshone captured by the Hidatsas five years earlier, and Lewis and Clark believed she might serve as an intermediary and interpreter with her people once their mountain homeland was reached. She was destined for high rank in American legend.

Throughout the summer the explorers worked their way up the Missouri, portaging around the Great Falls, pinpointing the source of the great river at the Three Forks, and naming its headstreams the Jefferson, Madison, and Gallatin. On the upper Jefferson, as the mountain ramparts lifted to the Continental Divide, they had to abandon their canoes. Fortunately they fell in with a band of Shoshones. They were Sacagewea's people and, as the captains had hoped, she helped cement friendly relations. From these Indians the expedition obtained horses with which to cross the mountains.

Geographical notions of the time pictured a narrow range of mountains giving way to a broad river that soon reached the Pacific. Instead, Lewis and Clark confronted a daunting tangle of rugged mountains piled range on range. Through these they picked their way during August and September 1805. From the Bitterroot River they crossed the craggy, snow-capped Bitterroot Range and, in the hardest trek of the journey, descended the Lolo Trail to the Clearwater River. Here, helped by friendly Nez Perce Indians, they exchanged their horses for canoes and once more embarked on navigable waters. Casting off on October 7, they dropped quickly down the Clearwater, the Snake, and the Columbia.

On November 18, 1805, Clark recorded at last arriving at "this emence Ocian."

The explorers erected Fort Clatsop at the mouth of the Columbia River and passed the winter of 1805–1806 there. Relentless cold rains, unfriendly Indians, and scarcity of game combined to make life miserable. In March, all welcomed the return trip. Following their trail of the previous autumn, Lewis and Clark led their men back up the rivers and the Lolo Trail to the Bitterroot Mountains. At their eastern base, the expedition divided. Lewis and nine men followed the Blackfoot River to the Missouri, detoured to explore the Marias River, then went down the Missouri. Clark and the remainder of the men retraced the outbound trail up the Bitterroot River, across to the Jefferson and down to the Three Forks. From there they traversed Bozeman Pass to the upper Yellowstone River and explored this main tributary of the Missouri.

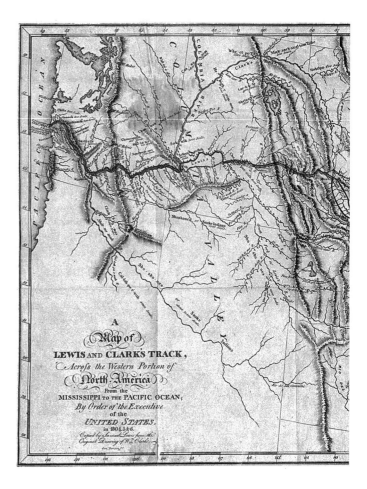

Lewis and Clark's route across the West.

On August 12 Lewis and Clark met at the mouth of the Yellowstone and turned down the Missouri. On September 23, 1806, two years and four months after their departure, the Corps of Discovery stepped ashore at St. Louis. Since they had long since been given up as lost, their appearance set off joyous welcomes in St. Louis. Jefferson was jubilant to learn of their safe return. He was even happier with the great store of knowledge the captains brought back.

In the short term, the Lewis and Clark expedition achieved limited results. Lewis's death and Clark's preoccupation with more pressing matters delayed publication of their findings. Not until 1814 was the report laid before the country. In the long term, the expedition had major consequences. Although it discovered no Northwest Passage, it made known the true character of the northern Great Plains and northern Rockies, and laid the cartographic groundwork for a series of maps that by midcentury had de-

lineated most of the trans-Mississippi West with fair accuracy.

The explorers compiled a solid foundation of knowledge about plants, animals, minerals, and other scientific aspects of the West on which later investigators built. Their descriptions of Native American tribes performed a notable ethnographic service. Their reports on the fur resources of the West inaugurated the fur-trade era in the Rocky Mountains. They established a solid American claim to the Pacific Northwest that culminated in 1846 with the resolution of the Oregon boundary dispute. In short, the Lewis and Clark expedition launched the westward movement of the American people, a movement that halted only when they had reached the Pacific and transformed the United States into a continental nation.

Finally, the Lewis and Clark expedition was one of the most exciting and dramatic adventure stories

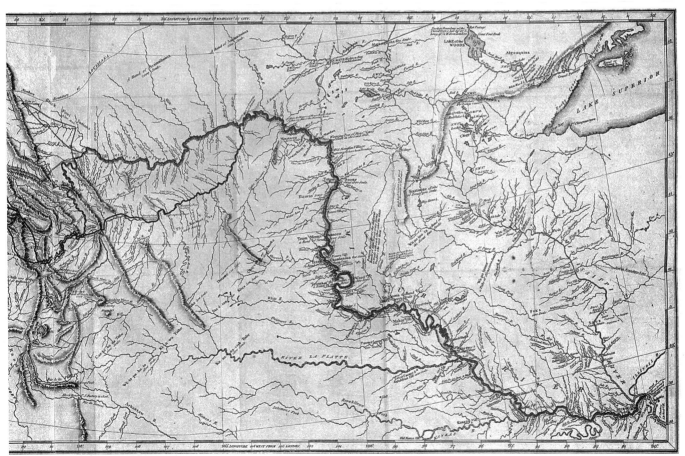

THE ACADEMY OF NATURAL SCIENCES OF PHILADELPHIA

in American history. In purely human terms, both physical and psychological, the story of the two captains and their followers became a great saga of the American past, one whose legacy lives on in the national memory.

Lewis, Meriwether

1774–1809

Meriwether Lewis was born in Virginia, not very far from Thomas Jefferson's estate. He had an excellent education and an eager mind, and he would put both to good use in his career as a soldier and explorer.

In 1794, Lewis entered the Virginia militia and served with the troops who suppressed the Whiskey Rebellion. He was appointed an ensign the following year and, while stationed at Fort Greenville, Ohio, met and became good friends with Captain William Clark. It would be several years before they met again, but they kept up a regular correspondence. By 1800, Lewis had reached the rank of captain and was the paymaster in the 1st U.S. Infantry.

On March 5, 1801, Lewis received a letter that would change his life and inscribe him forever in American history. President-elect Thomas Jefferson invited Lewis to come to Washington to serve as his private secretary. Jefferson probably had already decided on the young officer as a likely candidate to lead an expedition to explore the Northwest. The major goals of the expedition were to find a transcontinental water route to the Pacific in order to establish easier trade with Asia. At Jefferson's urging, Lewis received extensive training in the sciences. It was Lewis's suggestion that Clark be named co-leader of the unit, which became known as the Lewis and Clark expedition. His scientific training enabled Lewis to author much of the journal of their trip, although Clark also wrote extensively.

When Lewis returned from the westward trek in 1807, Jefferson appointed him governor of the Louisiana Territory. Unfortunately, Lewis was detained in the East on business and could not assume the post for a year. Jefferson's decision to reward Lewis in this way was not a sound one. Occasionally prone to rash judgment and given to severe depression, Lewis foundered in the governorship, quarrel-

ing with the territorial secretary, Frederick Bates, and alienating many of his constituents. After a year and a half, he headed back to Washington to defend his actions in office and to oversee the publication of the journals of the western trip. In an inn in the Natchez Trace of Tennessee, he died of a gunshot wound, probably self-inflicted.

Lincoln, Abraham

1809–1865

Although he was probably more strongly identified with the frontier than any other president in American history (except, perhaps, Andrew Jackson), it would be a stretch to say that Lincoln, the 16th president, was *of* the frontier. He was a child of the frontier in the most literal sense, having been born in a log cabin in Kentucky, the son of a wandering homesteader. He *did* grow up working the land on his father's farm, but he hated farming, and

Abraham Lincoln.

when he moved to New Salem, Illinois, in 1831, he had finished with the world of agriculture. He would spend the next thirty years in Sangamon County.

In 1832, Lincoln enlisted in his local volunteer militia in order to fight in the Black Hawk War. He was elected captain and served for 80 days, during which time he saw no action. (In fact, as he readily admitted, he saw no Indians.)

After an unsuccessful run for the state legislature in 1832, Lincoln won a seat in 1834 and held it until 1841, during which time he read for the law and was admitted to the bar. His political ambition drew him to the state capital, Springfield, where he became part of that city's social and intellectual circles.

Lincoln made his first appearance on the national political scene as a congressman, elected as a Whig in 1847. At this point Lincoln got his first national exposure, but not of the sort any politician would want. He spoke in opposition to the Mexican War, a position not calculated to endear him to other Black Hawk War westerners bent on expansion. In response to claims by President James Polk that the war began in response to the murder of Americans on American soil by Mexicans, Lincoln introduced a series of resolutions demanding that the president show the exact "spot" where the killing allegedly took place. For his efforts, Lincoln earned the nickname "Spotty" and lost his seat in Congress.

This setback was only temporary. When Stephen Douglas, one of the Illinois senators, spearheaded the passage of the Kansas-Nebraska Act, he forced residents of the state to make an open choice on slavery, and the bill, with its repeal of the Missouri Compromise, galvanized Lincoln. He spoke forcefully against the institution of slavery, and in 1858 was nominated to oppose Douglas by the fledgling Republican party. Lincoln engaged the "Little Giant" in a series of historic debates on the issue that established him as a national figure in the party, even though he lost the Senate race. In 1860, he was elected president.

As president, Lincoln's major preoccupation was, understandably, the Civil War. However, several measures that had an effect on the growth of the West were passed and signed into law during his five years in the White House, most notably the Homestead Act (1862), the land grants that made it possible for the transcontinental railroad to be built, and a law prohibiting slavery in all the territories. Lincoln also personally signed an order for the mass execution of 38 Indians at Mankato, Minnesota, in the

wake of the abortive uprising by the Sioux in 1862, although it is unclear how involved he was in formulating an Indian policy.

Lincoln County War

1878

The Lincoln County War illustrates the violence that characterized the frontier, where adventurous young men sought wealth by any means, habitually went armed, and frequently resorted to guns to settle disputes. "Wars" such as this outbreak in the mountains of southeastern New Mexico occurred when organized groups contended for gain, whether commercial monopoly, control of livestock ranges, or political power.

In Lincoln County "The House," the mercantile firm of Lawrence Murphy and James J. Dolan, domi-

LIBRARY OF CONGRESS

Billy the Kid escaping from the Lincoln County Jail.

nated the cashless economy of small ranchers and farmers and controlled government contracts at Fort Stanton and the Mescalero Apache Indian agency. In 1877 a newcomer challenged this monopoly. The new firm was headed by a young Englishman, John Henry Tunstall, who had teamed up with a Lincoln lawyer, Alexander McSween.

In a concocted confrontation in February 1878, a sheriff's posse shot and killed Tunstall under circumstances that amounted to murder. At once war broke out between his followers, headed by Mc-Sween, and the Murphy-Dolan establishment. Backed by the county sheriff and the district judge, the Murphy-Dolan group rode under color of law. So did the opposition, called the Regulators, for they were backed by the Lincoln justice of the peace and the town constable. Each side carried legal warrants for the arrest of the other. Among the Regulators was Henry Antrim, alias William H. Bonney, a youth of 17 destined to win fame as Billy the Kid.

A series of gunfights marked the four months after Tunstall's slaying, as the two factions maneuvered politically and legally as well as on the battlefield. On April 1, on Lincoln's single street, a group of Regulators who included William Bonney gunned down Sheriff William Brady from ambush. The conflict climaxed in Lincoln with the five-day battle of July 15–19, 1878. A sheriff's posse besieged the McSween house, defended by McSween and about a dozen men. The arrival of U.S. troops failed to stop the fighting, for the commander, Lieutenant Colonel Nathan A. M. Dudley, refused to do more than protect noncombatants. When the posse set the McSween house afire, Bonney organized a breakout that carried him and four followers to safety. Mc-Sween and three comrades were shot down in the backyard.

The deaths of Tunstall and McSween ended the challenge to the Murphy–Dolan monopoly. But since the war had forced that company into bankruptcy, no one won. Even so, lawlessness largely spawned by the war rocked Lincoln County for another year. Finally an amnesty and other measures undertaken by the territory's governor, Lew Wallace, restored a semblance of order.

Of all the combatants in the Lincoln County War, only William Bonney was convicted of crime—the murder of Sheriff Brady. The war thus launched the career of the youthful outlaw who came to be known as Billy the Kid; he died by a sheriff's bullet only three years later, at the age of 21.

Lisa, Manuel

1772–1820

Lisa was the first great developer of the western fur trade, a shrewd merchant, and a brilliant organizer who possessed almost boundless energy. Born in New Orleans, he worked the Mississippi and Ohio rivers as a trader, establishing a post at Vincennes in 1796. In 1802, he began to trade with the Osage. He was one of the suppliers for the Lewis and Clark expedition, and was one of the first to promote the idea of trade with Santa Fe.

Lisa's primary sphere of activity, however, was the Missouri River, particularly the fur country at its northern end; he made no fewer than 13 separate keelboat expeditions upriver. In spite of initial opposition from powerful St. Louis business interests, Lisa persevered, and eventually that city's traders realized it would be more lucrative to join him than to oppose him. In 1809, with local support, Lisa founded the St. Louis Missouri Fur Company. After a rocky first year, he found himself in a race against John Jacob Astor's American Fur Company for control of the Upper Missouri country. Eventually an amicable settlement was reached, and Lisa turned a substantial profit.

During the War of 1812, Lisa was a key figure in

MISSOURI HISTORICAL SOCIETY

Manuel Lisa.

keeping the Native American nations of the West neutral. After the war, he returned to the fur trade full time, prospering from his trips upriver. His last trip, in the winter of 1820, proved fatal; he contracted an illness of which he died in the summer of that year.

Little Bighorn, Battle of the

JUNE 25, 1876

This clash between about 2,000 Sioux and Cheyenne warriors and the 7th U.S. Cavalry under Lieutenant Colonel George Armstrong Custer, on the Little Bighorn River in southeastern Montana, resulted in the annihilation of five companies of the regiment personally led by Custer.

The Great Sioux War of 1876 grew out of a gold rush in 1874–1875 to the Black Hills, part of the Great Sioux Reservation guaranteed the Indians by the Fort Laramie Treaty of 1868. This treaty had divided the Sioux tribes into reservation and "nontreaty" factions. The former lived on the reservation (all of present South Dakota west of the Missouri River) and drew government rations. The latter lived in the "unceded" Powder River country to the west, scorning all relations with the whites. When the government in 1875 tried to buy the Black Hills from the reservation chiefs, the nontreaty chiefs objected, and the negotiations collapsed. To neutralize the influence of the obstructionists, officials ordered all Sioux and Cheyennes to settle on the reservation by January 31, 1876, or be considered "hostile." When few obeyed, the U.S. Army organized a military campaign to drive them in.

Exercising supreme command, General Philip H. Sheridan sent three columns to converge on the buffalo ranges of the Yellowstone River and its tributaries. General George Crook led the southern column, Colonel John Gibbon the western column, and General Alfred H. Terry the eastern column. The last included the 7th Cavalry under Custer, about 600 strong.

On June 17, 1876, Crook suffered a severe reverse at the Battle of the Rosebud, withdrew to his base camp, and appealed for reinforcements. Meantime, on the Yellowstone River to the north, Terry and Gibbon met at the mouth of Rosebud Creek and laid plans for finding and defeating the Indians, who were thought to be on the Little Bighorn River. Custer was to lead his regiment up the Rosebud and

BRADFORD BRINTON MEMORIAL

Fight on the Little Bighorn *by Frederic Remington.*

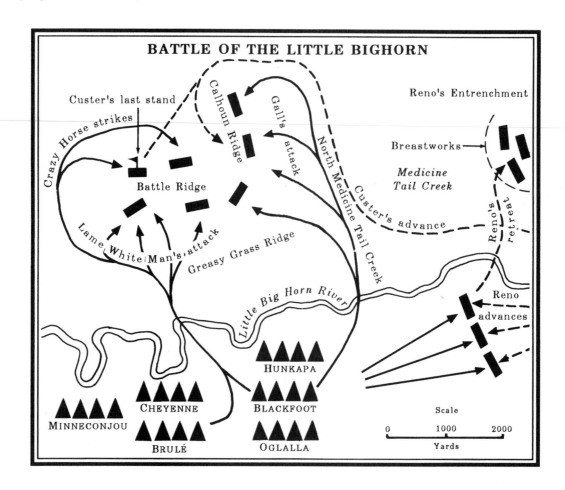

BATTLE OF THE LITTLE BIGHORN

swing north along the Little Bighorn. Terry and Gibbon, whose command included infantry as well as cavalry, would march up the Yellowstone and Bighorn to the mouth of the Little Bighorn, and there block any Indians fleeing from Custer's sweep.

By early morning of June 25, Custer had located his objective. As expected, it lay in the Little Bighorn Valley. It was a large village—six separate tribal circles, 1,000 tepees, 7,000 people, 2,000 warriors. The most prominent chiefs were Sitting Bull, Crazy Horse, Black Moon, and Gall. The tribes were angry at government actions, determined to fight for their freedom, and infused with a sense of power. They had only recently doubled their strength as reservation Indians came west to join their brethren in the war.

Custer had hoped to attack on June 26, after resting his men and scouting the country. But the Indians discovered his command, and fearing they would scatter, he advanced at once to the attack. He divided the 7th Cavalry into three battalions: one

under Captain Frederick W. Benteen, one under Major Marcus A. Reno, and the third and largest under his own command. Benteen departed on a mission to ensure that no Indians camped in the valley above the main village. Custer and Reno approached the village. Custer apparently intended to attack from two directions. He sent Reno with three companies to cross the river and strike the southern end of the village. With five companies, he himself turned north to hit the other end, three miles downstream.

Even though surprised by Reno's charge down the valley, the warriors rallied to protect their families and met the troopers at the edge of the village. Dismounting and fighting on a skirmish line in the open, Reno then withdrew his small command of 112 men into thick timber along the river. From here, after about 45 minutes of fighting, he retreated to high bluffs lining the east side of the river. The movement turned into a panic-stricken rout, with many killed and wounded.

Reno's retreat freed the warriors to concentrate

A Sioux artist's impression of Custer's Last Stand.

on Custer at the other end of their village. They kept him out of the village and confined to rough country east of the river. The fight raged along the crest and on both sides of a half-mile-long ridge overlooking the valley. On a hilltop at the northern end of the ridge, Custer and about 50 survivors gathered to make the "last stand" celebrated in history and legend. Within an hour all five companies, 210 men, had been wiped out. No one survived.

On the bluff four miles to the south, Benteen joined the battered remnant of Reno's command. Now some 350 strong, the troopers dug in and held out against attacks that evening and part of the next day. On the afternoon of June 26, as Terry and Gibbon approached from the north, the Indians struck their lodges and withdrew to the south. Counting Reno's casualties, military losses numbered 263 killed and 60 wounded. Indian losses probably did not exceed 40 to 50 killed, with many more wounded.

For the Sioux and Cheyennes, the Little Bighorn was a great triumph. For the United States, it was a terrible disaster. The death of Custer, a popular hero, and every man of his immediate command stunned Americans

and led to a renewed offensive. By the spring of 1877, most of the Sioux and Cheyennes had surrendered and settled on the reservation. The government forced them to give up the Black Hills.

Custer's Last Stand gave Custer and his troopers immortality while spawning both intense controversy and an imperishable legend. Whether a reckless fool or a victim of the failures of others, Custer remains an American icon. And the spectacle of his little band of troopers dying on their Montana hilltop is one of the most vivid and enduring images in the popular imagination.

Lone Star Republic

See Texas, Republic of

Long, Stephen Harriman

1784–1864

Long was born in Hopkinton, New Hampshire, and graduated from Dartmouth in 1809. After joining the Corps of Engineers in 1814, he taught mathematics at West Point for a year, then was appointed

Stephen Harriman Long.

major in the Corps of Topographical Engineers. In 1819 Long headed an expedition into the Far West, touted as the most ambitious since Lewis and Clark's. The Yellowstone expedition included both military and scientific personnel, and Long had direct command of the latter. His party included a botanist, a zoologist, a geologist, and the landscape painter Samuel Seymour. Their progress up the Missouri River, in a steamboat called the *Western Engineer,* was quite leisurely; after months of travel the party reached Council Bluffs, where they spent the winter of 1819–1920. Congress, impatient with the slow and costly expedition, cut off funding, forcing the men to return with disappointing results.

Long was given another expedition in 1820, this time to explore the Platte, Arkansas, and Red rivers. After departing from St. Louis in June 1820, he traveled up the Platte to the site that would become Denver, Colorado. The party then turned south and returned to St. Louis in October via the Red River and the Canadian River. In 1823 Long was charged with a third expedition, this one to explore the region between the Mississippi and Missouri rivers. He left Philadelphia on April 25 with a group of scientists and traveled west. They went down the Mississippi and then up the Minnesota and into Canada as far as Winnipeg. After following the Great Lakes to New York State, the party returned to Philadelphia on October 26, 1823. This was Long's most successful expedition, and he gathered much information about previously unexplored territory.

Long spent the remainder of his career on railroad surveys and other projects typical of a civil engineer. He retired from service at the age of 78 and died in 1864.

Longhorns

Longhorns are the breed of cattle most closely identified with the rise of the great Texas spreads, especially the King Ranch. They are immediately recognizable by the feature that gives them their name, a horn spread of 3 to 5 feet. Ironically, given their centrality to the growth of the Texas cattle industry, longhorns are known for their tough hides, stringy meat, and bad tempers. Believed to be descended from Spanish animals brought to the region by Juan de Oñate and others, the great advantage the

Cowboys driving Texas longhorns.

longhorns had for Texas cattlemen was their phenomenal stamina, which meant they could be driven the long distances to railheads. Some Texas ranchers actually drove longhorns all the way to California after the gold rush, when cattle were bringing $100 a head. Longhorns could go as long as 60 miles between waterings and were seemingly oblivious to heat and hunger, making them ideal animals for cattle drives, if not for eating. As the railroads spread across the country, the longhorn became less central to the industry. Angus cattle matured faster, produced tastier beef, and, with railheads closer, it was no longer necessary to drive them as far.

Los Angeles, California

Located on the coast of southern California, Los Angeles is the second most populous city in the United States. Its climate remains mild throughout the year, and rainfall averages only 12 inches annually. Pollutants from automobile and industry emissions hang in the trapped air above the city, causing its infamous smog.

For over 12,000 years, Native Americans inhabited the Los Angeles region. Before Europeans arrived, about 5,000 members of the Gabrielino tribe of Shoshonean Indians lived there. They were advanced and wealthy compared with their neighbors.

CENTER FOR AMERICAN HISTORY, THE UNIVERSITY OF TEXAS AT AUSTIN

The first published view of Los Angeles, made in 1853.

LIBRARY OF CONGRESS

Three wealthy young Angelenos—Ygnacio Sepulreda, Antonio Yorba, Andronico Sepulreda—as they left for school in Boston in 1850.

Unfortunately, little is known because they were soon displaced and their culture extinguished.

In 1781, Spanish Governor Felipe de Neve established a European settlement in what became Los Angeles. Los Angeles's current name stems from the original lengthy Spanish name, translated "Town of Our Lady the Queen of Angels by the Porciúncula River." The area's missions were turned into vast private landholdings under later Mexican rule. Since fresh water was scarce and the harbor was poor, cattle were raised. In 1848, the U.S. annexation of California, combined with the waves of gold seekers, caused the cattle industry to prosper. However, as the result of the stealing of ranches away from Mexican-Americans and years of alternating droughts and floods, only about 5,000 residents remained in the area by 1870.

When the Southern Pacific Railroad arrived in 1875, followed by its competitor, the Santa Fe, in 1885, cheap fares brought waves of new settlers. The discovery of vast oil fields fueled the city's growth; the population reached 100,000 by 1900. Completion of large aqueducts and pipelines, construction of a seaport, and the sprouting of Hollywood's movie business encouraged exponential population growth.

Lost Dutchman Mine

"The Lost Adams Diggings," "Tayopa," "Lost Nugget," "Peg-Leg," and "Glory Hole" are all names of "lost" gold mines of the Old West—rich treasure troves hidden by their discoverers and never again uncovered. All these, as well as the most celebrated of them all, the Lost Dutchman Mine, supposedly located in the Superstition Mountains some 35 miles east of Phoenix, have two things in common: there is little evidence they ever existed, and they remain lost.

The Lost Dutchman takes its name from Prussian-born prospector Jacob Waltz (in mining camp patois, *deutsch* translated to Dutch), who may have come to the United States in 1848 as one of the immigrant prospectors heading for the California goldfields. In

1870, legend has it (and legend is about all that has any part of the story), Waltz saved the life of one Miguel Peralta in a cantina fight in the Sonora, Mexico, town of Arizpe. Peralta is supposed to have rewarded Waltz with a map of a gold mine discovered by his grandfather in the Superstition Mountains, then located within a Peralta land grant.

Waltz and a partner, the story goes, found the mine and within a few weeks took out $60,000 in gold ore. Later, Waltz's partner was killed at the site by Apaches and Waltz covered the mine entrance, fearful of working it alone and distrustful of taking on another partner.

Waltz, who told many conflicting stories about his mine and its location, died in Phoenix in 1891. Nearly 150 years after it was allegedly discovered, treasure hunters continue to search for the mine. The Superstition Mountains have been part of the Tonto National Forest and a National Wilderness Area since 1940.

Louisiana Purchase

1803

With the frontier moving westward to the Ohio River at the end of the eighteenth and beginning of the nineteenth centuries, free use of the Mississippi to transport goods to the Gulf of Mexico, to the eastern seaboard, and to European markets became a critical issue for an expanding America. James Madison, President Thomas Jefferson's secretary of state, characterized the great heartland river as "the Hudson, the Delaware, the Potomac and all navigable rivers of the Atlantic states rolled into one stream." Indeed, even in the 1790s, the Mississippi had already become a pulsing artery of American commerce.

Spain, from its vast Louisiana province, controlled the Mississippi and its traffic. After 1786 and a royal order actively encouraging settlement, American emigrants came to both Upper and Lower Louisiana, trading with Indians, dealing in furs, and carving out farms and homesteads in Missouri, Arkansas, and as far south as New Orleans. By 1802 Spanish encouragement of the settlers had turned to fear—a fickle and ruinous policy Spain would soon pursue in its Texas province as well—and land grants to American citizens were halted.

But a more serious threat was now at hand. Unknown to Americans at the time the pact was made, in 1800 Napoleon had induced the king of Spain to cede the Louisiana province to France. By the time this momentous development became known to the U.S. government, two years after the fact, Spanish officials in New Orleans had closed the Mississippi to American traffic, thereby usurping a "right of deposit" treaty they had signed with America in 1795.

To Jefferson, a Francophile and normally a pacifist who abhorred foreign entanglements, the French advance in North America, especially under the military master of Europe, was a potentially deadly threat that might cause the United States, not strong enough to fight Napoleon's armies alone, to seek an alliance with its old enemy, England, against a common foe. In April 1802, Jefferson sent a letter to the U.S. minister in Paris, Robert Livingston, saying: "The day that France takes possession of New Orleans, fixes the sentence which is to restrain her forever within her low-water mark. It seals the union of two nations who in conjunction can maintain exclusive possession of the ocean. From that moment we must marry ourselves to the British fleet and nation."

Livingston, to whom Jefferson entrusted the opening negotiations with France, was a former chief justice of New York who had administered Washington's first presidential oath of office. In his talks with Napoleon's minister of foreign affairs, Charles Maurice de Talleyrand-Périgord, Livingston, hedging his words about the portions of Louisiana province east to the Floridas and speaking of a possible purchase of a "window" to the Gulf of Mexico (New Orleans), was startled to hear Talleyrand ask, "What will you give for the whole?" Livingston, who was partially deaf, was stunned. He had no instructions from his government on such a matter but said that the United States might give as much as $4 million for "the whole." Talleyrand answered quickly, "Too low! Reflect and see me tomorrow."

One thing was certain: Even before Jefferson, early in 1803, sent his friend James Monroe to France as minister extraordinary to assist Livingston in the negotiations, Napoleon had decided to sell Louisiana. Behind this decision lay another: his reluctant decision to abandon any dreams of expanding the French empire to the New World. His experiment in attempting to conquer sugar-rich Santo Domingo had ended in failure—a revolt by ex-slaves that had to be beaten down; then yellow fever that decimated the French forces on the island had forced a retreat from

United States territorial expansion in the 1800s.

those dreams. Moreover, Napoleon was waging a war against England and feared, given that enemy's undisputed mastery of the seas, that Louisiana might be too easy a plum to pick. To sell undefendable Louisiana to the United States, England's bitterest enemy only a few decades past, seemed the answer.

Livingston's negotiations with Talleyrand and Napoleon's various counselors had bogged down to the point that the U.S. minister had almost decided the territory would have to be taken by force and negotiated afterward. Then James Monroe arrived in Paris in April 1803. His orders were to assist in making a treaty with France "for the purpose of enlarging and more effectively securing our rights and interests in the river Mississippi and the Territories thereof."

A conference with one of Napoleon's counselors on April 13 revealed for the first time France's interest in selling the Louisiana Territory, but at about this time the issue of the legality of France's title arose. In ceding the territory to Napoleon in 1800, Spain had demanded and received a promise that France would not "alienate" the territory, that is,

cede it to any other power. Spain's formal protests to Jefferson on this matter were referred to Napoleon, who forced acquiescence to the treaty that was to follow. Haggling over the price took a week. The treaty was signed on April 30, 1803, and when the ceremony had ended, Livingston shook hands with the French negotiators and said, "We have lived long, but this is the noblest work of our lives."

For the Americans, this was patently true. The United States paid 60 million francs, $11,250,000, for the vast Louisiana Territory; adding the debts owed by France to American citizens for "spoliations"—goods lost through plunder and despoiling—the sum came to $15,000,000. For this the United States received over 500 million acres (529,911,680, to be precise) of territory, roughly five times the size of France, some of the richest, wildest land in North America.

Jefferson's bargain gave him momentary pause. He had authorized expenditure of $10 million to purchase New Orleans and, if possible, the southern coast of Louisiana east to Florida. Now he learned that he had purchased a wilderness so vast that its population of 80,000 was lost in it. He submitted the treaty to the

Senate for approval while privately admitting it was probably unconstitutional. Congress met in special session on October 17, and despite vigorous debate by the Federalists, who argued that the purchase was indeed unconstitutional, the treaty was enthusiastically ratified. Napoleon had ratified the treaty of cession five months earlier, on May 15, on the same day England declared war against France.

Although the boundary of the Louisiana Territory was not clarified until 1818, the Louisiana Purchase doubled the size of the United States, adding roughly the territory between the Mississippi River and the Rocky Mountains north as far as present-day Montana and North Dakota—today encompassing the states of Louisiana, Arkansas, Oklahoma, Missouri, Kansas, Iowa, Nebraska, and South Dakota, most of Wyoming and Montana, plus portions of southwestern Minnesota and South Dakota, northeastern New Mexico and eastern Colorado.

And even before there was a treaty, in a secret message to Congress in January 1803, Jefferson set forth his preliminary plans to explore the lands west of the Mississippi "even to the Western Ocean." In May 1804, just over a year from the signing of the treaty, Meriwether Lewis and William Clark launched their expedition into the unknown lands of the Louisiana Purchase and beyond it to the "Western Ocean."

Love, Nat

CA. 1854–19??

In his 1907 autobiography Nat Love, a black cowboy whose parents were slaves in Davidson County, Tennessee, apparently hoped he would earn recognition as the man on whom the "Deadwood Dick" dime novels were based. Love claimed to have left home in 1869. Since he was already a veteran horse breaker, he was able to join a cattle herd in the Palo Duro River area of north Texas as a cowboy. He wrote of hostile Indian tribes, breaking horses, trips up cattle trails to Kansas, traveling to Arizona and working on cattle outfits on the Gila River, learning to speak Spanish like a Mexican, and witnessing gunfights in Dodge City. He worked cattle and horses in New Mexico, Nebraska, Colorado, and the Dakotas, he said, and bragged of exploits involving whiskey, mustangs, and roping and shooting contests.

Love claimed to have won a shooting contest in Deadwood, Dakota Territory, in which he placed 14 of 14 in the bullseye with his rifle, and 10 of 12 with his Colt revolver. As the winner, he said, he was given the title "Deadwood Dick" by the appreciative Deadwood citizenry.

Love also claimed to have met Billy the Kid in a saloon in Anton Chico, New Mexico, in 1877, and to have known Pat Garrett and others in and on the fringes of the Lincoln County War.

He wrote proudly that he had ridden into the West on horseback and into the twentieth century on a train.

LIBRARY OF CONGRESS

Nat Love.

The place and circumstances of his death are unknown.

There were several other claimants to the title "Deadwood Dick," hero of a series of 33 Dime Novels written by Edward L. Wheeler for Beadle & Adams between 1877 and 1885.

Ludlow Massacre

APRIL 20, 1914

A major strike against coal operators in Colorado in September 1913 affected, among other employers, the Rockefeller-Gould-owned Colorado Fuel and Iron Corporation, the largest coal producer in the state. Prior to the strike, workers and their families had been living in miserable conditions in virtual tenements in the company town. When the strike began on September 23, 10,000 miners and their families packed their belongings and moved quietly into a tent colony in nearby Ludlow.

The miners' demands were simple: recognition of the United Mine Workers as their representative, a written guarantee of an 8-hour day, strict enforcement of state mining laws, an end to the requirement that miners live in company housing and buy all their goods from the company store, and a 10 percent wage increase to bring Colorado rates into line with those of neighboring Wyoming.

For months, a virtual state of siege existed, with the company sending guards to do battle with the miners and their families. Armed goons brought from out of state were deputized by local law enforcement officials and proceeded to harass and attack strikers and their families. The miners armed themselves and prepared for the worst.

Two companies of local militia were guarding the camp at Ludlow. These units of the Colorado National Guard were actually professional gunmen in the pay of the coal operators. On April 20, 1914, after setting off two bombs, the guardsmen opened fire on the tent city with machine guns and rifles. The miners returned their fire but were outgunned by the more heavily armed militia, who also had the advantage of being on higher ground. For 12 hours the two sides exchanged gunfire.

Then, under orders from officers, the guardsmen swept down on the colony, poured coal oil on the miners' tents, and set them ablaze. The militia looted the camp and killed three unarmed prisoners. Dozens of women and children were injured and killed.

For ten days, armed groups of miners fanned out from Ludlow, spreading word of what had happened. Fearing open rebellion, President Wilson sent federal troops to Colorado to restore order. The company finished the job of crushing the strike shortly thereafter.

Lynching

See Violence in the West

M

Mackenzie, Alexander

CA. 1764–1820

Mackenzie, a fur trader and explorer, was born in Scotland; in 1774 his family moved to New York. He began work with a Montreal-based fur trading company and by 1787 found himself a partner in the North West Company. In 1789, he set out from Fort Chipewyan in search of a navigable river to the Pacific. The river he chose to follow, which today bears his name, led him to the Arctic Ocean. He returned to Fort Chipewyan having learned that this route was not the right one.

On that first trip, Mackenzie quickly realized that he did not know how to calculate his position. During the winter of 1791–1792 he studied navigation in London before setting out again from Fort Chipewyan. As soon as the ice broke in 1793, he departed, this time following the Peace River. Following the Peace and one of its tributaries, the Parsnip, Mackenzie and his party crossed the Great Divide and followed the Fraser River west. Then, traveling overland, they followed the course of the Blackwater to the Bella Coola, down which they canoed to an inlet of the Pacific. Mackenzie had completed the first overland journey across America north of Mexico.

Perhaps the most important achievement of that trip, however, was that Mackenzie, armed with his new skill in taking astronomical readings, was able to draw a fairly accurate map of the westward journey he had successfully completed. That map became more

NATIONAL GALLERY OF CANADA, OTTAWA

Alexander Mackenzie.

widely available when Mackenzie published his journals of the trip. For his efforts, Mackenzie was knighted in 1802.

However, Mackenzie, in publishing his journals,

267

was not seeking either money or glory. Rather, he hoped to persuade the British government to grant him a charter that would give him a monopoly over the fur trade in all of Canada. His company would then be able to exploit the westward route in such a way that the increasingly greedy Americans would be warned off further encroachments into what Mackenzie believed was Canadian territory.

Mackenzie's book fired the imaginations of Thomas Jefferson and his private secretary, Meriwether Lewis. It undoubtedly helped inspire Jefferson's plan to send Lewis west with a party to explore the possibility of a water route to the Pacific and, not coincidentally, to establish American claims to the Northwest. And Mackenzie's map provided a rough guide for the Lewis and Clark Expedition on their own travels westward.

Mackenzie was elected to the Legislative Assembly of Lower Canada in 1805. In 1808 he returned to his native Scotland and spent the rest of his life there.

Mackenzie, Ranald Slidell

1840–1889

A native of New York City, Mackenzie graduated first in his West Point class of 1862 and compiled an outstanding Civil War record. Wounded twice, he ended the war a major general of volunteers and gained a colonel's commission in the postwar regular army.

As colonel of the 4th Cavalry, Mackenzie acquired a reputation as an outstanding Indian fighter. In 1871 he fought the Comanches in Texas and received a painful arrow wound. In 1873, without orders but backed by his superiors, Mackenzie led a foray into Mexico to punish raiding Kickapoo Indians. In the Red River War of 1874–1875, waged against Kiowas, Comanches, and Cheyennes to force their return to reservations, Mackenzie led a column that surprised a camp in the Palo Duro Canyon of the Texas Panhandle. In this action, September 28, 1874, his troopers killed few Native Americans but dealt them a severe blow by destroying their village and all its contents.

Shifted with his regiment to the Northern Plains following the Custer disaster of 1876, Mackenzie participated in a winter campaign under General George Crook. On November 25, 1876, Mackenzie surprised Dull Knife's Cheyenne village in a canyon of the Bighorn Mountains. In a repeat of the Palo Duro victory, he drove the Cheyennes out and destroyed their camp.

A harsh disciplinarian, tormented by wounds and often irascible, Mackenzie nevertheless was one of the most effective military leaders of the Indian Wars. His men idolized him, and President Ulysses S. Grant called him "the most promising young officer in the army." But shortly after promotion to brigadier general in 1882, Mackenzie became insane. Retired in 1884, he passed his remaining five years in an institution.

Mandan Indians

The Mandans, a Siouan tribe of Native Americans, lived on the upper Missouri River, where they grew beans, corn, squash, sunflowers, and tobacco. Early fur trappers, as well as Lewis and Clark, reported be-

JOSLYN ART MUSEUM, OMAHA, NEBRASKA

Mandan chief Mato-Tope drew this picture of himself battling and slaying a Cheyenne chief. Mato-Tope later died of smallpox, along with most of his people.

These two Mandans were the sole survivors of their village after the others died of smallpox.

ing impressed by their highly developed culture. In the 1830s, artist George Catlin immortalized them in painting and literature.

When the Mandans were first encountered by whites, they apparently had a number of albinos living among them. This fact, coupled with the tribe's cultural achievements, led early explorers to conclude that the tribe was descended from Europeans. One Welsh visitor even claimed that they spoke Welsh.

In 1750, there were nine Mandan villages. By 1800, there were only two. In 1837, a smallpox epidemic struck the 1,600 remaining Mandans. The exact number that survived is uncertain, though Clark Wissler's figure of less than 50 seems low. A better estimate is probably between 100 and 200. Later their numbers were further reduced by conflict with neighboring tribes.

Around 1845, the Mandans began affiliating with the Hidatsa and Arikara tribes. The Fort Laramie Treaty of 1851 defined a range of approximately 12 million acres for the three tribes, but when the Fort

Berthold Reservation in North Dakota was established, it contained only 8 million acres. Their land base has subsequently eroded to only 1 million acres.

Some ethnologists have declared the Mandans extinct, a claim that surprises surviving tribe members.

Mangas Coloradas

CA. 1791–1863

Mangas Coloradas, also known as Mangus Colorado and Red Sleeves, was a great war chief of the Mimbreño (eastern Chiricahua) Apaches and a

Chief Mangas, son of Mangas Colorado, carried on his father's work.

warrior in their combat against white encroachment.

Mangas had signed a treaty of friendship with the United States at Santa Fe in 1852, but became disillusioned as miners, soldiers, and settlers entered Apache territory. In 1861, by then around 70, he joined his son-in-law Cochise in fighting the whites after Cochise's brother and two nephews were executed by the U.S. Army.

In 1862, General James Carleton led a force of 1,800 soldiers through Apache country from California; his purpose was to confront the Confederate invasion of New Mexico. On July 15, 500 warriors under Mangas and Cochise attacked but were defeated by 300 soldiers at Apache Pass. During the engagement, Mangas was shot in the chest, and Cochise and a cadre of warriors carried their wounded chief 100 miles into Mexico, where he was treated by a Mexican surgeon. After recovering from his wound, Mangas returned to the Mimbres Mountains of New Mexico.

In January 1863, Mangas entered an Army encampment under a flag of truce to discuss peace. He was arrested, tortured, and killed. He was scalped, and soldiers cut off his head and boiled it so that the skull could be sold to a phrenologist in the East. Following Mangas's death, Cochise became chief of all the Chiricahuas and fought fiercely to avenge his murder.

the American character and remained a motivating force well into the twentieth century.

Thomas Jefferson's Louisiana Purchase anticipated the concept of a manifest destiny. Jefferson believed Americans were destined to expand all the way to the Pacific. John Quincy Adams and Albert Gallatin thought in similar terms, and the Monroe Doctrine of 1823, a warning to European powers against territorial ambitions in the Western Hemisphere, implied American designs on existing European possessions.

"Yes, more, more, more!" Editor O'Sullivan wrote, "till our national destiny is fulfilled and . . . the whole boundless continent is ours." As applied in the wake of his editorials, Manifest Destiny was a rallying cry for a broad program of expansion. It aimed at ending the long feud with Great Britain over the Oregon country, at incorporating independent Texas into the American union, at gaining the cession of the Mexican provinces of California and New Mexico, and at fighting a war if either nation resisted. Oregon champions vowed "Fifty-four Forty or Fight" but settled for a diplomatic accord that fixed the boundary at the 49th parallel. The Mexican War of 1846–1848 cost Mexico its northern provinces and its claim to Texas. Even so, extremists used Manifest Destiny to sanctify a demand for all Mexico. The war and the settlement of the Oregon dispute extended the boundaries of the United States to the Pacific and created a continental na-

Manifest Destiny

During the period of national expansion many Americans believed that manifestly—obviously—the destiny of the United States lay in peopling the entire North American continent. The term "Manifest Destiny" was coined in 1845 by New York editor John L. O'Sullivan, who wrote in his newspaper, the *Democratic Review*, of the nation's "manifest destiny to overspread the continent allotted by Providence for the free development of our yearly multiplying millions." Expansionists adopted Manifest Destiny as a slogan to justify the territorial aims of the Mexican War, and it achieved its greatest influence in the 1840s and 1850s. However, the ideas behind the term had long been a prominent feature of

LIBRARY OF CONGRESS

This 1872 painting shows a female embodiment of Manifest Destiny accompanying white settlers on their westward trek.

tion—not boundless, as O'Sullivan demanded, but continental nonetheless.

Not everyone subscribed to Manifest Destiny. Many believed that the nation should not expand, that it would grow too big to govern, that it would have to absorb "mongrel" peoples who would dilute the purity of the American character. The most determined opponents foresaw the impact it would have on the controversy over the extension of slavery. And in fact the issue of slavery in the territories hastened the coming of civil war.

Some who supported Manifest Destiny did so cynically; many more sincerely believed its message. In fact, Manifest Destiny was both an expression of altruism and a rationalization of greed. The altruism grew out of the belief of most Americans in the superiority of their civilization; to extend it conferred a blessing on peoples not so favorably endowed. The altruism also rested on a conviction that Manifest Destiny represented God's will. Providence decreed that the enterprising, freedom-loving Americans people the wilderness and exploit its riches. From these riches, of course, sprang the greed. Minerals, timber, grasslands, and farmlands beckoned a growing population seeking economic opportunity.

Manifest Destiny also afforded a rationale for American treatment of the Native American tribes. Indians did not make the full use of natural resources that God clearly intended. They were fated to yield to those who heeded the divine injunction to make the wilderness blossom. Manifest Destiny provided a comforting justification for what in reality was self-serving gain.

For the balance of the nineteenth century, the idea underlying Manifest Destiny found expression in projects to gain more territory: Mexico, Cuba, the Dominican Republic, Canada. In the Spanish-American War of 1898, it gave legitimacy to the acquisition of the Philippines. In the twentieth century, it lived on in a missionary impulse to spread American ideas and ways around the world.

Marshal

Although the title of marshal was often used without the proper distinction, there were town and

ARIZONA HISTORICAL SOCIETY

Arizona sheriff George Ruffner takes a break. Like modern police chiefs, he spent much of his time immersed in paperwork. At left is an early typewriter.

ARIZONA HISTORICAL SOCIETY

An array of sheriff, police, and marshal badges.

federal marshals in the Old West, each with distinct duties and legal powers.

The town marshal, essentially a chief of police, usually held office as a result of appointment by the town's administration—its mayor and city council. The marshal supervised a number of deputies and policemen and could deputize townspeople for temporary service, such as making up a posse or mob control force.

Famous town marshals include James Butler ("Wild Bill") Hickok in Abilene, Kansas (he had his headquarters at the Alamo Saloon's poker tables); Virgil Earp in Tombstone, Arizona Territory; Charlie Bassett in Dodge City (with Wyatt Earp as assistant marshal, Ed Masterson as policeman, and Bat Masterson as sheriff, an elected lawman with county responsibilities); Ben Thompson in Austin, Texas; and Henry Brown in Caldwell, Kansas.

The U.S. or federal marshal, often the beneficiary of political patronage and with little or no law experience, operated in districts that corresponded to those of U.S. District Courts in the states and territories. Federal marshals often were responsible for thousands of square miles. They were, at least technically, to enforce federal laws, pursuing such criminals as army deserters, mail or government payroll robbers, counterfeiters, and the like, and issuing subpoenas, conducting sales of federal property, gathering jurors, and executing warrants and writs.

The U.S. marshal's deputies did most of the actual field work; the marshal selected as many deputies as the district judge would permit. U.S. marshals and their deputies, who often served as town or county lawmen while holding their federal commissions, were, until 1896, paid from the fines and fees they collected.

Marshall, James Wilson

1810–1885

James Marshall's discovery of gold at Sutter's Mill in Coloma, California, on January 24, 1848, led to the California gold rush and changed the course of history not only for the American West but for the whole United States. Marshall himself profited little from his discovery, living out his later years as a gardener in Coloma County, California.

Marshall was born on October 8, 1810, in Hopewell Township, New Jersey. His father built coaches and wagons in Lambertville, New Jersey, and Marshall apprenticed in his father's shop, soon becoming an accomplished mechanic and an associate in the business. But Marshall grew restless and journeyed westward. As he traveled, he worked as a carpenter and wheelwright. In 1837 he settled in Platte County, Missouri, as a farmer. There he stayed until 1844, when, restless once more, he sold his farm and moved west to California.

Marshall was first employed at John Sutter's camp in July 1845 as a coachmaker and carpenter. The following year he fought in the Mexican War in Monterey, California, and when he returned to Sutter's camp in 1847, Sutter contracted him to build a sawmill on the south fork of the American River. Under Marshall's supervision the mill was nearly complete by January 1848. A first test revealed that the mill wheel did not turn properly because the tailrace had not been dug deep enough. Water backing up under the wheel did not provide sufficient force to set it in motion. To correct the situation, Marshall put his men back to work with explosives to deepen the channel. During the day the men would blast and dig; at night water was turned into the ditch to wash away dirt and gravel. On the morning of January 24, 1848, Marshall went out to inspect the ditch while his men were eating breakfast. Scattered along the bottom of the channel he

CALIFORNIA STATE LIBRARY

James Marshall posed next to the Coloma sawmill he built for Sutter.

saw glittering specks of metal, which he gathered up and tested. The metal was soft and malleable, and could be only one thing—gold. Marshall hurried back to the mill yard and exclaimed to the men, "Boys, I believe I have found a gold mine."

Sutter and Marshall agreed that it would be best to keep the discovery a secret until the mill was finished. By March only a small number of people in the area had heard of the gold, and many took the news with skepticism. However, by the end of May news of the gold had been published in several California newspapers, leading to a small rush of Californians to Coloma. Before long, stories of gold traveled first through the Midwest and finally throughout the country; the rush to California was on.

After his discovery, Marshall was sought out as a prospector by others but had little success. He prospected around California for several years, then returned to Coloma in 1857, where he lived on a vineyard. When he died in Kelsey, California, on August 10, 1885, his estate was worth less than $300.

Mason, Biddy

CA. 1830–?

Biddy Mason, a real estate entrepreneur and philanthropist, was a woman of rare courage and initiative, and one of pre–Civil War California's most intriguing success stories. Born a slave, she was brought west from Georgia by oxcart in 1852, first to Utah, then to San Bernardino, California. She traveled with another slave, a woman named Hannah, and their owner, Robert Smith, a Mormon convert originally from Mississippi.

In 1855, Smith decided to move with Biddy, Hannah, and their 12 children and grandchildren to Texas, a slave state, from California, a free state. Biddy, in an unprecedented step, proceeded to take Smith to court; a Los Angeles judge granted both women and their children their freedom.

Taking the last name Mason, Biddy began working as a confinement nurse and midwife for $2.50 a week. From each of her paychecks, she saved a little money and eventually bought a small building and two lots in Los Angeles. Her building had two stores at street level that she rented out. With the profits from that venture, she acquired another building, and so on. Her investments made Mason a wealthy woman, and she was a powerful and generous benefactor to the African-American community of Los Angeles. She turned her South Spring Street home into a travelers' aid center, helped to start the first elementary school for black children in the city, and was a founder of the Los Angeles African Methodist Episcopal Church.

LOS ANGELES COUNTY MUSEUM OF NATURAL HISTORY

Mason, in doorway, left, with friends and family in Los Angeles.

Masterson, Bartholomew ("Bat")

1853–1921

Masterson's history has the hallmarks of the most prominent of Old West lawmen: raised in the Midwest; worked as an Army scout; frequenter of saloons; prowess in gambling; troubles over women and drink; wandering from town to town. But of all his contemporaries, Masterson had the unique distinction of ending his career in New York City as a successful newspaperman.

He was born in St. George, Quebec, and grew up on farms in Illinois and Kansas. In his youth, for unknown reasons, he adopted the name William Barclay Masterson, but from his move to the West to the end of his life, he was known as "Bat."

In 1872, he and his brother Ed left the family home in Wichita, Kansas, to work on a Santa Fe rail-

KANSAS STATE HISTORICAL SOCIETY

Bartholomew ("Bat") Masterson.

road gang out of Dodge City. The following year he engaged in buffalo hunting, and when the outfit that employed him moved into Indian lands, he became caught up in the Battle of Adobe Walls (June 17, 1874), in the Texas Panhandle, when the hunters were attacked by Comanches and Kiowas.

Following the battle, Masterson served in the Red River War as a scout for General Nelson A. Miles. He stayed in Texas after his enlistment expired. In January 1876 he was wounded in a gunfight in Sweetwater, Texas, with an army corporal named King over the affections of a dance-hall girl named Molly Brennan. Both King and Brennan were killed. Masterson then moved back to Dodge City, served as a city policeman, and in 1877 invested in a saloon. That year he was elected sheriff of Ford County.

His tenure turned out to be hectic: He captured the outlaw Dave Rudabaugh and his accomplice Edgar West after the pair attempted a train robbery near Kinsley, Kansas; in April 1878, his brother Ed, a Dodge City policeman, was killed by marauding cowboys; and the following October, Masterson headed a posse (which included Wyatt Earp, Bill Tilghman, and Charlie Bassett) that wounded and captured James W. Kenedy, who was charged with killing a dance-hall girl.

In January 1879 Masterson was in Colorado chasing a horse thief when he was appointed a deputy U.S. marshal and delegated to bring seven Cheyenne prisoners to Dodge for trial for a series of murders committed during a raid in Ford County. When his term of office ended in defeat for reelection, Masterson headed for Leadville, Colorado, to gamble; then, in February 1881, he followed Wyatt Earp to Tombstone, Arizona Territory, and went to work for Earp at the gambling tables of the Oriental Saloon.

Masterson returned to Dodge in April to help his brother Jim, who was in trouble with his saloon-dance hall business partner and a bartender named Al Updegraph, and was involved in a gunfight with the bartender and two other men as he stepped off the train. Updegraph was shot in the lung (but later recovered), the fight was broken up by sheriff Fred Singer, and Masterson was fined $10 and released. He served for a time as deputy sheriff at Las Animas, Colorado, and in 1883 was instrumental in preventing the extradition of John H. "Doc" Holliday from Colorado to Arizona to stand trial for murder.

Back in Dodge City in 1884, Masterson launched a newspaper, *Vox Populi*, but published only a single issue. He became, for a short time at least, an ardent prohibitionist, then moved on to Fort Worth, Texas, in 1887 to work for Luke Short at the White Elephant Saloon. He was present when Short killed local badman "Long Hair" Jim Courtright.

Masterson returned to Colorado, married Emma Walters in 1891, and served as town marshal in Creede for a time, but mostly he gambled, drank heavily, and consorted with Denver's criminals. In 1902 he left Colorado for New York City, where he served briefly as a U.S. marshal and made acquaintances in the city's social set, including the journalist and novelist Alfred Henry Lewis, who wrote several stories about Masterson and even based a novel, *The Sunset Trail*, on the ex-lawman's career.

In financial straits, Masterson was persuaded to write a series of articles about his western experiences with such luminaries as Wyatt Earp, Doc Holliday, Ben Tilghman, Luke Short, Ben Thompson, and William Cody. These articles were published in 1907 in *Human Life* magazine. Masterson became a prominent New York journalist and sports editor for the *New York Morning Telegraph,* acknowledged as an authority on prizefighting. He died on October 25, 1921, of a heart attack at his newspaper office. On his desk was a sheet of paper on which he had written: "There are many in this old world of ours who hold that things break about even for us. I have observed, for example, that we all get about the same amount of ice. The rich get it in the summertime and the poor get it in the winter."

Maxwell Land Grant

1841

The grant of land that became known as the Maxwell Land Grant was originally made in 1841 to Carlos Beaubien, a New Mexico merchant, and Guadelupe Miranda, a customs collector for New Mexico, which was then a state of Mexico. The grant was made by governor Manuel Armijo, himself a land speculator. When Beaubien died in 1864, his holdings were taken over by his son-in-law, Lucien Bonaparte Maxwell, who bought out everyone else involved. Maxwell lived like a king on his land, but when gold was found there in 1867 and he was unable to protect himself from swarms of prospectors, he realized that he could turn a greater profit by selling out.

What followed was a textbook case of megalomaniac land speculation combined with corrupt political manuevering. Maxwell sold his grant of 97,000 acres to Jerome B. Chaffee and Stephen B. Elkins, who headed a joint Colorado–New Mexico-based group, for $1.35 million. They formed the Maxwell Land Grant and Railroad Company, hired surveyors, and claimed that their holdings were nearly 2 million acres. At the same time, before that survey could be confirmed, they sold the grant to English speculators bankrolled by Amsterdam bankers. But in 1871, Secretary of the Interior Columbus Delano ruled that the grant amounted to only 97,000 acres. Faced with financial ruin, Chaffee and Elkins acted

quickly and shrewdly. Each got himself elected as a territorial representative to Congress, and backed by the Santa Fe Ring, a group of powerful Anglo and Hispanic businessmen and politicians, they began behind-the-scenes manuevering to have Delano's decision overturned.

They couldn't move fast enough to avoid bankruptcy, which came in 1875, but Chaffee and Elkins were not about to be denied control over the land. By a series of clever manipulations, they were able to have the claim taken over by Thomas B. Catron, Elkins's former law partner, and to have Dutch bankers take over the New Mexico interest's holdings.

In the meantime, clashes between the speculators and farmer and miner squatter interests turned violent, precipitating the Colfax County War, a series of assassinations, lynchings and retaliatory attacks that would go on for a decade.

In 1879, the U.S. Land Commissioner ruled in the company's favor on the survey, a ruling that was upheld by the Supreme Court in 1897. Once again, the Maxwell Land Grant consisted of nearly 2 million acres, and the company, now run by the Dutch bankers, thrived well into the twentieth century.

McKenzie, Kenneth

1797–1861

Scottish-born Kenneth McKenzie was one of the boldest participants in the trans-Mississippi fur trade. So completely did he control the fur trade on the Missouri River that he was known by both rivals and colleagues as "King of the Missouri" and "Emperor of the West." He began his career modestly enough, as a clerk for the North West Company when he arrived in Canada in 1816. When that firm merged with the Hudson's Bay Company, he headed south to the United States to make his fortune with the Columbia Fur Company.

McKenzie enjoyed a meteoric rise in the company, becoming its president in 1825, when he had been there only four years. In partnership with William Laidlaw and Daniel Lamont, he came to dominate the Missouri, to the point that when the company merged with the larger American Fur Company, it was entirely on McKenzie's terms. The partners put him in charge of the Upper Missouri Outfit and told him to run it himself. McKenzie established Fort Union, near the junction of the Missouri and the Yellowstone, and blanketed the region with his employees. He also established trading relations with the hitherto hostile Blackfeet. By 1833, he was unchallenged on the Upper Missouri.

It was probably that near total control that led McKenzie to make his only mistake: erecting a whiskey still at Fort Union, in violation of U.S. government policy. He went to Europe until the uproar died down, and when he came back, he headed for St. Louis, where he had considerable success in the liquor business.

McLoughlin, John

1784–1857

John McLoughlin, fur trader, factor, and physician, was a remarkable figure in many ways. A giant of a man at 6 feet, 7 inches, he trained as a physician, was interested in natural science and anthropology, and was a shrewd businessman as well. He was also the nephew of Simon and Alexander Fraser.

McLoughlin was born and raised in Canada, and studied medicine from the age of 14 under the tutelage of his uncle Simon. Shortly after being licensed to practice, he went to work for the North West Company in 1803. By 1811 he had been made a partner, and was placed in charge of the post at Fort William, on Lake Superior, when the firm merged with the Hudson's Bay Company. He was made chief factor in 1824 and was appointed superintendent of the vast Columbia District. In that capacity he had to face an ever-increasing number of American trappers who were moving into the region. He struggled mightily to maintain a Canadian presence, attempting to steer missionaries south to the Willamette Valley.

McLoughlin was a committed Christian and a man of medicine; he felt a moral obligation to assist American missionaries even though their presence jeopardized his company's foothold in the Oregon/

OREGON HISTORICAL SOCIETY

John McLoughlin.

Washington area. He would remain in Oregon, near the mouth of the Columbia, until 1846. His outpost continued to be lucrative even after a massive influx of Americans into the Pacific Northwest ended his virtual monopoly in the interior. When revenues began to decline, McLoughlin retired to his home at Oregon City and became a U.S. citizen. His son Joseph, also a fur trader, died of tuberculosis in 1839.

Medicine Lodge Treaties

1867

Together with the Fort Laramie Treaty of 1868, the treaties negotiated at the Medicine Lodge coun-

Depiction of the 1867 meeting at Medicine Lodge Creek, Kansas, in which Kiowa leaders were pressured by U.S. officials to move their entire tribe to "Indian Territory" in Oklahoma.

cil in the autumn of 1867 were the principal accomplishment of the Peace Commission of 1867–1868. The commission was a reaction to the warfare that had swept the Great Plains during the Civil War years and culminated in the Fetterman Massacre of 1866. Its composition determined by Congress, it represented a new approach in Indian policy: conquest by kindness, an idea advanced by eastern humanitarian groups. Headed by Commissioner of Indian Affairs Nathaniel G. Taylor and including army generals as well as civilians, the commission sought to persuade the tribes of the Great Plains to abandon their traditional hunting grounds and move to designated reservations north and south of the principal overland travel routes. In return, the government would provide rations, goods, and other services to aid the tribes in the transition to a settled agricultural life.

Having failed to make contact with the northern tribes at Fort Laramie, in October 1867 the commissioners journeyed to Kansas to meet with the Cheyennes, Kiowas, Comanches, and Arapahos of the Southern Plains. The council was held under a brush arbor in a grove of trees along Medicine Lodge Creek. Some 5,000 Indians had gathered for the occasion, and a great pile of gifts encouraged them to agree to the government's plan. A series of treaties with the tribes established reservations in the Indian Territory (present-day Oklahoma) on which the tribes promised to settle once the buffalo had disappeared. Since this prospect seemed inconceivable, the chiefs all signed.

The Medicine Lodge treaties did not bring peace; almost at once another war broke out. It raged through 1868 and 1869 until the tribes were forced to begin gathering on the new reservations. Even so, still another war, the Red River War of 1874–1875, was necessary before the tribes finally went to the reservations and stayed on them.

Like most treaties, the Medicine Lodge treaties were accepted by people who did not fully understand what they were signing. They did not see that they were binding themselves to exchange their hunting grounds for a reservation and to give up their traditional way of life and become like white farmers. From the federal government's perspective, even though two more wars had to be fought, the treaties were a vital first step in transforming the Native Americans of the Southern Plains from nomadic buffalo hunters into "reservation Indians." On the Northern Plains, the Fort Laramie Treaty of 1868 achieved the same result for the Sioux and allied tribes.

Meek, Joseph L.

1810–1875

Joseph Meek was a mountain man and a politician. Born in Virginia, he traveled to Missouri as a young man and went to work as a trapper for William Sublette in 1829. For eleven years, Meek roamed the Far West from the Snake River to Utah. He survived numerous adventures, both comic and tragic. He traveled the Blackfeet country with Kit Carson, took part in the Battle of Pierre's Hole, fought grizzly bears, married three different Native American women (one of whom was killed by the Bannocks), was ambushed by Indians near Yellowstone Lake, and had a partner murdered by the Blackfeet.

Meek was a legendary spinner of tall tales and a man of considerable wit, some of it aimed at himself. For example, he told of the time he shot at a grizzly that was on a small river island. Believing the bear to be dead, Meek stripped and waded to the island to claim his prize—only to find the bear very much alive and very much annoyed. The naked hunter left hastily, pursued by the enraged bear, which might have caught him had his partner not been nearby with a rifle.

As the fur trade began to die out, Meek moved in 1840 to the Willamette Valley of Oregon with his third wife. He became a popular figure in the region and was first a sheriff, then a state legislator. A cousin of President Polk's wife, he was made marshal of the Oregon Territory when it was created. He served in the Yakima Indian Wars (1853–1855), attaining the rank of major. In spite of his Virginia heritage, Meek was strongly pro-Union, and helped found the Republican party in Oregon.

Mesa Verde

Mesa Verde is the site of prehistoric cliff dwellings and pueblos of the Anasazi Indians. The site, now Mesa Verde National Park, is located in southwestern Colorado, near Durango. One of the ruins, Cliff Palace, contains over 200 rooms and 23 kivas. Mesa Verde was designated as a national park on June 29, 1906.

The first Anasazi Indians, known today as Basketmakers, lived in caves and pit houses half in the ground and built of logs and mortar. These people were primarily farmers who grew beans, corn, and squash. Pottery was introduced in the period called Basketmaker III, which lasted from the fifth to the middle of the eighth century. In the Pueblo Period that followed, the Anasazi began constructing *pueblos*, rectangular apartmentlike buildings made of stone. The structures were often several stories high and grouped around courtyards.

In the latter part of the Pueblo Period, from the twelfth to the fourteenth centuries, the Anasazi began constructing the cliff dwellings at Mesa Verde. The dwellings were built on the ledges of cliffs high above the valley, protected by rock overhangs. They were constructed of mud mortar, stone, and wood, and were often reached by ladders or footholds carved into the rock. Some reached back into large caves deep within the canyon walls.

The Anasazi abandoned their dwellings after 1300. It is not known with certainty why they left, but most likely they were forced away by prolonged drought or raids by hostile nomads. Their dwellings were discovered by white men at the end of the nineteenth century, and soon thereafter they were excavated.

W.H. JACKSON/U.S. GEOLOGICAL SURVEY

Ancient Pueblo cliff dwellings in Mesa Verde, photographed in 1874.

Mexicans in the West

Natives of Mexico became some of the first residents in the southwestern American territories after the U.S. government took control of Texas, New Mexico, and parts of Colorado, Arizona, Utah, Nevada, and California. Their descendants are Mexican Americans, who are also known as Chicanos. Some Mexican Americans are part Indian, part South American, and/or part African.

As U.S. expansion girdled the territories just north of Mexico, these Mexican natives became part of the American population. Following the conclusion of the Mexican War in 1848, settlement in the

COLLECTION OF DAVID R. PHILLIPS

A Mexican-American couple and their baby pose for Joseph Smith.

Mexican War

1846–1848

James Knox Polk came to the presidency in March 1845 with three principal aims: to settle the Texas question (annexation and establishing Mexico's boundary with the new state at the Rio Grande), to establish exclusive U.S. rights to the Oregon Territory, and to purchase from Mexico the territories of California and New Mexico.

After the failure of the Slidell mission, Polk, hoping to pressure the Mexican government to negotiate the Rio Grande boundary issue, ordered Zachary Taylor to assemble an army between the Sabine and Nueces rivers. Taylor and a force of about 3,000 regular army troops left winter camp in Corpus Christi, Texas, and moved south to Port Isabel on the Gulf of Mexico. Supply ships followed the march, which then proceeded to the Rio Grande, in Mexican territory. Taylor arrived there on March 28, 1846, and immediately began construction of a fort opposite the Mexican town of Matamoros.

Taylor's army consisted of five under-strength regiments of regular infantry, a company of "flying" horse artillery under Seminole War veteran Major Samuel Ringgold, parts of two other artillery regiments, a regiment of dragoons, and, among the mounted volunteers, a unit of Texas Rangers. A few of the troops were armed with .54 caliber breech-loading rifles, but most carried Model 1822 flintlock muskets.

area by whites was essentially limited to U.S. Army troops. As the Indian Wars drew to a close in the late 1880s, white settlement of the Southwest began in earnest. By the end of the nineteenth century, as the policy of manifest destiny came to fruition, natives of Mexico were overwhelmed in population numbers and became a highly visible minority in the region.

White settlers employed native Mexicans on ranches, farms, and railroads, and in the mining industry. Like the Chinese, native Mexicans were considered by many whites as a plentiful source of cheap manual labor. Separated by language and culture, in addition to legal and social customs, native Mexicans were subject to much prejudice and exploitation.

BURT FRANKLIN PUBLISHERS, NEW YORK

At the beginning of the war, Mexican leadership was divided between General Pedro de Ampudia (right) and General Mariano Arista.

In Mexico City, President Mariano Paredes y Arrillaga, a vehemently anti-American former general who had taken the presidency by military coup only three months before, viewed the American presence in Mexican territory an act of war. Sending reinforcements to Matamoros, he announced on April 23 a "defensive war" against the United States. When the Mexican commander at Matamoros sent a patrol across the river to the east of the new fort and ambushed an American patrol on April 25, Taylor sent a letter to President Polk containing the words "Hostilities may be said to have commenced."

By the time this message was received in Washington, on May 9, and war officially declared four days later, Taylor had fought two battles. On the morning of May 8, Taylor's force of about 2,300 clashed with some 6,000 Mexican troops at a small elevation on the Texas plain called Palo Alto. This cannon duel, which set the prairie grass ablaze and covered the battleground with black smoke, resulted in a decisive American victory. The next morning a scouting party found the Mexican force a few miles down the road at a dry riverbed called Resaca de la Palma. A combination of cannon fire and charges by infantry and dragoons won the day for Taylor (who was promoted to major general after the battle). He lost 122 men; the Mexicans suffered more than 500 casualties, and many more drowned while crossing the river.

With war officially declared, Congress appropriated $10 million for waging it, doubled the strength of the regular army, and authorized a call for volunteer units to a strength of 50,000 men. The U.S. objectives also were clarified: they were, basically, to seize all Mexican territory north of the Rio Grande and Gila rivers, westward to the Pacific. To direct this formidable effort was the commanding general of the army, Winfield Scott, a veteran of the War of 1812 and the Black Hawk, Seminole, and Creek wars.

The battle plan that emerged under Scott's guidance called for a three-pronged invasion of northern Mexico: Taylor was to advance on Monterrey, another force was to march from San Antonio to Chihuahua, and a third, under Colonel Stephen Watts Kearny, was to go from Fort Leavenworth to Santa Fe, with the ultimate objective of invading California.

Taylor arrived at Monterrey on September 17 with a force of about 6,000 men; facing him was a Mexican army of some 9,000. The Americans attacked on September 20, and after two days of hard fighting, entered the city. After two more days of stubborn and bloody resistance in the streets, Monterrey surrendered. Kearny meantime had taken Santa Fe, and with a small force of dragoons was proceeding to San Diego, where an American naval squadron had seized the California port. Thus, 1846 ended with a large part of northern Mexico under American military control.

Meanwhile, Winfield Scott had begun assembling the transports, supplies, munitions, and men for a landing at Veracruz. He detached 4,000 regulars and about the same number of volunteers from Taylor's army on the Rio Grande, ordering them to Tampico and the mouth of the Brazos River for the journey by steamer to Veracruz and the march inland to the Mexican capital.

In February 1847 Taylor moved his depleted force into camp a few miles south of Saltillo, near the hacienda of Buena Vista, and joined forces there with General John E. Wool. On February 21, advance elements of a Mexican army approached—led by the American nemesis General Antonio López de Santa Anna, once again president of Mexico.

Wool had command of about 4,800 men to face Santa Anna's army of more than 20,000. At dawn on February 23, the Mexican infantry, marching forward by column, was met by Major Braxton Bragg's artillery and 360 men of the Indiana infantry regiment. The heavy fire broke the massed advancing columns. Santa Anna's reserves next came forward; they too were repulsed by Bragg's guns. Finally the Mexicans withdrew to San Luis Potosí. Taylor lost 267 killed and 456 wounded; Santa Anna, 1,500–2,000 killed and wounded. Buena Vista ended

NEW YORK PUBLIC LIBRARY

General Zachary Taylor's camp, Corpus Christi, Texas.

any further attempt by Mexico to retain its Rio Grande provinces.

Meantime, Winfield Scott, with a force of 13,660 men (about 6,000 regulars), landed at Veracruz after a reconnoitering in a small launch that narrowly escaped the shelling from the city's great fortress, the Citadel. (Had the launch sunk, American history, certainly its Civil War history, might have changed drastically: the boat carried Scott and such officers as Joseph E. Johnston, Pierre G. T. Beauregard, George G. Meade, and Robert E. Lee.) The city was taken on March 29 after assistance in capturing the Citadel from Matthew C. Perry, commander of the American naval forces, whose six heavy guns and their crews breached the walls.

On April 17–18, 30 miles inland from Veracruz, Scott and his force of 8,500 met Santa Anna's newly raised army of about 12,000 men at Cerro Gordo, an entrenched position in the mountain passes through which ran the road to Jalapa and Mexico City. Engineer Captain Robert E. Lee's discovery that the Mexican left flank was vulnerable helped win the day for Scott, who moved on to Jalapa, Santa Anna's birthplace. He was joined there by reinforcements led by General Franklin Pierce (the fourth future president to participate in the war: Taylor, Grant, and Jefferson Davis were the others).

Peace negotiations with Santa Anna failed in the summer of 1847, and Scott, his army dwindling as the result of sickness and the departure of volunteers whose enlistment had ended, decided he must push on to the capital. On August 7, leaving a small detachment in Puebla, he marched out with about 10,000 men. Since his army was not large enough to protect the road from Veracruz, Scott abandoned his line of communication with the coast.

On August 19–20, in the Valley of Mexico, Santa Anna had concentrated his forces in the villages of Contreras and Churubusco, guarding the southern approaches to Mexico City. General Gideon Pillow and 3,300 men attacked Contreras, held by about 5,000 Mexicans; his attack was repulsed, and the next day he was rescued by a force led by General Persifor Smith that routed the defenders and secured the town. At Churubusco, where the Mexicans had converted a church and convent into a fortress, the Americans stormed and took the positions under heavy fire. Mexican casualties in the two battles were one-third of Santa Anna's force—4,297 killed and wounded, over 2,500 prisoners taken. The Americans lost 133 killed and 900 wounded.

Scott and his army arrived at the outer defenses of the capital on September 6 and found Santa Anna's army deployed on steep hills rising from the marshy lowlands, across the roads leading to the city gates, and around the raised causeways on the city's perimeter. Among the most formidable of the impediments between Scott and the capital was the massive stone fortress called Chapultepec, perched on top of a 200-foot hill situated about a mile from the city proper.

With peace negotiations having failed, on September 8, with 3,450 men against 12,000 of the enemy, General William Worth attacked Molino del Rey, a place southwest of Chapultepec reported to house a gun foundry. The daylong fight ended with the American force overrunning the position, inflicting heavy casualties. On September 13, after a day's bombardment, the divisions under John Quitman and Gideon Pillow launched an assault on Chapultepec. By 9:30 A.M., Pillow's force had reached the summit despite stiff resistance from "Los Niños," the cadets of the military academy who defended the ramparts. American losses were about 130 killed and 700 wounded; Mexican casualties totaled 1,800. On September 14, with Santa Anna having escaped during the night, Mexico City surrendered.

For two months, the Americans under Winfield Scott served as de facto rulers of Mexico. When a government was finally organized with which U.S. Commissioner Nicholas Trist could negotiate, the Treaty of Guadalupe Hidalgo was signed on February 2, 1848. This document recognized the Rio Grande as the boundary of Texas and ceded New Mexico (including the present states of Arizona, New Mexico, Utah, Nevada, a corner of Wyoming, the western and southern portions of Colorado, and all of Upper California) to the United States. The United States agreed to pay Mexico $15 million and to assume the unpaid claims against Mexico.

On August 1, 1848, the last American soldier from Scott's army left Mexico.

Mexico

Long before the arrival of the white men, great civilizations flourished in Mexico. The original inhabitants probably crossed the Bering Strait into the North American landmass some 45,000 years ago.

By approximately 3500 B.C.E., they began to cultivate crops such as corn, abandoning a nomadic existence as hunter-gatherers to become an agricultural people. The earliest of the major pre-Columbian civilizations, the Olmec, reached its high point around 800–400 B.C.E. in the coastal areas around the Gulf of Mexico. The Mayas, who sprang up to the southeast, were clearly influenced by the art and religion of the Olmecs.

It was under Mayan rule that the first city-states began to emerge in Mexico, around 150 C.E., in what is now Guatemala. Gradually the Mayans moved north into the Yucatan Peninsula, abandoning their original city in the south and building urban centers in the central highlands. Eventually, the Mayan empire splintered into numerous tribal groups.

The Zapotecs developed their own civilization to the west of the Mayas, centered at first around the extraordinary mountaintop city of Monte Alban. They later abandoned the city, and the Mixtecs adopted it as their own. They were followed by the Toltecs and finally by the Aztecs, who came from northwestern Mexico to the central highlands and established the last great Indian empire before the coming of the conquistadors.

These pre-Columbian civilizations were highly sophisticated, but utterly unprepared for the arrival of Hernando Cortés and the Spanish. Although Spaniards had visited Mexico twice in the years immediately preceding Cortés's landing in 1519, it was Cortés, fresh from the conquest of Cuba, who would capture Moctezuma, the Aztec king, conquer Tenochtitlan, their capital, and subjugate the Aztec peoples. Under Nuño de Guzman, the Spanish realm was extended north to Nueva Galicia in 1528, and farther north by Antonio de Mendoza in 1535. Indian resistance was at times fierce (as in the Mixtan War of 1541), but the Spaniards, with their horses and superior weapons, prevailed.

The society that emerged was a highly stratified one, with Spaniards dominating the upper class, mestizos (mixed-bloods) and Indians the lower. In addition, there were class and ethnic tensions between Spanish-born whites and those born in the New World, who were called criollos. Under the mercantilist system, manufacturing on all but the most limited basis was not permitted in New Spain, so Indians were forced to labor in the mines and fields as the Spanish built an economy based on slavery and extractive industry. Although reforms would be enacted periodically, most notably by José de Galvéz in the 1780s, unrest grew.

When Napoleon occupied Spain in 1808 and placed his brother Joseph on the Spanish throne, it helped trigger a Mexican revolt against Spanish rule. The rebellion dragged on for several years with mixed success for the Mexican forces, but when liberals came to power in Spain in 1820, conservative Mexicans saw independence as an opportunity to maintain the status quo and their hold on power. A negotiated settlement with Spain was achieved in 1821, one that brought equality for the criollos under a monarchy, with the power of the Church untouched. A short-lived empire was established but in 1823, led by Santa Anna and Guadalupe Victoria, republican forces gained control of the government, drove out the imperial forces, and placed Guadalupe Victoria in the newly established presidency.

Mexico suffered through frequent turnovers in the presidency as various military leaders took turns overthrowing one another. Santa Anna emerged as the key figure in Mexican politics in this period, taking control of the presidency in 1832 and holding it until he was captured by the breakaway Texas Republic in 1836. He would resume the office from 1841 to 1844, and would find himself once more in command of the Mexican Army with the outbreak of the Mexican War in 1846. After the negotiated peace of the Treaty Of Guadelupe Hidalgo (1848) he resumed power as "perpetual dictator," a position he held until revolutionaries led by Benito Juarez and other progressives deposed him in 1855.

After Juarez and his compatriots drafted the liberal constitution of 1857 a virtual civil war broke out, with conservative forces opposing the secularization of Church property and reductions in the power and privilege of the army. They were aided by the French; Napoleon III had imperial designs on Mexico and installed the ill-fated Maximillian, a prince of the Hapsburg line, as emperor of Mexico. But French aid was cut off due to events in Europe, and Maximillian was unable to hold on to power. The result was that, once more, Juarez was president.

However, in a repeat of a familiar pattern in Mexican history that would recur, Juarez was unable to overcome domestic political turmoil to enact a program of much-needed reforms. In 1876, an armed revolt led by Porfirio Díaz brought that strongman to power. He would rule Mexico as president until 1911, except for a brief period from 1880 to 1884. Díaz brought growth to the Mexican economy, but his reactionary policies benefited only the large landowners and foreign investors. The plight of the Indians grew worse; as péones, they were no better off than the serfs in Russia.

Mexico, U.S. Policy Toward

Just as the "Texas Question" was to become the root cause of the Mexican War, so were Texas, and Mexico's volatile political climate, dating from its independence from Spain in 1821, the principal factors in the eroding relations between the two countries for the quarter-century preceding the war.

After 300 years of Spanish rule, Mexico's independence marked the advent of a long period of bitter political conflict between liberal anticlericals and conservative clerics, large landowners and high-ranking military. (Between 1821 and the rise of dictator Porfirio Díaz in 1876, Mexico was governed by two regencies, two emperors, numerous dictators, presidents, and acting or provisional leaders—some 74 separate governments in 55 years.) And nowhere in the vast new Republic of Mexico were there more problems than in the northern state of Coahuila Y Texas.

Between 1821 and 1835, after Mexico's eager invitation for Americans to settle there, some 25,000 American citizens swore oaths of loyalty as Mexican citizens in Texas. But almost from the outset, these "Texicans" established schools, traded with the United States, practiced non-Catholic religions, used English rather than Spanish, and in general flouted the laws and regulations they had agreed to live by in Mexico and resisted what they believed to be a corrupt, capricious, and stifling government based in Mexico City.

A particular thorn in the side of the Americans, as they most certainly were to him, was the perennial usurper General Antonio López De Santa Anna. This handsome, charming, but quite deadly opportunist from Jalapa had headed a revolution in 1832 and was elected president of Mexico in 1833. A year later he proclaimed himself dictator, decreed martial law, overthrew the Constitution of 1824, and drew

up a centralist constitution called the Siete Leyes (Seven Laws). These laws, among things important to the Texans, called for the states of Mexico to be converted to departments ruled by governors appointed from Mexico City. The Siete Leyes also greatly reduced self-government in and popular representation from the departments to the central government.

On March 1, 1836, at a settlement called Washington-on-the Brazos, Texas declared its independence from Mexico. Santa Anna, heading an army, came north. He had a brutal, no-quarter, no-prisoners success in capturing the Alamo on March 6, but was resoundingly defeated by Sam Houston, commander of the Texas Army, and his 800 men at San Jacinto on April 21.

With Houston as its first president, the Republic of Texas petitioned for statehood in 1836. But annexation, despite support from presidents Andrew Jackson, Martin Van Buren, and John Tyler, was delayed by those in Congress who opposed adding a slave state to the Union. James Knox Polk, a slave owner from Tennessee and an unabashed expansionist, won the Democratic nomination for president in 1844 on a platform that had annexation as a main plank. On December 29, 1845, President Polk signed the bill making Texas the 28th state of the Union.

While statehood had nearly universal approval north of the Nueces River (then the Texas boundary between American and Mexican soil), it produced heightened bitterness and hatred to the south. The Mexican government, which had publicly announced it would consider annexation of Texas an act of war, recalled its ambassador. In the Mexican capital, the United States was anathematized as arrogant, ruthless, power-mad, and on a determined course to conquer the continent.

President Polk's next move, sending John L. Slidell to Mexico City in the same month Texas was added to the Union, added to the growing tension and to Mexico's list of grievances: the United States now was also insolent and patronizing, and was willing to use whatever resources were necessary—whether coercion, economic blackmail, military force, or money—to seize more Mexican territory.

Slidell, a Democratic congressman from Louisiana who was fluent in Spanish, was named minister plenipotentiary to Mexico; the foremost objective of his mission was to secure recognition of the Rio

Grande as the northern boundary of Mexico. In return for this agreement, the United States would assume some $6 million in American claims for damages suffered during Mexico's periodic upheavals, a sum awarded in 1839 by an international commission. (Mexico, bankrupt, had defaulted on these claims, and American determination to collect them was another source of great annoyance to the government in Mexico City.) Slidell's other objective, to be abandoned if he felt it would jeopardize the Rio Grande boundary matter, was to offer to purchase the provinces of New Mexico (for $5 million) and California (for $25 million).

Slidell arrived in the capital in December 1845, but the Mexican government refused to receive him. He stayed on until the following March, hoping a change in the government might ease the rigid attitude toward the United States. This, however, was not to be, and the rebuff to Slidell was treated in many influential American newspapers and by Polk supporters and expansionist politicians in Congress as a calculated insult.

Meantime, Santa Anna, who had returned to power in 1841 and was overthrown in 1844 for malfeasances including extravagant personal spending, was in exile in Havana, awaiting his country's call. It came in December 1846, when he was elected president once again, this time to oppose the American invaders gathered on the Rio Grande.

In January 1846, President Polk, learning of the failure of the Slidell mission, ordered General Zachary Taylor, leading an army of nearly 3,000 regular troops plus some mounted volunteers, to assemble his force between the Sabine and Nueces rivers in Texas. This provocative move was exacerbated in March, when Taylor and his army marched out of Port Isabel. Supply ships followed them south to the Rio Grande, in Mexican territory, where they built a fort opposite the port of Matamoros.

On May 13, 1846, after Taylor's battles at Palo Alto and Resaca de la Palma, President Polk signed the declaration of war.

Miami Indians

Generally grouped with the Eastern Woodlands and Plains tribes, the Miamis, an Algonquian tribe, were found in both areas. At the time of their alliance with the French, they held lands in western Wisconsin, northeastern Illinois, and northern Indiana. Because of their relations with the French, they often found themselves under attack from the Iroquois, who were allied with the British. To avoid that rival tribe, the Miamis migrated to the area of the Miami River in northwestern Ohio. When the Treaty of Paris, ending the French and Indian War, was signed in 1763, they returned to Indiana.

In the following decades, when English settlers began to move west and increasingly encroached on Indian lands, the Miamis were among the tribes (including the Delawares, Ojibwas, Ottawas, and Shawnees) who engaged in armed resistance. Their chief, Little Turtle, was a particularly astute warrior and was instrumental in the defeats of British generals Josiah Harmar and Arthur St. Clair. Then General Anthony Wayne with greatly enforced troop strength mounted an inexorable offensive against the Indian forces. Little Turtle, realizing the futility of the situation, counseled peace. Resistance was finally broken in 1815.

The Miamis ceded their tribal lands in Indiana by 1827 and were removed first to Kansas and later to northeastern Oklahoma. Most surviving tribal members live there, although a small number still live in Indiana. In 1650, the Miamis were estimated to number 4,500. Within a century their population was reduced by two-thirds.

Mier Expedition

1842

Although Texas had won its war of independence with a decisive victory at the Battle of San Jacinto in 1836, Mexico still did not officially relinquish its claim on the now-sovereign republic. Throughout the rest of the 1830s, harassing raids across the Rio Grande were carried out by Mexican troops. They were often met by small detachments of Texas Rangers, who fought the larger forces to a standstill and chased them back across the border.

Late in 1842, Texas president Sam Houston, exasperated by these Mexican incursions, decided that a show of force was called for; he sent a 750-man unit, commanded by General Alexander Somerville, to attack Mexico. It was a dubious enterprise, made more so by the makeup of the "army," which contained only a small contingent of Rangers and actual militiamen. The remainder were freebooters and rabble who were mainly interested in looting.

After departing San Antonio on November 8, 1842, the army easily captured Laredo, whereupon most of the men began looting and raping. Somerville arrested some of the culprits and returned as much plunder as he could—only now he found himself with a rebellion on his hands. Two hundred of his men deserted and most of the rest simply decided to ignore all further orders. Somerville terminated the mission and marched home with some of the Ranger contingent, leaving about 300 men, including several prominent Ranger captains, to carry on the mission.

The remainder of the army pressed on to the Mexican town of Mier, where they were surrounded by Mexican troops. When the Texas commanding officer was wounded, order collapsed and the Texans took a vote and decided to surrender, demanding to be treated as prisoners of war.

The captives were marched deep into the Mexican interior. Ewen Cameron and Samuel Walker then led an escape, taking several Mexican soldiers prisoner; the Mexicans were released in exchange for promises that those Texans still in Mexican custody would be treated decently as prisoners of war. But the escapees became lost in the desert around Saltillo and were eventually recaptured by Mexican cavalry, after great suffering.

Santa Anna now demanded that all of the escapees be executed, and the order would have been carried out but for vociferous protests by both American and British ambassadors. Instead, every tenth man was shot. Those who survived were mistreated and kept imprisoned for years; their release was not obtained until just before Texas was annexed to the Union in 1846.

Miles, Nelson Appleton

1839–1925

A Boston crockery clerk, Nelson Appleton Miles took up arms for the Union at the outbreak of the

Civil War. Through ambition, hard work, and bravery he acquired a distinguished record in many battles, and rose from lieutenant to major general in the volunteer armies. At war's end, at the age of 26, he won a colonel's commission in the regular army.

Miles's first opportunity for field service came in 1874–1875. Kiowas, Comanches, and Cheyennes had left their reservations in the Indian Territory and taken refuge on the Staked Plains of the Texas Panhandle. Miles commanded one of General Philip H. Sheridan's columns that converged on the area. Miles fought just one successful battle, but his achievement lay in persistent campaigning throughout the rigorous winter that followed. This so demoralized the Indians that they drifted back to the reservation and surrendered. This ended the Red River War hostilities on the Southern Plains.

Miles's next chance for distinction came in 1876, following Custer's annihilation at the Little Bighorn. Miles's regiment was included in the reinforcements sent to the Northern Plains. Throughout the winter of 1876–1877, after all other troops had

Nelson Appleton Miles.

returned to their bases, Miles stayed in the field. His fur-clad soldiers kept the Sioux and Northern Cheyennes of Sitting Bull, Crazy Horse, and other chiefs so exhausted and offguard that by spring most of the Indian forces had given up. Noting Miles's winter gear, the Indians named him "Bear Coat." Promoted to brigadier general in 1880, Miles was then elevated to department commander.

In 1886 Miles again took to the field, this time in the Chiricahua Apache campaign in Arizona. General George Crook, Miles's old rival, had contended with the wily Geronimo for four years. Despite Crook's relative success in containing Geronimo, Miles regarded him as incompetent. In 1886, following Geronimo's second escape, Crook asked to be relieved of his command, and Miles took his place. Largely using Crook's unconventional methods of pursuit, Miles tracked Geronimo into the rugged Sierra Madre of northern Mexico and succeeded in persuading him to surrender. Thus ended a generation of bloody warfare with the Apaches.

Miles's final Indian service was in the ghost dance troubles among the Sioux in 1890. On the Sioux reservations of North and South Dakota, he exercised overall command and by an adroit combination of diplomacy and military force, he succeeded in persuading the ghost dancers to surrender. This campaign, tragically, climaxed with the terrible massacre at Wounded Knee.

Miles ultimately rose to the top command of the U.S. Army, which he headed during the Spanish-American War. Vain and ambitious, pompous, temperamental, rigid, and quarrelsome, these final years of his career were a dismal failure. President Theodore Roosevelt branded him the "Brave Peacock." Forcibly retired in 1903, Miles lived for another 22 years. He was primarily a field officer, not an administrator. Seen in this light, Nelson Miles emerges as perhaps the most effective and successful of all the military leaders of the Indian Wars.

Mines, Lost

See Lost Dutchman Mine

Mining Methods

The methods available to prospectors for extracting valuable ores were fairly simple ones. Placer mining, the foundation of several of the larger gold rushes, including those in California and the Yukon, required little more than a pick and shovel, a pan, and running water. Mining the ores and metals found in veins was more expensive and complicated, requiring the sinking of a mine and paying for workers and equipment.

Gold was often found in placers, washed into streambeds from veins that had been exposed to the elements. A prospector needed only to find a deposit and separate the gold from the dirt. The first of the forty-niners usually had only to put a shovelful of dirt in a pan of water and separate the heavier gold

This miner uses the simple method of panning for gold.

Forty-niners show off their equipment.

from the lighter debris. As the gold rush developed, larger, more efficient devices for making that separation came into use, from rockers and Long Toms to the sluice. Gold hunters also began using simple stamp mills to crush rock before it was run through a Long Tom or a sluice.

The biggest improvement introduced in California, which speeded the process of placer mining, was hydraulic mining. Large quantities of gravel were washed down with high-powered hoses, revealing the precious metals.

Vein mining required a considerably larger outlay of capital and involved greater danger. In this kind of mining the precious metals are encased in veins, embedded in solid rock. The vein must be traced,

the rock blasted, and the ore excavated. With the sinking of mine shafts and the digging out of chambers for mining, the danger of cave-ins is much greater. The Comstock Lode, with its enormous stamp mills and huge plants for treating crushed ore, was typical. A German mining engineer, Philip Deidesheimer, devised a method of shoring chamber walls with a "square-set" pattern of timbers. These worked so well at Comstock that this shoring method was copied all over the West.

With the shift from placer mining to "hard-rock" mining, there were new expenses, and suddenly mining was not a job for a lone prospector with a mule, a pick, and a pan. Railroad transportation, huge smelters, and work forces of hundreds of min-

A dipper gold dredge.

ers made vein mining a game for the very wealthy and for large corporations.

Finally, as the nineteenth century came to an end, mining companies shifted their attentions from precious metals to copper, lead, and iron. The growing industrialization that had reshaped the mining industry was now changing its focus.

Minnesota

Minnesota, the 32nd state to join the Union, is located in the north-central United States. St. Paul, its capital, is situated on the east bank of the Mississippi River near the confluence with the Minnesota River; the state's largest city, Minneapolis, lies on the opposite bank of the Mississippi. Together, the two are known as the Twin Cities.

The first European explorers in Minnesota may have arrived as early as the fourteenth century. The Kensington Rune Stone, found by a farmer in 1898, contains an inscription supposedly left by Norse explorers in 1362. Some consider the stone to be solid evidence of an early Viking presence in the area, while others dismiss it as a forgery. In the post-Columbian era, Minnesota was explored by European fur traders Pierre Radisson and Médart Chouart, Sieur des Groseilliers. Radisson and Chouart traveled west across the Great Lakes in 1654; knowledge of their travels is not extensive, but historians generally agree that they made contact with Minnesota Sioux. In 1678 Daniel Greysolon, Sieur Duluth attempted to reach the Pacific Ocean by way of the Great Lakes but hit land near the tip of Lake Superior. Pushing inland, he reached a Sioux village at Mille Lacs Lake, which he immediately claimed in the name of the French king. Territory east of the Mississippi came under American control after the American Revolution, while that west of the river was acquired as part of the Louisiana Purchase of 1803.

The first American settlement in Minnesota was Fort Saint Anthony, later renamed Fort Snelling. Built in 1819 on the site of present-day Minneapolis–St. Paul, the fort protected settlers in the region and their fur trade, and served as a base for western expansion. The first permanent settlers were farmers who lived and worked around Fort Snelling. Many of them came from Canada, seeking to escape the hardships of the Red River Settlement in Selkirk County.

The Territory of Minnesota was created on March 3, 1849. During the early 1850s, treaties negotiated between the Sioux and whites turned over much of the Indian land to white settlers. Although the gov-

Northfield, Minnesota. This photograph was taken shortly after the James gang robbed Northfield's First National Bank in 1876. The Younger brothers, at right, were captured by a posse.

ernment agreed to pay the Sioux, the Indians received little of the money promised to pay for their land. Statehood was granted to Minnesota in 1858. No Civil War battles were fought within its borders, but in the early 1860s war with the Sioux resulted in bloodshed for whites and Indians alike. The tremendous influx of white settlers to Minnesota drove the Sioux back into a narrow reservation along the Minnesota River. In the summer of 1862, annuities and food promised to the Indians by the U.S. government were diverted to the Civil War effort. This, together with a poor harvest and a decreased population of wild game, forced the Sioux to search for food in land off the reservation. When four Sioux killed five white settlers, the conflict quickly escalated. The four Indians were apprehended, and many other Sioux, frustrated by dishonest treatment from whites, armed themselves for war. Fighting over the next several days was intense; when it was over, more than 400 whites were dead, and 306 Sioux had been captured and sentenced to death. President Lincoln personally reviewed the court documents from the trial and commuted all but 39 of the death sentences.

In its early years Minnesota's economy was based primarily on farming, milling, and the lumber business. The mining of ore became increasingly impor-

tant in the late 1880s. Today agriculture in the state is concentrated in dairy products.

Missions

Spanish missionaries—Franciscan fathers accompanying the conquistadores north from their bases in Mexico—were the first churchmen to set foot in western America, the first to establish missions in the wild lands of the Southwest and California, and the most widespread and successful in their efforts to subjugate and convert the Indians, not only to the Catholic faith but also to an agricultural way of life.

In the period 1581–1608, explorer-missionaries under Franciscan Augustín Rodríguez and others with the Juan de Oñate expedition journeyed from northern Mexico across the Rio Grande to establish missions among the southwestern pueblos in a vast territory far to the north and west of El Paso del Norte. The effort was so successful with the fathers able to report such a strong conversion of Indians that Philip III of Spain canceled plans to abandon the far-reaching New Mexico territory. A demonstration of the pleasure with which the missionary efforts were received in Spain was the establishment in the winter of 1609–1610 of what would become the most important of the church's bases in New Mexico and later the most important trade center, the presidio and mission at Santa Fe.

By 1630, the Franciscans had 50 friars working in 90 villages, each with its own church, in New Mexico Province, and Santa Fe had a population of more than 1,000. By the mid-eighteenth century, the Franciscans had established 37 missions in New Mexico.

Out of these early efforts grew a mission-presidio system that pushed Spain and its church into the *terra incognita* of the American West. The presidios, forts garrisoned to protect the missions, provided safe harbors to the fathers and their converts despite the fact that there were always differences among the churchmen, the political appointees of the Crown, and the soldiers. The churchmen believed as an article of faith that even the most recalcitrant *indios* could be cajoled to come to the mission and learn to change their way of life; the political appointees and the military believed in subjugation by force first, conversion after.

Either way, Indian converts were essential to the missions and presidios, providing laborers and servants for the Church and ruling upper classes. By the end of the eighteenth century, the Spanish had built and garrisoned presidios from San José del Cabo, on the southern tip of Baja California, north to Monterey and San Francisco in Alta California, as far east as the Red River of Texas, as far north in the province of New Mexico as Santa Fe. There were 21 missions in Alta California alone, from San Diego (1769) 650 miles north to the San Francisco mission (established by Captain Juan Bautista de Anza in 1776 on the bay named for St. Francis of Assisi, the patron saint of Franciscans). Among the missionaries' most significant achievements was the work of the Jesuit astronomer and mathematician Eusebio Francisco Kino in southern Arizona (1687–1711) and the Majorca-born Franciscan Junípero Serra in Alta California (1769–1784).

From their bases in Chihuahua, Coahuila, El Paso del Norte, and New Mexico, Spanish expeditions with their attendant Franciscan fathers penetrated into Texas, and by 1722 had built and manned 10 missions and a permanent military establishment of about 300 soldiers scattered among four presidios.

Texas posed a special problem for the Spanish mission-presidio system in that many of its indige-

UNIVERSITY OF CALIFORNIA, LOS ANGELES

Mission, San Juan Capistrano, *by Carleton E. Watkins.*

nous Indian peoples, unlike those of the New Mexican pueblos, who were agricultural to begin with, were especially warlike and difficult not only to convert to Christianity but also to deal with in any way. One example of the Spanish troubles in Texas occurred in 1758, when a band of Comanches and Wichitas destroyed the San Saba mission on the river of the same name. The next year, the Spanish presidios in the vicinity mounted a punitive expedition against the Comanches. On the Red River, however, the Comanches routed the Spaniards and captured their cannon and supply train.

From that time and for over a century, the Comanches, in particular, subjected Texas settlements, missions, and presidios to incessant attack and siege.

The secularization of church lands in the 1830s by the Mexican government ended the era of the Spanish mission. Although such Jesuits as Jean-Pierre de Smet, who worked tirelessly among the Flatheads, Sioux, Blackfeet, and Yakimas, and established missions in Coeur D'Alene and in the Bitterroot country of Idaho and western Montana, exerted an influence in the Pacific Northwest, it was the Protestant missionaries who gained the strongest foothold in that region at about the time the Spanish mission lands were secularized.

In 1831, a delegation of Flatheads and Nez Perces traveled to St. Louis to visit the "Redhead Chief" William Clark of the Lewis and Clark expedition, who was now superintendent of Indian affairs, and to learn more about the white man's religion. Protestant religious leaders were quick to respond, and advertised for volunteers to go to the Oregon country. Soon a band of Methodist missionaries equipped themselves, and in 1835 they joined a trapper caravan bound for the Green River rendezvous. They pushed on west from Green River, were welcomed at Fort Vancouver, and settled in the Willamette Valley.

In 1836, Presbyterian missionaries Marcus Whitman, his new bride Narcissa, and another couple made their way to Oregon country—the wives becoming the first women to cross the Rockies to the Pacific, and established a mission for the Cayuse Indians near the Hudson's Bay Company post at Walla Walla, Washington.

Also successful in their missionary work were the members of the Church of Jesus Christ of Latter-Day Saints, the Mormons, under the leadership of the church president and prophet Brigham Young. In 1849, in order to attract settlers to the Great Basin area around the valley of the Great Salt Lake in Utah, Young established a Perpetual Emigration Fund and sent missionaries fanning out across the East and Europe to attract converts. Within six years after the establishment of the State of Deseret, the Mormons had founded missions to convert Native Americans and others to their faith from the Salmon River in Idaho to San Bernardino, California, and were undertaking missionary efforts in Canada and Mexico as well.

Mississippi River

The Mississippi River, the longest river in the United States, flows for 2,348 miles from north to south. The Mississippi, which means "Father of Waters" in the Algonquian language, drains 40 percent of the United States, an area covering approximately 1,250,000 square miles. The river has long been a major north–south route of transportation for inhabitants of North America.

The source of the Mississippi River is Lake Itasca in north-central Minnesota. From there the river flows to Minneapolis-St. Paul, where it is joined by the Minnesota River. South of this point the river valley widens significantly, and the bluffs on either side reach heights of 300 feet. At St. Louis, Missouri, the Mississippi is joined by its largest tributary, the Missouri River. The Missouri, which drains the Great Plains, constitutes 40 percent of the Mississippi's total drainage area and 20 percent of its total discharge. After being joined by the Ohio River farther downstream, the Mississippi swells to almost a mile in width.

The Mississippi and its tributaries provided a major network of transportation for Native Americans. Some of the tribes originally inhabiting the land along the river include the Ojibwas, Winnebagos, Foxes, Sauks, Choctaws, Chickasaws, Natchez, and Alabamas. The first Europeans to encounter the Mississippi (in 1541) were the members of Hernando de Soto's party. In 1673 Jaques Marquette and Louis Jolliet explored the river from the north, crossing Lake Michigan from Green Bay. Robert Cavelier, Sieur de La Salle, the most significant early European explorer of the Mississippi, reached the mouth of the great river in 1682 and claimed the whole valley for France. La Salle, a fur trader, envisioned a number of trading posts along its banks, with boats transporting supplies and furs up and down the river. Before long, French traders and missionaries had pushed far into the basin, establishing settlements such as New Orleans and St. Louis.

After the region passed into American hands with the Louisiana Purchase of 1803, the river became the primary route of north-south travel for Americans. Tributaries of the Mississippi provided a path for western exploration, such as the Lewis and Clark expedition up the Missouri River. With the coming of the steamboat in 1812, traffic on the river increased substantially, revitalizing the many towns that dotted the banks. Most of these, which had started out as trading posts, were located on the bluffs overlooking the river in order to avoid the spring floods that often overwhelmed the lowlands.

The U.S. Army Corps of Engineers began actively managing the river as early as 1837. Shortly after 1873 jetties were built throughout the delta, enabling oceangoing vessels to reach New Orleans. After the great flood of 1927, a project to control the flow of the river was undertaken; the river was straightened, and its navigational features were improved. Today the Mississippi is still widely used for transportation, and about 15,000 miles of the river system are navigable. The lower section is navigable for oceangoing ships up to Baton Rouge, Louisiana. Most of the cargo on the Mississippi is transported by barges and tugboats, and consists mainly of petroleum from the Gulf of Mexico and grain from the Midwest.

Missouri

Missouri, Algonquian for "people with big canoes," lies in the Midwest, with Iowa to the north and Arkansas to the south. The state capital is Jefferson City. During the nineteenth century Missouri was a starting point for pioneers heading west.

French explorers Jacques Marquette and Louis Jolliet traveled down the Mississippi in 1673. About a decade later Robert Cavelier, Sieur de La Salle named the Mississippi valley "Louisiana" and claimed it for France. The first permanent white set-

tlement was Sainte Geneviève, a trading post established in the 1740s.

Several Native American tribes inhabited the region before and during its occupation by the Spanish (1762–1800), the French, and later, the Americans. The Osages dominated the region, but the great westward push of white settlers following the Louisiana Purchase of 1803 forced them to cede their homelands by 1825. The Shawnees and the Delawares, who held Spanish land grants to the region, were ousted the same year, and most other tribes—the Sauks, Mesquakies (Foxes), Illinois, Otos, Iowas, and Missouris—left after the Platte Purchase of 1836.

The Louisiana Territory was renamed Missouri Territory in 1812. As a result of the Missouri Compromise in 1820, Missouri entered the Union as a slave state.

Even before the Lewis and Clark expedition set out from near St. Louis in 1804, Missouri's location had made it a major way station for westbound pioneers. Beginning in the 1820s, commerce thrived. Independence, Missouri, was at the head of both the Santa Fe Trail, leading to the Southwest, and the Oregon Trail, leading to the Northwest. The Pony Express left St. Louis along the Butterfield Trail. The Mississippi and Missouri rivers, and later the railroad, brought settlers and increased trade. The Russell, Majors and Waddell Company operated an immense freight line. Furs were shipped east, and tools and other necessities were sold to those heading for the frontier. Immigrants, particularly from Germany, arrived in large numbers, and by 1860 almost the entire state except for the region around the Ozark Mountains was populated.

Missouri was primarily a rural state, and the rift between the subsistence farmers growing wheat and raising livestock and farmers using slave labor to produce vast quantities of cotton and tobacco was reflected in the state's politics. In the early 1860s, Governor Claiborne F. Jackson, a proslavery Democrat and Nathaniel Lyon, an army officer who held antislavery and pro-Union views, kept the state divided between strong Union and Confederate loyalties. The Dred Scott case, heard in the U.S. Supreme Court in 1857, originated in Missouri. The legislature voted against secession in March 1861, then voted for it seven months later. After gaining control in 1864, the Radical Union Party emancipated Missouri's slaves in January of the following year.

The postwar era saw tremendous growth—progressive politics, development of manufacturing and mining, more extensive railways, and a surge of pioneers westward. By 1900 St. Louis was the fourth largest city in the nation. Four years later 20 million people flocked to the city for the Louisiana Purchase Exposition. Today Missouri's economy continues to rely on agriculture, mining, and especially manufacturing.

Missouri Compromise

1821

The Missouri Compromise was an agreement worked out between the North and South that allowed Missouri to enter the Union. Although the compromise, which was passed by Congress in 1821, did nothing to solve the moral issue of slavery, it represented the North's first large-scale assault on the institution of slavery.

When Missouri applied for statehood in 1818, there were an equal number of free and slave states in the Union. In early 1819 Congress began to consider admitting Missouri as a slave state, thereby touching off heated controversy between representatives from the North and South. In addition to antislavery sentiments based on moral considerations, free states were concerned that the entry of another slave state would upset the balance of power in the Union, because a constitutional clause allowed three-fifths of all slaves to be counted in determining congressional representation. Representative James Tallmadge of New York introduced an amendment to the Missouri statehood bill that eliminated the introduction of new slaves in the state and granted freedom to all children born to slaves when they turned 25. The amendment passed the House of Representatives, which was dominated by the North, but failed in the Senate, which was equally divided between North and South. A debate on slavery ensued, but Congress recessed before the issue was decided.

When Congress reconvened in December 1819, Maine applied for statehood as a free state. In March 1820 the Senate passed a bill granting statehood to Maine as a free state and to Missouri as a slave state.

The Tallmadge amendment was dropped from the Missouri statehood bill, but sectional balance was maintained in the Union. Illinois senator Jesse B. Thomas added an amendment to the bill, called the Missouri Enabling Act, that allowed Missouri to become a slave state but banned the creation of any additional slave states in the Louisiana Purchase north of Missouri's southern border (36°30').

A new crisis arose when Missouri's first constitution excluded free blacks and mulattoes from the state. Northern antislavery advocates objected to the racial exclusion, and Henry Clay was called on to draft a second compromise that would allow Missouri statehood as long as its exclusionary clause would never be interpreted in a way that violated the privileges of U.S. citizens. Missouri agreed, and officially entered the Union on August 10, 1821, as the 24th state.

Until it was repealed by the Kansas-Nebraska Act of 1854, and later declared unconstitutional by the Dred Scott decision of 1857, the Missouri Compromise temporarily settled the dispute over the western expansion of slavery. The debate it sparked represented the first time all elements of the slavery issue were brought under public scrutiny.

Missouri Fur Company

The Missouri Fur Company, the first large fur trading company in St. Louis, was founded in 1809 by Manuel Lisa, William Morrison, and Pierre Menard as the St. Louis, Missouri Fur Trading Company. In 1812, in the wake of mistrust among the partners and attacks by the Blackfeet, the company reorganized as the Missouri Fur Company. A devastating attack by the Blackfeet and increasing competition forced it to close in 1825.

In the winter of 1806, Lisa, Morrison, and Menard formed a partnership to send a trading and trapping expedition to exploit the uncharted region at the head of the Missouri River. Reports following the return of the Lewis and Clark expedition were extremely positive, and in the spring of 1807 the new partnership took action. Lisa commanded the expedition. Morrison and Menard stayed behind, sending George Drouillard, the famous hunter of the Lewis and Clark expedition, on their behalf. Lisa and Drouillard recruited about 60 men and set out from St. Louis on the first organized commercial expedition to ascend the Missouri River to the Rocky Mountains. The expedition was a success; after building Fort Raymond on the Yellowstone River, Lisa returned in 1808 with a handsome profit. This enabled him to secure additional investors for his venture, and with his original partners he formed the St. Louis, Missouri Fur Company.

As a result of Lisa's work, the company opened up the mountain fur trade. Lisa set up several posts along the Missouri River from which he sent out trapping parties. These posts eliminated the need to rely on annual expeditions dispatched from St. Louis. The many expeditions spread Americans throughout the northern Rockies and contributed significantly to the geographical knowledge of the region. Droulliard compiled a map of the Big Horn and Yellowstone rivers, and John Colter, who had joined Lisa on the first expedition, explored what eventually became Wyoming and Montana. Ezekial Williams, a hunter on many expeditions, was first to explore the central Rockies.

Lisa recognized that maintaining an amicable relationship with the Indians was vital to his fur trading interests. During the War of 1812, he was appointed Indian subagent and worked to maintain the loyalties of the western tribes. After Lisa died on August 12, 1820, Thomas Hempstead took charge of the company's financial concerns; Joshua Pilcher became field leader, then president of the company, which continued to prosper despite a decline in fur prices in 1820.

But a disaster in the spring of 1823 signaled its demise. A trapping party led by Michael Immel and Robert Jones was massacred by the Blackfeet. The incident took its toll on the company, financially and emotionally. Despite numerous efforts by Pilcher, the company was never able to recover fully. This, coupled with increased competition in the fur trade, forced the Missouri Fur Company to cease operations in 1830.

LIBRARY OF CONGRESS

Trappers on the Missouri River being attacked by hostile Indians.

ferson, Madison, and Gallatin rivers in southwestern Montana and flows 2,464 miles to join the Mississippi.

The upper Missouri River flows east across Montana's plains, where it is joined by the Yellowstone River. Continuing southward across the Dakotas, the river forms part of South Dakota's border with Nebraska. Tributaries include the Cheyenne, Kansas, Little Missouri, Platte, and Osage rivers from the west and south, and the James and Big Sioux rivers from the north. Farther to the southeast, the Missouri demarcates Nebraska's boundaries with Iowa and Missouri. After merging with the Kansas River, the Missouri heads to Saint Louis, Missouri, where it flows into the Mississippi.

Missouri River

The Missouri River, the principal tributary of the Mississippi River, begins at the junction of the Jef-

GILCREASE INSTITUTE

Indians gather on the banks of the Missouri River to await a supply boat or "fire canoe."

The river's drainage basin covers almost 580,000 square miles of mostly fertile soil. Its elevation ranges from 14,000 feet in the Rockies to 400 feet at its mouth, where the average discharge is about 64,000 cubic feet per second. Along its route the river carries a great sediment load from erosion, for which reason it has been popularly dubbed the "Big Muddy."

The Cheyenne, Crow, Mandan, Pawnee, and Sioux Indians lived in the Missouri River region. In 1673 Jacques Marquette and Louis Jolliet became the first nonindigenous people to set eyes on its murky waters. The area was explored by the Lewis and Clark expedition after the Louisiana Purchase of 1803.

Dams constructed in the Missouri River Basin Project provide flood control, power, and irrigation, and have made the lower river more navigable.

Modoc Indians

A Penutian tribe that inhabited a territory on the border of present-day California and Oregon, the

NATIONAL ARCHIVES

Captain Jack poses with some of his men.

Modocs' contact with whites began during the settlement of Oregon around 1830. After years of tension, they ceded all of their territory according to the Council Grove Treaty of 1864 and agreed to move to the Klamath Reservation in Oregon. The Modocs complied with the terms of the treaty, even though the agreement was not ratified until 1870.

In that year, believing that the government had no intention of abiding by the treaty, the Modocs, led by Captain Jack (Kintpuash or Keintpoos), left the reservation and returned to their homeland. In 1872, the Bureau Of Indian Affairs obtained permission to use force to compel their return to the reservation. The so-called Modoc War began on November 29, 1872, when federal soldiers arrived at Captain Jack's camp north of Tule Lake, in northern California. The Modocs established their defenses in the almost impregnable lava beds south of the lake. Fewer than 100 warriors defended themselves against a force that ultimately numbered 1,000 troops. On January 17, 1873, the federal troops attempted an assault but were repulsed.

Diplomacy came next. The Modocs proposed a reservation in their homelands: The United States demanded unconditional surrender. In April the talks broke down after Captain Jack shot General Edward Canby, the federal mediator.

The Modocs were eventually rounded up. Captain Jack and three others were hanged, and two others were sent to prison on Alcatraz. About 150 others were exiled to Indian Territory.

Moiety

"Moiety" is the scientific term for the division of a basically complementary group. A number of Native American tribes divide themselves into moieties, two more or less equal parts of a larger tribe. Other tribes maintain different social structures, such as phratries (clan structures with a number of subdivisions). Moieties are important for ceremonial functions, tribal governance, and familial relations. Often members of one moiety are required to marry someone from the other group.

Among the tribes structuring themselves into moieties are the Mandans, Omahas, and Poncas. Among southern California tribes, clans are divided into moieties. Many Pueblo groups structure themselves into moieties that manage religious ceremonies. The Osages divide into moieties known as Earth and Sky, and design their camps around these divisions.

Some tribes believe that animals also lived in villages and divided themselves into clans or moieties.

Mojave Indians

The Mojaves are a Native American tribe of the lower Colorado River region. In the seventeenth and eighteenth centuries, they lived along the river as an agricultural people, dependent, like the Egyptians along the Nile, on an annual flood to water their crops. In good years, the Mojaves could count on abundant crops—melons, pumpkins, corn, and beans were their staples. In bad years, they survived through a combination of hunting, gathering, and raiding neighboring tribes, particularly the Pimas and Maricopas. This lifestyle remained undisturbed even after the coming of the Spanish. However, white encroachment on their territory, in the form of ex-

OKLAHOMA HISTORICAL SOCIETY

Mojaves rafting on the Colorado River.

ploration, surveying, and trapping parties, marked the beginning of the end of this relatively idyllic existence. In 1865, the Colorado River Reservation was established for the Chemehuevi and Mojave peoples, and they were relocated to it. Almost 2,000 Native Americans still live on this reservation today.

BEN WITTICK, MUSEUM OF NEW MEXICO

A typical Mojave camp, around 1880.

MONTANA HISTORICAL SOCIETY

Cavalry barracks at Fort Keogh, Montana.

Montana

Montana, "mountain region" in Spanish, is one of the 10 least populous U.S. states. Borders are shared with Canada to the north, the Dakotas to the east, Wyoming to the south, and Idaho to the west. Montana's mountainous western edge evolves gradually into rolling plains on the east. Famed "cowboy artist" Charles M. Russell made his home in Montana. Known as the "Treasure State," "Big Sky Country," and "Land of the Shining Mountains," Montana has long been celebrated for its beauty and natural resources.

Following the Louisiana Purchase in 1803, Lewis and Clark spent more time in the Montana region than anywhere else. The area, they noted, supported an abundance of beaver and otter, and when European fashion created great demand for beaver hats, Montana's trapping and trading industries flourished. In 1807 Manuel Lisa established the first trading post, and others soon followed. However, a virtual monopoly in trade was enjoyed by John Jacob Astor's American Fur Company until the mid-1830s, when game grew too scarce to support the enterprise. By then the company had constructed Fort Union, Fort Piegan, and Fort Mackenzie for protection against the Blackfeet, into whose homeland the company intruded.

Francois Finlay found gold in Deer Lodge Valley in 1853, and prospectors soon scrambled to Montana's rugged west. The find at Camp Bannack yielded roughly $5 million in 1862 alone, and strikes at Alder Gulch (Virginia City), Last Chance Gulch (Helena), and Confederate Gulch (Diamond City)

COFFRIN'S OLD WEST GALLERY

A Montana sheepherder chops wood, surrounded by his flock.

flooded the frontier area with speculators. For a decade Montana's mines produced over $10 million annually.

The Territory of Montana was created on May 26, 1864, with Sidney Edgerton named first governor of the rowdy region. Lawlessness abounded—even Bannack's county sheriff, Henry Plummer, secretly led a band of outlaws. Settlers sought protection from the tribes who occupied the region—the Flatheads, Blackfeet, Gros Ventres, Assiniboin-Sioux, Rocky Boy-Crees, Cheyennes, and Crows—and several forts, such as Fort Smith on the Bozeman Trail and Fort Shaw on the Great Falls–Helena Road, were established. But Native Americans faced extreme hardship themselves, starting with the smallpox epidemic brought by a Missouri River steamship in 1837, which killed 15,000 Native Americans, and culminating with the Piegan massacre in January 1870, in which a peaceful and sleeping Blackfoot village was wiped out. Following General George Custer's overwhelming defeat at Little Bighorn on June 25, 1876, government troops pushed the Native Americans onto reservations.

The Great Northern and other railroads crossed the state during the 1880s and their presence helped expand the already well-established cattle and sheep ranching industries. The trains transported additional homesteaders, who in turn brought barbed wire and an end to the open range.

On November 8, 1889, Montana became the 41st state, but political battles continued. The "war of the Copper Kings"—Marcus Daly, William Andrews Clark, and "Fritz" Augustus Heinze—created political instability from the 1880s until well after the turn of the century. However, this volatile period was not bereft of progress—Montana spearheaded such reform measures as the eight-hour day for miners and an old-age pension law (the nation's first). Montana was the first state to elect a woman to Congress, Jeanette Rankin (terms served in 1916 and 1940).

Montana's population has always been sparse, and thanks to droughts in the 1920s, the state's growth rate even declined. Many mines closed during the Great Depression of the 1930s. But the state developed extensive irrigation projects and its substantial coal and petroleum resources to boost the economy. Montana encourages tourism to Yellowstone and other public parks, its 9.5 million acres of government forests, and its ghost towns and other historic sites.

LIBRARY OF CONGRESS

Thomas Moran.

Moran, Thomas

1837–1926

A panoramic landscape painter and etcher, Moran's work was critical in persuading Congress to create Yellowstone National Park. Like Albert Bierstadt of the Rocky Mountain School of artists, Moran painted enormous canvasses of western landscapes. Unlike Bierstadt, however, Moran remained a popular artist, in demand well into the twentieth century. His paintings and illustrations (over 1,500) tended to convey emotion, idealizing their subjects rather than depicting them realistically.

Born in Lancashire, England, Moran emigrated with his family in 1844 to Philadelphia, where he became apprenticed to a wood engraver. At the same time he studied painting under his brother, Edward; it was during a visit to England that both were inspired by the passionate painting style of William Turner.

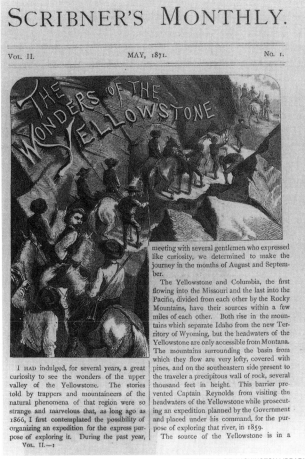

Moran's "The Wonders of the Yellowstone," as it appeared in Scribner's Monthly.

In 1871, at age 34, Moran accompanied geologist Ferdinand V. Hayden on an expedition to document and preserve the Yellowstone region. Overwhelmed by all he saw, the painter devoted the rest of his working life to capturing the majestic western landscapes on canvas. Moran's paintings, together with William Henry Jackson's photographs and Hayden's persistence, convinced a reluctant Congress to set aside two million acres in the Yellowstone region for a national park. A year later Congress paid $20,000 for two of Moran's Yellowstone and Grand Canyon paintings.

Moran traveled throughout the West, painting extensively. In 1884 he was named a member of the National Academy of Design. Moran's work was still in great demand when he died in California at the age of 89.

The largest collection of his work is located at the Thomas Gilcrease Institute of American History and Art in Tulsa, Oklahoma. Another collection is held by the U.S. Park Service.

Mormons

"Mormons" is the colloquial name for adherents to the Church of Jesus Christ of Latter-Day Saints (LDS). The LDS has the distinction of being the most successful religious movement to date to have been founded on American soil. The church was founded by Joseph Smith, a farmer's son from upstate New York. Smith, swept up in the wave of religious revivalism prevalent in that area in the 1820s and 1830s, prayed to God for guidance as to which group he should join. As he recounted it, God told him to join no church, and instead God would make the Gospel known directly to him. In 1823, the story continues, the 18-year-old Smith had a vision in which an angel, Moroni, appeared to him and revealed the existence of a set of golden plates. Smith would not receive them for four more years, even though he was told of their hiding place. In 1827, according to Smith, he was permitted to remove the plates so that he could translate them; the result was the Book of Mormon, a sacred text of the LDS.

In the Book of Mormon (which Smith said he was able to translate with the help of a magic sword and

A Mormon farmer poses in the doorway of his Utah cabin surrounded by his five wives and children.

Idyllic portrait of Mormon settlers stopping to make camp.

shield buried with the plates), the Native American tribes are revealed to be descendants of the Ten Lost Tribes of the ancient Hebrews. Smith said he continued to communicate regularly with the angel of God, who assisted in the translation.

In 1830, armed with his new-found knowledge, Smith founded the church. Understandably, he was greeted with skepticism, derision and, inevitably, persecution from his neighbors. Smith was forced to seek a more tolerant community from which to preach his religious beliefs. He began by moving to Kirtland, Ohio, the first step in a trek west that would eventually lead to the Great Salt Basin of Utah.

In Kirtland, revelations suggested to Smith that the future home of the Saints, the church's members, should be located in Jackson County, Missouri. By now he had hundreds of followers, and they traveled there, settling in the vicinity of Independence. Adopting a "Law of Consecration," which essentially established a communal property arrangement for the church's members, Smith found himself again running afoul of the locals. Their reception in Missouri was no doubt not helped by their comparatively liberal attitudes toward black slaves. Expelled from Missouri in 1833 by the governor, they were forced to return to Kirtland, where they built an imposing temple.

Eventually, they founded the town of Nauvoo, Illinois, in 1839, near Quincy. With a charter from the state that permitted them to form their own militia units, and courts controlled entirely by members of the church, the Mormons had great control over their lives.

But the situation did not last. Nauvoo grew fast as converts flocked to the town. Smith announced himself as a candidate for president of the United States. But as a fugitive from Missouri, where it was alleged he had masterminded a conspiracy to assassinate the governor, he was under constant physical threat. Rumors of the Mormon practice of polygamy increased anti-Mormon feeling throughout the state. Even more hostility derived from the LDS's seeking control of land and resources wherever the church set down roots.

The storm broke quickly and violently. In 1844, a dissident group within the church published a newspaper accusing Smith and his brother Hyrum of corrupt practices and polygamy. Smith ordered the paper destroyed. A near-riot resulted, with Illinois governor Thomas Ford calling out the militia. Smith and Hyrum surrendered to authorities and were

THE CHURCH OF JESUS CHRIST OF LATTER DAY SAINTS, SALT LAKE CITY

Mormon missionaries.

jailed in Carthage, Illinois. On the night of June 27, a mob stormed the jail and shot both Smith brothers to death.

The elders of the church, many of whom had been away on missions to encourage conversion, or on other church business, rushed back to Nauvoo. Brigham Young was named as the new head of the church. In the face of increasing violence, Young counseled a migration west to secure a permanent home and sanctuary. The town of Nauvoo was left virtually deserted, and an anti-Mormon mob bombarded the remaining inhabitants with cannon fire.

Followed by thousands of Mormons, Young began the trek west, with the first wagons eventually reaching the Salt Lake Valley in July 1847. The migration was not an easy one, and disease and the difficulties of travel took their toll on the pilgrims. At the request of President Polk, Young sent 500 members as a regiment of volunteers to serve in the Mexican War, which left the wagon trains even more shorthanded; undoubtedly, however, Young reasoned that sending the volunteers would make the administration in Washington more sympathetic to Mormon land claims when they finally decided on a location for their new home.

Legend has it that Young, who was suffering from mountain fever when the wagon train pulled into the Salt Lake Valley, looked at the land stretched out before him and said: "It is enough. This is the right place." His choice was not the best one he could have made. The area was dry, with few materials for building homes. But the Mormons were nothing if not industrious, and irrigation, planting, and home-building proceeded quickly.

With a settlement in the Great Basin secured, the population of the region burgeoned, as the activities of the Mormons grew in intensity and ambition. By 1852, there were more than 20,000 living in the Great Basin, a number that would increase fivefold by the time of Young's death in 1877. At that time, there were also more than 360 other settlements established by Latter-Day Saints in the states of Utah, Idaho, Arizona, Nevada, and California.

It was this Great Basin area, encompassing some 227,000 square miles, that Young named Deseret, and attempted to have recognized by the United States as a new territory. The Mormons elected Young the state's first governor, and filled the other offices with members of the faith. The legislature then petitioned the U.S. Congress to admit Deseret into the Union. Faced with a continuing sectional battle over slavery, Congress chose to use the land as a bargaining chip, organizing the Utah Territory on September 9, 1850, as part of the Compromise of 1850. Young was appointed territorial governor and superintendent of Indian Affairs.

In the meantime, Young's authority was being challenged by a series of events. News of the California gold rush reached Utah, and a floodtide of LDS adherents headed for the gold fields. Gold-seekers crossing the territory did business with the Mormons, exposing followers to an outside world from which they had always been isolated.

More significantly, the issue of the Mormon practice of polygamy was raised again, as were allegations of lawlessness and rebellion. President Buchanan sent an expedition to Utah in 1857 to suppress the alleged rebellion, and named Alfred Cumming of Georgia to replace Young as territorial governor.

In August 1857 a wagon train of non-Mormon immigrants was ambushed by Indians and whites at Mountain Meadows, Utah. John D. Lee, a Mormon Indian agent, and several other Mormon leaders organized a militia that took part in the massacre, allegedly under threat from the Indians. About 120 people were killed. Young subsequently excommunicated Lee and several others; Lee was executed by a federal firing squad in 1876 for his part in the bloodshed.

As for the predicted war between the federal government and the Mormons, it never materialized, thanks in no small part to negotiations on the Mormons' behalf by influential friends of the church.

Friction between the U.S. government and the LDS church was destined to continue intermittently for several more decades. In 1879, the Supreme Court upheld the constitutionality of antipolygamy laws clearly aimed at the Mormons. In 1882 Congress enacted the Edmunds bill, a federal law prohibiting polygamy. Mormon leaders were arrested, others went into hiding. Congress threatened to disenfranchise members of the church and to seize church property. Interestingly, another sore point for Congress was that the Mormons practiced female suffrage. Gradually, resistance ebbed, which is not surprising given that no more than 10 percent of LDS men actually practiced polygamy in the first place. Finally, in 1890, the LDS adopted a manifesto urging its members to comply with the law of the land regarding marriage.

Today, the LDS is one of the fastest-growing religious movements in the world, with more than two million members on five continents. Its economic and political clout in the West is substantial, a tribute to its members perseverance in the face of hardship, repression, and violence.

Morrill Act

1892

The Morrill Act, also called the Land-Grant College Act of 1862, provided 13 million acres of federal land to states to be used in supporting institutions of higher education. The bill, sponsored by Representative Justin S. Morrill of Vermont, gave 30,000 acres to a state for each of its congressmen. The land could be sold for funds to support at least one college or university in the state that taught agriculture, military practice, and the mechanical arts.

One of the goals of the Morrill Act was to encourage agricultural development west of the Mississippi River. When initially passed, the act applied only to states loyal to the Union, but after the Civil War Confederate states were included. With the Morrill Act, the United States came to be the first nation in the world to systematically commit its resources to higher education. The act ensured that educational control remained within the states yet at the same time promoted national interests. A second act was passed in 1890 that ensured further federal funds for land-grant colleges.

Mountain Meadow Massacre

See Young, Brigham

Mountain Men

Mountain men were beaver trappers who ranged the western mountains and played a vital role in the fur trade. The mountain men are colorful personalities in both history and folklore. Among the more notable were Jedediah Smith, Jim Clyman, Hugh

Glass, James Bridger, Tom Fitzpatrick, Kit Carson, Joe Meek, Doc Newell, Old Bill Williams, and Joe Walker. During the peak decades of the fur trade, roughly 1820 to 1840, probably 3,000 mountain men ranged the mountains in quest of beaver.

Topping the social scale of mountain men was the free trapper, so named because he worked for no one but himself. He bought his supplies from whoever offered the lowest price and sold his catch to whoever offered the highest price. Less prestigious than the free trapper was the *engagé,* who was equipped and salaried by a fur company and turned his catch over to the company. Of dubious claim to be called mountain men were the hunters and camptenders essential to the functioning of a trapping brigade but who did no trapping themselves. Almost beneath notice were the *mangeurs du lard,* the "pork-eaters" brought in to perform drudge labor, whose designation ultimately broadened to include any newcomer.

Mountain men were a diverse lot, but they shared a love of adventure and excitement, self-reliance, and absolute freedom from authority and social con-

straint. They came west for a variety of reasons—to find a world where they could live in freedom, to make money (which almost none did), to escape the law, or for a mix of all these motives. They celebrated their autonomy, boasted of their skill and prowess, delighted in extravagance, and gloried in their singular lifestyle.

The mountain men led a perilous existence, and few who did not develop great proficiency at their trade survived. The techniques of hunting beaver were the least of the required talents. Surpassing all others was "wilderness skill." In mountains and plains alike, extremes of weather and terrain could kill suddenly or in prolonged but no less deadly ordeals. Grizzlies, bison, moose, lions, rattlesnakes, and other denizens of the wilderness threatened life and limb. A highly specialized set of skills, fortified by an acute instinct drawn from experience, armed the mountain man against the hazards of the area, but for even the ablest the random misfortunes of the wilderness often proved fatal.

The mountain man maintained a unique relationship with the Native Americans, one that was decidedly based on borrowing from their culture. To cope with the wilderness and its human and animal adversaries, the mountain man adopted Native American techniques, tools and weapons, attire, practice, and even thought and belief. Many took Native American wives and reared mixed-blood families. While they did not entirely shed their own culture, the mountain men adapted to the Native American ways more than any other class of pioneers venturing west.

With different tribes, the mountain men developed different connections. Some, like the Flatheads, Snakes (Shoshones), and Nez Perces, welcomed them openly and never committed a hostile act. Other tribes were ambivalent, predatory when opportunity offered, amicable when it suited their purposes, like the Crows, Bannocks, and Utes. Still other tribes, like the Blackfeet and Arikaras, angry because the trappers harvested their meat and furs and armed their enemies, greeted them with belligerence.

The mountain man's costume, which copied Native American models, was both serviceable and susceptible to as much ornamentation as the wearer desired. Fringed buckskin pants and shirts—the fringes affording instant ties for any purpose—covered the body, while moccasins protected the feet. Headgear supported every variety of decoration. De-

A pair of buckskin-clad mountain men.

Black Beaver, a Delaware mountain man, worked as a trapper and guide for many years before settling on a Kansas reservation with the rest of his tribe.

parting from Native American design, many head coverings provided the shelter of a broad brim. A heavy wool cloak, called a capote, gave warmth in winter. Belts and slings held knife, hatchet, canteen, powder horn, shot pouch, rifle, sometimes a pistol, and a "possibles" sack to carry pipe, tobacco, pemmican, coffee, salt, and other "fixens."

Horses provided transportation—one to ride, one to pack, and possibly one or two spares. If the trapper claimed a Native American wife, she too rode a horse. The packhorse carried bedding, tipi or tent, utensils, and other baggage. Saddles and other horse gear bore gaudy ornaments of beads, feathers, embroidery, and fringes. Costumes sported similar embellishment. Native American wives strove to surpass all others in the richness and profusion of their adornment, which reflected the skills and prowess of their mates.

The mountain man's food also duplicated the Indian's. Red meat accounted for the overwhelming share. Buffalo, elk, bear, moose, mountain sheep, antelope, and deer were sought, and when they grew

scarce prairie chickens, ducks, geese, and other fowl, together with fish from lakes and streams, were supplements. Roots, fruits, and berries afforded a little variety. Portable rations consisted of another Native American food, pemmican—meat sliced thin, pounded, dried, mixed with berries, and encased in animal intestines. Like the Indians, trappers knew lean times. When the game disappeared, especially in winter, they ate anything they could find, including their own horses and mules and even their moccasins. Faced with starvation and freezing, they were known to kill and gut their pack animals and use the still-warm bodies as a last-ditch shelter.

Self-sufficient, the mountain man remained in the mountains year after year. Each summer he assembled with the others at the rendezvous, a prearranged site where the supply caravans spread their wares. Company trains of packmules came out from St. Louis and unloaded cargos of powder, lead, coffee, knives, utensils, and other goods needed in the mountains, together with ample stocks of pure alcohol. Diluted with water and more exotic additives, the alcohol fueled the debaucheries for which the rendezvous were noted. In exchange for the liquor and the next year's outfit, the mountain men turned over the last year's harvest of furs, which were transported back down to St. Louis and shipped to New York and foreign markets.

The summer rendezvous fell between the spring and fall hunts. Furs were best in spring after the animal's thick, luxurious pelt had protected it from the cold of winter. Fur was just adequate in fall, and poor in winter. Few mountain men pursued the hunt alone; it was too dangerous. Instead, the free trappers attached themselves to company brigades, composed of *engagés* and led by a company partisan, or "booshway" (*bourgeois*). The most powerful company in the mountains was the American Fur Company of John Jacob Astor. Smaller companies engaged AFC and one another in fierce competition. Most were transitory and financial failures. Some operated out of Taos, New Mexico, but most were based in St. Louis. The Rocky Mountain Fur Company, originally William H. Ashley's enterprise and then called Smith, Jackson, and Sublette, had the longest history.

The brigades ranged the mountains seeking the richest fur country. The men took many kinds of furs—fox, mink, otter, muskrat, marten—but the principal object was beaver. Beaver skins provided the finest felt for the world's hats. In prime beaver country, the brigade often paused for several days or weeks to stock up on game, while the trappers spread out in pairs to plant steel traps in the mountain streams. The trap was set underwater a short distance from the shore, where a willow wand was baited with castoreum (the beaver's glandular secretion). A chain ran from the trap to a pole thrust into the streambed in deep water. A beaver seeking the bait stepped in the trap, then in an effort to escape dragged the trap into deep water and drowned. Setting traps involved long periods of wading in cold water, both to fix the traps and chains and to avoid leaving a scent for the beaver. Years of such exposure took its toll on joints and muscles. Setting traps also took the trappers away from camp and made them vulnerable to Indian attack. Many a mountain man fell to a Blackfeet ambush while planting traps.

At the end of the fall hunt, the brigades sought a winter camp in some secluded valley where game was abundant and cottonwood groves provided bark to feed the horses. Typically, the winter camps moved and fluctuated in size, as game and weather dictated. With the spring thaw, another hunt preceded the rendezvous. Then, the skins were scraped, stretched on a hoop to dry, bundled, and loaded on packhorses. Eventually they reached market by way of the rendezvous.

No mountain man ever got rich. He was a prisoner of his St. Louis or Taos supplier. The caravans carried merchandise valued in beaver skins at prices set at the supplier's discretion. Rarely did the mountain men end the rendezvous without a debit in the suppliers' books. Yet they lived the free and adventurous life they treasured, and they prided themselves on being members of as select a fraternity of professionals as the West produced. By 1840 they had trapped out the streams, but by the same year the fashion world had replaced the beaver hat with the silk hat. The mountain man had to seek other employment. Some guided explorers and emigrants. Some went to Oregon and farmed. The rest simply vanished.

LIBRARY OF CONGRESS

Guide Elisha Stevens led the Donner party on their tragic trip.

Muir, John

1838–1914

John Muir was a naturalist, a conservationist, and a writer. An intellectual disciple of the Transcendentalists and a particular admirer of Ralph Waldo Emerson (whom he met in 1871), this Scottish-born writer came to the United States when he was 11 and was raised in Wisconsin on a farm. After four years at the University of Wisconsin, during which time he received no degree, Muir began the first of

THE SIERRA CLUB

John Muir.

narrowminded and unrealistic. The two men fought repeatedly over the possible uses of national forest lands. In 1908, they became locked in battle over Hetch Hetchy, a wild valley in Yosemite National Park that the city of San Francisco coveted as a site for a dam and municipal reservoir. For five years, Muir labored tirelessly to save the valley, but Pinchot and the city finally prevailed.

Perhaps, as some writers have suggested, the blow of that defeat led to Muir's death a year later. However, he is survived not only by his literary output, an extensive collection of beautiful nature writing and impassioned pleas for wilderness conservation, but also by the organization he founded and many others that he inspired. Finally, he is memorialized in the name of Muir Woods National Monument, Muir Glacier, and the extensive network of federal parks for whose creation he fought.

many lengthy hikes, walking to the Gulf of Mexico and then to California, where he arrived in 1868.

Muir was enthralled by what he found in California's Yosemite Valley and spent the next six years wandering there, keeping a journal of writings and sketches. During his rambles through the Sierra Nevada, he discovered 65 residual glaciers. He continued his exploring, extending his reach to Nevada, Utah, the Pacific Northwest and even Alaska, where he discovered the glacier that bears his name.

In 1880 he married Louise Wanda Strentzel and spent a lucrative decade managing a fruit orchard, a venture that gave him the financial independence to return to his first love, the wilderness. This time, however, he had a mission: to save as much unspoiled wilderness as possible. Muir also founded the Sierra Club in 1892 and would serve as its president until his death in 1914.

Muir brought to his conservation campaign a religious fervor, and he quickly achieved a reputation as one of the nation's foremost exponents of wilderness values. It was this position that inevitably brought him into conflict with Gifford Pinchot and the utilitarian wing of the conservation movement. In a clash of views that can still be seen in the environmental movement today, Muir stood for completely unspoiled wilderness and accused Pinchot of being little more than a covert exploiter of natural resources, bent on wringing the most efficient use out of the land. Pinchot, in turn, characterized Muir as

Murieta, Joaquin

1830–1853 (1878?)

Murieta was a legendary bandit and hero to Mexican Americans who lost land and social position after the conquest of California. A widespread sense of

Joaquin Murieta.

frustration and hopelessness prompted him to take action, and his exploits in the San Joaquin Valley represented destruction of the new establishment. Although historians debate his existence, many Mexican Americans have immortalized Murieta as an avenging angel.

A record exists of the baptism of one Joaquin Murieta in Sonora, Mexico, in 1830. In 1846 the area was ravaged by frequent rebellion against Mexico, Indian skirmishes, and an invasion by the U.S. Army. Two years later Murieta and his wife migrated to California with thousands of other weary Sonorans, most of whom joined the gold rush in the Sierra Nevada.

Murieta worked as a ranch hand near Stockton until he was falsely arrested for robbery and jailed. After his release, he settled in Sonora and began prospecting at Saw Mill Flat. Yankee miners, who terrorized the Mexican immigrants, raped his wife and drove him off his claim. Such miners pressed the legislature to pass the "Greaser Act" and "Foreign Miner's Act" to prevent the Mexicans from profiting from the land. Murieta's cry for vengeance magnified the voices of California's oppressed Mexicans. Legend holds that the Murieta, or several "Murietas," began raiding gold miners and stage coaches along the Sacramento and San Joaquin valleys.

Prosperous Anglo farmers feared Murieta throughout the 1850s, and the governor of California offered a reward for his capture, dead or alive. A visiting Texas Ranger supposedly beheaded the infamous outlaw and presented the head as proof of his death. Although the raids ceased, many believe that Murieta escaped and was later buried in a Jesuit cemetery high in the Sierra Madre in 1878.

N

Natchez Trace

The Natchez Trace was a famous road through the Southwest, running from Nashville, Tennessee, to Natchez, Mississippi. The road cut diagonally through Tennessee, the northern tip of Alabama, and through all of Mississippi. Much of the land traversed by the Trace was occupied by the Choctaw and Chickasaw Indians, and consequently treaties were negotiated with these tribes to permit the crossing of their territory. The Treaty of Chickasaw Bluffs was signed on October 24, 1801, with the Chickasaw, and on December 17, 1801, the Treaty of Fort Adams was signed with the Choctaw.

Congress appropriated $6,000 for the road, which was built between 1806 and 1820. Much of the Trace passed through rough swamp ground and heavy forest. Its most frequent travelers were flatboatmen returning north to Natchez and farmers journeying south to the New Orleans markets. Highway robbery was a problem on the road, as farmers returning from the markets often carried large amounts of money.

Natchitoches, Louisiana

Natchitoches, a town in northern Louisiana, often called "the New Orleans of the North," was the oldest permanent European settlement in the Louisiana Territory. It was established by the French under Louis Juchereau de St. Denis in 1714. He had first explored the region with Sieur de Bienville, a fellow Québecois, in 1700, but in 1713 Governor Cadillac sent him downriver to establish a post on the Red River. He left 10 men at an Indian village, the present site of the city, before pressing on to Mexico City himself, blazing the trail known as El Camino Real.

Spanish suspicion of French motives dogged St. Denis, even though he married the granddaughter of the Spanish commandant. After leaving her behind in Texas, he found himself imprisoned for two months on his attempted return to Natchitoches. However, he escaped and made it back to the outpost, of which he would remain commander until his death in 1744. The Spanish countered by establishing a military outpost, Los Adaes, about 14 miles away.

In addition to strained relations with the Spanish, St. Denis also had to contend with the Natchez Indians, who were if anything even more hostile. On one occasion in 1732, they erected a siege of the town that lasted 22 days. The outcome was decided by a pitched battle in which St. Denis, with 40 whites and 100 friendly Indians, counterattacked and killed 92 Natchez warriors.

Natchitoches was an important trade center in the colonial period. Pack trains traveled to and from Mexico, flatboats and pirogues traveled the Red River, and salt from the nearby Bayou Saline was brought to town overland. When the French ceded control back to Spain in 1763, trade continued to boom, in part because the Spanish left the French commandant, Athanase de Mézières, in charge of the outpost. An accomplished diplomat, he provided a smooth transition to Spanish rule. In 1803, the town was part of the territory ceded back to France, then sold to the United States in the Louisiana Purchase. Today, the city is home to Northwestern Louisiana State University and much of it remains a tourist attraction, not greatly changed from the way it looked in the early part of the last century.

Nation, Carry Amelia Moore

1846–1911

Temperance leader Carry Nation remains to this day the most famous (or infamous) spearhead of the dry movement, a woman known for using a hatchet to smash up saloons and stores that did a profitable side business in illegal whiskey.

Nation came from a troubled family background. Slaveowners in Kansas who fell on hard times during the Civil War, the Moores were on the move throughout Carry's childhood. Her mother was mentally ill and Carry herself was plagued with physical ailments and religious visions. Her husband, Dr. Charles Gloyd, was an alcoholic who drank himself to death, only more deeply embittering her against the demon drink.

KANSAS STATE HISTORICAL SOCIETY

Carry Nation.

After marrying David Nation, a lawyer and minister, and moving to Texas, she began claiming frequent visions and, after they settled in Medicine Lodge, Kansas, she became a local temperance leader, organizing a local chapter of the Women's Christian Temperance Union (WCTU). It was in 1899 that she finally declared war on the liquor business, smashing up a local drugstore that was dealing in whiskey under the counter. The success of this first foray started her on a path of violent attacks on saloons that would make her famous, get her arrested repeatedly, and cause the WCTU and other dry groups to distance themselves from her tactics.

Arrested over 30 times, Nation paid her fines and survived on donations from sympathizers, lecture fees, and the sale of souvenir hatchets. She gave much of the money to charity, establishing a home in Kansas City for the families of habitual drunkards. She also published numerous magazines, pamphlets, and tracts. She finally died in Leavenworth, Kansas of old age and exhaustion.

The long-term effects of her crusade are debatable. Certainly, her vigilance forced Kansas authorities to enforce the state's prohibition laws more stringently, but the fiasco of national prohibition probably reversed any lasting effect that her movement might have had.

National Farmers Alliance

The National Farmers Alliance was the forerunner of the Populist Party. In fact, there was a network of Farmers Alliances, with separate groups in the North and South and another for Southern African Americans. Like the Granger movement, the Alliances grew up in response to the conditions that had led to the collapse of agricultural prices in the Panic of 1873. Founded in the early 1880s, the National Farmers Alliance was strongest in the South, where it focused on the organization of farm owners.

The Alliance lobbied for railroad regulation, tax relief, and free coinage of silver. The Southern Alliance lobbied for its platform in the Democratic party, while the Northern Alliance worked toward the formation of a third party. Because of the Southern Alliance's segregationist policies and advocacy of secrecy, and because of disagreements over the formation of a third party, the two groups never formally united as a national organization, although an attempt at a merger was made at a St. Louis convention in 1889.

The groups reached the height of their power in 1890, particularly in the South, and won several local elections. They then turned their attention to national offices and issues, forming the People's party to counter what they perceived as the undue influence of Wall Street in the two-party system. Known as the Populist party, this group would enjoy its greatest influence when, led by William Jennings Bryan, it essentially took over the Democratic party in 1896.

As the prominent historian Richard Hofstader has observed, the Populist party is a landmark in American political history, "the first modern political movement of practical importance in the United States to insist that the federal government has some responsibility for the common weal."

Native American Dwellings

Like native cultures, dwellings exhibited a remarkable diversity. Different types of houses were built to adapt to the environment and to the lifestyles of their inhabitants. The many housing styles included wigwams, earth lodges, brush shelters, and lean-tos. Many tribes had both summer and winter villages. The tepee (tipi), which so many think of as the quintessential Native American dwelling, was not widely used except among the nomadic Plains tribes.

Among eastern tribes, thatched or bark houses were common. Often villages were surrounded by stockades for protection. The Iroquois built longhouses, Quonset-shaped homes 50 to 100 feet long, which often housed 8 to 10 related families. Eastern Algonquins built wigwams (or wikkiups)—oval, dome-shaped frames of wood covered with bark or cattail stalks. Sapling trees would be stripped of branches, bark and foliage then bent over and tied together to form a natural series of arches.

In the Southwest, the Pueblos and Hopis built houses of adobe and often lived in terraced, multistory "apartment" structures. In such a building, one family's roof was the patio of a family above. The Navajos built houses called hogans. These were

Framework of a tepee.

cone-shaped buildings constructed on a wooden frame made up of a log tripod surrounded by poles. The logs were then chinked or covered with bark and mud. There was a hole at the top to allow smoke from the fire to escape.

The tribes of the Pacific Northwest lived in gabled plank houses with wooden roofs. Boards were either tied together or held together by wooden pegs.

The tepee has come to symbolize life on the Plains, and it was used by many tribes because of its portability, and the fact that it could be put up and taken down relatively quickly. Its name is derived from a Dakota word meaning a place where one lives. The tepee was built by covering a pointed skeleton of poles, 12 or more feet high, with skins to form a tent. Sometimes the hide covering was decorated. As with the Navajo hogan, smoke was allowed to escape through a flap or hole in the top. When they were not on the move, however, many Plains tribes had permanent structures and villages.

JAMES JEROME HILL REFERENCE LIBRARY

Summer houses of the Dakotah Sioux.

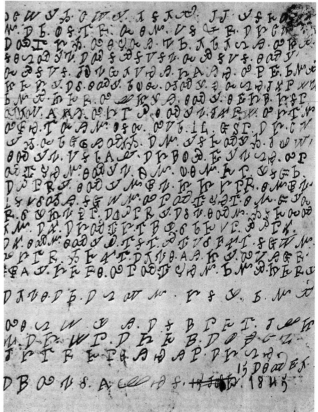

NATIONAL ARCHIVES

Letter written in Cherokee.

The Pawnees, for instance, lived in multifamily earth lodges built from a frame of wood covered with layers of willow branches, sod, and earth. The Osages, Omahas, Otos, and Winnebagos, when not on the march, lived in conical houses covered with earth. The Wichitas lived in similar houses, but instead of covering them with earth, they used grass. Some Apaches used tepees when in open country but brush shelters in the mountains.

Native American Languages

At the time of Columbus's arrival in the Americas there were, according to estimates, between 250 and 600 languages being spoken by the indigenous inhabitants of North America. To the bewildered Europeans, there seemed to be almost as many languages as there were tribes. Many of these languages, and the people who spoke them, no longer exist; others are still spoken by only a few people.

In 1891, J. W. Powell made the first serious attempt to classify Native American languages. He identified over 50 linguistic families. In 1929, Edward Sapir arranged Powell's families into six major groups. Others claim that the number of groups is actually 14. Today, although there is still no agreement, eight major language groups are commonly acknowledged. These groups (and representative tribes in each) are the Algonquian (Arapahos, Cheyennes, Ojibwas),

Athapaskan (Apaches, Navajos), Caddoan (Arikaras, Caddos, Pawnees), Iroquoian (Iroquois, Cherokees), Muskogean (Creeks), Penutian (Nez Perces, Maidus, Chinooks), Siouan (Lakotas, Assiniboins, Poncas), and Uzo-Aztecan (Comanches, Shoshones, Hopis). In addition to these eight major families, there are a number of smaller groups whose languages do not fit into the classifications. Tribes in these groups include the Zunis, Kiowas, and Keres.

Until the coming of Europeans, no tribe had a written language; writing was a gift the Creator had given only to whites. Most of the native languages were first recorded and then written down by whites. The Cherokees, however, developed their own written language. In 1821, Sequoyah perfected an 86-character syllabary, with each symbol representing a sound in the Cherokee language. Thereafter, the Cherokees became excellent recordkeepers and had a high degree of literacy.

Because language was viewed as the principal vehicle of a culture, the speaking of Native American languages was discouraged and even actively forbidden. Native American children at white-run boarding schools were prohibited to speak their own languages and were punished if they did so. Children from different tribes often were placed together as roommates so that, unable to communicate in their own languages, they would be forced to speak English. The destruction of Native American languages was seen as an important means of speeding assimilation.

Today it is estimated that approximately one-third of Native Americans speak their native languages. Over 100 languages are regularly spoken, with the Navajo, Iroquois, Inuit, Tohono O'odham (formerly the Papago), Pima, Apache, and Sioux tribes having the largest numbers of native speakers.

Navajo Indians

An Athapascan tribe of Native Americans residing in Arizona and New Mexico, the Navajos are the largest Native-American nation in the United States.

Sometime between 1000 and 1400 C.E., the Navajos, with their Apache relatives, migrated into the Southwest. Influenced by the neighboring Pueblos and the Hopis, they became gradually more sedentary and began to farm and raise stock. The earliest

European encounter was probably that of Coronado in 1541. Subsequent Spanish explorers called the people Apaches de Navahu (from a Tewa word meaning "cultivators of fields")—hence, Navajo.

In the eighteenth and early nineteenth centuries, Navajo villages suffered raids from the Spaniards and later from the Mexicans, as well as from the Comanches and Utes. In turn, they retaliated against the whites and raided the Hopis and the Pueblos. Following the Treaty of Guadalupe Hidalgo in 1848, the United States attempted to draw up treaties with the Navajos, but found the process difficult because of the tribe's structure, which lacked a central authority. In 1851, in an attempt to stop the raiding (and influenced by rumors of mineral wealth in the area), the U.S. Army established Fort Defiance (near present-day Window Rock, Arizona).

On April 30, 1860, more than 1,000 Navajos under Manuelito, Barboncito, and Herrero attacked Fort Defiance, nearly taking it. U.S. Army regulars and New Mexico volunteers retaliated, disrupting Navajo life and killing many of the tribe.

LIBRARY OF CONGRESS

Artist/naturalist Heinrich Mollhausen recorded a somber pair of Navajos in this print. Although the men have a romanticized, dreamy air, the detail of their dress is quite authentic.

CITY ART MUSEUM OF ST. LOUIS

Navajo chief Barboncito.

Navajo chief Manuelito was, along with Chief Barboncito, the last hold-out before surrendering in 1866 and being sent to Bosque Redondo, in New Mexico.

In 1863, General James Carleton placed Colonel Kit Carson in command of a campaign against the Navajo. The goal was to eliminate them as a threat to local ranching and mining operations. Although Carson reportedly believed that war against the tribe was unnecessary, he nevertheless waged the campaign with ferocity. He put a "scorched-earth" policy into effect—killing the Navajo's sheep, burning their crops, and chopping down their peach orchards—in order to starve them into submission. The plan worked.

Thousands of Navajos surrendered. They were then subjected to a forced march of hundreds of miles to a desolate reservation at Fort Sumner in the Bosque Redondo of southeast New Mexico. Hun-

dreds died on the way. The trek is remembered in Navajo history as the "Long Walk."

Conditions at Bosque Redondo were deplorable. About a third of the people died within two years from disease, hunger, exposure, and brutality. In 1868, faced with a scandal because of conditions at the reservation, the government executed a treaty with the Navajos, under which they were allowed to return to their homeland.

Adjustments to reservation boundaries throughout the remainder of the century led to tensions between the Navajo and Hopi that persist to the present day.

Nebraska

The first known human settlers of the Nebraska region were the Folsom people, although earlier inhabitants are believed to have existed. Folsom remains have been found along with mammoth and musk ox fossils near O'Neill.

The Native American tribes that populated Nebraska before white men arrived included the Pawnees, Sioux, Cheyennes, Poncas, Otos, Missouri, Arapahos, and Omahas, with the Pawnees being the largest group. The Sioux and Pawnees were almost constantly at war, and the more agricultural tribes were usually at the mercy of the warrior nomadic groups.

The first white men did not reach Nebraska until the eighteenth century. Both France and Spain claimed the land, but there was no significant white presence until Manuel Lisa established a fort bearing his last name as a fur-trading site in 1813. This site, near modern-day Omaha, later became the Army outpost known as Fort Atkinson. The nucleus of white settlement in the region was at Bellevue, at the southern edge of today's Omaha, primarily an outpost of the American Fur Company. Although, the state remained relatively unpopulated by white settlers, with thousands of people journeying west from Independence, Missouri, through Nebraska it was inevitable that some would settle down in Nebraska.

Bolstered by Stephen A. Douglas's interest in a transcontinental railroad, which he hoped would use Chicago as its eastern terminus, Congress created the Nebraska Territory in 1854 as part of the

LIBRARY OF CONGRESS

Platte River Basin, Nebraska.

controversial Kansas-Nebraska Act. Although it was assumed that Nebraska would be a free state and Kansas a slave state (under the doctrine of popular sovereignty), the resulting conflict led to protracted violence, with John Brown active in the region among antislavery forces. The state-to-be was also a site for the activities of the Underground Railroad. The creation of the Colorado and Dakota Territories by Congress in 1861 severely reduced the size of the Nebraska Territory.

With the passage of the Homestead Act of 1862, floods of settlers came into Nebraska. The decision in 1863 by President Abraham Lincoln about where to locate the eastern end of the transcontinental railroad further fueled the growth of the state. Lincoln chose a spot in Iowa directly across the Missouri River from Omaha. With the completion of the Union Pacific in 1869 and the erection of a bridge across the Missouri in 1871, Omaha became the premier city of the state, a status it has never relinquished.

Nebraska was admitted to the Union on March 1, 1867, as the thirty-seventh state. A farm state even today, it was a key source of support for the Populist movement and native son William Jennings Bryan.

After the death of the Populist Party, the state still manifested a residual interest in populist politics, which showed in its support for the Progressive Party early in this century.

Nevada

Lying almost entirely within the Great Basin, Nevada is one of the most sparsely populated states in the nation. Original inhabitants were nomadic Native Americans who survived in a harsh environment for thousands of years, until the arrival of Europeans. Tribes living in the Nevada region at the time of European arrival included the Northern Paiutes, the Southern Paiutes, the Washos, and the Shoshones. The first American to explore Nevada was Jedediah Strong Smith, a fur trader and part owner of the Rocky Mountain Fur Company. Smith opened up the area in 1826 when he reached the Walker River and central Nevada. Two years later Peter Skene Ogden and a party from the Hudson's Bay Company discovered the Humboldt River.

The first official exploration of the region was conducted by John C. Frémont from 1843 to 1845. Frémont led two expeditions into the Great Basin, forging new routes of travel into northern and central Nevada. When the Mexican War ended in 1848, the Treaty of Guadalupe Hidalgo transferred to the United States territory that included Nevada. The

U.S. GEOLOGICAL SURVEY

Timothy O'Sullivan's Sand Dunes, Carson Desert, Nevada.

following year the first permanent settlement, Genoa, was established by the Mormons in Carson Valley.

Major growth occurred in the years following the discovery of the Comstock Lode in the Washoe Valley. The lode, a rich silver deposit, was discovered in the spring of 1859 by Peter O'Riely and Pat McLaughlin. During its most productive years, between 1859 and 1880, the Comstock Lode yielded an amazing $300 million in silver. Nevada's population in that period grew from about 7,000 to over 42,000 residents. In its heyday the Comstock mines created individual fortunes for men such as George Hearst and John P. Jones and created boomtowns like Virginia City. In addition to its economic impact, the Comstock Lode had social and political implications for Nevada. Prosperity brought hotels, restaurants, and theater to Virginia City, and the lode was a major factor in territorial establishment and statehood.

Nevada was made the 36th state in the Union on October 31, 1864, just days before the elections of that year. President Abraham Lincoln wanted to ensure a majority of proreconstruction senators, and he knew that Nevada's three electoral votes would be Republican. The territorial governor telegraphed Nevada's constitution to Lincoln, who quickly approved it.

When mining at the Comstock Lode began to slow down, the state entered an economic depression that lasted from 1880 to 1900. Many blamed the Coinage Act of 1873 for Nevada's economic woes. Often called the Crime of '73, the act demonetized silver and brought an end to the coining of sil-

ver dollars, which naturally caused the price of the metal to drop.

The silver issue soon dominated Nevada politics, even prompting the creation of the platform-specific Silver party. When the population of the state dropped to 42,335 in 1900, there was talk of repealing Nevada's statehood. Relief came in May 1900 when Jim Butler discovered a silver mine in Tonopah. Prospectors rushed to the area, and similar discoveries soon followed at Goldfield and Rhyolite, sparking a new era of prosperity.

Over the past few decades, Nevada has witnessed a significant population growth in urban centers such as Las Vegas, which in turn has altered the focus of the state's economy. While tourism and gambling have become increasingly lucrative attractions, fostering a surge in the transient population, the increase in water demand has caused an undeniable shortage. The water table has lowered considerably since 1950, and irrigation efforts have not proved entirely successful. The outcome of this latest concern remains to be seen.

New Mexico

New Mexico is a region in which three distinct cultures, Native American, Spanish, and Anglo, have coalesced to form a distinctive lifestyle.

The land that New Mexico now occupies has been inhabited for over 10,000 years. The Anasazi Indians began forming permanent communities in northwestern New Mexico around the beginning of the Christian era. After their departure around A.D. 1500, the Apaches, Comanches, and Navajos moved in. (The Pueblo Indians, ancestors of the Anasazis, lived along the Rio Grande and built the cliff dwellings that can be seen today at Mesa Verde.)

Alvar Nuñez Cabeza de Vaca was most likely the first white man to explore the region in 1536. Three years later Fray Marcos de Niza entered the region of present-day New Mexico on his quest to find the seven golden cities of Cibola. Inspired by de Niza's stories, Francisco Vasquez de Coronado led an expedition in 1540 that explored almost the entire Pueblo region. Instead of finding the gilded cities he set out for, Coronado encountered the apartment-like adobe structures built by the Pueblos.

NEVADA HISTORICAL SOCIETY

Goldfield, Nevada.

CENTER FOR AMERICAN HISTORY, UNIVERSITY OF TEXAS AT AUSTIN

Northern New Mexico.

Several other explorations followed before the first permanent European settlement was established at San Juan Pueblo in 1598 by Juan de Oñate y Salazar, who colonized New Mexico when he led 130 families up the Rio Grande Valley. His successor as governor, Don Pedro de Peralta, founded the capital city of Sante Fe in 1610.

Conflict between civil and ecclesiastical officials dominated the early years of Spanish rule in the province. Forced conversion to Christianity led to a bloody revolt by Pueblo Indians, who in 1680 stormed across New Mexico, killing priests and colonists, and burning churches and ranches. Their attack on Sante Fe forced the Spanish to retreat south to El Paso. The province remained in the hands of the Pueblos until 1692, when General Diego de Vargas marched to a bloodless victory with 300 Spanish soldiers.

After the Louisiana Purchase of 1803, Spain felt the threat of Anglo-American pioneers pressing deeper into the Southwest. In 1806 Zebulon Pike embarked on an expedition to the headwaters of the Arkansas and Red rivers that took him (inadvertently or intentionally) into the Spanish province, where he was promptly arrested.

With Mexican independence in 1821, New Mexico's borders opened up, leading to increased contact with Americans. After the outbreak of the Mexican War in 1846, General Stephen Watts Kearny marched to Santa Fe and with little resistance claimed the New Mexican province for the United States. Two years later the Treaty of Guadalupe Hidalgo ended the war with Mexico and officially made New Mexico part of the United States; the territory was organized formally in 1851. During the Civil War much of New Mexico was captured by Confederate forces, who were forced to retreat after the Union army triumphed at Glorieta Pass near Sante Fe on March 28, 1862.

In the years following the Civil War, sheep raising dominated the economy in the territory, but the arrival of the Railroad in 1879 brought a boom in cattle ranching.

New Mexico's economy has grown considerably in recent years, largely because several federal research projects are based there, dealing mostly with weapons and nuclear energy, and employment opportunities abound. The huge multiple-disk space telescope is located in the desert outside Socorro, New Mexico.

Nez Perce Indians

The Nez Perces, a Penutian tribe of Native Americans, originally inhabited a territory ranging over southeast Washington, northeast Oregon, and western Idaho.

Lewis and Clark first encountered the tribe in 1805 and called them Chopunnish. The Indians were eager to trade for guns, a weapon they had first acquired a few months before from the Minitari in North Dakota. The first trader to reach the Nez Perces was David Thompson of the North West Company, sometime between 1807 and 1812. Thompson named them Shahaptians, the Flathead word for the tribe. Later French-Canadian *voyageurs* labeled them Nez Perces because of their custom of adorning their noses with small pieces of shell. They had adopted the custom from the tribes of the Columbia River, with whom they often traded, and though the habit was abandoned shortly after white contact, the appellation stuck.

In its earliest days, the Nez Perce culture, because of frequent trade dealings, closely resembled that of the tribes of the Columbia River. By the nineteenth century, however, the people had become essentially Plains Indians. Numbering around 5,000,

the tribe lived in small bands, each with its own leadership.

They strove to live in peace with the whites who entered their territory. Having heard of Christianity from the French, in 1831 the Nez Perces sent a delegation to St. Louis asking for teachers and books. The Presbyterians and Catholics responded. In 1836, the Reverend Henry H. Spalding and his wife opened a Presbyterian mission and school in Nez Perce territory. Most of the tribe became Christian, but in the 1840s, as increasing numbers of whites moved into the area, the Indians became disaffected, accusing the missionaries of helping to steal their country. In 1847, Spalding closed his mission after the neighboring Cayuses turned on and killed the missionaries who lived among them. Still the Nez Perces remained at peace and boasted that no member of their tribe had ever killed a white man.

The government made a Pacific railway survey of the area in 1852. In 1863, a treaty was concluded with the chiefs of a number of Nez Perce bands that divested them of their land and established a reservation. Other bands refused to sign. With pressure from white settlers mounting, in 1877 the entire tribe was ordered to surrender their land and move to the reservation. A nontreaty band, led by Chief Joseph, refused, and the U.S. Army was sent in. Joseph then led his people on a heroic but doomed 1,300-mile fighting retreat in an effort to

Raven Blanket, a Nez Perce warrior.

This painting by Frederic Remington entitled The Surrender of Chief Joseph *shows the Nez Perce chief making his famous surrender speech to General Howard and Colonel Miles.*

reach Canada where they thought they would be safe.

Joseph's band was confined first in Fort Leavenworth, Kansas, and then on a reservation in Indian Territory. So many of the Nez Perces died there, however, that those who survived were moved to the Colville Reservation in Washington in 1885.

Nicodemus, Kansas

Nicodemus was the most famous of the midwestern African-American agricultural towns that sprang up after the Civil War. Benjamin "Pap" Singleton spread word of great political and economic freedom in the Kansas prairies. Although the settlers of Nicodemus were, for the most part, much better off financially than the thousands of penniless migrating Exodusters, the town received a fair share of its population from the movement.

W. J. Niles, an African-American businessman, and W. R. Hill, a white minister and speculator who hoped to boost population around nearby Hill City, founded the town of Nicodemus in Graham County, Kansas, in 1877. Niles, Hill, and later Reverend Roundtree actively promoted the region, which covered about 12 miles of fertile land along the Salmon River and ran about six miles inland. April of 1877 saw the arrival of a group of settlers called the Nicodemus Town Company of Graham County. Nicodemus Colony followed, and then others arrived from Kentucky and Missouri, bringing with them farm equipment and livestock. By 1880 the town's African-American population exceeded 700.

Although the newcomers faced hostility from nearby white communities and battled to protect their crops from herds of roaming Texan cattle, the settlement thrived. Edward P. McCabe relocated there from Chicago and was later elected state auditor, the highest office in Kansas held by an African American in the nineteenth century.

The influx of settlers to Nicodemus peaked in the mid-1880s. After that, a period of drought and the failure of the railroad to continue service to the town slowed growth considerably. Despite this, Nicodemus remained a leader among midwestern African-American settlements.

Northern Pacific Railroad

The Northern Pacific Railroad was a transcontinental railroad that ran from St. Paul, Minnesota, to Seattle, Washington. Congress chartered the Northern Pacific Railroad in 1864 to be built from Lake Superior to a port on the Pacific coast. The railroad was originally deeded a land grant of 40 million acres, but inability to secure financial backing made progress impossible in the early years.

In 1869 Josiah Perham approached Philadelphia banker Jay Cooke, who agreed to become the financial agent for the Northern Pacific. However, an unfortunate involvement with the St. Paul and Pacific

Advertisements for the Northern Pacific enticed people west with free land.

Railroad, coupled with the depression of the 1870s, forced the Northern Pacific into receivership in 1873 (and Cooke into bankruptcy). Construction stopped for six years, and portions of the land grant were sold off in large lots in North Dakota and Minnesota. Henry Villard took control of the Northern Pacific in 1878 and began building it westward. Five years later he connected it with his Oregon Railway, thus completing the line to Seattle.

On the eve of the depression of the 1890s, the railroad was once more in financial difficulty and was again forced into receivership. This time it was acquired and reorganized by banker J. P. Morgan, who shared a controlling interest with James J. Hill of the Great Northern Railway. Hill tried to combine the Northern Pacific and the Great Northern with the Burlington and Quincy Railroad Company in 1904, but the Supreme Court ruled the merger to be in violation of the Sherman Anti-Trust Act. The three railroads were finally allowed to merge in 1970 to form the Burlington Northern Railroad.

Northwest Ordinance of 1787

JULY 13, 1787

The Northwest Ordinance of 1787 was passed by Congress to provide for a government for the territory northwest of the Ohio River and east of the Mississippi River. The ordinance also contained provisions for the establishment of new states in the territory.

After the Ordinance of 1784 was passed, settlements began to spring up in the Northwest Territory, especially in the area north of the Ohio River. No established system of government existed in the territory, and Congress thought it wise to outline a provision for government and transition of the territory to Union states. The Ohio Company of Associates, a group of New England investors, had just purchased a large amount of land in the Ohio territory from the government, and they too pushed Congress for the establishment of government there.

The Ordinance of 1787 was based largely on a plan drawn up by Thomas Jefferson three years earlier (the Ordinance of 1784). James Monroe headed the committee that drafted the bill as an amendment to the Ordinance of 1784. When Congress en-

couraged heavy revisions, two men from the Ohio Company were consulted.

The final bill, passed on July 13, 1787, stated that between three and five states would eventually be formed in the territory and laid out a three-step procedure for their establishment:

The first step involved government rule by a governor, a secretary, and three judges, all of whom were required to live in the territory and own freehold estates of varying sizes. The governor was to be appointed by the President and would serve a three-year term. The governor appointed all other civil officials and was entitled to establish counties and townships in the territory. The secretary, appointed by the President, was responsible for maintaining the acts and laws of the legislature, as well as for keeping public records, which were to be sent to the secretary of state every six months. The three judges were also appointed by the President. The government established in this first stage was authorized to adopt and publish criminal and civil laws from other states as it saw fit.

The second stage was to be launched once a census showed that 5,000 free males resided in one of the territories. At this point the men could elect a territorial legislature and send a delegate to Congress who could participate in debates but could not vote.

The third stage, reached when a territory boasted a population of 60,000 males, rendered the territory eligible to enter the Union as a new and equal state.

The compromise outlawed slavery in the Northwest Territory and guaranteed many civil rights, such as religious freedom and trial by jury. The legislation was considered one of the greatest successes under the Articles of Confederation, providing for a constitution and an orderly form of government for the Northwest Territory. The many Native Americans who occupied the area, however, believed the territorial expansionism of the United States threatened their way of life and saw the Northwest Ordinance as one more symbol of the political and social conquest of their homeland.

Northwest Passage

The Northwest Passage was the long-dreamt-of water route that would take merchant seamen across the North American continent to the Pacific and on to China for trade. Almost as soon as Columbus, Vespucci, and others had established that there was a land mass to the west of Europe that separated it from Asia, the search began for a way to cross the new continent by sea. John Cabot explored the coast of Newfoundland in 1497 in the mistaken belief that he had hit upon China. Jacques Cartier was the next to seek a way through, sailing as far as Montreal in 1535. With those expeditions, both the English and French staked claims to the North American continent. But neither found a route to Asia.

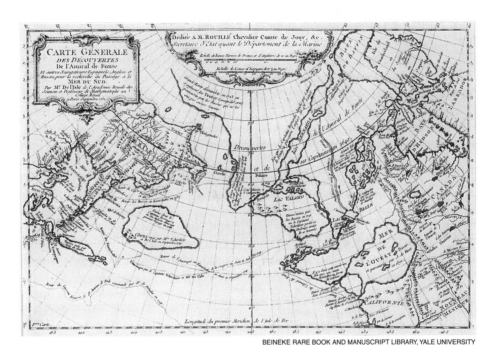

The ever elusive Northwest Passage, as drawn in 1752.

Two Spanish ships, the Sutil *and the* Mexicana, *were seeking the northwest passage when they arrived in Nootka Harbor.*

Over the next century, as the search continued, many more explorers found themselves in the frozen seas of the north. Martin Frobisher, Henry Hudson, William Baffin, Luke Fox, and Thomas James all sought the Northwest Passage unsuccessfully, but all helped to draw the map of the continent in the process. Juan Rodrigues Cabrillo and other Spanish and Portuguese explorers attempted to break through from the Pacific end, with similar results. One of the goals Thomas Jefferson hoped would be accomplished by Lewis and Clark was the establishment of a water route across the continent. It would not be until 1905, when Roald Amundsen finally completed the journey, that an all-water route was actually secured. By that time, people had been traveling from coast to coast on the railroads for 36 years.

Norwegian Settlers in the West

Like the Swedish immigrants, the great wave of Norwegians who came to America did so because of the scarcity of farmlands in their native country. Norway, which was under Swedish rule from 1814 to 1905, had little arable land; only 4 percent of the country was farmable. Moreover, between 1801 and 1845, the population of the country grew by 50 percent, making a terrible situation worse, especially as two-thirds of Norwegians lived in rural areas. The chance to go to America and secure farmland of one's own was irresistible.

Norway was also suffering from religious conflicts, and in fact, one of the first groups of Norwegians to settle in the New World was a party of 52 religious dissenters who sailed to New York in 1825 aboard the *Restauration,* often called the Norwegian *Mayflower.* The group's leader, Cleng Peerson, who had been involved in a similar Swedish settlement at Bishop's Hill, Illinois, would later found a community in Bosque County, Texas.

Most Norwegian settlers came to the United States after the Civil War, and settled in rural areas. After the passage of the Homestead Act in 1862, millions of pamphlets and posters extolling the virtues of America were circulated throughout Europe, and had a particularly strong effect in Scandinavia and Germany. In addition, Norwegians wrote home rhapsodizing over the beauty of the plains and the richness of the soil, which inspired still more emigration. The largest groups of Norwegians who came to the United States went to Wisconsin, Minnesota, and North Dakota, where they tended to settle in highly concentrated enclaves.

The Norwegians became active in the Populist party in the Midwest and in the Non-Partisan League in North Dakota; these organizations were the logical political outlets for those who brought strong egalitarian beliefs with them from their homeland. They also formed their own Norwegian synods of the Lutheran Church, rather than joining already existing German and Swedish groups. Norwegian-language papers flourished, particularly in the Midwest; but, as with other ethnic groups in America, by the second generation English had almost completely replaced the original native tongue.

O

Oakley, Annie

1860–1926

Annie Oakley (Phoebe Ann Moses), was a show-woman, champion sharpshooter, and a star performer for 17 years with "Buffalo Bill's Wild West" show. She was born in Darke County, Ohio, and by the age of 8 had learned to shoot. She practiced on her Quaker father's farm and supplemented the family's income by supplying a Cincinnati hotel with game.

In 1875, in a Cincinnati contest, she outshot the Irish-born marksman Frank E. Butler, and married him the next year. She adopted the name Annie Oakley and Butler became her manager and act partner and, for the next nine years, they toured with circuses and on the vaudeville circuit. In 1885, Oakley and Butler joined William F. Cody's "Wild West" traveling show, then performing in New Orleans.

Her act was an instant sensation, so much so that she received top billing as "The Peerless Wing and Rifle Shot," her portrait, bedecked with the marksmanship medals she had collected in contests and exhibitions, and renditions of some of her most famous stunts, depicted on colorful posters.

Oakley's 10-minute act, refined over the years and always carefully staged (even her costumes were homemade), included such crowd-pleasers as shooting a cigarette from her husband's mouth or a dime from his fingers at 30 paces; dividing a playing card by shooting through its edge (giving rise to the ex-

LIBRARY OF CONGRESS

Annie Oakley.

pression "Annie Oakley" for a complimentary ticket, commonly punched full of holes); breaking tossed glass balls with a rifle held upside-down over

323

her head or while lying across a chair. She hit targets with her back turned to them, using a mirror or shiny hunting knife, the rifle pointed backward over her shoulder. She hit as many as 11 glass balls thrown in the air and could leap over a table, grab a shotgun, and hit two clay pigeons released simultaneously.

Perhaps her greatest triumph came in 1887 when she performed in England during Queen Victoria's Golden Jubilee celebration. She was presented to the queen ("a gracious, very womanly woman," Oakley later said), along with Cody and others from the Wild West show. Victoria said to her, "You are a very clever little girl." (Oakley was five feet tall and weighed about 100 pounds.)

Independent of the Wild West, she toured Europe with her husband and later the two performed in Gordon W. "Pawnee Bill" Lillie's rival show before rejoining Cody in 1889 for another European tour and for the World Columbian Exposition in Chicago in 1893.

Oakley admired Cody, pronouncing him "the kindest-hearted, broadest-minded, simplest, most loyal man I ever knew," and counted among her "dear, faithful" friends, Sitting Bull. The Hunkpapa Sioux leader had seen her perform in St. Paul, Minnesota, in 1884, and gave her the nickname "Little Miss Sure Shot." During the 1885 Wild West tour, for which Sitting Bull was hired at $50 a week, he "adopted" her as his daughter and the two became fast friends.

Toward the end of the 1901 tour a freight train collided with the Wild West coaches as they attempted to cross the tracks and Oakley received severe internal injuries. She returned to work the following year and performed on stage and with the Wild West through 1913. During World War I she and Butler toured army camps giving exhibitions.

Oakley was crippled in an automobile accident in 1921 and died in her native Darke County on November 3, 1926. Her husband died 20 days later.

While a resolute and ambitious professional who "made her mark" in a man's world, Oakley was modest, sedate, and religious. She loved needlework and helping orphans, and came closest to anger when she missed a target and stamped her feet in the arena. She was nothing remotely like the boisterous and brash characterization of her in Irving Berlin's *Annie Get Your Gun.*

Obijay Indians

See Chippewa Indians

Oil

The oil industry in the West was born, not in Texas, the state that would become legendary for its oilfields, but in California, in the 1860s. Oil seepages noted in that state suggested to geologists that commercial development of California oilfields offered real commercial possibility. However, the crude oil from those deposits proved to be of too low a grade and too high a carbon content to be used as kerosene; this was the primary commercial oil product in the middle of the nineteenth century, before the advent of the internal combustion engine.

Geologists continued to search for oil in California, and in 1892 E. L. Doheny found an enormous oilfield in the Los Angeles area. Other large deposits were found near Coalinga and the Kern River. This oil could be used for boiler fuel for locomotives and steamships, and provided the basis for an entire new industry, as refineries and pipelines grew up to meet the new demand. Still, in 1900 California was ranked only fifth among oil-producing states, and the West accounted for only 9 percent of the nation's oil production.

All that changed in 1901. In January of that year, Captain Anthony Lucas, a wildcat oil driller, was looking for oil around Beaumont, Texas. Lucas punched through the top of a salt dome to what he hoped would be a pool of oil. The resulting geyser was so powerful that it ripped his drilling apparatus out of the ground; half a million barrels of oil shot into the air over a six-day period before Lucas and his crew could cap the well. Huge crowds assembled to watch; it was a harbinger of what was to come.

Spindletop Field, as the massive oil deposit came to be known, changed the face of Texas as dramatically as the 1849 gold rush had changed California. Almost overnight, thousands of would-be oil tycoons rushed into the Beaumont area, and Texas became as synonymous with oilfields as California once had been with goldfields.

Other major oil discoveries followed quickly.

Eventually oil would be found under the majority of Texas counties, with the East Texas oil boom of 1931 perhaps the largest of all. Major oilfields were tapped in Louisiana, Oklahoma, and California. In 1911, the West's share of American oil production had grown to over 72 percent. Four of the six largest oil-producing states were west of the Mississippi. By 1968, the West accounted for 95 percent of the nation's oil production, with the region's oil and natural gas production bringing in more than $13 billion.

As the oil industry grew, so did the economies of the western states that participated in the boom. In Texas, in particular, oil provided the basis for rapid industrialization and the growth of urban centers like Houston and Dallas. It also provided a new source of tax revenue, and oil royalties fattened up the state's educational endowment. In fact, it could be argued that virtually every great fortune made in this century in some way has been derived—directly or indirectly—from the petroleum business.

On the other hand, the negative side of the growth of the oil industry is self-evident, particularly in the West. The massive oil spill caused by the *Exxon Valdez* accident off the Alaska coast; the effects of offshore drilling in California, Louisiana, and in the Gulf of Mexico; the air pollution caused by emissions from automobile engines—these are but a few of the less desirable results of the success of the oil industry in the West.

THE HUNTINGTON LIBRARY, SAN MARINO, CALIFORNIA

Union Oil Gusher, Long Beach, California.

Ojibwa Indians

See Chippewa Indians

O.K. Corral Gunfight

1881

Eight men took part in the gunfight on Fremont Street near the O.K. Corral, Tombstone, Arizona Territory, on October 26, 1881. When it was over—probably in 30 seconds—three men were dead and three others wounded. The two chief antagonists, Wyatt Earp and Ike Clanton, were unharmed.

The gunfight was the culmination of a feud between the Earp brothers—Wyatt, Morgan, and Virgil—and the Clanton and McLaury brothers, who were involved in cattle rustling and other thievery from their ranches on the San Pedro River, west of Tombstone.

The sparks that ignited the gunfight occurred on October 25 when Ike Clanton was arrested by Tombstone town marshal Virgil Earp for carrying guns inside the city limits. Tom McLaury was accosted by Wyatt Earp, who "buffaloed" him by whipping the barrel of his pistol against the side of the outlaw's head, knocking him out. By the next morning, Ike Clanton had been joined by his younger brother Billy, and Tom McLaury by his brother Frank.

Virgil Earp, after deputizing brothers Wyatt and Morgan, and Wyatt's friend John Henry "Doc" Holl-

LIBRARY OF CONGRESS

The O.K. Corral

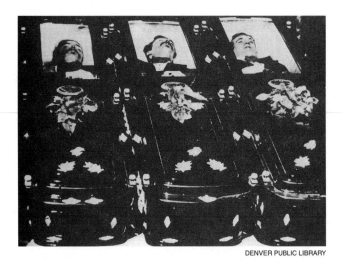

The bodies of those who did not survive the shootout at the O.K. Corral: Tom and Frank McLaury, and Billy Clanton.

iday, determined to arrest the Clantons, over the objections of Cochise County Sheriff John Behan, on the charge of carrying firearms within the city limits.

The Earps and Holliday met the Clantons, the McLaurys, and Billy Claiborne in midafternoon on October 26 in a vacant lot next to Fly's photographic studio and gallery on Fremont Street. In the quick exchange of gunshots, Wyatt and Morgan Earp's combined gunfire killed Frank McLaury; Billy Clanton died with wounds in his wrist, chest, and head. Holliday's shotgun blast killed Tom McLaury. Morgan and Virgil Earp, and Doc Holliday were wounded. Billy Claiborne and Ike Clanton had both hightailed it into Fly's studio when the shooting started, and so avoided injury.

Oklahoma

Oklahoma, first occupied as early as fifteen thousand years ago by nomadic tribes, became the destination of thousands of Native Americans on the Trail of Tears. The first European exploration of the area took place in 1541, when Francisco Vázquez de Coronado entered the western part of the state. Subsequent Spanish explorations followed, and soon French traders arrived, establishing posts along the Wichita and Caddo rivers. In 1806 the first Ameri-

can exploration of the region was led by James Wilkinson, who was part of the Zebulon Pike expedition. At this time Oklahoma was inhabited by a number of Native American tribes. Plains Apaches, Kiowas, and Comanches roamed the western part of the territory; Wichitas and Caddos occupied the southwest; Cheyennes and Arapahos predominated in the northwest; the Osages had settled in the northeast; and the Quapaws lived in the east. Most of the area had become part of the United States with the Louisiana Purchase of 1803, but the boundaries remained indefinite until 1819, when the United States and Spain agreed on the 100th meridian and the Red River as the international border. Traders settled in the region and established posts at the confluence of the Arkansas, Verdigris, and Grand rivers, which became known as Three Forks.

In the 1820s pressure was placed on The Five Civilized Tribes—the Cherokees, Creeks, Choctaws, Chickasaws, and Seminoles—to give up their fertile land east of the Mississippi and relocate to a "permanent" home east of the 96th meridian. In 1828 the federal government prohibited new settlement in the Oklahoma territory to make room for these Native Americans, who in the early 1830s were forced to move and were escorted to their new location. During the removal, the U.S. Army burned Native American homes and farms, shot resisters, and even looted Cherokee graves. Of the 13,000 Cherokees who traveled the Trail of Tears to Oklahoma, at least 4,000 died before arriving. A group of 1,000 Chocktaws was ravaged by cholera; only 88 survived the journey.

The tribes were settled on the eastern half of what is now Oklahoma. Eventually the Five Civilized Tribes established their own governments and capital cities, began farming, and started educating their children at mission schools. During the Civil War, loyalty among the tribes was split, but most sided with the Confederacy. Oklahoma was hit hard by the war, which destroyed the homes and villages of most of the Native Americans. After the war, the federal government insisted that the tribes yield right of way to the coming railroad. Moreover, governmental petitions were issued again and again, asking the settled groups to give up portions of their land to newly relocated tribes. By 1885 representatives from at least 50 tribes inhabited the territory that had been promised to the Five Civilized Nations as a permanent home.

Although the territory was designated as exclusively for Native Americans, many white settlers moved there too. They soon outnumbered the Indians. (It was because of these settlers who scrambled to Oklahoma *sooner* than it was legal to do so that Oklahoma became known as the Sooner State.) In 1889 President Benjamin Harrison opened up some of the unoccupied land to white settlement, and on April 22 an estimated 50,000 to 60,000 white immigrants rushed in. Towns such as Norman and the capital, Oklahoma City, sprang up overnight, and within two months Congress established the territory of Oklahoma. By the early 1900s two territories actually existed in the area, the Oklahoma territory and the Indian Territory to the east. Although both fought for statehood separately, in 1906 they combined to form the state of Oklahoma.

Omaha, Nebraska

The largest city in the state of Nebraska, Omaha is located on the west bank of the Missouri River.

Omaha takes its name from the Omaha tribe, the word meaning "upstream." The Lewis and Clark expedition passed through what is now Omaha in 1804. The fur trade in the region became very active shortly thereafter, and from 1820 to 1827, the Army operated Fort Atkinson just north of the current city. The Mormons fleeing Nauvoo in 1846 wintered just across the river in what became Florence and has since been incorporated into Omaha. The encampment became a major departure point for Mormon wagon trains heading for Utah.

In 1854, the Omaha Indians ceded their land to the United States, and after the creation of the Nebraska Territory, the land adjacent to Council Bluffs was opened to settlers. The Council Bluffs and Nebraska Ferry Company, a land speculation outfit, created the town of Omaha to attract settlers, building a territorial capital there. Omaha remained the capital until 1867.

However, the city's importance in the growth of the state did not stem from its political centrality but from its location. In 1858 a road was opened between Omaha and Fort Kearny that quickly became a major transfer point for passengers and freight

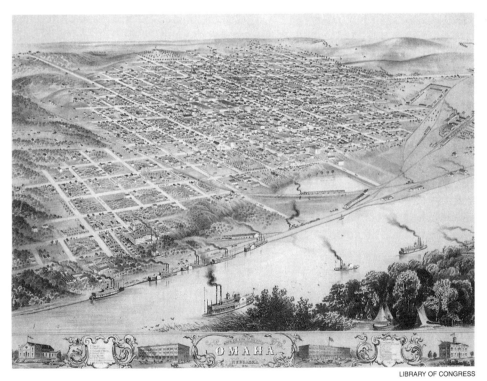

Aerial view of Omaha in 1868.

coming up the Missouri and then traveling west overland. Omaha's importance as a shipping and passenger transportation center was cemented with the completion of the Union Pacific Railroad. Omaha quickly became a major center for processing food, which it continues to be today.

Omaha Indians

The Omahas are a Siouan tribe of Native Americans, now residing in Nebraska, about 80 miles from the city that bears their name.

According to traditional lore, the Omaha, Kansa, Osage, Ponca, and Quapaw tribes were once all a single people, living east of the Ohio River Valley in Indiana and Kentucky. Similarities in their languages, tribal organization, and customs seem to confirm this idea. The five tribes gradually split apart. At the time of first white contact, the Omahas ranged over an area between present-day Minnesota and South Dakota. They gradually withdrew into Nebraska, which they consider their traditional home. They did a certain amount of farming, but, as with other Plains tribes, hunting was their major means of subsistence.

In 1854, the tribe ceded its lands to the United States and moved to a reservation at its present location. In 1882, the Omaha Allotment Act (a forerunner of the Dawes Act) was passed by Congress. Despite some opposition from traditionalists, Omaha land was individually allotted. Subsequently, Alice Fletcher, an ethnographer hired to administer the program, collaborated with Francis La Flesche (an Omaha, a lawyer, and one of the earliest Native Americans to engage in modern-day ethnography) in producing a voluminous report on the history and customs of the Omahas for the Bureau of American Ethnology of the Smithsonian Institution.

Oñate y Salazar, Juan de

CA. 1550–1630

Juan de Oñate y Salazar was a Spanish colonizer and the founder of New Mexico. He was born to wealth and prestige, the son of a conquistador who had served in Nuevo Galicia and founded Zacatecas. His wife was a granddaughter of Cortez.

In 1595, Oñate was granted a contract for the conquest and settlement of what would become New Mexico. Under the contract he was to mount an expedition at his own expense, and then run the colony as a business for profit. After numerous delays, he launched his expedition on February 7, 1598. Traveling north from Mexico with over 500 people—130 soldiers, their families, and servants—he paused at El Paso before proclaiming Spanish rule over the territory, and then moved up the Rio Grande and into the heartland of the Pueblo Indians.

Oñate established his headquarters near what is now Santa Fe, dispossessing the Pueblos who lived there and announcing their subjection to the Spanish crown. The Pueblos, who had already suffered from their dealings with Coronado and later conquistadors, reluctantly acceded to his demands. If some had thoughts of resistance, Oñate quickly helped them see the error of their ways. After a Pueblo group ambushed and killed eleven Spaniards not long after his arrival, Oñate sent a small expeditionary force to Ácoma, where the massacre had taken place. They destroyed the settlement, killing 500 men and 300 women and children, and taking 80 men and 500 women and children captive. After trying the adults for murder and finding them guilty, Oñate sentenced all between the ages of 12 and 25 to 25 years of servitude; males older than 25 had one foot amputated, a sentence that was carried out in public.

Oñate sent prospecting expeditions out in all directions in search of gold and silver, in order to make his contract for colonization a profit-making venture. It is believed that his parties went as far west as the Gulf of California, but no one found any of the elusive mineral riches that the Spanish craved. After growing disillusionment led to a mutiny by his followers, Oñate tendered his resignation from the governorship in 1607, although he remained in New Mexico for another two years. He was ordered back to Mexico City to stand trial for misrepresenting the value of the colony to authorities in Spain, was cleared of some but not all of the charges, and was stripped of his titles in 1614. He spent the remainder of his life petitioning the crown for recognition of past services rendered, and successfully reversed the verdict in his case shortly before his death.

Open-Range System

Much of the mystique that grew up around the business of cattle ranching in the first 75 years of the nineteenth century American West was the result of a simple fact of climate and topography. The Great Plains and flatlands of the Southwest did not offer any means of fencing off land, and so livestock had to be allowed to wander in the open; those whose job it was to look after the cattle became romanticized as lonesome herders riding the range. There were neither rocks nor timber for fencing, as there were in the East, but there was plentiful grass for cattle.

Even in the days of Spanish dominion over the Southwest, mission-raised cattle were allowed to run free. But the mingling of so much livestock from different owners necessitated some system of identification; so branding and ear-notching systems were developed. Calves were branded according to the markings of their mother. Ownership of land was less important.

When southern immigrants came to Texas before the Civil War, they adopted this system as well. Cattle droving in the Southwest had its beginnings in the 1830s, and techniques used elsewhere had to be adapted to the open-range system. The roundup, for example, was a direct product of this system, with all the herds within a certain range being gathered and driven to a central point for sorting and branding. The owner who hosted the roundup would be given first cut of the cattle.

Among the Mormons of Utah, cattle-raising was done differently. Stock was raised by villagers and hay was produced on irrigated farmland. With that exception, the open-range system was the norm all over the West until the advent of barbed wire in the 1880s. Although wire had been used for fencing in the past, without barbs it wasn't sufficient to keep livestock penned in. When Joseph Farwell Glidden invented barbed wire in 1873, his creation brought about changes that would remake the cattle industry in the next decade.

In some ways, his invention was a logical step. After the Civil War the cattle industry had expanded almost exponentially as the demand for beef grew. Because the sheep industry was also growing, competition for grazing lands was becoming intense. Urbanization in the Great Plains was encroaching on grasslands, too. The Homestead Act of 1862 was bringing farmers west in large numbers. And ranch owners were being offered the possibility of purchasing public lands.

As a result, ranches became large areas of enclosed land, rather than an island in a sea of grazing land. Eventually, the result would be friction between large and small cattle owners, between cattle owners and farmers, and between cattle owners and sheep owners. Most of all, barbed wire was leading to more controlled breeding and the end of the long cattle drive. By the late 1880s, the grasslands of the plains were entirely under private ownership and the era of the open range was over.

Oraibi, Arizona

See Hopi Indians

Oregon

The 33rd admitted to the Union, Oregon was populated by many Indian tribes when the first white explorers sighted it. The first Europeans to land on the coast of what is now Oregon were probably the Spanish group led by Bartolome Ferrello in 1543. Sir Francis Drake sailed north along the coast in 1579 and claimed it for England, but the real basis for an English claim was Captain James Cook's landing there in 1778. The first white man to set foot in the present state, though, was the American sea captain Robert Gray, who put ashore in today's Tillamook County in 1788. Gray also discovered the mouth of the Columbia River four years later, thereby establishing an American claim to Oregon.

By the early part of the nineteenth century, the English, Spanish, Americans, and Russians had all laid claim to this region which was rich in furs, wildlife and timber. After the reports of the area's great natural wealth brought back by Lewis and Clark, Oregon became prime territory for the battling fur companies, with John Jacob Astor's men establishing Astoria in 1811 as the base for a Pacific empire, and spirited competition ensuing that included Hudson's Bay Company, the North West Company, and others. Much of this turf battle was

During his 1845 trip to the Oregon territories, Englishman Henry James Ware captured the splendor of the Northwest in his picture Oregon City, The American Village.

decided by the Convention of 1818, in which Great Britain and America agreed to have equal trade and settlement rights in the entire Oregon Territory, and by the merger of the North West and Hudson's Bay companies, a transaction that brought Dr. John McLoughlin to prominence as the region's governor and factor for the fur traders.

In the 1830s, missionaries began to arrive in Oregon, led by Rev. Jason Lee, who established a mission near present-day Salem in 1834. Two years later, Dr. Marcus Whitman and his wife Narcissa Prentiss Whitman and Rev. H. H. Spalding and his wife Elizabeth made the trip over the Oregon Trail to establish a mission further east, a trip that proved that women could weather the long and difficult overland journey. By the early 1840s, settlers were flooding into the territory, alarming the Indians, who attacked and killed the Whitmans and other settlers in 1847. In 1848, Congress created the Oregon Territory, an area that included present-day Washington, parts of Idaho, Montana and Wyoming, as well as the current state of Oregon.

Nine years later, Oregonians voted to outlaw slavery in the territory, an early example of popular sovereignty in practice. Oregon was admitted to the Union on February 14, 1859, as the thirty-third state. After the outbreak of the Civil War, Edward Dickinson Baker, the state's first senator, resigned his seat in the Senate to join the Union Army and was one of the first U.S. officers killed. The Union erected Fort Stevens at the mouth of the Columbia River to protect its interests in the state but no combat occurred in the Pacific Northwest.

Indian wars, however, remained a common occurrence. The most famous of these was the Modoc War, fought in 1872-1873, between members of the Modoc nation, led by Captain Jack, and white settlers over the Lost Valley area. The outcome of the war included the death of Civil War hero General Edward Canby, the only regular army general ever killed by Indians, and the eventual hangings of the leaders of the uprising, including Captain Jack. In the northern part of the state, the Nez Perces, led by Chief Joseph, began their 1,300-mile fighting retreat to Canada (to which Chief Joseph never made it).

Oregon Question

The ownership of the Oregon territory was a subject of controversy for more than 50 years, with both the United States and Great Britain claiming title. Until the border was finally set by the Oregon Treaty of 1846, which put the boundary between American and British territory at the 49th parallel, it had been a source of contention. Since 1789, the British and the Americans, along with the Spanish and the Russians, had claimed parts of this territory.

In fact, the first stage of the controversy involved England and Spain. In 1789, the two European powers clashed over the right of British fur traders to establish a trading post at Nootka Sound on the west side of Vancouver Island. A Spanish man-of-war broke up the settlement and arrested the trappers, taking them to Mexico. Spain and England worked out an amicable agreement, while the United States told the English that they should not cross American territory in any attack on Spanish interests in Louisiana. Spain lost interest in the Pacific Northwest, leaving the field to other players. In 1819, John Quincy Adams negotiated the Adams-Onis Treaty with Spain, which set the California-Oregon border at the 42nd parallel.

When Captain Robert Gray sailed into the mouth of the Columbia River in May 1792, naming the river for his ship, he not only became the first to sail past the estuary to the actual mouth of the river, he also established the first American presence in the territory. His claim was a dubious one, however, since no Americans were settled there yet and it would be several years before the United States would press for its rights against the English. In 1818, the English and Americans concluded an agreement that Oregon would be "free and open" for the next ten years. (A similar agreement, extending the arrangement indefinitely and with one-year's notice required for termination by either side, was signed in 1827.)

The Russians came into the picture briefly five years after the Adams-Onis Treaty was signed. In 1824, they negotiated an agreement with the United States setting the southern boundary of Alaska at 54°40'. The next year, they reached a similar agreement with England. The Oregon Territory could now be defined as lying between the 42nd parallel in the south and the 54-40 line in the north. But where did England's territory end and American territory begin?

In 1845 President James K. Polk was elected on a Democratic platform that called for the reannexation of Texas and the reoccupation of Oregon. Polk was giving his attention to the looming war with Mexico and didn't want to be forced into a conflict with England at the same time, so Texas, and not Oregon, was his priority. He would have been happy to compromise with England on a northern border set at the 49th parallel, but he was being pushed by members of his own party, whose slogan was "Fifty-Four Forty or Fight."

After considerable discussion within Congress and a certain amount of diplomatic confusion with England, Polk was able to get both American and English officials to agree to the 49th parallel. In the final treaty, England was also guaranteed the right of navigation on the Columbia River. The 54–40 faction in Congress was not happy, but Polk had effectively resolved the dispute with England and could now turn his attention to the approaching war with Mexico.

Oregon Trail

Overland migration to the Oregon Territory began in May 1841, when a pioneering party of 70 people left Independence, Missouri, to follow the Platte River through the South Pass of the Rocky Mountains and northwest to the Columbia River. This and subsequent emigrant trains—some of them a mile long, with 40 or more wagons loaded with foodstuffs, farm implements, clothing, and household belongings and pulled by horse, ox, and mule teams—reblazed an old trapper–missionary route into what became known as the Oregon Trail.

At its peak of use, the trail, 2,000 miles in length, was the longest road in the United States and the most difficult to travel. At its terminus lay a tract of wilderness extending north of California to Alaska and from the Pacific Coast eastward to the Continental Divide, encompassing all of present-day Oregon and Washington and parts of Canada, Montana, Idaho, and Wyoming.

In 1842, 100 emigrants and 18 wagons were guided over the Trail by Dr. Elijah White, who brought with him the news that the Presbyterian

Settlers camped out overnight on the Oregon Trail are awakened by a trumpeter alerting them that it's time to move on.

missions of the Pacific Northwest were to be discontinued. Missionary Marcus Whitman, who had made his first journey to Oregon in 1835, returned east and won a reversal of this decision, and after he returned to Oregon in 1843 a significant movement to the territory began.

The same year Whitman returned, a Missouri lawyer named Peter H. Burnett took an emigrant train of 1,000 men, women, and children, gathered in western Missouri from Ohio, Illinois, Kentucky, and Tennessee, plus 100 wagons and 5,000 head of oxen and cattle, over the Oregon Trail. It is estimated that by 1845 upwards of 3,000 emigrants used the trail; by 1847, 4,000 to 5,000.

From its eastward jumping-off spots, Westport Landing (Kansas City), Independence, and other Missouri frontier towns, pioneers traveled northwest to Fort Kearny on the southern bend of the Platte, followed the south bank of that river to Fort Laramie (a trapper's post inside a tall adobe wall, its only tie to civilization the old trail used by fur traders and a scattering of missionaries), the North Platte across present-day Wyoming to the mouth of the Sweetwater River, then to the South Pass, 950 miles from Missouri, and the gateway to what became, in 1846, Oregon Territory.

From the South Pass, the emigrants crossed the Green River Valley southwest to Fort Bridger, 1,070 miles out, then turned northwest to Fort Hall on the Snake River, following the Snake past Fort Boise to the Blue Mountains and Marcus Whitman's mission on the Columbia River, 1,835 miles from Missouri. By the time the travelers reached the Willamette Valley they had covered 2,000 miles in a journey of four to six months.

The great obstacles to travel on the Oregon Trail were the fording of swollen rivers and streams and the necessity of timing the travel to avoid the winter snows and to give livestock the best opportunity to feed off spring and summer grass. Indian raids were feared but were never a real danger since even the most hostile tribes hesitated to attack a large caravan.

The Oregon Trail continued in use until the Union Pacific Railroad established a route from Granger, Wyoming, to Portland, Oregon, in the early 1880s. Thereafter the trail was used to drive cattle and sheep to the Pacific Coast.

The old emigrant route was immortalized in 1849 with publication of *The Oregon Trail* by Francis Parkman, published originally in *Knickerbocker Magazine* as "A Summer's Journey Out of Bounds." Parkman, son of a Boston Unitarian minister, graduated from Harvard in 1846 and headed west for the purpose of extending his research for a history of the French and Indian Wars to the tribes of the western plains. He traveled to Kansas City, and with a guide, struck out on horseback along the path favored by Oregon emigrants. They reached Fort Laramie where through the efforts of his fur trapper guide, who was married to a daughter of an Oglala chief, Parkman moved into the tepee of a Sioux warrior named Big Crow. He lived there six months, then returned to Boston to write *The Oregon Trail* and other works.

Osage Indians

The Osages are Siouan tribe of Native Americans who were once the wealthiest people in the world on a per capita basis.

According to Osage tradition, the tribe migrated from the Ohio River Valley to present-day Missouri. They were first encountered by Europeans in 1673,

An Osage battle hatchet with a forged blade acquired from white traders.

living along the Osage River. In 1825, they were resettled on a large reservation in Kansas. In 1871, the Osages moved again, this time relocating to a one-million-acre reservation in the Cherokee Outlet, having purchased the land from the Cherokee Nation pursuant to the post–Civil War treaties of 1866. The move helped free all of Kansas for white settlement.

In 1895, the secretary of the interior authorized oil and gas exploration on the Osage Reservation, and oil was discovered the following year. By 1900, it was clear that the find was one of the largest reservoirs of oil yet tapped. Pressure for allotment mounted, and in 1906 Congress enacted the Osage Allotment Act.

The royalties generated from oil production made the Osages a wealthy people, and between 1920 and 1970 they received approximately $500 million. These new-found riches led to what is known as the Osage Reign of Terror, when many were murdered and many more were swindled. During the Reign of Terror, one percent of the Osage were killed. The events were largely covered up.

In 1894, John Joseph Mathews, a major Native American novelist and writer, was born on the Osage Reservation.

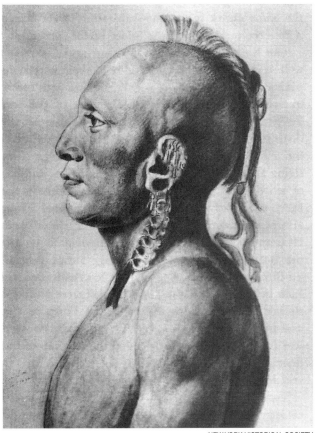

An Osage warrior.

Outlaws

See Dalton Gang; James, Jesse Woodson; Parker, Robert; Wild Bunch

P

Paiute Indians

Paiute is an overall designation for three related groups of Uzo-Aztecan Indians who live in areas ranging from Oregon and Idaho to Arizona.

Considerable confusion has arisen concerning usage of the name *Paiute.* The names Monos, Snakes, and Bannocks are sometimes erroneously applied to various Paiute bands. *Monos,* used to designate Paiutes living around Mono Lake, is more properly applied to a tribe living in the southern Sierra Nevada; *Snakes* more correctly refers to certain

NEBRASKA STATE HISTORICAL SOCIETY

A Paiute woman goes about her daily work of preparing food for her family.

JOHN K. HILLERS, UTAH STATE HISTORICAL SOCIETY

Two Paiute pose in front of their summer dwellings in Utah, around 1870. The Paiutes were gifted weavers, which is evident in the basket to the left of the seated couple.

Northern Shoshones; and the *Bannocks* are Northern Paiute speakers who moved from Oregon to Idaho by the middle of the eighteenth century. Correctly used, *Paiutes* refers to the Northern Paiutes of

335

NATIONAL ARCHIVES

Sarah Winnemucca, pictured with her father, a Pauite chief, served as an interpreter and scout for the U.S. Army. She was known as "Princess Sarah," and went on to marry a white lieutenant.

Nevada, California, and Oregon; the Owens Valley Paiutes in southern California; and the Southern Paiutes of Nevada, Utah, and Arizona. The terms have been muddled since first European contact in the eighteenth century, and the people themselves often refer to themselves as Paiutes without any modifier, adding to the confusion.

Increasing white settlement led to pressure to move the various Paiute groups to reservations in the nineteenth century, and four reserves were established for the Northern Paiutes between 1859 and 1891. Many, however, refused to move. Instead they made themselves useful as low-wage laborers for whites, whose eagerness for their relocation soon subsided.

In the mid-nineteenth century, the Southern Paiutes ranged over a vast territory in Arizona, California, Nevada, and Utah. The arrival of the Mormons, who urged Paiutes to become indentured servants, led to the tribe's decline. Eventually, the Paiutes were reduced to 10 widely separated groups, on and off reservations. Today, the three Paiute divi-

sions possess less than 5 percent of the land they controlled before contact with whites.

Parker, Isaac Charles

1838–1896

Isaac Charles Parker was a judge and congressman who became famous as the "Hanging Judge" and the "Law West of Fort Smith." Parker was a self-taught lawyer who was admitted to the bar in Missouri in 1859. After serving briefly in the Civil War, he became city attorney for St. Joseph, Missouri in 1862, then rose to circuit attorney, a post he held from 1864 to 1867. After three terms as a congressman (during which time he served on the Committee on Territories), he was offered the position of chief justice of the Utah Territory, which he declined.

Instead, he accepted an appointment as judge of the U.S. district court for western Arkansas, and it was there that he made his reputation. Headquartered at Fort Smith, Arkansas, his jurisdiction extended over the Indian Territory, at the time an almost completely lawless region. Faced with a large area to oversee and few law enforcement officers, Parker proceeded to appoint 200 deputy marshals, and urged them to go out and bring back malefactors in quantity. Over the 21 years he served, 65 of his marshals would be killed, which suggests how violent the era and the territory were.

Parker was not a criminal-hunter himself, but he was a dedicated and highly successful jurist. In his initial term at Fort Smith, he tried 18 murder cases, 15 of which ended in convictions. Overall, he sentenced 162 men to death, 80 of whom were hanged, generally in public executions. "This court is but the humble instrument to aid in the execution of that divine justice which has ever decided that he who takes what he cannot return—the life of another human being—shall lose his own," Parker said.

For all that, he was actually something of a progressive, an early advocate of women's suffrage and a supporter of liberal measures regarding the status of Native Americans. While in Congress, he drew up a bill to donate the U.S. Reservation in Fort Smith to the city for schools rather than to a railroad corporation which coveted it.

Parker, Quanah

1845–1911

Born into the Nocona band of the Comanches near modern-day Wichita Falls, Texas, Quanah ("fragrant" in Comanche) Parker was the son of chief Peta Nocona and Cynthia Ann Parker, a white captive taken by the Noconas in a raid into eastern Texas in 1836.

Quanah spent his youth as a raider against buffalo hunters and other whites in eastern and northern Texas, and he is believed to have killed a white man at the age of 15. He was described in his youth by a U.S. cavalry captain as "a large and powerfully built chief on a coal black racing pony. . . . He seemed the incarnation of savage, brutal joy."

In 1860, the Noconas were camped near the Peace River when a force of Texas Rangers and U.S. cavalry attacked them, killing a number of the band. Peta Nocona was mortally wounded and Cynthia Ann Parker was taken back to the Parker family in east-

LIBRARY OF CONGRESS

Quanah Parker and his youngest wife, Tonacey.

ern Texas. She tried repeatedly to rejoin the tribe, but was thwarted. In 1864, after the death of her daughter Prairie Flower, she starved herself to death.

With the loss of his mother and the death of his father, Quanah and his brother Pecos joined the Kwahadi band of Comanches. With the Kwahadis and Kiowas, they took part in raids throughout central Texas, attacking frontier forts that had been stripped of manpower, as some 60,000 Texans were fighting in the Confederate Army.

In 1867, when the U.S. government called a peace council at Medicine Lodge Creek, Kansas, most of the Comanches, Arapahoes, Cheyennes, and other tribes were represented. However, the Kwahadis and Kotsotekas—two of the strongest Comanche bands—were notably absent. When 10 Comanche chiefs signed a treaty that was interpreted to include all the Comanche people, the Kwahadis ignored the paper and continued their raids.

In 1870 Colonel Ranald S. Mackenzie set up patrols out of forts Richardson, Griffin, and Concho to invade Kwahadi homelands along the Llano Estacado—the Staked Plains of the West Texas plateau. In the spring of 1872, after Mackenzie's troops struck a large Kotsoteka camp, killing 23 and taking 124 captive, the Kwahadi were the last of the hostile Comanches yet to be conquered.

The standoff between the Kwahadis and the army was broken in 1874, when white buffalo hunters set up a base near the deserted trading post of Adobe Walls on the South Canadian River. On June 26, after Kiowa, Arapaho, and Cheyenne bands of about 700 warriors rallied around Quanah and the Kwahadi medicine man Isa-tai, Quanah's forces attacked the Adobe Walls post, in which 28 men (including young Bat Masterson) were lodged. A chance gunshot ruined the surprise element of the nighttime attack, and the Adobe Walls defenders, with their Sharps rifles and telescopic sights, won the battle after three days, losing only three men. The victors mounted the heads of 13 Indian raiders on poles.

On September 28 that year, Mackenzie, with a force of 600 soldiers, made his way into Palo Duro Canyon in the Texas Panhandle and swept through the Comanche-Kiowa-Cheyenne village, burning it to the ground and capturing 1,000 horses and numerous tribesmen. Quanah was not among them, but the raid broke the back of the Indian resistance. In April 1875, the Kwahadis began surrendering at Fort Sill. Quanah and 400 others held out until June 2, when he marched his band and 1,500 horses into the fort.

Quanah, who spoke little English when he surrendered, became the leading spokesman for his tribe. In the next 35 years he rose rapidly in reservation politics, becoming a model of the white man's idea of citizenship and deportment and a favorite among the Indian agents and the cattlemen whose herds grazed on reservation lands. He became the principal Comanche chief in 1890 and amassed considerable wealth and property. As time passed, despite his being called a half-breed and traitor by a dwindling number of adherents to the old tribal ways, he was viewed not as a white man's Indian but as a free and independent thinker, a progressive who often opposed white programs but who negotiated compromises.

Quanah was a devotee of mescal and peyote, the hallucinogenic drugs. He described the peyote ceremony by saying, "The white man goes into his church and talks about Jesus; the Indian goes into his tipi and talks *to* Jesus." A polygamist in his early life, Quanah had a total of 8 wives and 25 children over the years. A commissioner of Indian affairs once told him he could have but one wife and that he should tell the others to go away. "You tell them, " Quanah replied.

In 1902 Quanah was elected deputy sheriff of Lawton, Oklahoma (near Fort Sill), and was later chosen chief judge of the Court of Indian Offenses. Toward the end of his life he was a celebrity, believed to be the wealthiest Indian in America. He traveled widely and entertained visiting dignitaries in his fine 12-room home—known as the Comanche White House—near Cache, Oklahoma, purchased for him by Texas cattleman Burk Burnett.

Quanah died of pneumonia near Fort Sill on February 22, 1911.

Parker, Robert Leroy

1866–CA. 1909

Better known as "Butch Cassidy," Robert Leroy Parker was a train robber and outlaw. Parker's father and grandparents came across the Great Plains to Utah as Mormon "handcart pioneers"—walking and pulling carts carrying their belongings—in 1856. They settled in the Sevier River country, and Robert was born near Beaver and raised on his father's ranch near Circleville. As a teenager he fell under the influence of a cowboy-rustler named Mike Cassidy who taught his young protégé to ride, rope, and shoot—and mastery of the finer points of cattle and horse thievery. By his late teens, Robert had left home with Cassidy and traveled to the mining town of Telluride, Colorado, where, after a period of honest employment, he fell in with the bank robbing group of Tom McCarty and Matt Warner.

Parker took part in an aborted train robbery in Colorado in 1887, the robbery of a bank in Denver, and the San Miguel Valley Bank in Telluride in 1889. For a time following his debut as an outlaw Parker used the alias "George Cassidy." After a time working in a Rock Springs, Wyoming, butcher shop, he became known as "Butch Cassidy," the sobriquet he lived with to the end of his life.

Periodically, Cassidy shifted to honest work—he was at various times a mine employee, butcher, and cowboy—but he soon returned to the "Owlhoot Trail," becoming a familiar figure in the outlaw stronghold of Brown's Hole, a rugged mountain camp along the Green River at the borders of Utah, Colorado, and Wyoming. There he met Harry Longabaugh ("Sundance Kid") and others who were to become members of the Wild Bunch gang, with which Cassidy's name is indelibly and historically joined.

LIBRARY OF CONGRESS

Butch Cassidy.

Cassidy's name first appeared in court records in 1892 when he was sentenced to two years in the Wyoming State Prison for cattle rustling. He began the sentence, after court delays, in 1894 and was released in January 1896. Prison, if anything, only convinced Cassidy that there was no future in cattle rustling. He returned to Brown's Hole, collected some men, and, beginning with the robbery of a Montpelier, Idaho, bank in August 1896, began a five-year run of looting banks and trains. The gang's retreats, the "Hole-in-the-Wall," and "Robber's Roost," lay in the remote canyons of northern Wyoming and southeastern Utah.

The train robberies—in one instance they used too much dynamite and blew the baggage car to smithereens—such as those near Wilcox, Wyoming; Folsom, New Mexico; Tipton, Wyoming; and Wagner, Montana, brought Pinkerton detectives on the trail of the Wild Bunch. In an 1897 wanted poster, the Pinkerton Detective Agency described Cassidy as being 5'7" tall, weighing 165 pounds, having a light complexion, flaxen hair, and deep-set blue eyes.

In September 1901, Cassidy and two others robbed the First National Bank in Winnemucca, Nevada, of $32,000, then rendezvoused with other Wild Bunch members 1,000 miles to the east, in Fort Worth, Texas. It was in Fort Worth that Cassidy, Longabaugh, and other gang members, dressed in fine suits and derbies, had their famous photograph taken. Cassidy sent a print of the picture to the Winnemucca bank, thanking its proprietors for making it possible for him to dress so elegantly, and the Pinkertons made good use of the photo to close in on Cassidy and his gang.

In late 1901, Cassidy, Longabaugh, and the latter's mistress, Etta Place, sailed from New York for South America (Cassidy probably traveled separately and rejoined the others in Montevideo, Uruguay). Although there is little evidence for their activities in South America, it appears that the three operated a ranch in Argentina for a time, then resorted to bank and train robbery, ending up in Bolivia in 1908. In the town of San Vicente in 1909 (or perhaps 1911), legend has it, Cassidy and Longabaugh, who had robbed a mine payroll, were killed by Bolivian soldiers.

In light of the fact that there is no compelling evidence of the death of either man in South America or anywhere else, there is at least the possibility, as the families of each maintained, that both men returned to the United States and lived out their lives. In the least convincing of these stories, Longabaugh is said to have married Etta Place, lived for years in Mexico and New Mexico, and died as recently as 1957 (when he would have been 96 years old). Cassidy's sister, in a book published in 1975, claimed her brother visited his family in Utah in 1925. An independent researcher claims Cassidy returned to the United States, served as a mercenary in the Mexican Revolution, and later lived in Spokane, Washington, under the name William T. Phillips, where he operated a successful business and died in 1937.

Pawnee Indians

The Pawnees are a Caddoan tribe of Native Americans who are closely related to the Arikaras and Wichitas. They are divided into four bands: the Chaui, Kitkahahki, Pitahawirata, and Skidi.

The Pawnees may have been encountered by Coronado's expedition, but the evidence is sketchy. By the early eighteenth century, the period of the earliest confirmed contact, they occupied a territory from eastern Wyoming, through Nebraska, to Kansas, and numbered around 10,000. They raised corn and raided the Comanches for horses. They waged war against the Sioux and Cheyennes and raided east of the Mississippi into the western edge of territory controlled by the Iroquois.

The Pawnees never made war with the United States, although they frequently raided trains on the Santa Fe Trail. During the War of 1812, William Clark, then serving as Governor of the Missouri territory, subsidized raids by the Pawnees against pro-British Indians. They concluded their first treaty with the American government in 1818.

In the 1830s, the removal of eastern tribes to the West coincided with Sioux pressure upon the Pawnees from the north. The Pawnees raided south into Indian Territory and became a terror to the immigrant tribes. Beginning in 1833, they ceded all their territory except for a small reservation in Nebraska.

During the Indian Wars of 1865–1885, the Pawnees served as scouts for the U.S. Army. They were eventually recognized as their own Army unit

Pawnees, as depicted by A. J. Miller.

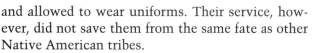

Particular Time of Day, Pawnee

Pawnee chief Particular Time of Day.

and allowed to wear uniforms. Their service, however, did not save them from the same fate as other Native American tribes.

In 1876, the Pawnees were removed to a reservation of roughly 200,000 acres in northcentral Indian Territory. In 1893, under the terms of the Dawes Act, their reservation was divided into individual parcels. During the early 1890s, as allotment became inevitable, the Ghost Dance spread among the Pawnees. Their leaders were imprisoned, and the movement was forced underground. Later, in an effort to gain acceptance of allotment, whites told the Pawnees that, if the breakup of their reservation proceeded, the tribe would no longer be subject to federal government supervision and that they would be free to practice the Ghost Dance religion. During the same period, the religious use of peyote gained many adherents.

By the time of allotment, disease and exposure in Indian Territory had reduced the Pawnee population

to 821. By the turn of the century, their numbers had continued to decline to only around 700. Today the Pawnees hold less than one-tenth of what had been their reservation prior to allotment.

Payne, David

DIED 1884

Indiana-born David Payne went west in 1857 with his brother Jack, hoping to join Albert Sidney Johnston's "Mormon" army. Instead, he farmed a homestead in Kansas for a short time, then joined the Union army, serving on the western front and in the Indian Wars where he rose to the rank of captain. Once discharged from the army, he drifted aimlessly from job to job, enjoying little success in various business dealings. He even ended up briefly in Washington, D.C., where he served as doorkeeper to the House of Representatives.

In 1879, encouraged at prospects of making a killing in land development, Payne drifted back west and organized the Oklahoma Colony and the Oklahoma Town Company. Under the guise of these organizations, he and hundreds of "boomers" began a series of invasions of Native American lands. They claimed that the lands in question had been ceded to the federal government by the tribes in 1866 and were therefore covered under the Homestead Act of 1862. Payne received funds not only from would-be homesteaders but also from railroad interests who stood to profit if the territories were opened and rail lines established. However, his financial irresponsibility, as had happened in his earlier business ventures, often left him very close to bankruptcy and the frequent target of lawsuits.

The federal government did not recognize the legality of the boomers' claims and repeatedly had to remove them from Native American lands by force. Ironically, although Payne was personally unable to secure title to these lands, in 1884 Congress was moving toward opening what is present-day Oklahoma to settlers. But for David Payne it was too late. He died of an apparent heart attack or stroke at his breakfast table on November 27, 1884.

Pecos Bill

The legendary hero Pecos Bill is a fictional folk hero who has taken on a life of his own. As such, he is a good example of a classic strain in American folklore—the "occupational" hero. Bill is a larger-than-life version of the working cowboy, much as Paul Bunyan (another manufactured icon) is a blown-up model of the northern woods lumberjack.

Bill is a giant who rides a mount that is part mountain lion, part mustang, part tornado, part bolt of lightning. He uses rattlesnakes as lariats and can unbend a frozen river with a snap of his wrist.

For all his mythical qualities, however, Pecos Bill is not the product of real folklore. Rather than being the creation of real cowhands trying to evoke and satirize the daily routine of their job, he is the stuff of advertising copy, again like Paul Bunyan, who

was apparently created by the Red River Lumber Company in the 1910s.

Picket, Bill

CA.1860–1932

Bill Pickett was a cowboy and rodeo performer. The son of African-American and Choctaw parents who was born on the San Gabriel River in Texas, Pickett is credited with "inventing" what was to become the rodeo event of bulldogging (steer wrestling) in the 1890s when he worked as a cowboy on the Miller 101 Ranch in Oklahoma. Pickett, described by Zack Miller, one of the owners of the 101, as "the greatest sweat-and-dirt cowhand that ever lived—bar none," perfected bulldogging in fairs and rodeos and in the 101 Wild West Show, organized by the Miller Ranch in 1900.

Pickett became a star attraction of the 101 show for many years, performing with such other stars as Will Rogers and Tom Mix. He later demonstrated bulldogging at Madison Square Garden in New York, and in England.

He died on the 101 Ranch on April 2, 1932, 11 days after being thrown from a horse and fracturing his skull.

Pike, Zebulon Montgomery

1779–1813

Zebulon Pike was a soldier and explorer who led an expedition second only to that of Lewis and Clark in its importance in the exploration of the American West. Pike was born in Lamberton, Somerset County, New Jersey, and enlisted in the army at age 15. He was largely self-educated, and read deeply in military history, mathematics, science, and languages.

Pike served under General Anthony Wayne in the Ohio Valley and in 1799 was promoted to a lieutenancy, serving over the next six years at various frontier forts. In August 1805, on orders from Gen-

INDEPENDENCE NATIONAL HISTORICAL PARK

Zebulon Pike.

eral James Wilkinson, military governor of the Louisiana Territory, to make a reconnaissance of the Upper Mississippi and find its headwaters, Pike gathered 20 men at Fort Belle Fontaine, near St. Louis. The expedition used a 70-foot keelboat and smaller craft to explore the river and to collect data and investigate sites for military posts. Its winter camp was near Little Falls, Minnesota. The men then proceeded up the Mississippi and, in an overland journey, reached Cass Lake, which they wrongly thought to be the source of the river. (Actually they had fallen short of reaching the headwaters at Lake Itisca by 25 miles.)

By the time Pike returned to St. Louis in April 1806, he had succeeded in writing a treaty with the Sioux for the site of Fort Snelling, building a stockade near the mouth of the Swan River, and writing a journal and drawing a map of the upper Mississippi.

On July 15, Pike set out again from Belle Fontaine with 21 men, again under orders from Wilkinson. This time Pike was to determine the extent of the Louisiana Territory's southwestern lands. Pike and his men explored the Republican River near the present Kansas-Nebraska border, then the headwaters of the Arkansas River. The party moved on into Colorado where, on November 15, 1806, he discovered the mountain peak, east of present-day Las Animas, Colorado, that would ultimately bear his name.

Pike and his party crossed the Sangre de Cristo Mountains and reached the Rio Grande a few miles south of modern Alamosa, Colorado. At Conejo, on the Rio Grande, where the explorers constructed a stockade, a Spanish patrol of 100 men took Pike into custody on February 26, 1807. They conducted him to Santa Fe where his papers were confiscated. (The papers were discovered in a Mexico City archive in 1907 by an American historian.) Pike was escorted to Chihuahua for questioning, then returned to the United States near Natchitoches, Louisiana, where he arrived in July.

In his absence he had been promoted to captain. There has been speculation, unsubstantiated by historical documentation, that Pike was not "lost" in mistaking the Rio Grande for the Red River in his year-long exploration, but was acting as Wilkinson's intelligence agent to gather information on Spanish-held territory around Santa Fe. He was also accused of being involved with Wilkinson and Aaron Burr in a scheme to gain control of western territory that belonged to the United States, but he was exonerated by the secretary of war. Pike's narrative of his explorations was published in 1810. He was promoted to major in 1808, lieutenant colonel in 1810, and helped train forces that won the Battle of Tippecanoe against the Shawnees.

By 1813, he was a brigadier general. In the War of 1812, Pike won a brilliant victory at York (Toronto), Ontario, in which he captured the city, but as he was standing outside the British fortifications conferring with his staff, a nearby powder magazine exploded and a huge stone struck him in the back. He died on April 27, 1813, on the deck of an American warship in Lake Ontario, with a captured Union Jack under his head.

Pima Indians

Also known as Akimel O'odham, the Pimas are an Uzo-Aztecan tribe of Native American dwelling in central Arizona and closely related to the Papago.

Descended from the Hohokam culture, from earliest times the Pimas have used the same system of irrigation canals that their ancestors established around 300 B.C.E. (before the common era). Peaceful farmers, they raised beans, corn, and squash. The addition of winter wheat made Piman fields productive year round. A member of the expedition of

Padre Eusebio Kino in 1687 described them as "haughty and proud." Their ethical code was simple: "Do not steal, get up early and go to work, always kill Apaches, and help everyone who needs anything."

During the period of Spanish and Mexican rule, the tribe lived beyond the frontier of settlement and was allowed autonomy. The government viewed the Pimas as a good buffer between settlers and Apaches, and when the United States took possession of the region, the situation changed little. The Pimas' main interest on the other hand was to obtain protection for themselves from both the Apaches and the Navajos.

In the 1850s, at the request of the U.S. Army, a military alliance of the Pimas and the Maricopas protected white immigrants from the Apaches. Pimas wheat fed thousands of settlers as they crossed through the tribe's territory on the way to California. During the Civil War, companies from the Pima-Maricopa confederation served in the Arizona Volunteers. In 1862 alone, the United States purchased 1,000 tons of Piman wheat to feed troops west of the Mississippi.

The first reservation for the Pimas and the Maricopas was created in 1859. A second was established in 1879. By 1867, increasing white settlement led to the first of a series of disastrous diversions of Piman water, and by the late nineteenth century, these appropriations forced the Pima to shift from farming to a largely service wage economy.

Pinchot, Gifford

1865–1946

Gifford Pinchot was a conservationist and a politician. In the battle between pure-wilderness advocates and utilitarian conservationists, Pinchot played utilitarian to John Muir's preservationist in the early days of the twentieth century. Pinchot was born to a wealthy family in Connecticut, studied at Yale and the French Forest School in Nancy, and came back to the United States in the early 1890s with new ideas about managing forests as a sustainable resource. He first put those ideas into practice in 1892 on the Vanderbilt estate in North Carolina. He was named a member of the National Forest Commission in 1896 and was made chief of the federal Forestry Division (which would later become the U.S. Forest Service) in 1898, a position he would hold until 1910.

Pinchot was a close friend of Theodore Roosevelt's, and when Roosevelt became president, the two like-minded conservation advocates were uniquely positioned to advance their cause. In fact, Pinchot asserted that he coined the word *conservation* in 1907, and in 1908 he launched the movement as head of the White House Conservation Conference.

Pinchot would find himself at odds with Interior Secretary Richard Ballinger over the private acquisition of Alaskan coal lands, and in 1910 President Taft fired him from the Forest Service. It was a move that exacerbated tensions within the Republican party, and Roosevelt, supported by Pinchot, soon broke away to form the Progressive party.

In 1913, Pinchot clashed with Muir over the disposition of Hetch Hetchy Valley in Yosemite National Park, which was being proposed for a dam and reservoir site. Muir opposed the project, but Pinchot and the advocates of the development triumphed, leading Muir to dismiss him as an exploiter and profiteer.

Pinchot continued to serve as president of the National Conservation Association even after being

LIBRARY OF CONGRESS

Gifford Pinchot.

fired from the Forest Service in 1910. He helped found the Yale School of Forestry, where he taught from 1903 to 1936, and ran for public office several times. He was elected governor of Pennsylvania twice, in 1923 and 1931, and spent the remainder of his life writing on land use and forestry and advising government and advocacy groups on conservation issues.

Pine Ridge Campaign

The Pine Ridge campaign involved the eruption of hostilities on one of the smaller reserves in Pine Ridge, South Dakota, that were the product of the division of the Great Sioux Reservation under the Dawes Act of 1887.

In late 1889, the Sioux sent delegates to see Wovoka and learn of his newly proclaimed Ghost Dance. The emissaries returned in the spring of 1890 and began teaching the dance on the Sioux reservations. Misunderstanding its nature, whites feared that the new religion would lead to uprisings. By November 1890, near anarchy prevailed at Pine Ridge. The problem was largely the creation of the Indian agent Daniel F. Royer, "a newly appointed mediocrity both ignorant and fearful of Indians." He repeatedly urged the U.S. Army to intervene on the reservation to halt the dancing. On November 15, Royer telegraphed Washington, "Indians are dancing in the snow and are wild and crazy. We need protection and we need it now."

On November 20, cavalry and infantry arrived at Pine Ridge and at Rosebud, a neighboring reservation. Confusion ensued as some Sioux rushed to the Indian agency and others fled to a remote area of Pine Ridge where they performed the Ghost Dance with even greater vigor. The U.S. Army commander, General John R. Brooke, peacefully attempted to persuade the fugitives to return to their homes. However, his superior, General Nelson A. Miles, believed the situation called for him to assume direct command in the field. He established his headquarters in Rapid City on December 17.

On December 23, a band of Sioux under Big Foot abandoned their village on the Cheyenne River and headed for Pine Ridge. They were intercepted by the 7th Cavalry on December 28. The following day,

tension and confusion resulted in the Wounded Knee tragedy. Outraged by the slayings, about 4,000 Indians united north of the Pine Ridge Agency. On December 30, they attacked the 7th Cavalry, which was finally relieved by the black 9th Cavalry.

Miles drew a circle of about 3,500 troops around the large village and began to move slowly toward Pine Ridge, sending conciliatory messages to the chiefs as he maneuvered. The Sioux surrendered on January 15, 1891.

Pinkertons

For six decades the Pinkerton National Detective Agency was the leading law enforcement group of the United States, the name Pinkerton synonymous with criminal detection, and the company's slogan, "We Never Sleep," under a picture of an open eye, the origin of the term private eye.

The agency was the brainchild of Scottish immigrant Allan Pinkerton (1819–1884), a cooper (barrel maker) who emigrated to Canada in 1842 and then moved to Illinois, settling in Dundee, 40 miles west of Chicago, where he established a barrel works. He became something of a local hero in 1847 when, while searching for wood for barrel staves along the Fox River, he came across a gang of counterfeiters and helped arrest them. He then became a deputy sheriff and a city deputy in Chicago and, in 1850, the first detective with the Chicago Police Department.

By the outbreak of the Civil War, Pinkerton had established himself as a private operative, working undercover on U.S. mail-theft cases, providing security for Illinois Railroads, and setting up patrols to protect Chicago businesses from theft. Just before the outbreak of the war, Pinkerton, an ardent abolitionist, was hired to protect the only railroad line out of Washington, D.C. He and his agents uncovered a plot to assassinate president-elect Lincoln in Baltimore, through which Lincoln had to pass en route to the capital.

During the war, Pinkerton became the chief intelligence officer for his friend (and former railroad executive), Major General George McClellan. He was successful in arresting Southern spies but less so in running his own network of spies inside enemy lines.

PINKERTON SECURITY AND INVESTIGATION SERVICES

The Pinkerton Agency logo.

By the end of the war, the Pinkerton Agency had offices in Chicago, Philadelphia, and New York. The company's reputation grew enormously in the decade that followed as it infiltrated the Molly Maguires, the Irish gang in the Pennsylvania coalfields; solved a national stock-fraud scheme and the 1876 looting of $1.25 million from a Northampton, Massachusetts, bank; plus numerous other train and bank robberies, safecrackings, forgeries, and burglaries. Pinkerton methods and practices—the use of a network of informants, undercover work, extensive files on career criminals (the famous Rogue's Gallery), use of fingerprinting—became standard police practices.

Among the Pinkertons' most celebrated, if unsuccessful, cases was the pursuit of the Jesse James gang after it robbed the Iron Mountain railroad outside Gads Hill, Missouri, in January 1874. In March, two Pinkerton operatives and a sheriff's deputy were shot to death in Clay County, Missouri, by James gang associates Jim and John Younger. The following January, Pinkertons received information that the James brothers were hiding out in the Clay County home of Dr. Reuben Samuel, their stepfather. On January 25, a Pinkerton posse surrounded the home and an agent tossed an incendiary device into the house. It exploded and killed the James's 9-year-old half-brother Archie and wounded their mother. The James brothers were not there. (Jesse James later reportedly said, "I know God will some day deliver Allan Pinkerton into my hands.")

Other Pinkerton pursuits of the period 1877–1900 included that of train robbers Sam Bass and Rube and Jim Burrows, and the ever-elusive Butch Cassidy and the Wild Bunch, who robbed at least 10 trains and banks in this period. The Pinkertons were able to arrest Wild Bunch members Bob Lee in Harlem, Montana, in November 1899, and Ben Kilpatrick in Nashville in April 1902, but their main targets—Cassidy and Harry "Sundance Kid" Longbaugh—eluded them.

The Pinkerton Agency suffered considerable damage to its reputation by its involvement in labor problems. In 1892, agent Charlie Siringo spied on union activities during the violent strike at the Coeur d'Alene mines in Gem, Idaho. In the same year, during a major uprising at the Carnegie steel plant at Homestead, Pennsylvania, strikers forced a 300-man Pinkerton security force to surrender. Congressional hearings and press reports after the Homestead incident created the popular perception that the Pinkertons were little more than strikebreakers and management spies—a perception based on considerable evidence.

After 1900, the agency concentrated its work in the eastern part of the country, rising again to public prominence during World War I when it was hired by the French government to investigate the bombings of French vessels anchored off New Orleans. After Allan Pinkerton's death, the agency was headed by his sons Robert and William; William died in 1923.

The Pinkerton Agency's work was eclipsed by creation of the Federal Bureau of Investigation in 1924; the company exists today principally as a security agency guarding industrial plants and businesses.

Pleasant Valley War

See Graham-Tewksbury Feud

Ponca Indians

A Siouan tribe of Indians, the Poncas are closely related to the Kansas, Omahas, and Osages. Tradition common to these and the Quapaws maintains that once the tribes were a single people, and their language, organization, and customs bear this out. They probably appeared on the Plains between 1,200 and 1,300 C.E. According to legend, the Poncas separated because of a quarrel over a game. After the split, the tribe settled around present-day Niobrara, Nebraska. They were encountered by Lewis and Clark in 1804.

In 1858, the Poncas ceded their 2.3 million-acre territory to the United States in exchange for a reservation of 96,000 acres near Niobrara. The treaty was reconfirmed in 1865. In 1868, however, the Fort Laramie Treaty inadvertently assigned the Ponca reservation to the Sioux, and in 1876–1877 the Poncas were ordered to move to Indian Territory.

In Oklahoma, many Poncas died of disease and exposure. One of the deceased was the son of Standing Bear. In January 1879, Standing Bear and 66 other Poncas set out to walk back to their traditional home to make the burial, traveling as far as the Omaha reservation before they were arrested. Standing Bear then brought suit against General George Crook (with Crook's cooperation), asking that they be allowed to remain in Nebraska. The now almost forgotten civil rights case of *Standing Bear* v. *Crook* ended with the Indians being released and permitted to stay. Other Poncas in Indian Territory, however, were not permitted to return, and the tribe was split between their Oklahoma and Nebraska settlements.

Pony Express

A response to California's demand for faster mail service from the East, the lure of government mail contracts, and a determination to establish a better freight route from the Mississippi River to the Pacific Coast were the background for the brief but spectacular life of the Pony Express.

The concept originated with William Hepburn Russell (1812–1872), partner in the West's largest wagon-freight operation, Russell, Majors and Waddell, headquartered at Fort Leavenworth, Kansas. Russell sought to capitalize on the suspension of the Butterfield Overland Mail Operation that since 1858 had carried mail from St. Louis to San Francisco along a three-week, 2,800-mile route that dipped as far south as El Paso. Because the Civil War put Texas in the Confederacy, the Butterfield Operation ended its service in 1861, leaving mail delivery open to new bidders.

More important to Russell and his partners was

LIBRARY OF CONGRESS

A Pony Express Rider en route.

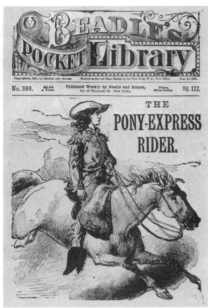

NEW YORK PUBLIC LIBRARY

The Pony Express Rider as mythologized in the dime novel. Buffalo Bill was the model for this particular epic.

establishing a central route to California for mail and freight from the East, as preferable to the route used by the Butterfield company. Russell convinced his reluctant partners that since a $600,000 government mail contract was at stake, they should finance a scheme to use express riders to deliver mail from a staging area in St. Joseph, Missouri (then the farthest western point reached by telegraph and railroad), to San Francisco, in half the Butterfield time.

A few months after his partners issued the needed notes of credit, Russell set up his Pony Express. He advertised in newspapers along the Missouri frontier ("Wanted—Young, skinny, wiry fellows not over 18. Must be expert riders to risk death daily. Orphans preferred"), and from hundreds of responses, he hired 80 young men. Each was required to take an oath swearing to remain sober and not use profanity, gamble, treat horses cruelly, or interfere with the rights of citizens or Indians. Each man was presented with a Bible and a pair of Colt revolvers and was paid $125 a month.

Russell established 190 stations in 5 divisions along the route. The bigger stations, 40 to 100 miles apart depending upon the terrain, had bunks and mess facilities; the relay stations, every 10 to 20 miles, had small shelters, horses, and stables. He bought 500 grain-fed undersized horses (which he reasoned could outrun the grass-fed ponies of the Indians), hired station keepers and stock tenders, and on April 3, 1860, the Pony Express began.

At about 5 P.M. on that day in St. Joseph, a rider named Johnny Frey (or Frye) mounted a bay horse to ride out to board a Missouri River ferry to Elwood, Kansas, and the opening leg of the 2,000-mile journey to San Francisco. He was dressed in a red shirt and blue pants (supplied by Levi Strauss of San Francisco) and shiny black high-topped boots. Across his horse's pommel was a rectangular saddlebag called a *mochila* (Spanish for "knapsack") that was divided into four padlocked mail compartments. The whole thing fitted over pommel and cantle, so that the rider would have a pouch in front and back of each leg. The mail, costing the sender $5 per half-ounce plus the regular 10 cents in U.S. postage, consisted of about 85 pieces—telegrams, letters, bank drafts, newspapers, a message of congratulations from President James Buchanan to the governor of California—weighing 15 pounds.

At about the same time as Frey rode out of St. Joseph, an eastbound rider named Billy Hamilton left San Francisco for Missouri. The riders were expected to change mounts and transfer the *mochila* in two minutes. The stationkeeper would provide a cup of water or coffee and some bread and meat as the rider prepared for the next 10- to 20-mile run.

The westbound route cut across northwestern Kansas into Nebraska, followed the Platte River Valley to Fort Kearny, then on to Fort Laramie, the South Pass of the Rocky Mountains to Fort Bridger, across the Wasatch Range to skirt the southern edge of the Great Salt Lake, and then across the alkali flats to Nevada and Lake Tahoe, through the Sierra passes to Sacramento, and then by boat to San Francisco.

Although the Pony Express lasted only 19 months, it was a notable success despite the heat, rains, blizzards, and occasional Indian attacks. As the Civil War went on, 40 additional riders were hired and the mail rate dropped to $1 per letter. But despite its achievement in establishing the central route to California as quicker and more reliable than Butterfield's, the cost of the Pony Express operation soon grew to $30,000 a month. Russell and his partners were losing money rapidly. By October 1861, soon after the transcontinental telegraph reached California, Russell, Majors and Waddell announced that the Pony Express would be discontinued. The next year the partnership was dissolved and the company was sold.

In its 19-month existence, the Pony Express carried 34,743 pieces of mail (including news of Abraham Lincoln's election and his inaugural speech) and earned about $90,000 for its efforts—about a tenth of its cost. The record endurance ride was held by Jack Keetly, who rode 340 miles in 31 hours; its speed record by Jim Moore, who covered 280 miles in 14 hours 46 minutes. And its most celebrated rider was William F. Cody, who at the age of 14 or 15 rode the 116-mile section of the route between Red Buttes and Three Crossings in central Wyoming.

Populists

Members of a political party in the United States, the Populists attained power during the height of agrarian discontent in the 1890s. During this period the nation was undergoing a difficult economic transformation that would transfer the base of power from agriculture to industry. The party's position against big business and industry gained additional support from laborers and small-business owners who felt threatened by powerful industrial giants.

During this transition in the late nineteenth century, the frontier was being sold and settled at a frenetic pace, railroad monopolies stretched aggressively across the continent, and research and technological advances had revolutionized agriculture and industry. Older democratic values touting such concepts as "the individual" and "equality" were being replaced with ideas associated with capitalism, such as mass labor and production, and an unequal distribution of wealth.

The Populist Party essentially sprang out of the farmers alliances, which formed in the 1870s in the South and West. These granger organizations, such as the great National Farmers Alliance in the North and the National Farmers Alliance and Industrial Union in the South, advocated democratic ideals and therefore pushed for such measures as the regulation of railroads. All together the alliances claimed several million members. They funneled their political efforts into controlling the Democratic and Republican parties. When they were unsuccessful,

many granges soon combined with labor groups and other sympathizers to form a third state party, the People's Party. With the election of 1890, numerous candidates advocating alliance objectives moved into local, state, and even national office, with senators from Kansas and South Dakota elected. Encouraged by their success, alliance leaders formed a national political party in 1892, known officially as the People's Party but usually hailed as the Populist Party.

At a convention in Omaha, Nebraska, in 1892, the Populist Party's newly formed national committee nominated James B. Weaver of Iowa as its presidential candidate. Their platform, aimed at southern and western farmers, gained support from northeastern industrial workers as well. Among other reforms, the Populists championed government ownership of the railroads and the telephone and telegraph systems; a national, stable currency and free silver; a graduated income tax to more equally distribute the national wealth; a system whereby farmers could withhold crops from the market when prices dipped; immigration restriction; and an eight-hour day for industrial workers. In the election of 1892 Weaver received over a million popular votes and 22 electoral votes—substantial, but not enough to beat Democrat Grover Cleveland.

Cleveland made the silver issue—one that concerned many Populists—a major concern during the election of 1896. Since the Democratic platform supported this and other Populist goals, the Populists supported the Democratic presidential candidate, William Jennings Bryan, and their own Thomas Edward Watson for the Democratic vice presidency. However, Republican William McKinley won the election, which furthered urban-rural polarization and conflict. In 1900, already much weakened, the Populist Party divided over the issue of joining with the Democrats. Watson ran again in 1904 and 1908 as a Populist candidate, but the party had largely dissolved by that time, and the agrarian-based society and its value system had become part of the nation's past.

Posse

From posse comitatus ("authority of the county"), a posse is any group of people, usually deputized, that has been called upon by a law officer to assist in keeping the peace, making arrests, and serving writs. In the American West, a county sheriff generally had a small force, sometimes only one or two men, of full- or part-time deputies to assist in peacekeeping. A posse, therefore, was often formed to sweep a large territory to locate lawbreakers, serve warrants, and make arrests.

Potawatomi Indians

An Algonquian nation of Indians, the Potawatomis divided into many tribes, owing to forced removals and relocations by the U.S. government. Prior to contact with white people, the Potawatomis claimed a region on the north shore of Lake Huron, where they were closely associated with the Ojibwas and Ottawas. At the end of the sixteenth century, they lived in the vicinity of modern-day Green Bay, Wisconsin. Shortly thereafter, however, they settled in southern Michigan and Illinois, eventually occupying an area around Lake Michigan in what now constitutes Illinois, Indiana, Michigan, and Wisconsin.

The tribe took an active part in Pontiac's Rebellion, which united the Ojibwas, Ottawas, and Potawatomis against the British in the 1760s. Nonetheless, they fought with the English during both the American Revolution and the War of 1812.

Throughout the early nineteenth century, the Potawatomis engaged in sporadic and disorganized resistance against white encroachment. By the Treaty of Chicago of 1833, however, they ceded 5 million acres in Illinois and Indiana. They then moved across the Mississippi into Iowa, Missouri, and later Kansas. Some Potawatomis, however, remained in Michigan, Wisconsin, and Ontario (Canada). A reservation was established in Kansas for the United Band of Potawatomis, Chippewas (Ojibwas), and Ottawas. In 1861, an assimilationist group of Potawatomis split from the United Band, accepting both allotment and U.S. citizenship. During the 1870s, this Citizen Band was resettled to a reservation in Indian territory. Today, both recognized and unrecognized groups of Potawatomis live in Kansas, Michigan, Oklahoma, Wisconsin, and Ontario.

Powell, John Wesley

1834–1902

A self-taught naturalist and explorer of the Colorado River, John Wesley Powell was born in Mount Morris, New York, the son of a circuit-riding Methodist preacher, and worked with his seven brothers and sisters on his father's farms in Ohio, Wisconsin, and Illinois. In what leisure time he had, Powell learned basic science and the wonders of the natural world from another self-taught scientist, George Crookham.

By 1852 Powell was teaching in country schools, attending college—Illinois College, Wheaton, Oberlin, wherever his father's travels took him—and exploring the Mississippi River and its tributaries, collecting specimens along the way. In Wheaton, where his family settled for a time, he became secretary and curator of collections for the Illinois Natural History Society.

US GEOLOGICAL SURVEY

John Wesley Powell, photographed with Paiute Chief Tau-gu.

At the outbreak of the Civil War, Powell enlisted in the 20th Illinois Infantry and became a Union officer and artillery battery commander. He lost his lower right arm at Shiloh, was nursed back to health by his new wife Emma (Dean), promoted to major, and again distinguished himself at the siege of Vicksburg. In 1865 Powell returned to teaching, this time as professor of geology at Illinois State Normal University, but by now he was thinking of a journey to the Rocky Mountains. His trip there with students and other amateur scientists in 1867–1868 was followed by a more serious geological and geographical survey of the Rockies in 1868. In August of that year, he and six others made the first ascent of 14,250-foot Long's Peak in Colorado. During this period he conceived the idea of a boat exploration of the Colorado River.

Funded by the Smithsonian Institution and Congress, the Colorado River Scientific Exploring Expedition left Green River, Wyoming, on May 24, 1869. (The beginning of this momentous venture followed by only two weeks the Central and Union Pacific lines' reaching Promontory Summit, Utah, marking the completion of the first transcontinental railroad.) Powell's party of 11 men in 4 small boats navigated the Green and Colorado river rapids and emerged on August 29 a thousand miles downstream. One man had left the expedition early; three others refused to try the wild waters of the Colorado, climbed the canyon walls, and were killed by Indians.

Despite this tragedy, the success of his expedition gave Powell the determination to fight for federal funds to continue his work. In 1871, with a $12,000 congressional appropriation, he led an expedition to map the Colorado Plateau and to study the arid regions drained by the Colorado River. Further expeditions followed, including those in 1874 and 1875 to the Uinta Mountains, the 120-mile range of the Rockies in northeastern Utah.

After 1875, Powell remained in Washington, D.C. At the urging of his friend James A. Garfield, then a congressman from Ohio, he published his *Explorations of the Colorado River*, a work today regarded as among the classics of exploration accounts. His other books included *Geology of the Uinta Mountains* (1876) and *Report on the Lands of the Arid Region of the United States* (1878). Powell served as head of the new U.S. Bureau of Ethnology and for 13 years as head of the U.S. Geological Survey, during which time he often addressed Congress on the need for government support of scientific efforts.

By the time of his death on September 23, 1902, Powell was recognized not only as the father of the reclamation movement in the United States but as a pioneer environmentalist.

Preemption Act

1841

A forerunner of the Homestead Act of 1862, this legislation was a response to a problem that had plagued the United States since the 1750s: what rights to the land did squatters have? There had always been a number of people who had "preempted" federal lands by settling on them before they had been surveyed or auctioned by the government. On more than one occasion, violence had broken out, and there was growing agitation for establishment of a new policy regarding the distribution of public lands. In fact, there had been at least four temporary measures, passed between 1820 and 1834, in response to pressure from settlers moving onto the frontier.

The dispute over land centered on sectional rivalries between the conservative East, which feared the loss of its labor force to the rapidly expanding West, and the South, which wanted to make sure that any change in the law would have no weakening effect on the institution of slavery. In August 1841 Congress passed a law that permitted settlers to stake claims of up to 160 acres and, after a minimum term of residence, to purchase the land from the federal government for as little as $1.25 an acre. Although it was a major victory for the West and for small homesteaders, easterners were able to claim some points too, as the bill called for the proceeds from these sales to be distributed back to the states by a formula based on population.

Promontory Summit, Utah

Located north of the Great Salt Lake, Promontory Summit is where the Central Pacific Railroad and

Engineers Grenville Dodge and Samuel Montague shake hands after tracks are joined in Promontory Summit.

the Union Pacific Railroad met on May 10, 1869, to form the first Transcontinental Railroad in the United States. The location for the meeting was not decided until a month before completion of the project. Mormon leader Brigham Young wanted the meeting point to be at Ogden, Utah; however the Gentiles of Utah, along with miners and traders to the north, insisted on Corrine, where stagecoaches and wagon freighters departed for Idaho and Montana. Congress settled the debate with a joint resolution on April 10, 1869, which established Promontory Summit as the rendezvous.

The entire nation joined in celebrating the historic event on May 10, but the largest celebration took place at Promontory. To commemorate the event, California supplied a gold spike, Nevada provided one of silver, and Arizona's contribution had been forged of iron, silver, and gold. The last spikes were driven by Leland Stanford of the Central Pacific and Thomas Durant of the Union Pacific. The tie into which the last spikes were driven was made of California laurel and had a silver plaque mounted

on it with a dedicatory inscription. The last spike was attached to a telegraph wire, which carried news of the historic meeting to both coasts. After the ceremonies were completed, two engines that stood facing each other inched forward and touched noses, officially uniting the two coasts for the first time by rail.

Pueblo Indians

Denoting a number of Indian tribes inhabiting the Southwest, the name is derived from their traditional style of village. Although the tribes do not speak the same language, there are enough similarities in their history and cultures that they can be considered together. The Pueblo Indians are believed to be the descendants of the ancient Anasazi culture.

Nineteen of the 22 Pueblo villages (Acoma, Con-

Journalist Ernest Ingersoll, seated, and his guide relax next to ruins of Pueblo cliff dwellings he discovered in Mancos Canyon, Colorado, in 1874.

chiti, Isleta, Jemez, Laguna, Nambe, Picuris, Pojoaque, San Felipe, San Ildefonso, San Juan, Sandia, Santa Ana, Santa Clara, Santo Domingo, Taos, Tesuque, Zia, and Zuni) are located in New Mexico and are normally referred to as the Northern and the Southern Pueblos. Tortugas is also located in New Mexico, immediately south of Las Cruces. It was founded in the late nineteenth century, primarily by Indians from the Mission of Nuestra Señora de Guadalupe in present-day Juarez, Mexico. The Hopi are located in Arizona. Ysleta del Sur Pueblo (also known as the Tigua Indians or Tigua Pueblo) is located in El Paso, Texas, and was founded in the aftermath of the Pueblo revolt of 1680.

As the Spaniards moved into New Mexico in the sixteenth century, the first pueblo they encountered was Zuni. The sun glinting off the adobe village fueled reports of the Seven Cities Of Cibola, villages literally made of gold. Coronado passed through the area in the 1540s. It was not, until 1598, however, when Don Juan de Oñate arrived with settlers and missionaries, that the Spanish had any lasting im-

pact on the Pueblos. By the end of the year, all the Pueblo Indians had been subdued.

Peace was not maintained long. Late in 1598, some Acomas killed one of Oñate's aides, along with some of his men. The Spaniards retaliated, killing hundreds, wrecking much of the pueblo, and sentencing 500 men to have one foot chopped off and serve 20 years of "servitude." Oñate was subsequently relieved of his governorship and banned from the territory for his wanton brutality. Very little changed for the Pueblo people. Churches were built at each pueblo, and Catholic missionaries believed that they had converted all the Pueblo people. By the mid-seventeenth century, however, they realized that the Indians' traditional religions were being maintained in the secret, underground kivas. In 1660, priests raided the kivas, seizing many ritual objects. In 1675, authorities hanged 3 tribespeople and whipped 43 others they had accused of sorcery.

By 1680, the Pueblos had had enough. On August 10, they launched a carefully planned revolt, killing many priests and colonists and forcing the remainder out of the territory. The Spanish did not succeed in reconquering New Mexico until 1692, when Santa Fe was retaken under Diego de Vargas.

In 1821, Mexico declared its independence from Spain and claimed its domains in the Southwest, making the Pueblos Mexican citizens. In 1837, citizens of New Mexico (both white and Indian) rebelled against Mexico because of heavy taxation. They succeeded in capturing Santa Fe, and Jose Gonzales of Taos pueblo was installed as governor. He ruled for a few months, until the Mexicans retook the city and executed him. In 1848, the Treaty of Guadalupe Hidalgo formally ended the Mexican War. Under the terms of the treaty, residents of New Mexico were given the choice of retaining their Mexican citizenship; not a single Pueblo Indian chose to do so.

Pueblo Revolt

1680

A rebellion by the Pueblo Indians of New Mexico and Arizona against the Spanish, this event has been called the "First American Revolution."

After the Spanish conquest of New Mexico in

1598 by Don Juan de Oñate, the Pueblo Indians were subjected to severe brutality by a succession of governors. Likewise, Catholic missionaries forcibly attempted to convert the Indians to Christianity and to suppress their indigenous religions. In 1675, 3 Pueblo men were hanged for practicing their traditional faith (a fourth hanged himself in his cell) and 43 others were flogged. Among those who were whipped was one known as Popé.

Pueblo *caciques* (medicine men) and war leaders began considering the possibility of an uprising against the Spanish. Although more than a dozen prominent leaders were involved, tradition states that Popé of San Juan Pueblo emerged as the prime motivator. Over the next five years, the many different pueblos in New Mexico and Arizona forged an alliance.

By the summer of 1680, the planning was completed, with August 10 as the date for the revolution to commence. Leaders whose loyalty was suspect (particularly because they were Christians) were told that the date was three days later. Popé passed knotted ropes along to conspirators in each pueblo. One knot was to be untied each day leading up to the event. When the last knot was unraveled, it would be time to act.

At 7:00 A.M. on Saturday, August 10, word reached Governor Antonio de Otermin that Tesuque pueblo, nine miles from Santa Fe, had risen up, killing its priest and burning the church. The Indians had also murdered a white trader. Otermin dispatched troops to Tesuque, but it was too late. The entire territory was at war. Priests had also been murdered at San Ildefonso and Nambe. Smoke from the church at San Juan was clearly visible; outlying farms were attacked. The Pueblos then laid siege to Santa Fe. On August 21, after intermittent fighting, Otermin abandoned the capital. Gathering the remaining colonists at Isleta, the only surviving pueblo not part of the revolt, the Spanish left. With some friendly Indians along with them, they founded Ysleta del Sur Pueblo in El Paso, Texas. Twenty-one missionaries, more than 400 Spaniards, and untold numbers of Indians had died during the revolt. Following the revolt, the Pueblos enjoyed 12 years of freedom. In 1592, however, Diego de Vargas succeeded in completing a reconquest of the territory.

The Zuñi pueblo of Hawikuh. Hawikuh was the first town that Coronado reached. He thought that it was one of the seven golden cities of Cibola.

Pueblos

The Spanish word for "village" was employed in the Americas to designate Mexican villages or towns. It was applied as well to certain Indian villages of the Southwest, in which the dwellings were made of adobe or stone. In time, the Spaniards extended the term to mean the dwellings themselves, and it eventually became the name for the Indians who lived in such villages. These persons were also called Pueblos (Pueblo Indians) or Pueblenos.

The Pueblo people are descendants of the Anasazi Culture that flourished from about 600 to 1,300 C.E. These Anasazi built great cliff dwellings, up to five stories high, at several locations in the area. Though these structures were abandoned beginning around 1,200 C.E., they formed the model for later adobe pueblos.

The typical pueblo was a multistory terraced apartment house of adobe. One family's roof served as a patio for the family above it, with upper stories reached by means of wooden ladders. Today most pueblo villages resemble more modern Mexican villages. Only Taos in New Mexico keeps the terraced dwellings.

Q

Quakers

Also known as the Society of Friends, this protestant sect was founded in England in 1647 by George Fox. His followers rejected clergymen and conventional churches in line with Fox's philosophy that "there is God in every man." The victims of considerable persecution in the Old World, many Quakers came to the North American colonies, where they found themselves equally abused by the Puritans of New England. Pacifists who preached simplicity and tolerance of others, they endured quietly, but when their leader William Penn was granted extensive lands in return for his father's service to the crown, they were finally able to establish a home for themselves in what became Pennsylvania.

The Quakers were one of the rare groups of white settlers who consciously sought out friendly contact with Native Americans. Even before he sailed for North America, Penn sent a letter containing a message of brotherhood intended for them, proclaiming, "I have great love and regard toward you, and I desire to win and gain your love and friendship by a kind, just, and peaceful life."

He was as good as his word. In the three years in which Penn lived in America, he made at least seven land purchases from the Indians, based solely on spoken assurances of just treatment for both sides. He traveled through Indian country unarmed, studied the languages of neighboring tribes, and kept the peace. Virtually alone among the colonies, Pennsylvania was spared the frontier wars that ravaged other white settlements.

Regrettably, his son Thomas was less scrupulous. In 1737, he persuaded the Delawares to sell him as much land along the Delaware River "as a man could walk in a day." The Delaware assumed that the walk, starting at Wrightstown, would end at the Lehigh River, but Penn handpicked trained woodsmen, who ran much of the way. The resulting parcel of land was some 1,200 square miles in size and the Delawares were understandably angry. The so-called Walking Purchase created so much ill will that it is generally considered the primary motivation behind the Delawares' decision to attack Pennsylvania settlements during the French and Indian War.

With the occasional exception of a Thomas Penn, however, the Quakers were humanitarian in outlook. Quaker writer John Woolman was an early advocate of the abolition of slavery and an eloquent champion of African-American equality. Members of the Society of Friends were frequently in the forefront of other movements for social betterment.

In 1868, two committees of Quakers approached newly elected President Ulysses S. Grant to urge him to reform the nation's Indian policies. The result was Grant's Peace (or Quaker) Policy. Under this new plan, Indian rights were to be safeguarded by church-selected Indian agents and a nonpolitical Board of Indian Commissioners, with the goal of "civilizing" the Indians through education and religious instruction. At the end of that process, the Indians were to be full citizens, culturally assimilated into white society. In the meantime, they were to live on reservations administered by the federal government.

Needless to say, many Western tribes viewed this new policy with dismay, and the result was actually an escalation in tensions between whites and Native Americans. The Quaker-run missions were of uniformly high quality and the agents they selected were well motivated and well intentioned. But interference in the activities of the church-led mission boards by the Bureau of Indian Affairs thwarted their efforts and in 1880 the Orthodox Friends, one of the two Quaker groups involved, withdrew in protest. By the time President Arthur took office, the Secretary of the Interior was declaring that there was no such thing as a peace process.

The Quaker role in Native American affairs did not end there, however. Albert K. Smiley, a devout Quaker and co-owner with his brother Alfred of the Mohonk Lodge, near Poughkeepsie, N.Y., convened a conference on Indian rights at the Lodge in 1883. It would be the first of a series of such three-day conferences, often drawing as many as 200 participants. The platforms that emerged from these meetings, known as the Lake Mohonk Conference of the Friends of the Indian, became an important source of ideas on the "Indian problem." President Cleveland, for example, credited the Mohonk group with convincing him to abandon an ill-thought-out plan to confine all the Native Americans onto a single reservation. The conference published a detailed annual report, and continued to meet for 30 years.

Quantrill's Raiders

1837–1865

This Confederate band of guerrilla raiders ravaged abolitionist and loyal Union communities and Union forces along the Kansas-Missouri border during the Civil War. The band's leader, William Clarke Quantrill (1837–1865), settled in Kansas in 1859, where he taught school and got involved in horse stealing and murder. He fled to Missouri, where in 1861 he became the leader of a small irregular force of guerrillas. His Raiders skirmished with the Jayhawkers, a band of antislavery guerrillas from Kansas, and burned and pillaged pro-Union communities. Declared an outlaw by the Union, his force aided in the capture of Independence, Missouri, on August 11, 1862, after which he was commissioned as a captain in the Confederate regular army. Quantrill's Raiders could operate cohesively or as small highly mobile units with specific tactical objectives. Each man was a skilled horseman, handy with either a rifle or a Colt .45 pistol, and completely at home on the terrain. Young Frank and Jesse James and Cole and Jim Younger, later part of infamous outlaw bands, learned hit-and-run warfare as Raiders.

On August 21, 1863, Quantrill led almost 400 of his men against the free soil (slavery not permitted) stronghold of Lawrence, Kansas. One hundred-eighty men, women, and children were slaughtered, and most of the town was burned. Wearing Union uniforms, his forces then ambushed and killed approximately 100 Union soldiers at Baxter Springs, Kansas, and continued to massacre small garrisons and runaway blacks. In the spring of 1864 Quantrill lost command when dissension split the Raiders into small independent raiding units. In a raid on Taylorsville, Kentucky, Quantrill was mortally wounded and captured by Union troops. He died in prison. He is credited with the deaths of 1,000 people in 1863 alone, but Union forces also committed guerrilla raids, and, in retribution, northern Missouri became popularly known as the "Burnt District."

R

Railroads

In 1829 the first steam-powered locomotive, a British-made engine, made its maiden run on a three-mile stretch of track in Pennsylvania. In 1830, the Baltimore and Ohio Railroad began carrying freight and passengers, and five years later it became the first railroad to enter Washington, D.C. In 1833, the first interstate rail line was opened between Petersburg, Virginia, and Blakely, North Carolina, a distance of 59 miles.

By the 1840s, eastern North America was in the grip of railroad fever. It was during this momentous time—the decade of the Mexican War, the acquisition of California, and the great gold strike there—that private and corporate railroad financiers, state legislatures, and the federal government began turning their attention to the West and to the potential in binding that vast part of the nation to the East.

While the eastern states were all being connected by rail, the far West could communicate with the Atlantic Seaboard only by the great sailing ships that laboriously beat their way around Cape Horn or that portaged freight and passengers across the Isthmus of Panama. (A railroad across the isthmus from

An early passenger train makes its way on a shelf cut through a granite gorge in the Rockies.

A train inches along a bridge over a canyon in Arizona. The track was perched far above the canyon in case of flash flooding.

Aspinwall—Colón today—on the Atlantic side to Panama City on the Pacific side, a distance of 48 miles, opened in 1855, delivering passengers and freight to the Pacific Mail Steamship Company's vessels bound for San Francisco. In its first four years of operation, the railroad carried 200,000 passengers, for the astronomical sum of $25 one way.)

With St. Louis, Independence, and other Missouri and Iowa towns as jumping-off places, great wagon caravans crawled across the plains or through the northern passes, carrying freight and settlers. Stagecoaches offered faster, lighter travel, but either method took months, and the journey was arduous and dangerous every step of the way. But soon there were signs that all this was about to change.

The 1850s began with an Act of Congress granting railroad companies six sections of public land for each mile of track they built. (In the next 20 years, the federal government would give away 180 million acres of land in railroad construction grants.) In 1852, the first railroad to run west of the Mississippi—the grandly named Pacific Railway of Missouri—began operating within the state; in 1854, the Chicago and Rock Island reached the Mississippi; and Chicago, where a dozen rail lines converged, became a railroad hub for the nation.

Perhaps the most important development of the 1850s was the launching, amid considerable confusion, of surveying expeditions to map routes for a transcontinental railroad. Influential politicians such as Senators Thomas Hart Benton of Missouri and Stephen A. Douglas of Illinois, and President Pierce's secretary of war, Jefferson Davis of Mississippi, became deeply involved in these surveys and routing issues, as all hoped to see the route established where it would benefit the regions they represented.

Benton favored the "Buffalo Route," which would originate in St. Louis and run north, then roughly follow the 38th parallel west to San Francisco. The Missouri senator sponsored an 1848 expedition by his son-in-law, John C. Frémont, to search for a route through the Rocky Mountains along the 38th. Frémont was stopped in the mountain passes in the winter and lost ten of his party before turning back, but his disappointing expedition did not dampen enthusiasm for the route.

Douglas favored a course from the Great Lakes along the Missouri River into Washington Territory; Jefferson Davis liked the idea of a southern route, one which would trade the problems of mountain passes for the problems of desert travel. As it turned out, none of these paths were ultimately adopted.

The pivotal figure in the development of the transcontinental railroad was Theodore D. Judah (1826–1863), a pioneer engineer from Connecticut who went to California in 1854 to built the Sacramento Valley Railroad. It was Judah—who had personally explored the Sierras—who influenced the Central Pacific Railroad and its "Big Four" financiers to build from Sacramento through the Donner Pass in the Sierra Nevada and who drafted the entire west-east portion of the transcontinental plan.

In 1869, at Promontory Summit, Utah, the tracks of the Central Pacific and the Union Pacific Railroads joined. But between 1860 and 1870, while the nation's railroad trackage increased from 30,626 to 53,000 miles, only the original transcontinental line—the Union Pacific from Omaha to Promontory Summit and the Central Pacific from Sacramento to Promontory Summit—figured in that number. Not until 1893 was the entire Mississippi Valley linked to the Pacific—by James J. Hill's Great Northern Railway from the Great Lakes to the Puget Sound, and by the Southern Pacific, Northern Pacific, and Atchison, Topeka & Santa Fe.

The effect that the railroads had on the West cannot be overstated. The pace of life was suddenly quickened up to and beyond the speed of the locomotives. Railroad companies offered inducements

SMITHSONIAN INSTITUTION

A luxurious private Pullman compartment like this would cost $50 a day in the 1890s.

dians of New York or Massachusetts." The commissioner knew his business: the western railroads absorbed Indian lands and gave the army greater mobility. They also made it easy to kill off the buffalo herds. At first the animals were hunted for meat for the rail crews; later the goal was to harvest hides for eastern tanneries and bones for carbon and fertilizer; or simply to provide sport for hunters and visiting dignitaries. By 1900 the buffalo herds had been reduced from an estimated 75 million before the advent of whites to perhaps 1,000. It would take 75 years for the buffalo population in the West to reach 10,000 again.

Rain-in-the-Face

CA. 1835–1905

A Sioux warrior who was among the most feared Indians of his day, Rain-in-the-Face was probably

NATIONAL ARCHIVES

Sioux warrior Rain-in-the-Face.

to potential émigrés to the West, allowing settlers to inspect the lands that speculators—and the railroads themselves—hoped to sell. The railroads carried stock to market, bringing to a close the era of the great cattle drives. They shipped produce and other farm goods, mail, machinery, people, and their belongings, thereby ending the long sea voyages and the era of the conestoga wagon and stagecoach.

A generation earlier, a pioneer family might have taken six months to sail from the East Coast to California, and as long to cross the West by wagon train. Now, they could travel by railroad coast-to-coast in eight short days.

At the same time, the railroads spelled doom for the ancient way of life of the Indian. In 1872, a commissioner of Indian affairs reported that building the Northern Pacific would "leave the 90,000 Indians ranging between the two transcontinental lines as incapable of resisting the government as are the Inborn around 1835 near the Cheyenne River. As a young man he participated in war parties against the Crows, Gros Ventres, Mandans, and Pawnees.

There are alternate tales regarding the origin of his name. In one account, it was said that as a youth he was hit in a fight with a Cheyenne, and that blood ran down his face like rain. In another version, it was said that when he painted his face for war, the half red, half black paint (representing an eclipsing sun), when freshly applied, would run down his face as if streaked by rain.

Rain-in-the-Face fought in the attack on Fort Totten in the Dakota Territory in 1866, and he was also present at the assault of Fort Phil Kearny the same year. In this latter engagement, by his own account, he was one of the decoys who lured Captain W. J. Fetterman to his death. In 1874, he was arrested by Tom Custer (upon orders from his brother, George Armstrong Custer) for the ambush of stragglers from the Yellowstone Expedition of 1873. He was taken to Fort Abraham Lincoln, but he managed to escape.

He later took part in the Battle of Rosebud. He also participated in the Battle of the Little Bighorn. In that encounter, some contended that it was he who killed Custer; others asserted that he cut out Tom Custer's heart because he was so angered at being arrested. This latter story was popularized by Elizabeth Custer. However, shortly before his death, the aged warrior denied both versions to the writer Charles Eastman, terming them "lies."

Ranchero

See Rancho System

Ranches

The word ranch comes from the Spanish word rancho. The original North American ranches were Mexican and often built on huge Spanish land grants.

Although many of these were, and are, sheep ranches or ranches for dairy cows and other animals, the Old West ranch generally was devoted to the raising of beef cattle, and was patterned after the livestock outfits of Texas, which had their greatest impact on the development of the West in the two decades following the Civil War. During this period, grazing land was cheap and many ranches that began as mustanging enterprises—capturing and breaking wild horses—turned to raising beef by using the horses to corral small wild herds of free-roaming cattle.

In the post–Civil War boom, when the American taste for beef created an industry that attracted capital from East Coast financiers, it was quite common for ranches to cover several hundred thousand acres. Among the "cattle kings," Charles Goodnight controlled a million acres in the Texas Panhandle,

DENVER PUBLIC LIBRARY

Cowboys at a roundup.

Richard King's Santa Gertrudis Ranch of south Texas, begun in 1853, became the world's largest stock operation, controlling 1.25 million acres at its peak; and on the Pacific Slope, Henry Miller's 800,000-acre ranching empire spread across Oregon, California, and Nevada. Similar huge spreads could be found in New Mexico, Colorado, Wyoming, Montana, and the Pacific Northwest.

Life for the early stockmen was fraught with uncertainty. Among natural disasters, the droughts played havoc with the grasslands on which the ranchers' cattle were fattened. Manmade enemies included whipsawing market prices, and eastern financial panics. More immediately, Indian raiding parties and bands of rustlers made constant vigilance necessary. Farmers and sheepherders were perhaps the cattlemen's bitterest enemies, because they all vied for the same land.

Rancho System

In Mexican California, it quickly became abundantly clear that the mission system would not prevent encroachment by the Russians and English in the north or Americans in the north and east. More-

over, the 21 missions with their all-powerful Franciscan padres were a Spanish holdover, and the Mexican government wanted to make it clear that this area was now part of Mexico, not Spain—it was a republic, not a colony. The Mexican Constitution of 1824 authorized secularization of the missions, and Governor José Maria Echeandia began the process in 1831, although the effects would not be fully felt until 1836.

In response to the changing situation, and in conjunction with the secularization of the missions, Mexico gave over great tracts of land to local residents of wealth and position, so-called *gente de razon* or "rational people." These "rancheros" ran their spreads, or "ranchos" (from which the English word *ranch* is derived), essentially as feudal empires controlled by their families. Holdings could be enormous; for example, the Nieto family received a grant of 200,000 acres in 1844. For the workers, all bounty came from the ranchero, whether it was food to eat or a roof to sleep under.

Unseating the padres drastically altered the social order of California, making the *gente de razon* the new ruling class. These were the landed gentry, the rancheros whose large holdings comprised a sizable part of the territory. Indeed, more than 800 rancheros divided among themselves some 8 million acres of prime land; a contemporary source esti-

LIBRARY OF CONGRESS

Elegant portrait of a California vaquero, circa 1830. These Spanish horsemen were the original American cowboys.

mates that some 46 owners ruled virtually all of California. The result was a social structure essentially feudal in nature, with power and patronage radiating from the ranchero and family ties taking precedence over priorities. The ranchero was the source of all bounty to the common people; the provider of housing, food, and work.

It was an easy life for the ranchero, owing to a good climate, plenty of arable land, and cheap Indian labor. But it also left the rancheros unprepared for the conditions that would threaten and, eventually, destroy the system. For example, the economics of the rancho system depended on trade in cattle hides and tallow. Although most rancheros grazed sheep and horses and raised grain crops or wine grapes, very few finished products were produced on the rancho. As trade with the British and Americans increased, such products were introduced by outsiders.

In the north, the gold rush brought a huge influx of Anglos into California. Pressure to reach a more urban, industrial system led to new patterns of land use. The 1848 Treaty of Guadalupe Hidalgo guaranteed the rights and land titles of all, but the Land Law of 1851 called for a close reading of all prior land grants. Needless to say, the new reading was done by Anglos and the result was an increasingly heated series of battles between rancheros and white squatters.

The rancho system was still in place in the south, where land use was still largely pastoral. Most Anglos were just passing through on their way to the gold fields. There wasn't enough rainfall for farming. The Land Commission recognized more of the southern California land grants, and there was less squatter violence. However, under the new federal law it became increasingly difficult for the rancheros to pass on their land to their heirs. Moreover, a tendency to overspending in good times left the rancheros ill-equipped to deal with changes in the social system, and gradually the land-rich, cash-poor Californios lost their land in the South as well, bringing the rancho system to an end.

Red Cloud

CA. 1822–1909

A Sioux chief, Red Cloud's successful war against the United States led to the Fort Laramie Treaty of

SMITHSONIAN INSTITUTION

Red Cloud.

1868. Red Cloud was born around 1820 on the Platte River, the son of a respected warrior. His family opposed the Fort Laramie Treaty of 1851, which allowed roads and military posts across Sioux territory. In fact, his father and brother were reportedly killed by Bull Bear in an intratribal dispute over the pact, and Red Cloud avenged their deaths. According to Indian accounts, the incident immediately gave him stature as one who defended his people and their land.

A gifted orator, Red Cloud became an outspoken critic of white encroachment, especially in his opposition to the Bozeman Trail. In 1866, he arranged a truce with the Crows, so that the Sioux could turn their full attention to the soldiers building forts along the disputed trail. He then orchestrated and led the campaign against Fort Phil Kearny, which culminated in the massacre of Captain W. J. Fetterman and 80 soldiers on December 21 of that year.

The battles that followed came to be known as Red Cloud's War, and resulted in the Fort Laramie

Treaty of 1868. In April of that year, several Indian leaders signed the treaty, whereby they agreed to live on reservations and secured the right to hunt buffalo so long as they roamed "in numbers sufficient to justify the chase." However, Red Cloud refused to sign as long as the Bozeman Trail and its string of protective forts remained. The United States capitulated and abandoned both. Red Cloud then signed the treaty on November 6, 1868. He thus became the first and only western chief to win a war with the United States.

In 1870, Red Cloud traveled to Washington, D.C., to meet with Donehogawa, an Iroquiois Indian who had become Commissioner of Indian Affairs under President Ulysses Grant. This would be the first of many trips Red Cloud made to the east and had the unfortunate effect of helping foster suspicion among fellow Sioux that he was more interested in his own ambition than in what was best for his people. Red Cloud tried as best he could to accommodate his people's needs to the government's ever-changing plans for the Sioux, which took them from agency to agency.

Ultimately, Red Cloud and the Sioux were permanently placed at the Pine Ridge Reservation in South Dakota in 1877. While at Pine Ridge, Red Cloud helped his people through turbulent times, including the murder of Sitting Bull and the Wounded Knee massacre that was the culmination of the government's inability to deal with the Ghost Dance religion.

Red River War

This is the name given to the Indian outbreak following the Battle at Adobe Walls. By the early 1870s, millions of buffalo were being slaughtered, not only for their hides and tongues but also as a means of waging economic war against the Plains tribes. When General Philip Sheridan was asked if something should be done to halt the massive buffalo kills, he is reported to have replied, "Let them kill, skin, and sell until the buffalo is exterminated, as it is the only way to bring lasting peace and allow civilization to advance."

In 1874, Quanah Parker, a mixed-blood Comanche war chief, inspired by a mercurial prophet named Isatai, called for a war against the whites to save the buffalo. The first assault was against the hunters' base, a trading post known as Adobe Walls in the Texas Panhandle. The attack on June 27 failed to destroy the outpost, and the Indians withdrew. Soon thereafter, however, a decision was made to abandon the installation.

Following the Battle of Adobe Walls, more Indians from several different tribes began leaving their reservations. They struck far from home in Colorado, Kansas, New Mexico, and Texas, as well as in Indian Territory. In July, General Sheridan gave orders to punish the Indians and to herd them back onto their reservations.

Cheyennes, Comanches, and Kiowas had set up a large village in Palo Duro Canyon on the Staked Plains of the Texas Panhandle. They were living not as war parties but as families. Five columns of troops set out (from Fort Lyon in Colorado, Fort Union in New Mexico, Forts Griffin and Concho in Texas, and Fort Sill and Camp Supply in Indian Territory) to converge on the Staked Plains in search of the so-called renegades. One of the separate columns was under the overall command of Colonel Nelson A. Miles (brevet major general).

In late September, the 4th Cavalry, out of Fort Concho and under the command of Colonel Ranald Mackenzie, was the first to spot the Palo Duro encampment. Lone Wolf's Kiowas were hit first. They scattered; their teepees were burned, their winter supplies destroyed, and their horses killed. Although the chief and 252 of his people escaped, they surrendered at Fort Sill on February 25, 1875. Three months later, Quanah Parker and his Comanches also turned themselves in and the Red River War came to a close. With its conclusion there were no more free Indians on the southern plains.

Remington, Frederic Sackrider

1861–1909

An artist and author, Frederic Remington produced paintings, magazine illustrations, and sculptures for close to a quarter-century, establishing him as one of the greatest artists of the Old West.

Remington was born in Canton, New York, the son of a newspaper publisher and Civil War cavalry colonel. He spent his boyhood in Ogdensburg on the St. Lawrence River, then studied at military academies in Massachusetts and Vermont (where he made his first sketches of soldiers). He entered the Yale School of Fine Arts in 1878, played football under Walter Camp—the "father" of the game—but dropped out of Yale in 1880 when his father died and left him a modest inheritance.

That year Remington went to the Montana Territory, and while camping on the Yellowstone River was told by a pioneer that the West was dying. "I knew the wild riders and the vacant land were about to vanish forever," Remington later wrote. "Without knowing exactly how to do it, I began to try to record some facts around me, and the more I looked the more the panorama unfolded around me."

Using his inheritance money, Remington bought a 160-acre sheep ranch in Kansas. The ranch failed and he wandered through the Southwest, sketching cowboys, *vaqueros* in Mexico, Cheyennes and Comanches in Indian Territory, and making extensive notes. After a brief stint as a saloon-keeper and after selling his sketches in Kansas City, he returned to New York in 1884. There he married Eva Caten, whom he had met in his college days, then the couple returned to the West. Between 1884 and the end of 1885, when he came back to New York (with $3 in his pocket, he said), he wandered frontier military posts and was even permitted to ride along

with the army during several of its Indian campaigns.

Reunited with his wife (who had left him in Kansas City to return home to her parents), Remington took an apartment in Brooklyn and within a year had launched a career as a magazine illustrator. His first sketch, "Indian Scouts on Geronimo's Trail," was published in January 1886 as a cover illustration for *Harper's Weekly*. It is said that the artist appeared in the *Harper's* office in full cowboy regalia to show his work. *Harper's* was apparently impressed with the work if not the costume and published 37 Remington drawings in 1887 alone. After the initial *Harper's* sale, he took a portfolio of his work to *Outing Magazine*, edited by his Yale classmate Poultney Bigelow. Bigelow bought all the sketches and asked for more. There followed sales to *St. Nicholas, Century Illustrated Magazine,* and others.

By 1887, Remington's annual income was $8,000 and he had added watercolors and oils to his pen-and-ink repertoire. He thereafter enjoyed a rising popularity with exhibitions of his work and major commissions that sent him back to the American West as well as to Europe and North Africa in the 1880s and 1890s. In 1895 Remington produced his first sculpture, "Bronco Buster," and saw his first book, *Pony Tracks,* published.

As a war correspondent-artist he is best known for

A Remington drawing depicting everyday life in a frontier town.

his work in Cuba during the Spanish-American War of 1898. Enthusiastic over the war, he was sent to Cuba on assignment for William Randolph Hearst's *New York Journal*, but he came home disillusioned by the experience. Expecting glory and romance, he saw nothing but disease and misery. He painted and sketched the army in camp and in the trenches and the Rough Riders in action and wrote some of the best and most baldly honest dispatches to come out of the war. (He had gone to Cuba for the first time in 1897 and reportedly cabled Hearst, "Everything is quiet. . . . There will be no war." Hearst—although he later denied it—cabled back, "Please remain. You furnish the pictures and I'll furnish the war.")

Remington amassed wealth and property and enjoyed success to the end of his life. He died from a ruptured appendix on December 26, 1909, at his home in Ridgefield, Connecticut. Remington, whom his wife described as "my massive husband" (he weighed 300 pounds toward the end of his life), loved food, cigars, scotch, and martinis and was an affable man described by one of his western friends as "a big, good-natured, overgrown boy."

His works remain celebrated for their authenticity. His human figures have character; his mules, buffalo and cattle, and uniforms, guns, and saddles are true to the life and times he witnessed. He took special pride in being the first artist to depict the horse in action, all four legs in the air at times, and once suggested that his own best epitaph might be "He knew the horse."

Rendezvous

At the end of the fur-trapping season, in early summer, trappers came together in a gathering known as a rendezvous, from the French word for "meeting." The purpose was to settle their accounts, to pool their resources, to share any newly acquired knowledge of the land, and just to have some fun and games. The tradition was begun by General William Ashley during the 1824–1825 season. Ashley's veritable army of trappers had been

HARPER'S WEEKLY

Remington's Thanksgiving Dinner for the Ranch.

Indians gather at a rendezvous for fur trappers.

flung across the Trans-Mississippi fur grounds, covering some 20,000 square miles of western America; he brought them back together in July 1825. All of the various parties reunited in the Green River Valley. As a number of the trappers had not seen each other in three years, they proceeded to spend several days partying, storytelling and holding athletic contests, as well as conducting some serious trading. The rendezvous became a more or less annual occurrence, with the last one held by the American Fur Company in 1839 as the great days of the fur trade were fading.

Reservations, Indian

Reservations were lands reserved for various Indian tribes; as such, they formed the cornerstone of U.S. federal Indian policy during the second half of the nineteenth century.

In 1763, as pressure upon Indian lands grew, the British established the Appalachian Mountains as the western boundary of white habitation. Territory beyond that line was designated as "Indian Country." The policy was probably unworkable from its inception, but the idea behind it became the guiding principle of Indian policy in the new republic.

Between 1820 and 1840, numerous Indian tribes in the East and Midwest (most notably the Five Civilized Tribes) were removed from their traditional homelands to new territories west of the Mississippi. Policymakers now viewed that area, roughly a line extending from Fort Snelling, Minnesota, along the western borders of Iowa, Missouri, and Arkansas, to Fort Jesup, Louisiana, as the "permanent" Indian frontier. The Indians were moved to "Indian Territory." Originally this was an ill-defined area encompassing most of modern Kansas, Nebraska, and Oklahoma. Eventually, however, the term came to mean only Oklahoma.

As non-Indians moved west in increasing numbers, it became apparent that the idea of a permanent Indian territory, protected by the single boundary of the Mississippi, was not feasible. By the middle of the nineteenth century, the idea began to emerge of forcibly consolidating Indians onto reservations. These islands of land would be "reserved" for the Indians and administered by white officials.

Over time, the reservation system evolved as the best means of "civilizing" and assimilating the Indian population. At the time, the Indian societies were perceived by the white settlers as backward and pagan. Few whites recognized the differing values of the various Indian cultures. Many truly believed that "civilizing" and converting the Indi-

Apaches receive their rations of cloth.

ans as fast as possible was in everyone's best interests. Of course, some did see the Indians as mere obstacles to their own desires who could be swept aside with no concern. One of the earliest proposals came from Indian Commissioner William Medill, who envisioned two concentrated "colonies" of Indians in the West. In 1848, Medill wrote, "The policy already begun ... is, as rapidly as it can safely and judiciously be done, to colonize our Indian tribes beyond the reach, for some years, of our white population; confining each within a small district of country, so that, as the game decreases and becomes scarce, the adults will gradually be compelled to resort to agriculture and other kinds of labor . . ." The Indian commissioner went on to suggest financing the operation with funds from the sale of their former lands. As he foresaw it, schools would be set up to teach male children vocations and females "housewifery." Missionaries were to be used to convert the tribes to Christianity.

In 1858, Commissioner of Indian Affairs Charles E. Mix cited three "fatal errors" that previously had been made in federal Indian administration. These were the frequent removal of tribes from place to place as settlement advanced, the assignment to them of too great a territory, and the promise of large annuities in exchange for lands ceded. According to Mix, the current policy was "entirely the reverse" of the one previously pursued with regard to these matters. Indians were to be permanently settled on lands just large enough for their actual occupancy. Instead of cash payments, they were to be given livestock, agricultural implements, tools, and schools.

San Carlos, an infamous Apache reservation in Arizona, was located on 5,000 acres of desert. Eight different bands of warring Apaches were forced to live together in a society where everything was rationed, even horsemeat. The picture shows a horse being divided up.

However, along with other federal officials, Mix viewed these reservations as an interim measure. After the Indians had been civilized, their land would be awarded in "severalty." In 1862, in his annual report, Commissioner William P. Dole endorsed this emerging reservation policy as a first step toward in-

Apache women collect mesquite and cottonwood to use as fuel.

dividual land holdings and the ultimate assimilation of Indians as U.S. citizens.

The confinement of Indians to reservations was accomplished through an intense period of treaty-making between the federal government and the tribes. Between 1778—the date of the first federal treaty with the Delawares—and 1871—when Congress unilaterally ended the treaty process—approximately 370 treaties brought Indian tribes under the guardianship of the federal government. Millions of acres of land were ceded and made available for settlement. The reservation system ushered in an era of increased Indian dependency, economic collapse, and erosion of traditional authority.

When it became apparent that the reservations were not accomplishing their designed purpose, a new solution was sought to "the Indian problem." In 1887, Congress passed the Dawes Act, providing for allotment of the Indian reservations, held in common among all members of a given tribe, into individual parcels. The goal was the destruction of tribal sovereignty through reduction of its land base and increased non-Indian settlement on lands that had once been part of reservations. Theodore Roosevelt described the act as "a mighty pulverizing engine to break up the tribal mass."

This policy was again reversed in 1934, when the Indian Reorganization Act ended the allotment era. Part of the so-called Indian New Deal, the act and other actions by the federal government sought to encourage tribal self-government and culture rather than to discourage them.

Today less than five percent of aboriginal lands remains under Indian control, so it can be safely said that the reservation system and allotment policy achieved their primary objectives—the freeing of Indian lands for non-Indian settlement.

Revolver

See Colt, Samuel

Ridge, John

1803–1839

John Ridge was a noted Cherokee lawyer and political leader, whom Sam Houston described as "not inferior in . . . genius to John Randolph."

The son of Major Ridge (a prominent Cherokee leader) and the cousin of Elias Boudinot, Ridge had his first political experience when he served as an interpreter at the annual Cherokee council meeting in 1823. In 1825, he was hired by the Creeks to help negotiate a treaty with the federal government. He was subsequently elected to the Cherokee National Council.

Ridge originally opposed the removal of Cherokees from their traditional homelands to the West. When gold was discovered on Cherokee land in 1829, he helped draft a law making it a capital offense to sell any of the tribe's land without permission from tribal authorities. However, after the Cherokees lost their court battles to prevent white encroachment, and after he had had an audience with President Jackson, who knew his father, Ridge became convinced that removal was inevitable.

Ridge was a leading figure in the party that favored a treaty of removal with the federal government. In 1835, he signed the infamous Treaty of New Echota, which ceded Cherokee lands for new territory in the West and $5 million. That treaty led to the Trail of Tears. Ridge moved to Indian Territory in 1837. On June 22, 1839, he was dragged from his bed and executed, condemned under the very law he had helped craft.

Ridge, John Rollin

1827–1867

John Rollin Ridge, a Cherokee writer and journalist, was the author of the first novel written by a Native American.

The son of John Ridge, John Rollin Ridge was only a child at the time of the Trail of Tears. At 12 years of age, he witnessed the execution of his father, who was killed for signing the Treaty of New Echota. John Rollin's mother then moved the family to Arkansas.

Ridge spent his teenage years involved in the guerrilla warfare between the factions of the Cherokee Nations supporting the Ridges, on one hand, and Principal Chief John Ross, on the other. In 1850, after killing a pro-Ross partisan, he fled to California, where he worked as a clerk in the gold fields.

Writing poetry and essays under the pen name Yellow Bird (the literal translation of his Cherokee name, *Cheesquatalawny*), Ridge became a regular contributor to several San Francisco periodicals. He was later the owner and editor of several newspapers in California. In 1854, he published *The Life and Adventures of* Joaquin Murieta: *The Celebrated California Bandit*, a novel about a California Robin Hood. Though the work was purported to be "strictly true," it was in fact a literary creation in which Ridge poured out his desire for revenge for the deaths of his father and his grandfather, Major Ridge. He continued to be active in Cherokee politics and affairs until his death.

Ringo, John

CA. 1844–1882

Outlaw John Ringo's life is shrouded in mystery from his birth to his death. Although there are vir-tually no records of his early years, he is believed to have been born and raised in the East and to have been college-educated. People who knew him in Tombstone, Arizona, his base of operations, spoke of him as a gentleman and an intellectual. Others say that he was born in the border states, left school at the age of 14, and that his name was originally Ringgold, but really was Ringo.

The first verifiable appearance Ringo makes is in the "Hoodoo War," one of the many Texas feuds of the post–Civil War era. During this fracas, he rode with Scott Cooley and supposedly murdered at least two men. He was arrested on murder charges but escaped from jail. Then he was rearrested, released, and reported dead.

After some time had passed, Ringo turned up in New Mexico, where he became part of the Clanton-Curly Bill Brocius gang of rustlers. Known as a loner, a hard drinker, and a deadly shot, he managed to avoid the Clantons' feud with the Earps, but became fully embroiled in the vendetta that followed the O.K. Corral shootout. He almost shot it out with Doc Holliday in January 1882, but both men were arrested before any shots were exchanged. Wyatt Earp firmly believed that Ringo was a party to the murder of Earp's brother Morgan two months later, although there was no substantiating evidence. Ringo was a member of the Tombstone posse that pursued the Earps after they left Tombstone.

During the summer of 1882, Ringo became despondent for unknown reasons and started drinking more heavily. On July 14, 1882, he was found dead, apparently of a self-inflicted gunshot wound to the head. Although his death was ruled a suicide, Wyatt Earp claimed to have killed him in revenge for his brother's murder. To add to the mystery, Ringo's body had also apparently been scalped.

Rio Grande

Also called the "Great River," the Rio Grande is the fifth longest river in North America. Rising in the Rocky Mountains of western Colorado near Stony Pass, the river begins its descent from an elevation of more than 12,000 feet. It flows in a southeasterly direction through Colorado and New

Mexico to Texas, where it marks the border between the United States and Mexico. When it finally empties into the Gulf of Mexico near Brownsville, Texas, it has traversed 1,880 miles. The river's water level fluctuates from great torrents in early spring and late summer to mere trickles in the summer that leave the winding riverbed cracking in the sun.

From the Rio Grande Reservoir at its headwaters in Colorado to its mouth at the Gulf of Mexico, tributaries augment the water flow. Most important are the Pecos, Devils, Chama, and Puerco rivers in the United States and the Salado, San Juan, and Concho rivers in Mexico. The river drains an area of approximately 172,000 square miles, largely arid country used only for grazing cattle. The limited water supply of the Rio Grande is in great demand, and it was not until 1944 that Mexico and the United States reached an agreement on how the supply should be divided. Today, most of it is used to irrigate thousands of acres of rich farmland around the Gulf of Mexico in Texas and Mexico; various grains, vegetables, citrus fruit, and cotton are grown in the fertile ground. Large irrigation projects also provide flood control and hydroelectric power.

For centuries the Pueblo Indians and their ancestors lived along the river and its tributaries in the region now known as New Mexico. The first Europeans to explore it (in the early 1500s), were the Spanish, who later settled there. In 1598 Juan de Oñate named this magnificent river, and the Spanish created their first North American capital, San Juan de los Caballeros, near where the Rio Grande meets the Chama River. U.S. exploration began in the early nineteenth century.

Tourist attractions in the Rio Grande area include Big Bend National Park, in southwestern Texas, and the Rio Grande Gorge. A curve in the Rio Grande, the "big bend," creates a dip toward Mexico in the Mexican-American border. The park, located inside the bend, was established in 1944, and its 1,107 square miles are mostly desert. Just below the border the Rio Grande plummets into the Rio Grande Gorge. Here it winds for almost 75 miles between dark, volcanic walls up to 1,000 feet high.

Petroleum, gas, coal, silver, gypsum, and potash are mined in the Rio Grande region, but the river cannot be navigated for commerce. Major cities along its course include Albuquerque, Brownsville, and El Paso in the United States and Ciudad Juarez, Matamoros, Nuevo Laredo, and Reynosa in Mexico.

Rocky Mountain Fur Company

Although the formal name was not adopted until 1830, the Rocky Mountain Fur Company was the offspring of the early fur trade in the Rocky Mountain region under the leadership of William H. Ashley (1778–1838) of Virginia, who came to Missouri after the Louisiana Purchase and who formed a partnership with Andrew Henry (1775–1833), a Pennsylvanian involved in the St. Louis fur trade since 1809. The two men launched a trapping enterprise on the upper Missouri River in 1822. Among their notable employees were Jedediah S. Smith—among the greatest trailblazers in western history—and Thomas Fitzpatrick, who opened up rich beaver grounds on the Green River.

Ashley retired in 1826 a wealthy man, and sold his part of the business to a trio of partners—Jedediah Smith, William Sublette, and David Jackson—who continued to explore the Rockies, combing the region from Canada to Sonora and from the eastern base in the Rockies to the Pacific Coast in search of new trapping areas.

In 1830, Smith, Jackson, and Sublette sold their fur enterprise for $16,000 to Thomas Fitzpatrick, James Bridger, Milton Sublette (William's brother), Henry Fraeb, and Jean Baptiste Gervais, all experienced trappers. These men adopted the name Rocky Mountain Fur Company.

Until the 1830s, the company had little competition in the central Rockies other than the Hudson's Bay Company fur traders and a scattering of free trappers who came north from New Mexico. But almost from the outset of its new ownership and new name, the Rocky Mountain Fur Company suffered serious problems. Overtrapping had thinned out the beaver population in the Rockies and, in any event, the trade was in decline with the silk hat replacing beaver headgear in the east and in Europe. Many trappers turned to other work, such as buffalo hunting.

Added to these factors, the new owners suffered from the inroads being made in the fur trade by John Jacob Astor's powerful American Fur Company, which before 1830 had confined its work to the upper Missouri country. Astor's trappers now began dogging the footsteps of the Rocky Mountain Fur Company's men throughout the Missouri River beaver grounds. This situation resulted in at least one fatal encounter: In October 1832, Jim Bridger and Tom Fitzpatrick are believed to have lured Astor's chief field man, William H. Vanderburgh, and his partner, Alexis Pilou, to the juncture of the Shoshone River and Alder Creek, in Blackfoot country, where they were attacked and killed by Indians.

In 1832, the Rocky Mountain Fur Company partners were joined by William Sublette who by advancing needed supplies to the various outposts became financial director of the company. At the 1834 Green River rendezvous, Sublette demanded the company pay its debts, and when they could not, he bought out the partners. He dissolved the enterprise on June 30, 1834, and its remnants were subsequently absorbed by Astor's American Fur Company.

Rocky Mountains

The Rocky Mountains are a major mountain system in North America. They received their name in the nineteenth century, a reference to their rugged terrain and the large amounts of bare rock that cover the mountains. The continental divide runs along the Rockies, making them a major barrier to west-ern travel for early migrants, who were forced to find routes around them. The discovery of gold in 1858 boosted the economic development of the area. Today the Rockies draw thousands of tourists to their national parks and many resorts.

The diverse Rocky Mountain range is often divided into four sections: the Southern Rockies, the Wyoming Basin, the Middle Rockies, and the Northern Rockies. The Southern Rockies, stretching from western New Mexico across Colorado into southern Wyoming, contain the highest peaks, including Mount Elbert in Colorado, at 14,432 feet the highest peak in the Rocky Mountain system. Five major rivers have their source in the Southern Rockies: the Arkansas River, North Platte River, and the South Platte River, all running east; the Rio Grande, running south; and the Colorado River, running west.

The Wyoming Basin is located in northwestern Colorado and southwestern Wyoming. With a topography and altitude similar to the Great Plains, the basin provided an easier route for travel westward, forming a corridor for the Mormon, Overland, and Oregon Trails. The basin is largely desert land, and annual precipitation is less than 10 inches.

The Middle Rockies, separated by the Wyoming Basin, are divided into eastern and western segments. The eastern section, lying in western Wyoming, contains the Beartooth, Bighorn, Laramie, and Wind

View of the Chasm Through Which the Platt Issues from the Rocky Mountains *by I. Clark.*

A church meeting taking place amid the natural beauty of the Rocky Mountains.

River mountains. The western section in northern Utah, southwestern Wyoming, and southwestern Idaho, includes the Teton and Wasatch ranges.

The Northern Rockies are located in British Columbia and Western Alberta in Canada and in northwestern Montana and northern Idaho in the United States. The Cariboo and Selkirk ranges are found in the Canadian Rockies; the Bitterroot, Clearwater, and Salmon River mountains are in the United States. Beautifully sculpted by glacial formations, the Northern Rockies contain many majestic sights, particularly at Glacier National Park. Water is abundant in the Northern Rockies, and the area is widely used for grazing.

Early economic development in the Rockies centered on mining and forestry. Gold was discovered in the Southern Rockies in the late 1850s. Further exploration led to the discovery of significant lode deposits of gold, lead, and silver. One of the nation's largest copper mines can be found in Butte, Montana. Forestry is still a major industry in the region. Today tourism bolsters the economy. The Rocky Mountains provide some of the nation's most dramatic scenery. Glacier, Grand Teton, Yellowstone, and Rocky Mountain national parks are all located there. Recreational opportunities abound in numerous resorts and ranches. Population is sparse; permanent residents number fewer than 1 million. Most of the towns and villages are either mining or resort towns, while isolated farmsteads and ranches are interspersed throughout the mountains.

Rodeo

From the Spanish rodear, meaning "to encircle," the rodeo grew out of cattle ranch activities. Long before public demonstrations of their prowess with horse and rope, cowboys from neighboring ranches gathered periodically for massive sortings-out of cattle in unfenced grazing lands and as an extension of their work held cow camp exhibitions and contests involving bronco riding, horse racing, roping, and similar events.

The first public rodeo (although the word was not yet in use) was probably the one held in Pecos, Texas, on July 4, 1883, and the first such exhibition to offer prizes for champion events was the cowboy contest held in Prescott, Arizona Territory, on July 4, 1888.

These shows and others that followed, together with the cowboy riding and roping events of Buffalo Bill's Wild West and other traveling extravaganzas, proved to be so popular that many western cities and towns launched annual Cowboy Tournaments, Roundups, Frontier Days (such as the one held in Cheyenne, Wyoming, since 1897), and Stampedes (such as the Calgary, Alberta, Stampede, dating from 1912). The word *rodeo* was first applied to these cowboy exhibitions in 1916, the same year that the first of such events was staged east of the Mississippi, at the Sheepshead Bay Speedway in Brooklyn, New York. The first indoor rodeo was held in 1917 at the Stockyards Coliseum in Fort Worth, Texas.

Early rodeos included such events as chuckwagon races, relay horse races, and even marksmanship

Like many "rodeo cowgirls," these women learned their riding and roping skills on a real ranch. They also helped to popularize practical riding clothing such as the divided skirts they wear in this 1907 photograph.

matches and wrestling. The standard program today consists of saddle or bareback bronco riding, bull-dogging or steer wrestling, calf roping, and bull riding. In 1929, the Rodeo Association of America was formed in Salinas, California, to promote the rodeo and to establish schedules and uniform judging and rules.

Among the great names in rodeo are Enos "Yakima" Canutt of Colfax, Washington, who later became the celebrated Hollywood stunt man; Okla-homan Will Rogers; bronco rider Casey Tibbs of South Dakota; and bronco and bull rider Jim Shoulders of Henryetta, Oklahoma.

This 1889 illustration from Leslie's Weekly *magazine shows how cowboys went about training bronco ponies. The breaking of these wild horses would eventually develop into rodeo competitions.*

Roman Nose

DIED 1868

Roman Nose, also known as Bat, was a Cheyenne war chief; he died at the Battle of Beecher's Island.

Roman Nose made his reputation defending Native American lands in western Kansas and eastern Colorado. He was probably responsible for more attacks than any other chief on settlers headed west between 1860 and 1868. According to most sources, he could be boastful and pompous. He was also a brilliant and inspiring leader, and it is reported that, because of his tendency to make reckless charges on the enemy, he caused the deaths of more young warriors in battle than any other chief.

On September 16, 1868, a small group of federal troops and civilians under the command of Major George Forsyth (a brevet brigadier during the Civil War) came upon a village of Sioux, Cheyennes, and Arapahos on the Arikaree River in Colorado. Attacked by about 600 warriors, Forsyth withdrew his men to an island in the river. A series of charges en-

LIBRARY OF CONGRESS

This painting depicts the Battle of Beecher's Island, which the Cheyenne came to call the Fight When Roman Nose Was Killed.

sued. Roman Nose, however, had not yet entered the fray. The chief believed that he possessed magical protection from bullets and arrows. On this day, however, he had violated one of the taboos of his medicine by eating food that had been touched by metal after being cooked. Finally compelled to join the battle, he led another assault on the soldiers and was killed.

Roosevelt, Theodore

1858–1919

Theodore Roosevelt, twenty-sixth president of the United States (1901–1909) successfully labored to curtail the power of big business and advocated conservation through his progressive domestic policies.

Born in New York City on October 27, 1858, Roosevelt graduated from Harvard in 1880 and married Alice H. Lee. Winning a position in the New York State Assembly in 1882 launched his political career as an independent Republican. However, when his wife died in 1884, Roosevelt headed for Dakota Territory and explored ranch life. He returned two years later, and married Edith Carow in 1887. A writer as well as a politician, Roosevelt published several works on the West, the best known being the four-volume *Winning of the West* (1889–1896).

In 1889, Roosevelt's political career regained momentum when President Harrison named him a civil-service commissioner. He became president of New York City's Board of Police Commissioners in 1895, and assistant secretary of the navy under President William McKinley two years later. His decision to command the western volunteer cavalry, the Rough Riders, during the Spanish-American War, led to fame and the position of Governor of New York in 1898. Roosevelt became vice-president under President McKinley in 1900, and McKinley's assassination in September 1901 put him in the executive chair.

LIBRARY OF CONGRESS

Roosevelt, center, was most comfortable in the great outdoors.

His policies supported the developing reform movement, which raised the ire of conservative Republicans. In deflating the immense power of large corporations, Roosevelt earned the nickname "Trust-buster." His crusade began in 1902 when he brought suit against the Northern Securities Company, a railroad monopoly, under the Sherman Anti-Trust Act of 1890. He pursued this further in 1903 by establishing the Bureau of Corporations, an investigative agency of interstate corporations. In 1902, "Teddy" became the first president to intervene in a labor-management dispute, when he threatened to seize coal mines if the owners refused mediation with the striking workers.

Drawing on his Dakota days, Roosevelt avidly pushed conservation measures. He backed the Newlands Bill of 1902, which advocated irrigation of the west, and established the Public Lands Commission in 1903. Working with Forest Service Chief Gifford Pinchot, he expanded the nation's forest reserve by 16 million acres and encouraged state-level conservation.

In 1904, after defeating Democrat Alton B. Parker, Roosevelt launched a second term of progressive reform. During this administration, Congress passed the Hepburn Act to further undermine the power of the big railroads, and both the Meat Inspection and Pure Food and Drug bills.

His foreign policy was equally aggressive, and he is well-remembered for his political maneuvering to construct the Panama Canal; for justifying U.S. intervention in Latin American affairs; and for mediating between the Russians and Japanese, which earned him the Nobel Peace Prize in 1905.

By the end of Roosevelt's presidency in 1909, the Republican party had become greatly divided between conservatives and progressives. His frustration with his chosen successor, William Howard Taft, grew so intense that Roosevelt reentered politics to challenge Republican presidential nomination in 1912. Taft won, but Roosevelt established the National Progressive Party, often called the Bull Moose Party, to advocate the ambitious reforms of his New Nationalist platform. However, his splinter group divided the Republicans and allowed Democrat Woodrow Wilson to win the presidency.

Still a prolific writer, Roosevelt finished his autobiography in 1913. He hoped to win the Republican presidential nomination of 1916, but the party backed Charles Evans Hughes instead. Roosevelt died in Oyster Bay, New York, on January 6, 1919.

Rosebud, Battle of the

An engagement between Sioux and Cheyenne warriors and federal troops during the military campaign leading up to the Battle of the Little Bighorn.

In the spring of 1876, the United States launched a military campaign designed to bring all Indians on the northern plains onto reservations. As part of the operation, General George Crook moved out of Fort Fetterman in May. He had already attempted one sortie, at the beginning of March, only to have to retreat to the outpost after some of his force was defeated on March 17. Now he departed with almost 1,300 men (including cavalry, infantry, Indian scouts, and assorted civilians). By the afternoon of June 16, scouts began reporting back a "very great village" ahead on Rosebud Creek.

The Sioux and Cheyennes were aware of Crook's movements, but they were confident of victory because Sitting Bull had foreseen the soldiers' defeat a week earlier during their sun dance. On the morning of June 17, as Crook's army rode out, they were attacked by about 500, led by Crazy Horse and other chiefs.

The battle became a swirling melee, and the Indians kept up constant pressure until the early afternoon, when they broke off. At midday, Crook dispatched Captain Anson Mills with eight companies of cavalry to assault the reported village, but recalled his subaltern when it appeared to him the terrain was well suited for an ambush. In any event, the village described did not exist. In official reports, Crook termed the battle a victory, but his withdrawal to base camp neutralized his large force during the movements leading to Custer's disaster on the Little Bighorn a week later.

Ross, John

1790–1866

John Ross was principal chief of the Cherokee nation; despite being only one-eighth Cherokee, he was the leading figure in that tribe's politics for more than 35 years.

During the first half of the second decade of the nineteenth century, Ross served sporadically as clerk to chiefs Path Killer and Charles Hicks and as liaison to the tribe's federal Indian agent. In 1816, he accepted an appointment as one of the tribe's delegates to Washington. Three years later, he was elected president of the Cherokee National Committee (their legislature). In 1827, he became the president of the constitutional convention that drafted the new Cherokee constitution, modeled on that of the United States. In October 1828, he was elected principal chief.

As Ross assumed his new position, the problem of removal to the West was looming. The new chief proved an implacable foe of cession of Cherokee lands. After gold was discovered and whites began to encroach increasingly on the tribe's land, Ross and the Cherokees turned to the courts. When they lost their case before the U.S. Supreme Court, the tribe split into a faction led by Major Ridge, John Ridge, and Elias Boudinot, which favored removal, and a pro-Ross group that opposed it.

After the so-called Treaty Party (the Ridge faction) signed the Treaty of New Echota in 1835, President Martin Van Buren sent federal troops to forcibly dispossess the Cherokees of their homes and move them to Indian Territory. In an effort to mitigate the suffering, Ross asked for and received permission to organize the emigration himself. During the ensuing march, known as the Trail of Tears, at least one-fourth of the Cherokee nation perished.

In Indian Territory, Ross oversaw the rebuilding of the tribe, shepherding it through a period of intense civil strife. The Civil War again rent the tribe. Ridge supporters favored the Confederacy and Ross supported the Union, but once again Ross managed to prevent the actual division of the tribe.

Russell, Charles Marion

1864–1926

A painter, illustrator, and sculptor, Charles Russell is known as "the cowboy artist." Russell's action-filled and often comical work reflects his enthusiastic embrace of the great freedom of the American West. A shift in interest from the grand landscape paintings of the Rocky Mountain School to the human experiences of the western wilderness enhanced the popularity of his frontier characters.

With an adventurous spirit, Russell left his home

John Ross.

Russell at work in Great Falls, Montana, 1897.

in St. Louis, Missouri, at the age of 16 to explore the rough frontier region that filled his imagination. After working briefly as a sheepherder and then rambling the range with a hunter and trapper, Russell settled in the Judith Basin of Montana in 1881. Working as a night wrangler for 11 years, he honed his self-taught sketching and painting skills.

Russell's drawings—such as the ones showing a gun-brandishing gang driving their horses into a bar, titled, *In Without Knocking,* or *Indians Discover Louis and Clark*—were often comical. The tough-looking cowboy soon gained an artistic reputation when his work was published in *Harper's Weekly* in 1888. Russell created thousands of pictures. His life with the Blood Indians of Alberta, Canada, for six months during 1888 inspired many paintings of Indian life, rendered with great sympathy and understanding. Native Americans were his favorite subject.

Saloon keepers were his main patrons when he married Nancy Cooper in 1896. But spurred by his wife's business savvy, by 1904 Russell was sculpting in bronze for such exalted patrons as Tiffany and Company in New York City.

Rustlers

See Cattle Rustling

S

Sac and Fox Indians

The Sacs and the Foxes are two allied Algonquian tribes of Native Americans who originally occupied the Great Lakes area. The two tribes have been closely related for almost 300 years and are often referred to as a single entity.

At the time of the first European contact around 1667, the Sacs and the Foxes were two separate and distinct tribes living in what is now Michigan and Wisconsin. The Sacs were originally called the Sauks (a name still occasionally seen today) and referred to themselves as *Asa ki waki* ("Yellow Earth People"). The Foxes were the Mesquaki, after their own name meaning "Red Earth People." After the two were nearly wiped out in wars with other tribes and with the French, they came together in the early eighteenth century, but maintained their separate tribal identities.

In 1727, the Sacs and Foxes joined with the Dakotas to wage war against the French. The French bought peace by establishing traders among the Indians and equipping the tribes with firearms. This action only served to intensify the warfare between the Sioux and the Ojibwas. Pressure from the French led the Sacs and Foxes to retreat into Illinois. They fought with Pontiac in his rebellion in the 1760s.

In 1803, the United States acquired the Louisiana Purchase. In March 1804, a detachment of soldiers reached St. Louis and took possession of the region. That year, a skirmish between Sac warriors and white settlers north of St. Louis led to hysteria and demands by whites that the Sacs and Foxes be

LIBRARY OF CONGRESS

Sac chief Black Hawk.

brought to heel. By a treaty signed in St. Louis on November 3, 1804, the allied tribes agreed to cede all of their land east of the Mississippi, and some of their hunting grounds on the west bank of the river as well. The cession surrendered large sections of Illinois and Wisconsin and part of Missouri. In exchange, the United States paid the paltry sum of $2,234.50 (the amount already expended entertaining the Indian treaty delegation) and promised a pitiful annuity of $600 to the Sacs and $400 to the Foxes.

The tribes protested the treaty but to no avail. Though there was no immediate move upon the ceded territory, anger over the treaty never subsided. The Sacs and Foxes were eventually confined to an area in what is now Iowa.

About 200 warriors under Black Hawk joined with Tecumseh and the British during the War of 1812. This marked the beginning of a split within the tribes between Black Hawk and a rival chief, Keokuk. The split led to the so-called Black Hawk War in 1832 and tensions remained until Black Hawk's death in 1838.

In the mid-nineteenth century, the tribes were removed from Iowa to Kansas. A number of Foxes remained behind, forming the Mesquaki nation (today officially recognized as the "Sacs and Foxes of the Mississippi in Iowa"). In 1869, the Sacs and Foxes were removed again, this time to Indian Territory. And on September 22, 1891, the Sac and Fox land run opened 759,000 acres of tribal lands to non-Indian settlers.

Sacagawea

CA. 1786–1812

Sacagawea, also called Sacajawea and Bird Woman, was a Shoshone Native American who helped guide Lewis and Clark on their expedition. Because of that assistance, she has attained legendary stature—like Pocahontas, Squanto, or Keokuk—as the paradigm of the "good" Indian.

Sacagawea was captured by a raiding party of Hidatsas, who sold her to the Mandans. They, in turn, sold her to a French-Canadian fur trader named Toussaint Charbonneau. In 1804, when Sacagawea was about 18 years old, Charbonneau took her for his second wife.

Lewis and Clark spent the winter of 1804–1805 with the Mandans, and met Charbonneau. They hired him as their interpreter, and Sacagawea and her infant son, Jean-Baptiste, went along on the journey.

In August, near the present-day site of Armsted, Montana, the expedition met a group of Shoshones led by Sacagawea's brother, Cameahwait. Their reunion produced a favorable climate for the negotia-

MONTANA STATE CAPITOL BUILDING

Clark, Lewis, and Sacagawea.

tion of provisions, horses, and guides. Apparently, the presence of a woman and child in the expedition also led other tribes they encountered to view them with less suspicion.

Sacagawea died in 1812 at Fort Manuel. Over the years, it has become difficult to separate myth from fact in the story of her life.

Sacramento, California

The city of Sacramento has been the state capital of California since 1854. The site was originally chosen by John Sutter (of Sutter's Mill fame) in 1840 for his new trading post, which he called New Helvetia. It was a well-chosen spot; situated at the junction of the American and Sacramento rivers, it had access to the valleys of the interior by river, and a passage to the sea through the delta. Moreover, it was located on what would become the trail across the Sierra Nevada Pass.

When gold was discovered at Sutter's Mill in 1848, that location became even more advanta-geous, with would-be miners coming from all directions, and New Helvetia's population swelled to 10,000. The town's structures increased from two shacks to 300 canvas and wooden buildings by August 1849.

Shortly thereafter, the once-modest trading post of New Helvetia had become the burgeoning city of Sacramento. It now served as one of the shipping centers for supplying the goldfields, and as it was near the fertile river valleys, it also became a major marketplace for the farmers who came along behind the Forty-Niners looking for good land and a ready market.

Sacramento's location served it well again in the 1860s. When the Pony Express service was begun, Sacramento was its western terminal point. When the Central Pacific Railroad came over the Sierras, Sacramento became the terminus for the Transcontinental Railroad. The gold miners were long gone by then, but Sacramento would continue to thrive at the heart of a rich agricultural area.

LIBRARY OF CONGRESS

Arrival of the Pony Express in Sacramento.

Sagebrush

Sagebrush is a deciduous shrub, a member of the aster family. It is among the most abundant forms of plant life in the drier parts of the American West. The common sagebrush is a low, silver-gray shrub. It gets its name from its aroma, which strongly resembles that of fresh herb sage, although the plants are not related. The shrub is important as a forage plant, and its presence is believed to be indicative of good soil. The wood burns readily, and can be used to start fires by friction. Where available, two sagebrush sticks rubbed together over tinder or wood shavings can take the place of matches. Valued by many Native Americans for its medicinal properties, the sagebrush is also the state flower of Nevada.

San Antonio, Texas

Located in south-central Texas on the San Antonio River, San Antonio is the only present-day Texas city that existed before the state won independence from Mexico in 1836.

In 1718 Governor Martin de Alarcón of Texas arrived in Texas Hill Country, home of the Payaya and Coahuiltecan Indians. He and his group erected a Spanish presidio and Mission San Antonio de Valero, whose chapel, the Alamo, would later become the stuff of legend. In 1731 the first civilian settlers—15 families—arrived from the Canary Islands after an exhausting year-long journey.

By 1773, San Antonio had become a main frontier trading post and capital of the province of Texas. After the turn of the century, the population had increased to about 25,000. Following the outbreak of the Texas Revolution in 1835, a group of Texas volunteers managed to defeat Mexican general Martin de Cos. The most memorable action of the war centers on the 187 Texans who set out to defend San Antonio against Santa Anna's Mexican troops. For 13 days they held out in the Alamo against a Mexican army of thousands before being overrun and annihilated.

After Texas gained independence, San Antonio was no longer the capital. Because it was situated at the beginning of the Chisholm Trail, San Antonio grew into a major cattle town where rangers traded and gathered supplies. After the railway reached San Antonio in 1877, the city quickly expanded. It also remained a great military stronghold. Fort Sam Houston, built in 1879, was the largest U.S. military

Mexican soldiers defending San Antonio in their struggle against Texas volunteers.

establishment of its time. Today, tourists visit the Alamo and other historic sites of Hispanic influence and design. The beautiful River Walk, begun as a WPA recovery project during the Great Depression, meanders for over two miles through the city's heart and is the reason that many people refer to San Antonio as "the Venice of Texas."

San Diego, California

The second largest city in California, San Diego lies about 100 miles south of Los Angeles and 12 miles from the Mexican border. The metropolitan area's population exceeds 2.5 million. San Diego's economy hinges on a variety of industries, such as fish canning and the manufacture of electronic equipment. A major commercial fishing fleet and the U.S. Navy, Marine, and Coast Guard have bases by the San Diego Bay.

The Dieguenos, Kamia, and Shoshone Indians lived in the San Diego area. The first known European to arrive was Juan Rodriguez Cabrillo, who touched shore in 1542 and named the region San Miguel. In 1602 Sebastian Vizcaino renamed it after a Franciscan saint, San Diego de Alcala. On July 16, 1769, Governor Gaspar de Portola led an expedition northward from Baja California and established a Spanish base at San Diego from which to further explore the coast. Father Junipero Serra, who had accompanied the party, founded the first of a string of missions at San Diego.

The town grew slowly under Mexican rule and was captured by U.S. forces in 1846. Only after a gold strike in 1870 and the arrival of the Santa Fe Railroad in 1884 did San Diego experience real growth. With the opening of the Panama Canal and the establishment of a key military base there during World War I, San Diego's economy strengthened. Tourism also supports the city economically, and attractions include the San Diego Zoo in Balboa Park, Mission San Diego, and Cabrillo National Monument, which commemorates the first European landing on the West Coast of the United States.

San Francisco, California

Situated on the coast of California, San Francisco occupies a peninsula and 43 hills on the beautiful San Francisco Bay, which extends 45 miles in-

An 1853 picture of the mission that dominated San Diego in the mid-nineteenth century.

San Francisco in 1851.

land. The Golden Gate Bridge, which spans the channel, is one of the city's greatest tourist attractions. San Francisco's metropolitan area boasts over 1.6 million inhabitants who can enjoy mild weather throughout the year.

The Tamal Indians had lived in the bay area for centuries before the Spanish established a fort and a mission in 1776. The first civilian settlement, Yerba Buena, was founded in 1835 and grew as a trading port. During the Mexican War, U.S. forces captured the area and renamed it San Francisco. The 1848 discovery of gold in the Sierra foothills drove the population from less than 1,000 in 1847 to over 56,000 by 1860. The city sprawled lively and wild, and by 1902 its population exceeded 400,000. On April 18, 1906, an earthquake rocked San Francisco, and the three-day blaze that followed destroyed almost 500 city blocks—one-third of the city. Ashes were still cooling when new structures were erected, and the city sprouted almost as wildly as it had during its initial gold-rush days. The more recent earthquake of 1989 damaged the Marina district and the major Embarcadero Freeway.

San Francisco has been a haven for such counterculture groups as the Bohemians of the 1890s, beats of the 1950s, and hippies of the 1960s. Tourists ride the historic cable cars and visit Fisherman's Wharf and the bay's now empty former federal prison, Alcatraz, among other sites.

San Jacinto, Battle of

See Houston, Samuel

San Francisco residents avoiding puddles by hopping from plank to plank along the unpaved streets.

San Joaquin Valley

Located in California's Central Valley, the San Joaquin waters some of the world's most fertile soil. Named after its main river, the San Joaquin Valley comprises the southern two-thirds of the Central Valley, which stretches between the Sierra Nevada and the Coast Range, and extends from the Sacramento River in the north to the Tehachapi Mountains in the south. The largest cities in the region are Stockton, Fresno, and Bakersfield. The San Joaquin River flows 100 miles northward to empty into the San Francisco Bay, and the Sacramento–San Joaquin Delta contains over 1,000 miles of waterways.

The first nonindigenous person believed to have arrived in the valley was Pedro Fages, who set out searching for army deserters in 1772. Missions were not established here, unlike in other areas of California, and the region remained relatively ignored for decades. In 1805 or 1806, Gabriel Moraga named the river after Saint Joachim, and the valley soon began to buzz with the trapper and trader activity of such well-known mountain men as Jedediah Smith. The Hudson's Bay Company established a post near present-day Stockton.

If few settlers trickled in to the San Joaquin Valley during the California gold rush, the arrival of the Southern Pacific Railroad in the 1870s and the Santa Fe in the 1880s brought them in waves. Cattle ranching made room for wheat farming as settlers realized the potential of the flat, rock-free, moist soil. Great irrigation systems were eventually constructed. In addition to wheat, wine grapes, apples, rice, and cotton were also well-established crops by 1920. Petroleum, discovered in 1868, and cattle ranching continue to support the economy today.

Sand Creek Massacre

The Sand Creek Massacre was an attack by whites upon a peaceful Cheyenne and Arapaho camp. General Nelson Miles called it "the foulest and most unjustifiable crime in the annals of America."

The influx of settlers into Colorado following the discovery of gold at Pike's Peak in 1858 led to a series of altercations between whites and Native Americans. In June 1864, the governor called out the militia and ordered all Indians to report to designated forts, but minor clashes continued to occur. In September, after a conference at Fort Weld, Chief Black Kettle of the Cheyenne, upon the promise of complete safety, brought his band in. They eventually made winter camp on Sand Creek, where they

RALPH L. MILLIKEN MUSEUM

Henry Miller's Colony Farm, located in San Joaquin Valley.

The Sand Creek Massacre.

were joined by some Arapahos. As a sign of friendship, the Cheyenne chief flew an American flag, presented to him by President Abraham Lincoln in Washington, above his lodge.

On the morning of November 29, 750 men of the 1st and 3rd Colorado Volunteers led by Colonel John Chivington, a former Methodist preacher, attacked the village. Chivington instructed his men to kill all the Indians they found, including the children because "nits make lice." Black Kettle rushed from his lodge and tried to halt the assault, raising a white flag on the pole with the Stars and Stripes. Chivington's men nevertheless swept through the village, killing 28 men and 105 women and children.

When word of the massacre reached the East, it provoked a public outcry. Chivington assuredly would have been court-martialed but wisely chose to leave the service. To the end, however, he maintained, "I stand by Sand Creek."

Santa Anna, Antonio López de

1792–1876

Mexican soldier, president, and dictator, Santa Anna served as president five times (1833, 1839–1840, 1841–1845, 1846–1848, 1853) and was exiled four times. Self-named the "Napoleon of the West," he was born Antonio López de Santa Anna de Lebrón in Jalapa, near Vera Cruz, Mexico, less than a year after the birth of his nemesis, Sam Houston. After a rudimentary education, Santa Anna joined the Royal Army in 1810 and served in Texas, Vera Cruz, and Tamaulipas until 1821.

During the Mexican War of Independence, he backed Augustín Iturbide, when Iturbide declared himself emperor in May 1822 and occupied Vera Cruz. Later, when Iturbide's empire fell, Santa Anna

Antonio López de Santa Anna.

supported the republican government and served in San Luis Potosí and in Yucatán as governor and military commander. During this period, he helped subvert elections and assisted in defeating an attempt by Spain to recapture Mexico in 1829. After the aborted Spanish invasion, he retired to his *hacienda* in Jalapa until he was named president in 1833.

As president and de facto dictator, Santa Anna took personal command of the Mexican forces against the insurgent Texans in 1835–1836, and was responsible for the massacres at the Alamo and Goliad. He was captured after the debacle of the battle at San Jacinto on April 21, 1836, but was soon released, and in November 1836 traveled to Washington, where he was entertained at a state dinner by President Andrew Jackson. In 1837, he was recalled from retirement to command forces against a French invasion and lost a leg in battle at Vera Cruz.

In the Mexican War, after two other brief tenures as interim president, Santa Anna led his troops in the battles of Angostura and Cerro Gordo and once more assumed the presidency in 1846. After being defeated in General Winfield Scott's siege of Mexico City, he retired in exile. In April 1853, Santa Anna returned as dictator and was again exiled, for the final time, in 1855. In 1874, Santa Anna was permitted to return to his home country, but by then he was broken, blind and poor. He died in Mexico City on June 20, 1876, in penury and squalor.

In his prime, he was regarded as handsome and dashing, with dark hair and black whiskers, courtly, gracious and charming, but also ruthless and cruel. His vanity was legendary. He wore gaudy uniforms and cocked hats. He was amoral in his relations with women, and an opium addict. His opponents acknowledged his skill as a general, tactician, and charismatic leader, but were ever wary of his unscrupulous, unprincipled ambition.

"Were I made God," Santa Anna once said, "I should wish to be something more."

Santa Fe, New Mexico

Capital of New Mexico, Santa Fe was founded in 1610 by the Spanish governor of the territory, Pedro de Peralta. Most of the city's construction was performed by conscripted Pueblo Indians and Indian

NATIONAL ARCHIVES

Santa Fe, 1886.

servants brought from Mexico. The Indian laborers were housed in a suburb called Barrio de Analco, and the church built for them, the San Miguel Chapel, is considered to be the oldest in the United States.

Missionary efforts to convert the Indians to Christianity often involved assaults on the tribal culture and religion, and in 1680 this led to a bloody revolt by the Pueblos. The Indians ravaged the entire province of New Mexico, killing priests and colonists as well as burning down churches. On August 15 Santa Fe was attacked and the residents forced to flee south. The Indians remained in occupation there until 1692, at which time General Diego de Vargas led a force from El Paso to reclaim the city. Once the Indians had been driven out, Spanish settlers returned and began to rebuild.

The New Mexico province was relatively isolated from Americans under Spanish rule. When Zebulon Pike strayed into the territory on an expedition to explore the headwaters of the Arkansas and Red rivers in 1807, he was arrested and brought to Santa Fe. Once Mexican independence was granted in 1821, however, the territory opened to American trade. The increased commerce in and through Santa Fe stimulated the city's economy, and soon the Santa Fe Trail was blazed from Missouri.

In 1846, after the outbreak of the Mexican War, General Stephen Watts Kearny invaded New Mexico and easily captured Santa Fe. Kearny proclaimed the

Santa Fe is seen as a lush paradise in this railroad poster.

province an American territory, and the Treaty of Guadalupe Hidalgo, which ended the war in 1848, officially transferred New Mexico to America. During the Civil War Santa Fe was captured by Confederate forces but was soon restored to Union command. By the time New Mexico gained statehood in 1912, Santa Fe was a fully developed American city with a rich Spanish-Indian heritage.

Santa Fe Trail

Although the Santa Fe Trail (the commercial road that ran from Missouri to Santa Fe), was traversed for the first time by William Becknell in 1821, the first Santa Fe traders were two brothers from Montreal who had come down from Canada 80 years earlier. Pierre-Antoine and Paul Mallet were drawn to the fabled town (founded by Spanish conquistadores in 1610) by reports of its great riches.

The Mallets and their company of traders came by way of the Missouri and Platte rivers, lost most of their trade goods in a river crossing, and arrived at Santa Fe in the summer of 1739. To their great disappointment they found a dreary collection of wooden and adobe buildings housing a few hundred people, a pitiful garrison of poorly armed soldiers, and local authorities who treated foreigners with great suspicion. The Mallet party was not allowed to leave until instructions came from the viceroy in Mexico City, a process that took nine months. Several of the traders decided to settle in Santa Fe, and the others, including the Mallet brothers, were finally permitted to leave in May 1740.

Occasional outside adventurers, wanderers, and traders made their way to Santa Fe over the eight decades that followed. (These included explorer Zebulon Pike and his party of soldiers, who were captured and imprisoned there briefly in 1806.) But the turning point in the Santa Fe trade—and the trail that opened it up—came in 1821.

In that year, Captain William Becknell, a young veteran of the War of 1812 who had emigrated from his native Virginia to Franklin, Missouri, learned of Mexico's independence from Spain and that American traders would now be welcomed in the Mexican province of New Mexico. In September 1821 Becknell, with four partners and a pack train of trade goods, left Franklin, crossed the Osage River to the

Pioneers on the Santa Fe Trail show their weapons to ward off hostile Indians.

Arkansas, and followed it into Colorado, where he proceeded south across Raton Pass to Santa Fe. The five-month venture was spectacularly successful. Becknell returned to Missouri with a canvas sack filled with silver coins and the following spring advertised in St. Louis newspapers for a company of men "to go Westward for the purpose of trading for Horses and Mules."

Thirty men answered the call. Equipped with several wagons to carry $5,000 in trade goods, Becknell's party left Missouri in August and explored a new and shorter route into Santa Fe. The traders left the Arkansas River at a point near present-day Dodge City, Kansas, and followed the Cimarron River into New Mexico. They reached Santa Fe on November 16. The new alternate trail, known as the Cimarron Cutoff, was shorter than the one through Raton Pass but more hazardous, because water was scarce and there was constant danger of Indian attacks.

By 1824, the Santa Fe Trail and both its alternate routes were well established, and the Santa Fe trade flourished. For the first decade of the trail's existence, Becknell used Franklin, Missouri as the starting point for the 800-mile journey to Santa Fe. In 1830 he changed it to the newly founded town of Independence, 100 miles west.

From Independence, the trail led across the prairie 150 miles west to Council Grove. This was a point of final rendezvous for those who wished to join the caravans for the 575-mile trek to San Miguel, the only sizable town in New Mexico between Independence and Santa Fe. After fording the Arkansas River, those taking the Cimarron Cutoff proceeded across 60 miles of desert to the Cimarron River, crossed the Canadian and Pecos rivers and filed into Santa Fe across Glorieta Pass. The other route, which avoided the more dangerous desert country, ran westward to Bent's Fort (completed in 1833) on the Arkansas near modern-day La Junta, Colorado, then dropped over Raton Pass, and rejoined the Cimarron trail at the Mora River.

The trade caravans were made up of mule- or ox-drawn wagons, four to six animals yoked to a single wagon. These enormous "prairie schooners," many of them conestogas manufactured in Pittsburgh, were capable of carrying two tons of goods—soap, cloth, ribbons, shoes, molasses, cider, flour, sugar, whiskey, coffee, cured meats, tools, and farm implements.

Josiah Gregg, a 25-year-old lawyer in Independence who knew the Santa Fe trail from first-hand experience as a trader, wrote a classic account of the "commerce of the prairies." In it, he described the grand departures of the trade caravans out of Independence—the wagon masters crying out "All's set!" and "Stretch out!," the bellowing "Hep! Hep!" of the drivers as they snapped their long bullwhips, the creak and rumble of the cart and wagon wheels as they began their journey.

On a good day, the caravans managed to travel a

dozen miles or so. The entire trip took an average of three months, the return half that time because the wagons had been emptied of their burdens. (In 1848, a trader named François Aubrey made the return trip from Santa Fe to Independence in 8 days and 10 hours and later, traveling alone, cut that record to 5 days and 16 hours.

As the Santa Fe trade increased, Mexican government officials in the town began leveling higher taxes on the traders—as high as $500 per wagon, regardless of its size—and in 1840 they tried to restrict the trade altogether. But when Stephen Watts Kearny marched into Santa Fe in the summer of 1846 and claimed it for the United States, a new era of prosperity was inaugurated. By 1855, trade reached $5 million annually, the heaviest traffic coming during the California gold rush and the Civil War.

In the 1860s stagecoaches carrying mail and passengers made the run from Independence to Santa Fe. Traffic on the trail continued until the late 1870s, when Atchison, Topeka & Santa Fe railroad crews laid tracks over Raton Pass and into the village of Lamy. A spur line was then constructed into Santa Fe. The first AT&SF trains rolled into Santa Fe in January 1880 and the town's newspaper, *The Territorial New Mexican*, announced

OLD SANTA FE TRAIL
PASSES INTO OBLIVION.

Sarsi Indians

The Sarsis, also called Sarcees, are an Athapaskan tribe of Native Americans related to the Apaches and historically allied with the Blackfoot tribe.

Probably around the end of the seventeenth century, the Sarsis moved south across Saskatchewan in Canada and took up the buffalo hunt. When they were first encountered by whites in the middle of the eighteenth century, they were a small tribe living under the protection of the Blackfeet. The name Sarsi derives from the Blackfoot word for "no good." Though they often traveled south into Montana, the tribe continued to regard Canada as their home. They suffered constant attack by other tribes, particularly the Crees, and their numbers were further

reduced by smallpox and scarlet fever epidemics in the nineteenth century. Though they retained their separate tribal identity and language, the Sarsis adapted closely to the Blackfoot customs and ceremonies.

In 1877, the Sarsis, together with the Blackfeet and the Assiniboins, ceded their territory in Canada to the government. They were placed on a small reservation near Calgary, Alberta in 1880.

Sauks

See Sacs and Foxes

Scott, Winfield

1786–1866

Born in Virginia and educated in law at William and Mary College, Scott was commissioned as an artillerist in the regular army in 1808. By the end of the War of 1812 he had risen to the brevet rank of major general, an astonishing advance for a 28-year-old with only six years' service in the regular army.

Named commanding general of the army in 1841, Scott was highly political but a loyal officer, and a daring and innovative field commander, who planned his campaigns meticulously. He was also merciless to the incompetent, whose faults he felt ought to be "equally punished with cowardice, or giving aid and comfort to the enemy."

A skilled diplomat who negotiated Indian treaties, he helped effect the compromise over the Maine-Canada border issue with England, was influential in calming crises with the Seminoles in Florida, and assisted in the peace negotiations with Mexico. He advised presidents (including Abraham Lincoln during the Civil War) until well past his retirement in 1861. (Scott always remained loyal to the Union.)

In 1852, he became the Whig party's presidential candidate, but lost the election to Franklin Pierce, one of his subordinate officers in the Mexican War. Scott is perhaps best remembered for his command of the army in that war and the march with his 10,000-man force from Veracruz to conquer Mexico City in 1847.

Standing 6 feet 5 inches tall and wearing the resplendent dress uniform of braid, stars, and medals, Scott was a physically impressive man who earned the affectionate nickname of "Old Fuss and Feathers" from his men. He died at West Point on May 29, 1866, and is buried there.

Seattle, Washington

The largest city in the state of Washington, Seattle was settled in November 1851 by a small party of Americans who set out from Portland, Oregon, on the steamship Exact. The group landed on what is now Alki Point in West Seattle, and within a few months some of the colonists moved up to Elliot Bay on a site more suitable for permanent settlement. The town was originally called Duwamp, but this was soon changed to Seattle, after an Indian leader named Sealth. The town thrived early on in the lumber business, particularly after 1853, when Henry M. Yesler built a sawmill there that became the main source of employment.

Conflict with displaced Indians discouraged some white settlers, who departed from Seattle in the mid-1850s. Skirmishes had broken out along Puget Sound in 1855 and 1856, and in January 1856 Indians from the White River Valley attacked the city. Many Seattle citizens blamed the territorial governor, Isaac Ingalls, for Indian discontent, and in response the city ignored his proclamation of martial law. In retribution Ingalls arranged a dishonorable discharge for the entire troop of Seattle Volunteers.

The arrival of the railroad in Seattle in the 1880s helped diversify the city's economy. No longer relying solely on the timber industry, Seattle became a major port of commerce, trading heavily with Asia and Japan. Growing industrialism during World War I led to labor unrest, and in 1919 Seattle was the site of the first major general strike. Today the economy is driven primarily by the Boeing Aircraft Company, which is the largest employer in the state of Washington.

SEATTLE HISTORICAL SOCIETY

Loggers in the streets of Seattle, ca. 1880.

Seminole Indians

The Seminoles, a Muskogean tribe of Native Americans, fought three celebrated wars against the United States in an effort to prevent being removed from their tribal lands.

The Seminoles, who moved into northern Florida around 1750, are an offshoot of the Creeks. In the aftermath of the War of 1812, Andrew Jackson forced the Creeks to cede their lands in Alabama and along the Florida border in Georgia. This left the Seminoles totally isolated.

In 1817, General Edmund Gaines, commanding federal troops on the Florida border, crossed into the Spanish territory to arrest a Seminole chief accused of harboring fugitive slaves. Skirmishes ensued, and in March 1818, Jackson invaded with more than 2,000 regulars and militia. At year's end the First Seminole War was over. Spain ceded Florida to the United States in 1819.

In 1830, after the passage of the Indian Removal Act, Jackson, now President, made plans for removal of the Five Civilized Tribes, including the Seminoles,

These scouts for the U.S. Army were descended from Seminole Indians and runaway slaves.

to Indian Territory. In 1832, the Seminoles signed a removal treaty, but when removal was scheduled to commence in 1835, the Seminoles, under Osceola, resisted. The Second Seminole War (1835–1842) was one of the costliest to U.S. military forces in American history.

By 1842, most of the Seminoles had been successfully removed. A significant number, however, remained in Florida. From 1855 to 1858 the Third Seminole War was waged as the U.S. government sought to bring those who still held out under federal control. A tiny remnant, however, eluded capture and remained in the Everglades. They formed the basis of what is the Seminole tribe of present-day Florida.

Sequoyah

1755 (1775?)–1843

Sequoyah, also called George Gist, Guess, or Guest, was a national hero of the Cherokees; he developed the alphabet that allowed Cherokee to be written as well as spoken. Over the years, he has achieved mythic stature, and it is very difficult to separate fact from fiction in accounts of his life.

The son of a white father and a Cherokee mother, Sequoyah grew up to become a silversmith. Some time around 1809 he began work on a syllabary to

SE-QUO-YAH

157

Sequoyah.

put his language into written form. He fought in the Creek War (1812–1814), and afterward he became active in politics, signing one of the land cession treaties made between 1816 and 1817. He also became involved in a conspiracy to sell more land. Sometime thereafter he left the Cherokee Nation and moved to Arkansas with a group that became known as the Western Cherokees. In Arkansas he completed work on his 86-character syllabary.

Sequoyah returned to the Cherokee Nation in 1821–1822 and presented his tribe with what he called his "talking leaves." Though his people resented him for his involvement in land cessions, they nevertheless adopted his syllabary. With it, a person could learn to write in two or three days, and soon almost two-thirds of the Cherokees were literate. Sequoyah returned to the West around 1824. In 1839, he was instrumental in reuniting the Western Cherokees with the recently removed eastern band.

Very late in his life, Sequoyah undertook a journey to Mexico to persuade a band of Cherokees living there to return to their original tribal lands. He died in Mexico in August 1843.

Serra, Junípero

1713–1784

Junípero Serra was a Spanish priest who founded missions in California from San Diego to San Francisco in order to convert Native Americans to Christianity.

In 1749, Serra gave up a position as professor of theology in Mallorca to come to the Americas as a missionary. For the next nine years, he worked with the Pame Indians in the Sierra Gorda. In 1752, the Inquisition appointed him to be an inquisitor, a position he held for the next 18 years.

In the spring of 1769, despite his age and an almost crippling illness, Serra joined the Spanish expedition into California as head of its missions team. On July 1, he founded the mission of San Diego. Over the next 15 years, he blazed a bold mission-building trail, and by the time of his death there were nine missions and 18 friars in California.

Serra was pious, brave, and sincere in his efforts

Junípero Serra receiving his last communion.

with California's indigenous peoples. He often sought to mitigate the worst Spanish abuses against them. Nonetheless, he supported and authorized an evangelical system that included forced conversions, corporal punishment, and involuntary labor. Indian converts suffered a death rate of around 70 percent owing to the harsh conditions of their lives.

Serra was beatified on July 1, 1988, the anniversary of the founding of San Diego, and currently is being proposed for sainthood. But because of his record and the cruelty of the system he espoused, many Native Americans and other groups sympathetic to their feelings oppose his beatification.

Shafter, William Rufus

1835–1906

Born in Kalamazoo, Michigan, William Shafter, after a halfhearted teaching career, was commissioned a first lieutenant in the 7th Michigan Infantry in 1861. At the Battle of Fair Oaks, Virginia, on May 31, 1862, he was wounded and his horse shot from beneath him during a charge across an open field. The charge resulted in the deaths of 18 of the 22 men he led. Despite the wounds he received, he

William Rufus Shafter.

remained in the fight for two more days. For his valor he was decorated with the Medal of Honor. By war's end, Shafter had served time in a Confederate prison camp and after release was made a colonel of volunteers. He returned home, married Harriet Grimes, and while awaiting a regular army appointment, hauled firewood for a living. In 1866, he was made a lieutenant colonel.

For over a decade, beginning in 1869 when he was assigned to the black 41st Infantry in Texas under Colonel Ranald Mackenzie, Shafter served in the Southwest, fighting Indians. After the 41st merged into the new 24th Infantry and with Mackenzie's leaving to command a cavalry regiment, Shafter took command of the unit. Their mission was to fight the Comanches and Apaches raiding Texas settlements in the Staked Plains and Pecos River country. For five years he led expeditions against these raiders and explored and mapped the seldom-traveled region.

In the 1870s he was already heavy—weighing 240 pounds—and had the abrupt and abrasive manner, coarse tongue, and fiery temper that would cause him constant problems with subordinates and the press throughout his career. But he was tireless, maintained strict discipline, and established a tough schedule on the march for his officers and men. Disliked but respected by his men, who called him

"Pecos Bill," he was greatly admired by Ranald Mackenzie, whom he resembled in manner.

In 1875, Shafter commanded major expeditions against the Indians from travel routes across Texas. Two years later he led another large force against Lipan and Mescalero Apaches who rode across from Mexico to raid U.S. settlements on the border. He asked for and won permission to pursue the raiders into Mexico on the condition that he avoid Mexican troops and towns. He set a fast pace in the heat and rough country, and covering more than 100 miles in 72 hours, struck Indian camps in northern Mexico. He was sometimes pursued by Mexican troops while his superior, Brigadier General Edward O. C. Ord, watched nervously from his headquarters in San Antonio.

Shafter's hit-and-run tactics kept the West Texas frontier pacified, and the situation improved when Mackenzie returned to the border in 1878 with his cavalry regiment. Shafter was promoted to colonel of the 1st Infantry in 1879. He was assigned to Dakota Territory, returned to West Texas in 1880, and the next year played a significant role in the Lt. Henry O. Flipper affair.

Flipper, the army's first black West Point graduate, was among the officers in Shafter's command at Fort Davis, Texas. He was charged with embezzling post funds and with conduct unbecoming an officer and gentleman. (Flipper was found guilty and left the army. Later evidence seems to indicate that Flipper was innocent of the actual embezzlement but had tried to cover up the incident.)

In 1897, Shafter was promoted to brigadier general and then to major general at the outbreak of the war with Spain, when President William McKinley, Secretary of War Russell Alger, and General Nelson Miles chose him to command the Army's 5th Corps for the capture of Santiago de Cuba. Although Santiago fell after brief fighting in July 1898, the Cuban campaign was controversial. Shafter, who by now weighed over 300 pounds and was ill with gout during most of the campaign, was a target of ridicule by newspaper correspondents and cartoonists. He retired in 1901, to his ranch in Bakersfield, California. He died there from pneumonia on November 12, 1906, and was buried at the Presidio in San Francisco.

Shawnee Prophet

CA. 1774–?

Tenskwatawa (also known as Laulewasikau) was the younger brother of Tecumseh. He is most often referred to simply as the Prophet or the Shawnee prophet.

Throughout the centuries, the role of prophet has played a crucial role in the belief systems of Native American peoples. In 1762, a nameless prophet appeared among the Delawares and exhorted them to form a confederation of all Indian nations to drive whites from the land. Indians were to give up everything they had gotten from whites and return to the old ways. The Delaware prophet stated that he received this vision from the Master of Life, who promised success to all who embraced his vision. Taken to heart by the great leader Pontiac, the prophecy led to a widespread rebellion in the Great Lakes region.

In 1805, the young Laulewasikaw claimed to have had a new revelation from the Master of Life. His message was essentially the same as that of the nameless Delaware prophet. If Indians forsook white ways and drove whites from their territory, they would find favor with the divine. Game would return to their land, and their dead friends and rela-

tives would be restored to them. Laulewasikaw now took the name Tenskwatawa, meaning "the open door." (Ironically, the name derives from Jesus' saying "I am the door" in the Christian Bible.) He claimed to be the incarnation of Manabohzo, a fabled Algonquin hero. Tenskwatawa's teachings received wide acceptance. He inspired a religious revival, and gained adherents from Florida to Saskatchewan. He and his brother established a community on the Tippecanoe River, which came to be called "Prophet's Town." Tecumseh used his younger brother's words to inspire their people to revolt, eventually resulting in the Battle of Tippecanoe.

During the rebellion, Tenskwatawah sought refuge in Canada. After hostilities had ceased he returned to his Shawnee people in Ohio and moved West with them in 1827.

Sheridan, Philip Henry

1831–1888

An Ohioan, son of Irish immigrants, Philip Henry Sheridan graduated from West Point in 1853. For the next seven years he gained extensive experience in

The Shawnee Prophet, Tenskwatawa.

General Philip H. Sheridan (second from left) seated with President Chester Arthur (center) during a hunting trip to Yellowstone.

military campaigns against the Indians of Washington and Oregon. In the Civil War he made a name for himself as one of the Union's most famous and successful generals. After the war he returned to the West, leading the successful campaign of 1868–1869 against the tribes of Kansas and the Indian Territory. When William T. Sherman became commanding general of the U.S. Army in 1869, Sheridan took his place as lieutenant general heading the Division of the Missouri, headquartered in Chicago. This division embraced the Great Plains as far west as the Rocky Mountains, and to Sheridan fell the task of maintaining and enforcing the will of the U.S. government in this vast and hostile environment.

Throughout his Indian service, Sheridan feuded with the Indian Bureau and insisted on using forceful measures against any Indian resistance. In the Red River War of 1874–1875, his columns defeated the Kiowas, Comanches, and Cheyennes and ended warfare on the Southern Plains. In the Great Sioux War of 1876, after the disaster at the Little Bighorn, Sheridan's columns forced the surrender of the Sioux and Northern Cheyennes. Other hostilities under his direct supervision included the Nez Perce War of 1877, the Bannock War of 1878, and the Ute War of 1879. With Sherman's retirement in 1884, Sheridan moved to Washington as commanding general of the Army, a post he held until his death four years later.

Sherman, William Tecumseh

1820–1891

Born in Ohio on February 8, 1820, and a West Point graduate in 1840, "Cump" Sherman is remembered chiefly for his Civil War service, second only to Ulysses S. Grant among Union generals. Even so, Sherman also played an important role in the history of the West. In the years following the Mexican War, 1847–1850, he served as a young officer in newly annexed California. After his resignation from the army in 1853, he returned to pursue an unsuccessful career as a banker in San Francisco. Later he did no better as a lawyer in Leavenworth, Kansas. His western experiences, however, gave him a deep interest in the future of the West, and after

the Civil War he was in a position to influence its fortunes.

From 1866 to 1869, as lieutenant general, Sherman commanded the Division of the Missouri and oversaw the opening stages of warfare with the Indians of the Great Plains. After Grant's inauguration as president, Sherman was promoted to full general and commanded the U.S. Army until his retirement in 1884. In this post, as Indian troubles spread throughout the West, he resisted advocates of peaceful measures and urged forceful treatment of rebellious tribes. Sherman's sympathies and affections lay with the men of his little army stationed on the frontier, and he labored diligently for their welfare. In spirit as well as composition, the army in the West became uniquely "Sherman's Own."

William Tecumseh Sherman.

Sibley, Henry Hastings

1811–1891

The Detroit-born soldier and politician Henry Hastings Sibley began his career as a fur trader with the American Fur Company, after he completed his studies in law. He first clerked for the company for five years, before setting out in 1834 with Hercules Dousman and Joseph Rolette on a trading expedition for the firm, which took them to Minnesota. He built a stone house near Mendota, said to be the first residence in the state built by a white person, and from there he ran the AFC's upper Mississippi operations. Sibley became well regarded for his dealings

MINNESOTA HISTORICAL SOCIETY

At the end of the brutal Minnesota Sioux uprising of 1862, Henry Hastings Sibley sentenced approximately 400 Sioux warriors to death, after giving them extremely brief trials. President Lincoln intervened, and pardoned all but 38 Sioux, who were sentenced to hang. Their deaths are immortalized in this panorama.

at that outpost, maintaining cordial relations with the Sioux as well as with the traders who passed through.

Sibley's establishment in the fur trade served as a useful political base, as well; he was elected to Congress from Wisconsin in 1848 and from Minnesota thereafter, serving until 1853. His principal charge from his constituents was to get Minnesota organized as a territory, and he did. He was also intimately involved in the 1851 treaties in which the Sioux ceded their lands in the region to the control of the U.S. government. He would be rewarded for his efforts by being elected first territorial governor in 1857.

In 1862, Sibley was asked by Governor Alexander Ramsey to head the state militia in fighting the Sioux uprising led by Little Crow. As a colonel in the militia, he enjoyed quick success against the Indians despite a lack of cavalry forces at his disposal. He was commissioned a brigadier general of volunteers by President Lincoln, placed in command of the military district of Minnesota, and ordered to pursue the Sioux on the upper prairies of the Dakotas. He did so, routing the Indians in three separate battles in one week in July 1863. After serving on the commission that negotiated the peace treaty with the Sioux, he retired from public service, but remained active in business and civic affairs. He served as president of the state's historical society, chairman of the board of regents of the University of Minnesota, and president of the St. Paul Gas Light Company.

Sibley, Henry Hopkins

1816–1886

Henry Hopkins Sibley was a West Point graduate who fought in Florida with the 2nd Dragoons in the Seminole War in 1838–1839. He also fought effectively in the Mexican War, winning honors for his actions at Medelin. He served in the Mormon War (1857–1859) and battled the Navajos in 1860.

When the Civil War broke out, the Louisiana-born Sibley, a friend of Jefferson Davis, accepted a commission as a brigadier general in the Army of the Confederacy. Sibley had concocted a scheme to seize control of the Southwest for the Confederacy, not only securing Arizona and New Mexico, but annexing portions of northern Mexico as well. He raised an outfit called the Texas Brigade, a mixture of old frontier hands and raw recruits.

In their first encounter with Union troops, at Valverde, Sibley's men won a hard-fought and bloody victory. Rather than press their advantage and seize neighboring Fort Craig, Sibley and his men went on to Albuquerque. There the men engaged in widespread looting, which failed to endear them to the local population. The Union sent Colonel John P. Slough and his seasoned Colorado territorial troops to confront the Texas Brigade, and they defeated them soundly at the Battle of Glorieta Pass. The Texans retreated back to their home state, and Sibley spent the rest of the war as a subordinate to other general officers.

Sibley's one other contribution to American military history was a tepee-like device called the Sibley tent. It was favored by both sides during the Civil War, until it was replaced by more modern types of shelter.

Sierra Nevada

Sierra Nevada is the name of a mountain range in eastern California running 400 miles from Lassen Peak in the north to Tehachapi Pass in the south. The highest peaks are in the southern part of the range, in a region known as the High Sierra. There Mount Whitney, the highest peak in the conterminous United States, rises to over 14,000 feet. Other peaks in the range reach heights between 12,000 and 14,000 feet.

Mostly granite, the Sierra Nevada mountains were formed by a geological uplift in the Tertiary period, which caused abrupt faces of rock in the range's eastern terrain but gradual slopes in the west. The west side of the Sierra Nevada receives much more precipitation; this has sculpted deep valleys such as Yosemite and Kings Canyon. While the Sierra Nevada is drained by the Feather, Yuba, American, Merced, and Kern Rivers, no rivers actually cross it.

The Sierra Nevada ("Snowy Mountains" in Spanish), was not only an awesome spectacle for early immigrants to the Pacific Coast, but also a formidable barrier. The most popular crossing point was Donner Pass, located opposite the Nevada lakes on the route across the Great Basin. This was the site of the tragic Donner party crossing of 1846, where a group of 81 settlers were trapped in the mountains by early snowfall. Forced to camp for the winter at Donner Lake, they endured the rigors of a harsh climate and inhospitable terrain, and by spring of 1847 only 36 were still alive. Those who did survive had been forced to eat the flesh of their dead companions. Today Donner Memorial State Park commemorates the site. Other national parks in the Sierra Nevada include Yosemite, Sequoia, and Kings Canyon. Gold found in the mountains on the banks of the American River in 1848 led to the famous Gold Rush of 1849.

Singleton, Benjamin "Pap"

1809–CA. 1887

Benjamin Singleton was a prominent figure in the Exoduster movement, rallying blacks as early as 1869 to leave the South for the Kansas prairies. His "Singleton" Cherokee Colony was the first of many midwestern all-black agricultural towns, which formed as blacks sought economic and political opportunity after the Civil War.

Born in 1809 in Tennessee, Singleton spent most of his life in slavery. He escaped to Canada, then worked in Detroit, Michigan, housing fugitive slaves until the end of the Civil War. Singleton believed that he had a divine-ordered mission to remove blacks from the former slave states. He visited southeastern Kansas in 1873 and, believing that owning and cultivating land was the key to economic freedom, bought 1,000 acres of former Indian Territory. Working with the Edgefield Real Estate and Homestead Association, Singleton spread word of the new colony. In 1878 and 1879 he began conducting southern blacks to the Cherokee "Singleton" colony in Norris County, Kansas, and later claimed to have led 7,432 individuals to Kansas.

In 1881 Singleton formed and directed the United Colored Links, devoted to uniting all blacks and improving their situation. At this time, friends and family began providing annual financial support for the elderly and poor "Old Pap." This "Father of the Migration," as he called himself, believed that his mission extended to leading the migrants back to the South after it had "learned its lesson" as to how to treat its fellow brothers and sisters. Sadly, this end was never realized.

Benjamin "Pap" Singleton.

Sioux Indians

One of the largest and best known of the American Indian tribes, the Sioux appear in the popular mind as the archetype of the horse-mounted, buffalo-hunting nomads of the Great Plains. Nearly half the Sioux, however, were not Plains peoples but inhabitants of the lake-and-forest country around the headwaters of the Mississippi River. In this area, rather than the Plains, these people had achieved their identity as Sioux by the time French traders made contact with them in the seventeenth century.

They did not call themselves Sioux; that was a French corruption of what the Sioux's enemies the Chippewas called them—*nadowe-is-iw*, meaning "snake" or "adder," and thus "enemy." They called themselves *dah-kota*—Dakota in English—"friends" or "allies." For more than two centuries after the French first opened European relations with the Sioux, these people underwent cultural and demographic changes. By the early decades of the nineteenth century, the Dakotas had evolved into the people white Americans came to know during the period of the westward movement.

The Eastern Sioux, the true Dakotas, still lived in the country that later became Minnesota. From their earlier homeland, they had shifted southwest to the Minnesota River. Here they hunted the animals of the prairie and forest, fished the rivers and lakes, and harvested wild rice. They moved about mostly on foot or by canoe, relying on dogs to transport their belongings, and led a semi-sedentary exis-

Sioux women playing the "plum stone" game, similar to a modern dice game.

A Sioux encampment, with wagons captured during their many wars with the U.S. Army.

Two more distinct Sioux groupings resulted. One was comprised of the Yankton and Yanktonai tribes, sometimes known as the Nakotas from their variation of the Dakota language. Ranging the prairies east of the Missouri River, the Yanktons and Yanktonais followed the buffalo on horseback but also retained many customs of their kinsmen in Minnesota. These middle tribes were a bridge between the Eastern and Western Sioux and shared the traits of both.

Still farther west, beyond the Missouri River, the seventh of the original "council fires" of the Dakotas in turn divided itself into seven tribes. In their dialect, these Western Sioux called themselves Lakotas. They were also *titonwan*, "dwellers of the prairie," or Tetons in English. The seven Teton tribes were the Oglala (Scatters Their Own), Brule (Burned Thighs), Miniconjou (Planters by the Water), Two Kettle (Two Boilings), Sans Arc (Without Bows), Hunkpapa (Campers at the Opening of the Circle), and Sihasapa (Blackfeet—not the Blackfeet tribe that claimed lands farther to the northwest). Population statistics can only be roughly estimated for the period before the Sioux were placed on reservations. In 1780, an approximate count arrived at a figure of 25,000 people in all the Sioux groupings, while in 1904 a census counted more than 27,000.

Despite the differences between Eastern and Western Sioux, the tribes shared similar cultural traits. Society focused on kinship ties, which bound individuals in intimate personal relationships, strengthened feelings of group identity, and established families and extended families as the basic social organization. Political institutions were rudimentary, with individual freedom highly prized and governance resting on consensus and example set by the leadership rather than on a hierarchy of authority. Chiefs did not rule; they met in council and, if they could not agree, then no decision was made at that time. A well-developed spiritual life centered on the natural environment, a quest for personal awareness and strength to guide one's journey through life, and an elaborate body of rites and ceremonies. The quest for food was a constant preoccupation and was at the core of a host of beliefs and practices, both spiritual and temporal. So too with war. The Sioux fought rival tribes and later encroaching whites. Warfare gave form and direction to cultural institutions and spawned a system of honors and rewards that determined a man's station in life (for instance, the prac-

tence. Of the original seven autonomous but related Dakota groups, the Eastern Sioux included four: Mdewakanton, Wahpekute, Wahpeton, and Sisseton. Collectively, the Eastern Sioux were known as the Santees.

There were three reasons that the Sioux moved southwest. First, the food resources of their original homeland began to grow scarce. Second, the prairies to the southwest teemed with game, including buffalo. Third, their enemies the Chippewas pressed them hard. As the Sioux migrated, they acquired horses, which were spreading northwest from tribe to tribe from their source in Spanish New Mexico. Horses allowed for greater mobility and speed of travel farther west, out onto the open plains and even across the Missouri River as far as the Black Hills and the Powder River. Horses fostered the nomadic way of life and made possible a major cultural evolution. While the Dakotas retained their traditional lifestyle, the lives of the people who moved to the plains were vastly changed. Horses and buffalo made the difference.

The most intense warfare involved the people who became the Lakotas. In the late eighteenth and early nineteenth centuries, their westward surge onto the buffalo plains from Minnesota brought them into collision with one tribe after another. Mandans, Arikaras, Hidatsas, Pawnees, Omahas, Poncas, Crows, Shoshones, Assiniboins—each yielded to the powerful thrust of the Lakotas.

As these wars raged, the tribes also established trading relations with whites. Either directly or through intermediary tribes, the Dakotas of Minnesota bartered skins and furs with French traders in exchange for European manufactured goods. When the French were expelled from North America in the middle of the eighteenth century, trade continued with the British and then with the Americans. After the founding of the military post of Fort Snelling on the upper Mississippi in 1819, fixed trading posts operated by American firms served the Dakotas.

In the closing decades of the eighteenth century, traders also appeared on the upper Missouri River and opened trade with the Lakotas and Nakotas. Here the prime medium of exchange was the buffalo robe. The Sioux could trade at any one of half a dozen posts belonging to American companies on the Missouri. Fort Pierre was the most important. After 1834, the Lakotas of the Platte River country traded at Fort Laramie.

From traders the Sioux obtained arms and ammunition, metal utensils and containers, personal adornments, and other manufactures that eased the traditional way of life. By the middle of the nineteenth century, they had grown dependent on the white traders, who they generally welcomed. But the Sioux resented the growing number of settlers who followed. With the settlers came treaty commissioners. A series of treaties in the 1840s and 1850s forced the Dakotas to relinquish all their hunting grounds and withdraw to a reservation along the Minnesota River. To the west, treaties with the Nakotas and Lakotas had opened official relations with the federal government, but by 1860 only the Yanktons had given up their homeland in exchange for a reservation.

On the Minnesota reservation, the Dakotas grew increasingly dissatisfied as greedy traders and corrupt or incompetent officials made life more and more difficult. The grievances erupted in the Minnesota Uprising of 1862, which took the lives of about 400 whites. Little Crow led the outbreak and eventually paid with his life. Military forces quelled

NATIONAL ARCHIVES

An 1851 sketch of the treaty meeting during which the Santee Sioux sold their hunting grounds for $3 million.

tice of counting *coup* in battle—literally the degree to which a man put his life on the line).

War with enemy tribes was also a constant. The Chippewas pressed the Dakotas from the north and east and sparked constant fighting until the intervention of whites separated the combatants. At first the Chippewas had the advantage, with firearms obtained from French traders. Later the Dakotas armed themselves from American traders, and the conflict resolved itself into raid and counterraid.

the rebellion, hanged 38 Dakotas who were judged guilty of atrocities, and exiled the rest to bleak reservations in Dakota Territory.

The Minnesota hostilities spilled over into Dakota and involved the Lakotas. Already in 1854 the Lakotas had stood up to the U.S. Army and had been forced to back down. In 1863–1865 they fought the armies of generals Henry H. Sibley and Alfred Sully in the badlands and plains west of the Missouri River. In 1866, under Red Cloud and other chiefs, they blocked the Bozeman Trail to the Montana goldfields and wiped out the command of Captain William J. Fetterman. The Treaty of 1868 ended the Red Cloud War and set up the Great Sioux Reservation for all the Lakotas. Many, however, under Sitting Bull, Crazy Horse, and other "nontreaties," remained in the buffalo ranges to the west. Here in 1876 they fought the last of the Sioux Wars. At the Little Bighorn they triumphed by destroying the command of Lieutenant Colonel George A. Custer, but in the end were forced to surrender by U.S. Army troops swarming over their domain.

By 1881 all the Sioux had been confined to reservations in Dakota Territory. Here the government tried without success to transform them into copies of white farmers. The once great Sioux nation's last gasp of protest occurred in the Ghost Dance of 1890, which ended with the terrible bloodletting at Wounded Knee. Today, the Sioux still live on these reservations, a proud but impoverished people who continue to nurture their tribal identity and preserve many of their rituals and traditions.

DENVER PUBLIC LIBRARY

Charles A. Siringo.

Siringo, Charles A.

1855–1928

Charles Siringo was a cowboy, a Pinkerton detective, and an author. Born in Matagorda County, Texas, Siringo, by his own account, worked as a cowboy from the age of 16 when he got a job on Abel H. "Shanghai" Pierce's Rancho Grande spread in Wharton County, Texas. Siringo joined the Pinkerton Detective Agency in the 1880s and spent 20 years as a range detective. Among his famous exploits were chasing Butch Cassidy's Wild Bunch and testifying during the Coeur d'Alene, Idaho, labor riots of 1892.

Siringo wrote the first cowboy autobiography, *A Texas Cowboy, or Fifteen Years on the Hurricane Deck of a Spanish Cow Pony,* in 1885, a book the author claimed eventually sold a million copies, and followed it with such other popular, self-published reminiscences as *The Cowboy Detective, A Lone Star Cowboy,* and *Riata and Spurs.*

He died in Hollywood, California, on October 19, 1928.

Sitting Bull (Tatanka-Iyotanka)

CA. 1831–1890

Hunkpapa Lakota Sioux chief Sitting Bull was widely admired by all the Sioux people for his military, political, and spiritual leadership. In the late nineteenth century he emerged as the symbol of Indian resistance to the white westward movement. He remains today one of the best known and most significant Native American leaders.

Sitting Bull was born into the Hunkpapa tribe of the Lakota (or Teton) Sioux, one of the seven separate tribes that made up the Lakotas, who ranged the buffalo plains west of the Missouri River and north of the Platte River. Sitting Bull's birthplace was probably on Grand River in present South Dakota. Initially named Jumping Badger, Sitting Bull took his father's name at age 14 after counting his first coup on a Crow Indian and entering the warrior ranks. (Counting coup was a system of acknowledging bravery in the face of danger. Indian braves carried coup sticks. To touch an enemy with a coup stick counted so many points. To wound an enemy counted for so many more. To kill an enemy in face to face combat and remove his scalp counted for even more.) In warfare with enemy tribes, he compiled a superior record that led to his designation, in 1857, as a war chief of the Hunkpapa tribe. At the same time, he mastered the sacred mysteries and ceremonies and became a holy man. His life was characterized by a profound spirituality. He exemplified the four cardinal virtues of the Lakotas: bravery, fortitude, generosity, and wisdom. His name, fame, and influence spread to the other six Lakota tribes.

Sitting Bull first caught the attention of whites in the 1860s. With the discovery of gold in 1862 in western Montana, whites appeared on Hunkpapa lands in increasing numbers, and the Lakotas were provoked into war. In 1863–1864 Sitting Bull and his warriors fought Generals Henry H. Sibley and Alfred Sully in Dakota, and in 1865 they skirmished with columns of General Patrick E. Connor in the Powder River country to the west. From 1865 to 1870 Sitting Bull directed special venom against the military posts of the upper Missouri River.

The Treaty of 1868 divided all the Lakota tribes into factions, one which advocated accommodation to white authority, the other resistance. The more

DENVER PUBLIC LIBRARY

Sitting Bull.

peaceful faction settled on the Great Sioux Reservation in western Dakota and accepted government rations regulations. Those who chose the path of resistance remained in the unceded Indian territory to the west, the buffalo ranges of the Powder River country. Sitting Bull was the leading chief of the "nontreaty" Lakotas, who government officials labeled "hostiles."

A staunch foe of all government programs, Sitting Bull disdained treaties, agents, rations, or anything that interfered with the old life of following the buffalo and warring against enemy tribes. His friends designated him head chief of all the nontreaty Lakotas. For eight years, with the staunch backing of the Oglala war chief Crazy Horse, Sitting Bull held together an alliance of Lakota and Northern Cheyenne tribes that pursued the ancient free way of life.

After 1870, Sitting Bull and Crazy Horse adopted a purely defensive policy. They would fight only when their homeland was invaded. In 1873, in the

Yellowstone Valley, they warred on surveyors of the Northern Pacific Railroad and their military escort. The next year, the discovery of gold in the Black Hills and the resulting gold rush infuriated the Sioux. The Black Hills lay within the Great Sioux Reservation, which until then had been guaranteed by treaty; the Indians turned aside government efforts to buy the hills and vowed to fight in their defense. The Black Hills issue led directly to the Great Sioux War of 1876.

In the face of three armies converging on the Sioux country, Sitting Bull reached the zenith of his power and leadership. At a sun dance early in June 1876, he experienced a mighty vision of enemy soldiers falling upside down into camp, an image that anticipated a stunning defeat for the U.S. Army. At the Battle of the Rosebud on June 17 the Sioux dealt General George Crook a severe setback. Then, in the Battle of the Little Bighorn, Sioux and Cheyenne warriors wiped out Lieutenant Colonel George A. Custer's command and achieved the great triumph Sitting Bull had foretold. As an "old-man" chief, Sitting Bull did not play a major role in this battle. His significance lay in holding together and imbuing with his spirit of resistance the tribal alliance that defeated Custer.

In this victory lay the seeds of defeat. The Little Bighorn disaster shocked white Americans and led to a massive counteroffensive. By the spring of 1877, most of the fugitive tribes had surrendered. Not Sitting Bull. He and other diehards sought refuge in Canada. He remained there for five years. Oddly enough, he got along well with the redcoats of the Northwest Mounted Police. But the buffalo were vanishing, and the Sioux experienced increasing hunger and finally starvation. His ranks thinned by defections, Sitting Bull surrendered at Fort Buford, Dakota Territory, on July 20, 1881.

After two years as a prisoner of war, Sitting Bull was allowed to rejoin his people at the Standing Rock Agency. There he encountered the government's "civilization" programs, which sought to force Native Americans into a white lifestyle. For seven years Sitting Bull stubbornly insisted on his right to remain an Indian, while Indian Agency representative James McLaughlin just as stubbornly demanded that all his charges embrace white ways. This turmoil, combined with the loss of still more reservation land, led to the culmination of the Ghost Dance resistance movement of 1890. Sitting Bull emerged as the leading apostle of the Ghost Dance at Standing Rock. McLaughlin and the military authorities decided that he had to be removed from the reservation. On December 15, 1890, Indian police surrounded his cabin on Grand River. His followers resisted, and in a bloody shootout Sitting Bull and others were killed. Today Sitting Bull is remembered as one of the greatest of all Indian chieftains—

SITTING BULL IS DEAD.

The Old Chief and Seven of His Followers Killed in an Engagement with Police.

Sitting Bull was Preparing to Start for the Bad Lands and His Arrest was Ordered.

The Indian Police Start From Yates, Followed by Two Companies—Cavalry and Infantry.

When the Arrest was Made, Sitting Bull's Followers Attempted a Recapture.

In the Fight That Ensued, Sitting Bull, His Son and Six Indians were Killed.

On the Other Side, Four of the Police were Killed and Three Wounded.

The Cavalry Then Arrived on the Scene, and the Indians Fled Up Grand River.

A Lengthy Account of Major McLaughlin's Last Trip to Sitting Bull's Camp.

He's a Good Indian Now.

CHICAGO, Dec. 15.—At 9 o'clock to-night, Assistant Adjutant General Corbin of General Miles' staff received an official dispatch from St. Paul, saying Sitting Bull, five of Sitting Bull's men and seven of the Indian police have been killed. Thirteen casualties were the result of the attempt by the Indian police to arrest Sitting Bull.

HOW IT HAPPENED.

ST. PAUL, Dec. 15.—The report was received in this city this afternoon that Sitting Bull had been killed by the Indian

BISMARK, NORTH DAKOTA DAILY TRIBUNE

A North Dakota newspaper rejoices at the demise of Sitting Bull.

a leader of distinction and a patriot whose refusal to surrender his principles cost him his life.

Slavery in the West

Slavery was an accepted institution on the frontier from the arrival of the first black slaves at Jamestown in 1619. Black slaves had accompanied the conquistadors on their inland journeys, but those "imported" to the Jamestown colony represented the first permanent slave presence in America.

In colonies where slaves were numerous, they worked in gangs under an overseer, at a social and sometimes even physical remove from the slave-owners. As the United States grew and the frontier moved west, the institution of slavery in the South evolved toward its more familiar plantation-based character.

But western frontier conditions were different. On the early American frontier, most settlements were embattled and hence needed defense. This reality affected the forms that slavery took. After a brief experiment in which slaves were used as militiamen against Indian attack, white Southerners reasoned that arming slaves was not in their best interest. So, they drastically curtailed their freedom, particularly in those areas of the South where Spanish colonists were encouraging slaves to run away to Florida. Instead, in areas where slaves were few in number, they worked under conditions similar to those of free labor, often side by side with white laborers.

In the West the economic stability that existed in the South was absent, and there was no great need for a large body of slave labor. Moreover, western white laborers argued that slave labor took their jobs and depressed wages. Particularly during the California gold rush—where there was no entrenched local slave-owning political base—this argument had considerable weight.

Among Native Americans, many Creeks and Seminoles were slaveholders; but Native American slaveowners exerted little control over their slaves, and runaway slaves from the white South lived independently among the Native Americans in Florida. When the Seminole Wars broke out (the First Seminole War was ostensibly triggered by the fact that Spanish-held Florida was serving as a refuge for runaway slaves), former black slaves allied with the Creeks and Seminoles were among the most tenacious opponents that the U.S. Army would face.

Even before the birth of the United States as a nation, there was argument over whether the newly formed federal government would have the power to regulate or prohibit slavery in the West. In 1787, the Continental Congress concluded a five-year debate over whether slavery would be permitted in the Ohio and Northwest Territories and arrived at a complicated compromise measure, the "Ordinance for the Government of the Territory Northwest of the Ohio River."

Between the 1820s and the Civil War, the status of slavery in the western territories became the single most divisive political issue in the nation, especially as westward movement came to dominate the economic life of the United States. Various attempts at compromise, all ultimately unsuccessful, are well documented.

From the Missouri Compromise in 1820 right up to the Kansas-Nebraska Act of 1854, every attempt to legislate a solution to the slavery question in the West served only to exacerbate regional conflict between the North and the South, and to postpone the inevitable day when the nation was forced to choose slavery or to oppose it.

Smith, Jedediah

1799–1831

The West's greatest trailblazer was born in Bainbridge, New York, and raised in Erie County, Pennsylvania, and the Western Reserve of Ohio. He received some rudimentary education and a strong Methodist upbringing and was working as a clerk on a Lake Erie freighter when he decided to go west.

He reached St. Louis in 1822 and read William H. Ashley's advertisement in the St. Louis *Missouri Gazette* seeking "Enterprising Young Men" to ascend the Missouri River. Smith was taken into the group of trappers formed by Ashley and his partner, Andrew Henry, that included Thomas Fitzpatrick, Hugh Glass and Robert Campbell.

In the spring of 1823, after the group had wintered at Fort Henry at the mouth of the Yellowstone River, Smith was sent back to St. Louis to gather

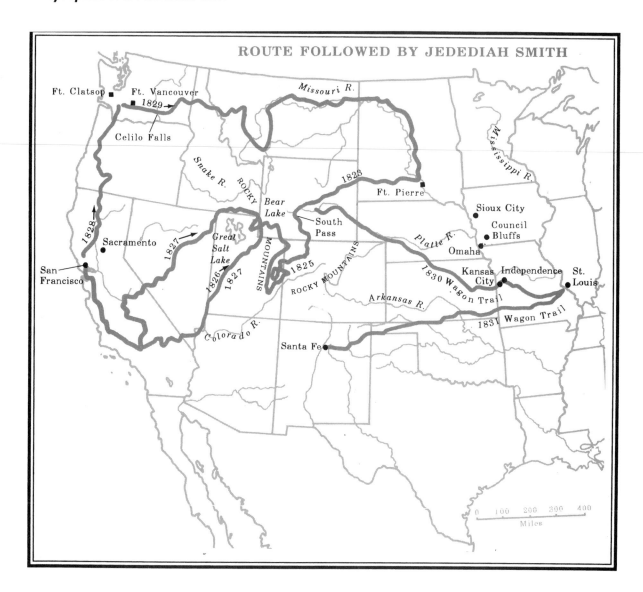

ROUTE FOLLOWED BY JEDEDIAH SMITH

supplies and horses and to bring Ashley back to Fort Henry. During the return trip, the group poled two keelboats up the Missouri and stopped to trade with a band of Arikaras, then were attacked by the Indians. Twelve of Ashley's men were killed, 11 wounded. Smith, sent ahead to inform Henry of the attack, joined the band of trappers that returned and attacked the Arikaras on June 1, 1823.

In the fall of that year, Smith and a party of 12 of Ashley's trappers, including James Clyman and Tom Fitzpatrick, crossed the plains south of the Yellowstone to search for new beaver grounds. During this expedition, Smith was mauled by a grizzly bear, had his ear sewn back in place by Clyman, and bore the scars of the encounter the rest of his life.

In subsequent ventures, Smith and other Ashley men pioneered what became known as the Oregon Trail, and after several successful trapping seasons, joined David Jackson and William Sublette in a partnership after Ashley's retirement.

Smith's explorations included the great venture in August 1826 from Utah to the Colorado River, then across the Mojave Desert and into the San Gabriel Mission in southern California, the first overland crossing of the southwestern route to California. Although he was ordered by Mexican authorities to leave California, he stayed the winter of 1826–1827 in the San Joaquin Valley, trapped along the Stanislaus River, and with 15 men crossed the Sierra Nevada and the Great Salt Desert in time to attend the July 1827 rendezvous on Bear Lake on the present-day Utah-Idaho border.

In 1827, Smith and 18 others again headed for California. At a Mojave Indian village on the Colorado River crossing, half his party was killed. The others pushed on, retracing their earlier trail, arriving on the Stanislaus on September 18. After being jailed briefly at the San José Mission and spending the 1827–1828 winter in southern California, Smith and his men resumed their journey northward, reaching the Klamath River in Oregon in May 1828. In July, on the Umpquah River, Kalawatset Indians attacked Smith's party and killed 14 of his men. The remnants of his expedition reached Fort Vancouver in August and returned to the upper Rockies the following spring.

After he and his partners sold their trapping interests in 1830, Smith returned to St. Louis and lived in semi-retirement. But in 1831 he organized a caravan of 22 wagons and 74 men for a trading venture to Santa Fe. In late May, in the desert country between the Arkansas and Cimarron Rivers, Smith and his old friend Tom Fitzpatrick rode ahead of the wagon train to search for water. At some point, Smith split off from Fitzpatrick and disappeared. Indians in Santa Fe later reported Smith had been attacked by a party of Comanches and killed.

Jedediah Smith was a tall, clean-shaven, humorless man who neither smoke, drank, or used profanity. His constant companion was his Bible, from which he frequently read aloud when on the trail. So compelling was his personality he was referred to as Mr. Smith or Captain Smith even by his trail-hardened comrades. He was the greatest of all the mountain men and his pioneering expeditions opened the gateway from the South Pass of the Rocky Mountains to the Pacific Coast and blazed the trails from the Colorado River to California and from California to the Columbia River.

Smith, Joseph

1805–1844

Founder of the Church of Jesus Christ of Latter-Day Saints (Mormons), Joseph Smith was born in Sharon, Vermont. He moved with his parents to Palmyra, New York, in 1815, and to a farm in Man-

LIBRARY OF CONGRESS

Missouri locals attack a Mormon settlement in Independence, Missouri, forcing Joseph Smith and his followers to leave.

chester, New York, a center of religious revivalism, in 1819.

About 1823, Smith testified that he was visited by an angel named Moroni who gave him the task of finding and deciphering certain ancient texts he discovered in the form of golden plates on a hill called Cumorah on the outskirts of Palmyra in 1827. These plates, written in what he said was "Reformed Egyptian," when translated by Smith with the aid of certain optical relics buried with them, told the story of an ancient people who lived in North America before the time of Christ.

Smith said he had been commanded by God to publish the translation and "bring forth and estab-

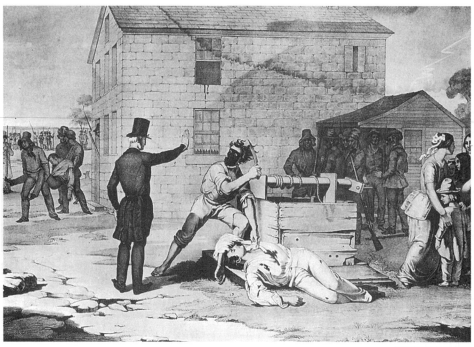

The murders of Joseph and Hyrum Smith, as imagined by artist G. W. Fasel.

lish the cause of Zion." He dictated the text, sitting behind a screen, to several friends who served as scribes. The *Book of Mormon* (Mormon was the angel Moroni's father and historian of the lost Israelites who, the golden plates revealed, had colonized North America in 600 B.C.) was published in March 1830, and created a sensation: Smith was accused of being a liar, a false prophet and a fake, but a month after the publication, he and his small band of followers founded the Church of Jesus Christ ("Latter-Day Saints" was added later) in Fayetteville, New York.

As the church grew, Smith moved his headquarters to Kirtland, in the Western Reserve of Ohio, then to Jackson County, Missouri, then back to Kirtland. In 1839, a move was made to Nauvoo, north of Quincy, Illinois, on the Mississippi River. The migrations were usually preceded by new revelations on the direction of the new religion and the conduct of its members (such unorthodox ideas as communal property and theocratic governance), by divisiveness among the church's members and leadership, and by persecution from "gentiles," non-followers of the religion.

It was in Nauvoo that Smith revealed to his inner circle the most controversial of all the church's early doctrines, that of plural or "celestial" marriage—that a man might have as many wives as he could support. It was a doctrine which, although not publicly revealed for several years, was an open secret and practice and which alienated members and brought public wrath down on the heads of Smith and his Mormon followers. (Smith himself married Emma Hale, who was to bear him eight children, in 1827. He was said to have been "sealed" to as many as 60 other women.)

The 1837 failure of a bank he founded in Kirtland, Ohio, his announcement that he intended running as a candidate for the U.S. presidency in 1844, the actions of disaffected former church members and other controversies over his leadership caused Smith and his loyalists great turmoil in the first decade of the Mormon movement. But the church prospered and is believed to have had about 35,000 members by the time of his death.

In Illinois, when former church members began work on a newspaper, the *Nauvoo Expositor*, that exposed the practice of polygamy, Smith ordered the paper destroyed. He and his brother Hyrum were arrested on charges of arson and jailed in the nearby town of Carthage. There the two were killed by a mob of state militiamen on June 27, 1844.

Brigham Young, president of the church's Quorum of Twelve Apostles, led an exodus of some 16,000 church members—popularly called "Saints"—from Illinois in February 1846. After spending some time in Iowa and Nebraska, Young and his people arrived in the Salt Lake Valley on July 24, 1847, where the church has its headquarters to this day. Young was named president and prophet of the church in the year it found its "Zion."

Smoky Hill Trail

This trail was one of the three important routes (along with the Platte and Santa Fe trails) to the gold fields used by the prospectors of the Colorado gold rush of the late 1850s. Although the shortest, the Smoky Hill Trail was in many ways the least hospitable of the three, crossing arid plains from the Smoky Hill River, along the Big Sandy Creek, to Cherry Creek and down into Denver. The trail was forged by would-be prospectors in 1858, and had no landmarks, water, or food along its entire length. Travelers quickly nickname it "the Starvation Trail."

The land on which much of the trail was located ostensibly belonged to the Cheyennes, and had been their prime hunting ground. With hordes of gold-seekers constantly encroaching on the land, the buf-

falo herds that had once been plentiful in the area moved elsewhere. Any pretense of co-existence between the miners and the indigenous peoples ended when a group of miners raped the women in a neighboring Arapaho camp.

A government report (drawn up well after the encroachment of prospectors was well under way) stated that the use of the trail by whites was based on the Fort Laramie Treaty of 1851, which guaranteed right of transit over Indian lands. However, the so-called travelers often blatantly seized possession of the land, on the pretext of looking for gold, then established towns, farms, and roads. The inevitable result was violent conflict, with stage stations on the trail repeatedly attacked and burned and wagon trains devastated. When the Kansas Pacific began to lay track along the trail's route, General William Sherman and the U.S. Army took up the role of protecting it from further Indian attacks.

The completion of the railroad served an even more important purpose for the U.S. Army. It allowed for the swift movement and deployment of troops, and these troops would eventually contribute to the demise of the Plains Indians.

Snake River

The Snake River, the largest tributary of the Columbia River, rises in Yellowstone Park and flows through Wyoming, Idaho, Oregon, and Washington.

Shoshone Falls in the Snake River.

As the river runs along the border between Idaho and Oregon, it flows through Hell's Canyon, the deepest gorge in North America and one of the deepest in the world. The canyon stretches for 125 miles; it averages 5,500 feet in depth, reaching a maximum of 8,000 feet in certain areas.

Lewis and Clark were the first white men to encounter the Snake River when they traveled it from the Clearwater to the Columbia River during their expedition to the Pacific coast in 1805. American and Canadian trappers soon followed to exploit the rich trapping lands of the Northwest. Fort Henry, built in 1810, was the first trading post built on the Snake. It was constructed by Andrew Henry near present-day St. Anthony on a small tributary that now bears his name. Several other posts followed, including one built by fur trader Nathaniel Wyeth. Named Fort Hall, it was located on the Oregon Trail route and became an important outpost for emigrants making the journey to Oregon and California.

Settlement in the Snake River basin increased significantly after gold was discovered near Boise in 1862. The area's Mormon population also grew when many Mormons traveled north to obtain land made available through the Homestead Act of 1862.

Today, wildlife abound in and around the river. Several national parks along wildlife migration routes serve as game preserves. The Snake River, which is dammed in several places, is also used for irrigation and is a source of electric power.

An acre of turf was usually needed to construct a sodhouse.

stances, shingles would be used for a roof if the home builder had them. Sometimes wood would be used for floors or interior supports, on those rare occasions when a farmer had access to lumber.

Sod houses had both advantages and disadvantages. In the extreme hot and cold climates of the prairie, the soddies provided good insulation. The earthen bricks kept the homes cool in the summer and warm in the winter. However, there was no natural lighting inside sod homes and they were generally damp as well. Families living in sod houses were usually not the only residents. The sod bricks made a good home for insects, mice, and snakes. Cleaning the area surrounding the sod home helped eliminate mice, but not much could be done to stop fleas or lice from moving in.

When wood became more easily available for house building on the prairie, sod homes were generally turned into storage facilities or stables.

Sod Houses

Sod houses were homes on the prairie that were built out of sod.

With no plentiful source of wood for constructing homes on the vast, open expanses of prairie, resourceful pioneers learned how to make houses out of sod from the earth. Building sod houses—also known as "soddies"—was a simple process. First the ground would be plowed in furrows to loosen the earth. Sod bricks, generally measuring one foot by two feet (and sometimes one foot square), would then be cut. These earthen bricks were piled up like standard bricks to form the walls of the soddy. The roof was made of grass or hay thatching. In some in-

Sooner

The term "Sooner" was applied to someone who moved into federally released lands before it was legal to do so; usually these were reserved lands in Oklahoma.

The term predates the great Oklahoma land "run" of 1889. It originally referred in a derogatory manner to those people who jumped the gun on the release of what had previously been Indian lands.

A couple poses proudly in front of their sod home.

Today, the term has lost its pejorative connotation, and in fact, Oklahoma proudly carries the nickname of the "Sooner State," which suggests that this sort of early-bird initiative fits squarely in with the American frontier pioneer tradition.

Sourdoughs

Of all the important gold and silver rushes in western history, perhaps none exacted a greater toll in physical suffering on its participants than the Klondike gold rush of 1898. Would-be prospectors faced brutal cold and hazardous mountain routes to the goldfields. To stick it out under such conditions took an iron will and a strong constitution. Yukoners only gave the honorific "old-timer" to those who had been in the territory prior to 1898, and all newcomers were known as Cheechakos—tenderfeet—until they had seen their first winter. Forced to sit out the winter in their cabins, prospectors were heavily reliant on sourdough as a baking ingredi-

ent, as the fermented dough was kept from one baking to start the next (instead of using fresh yeast). Therefore, those who lived through the rugged Yukon winter and saw the break-up of the Yukon River icepack, heralding the arrival of spring, earned the respect of other Yukoners and the nickname "Sourdoughs."

South Pass

South Pass, a 20-mile-wide pass across the Continental Divide, was a crucial gateway to the far West through which hundreds of thousands of settlers passed.

Situated in Wyoming's Rocky Mountains, South Pass rises gradually from the Wyoming Basin to an elevation of 7,550 feet above sea level. The first whites to travel through South Pass were a party of Astorians led in 1812 by Robert Stuart, all of whom were returning from the Pacific Coast. However, the pass remained unknown to most white travelers until 1824, when friendly Crow Indians introduced it to Jedediah Smith. Smith's discovery of South Pass made it possible for supply wagons to reach trappers along the Green River and beyond.

The pass was used extensively by settlers traveling to Oregon and California. B.L.E. Bonneville drove the first wagon train through in 1832. Between the years 1841 and 1853 an estimated 150,000 people crossed through South Pass, including Mormons en route to Utah and Forty-niners rushing to the gold fields of California. Many thought that the first transcontinental railroad would use the pass to cross the Great Divide, but a more suitable location was found farther south by an expedition Jim Bridger conducted in 1849–1850.

When gold was discovered in the Sweetwater district in 1870, South Pass City sprang to life. Although its days as a boom town were short-lived, the city gained fame when Esther Morris became the first female justice of the peace in America.

Southern Pacific Railroad

The Southern Pacific Railroad extended all the way from New Orleans to California. Upon the Central Pacific's completion, Collis P. Huntington, Charles Crocker, Leland Stanford, and Mark Hopkins (the Big Four) decided that rather than get out of the railroad business, they would turn their attention toward developing the western region of their railroad empire. To this end they acquired first the California Pacific, an important link from Sacramento to San Francisco, and then the Southern Pacific.

The Southern Pacific was originally chartered in 1865 to run from San Francisco to San Diego. In 1870 Huntington took control and began building southeast to San Bernardino; the railroad reached Los Angeles in 1876. By the end of the following year the Southern Pacific controlled 85 percent of all railroad mileage in California. When the Southern Pacific connected with the Sante Fe in Demming, New Mexico, in 1881, it became the nation's second transcontinental railroad. Subsequently the company gained control of several smaller railroads and acquired direct access to New Orleans.

The Southern Pacific, with its many branches, wound its way into almost every phase of California's economy and consequently acquired the nickname "the Octopus." The West Coast could be reached easily from the East via water, a competitive alternative to transcontinental rail. But inland and mountain routes lacked such an alternative, which gave the Big Four a transportation monopoly in the form of the Southern Pacific. The concentration of economic control in one company gave rise to strong commission regulation in California beginning in 1880.

After Huntington's death in 1900, Edward Harriman acquired a controlling interest in the Southern Pacific. The railroad continued to grow, and today operates as one of the most prosperous in the industry.

St. Vrain, Ceran de Hault de Lassus de

1802–1870

St. Vrain was a fur trapper and trader. Born in St. Louis County, Missouri, St. Vrain began his career as a clerk for Bernard Pratte and Company before forming a partnership with François Guerin and entering the New Mexico fur trade. After a successful trip to Taos, St. Vrain dissolved the partnership and returned to St. Louis, then went back to Taos for more trading. He pursued his career in the New Mexico trade successfully for several years, and in 1832 went into partnership with Charles Bent.

The firm that was born of that pairing, Bent, St. Vrain and Company, became one of the most successful in frontier history. Their business amounted to as much as $40,000 annually, ranking them second only to the American Fur Company. In 1834, they erected Bent's Fort, one of the most famous outposts of the fur trade, ten miles above the mouth of the Purgatoire River. It quickly became a major commercial center for the military, the trappers, and the Native Americans of the Southwest, in no small part because of its proprietors' reputation for honest and intelligent business dealings.

St. Vrain acquired a huge land grant in New Mexico in 1844, and he later helped organize a force at Santa Fe to put down the Taos rebellion. He and

Ceran St. Vrain.

William Bent, but he left the partnership in 1850 as he began to diversify his interests. He invested successfully in real estate, banking, mills, and even publishing. He also served with mounted volunteers against the Jicarilla Apaches in 1855 and as a colonel in the 1st New Mexican Cavalry in 1861.

Stagecoach

The stagecoach (a "stage" being a fixed point on a route) of the Old American West was an outgrowth of the English-styled coaches in use in the East from colonial times to carry passengers, mail, and freight. Although western stagecoaches were manufactured in Troy and Albany, New York, Salem and Worcester, Massachusetts, and elsewhere, the famous Concord model, first made by the Abbot, Downing & Company of Concord, New Hampshire, in 1826, was considered the Cadillac of coaches, the one Mark Twain described as "a cradle on wheels." The firm manufactured up to 2,000 coaches a year in peak years, and each cost from $1,200 to $1,500.

The Concord, made of hickory and steel with

Bent also gave considerable information to General Stephen Kearny when the general was en route to New Mexico at the outset of the Mexican War.

After Charles Bent was murdered in 1847, St. Vrain reorganized the firm in partnership with

Stagecoach travel, in the days before railroads.

Poster advertising the Oregon Line's Portland, Oregon, to Sacramento, California, overland route.

brass trimmings, typically weighed 3,000 pounds. Its boatlike body swung on four 3"-thick leather shock-absorbing "thoroughbraces." Two-horse teams of four to six horses drew the coach. The reins were split at the forward end and attached to each side of the horse's jaw so that a single pull directed the two-horse team at once. The driver used the reins as whips and also often carried a long-lashed whip to pop above the heads of his teams.

The driver sat on the right-hand side of the "box," the prowlike point of the coach body, six feet off the ground, where the handbrake was located. The front edge of the coach served as a backrest and the seat was built into the body to give the driver the benefit of the thoroughbracing. The left side of the seat was for an armed guard, who generally carried a shotgun. To provide some light for night travel, oil lamps were set in brackets on either side of the driver.

There were three bench seats inside the coach: two facing forward and one facing back, and each capable of seating three passengers. The middle seat had no backrest; its occupants hung on to leather straps attached to the ceiling. Middle seat passengers dove-tailed their feet with those across from them.

Passengers were generally limited to 25 pounds of baggage (and paid extra for more). It was carried on the railed roof, on a hinged platform at the rear of the coach, and in a leather "boot" under the driver's feet. A compartment under the driver's seat contained a strongbox.

The passenger coaches were varnished or painted, Concords typically in red and gilt. The coach was entered via hanging steps. Some models had glass windows, but most had open windows with canvas curtains.

Travelers were cautioned not to smoke strong tobacco, spit on the leeward side, use profanity, or lean on neighboring passengers. Suggestions for stagecoach travelers: carry a heavy blanket, do not discuss politics or religion, do not overgrease your hair before boarding (dust will stick to it).

A stagecoach traveling from St. Louis to San Francisco commonly made the trip in about three weeks, traveling night and day, and stopping at inns and stations along the route for meals, rest, and change of horse teams. Average speed was 4–5 miles an hour. Passenger fare for this trip was $200.

The great era of the stagecoach effectively ended with the arrival of railroads in the West, but the coaches remained in use in remote areas, for both passengers and freight, until after the turn of the century.

Stampedes

One of the most feared of the hazards encountered during a cattle drive was a stampede; a sudden and uncontrolled run by the herd. It was also one of the most difficult problems to avoid; all it took to start a stampede was one frightened animal, and the rest of the herd would follow in a frantic dash. Stampedes could happen anytime on the trail, day or night. There were even stampedes at the end of a cattle drive. Uncontrolled animals would run madly through town streets, much to the terror of local citizens. Once it had started, it was up to cowhands and their horses to slow the stampede down and to contain it.

Almost any unexpected movement, sight, or sound could set a nervous steer off and running. A bolt of lightening or clap of thunder was a common cause of stampedes. Even such seemingly innocent factors as a honking flock of geese, the flare of a lit match, or the clank of a cooking pan, all could start a stampede. Western artist Charles Russell wrote of stampeding herds "Nobody knows why they run but the cows, an' they won't tell."

Once a stampede had begun, all the cowhands whipped into action. The raced their horses to the front and sides of the herd in an attempt to slow down the cattle and bring them under control. Surprisingly, stampeding cattle made little noise, other than the enormous thundering of their hooves.

It was rare for range riders to be killed in stampedes. Generally, if a man fell off his horse, the cattle would run around the fallen cowboy rather than trample him.

Cowboys took certain precautions to curtail stampedes. One unusual approach was to sing lullabies to the cattle at night, soothing them with soft music. Another method was to try to identify the cattle most easily spooked. It was not unusual for these animals to congregate together. Cowhands would separate these nervous animals from the herd and in some instances even sew their eyelids shut to prevent the steer from seeing anything unexpectedly. The stitches usually came apart and healed by the time the cattle drive was over. If nothing else worked, the animals were destroyed.

Stanford, Leland

1824–1893

Leland Stanford was a railroad magnate, governor of California, a U.S. Senator, and a philanthropist. Born Amasa Leland Stanford in Watervliet, New York, to a prosperous and large family, Stanford was admitted to the bar in 1848 and began private practice in Wisconsin. At that time, his father presented him with a private law library that was reputed to be the finest in the United States north of Milwaukee.

In the meantime, his brothers migrated to Cali-

fornia, where they were successful in the mercantile trade. When a fire destroyed his office and library, Stanford decided to join them. He was moderately successful in business, then embarked on a career in politics, and attained the governorship of the state in 1861. His chief task as governor was to keep California in the Union. He also approved several public grants to the transcontinental railroad.

It was in this venture that Stanford made both his reputation and his fortune. Leaving office in 1863 (at the time, governors only served two-year terms), he turned his attention to the Central Pacific Railroad, eventually becoming its president, a position he held until his death. He also was one of the organizers of the Southern Pacific in 1884, and served as its president for five years. A key figure in the building of the transcontinental railroad, he contributed immeasurably to the success of the two companies he headed. In 1885 he returned to politics, winning election to the U.S. Senate, where he served until his death. In 1885, he founded and endowed Leland Stanford Junior University—today Stanford Univer-

STANFORD UNIVERSITY MUSEUM OF ART

Leland Stanford, seated, left of tree, and his family.

sity—which was named for his son, who died at age 15.

Starr, Belle

CA. 1848–1889

Outlaw Belle Starr was born Myra Belle Shirley in Carthage, Missouri, where her father was a farmer and tavern owner. Her twin brother Ed was allegedly a captain under Quantrill and sought after by Union troops. Belle was arrested as a courier for the Confederate irregulars on her birthday in 1862. She was released and tried to warn her brother, but he was ultimately killed.

In 1864, the Shirleys moved to Dallas, where

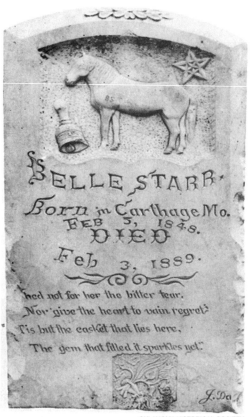

Belle Starr's gravestone, decorated with a horse, bell, and star.

Belle took up with Cole Younger, and bore him a child. Much to her father's dismay, Belle then married bank robber Jim Reed in 1866, had a daughter by him in 1869, and helped him in his criminal career. The couple moved to escape the law in 1870 after Jim was implicated in a killing. They went to Los Angeles, where she bore him a son, and after they returned to Texas, he was killed by a fellow gang member in 1874 or 1875.

Belle left her children with her mother and pursued an outlaw life. She was arrested for horse theft in Dallas and lived with a succession of male outlaws before marrying Sam Starr, a Cherokee. They moved to the Indian Territory where she ran a hideout for fugitives and served as a "fixer" with local authorities. She and Sam were arrested for horse theft in 1883 and she had the dubious distinction of being the first woman ever tried by "hanging judge" Isaac Parker for a major crime. She served five months in a federal prison in Detroit. In 1886, Sam was killed in a gunfight in Oklahoma. Belle took up with another outlaw, Jim July. When he was arrested and brought to trial in Fort Smith, Arkansas, Belle followed him part of the way there, but abandoned the pursuit. On her way back home, she was ambushed and killed by persons unknown.

Since her death, Belle's reputation has rested largely on the heavily fictionalized story of her life written by Richard K. Fox, a dime-novel author. He compared her to Cleopatra and Joan of Arc. Hollywood treatments of her life have been no less fanciful.

Steamboat

These were the boats that plied the great inland waterways and rivers of the United States in the late eighteenth and early nineteenth century. They were powered by steam engines attached to huge side or stern paddle wheels.

In 1787, a man named John Fitch developed the first steamboat for use on America's waterways. Within three years, Fitch was transporting passenger and freight between Trenton, New Jersey and Philadelphia, Pennsylvania. Although Fitch ultimately went bankrupt, America had already begun to rely on his invention. By 1807, designer Robert

This steamboat, Far West, *delivered supplies to General Custer.*

Fulton adapted the paddle wheel to his own fleet of ships. Fulton's business was a success and his name became synonymous with the steamboat.

With many rivers to be found in the western territories, steamboats quickly became an essential mode of transportation and spawned a vast network of trade and burgeoning cities. The Mississippi River, stretching from Minnesota to New Orleans, was crowded with steamboats traveling from one end to another. Canals were dug to connect the rivers, thus easing the way to transport goods out West. Small towns for receiving and shipping freight sprang up along rivers in their wake. Steamboats carried all sorts of goods ranging from cotton to whiskey to cattle. Because of the enormous amount of steam belched out by the engines, steamboats were nicknamed "floating volcanoes." They relied on wood to fuel their voracious steam engines, and many enterprising waterside dwellers up and down the rivers sold lumber to the steamboat crews. This much-needed source of power usually went for $3 a cord.

Steamboats were a prized way for the wealthy classes to travel. The most extravagant steamboats were more like floating hotels, complete with a variety of amenities. Many steamboats served as floating casinos. Professional gamblers often worked boats on the Mississippi River before heading West to ply their skills.

Steamboat expedition on the Colorado River.

The boilers that powered the ships occasionally exploded, posing a danger to both passengers and crew members. Lawsuits were often filed by survivors when loved ones perished during these steamboat explosions.

Piloting a steamboat was considered an art as much as a science. A good steamboat captain knew what to expect from river currents and depths and how to approach coming shallows and rapids. A good pilot could expect to make between $150 to $250 per month, which was considered a handsome salary for the times.

Many legends have built up around steamboats, thanks in large part to the writings of American novelist Mark Twain. Twain even took his pen name from the depth soundings made by river pilots. "Mark Twain" meant a two-fathom depth. In addition to the steamboat lore in his classic books *The Adventures of Tom Sawyer* and *The Adventures of Huckleberry Finn*, Twain penned an autobiographical account of his own days as a cub steamboat pilot, *Life on the Mississippi*.

Sublette, Milton Green

1801–1837

A mountain man and one of the five Sublette brothers associated with the fur trade, Milton Sublette, the second eldest, was born in Kentucky in 1801. The Sublette family migrated to Missouri Territory around 1817 where Philip, the father, was a tavern keeper. Milton started as a fur trader by accompanying Ewing Young on the Gila River expedition in 1826. During the expedition, the governor of New Mexico, Manuel Armijo, confiscated their pelts based on questionable legal charges. Sublette, a large, muscular man, managed to escape with his share of the pelts. The following year he joined the Pratte-St. Vrain expedition which ventured into the Rocky Mountains.

In August 1830 Milton Sublette formed the Rocky Mountain Fur Company with four partners, Thomas Fitzpatrick, James Bridger, Henry Fraeb, and Jean Baptiste. In the following years he fought in the battle of Pierre's Hole in 1832, and married a

Shoshone Indian, Mountain Lamb. He joined trader Nathaniel Wyeth, traveling with him extensively in Blackfoot country. In April 1834, Wyeth called upon Sublette to captain a caravan of 70 men from Independence, Missouri, but Sublette was forced to turn back due to an aggravated leg injury. The Rocky Mountain Fur Company dissolved that year, but Sublette maintained a partnership with Fitzpatrick and Bridger.

Sublette sought medical treatment for his leg in St. Louis in 1834, but the following year it was amputated. Within a few months, however, he was off on another fur expedition in the mountains. He died at Fort Laramie, Wyoming on April 5, 1837.

Sublette, William Lewis

1799-1845

Born near Stanford, Kentucky, William Sublette was the eldest child in a family of mountain men. He began his long career in the fur business by going along with General William Ashley's 1823 trapping expedition on the Missouri River. William luckily escaped an attack by Arikara Indians on the expedition which took the lives of 15 trappers. He returned with Colonel Henry Leavenworth's 200-man punitive army that did not completely resolve the problems with Arikaras.

Later in 1823, William Sublette joined Jedediah Smith's pathbreaking trip to the Rockies, which did not proceed along the known routes on rivers but instead found new overland trails. Their journey brought fur trading to new areas. In 1824, Sublette accompanied Smith's expedition that took them to South Pass, a trip which opened up the Green River to trappers. By 1825, William and the rest of Smith's party travelled all the way northwest to areas controlled by the Hudson's Bay Company. In 1826, General Ashley sold his fur company to Sublette, Smith, and David Jackson.

From 1827 to 1830, he travelled northwest from St. Louis several times to trap. In 1830, he became the first person to bring wagons to the northern Rockies when he returned to his trapping territory there with supplies loaded in them. In 1832, he was wounded in a battle with Blackfeet Indians at Pierre's Hole. He left trapping behind in 1836 when he settled down in St. Louis on a farm and later became involved with politics. He died of tuberculosis in Pittsburgh on July 23, 1845.

Suffrage

See Women's Suffrage

Sutter, John A.

1803–1880

John Sutter's story is a hybrid of two American classics: European immigrant makes good in the New World, generous man is destroyed by the greed of others. Sutter was born in Germany of Swiss parentage. After a term in the Swiss Army, he went into the dry-goods business and married. Unfortunately, both of these ventures turned out badly: His

OAKLAND MUSEUM

John A. Sutter.

marriage was unhappy and his business failed, leaving him with large debts. In 1834, he emigrated to America.

Traveling first from New York to St. Louis, then to Santa Fe, Oregon, Honolulu and Sitka, he finally arrived in San Francisco in 1839. At the time, northern California was the farthest piece of Mexican territory, and Sutter offered his services to the Mexicans to establish a fort at the junction of the American and Sacramento Rivers. He became a Mexican citizen and Governor Alvarado made him the largest land grant possible, nearly 50,000 acres.

Sutter was nothing if not industrious. He planted wheat, fruit trees, and vineyards, built an impressive fortress, and encouraged immigrants to join him at what he now called New Helvetia. He was somewhat less than true to his word to Alvarado, offering military aid to his chief political opponent, Micheltorena, in exchange for a further land grant, twice the size of the first one. In addition, he bought up Russian holdings at Bodega and Fort Ross.

From 1841 to 1848, Sutter's Fort was a key stopping point for wagon trains from the East. Sutter's growing power and his endorsement of American interests (after a brief contretemps with John Frémont, in which that impulsive general seized the fort), led to growing suspicion of him in Mexican circles. But it was not his political intrigues or his own expansionist dreams that destroyed Sutter.

His downfall began simply enough, with the decision to construct a sawmill on the American River. His partner, carpenter James Marshall, found some bright, metallic stones in the stream behind the mill, still under construction. After consulting his library, Sutter realized that Marshall had found gold. As soon as word of the find leaked out, a mad international dash for promised riches began. Sutter's workmen deserted him to look for easier money, and the *rancho* was ruined by squatters who killed his cattle and destroyed his fields.

By 1852, Sutter was bankrupt, too broke even to reclaim his stolen land. He petitioned Congress repeatedly—though unsuccessfully—for redress. From 1862 to 1878, he received a pension of $250 a month from the California State Legislature, which he regarded as only fair since he had helped bring so many people to the state. Sutter died, impoverished, but his memory is kept alive by the state historical monument that was his fort, now in Sacramento.

Sutton-Taylor Feud

Also known as the DeWitt County War, the Sutton-Taylor feud was a lengthy and bloody series of altercations that broke out in 1869 when someone killed rancher Buck Taylor and another family member near Cuero, Texas. The killings triggered a factional war that divided DeWitt County for another seven years, long after both the Suttons and Taylors had ceased to be involved directly. As the *WPA* (Works Project Administration) *Guide to Texas* notes, "Men were killed in their fields, on the roads and in their homes. There were shootings and hangings in all sections of the county, and many citizens were aligned with one faction or another."

Two forces for peace intervened repeatedly in the running battle. The first was Judge H. Clay Pleasants, one of the few neutrals in the county. On more than one occasion, Pleasants dispersed mobs from one faction or the other with nothing more than a shotgun and his own nerve.

The second force came from outside the county: the Texas Rangers. Led by Captain Leander McNelly, a soft-spoken Confederate veteran who suffered from consumption, a detachment of Ranger volunteers rode into DeWitt County in 1874 to enforce the courts work fairly and put a damper on the violence. McNelly found himself facing two veritable armies, with each side able to produce 150 or more armed men on short notice. McNelly, by his own account, felt that he had achieved little in DeWitt County, but the brief presence of the Rangers meant that someone was willing, for however short a time, to enforce the law evenhandedly.

Perhaps the most infamous name to emerge from the Sutton-Taylor feud was John Wesley Hardin. Hardin, a notorious killer, was briefly aligned with the Taylor faction in the feud.

Swedish Settlers in the West

One could argue that the very first immigrants to the Americas were either Swedish or Norwegian, as Norse sailors came to these shores at the end of the first millennium B.C.E. (before the common era). However, these voyagers didn't stay long enough to qualify as permanent residents, and it would be almost 700 years later that another Swedish attempt was made to establish a presence in North America.

Sweden enjoyed a brief period as a major force in European politics during the Thirty Years War. It was at that time that the Swedes made a brief effort to colonize America—in 1638 a settlement called Fort Christina was founded on the Delaware River near what is now Wilmington. The first arrivals were soldiers and traders, but the following year the Swedes sent some farmers down the river valley. However, in 1655 the Dutch conquered New Sweden, such as it was. Sporadic Swedish immigration would continue through the colonial period. The primary contribution that Swedish (and Finnish) immigrants made to colonial life was the construction method by which log cabins were built, adopted from similar means used in Scandinavia.

It was in the nineteenth century that a Swedish influx occurred that would have a lasting effect on

LIBRARY OF CONGRESS

Swedish-American railroad workers.

the frontier. Unlike the earlier colonial immigrants, the nineteenth-century arrivals were mostly middle-class people, mixed with a scattering of soldiers and adventurers, who traveled to America on Swedish ore ships in the 1840s. Toward the end of the decade, another influx, this time of land-owning farmers, took place, lasting into the middle of the 1870s. The nature of the Swedish immigrant population changed again in that decade, when more agricultural laborers arrived; then as the century drew to a close, a more urbanized type of Swede made its way to American shores. The vast majority of these men and women settled in the wheatbelt of the Midwest, particularly in Minnesota and Illinois, although there were large urban enclaves as well.

What drove Swedish immigration was economic pressure in the old country caused by a rapidly expanding population coupled with a limited supply of arable land. The vastness of the Plains states must have been very inviting to ambitious young Swedes dreaming of farms of their own. The passage of the Homestead Act of 1862, with its promise to the set-tler of affordable land, served as an additional spur. After that, the familiar pattern of "chain emigration" occurred, with one set of immigrants encouraging the next wave to come over and settle.

Swedish-Americans fought valorously for the Union during the Civil War. They were particularly well represented in Minnesota's volunteer units, many having been recruited by Colonel Hans Mattson. One of Sherman's subordinate generals was a native Swede from Illinois, Carl Stohlbrand. Undoubtedly the most famous Swedish name of the period was that of Captain John Ericsson, who designed the Union ironclad, the *Monitor.*

The Swedish-American population played an active part in the general westward movement of settlers from the 1849 Gold Rush on. However, the most familiar contribution that the nineteenth-century frontier Swedish-American made was in agriculture. To a large extent, it was Swedish men and women who farmed the frontiers in Minnesota, Wisconsin, and Illinois, feeding a growing nation as it expanded to the West.

T

Tabor, Horace Austin Warner

1830–1899

A mining magnate who amassed a huge silver mining fortune in Colorado, Horace Tabor built extravagant opera houses in Denver and Leadville, and erected the first skyscraper in Denver, called Tabor Block. After being mayor of Leadville he became lieutenant governor of Colorado from 1879 to 1883, and finally served as a United States senator in 1883.

Tabor was born in Orleans County, Vermont, in 1830. He grew up in the East and learned the stone-cutting trade from his brother. In 1855, he went to Kansas, ran for the legislature on the Free Soil Party ticket and won. He married Augusta Pierce in 1857, and inspired by tales of the Pike's Peak gold rush traveled to Denver two years later with his new wife and son. Tabor enjoyed some mining success, and soon opened stores in Buckskin Joe and Oro City. During the Leadville rush of 1870, two miners financed by Tabor discovered the Little Pittsburgh mine, and gave Tabor one-third of the find. Other mining investments flourished and he became a multimillionaire. During his time of prosperity, Tabor divorced his first wife Augusta and married Elizabeth McCourt ("Baby") Doe.

Tabor's mines remained prosperous during the 1880s, but poor investments in Mexican and South American mining ventures took a toll on his fortune. By the end of the decade, reduced production in his mines, together with the crash of 1893 and the repeal of the Sherman Silver Purchase Act (which

LIBRARY OF CONGRESS

Horace Austin Warner Tabor.

had committed the government to buy 4 million ounces of silver a month), forced Tabor into bankruptcy. He managed to secure a position as the Denver postmaster in 1898, in which he served until his death one year later.

Taos, New Mexico

Taos is a Pueblo village in north-central New Mexico; it is also known as San Geronimo de Taos.

Inhabited since about 1350, the pueblo is only three miles from the New Mexico town of the same name. By the eighteenth century, it was one of only four pueblos (along with the Acoma, Isleta, and Picuris) that had not had to relocate due to incursions by the Spanish. Taos Pueblo was in the forefront of opposition to the invaders, however, and took an active role in the Pueblo revolt of 1680.

In 1847, a few members of the pueblo revolted against the United States and killed the new American governor, Charles Bent. The gesture was seen as support for the Mexicans. The United States, which was generally more involved with the Apaches and Navajos, retaliated, killing 150 Taos Indians and burning their church.

Around the turn of the twentieth century, Taos learned that some of their land was to be set aside as a national forest, and they petitioned the government for its exclusive use. In 1906, 130,000 acres of the pueblo's most sacred lands were set aside for the preserve. To the horror of the Taos people, these lands were used by non-Indians for grazing and tourism. They engaged in a legal battle that lasted more than 60 years for the return of Blue Lake, their most sacred site. In 1970, the Taos people regained Blue Lake by an act of Congress.

Taylor, Zachary

1784–1850

A military leader and 12th president of the United States, Zachary Taylor gained notoriety in the Mexican War, and his military successes helped boost him from relative obscurity to the presidency.

Born in Montebello, Virginia, on November 24, 1784, Taylor was fortunate by birth—his family was prominent throughout the state—but received little benefit from the connection: he was raised on the frontier and received little formal education. In 1808 he joined the army and served initially in Virginia. During the War of 1812 he gained distinction in the Indiana Territory for turning away a large force of Indians in defense of Fort Harrison. This led to his appointment as commander of various frontier posts, following which (in 1832) he led the First Infantry Regiment in the Black Hawk War. In 1837–1838 Taylor served in the Seminole War, winning a key

WEST POINT MUSEUM

General Zachary Taylor, third from left, with his troops near Monterrey.

victory at Lake Okeechobee. This achievement earned him a promotion to brigadier general, along with the nickname "Old Rough and Ready."

After serving at Fort Smith, Arkansas, from 1841 to 1844, Taylor commanded the military department of the Southwest. In 1845 President Polk ordered him to defend the newly annexed Republic of Texas against Mexican invasion, and on July 23 he sailed with 1,500 troops from Louisiana to Corpus Christi, where he built a camp on the Nueces River. In the spring of the following year Polk ordered Taylor to advance his forces into the disputed area between the Nueces River and the Rio Grande. Within a few weeks the Mexican army crossed the Rio Grande and attacked Taylor's troops, prompting Congress to declare war on May 13, 1846.

Taylor won several unexpected victories in the early stages of the war, and on June 29, 1846, he was given a gold medal and promoted to major general. From this point on, however, throughout the rest of the war, his military strategy was questionable. After capturing Monterey, Mexico, in August, Taylor found that he had depleted his supplies. Consequently he granted Mexican general Pedro de Ampudia an eight-week armistice and allowed him to retreat with most of his arms and ammunition. This move was considered a major strategic error, drawing intense criticism from Polk. Then, although Polk ordered him to assume a defensive position, Taylor pressed on and won an unexpected victory at Buena Vista when attacked by Santa Anna.

When the Mexican War ended, Taylor emerged a national hero despite Polk's disfavor. Campaigning on the Whig ticket with Millard Fillmore, he won the November 1848 presidency in a three-way race with Democrat Lewis Cass and Free Soil candidate Martin Van Buren. Taylor had little political experience and was soon at odds with many members of Congress over the annexation of New Mexico and California, particularly following his support of the Wilmot Proviso, which stated that the territory annexed from Mexico should be closed to slavery; Southern states were especially angered when he encouraged New Mexico and California to enter the Union as free states. After attending a ceremony to lay the cornerstone of the Washington Monument, Taylor died suddenly on July 9, 1850. The cause of death was originally given as cholera, but a theory of arsenic poisoning led to the testing of his exhumed remains in 1991 (the tests proved negative).

Tecumseh.

Tecumseh

CA. 1768–1813

Tecumseh (also spelled Tekamthi and Tecumtha) was a Shawnee leader whose resistance to settlers and the western frontier from Kentucky to the Indiana Territory in the early nineteenth century was so fierce it has been called the "First American Civil War."

The son of a chief, Tecumseh lost two brothers fighting against the white settlement. He became an unrelenting foe of white expansion and is reported to have declared that the very sight of a white man made his skin crawl. As soon as he was old enough, he too became a warrior, fighting settlers on the western frontier.

In 1805, Tecumseh's brother, Laulewasikaw, had a vision, which he said came from the "Master of Life." Its message was similar to the revelation of the Delaware prophet in 1762, which declared that Native Americans were to forsake white ways and

to drive all whites from their territory. If they did this, the vision promised that they would find favor. Game would return to their land, and their dead friends and relatives would come back to life. After his vision, Laulewasikaw changed his name to Tenskwatawa, "The Open Door," but he is most often called simply the Prophet or the Shawnee Prophet. His message spread rapidly and gained adherents from Florida to Saskatchewan in Canada, changing to accommodate the beliefs of local tribes.

The Prophet's teachings also inspired his brother, Tecumseh, who envisioned a grand confederacy of all the Native American tribes united to fight further white encroachment. A gifted orator, whom whites likened to Henry Clay in "fiery eloquence" and to Daniel Webster in "clear-cut logic," Tecumseh made long trips to proselytize for the Prophet's message and to seek allies. He met with the Delawares, Iroquois, Miamis, and Wyandots in the Ohio Valley; the Ojibways, Ottawas, Sac and Foxes, and Winnebagos around the Great Lakes; the Five Civilized Tribes in the Southeast; and the Iowas, Kickapoos, Osages, Potawatomis, and Sioux on the Plains. He traveled to Canada several times and crossed over the Mississippi. Not all the tribes agreed to join him. Some felt that to resist the whites was suicidal. Others refused to surrender some of their individual tribal sovereignty to become a part of such a diverse confederation. Still, he made remarkable progress, and from the Great Lakes to the Gulf of Mexico he laid the foundation for the broadest alliance in Native American history.

In late 1809, William Henry Harrison, governor and Indian superintendent of the Indiana Territory, forced a treaty on the tribes of that area. The land cessions it dictated infuriated Tecumseh. Hundreds of Native Americans converged on his homeland at Tippecanoe in the Territory. In August 1810, Tecumseh met with Harrison to protest the agreement. A series of meetings ended inconclusively, and Tecumseh undertook another journey to rally support among Native American tribes. During his absence, in late 1811, Harrison marched Prophet's Town, his village, and destroyed it. This success made the governor a national hero (years later he would be elected President on the slogan "Tippecanoe and Tyler too").

Isolated pockets of resistance resulted, but the massive campaign Tecumseh envisioned never materialized. When the War of 1812 began, Tecumseh joined the British, commanding a force that fluctuated between 1,000 and 3,000 warriors. He was instrumental in the capture of Detroit. In 1813, Tecumseh was killed in action at the Battle of the Thames River in Canada.

Tepee

See Native American Dwellings

Teton-Dakota Indians

See Sioux Indians

Texas Rangers

In the mid-1820s, after Stephen F. Austin established his colony of emigrants at the confluence of the Brazos and Colorado rivers in newly independent Mexico's northern province of Coahuila y Texas, settlers formed "ranging companies" for protection against Karankawas, Cherokees, and later the most feared of all the Texas tribes, the Comanches. These Indian-fighting militiamen, many of whom subsequently served in the Texas war of independence of 1835–1836, were the first Texas Rangers.

In 1835, the year Mexican president Antonio López de Santa Anna proclaimed himself dictator and overthrew the Constitution of 1824 which had opened the door to colonization of Texas, the Rangers were officially organized in the colony's capital of San Felipe de Austin. In the "Consultation" of November 3, 1835 (a month before the defeat of Mexican forces in San Antonio and less than four months before the battle of the Alamo), 58 prominent Texans declared their intent to seek restoration of the 1824 Constitution and, among lesser matters of business, formally organized the Texas Rangers.

The original force of 25 men was soon expanded to three 56-man companies to be deployed on the Indian frontier between the Brazos and Trinity rivers. Their territory was later expanded westward to the Guadalupe River. They were paid $1.25 a day, provided their own horses and arms, and patrolled their vast territory as soldiers and law enforcers to protect Texans against Indian and Mexican raiders.

The Rangers played a notable role in the defense of the fledgling Republic of Texas, and the Republic period gave rise to some of the great heroes of Ranger history: Ben McCulloch (1811–1862), the Tennessee frontiersman and friend of Davy Crockett's who fought at San Jacinto and died in the Civil War battle at Pea Ridge, Arkansas; William A. A. "Big Foot" Wallace (1817–1899), a huge Virginian (6 feet 6 inches tall, 240 pounds in his prime, and wearing a size-12 boot) who became a Comanche captive, buffalo hunter, Mier Expedition veteran, stagecoach driver and authentic Texas legend; and John Coffee "Jack" Hays (1817–1883), another Tennessean who fought Comanches at Plum Creek in 1840, Mexicans at Monterey in 1847, and became sheriff of San Francisco and a founder of the city of Oakland, California.

A detachment of Rangers took part in the disastrous Mier Expedition of 1842. In this venture 700 Texans under General Alexander Somerville captured the north Mexican towns of Laredo and Guerrero. In retreating to the Rio Grande, about half of Somervell's army advanced on the obscure village of Mier near Camargo. The commander of this force ignored warnings that the town was garrisoned by 2,000 Mexican soldiers. The Rangers—experienced in being outnumbered and wise to impossible odds—quit the field and returned to Texas before the fighting started on Christmas Day. Those who remained were forced to surrender: 17 were executed by Santa Anna's order and the 158 others were marched to Mexico City, where they imprisoned for nearly two years.

Colonel Jack Hays organized and commanded the Rangers who fought with Zachary Taylor and Winfield Scott in the Mexican War, and it was Hays who was ultimately responsible for the reputation for brutality the Rangers earned in the war. Samuel Chamberlain, a Bostonian and dragoon private in Taylor's

E.A. WRIGHT

Texas Rangers.

army, described the Rangers in his postwar memoirs as men with "uncouth costumes, bearded faces, lean and brawny forms, fierce wild eyes, and swaggering manners," who were "fit representatives of the outlaws which make up the population of the Lone Star State."

To the Mexicans, the Rangers were *Los Tejanos Diablos* (Texas Devils), a name especially appropriate after the capture of Mexico City in September 1847, when, after one of their number was killed on a city street, the Rangers rampaged throughout the capital, killing 80 citizens in retaliation. One significant development in the war and its aftermath came about from the efforts of Ranger Captain Samuel H. Walker. In 1846 Walker, a San Jacinto veteran, was sent by Hays to Paterson, New Jersey, to work with Samuel Colt on refinements to the handgun Colt had patented in 1836, modifying the weapon into a quicker-firing, easier-loading, and more dependable sidearm. The Walker Colt was introduced in 1847 and used by the Rangers in the Mexican War. Samuel Walker, who had fought with the Rangers throughout the war, was at the besieged city of Puebla in September 1847. On October 9, leading four companies of Rangers in a charge against Santa Anna's army in the village of Huamantla, Walker was killed.

After the Mexican War the Rangers returned to patrol the new state of Texas as they had patrolled it as a Republic, concentrating on ending the persistent Comanche threats in the east, south, and north. One spectacular example of this work involved another Ranger legend, Captain John S. "Rip" Ford (1815–1897), a tough frontiersman, newspaperman, state senator and sometime physician from South Carolina who commanded scouts for Jack Hays in the Mexican War and whose nickname (from R.I.P.—Rest in Peace) came from the death notices he sent to families of Rangers killed in the war.

In 1858 Ford, with a force of 215 made up of Rangers, militia, and Indian "friendlies," tracked a party of raiding Comanches to the Canadian River in Oklahoma and attacked a village of 300 Comanches, killing 76, taking 18 prisoners and 300 horses while only two of his own men were killed.

Rangers were also involved in bringing to an end the border raids by the renowned "freebooter" and rustler Juan Nepomuceno Cortinas, a Mexican who fought against Zachary Taylor, and who gained notoriety as a sort of Robin Hood of Mexico for his breaking Mexican citizens out of Texas jails. In 1859,

Texas Rangers, with Colonel Hays, center front, in a white shirt.

Cortinas and his small band took the Texas town of Brownsville and were chased by Rangers under Captain W. C. Tobin who captured and hanged a Cortinas lieutenant. After Brownsville was recaptured, a force of Texas troops, including 120 Rangers, routed Cortinas and his 350-man force at Rio Grande City, killing 60 of the insurgents. Cortinas escaped but was defeated again the next year by a Ranger force under Rip Ford. (The ever-elusive Cortinas subsequently became governor of Tamaulipas and died in Mexico City in 1894.)

In the Civil War and Reconstruction era, the Rangers, seldom numbering more than 500 men, continued their pursuit of Indian raiders, outlaws, cattle rustlers, bandit gangs, train and stagecoach robbers, and various feuding Texans, bringing to bay such notable outlaws as Sam Bass, King Fisher and, trailed all the way to Pensacola, Florida, John Wesley Hardin.

In this era, the Ranger legend grew. One of many stories about them concerned a town so terrorized by an outlaw gang that the town fathers called in the Rangers. A single Ranger rode into town and was asked, "Where are your men? We need at least a company of 'em." "Why?" the lone Ranger asked, "You've only got one mob."

The Texas Rangers were reorganized in 1935, in their centennial year, as a branch of the Texas Department of Public Safety. They remain active today, the oldest law enforcement agency in America.

Texas, Republic of

1836–1845

On March 1, 1836, five days before the fall of the Alamo, at the town of Washington-on-the-Brazos, northeast of San Antonio de Bexar, a group of influential Texans declared the independence of Texas from Mexico. A few days later, this group elected Sam Houston commander-in-chief of the Texas Army (which was virtually nonexistent), drafted a constitution, and named an interim government with David G. Burnet as president and Lorenzo de Zavala as vice president.

On the following April 21, Houston defeated Santa Anna at San Jacinto in a battle that ensured independence, and in October Houston was elected president of the Texas Republic and gained U.S. recognition for the new "nation" the following year.

Austin, Texas, in 1840.

The Farmersville, Texas, booster club promotes its town.

The republic claimed 242,594,560 acres of land (about 180 million of which was unoccupied) stretching from the Sabine to the Red rivers in the east and the Rio Grande in the west. The occupied territory had a population of about 30,000.

Houston's problems as president of this vast and largely uninhabited land included food shortages, Indian depredations, fear of a counterattack from Mexico to reclaim the territory, and governmental bankruptcy. His primary goal was to win annexation by the United States—a more formidable task than Houston and the other fathers of Texas independence imagined. From the beginning, annexation was opposed in the U.S. Congress by abolitionists who characterized Texas as a southern slavocracy. (There were about 5,000 slaves in Texas in 1836, most of them laboring in cotton growing and ginning.) President Andrew Jackson extended diplomatic recognition to Texas on his last day in office, but the question languished during the term of office of his successor, Martin Van Buren, who rejected all annexation petitions.

Houston was succeeded as president in 1838 by Mirabeau B. Lamar, who believed Texas would prosper independent of the U.S. government. He secured diplomatic recognition from England, France, the Netherlands, Belgium, and several German states, attempted to strengthen the republic's army to defend against Indian raiders and possible Mexican invasion, concentrated on building roads and schools, negotiating loan and trade treaties, and laying out

the new capital city of Austin. Despite these efforts, Lamar's administration was largely a failure and the republic's finances were in desperate straits when Houston was reelected president in 1841.

Some of Houston's acts in his second administration were more symbolic than effective—he cut his salary in half and refused to live in the two-story mansion Lamar had built in Austin—but he also cut spending by a tenth of what his predecessor had authorized, from $5 million to $500,000 in the three-year presidency, and renewed the petitioning for annexation. (During Houston's second presidency, Mexico made a last attempt to win back its lost province. In September 1842, a Mexican army of 1,400 men under General Adrian Woll (1795–1875), a French-born soldier-of-fortune, captured San Antonio de Bexar and held it for nine days until a force of 600 Texas Rangers commanded by Captain Jack Hays decoyed Woll from the city and into an ambush on Salado Creek. The Mexicans lost 60 men and retreated across the Rio Grande.)

Houston was succeeded as president in 1844 by Anson Jones, who worked assiduously on two compelling problems: pacifying the Indian tribes, particularly the Comanches, and working toward securing annexation. The outlook on annexation problem improved markedly with the election of President John Tyler, a southerner and outspoken supporter of bringing Texas into the Union. But a treaty of annexation presented to the U.S. Senate in April 1844, providing for Texas to be admitted to the Union as a territory, was rejected.

When James Knox Polk of Tennessee was elected president on November 5, 1844, Tyler interpreted this as a mandate for annexation and recommended that Congress adopt Texas as a state of the Union by a joint resolution. This measure passed both houses of Congress and Tyler signed the document on March 1, 1845, a few days before leaving office. On October 13, the annexation ordinance and state constitution were approved in Texas. President Polk signed the act admitting the State of Texas into the Union on December 29, 1845. Anson Jones, last president of the Texas Republic, relinquished office on February 19, 1846, to J. Pinckney Henderson, a lawyer who had served as Houston's attorney general and who was now first governor of the state.

Timber (Lumber) Industry

Prior to 1900, the timber industry was concentrated in the timberlands of the Great Lakes and the southern states; even as late as the post–Civil War era, massive lumbering interests were centered around the immense pine forests of Michigan and Wisconsin. The lumber industry also thrived in the eastern states, if on a smaller scale, as it had from the beginning of settlement in the eighteenth century.

In the early development of the western lumber industry, empires were often built by buying from public lands for as little as 10 cents an acre, or simply by squatting on public lands, cutting trees, and moving on to new forested areas. Awaiting the axes and saws of the lumberjacks and the rapacious eye and deep pockets of the lumber magnates were the seemingly endless forests of the Pacific Slope. Here, stretching from Canada into northern California, was a 1,200-mile-long, 20-to-150-mile-wide belt of lush forests of pine, fir, cedar, hemlock, spruce, redwood, and other usable trees, with another vast region of forest lands running along the western slopes of the Rocky Mountains.

While the lumber business was prominent and profitable on the Pacific Coast for decades before its boom years after 1900, there were no truly large-scale operations in this region until railroad magnate James J. Hill sold 900,000 acres (1,400 square miles) of tim-

A log boom on a Oregon slough.

berland, mostly Douglas fir country, to the Weyerhaeuser Timber Company in 1900 for $5.4 million.

After this the Pacific Slope—the western Rocky Mountains, the Sierra Nevada and Cascade ranges and on to the Pacific coast—became a lumberman's heaven. By 1905, 52 million more board feet of lumber—Douglas fir, Ponderosa pine, and redwood chief among the trees cut—was shipped from this region than from the Great Lakes.

Public and governmental criticism of the ex-

Loggers at work on a redwood.

UNIVERSITY OF OREGON LIBRARY

A log train in Washington.

ploitation of American forests by rapacious lumber companies began in the 1870s, after a half-century of uncontrolled cutting. In 1878, for example, the U.S. Department of Agriculture reported that eastern lumber companies were responsible for fires that consumed 25 million acres of timberland annually through such careless operations as leaving behind the waste of deforested areas—sawdust and dried branches—which acted as tinder for lightning or any errant spark. (In 1871, around Peshtigo, Wisconsin, a forest fire with just such an origin killed 1,000 people as it devastated the area.)

Similar findings blighted the reputations of large-scale lumbering operations from coast to coast in the early era of the industry. Water-powered mills built on rivers and streams were polluting and clogging the waterways with flumes built to channel logs to the mills and finishing plants and by dumping tons of sawdust into streams and rivers. (Rivers as large as the Sacramento and Columbia were often clogged in this manner.) Other criticism centered on the trails slashed through virgin forests for the traffic of men and wagons, the lack of replanting, and, most of all, the assumption that the forest lands would last forever.

The movement to preserve forest lands and force conservation practices by the lumber companies which began in the 1870s resulted in the formation of the forestry division in the Department of Agriculture in 1886. In 1891, Congress authorized the setting aside of forest reserves and the first of these, the Yellowstone National Park Timberland Reserve, was created that year, the bill signed by President Benjamin Harrison.

By 1939 there were 217 national forests, experimental forest stations, and reserves.

Timber and Stone Act

JUNE 3, 1878

The Timber and Stone Act, passed by Congress on June 3, 1878, made additional public land available to farmers. Although conceived to transfer these public lands to private individual ownership, the act was exploited by corporations and timber companies who stripped millions of acres of western forests.

Superintendent of the Census Bureau Franklin B. Hough collected the first statistics of American forestland in 1870 and sounded the alarm when he discovered how rapidly this "vast" bounty was disappearing. In 1876 John Muir proposed the creation of a national commission to recommend conservation measures. The following year Secretary of the Interior Carl Schurz pressed Congress to prevent all public timberlands from being liable to the homestead and pre-emption laws. Unfortunately the Timber and Stone Act of 1878 made it easier than ever for land to pass from public to private hands.

The act allowed individuals to purchase up to 160 acres of public land for $2.50 per acre, a price unrelated to the value of timber. Purchase was applicable only to lands "unfit for cultivation" in Washington, Oregon, Nevada, and California. Although the act was targeted for individual settlers, many timber companies and land speculators took advantage by means of fraudulent and abusive tactics. One commonly employed strategy was to pay men $50 to purchase 160 acres through the General Land Office; combined, these individual purchases represented vast land holdings for an unscrupulous dealer. A staggering 15 million acres of the nation's finest timberland was accumulated by a few large companies while many legislators looked on silently. The 300-foot-high Olympic Forest Reserve in northwest Washington was reduced to a quarter of its size in less than two and a half years; 126 square miles was hoarded by the Milwaukee Railroad alone.

Timber Culture Act

MARCH 13, 1873

The Timber Culture Act, passed by Congress on March 13, 1873, was enacted to accelerate the settlement of the arid High Plains region, referred to as the Great American Desert. The act also helped make the Homestead Act of 1862 more applicable to the western region.

Heavy advertising by both government and railroad companies drew hardy settlers to the least desirable of the frontier regions. Under the homestead legislation, for a $10 fee any adult was entitled to 160 acres of public land, provided that he occupied the land for five years. While farmers who worked the land often needed to irrigate and therefore found 160 acres more than sufficient, ranchers found the 160 acres inadequate for their needs. They were assisted by the Timber Culture Act, which allowed a homesteader to receive an additional 160 acres if he planted trees on at least 25 percent of the property within four years. In 1878 the minimum tree-growing requirement was reduced to 10 acres, which aided both ranchers and homesteaders. Altogether the law enabled 65,000 individuals to acquire about 10 million acres. But corruption and fraud allowed investors and corporations to circumvent the law and accumulate vast land holdings.

When the act was repealed in 1891, the future of the nation's conservation policy was altered to allow the President to set aside any public lands, regardless of commercial value, for the creation of public preserves.

Tippecanoe, Battle of

See Tecumseh

Tombstone, Arizona

The town of Tombstone is so inextricably tied to the moments of its history when such figures as the Earp brothers, Doc Holliday, John Ringo, Curly Bill

Brocius, Luke Short and others walked its streets that its genuine history and significance as a mining boomtown has been overshadowed if not forgotten.

Tombstone lies in the San Pedro Valley of Arizona, about 70 miles southeast of Tucson, and had its origins when Oregon-born prospector Edward L. Schiefflin began roaming the Apache lands east of the San Pedro River. Legend has it that he was warned that all he would find there was his tombstone.

Schiefflin was a veteran goldseeker, used to the backbreaking work of placer mining, and he persisted. North of the Mule Mountains in the San Pedro Valley he found an area of upthrust limestone and porphyry which signaled some body of ore beneath. In the summer of 1877 he staked out two claims which he named the Tombstone and the Graveyard. He then traveled 250 miles west to the town of McCracken, near the Colorado River, where his brother was working as a miner. In McCracken an assayer examined Schiefflin's ore samples and guessed that the claims might produce as much as $2,000 in silver per ton of ore.

With his brother Al and the assayer, Richard Gird, Schiefflin returned to his claims and eventually uncovered a ledge of ore-bearing granite that assayed at $15,000 a ton in silver and about a tenth that amount in gold. The story goes that Gird told Schiefflin, "Ed, you are one lucky cuss," giving rise to the naming of the rich mine as the "Lucky Cuss." Two nearby silver-bearing ledges were named the Tough Nut and the Grand Central. Together they formed the biggest silver strike in Arizona history.

Schiefflin and his brother sold their interests in the mines in 1880 for $600,000. Ed married and settled down in San Francisco but resumed prospecting, as far north as the Yukon, as far south as South America, and died in the wilds of Oregon in 1897 searching for gold. He was buried, as he wished, with his pick and canteen, about three miles west of Tombstone on the spot where he had camped on the eve of his great discovery.

Tombstone, the town that sprang up in 1879 on the heels of Schiefflin's strike, at one time had a population (10,000 in 1881) greater than San Francisco's, and while it was never the Sodom and Gomorrah of boomtowns that its name seemed to indicate, it earned its reputation as "the town too tough to die." Tombstone's main thoroughfare was Allen Street (named for one of the town's early merchants) and along its south side were a row of stores and cafes.

On the north side was a string of saloons, casinos, and brothels. When the Earp brothers arrived there in December 1879, the town, then less than a year old, consisted of a collection of shacks and tents perched on a high plateau between the Dragoon and Whetstone mountains. Only a year later, Tombstone had gas lights and a telegraph office.

The town's business district burned to the ground in June 1881 when a bartender tried to measure the contents of a whisky barrel with a cigar in his mouth. The resulting fire destroyed 60 stores, saloons, and other businesses. A second fire, in May 1882, again started in a saloon and again destroyed the Allen Street district. In 1881, despite the fire, the famous Bird Cage Theater (said to be the inspiration for the song "She Was Only a Bird in a Gilded Cage") opened. It was a combination saloon, brothel, burlesque theater, and dance hall. Comedian Eddie Foy, who played there, likened it to playing in a coffin. The October 26, 1881, gunfight off Allen Street near the O.K. Corral, while not the end of the town's violence, was the most celebrated of Tombstone's—or any other western town's—conflicts between law and outlaw.

Tombstone's boomtown era began eroding in the late 1880s when water was struck in the mines at 500 feet and after a pumping system was destroyed by fire in 1886. The financial Panic of 1893, the demonitization of silver, and similar economic factors spelled the end. By 1911, ore production had ceased.

Tombstone today, rich in historical restorations and museums, has a permanent population of about 2,000 citizens. Its famous newspaper, *The Tombstone Epitaph*, founded in 1880 by Indian agent, lawyer, and Arizona pioneer John P. Clum (1851–1932), continues publication as a national historical periodical.

Trail of Tears

The Trail of Tears was the name given to the forced removal of the Cherokee Indians from the southeastern United States to Indian Territory, from a Cherokee phrase meaning "trail where they cried." The term is sometimes loosely applied, as well, to the removal of the other tribes of the Five Civilized Tribes.

The idea to remove and relocate Indians west of the Mississippi began to take shape as early as 1802, when President Jefferson agreed to obtain the extinguishment of Indian title to any lands lying within the state of Georgia. The question remained, however, of what to do with the Indians who lost their lands. The Louisiana Purchase of 1803 was the answer. Jefferson justified the purchase in part by claiming that it would provide a location to which to remove all Indians from the East. Little was done, however, and whites grew increasingly adamant in agitating for Indian land.

Andrew Jackson, who favored removal, was elected president in 1828. Georgia responded by passing legislation extending its authority over the Cherokee Nation. The discovery of gold in the area exacerbated the problem as prospectors rushed into Cherokee country. On May 24, 1830, Congress passed and President Jackson signed the Indian Removal Act of 1830, authorizing the President to move the Indian tribes west.

Meanwhile, the Cherokees brought a suit in federal court to enjoin Georgia from carrying out its laws against them. The action, *Cherokee Nation v. Georgia*, was decided against the Indians by the U.S. Supreme Court in 1831. The following year, however, in *Worcester v. Georgia*, a case involving the

The Trail of Tears, portrayed by artist Robert Lindneux.

arrest of a missionary friendly to the Cherokees, Chief Justice John Marshall asserted the unconstitutionality of the state enactments. Jackson refused to take action and is reported to have remarked, "The Chief Justice has made the law; now let him try to enforce it."

The failure of their legal actions convinced some Cherokees that removal was inevitable, and the tribe split into pro-treaty and anti-treaty factions. The Treaty Party was led by John Ridge and Elias Boudinot. Those opposed to removal rallied around principal chief John Ross. It was made a capital offense to sell any Cherokee land.

In late 1835, a meeting was convened by the United States at New Echota, Georgia. Federal representatives negotiated a treaty with the Treaty Party, providing for removal of the Cherokees in exchange for 7 million acres in Indian Territory and $5 million. Ross's party refused to recognize the agreement and urged resistance.

In May 1838, President Van Buren ordered the U.S. Army into the Cherokee Nation. Troops rounded up Cherokee men, women, and children at bayonet point, dragging them from their homes without notice and imprisoning them in stockades. Crops were burned, and a number of women were raped. By June, about 5,000 Cherokees had been shipped out. Drought and hot weather halted further removals until the fall. At that time, the bulk of the Cherokees began an 800-mile journey to Indian Territory under John Ross. By the time the Trail of Tears concluded in March 1839, one quarter of the 16,000 Cherokees, including Ross's wife, had died of disease, hunger, and exposure.

Transcontinental Railroad

The earliest European explorers to make landfall on the continent of North America were seeking a shorter marine route to China and India for trading purposes. What they found was an entirely new (to them) continent. New World or not, it was still in the way. The dream of a quicker route to the Far East didn't die easily, and explorers continued to seek a faster way to cross the American landmass, in the mistaken belief that it would lead them to Asia. Eventually, of course, they realized that there were

riches enough in North America, and as the West Coast was settled, it quickly became obvious that a railroad route linking the two coasts of the United States would be as lucrative and as essential to the economic expansion of the nation as any route to China. (Ironically, Thomas Hart Benton, one of the great proponents of western expansion and the transcontinental railroad, still couched his advocacy in terms of a trade route to India.)

In 1845, wealthy businessman Asa Whitney brought before Congress a plan for the federal government to subsidize the construction of a railroad between Lake Michigan and the Pacific Ocean, providing a technological basis for Asiatic trade. As the West Coast became more heavily settled, support for the concept grew. The discovery of gold in California in 1849 was a particularly strong spur. Congress appropriated funds for surveyors to evaluate various possible routes in 1853.

The rivalry between supporters of different prospective routes was intense, reaching its peak with the passage of the Kansas-Nebraska Act, initiated by Senator Stephen Douglas as part of his efforts to win a Chicago-based route. However, the sectional rivalry between North and South that this legislation triggered forced a postponement in railroad surveying and construction.

With the outbreak of the Civil War, Congress took on a Republican cast, and passage of a bill to construct a transcontinental railroad took place on July 1, 1862. Under the legislation, two railroads were to participate in the building of the transcontinental line, each receiving massive land grants from the federal government and a 30-year loan for each mile of track constructed.

The Union Pacific began construction from the eastern end in 1863, starting from Omaha, Nebraska. At the same time, the Central Pacific began work at Sacramento, California. On May 10, 1869, the two lines met at Promontory Summit, Utah, and were joined by the symbolic driving of a golden spike. At last, the vision of the poet Walt Whitman was realized:

> The oceans to be cross'd, the distant brought
>   near,
> The lands to be welded together.

Three more lines were finished in 1883. The Northern Pacific ran from Lake Superior to Portland,

Oregon; the Santa Fe from Atchison, Kansas to Los Angeles; and the Southern Pacific from New Orleans to Los Angeles. Ten years later, the Great Northern was completed, for a total of five railroads in all. All of the companies involved received extensive grants of federal lands, although only the original line received loans.

The advent of the transcontinental railroads greatly hastened the economic development of the West and the closing of the frontier. It also turned railroad magnates like Leland Stanford into multi-millionaires. Ironically, the one thing it did not do was to increase Asian-American trade; American imports from Asia were a negligible part of the rail-roads' business in the nineteenth century.

Frederick Jackson Turner.

Turner, Frederick Jackson

1861–1932

Frederick Jackson Turner, an American historian and a graduate of the University of Wisconsin, began his career as a journalist but quickly turned his attention to history, under the influence of William Francis Allen, an apostle of the application of scientific methods to the study of history. Turner taught at his alma mater from 1885 to 1910 (except for a year of graduate study at Johns Hopkins in Maryland); then at Harvard until 1924. He then became a research associate at the Huntington Library.

Although he began his teaching career in rhetoric and oratory, Turner quickly found his interest shifting to American history, and particularly to the history of the American West. At the 1893 meeting of the American Historical Association, he delivered the paper that would secure his reputation, "The Significance of the Frontier in American History."

Turner's famous "Frontier thesis" argues that the existence of the frontier was a determining factor in the shaping of the American character. The thesis explains that the frontier caused America to develop differently from European nations. As he wrote in his *The Frontier in American History*, "The existence of an area of free land, its continuous recession, and the advance of American settlement westward, explains American development." The influence of his theory cannot be overstated; in some form, it has been incorporated into virtually

all standard histories of the United States, and all historians of the American West have had to grapple with it, pro or con.

Twain, Mark

See Clemens, Samuel Langhorne

Tyler, John

1790–1862

John Tyler, the tenth president of the United States (1841–1845), was the first man to succeed to the presidency following the death of an incumbent president. Under Tyler's administration the Webster-Ashburton Treaty was signed, ending the Maine border dispute, and the annexation of Texas was completed.

Tyler was born in Charles City County, Virginia, on March 29, 1790. Having set his sights on a career in law and politics, he attended the College of

William and Mary and in 1811 ran for and was elected to the Virginia State Legislature. As a moderate states' rights Democrat, he believed in limiting federal powers to those specified in the Constitution. Following his term of office in the legislature, he was voted a member of the U.S. House of Representatives (1817–1821); his opposition to the Missouri Compromise during his tenure was commonly known. From the House Tyler proceeded to serve as governor of Virginia from 1825 to 1827 and then as a senator from 1827 to 1836.

After resigning from the Senate in 1836, Tyler severed his ties with the Democratic Party and allied himself with the Whigs, who selected him as their vice-presidential candidate in 1839 to run on a ticket with William Henry Harrison as president. After campaigning with no official platform, amid mass rallies, songs, and slogans such as "Tippecanoe and Tyler, too," the Whigs won the 1840 presidential race.

One month after he took office the 69-year-old Harrison died, and Vice President Tyler took the presidential oath on April 6, 1841. Tyler's succession to the office caused uneasiness in the Whig Party, whose proponents recognized that he had never been particularly close to them. In September 1841, after Tyler vetoed two bills, sponsored by Henry Clay, that called for the establishment of a new Bank of the United States, the Whig cabinet (with the exception of Secretary of State Daniel Webster) resigned.

Tyler subsequently alienated most of the rest of the Whigs, and when they expelled him, he became a president without a party. In 1845 Tyler became the first U.S. president to have Congress override his veto.

Perhaps Tyler's greatest success as president was the Webster-Ashburton Treaty, which settled the Maine boundary dispute. Secretary of State Daniel Webster, the only remaining Whig in Tyler's cabinet, negotiated with Great Britain's Lord Ashburton, and the treaty was signed in 1842. Tyler's administration also ended the Seminole War, extended the Monroe Doctrine to Hawaii, and opened the first American trade mission to China.

With his term as president coming to an end, Tyler realized that gaining Democratic support would be essential to his reelection efforts. One surefire tactic, he realized, would be to lobby in favor of annexing Texas (a politically sensitive issue), and this he did, forcing the issue into national politics. The treaty was originally rejected, but in March 1845 Tyler signed a joint resolution of Congress, annexing Texas as a state. Ironically, Tyler did not run for reelection, and James Polk won the presidency on an annexation platform.

In 1845 Tyler retired to Virginia. In subsequent years he served in the provisional Confederate Congress (1861) and was elected to the Confederate House of Representatives; however, he died in Richmond, Virginia, on January 18, 1862, before he could take office.

U

Union Pacific Railroad

The Union Pacific was created by Congress on July 1, 1862, to build the eastern section of a transcontinental railroad. The act also provided for assistance to the Central Pacific for the west-east portion of the line.

Federal loans for laying track were at first fixed at $16,000 per mile across relatively flat land, up to $48,000 per mile in mountainous terrain. These amounts were quickly found to be too little, so concessions were given: land grants to the railroad company were doubled and initial loans made in effect second mortgages, permitting the companies to make new "first" loans.

In the early 1860s Thomas C. Durant, a Massachusetts-born railroad builder who was instrumental

Workers in front of a Union Pacific train.

Workers laying ties for the Union Pacific.

in the passage of federal Railway Acts, became chief executive of the Union Pacific. Ground was broken on December 2, 1863, in Omaha. But because of the Civil War, it was not until July 10, 1865, that the first rail was placed. By the end of the year, 40 miles of track had been laid.

After the end of the war and with labor again abundant, Durant won additional financial backing from Boston capitalists. He then set up the Crédit Mobilier of America as a construction company; its stockholders were made up of Union Pacific backers, U.S. congressmen, and others of wealth and influence. The Crédit Mobilier was given lucrative construction contracts, became a national scandal in 1873, and contributed to turning public sentiment against railroads and to the end of government support of them after 1870.

By November 13, 1867, the Union Pacific tracks reached Cheyenne, Wyoming Territory, and under the supervision of the chief engineer, General Grenville Dodge, Indian problems were kept at a minimum. After joining the Central Pacific at Promontory Summit, Utah, on May 10, 1869, control of the Union Pacific was acquired by financier Jay Gould, who merged it with his Kansas Pacific line. The company declared bankruptcy in 1893 and was rebuilt by Edward H. Harriman in the late 1890s into a powerful and profitable enterprise.

Utah

Utah lies in the Rocky Mountain region and is bordered by Colorado, Arizona, Nevada, and Idaho.

The state was settled by Mormons, who now constitute over two-thirds of the population. "Utah" derives from the Ute Indians, who inhabit the Uinta Basin southeast of Salt Lake City, the state's capital.

The Wasatch Mountain range cuts the state in half, with the Colorado Plateau to the east and the Great Basin on the west. The Uinta Mountains, which form the longest east-west range in the United States, are located just below the state's border with Wyoming. King's Peak, Utah's highest point at 13,528 feet, rises from this range.

Evidence exists that a desert nomadic culture inhabited the region about 10,000 B.C. The Anasazi Indians lived there approximately 1,700 years ago, and when Europeans originally explored the region, they encountered Ute, Paiute, Gosiute, and Navajo Indians.

In 1776 Franciscan missionaries ventured into what is now Utah, hoping to forge a trail from Santa Fe to the Spanish missions in California. The region soon captured the interest of the Hudson's Bay Company and John Jacob Astor's American Fur Company, which spurred trappers and traders such as William H. Ashley, Jim Bridger, and Jedediah Smith to explore it in the 1820s. Fort Davy Crockett (1834) and Fort Bridger (1841) were among the first of many Anglo settlements. John C. Frémont conducted several expeditions into the Great Basin region in the early 1840s. At that time great caravans bound for Oregon and California were already crossing Utah.

Midwestern persecution drove the Mormons to seek a new promised land out west. Led by Brigham Young in 1847, a large group of Mormons arrived in the Great Salt Lake region, where they established the state of Deseret. Congress greatly reduced its boundaries before admitting it to the Union in 1851 as the Territory of Utah. Brigham Young served as governor, and Salt Lake City became the capital in 1856.

Although the Mormons coexisted peacefully with the thousands of Native Americans, tension ultimately erupted in the area, climaxing in 1853 with the Walker War and in 1865 with the Black Hawk War. By 1867 most Indians were resettled on reservations.

Friction with the U.S. government developed over the Mormon practice of polygamy and rumors of Mormon intolerance toward non-Mormon settlers. Uneasiness over the situation peaked when President James Buchanan dispatched troops to Utah during the Utah War of 1857–1858, although

The natural beauty of southern Utah.

With the beginning of the twentieth century Utah ushered in extensive progressive reforms, such as the eight-hour working day, minimum wages for women, and workers compensation. Education became a major issue when the state attempted to bounce back from a depression following World War I. But true prosperity did not occur until the industrial boom of World War II. Irrigation projects, uranium mining, and manufacturing have supported Utah's economy into the late twentieth century.

an amicable settlement was reached without bloodshed. Despite frequent requests, Congress did not grant Utah statehood until 1896, after the Mormons renounced their practice of polygamy.

The transcontinental railroad was completed in Utah in 1869 when the Golden Spike was driven at Promontory Summit. This brought a wave of Mormon and non-Mormon settlers and boosted the state's agriculture and industry. The mining industry, especially copper mining, developed around the turn of the century and further strengthened the economy.

Utah War

Tensions in Utah between the United States government and Mormon leader Brigham Young culminated in 1857 in the Utah War, also known as the Mormon War.

Brigham Young and his followers in the Mormon Church constantly found their beliefs disapproved of by others, and they were often the victims of physical violence. Once settled in Utah, Young thought they had found peace at last. However, the religious leader's old troubles eventually caught up with him.

After establishing his "state" of Deseret, Young made himself governor. He ran the state as a theocracy and appointed his close aides to key political offices. The U.S. Congress barely acknowledged Young's efforts. When the area was officially made a

An 1853 drawing of Salt Lake City by Frederick Piercy.

territory in 1850, much of the Deseret land was excluded from Utah's boundaries.

Young, however, was named as Utah's governor. He continued to run official business according to Mormon doctrine. Young's policies (particularly the Mormon practice of polygamy), conflicted with those of American authorities. Young's followers openly defied federal officials in Utah. Concerned over the power of this Mormon-run government, President James Buchanan decided to take action.

In 1857, Buchanan appointed Alfred Cummings as Utah's new governor. Young ignored this threat to his authority, saying "No man they can send here will have much influence with this community." In July, Colonel Albert Sidney Johnston at Fort Leavenworth, Kansas, was ordered to take his troops to Utah and quell the Mormon uprising. When Young learned of this new attack he ordered all Mormons to repel the coming army. Young's "Nauvoo Legion" defended their territory by stealing Johnston's horses and then burning grass and destroying supply wagons so that the enemy's livestock would have nothing to eat. These actions, coupled with severe weather, succeeded in delaying any confrontation. Meanwhile Young declared martial law and began to refer to himself as "president."

By November, the Mormon guerrillas had stopped the U.S. government forces. Johnston and his troops spent the winter at Fort Bridger, Wyoming. They prepared for a spring attack. Before the attack could happen, however, Buchanan sent negotiators to work out a peaceful agreement with Young. Wanting to avoid an all-out war, Young finally came to terms with the U.S. government. Federal troops remained in place to make sure peace was maintained.

Ute Indians

The Utes are a Uzo-Aztecan tribe of Indians, historically divided into 11 bands, who now occupy reservations in Colorado and Utah.

Prior to contact with whites, Ute bands occupied most of Colorado and Utah, and parts of New Mexico and Wyoming. They were one of the first tribes to acquire horses, having captured them in raids against the Spaniards before 1640. Within 10 years, they were mobile and had taken up the buffalo hunt. Although they raided the Pueblo Indians, they main-

LIBRARY OF CONGRESS

A Ute warrior and young boy begin their summer migration into the mountains of Utah.

tained peace with the Spanish, with whom they traded until the eighteenth century. In the 1700s, however, they allied themselves with their relatives, the Comanches, and the Spanish moved against them. Finally, in 1750, the Utes again sued for peace.

In 1851, the first white settlement in Colorado was established at San Luis. The following year, the U.S. Army built Fort Massachusetts to protect the town. The Pike's Peak gold rush in 1858–1859 led to a tremendous influx of prospectors and settlers. Though increasingly pressured, the Utes kept the peace and agreed to a series of land cessions. The discovery of more gold and silver in the San Juan Mountains in the 1870s caused further encroachment into Ute land.

In 1874, Felix Brunot, one of President Grant's peace commissioners, persuaded the Colorado Utes to cede the San Juans, which comprised one-fourth of their reservation. Brunot promised them that this cession would be the "last request the government would ever make of the Ute." When Colorado be-

Ute horsemen, Colorado.

Ute men pose with their attorney in 1910.

came a state in 1876, however, the demand increased to open the remainder of the reserve for settlement.

In 1878, the federal government appointed Nathan C. Meeker as Indian agent for the northern Colorado Ute bands. "Wildly unqualified," narrow, and rigid, Meeker tried to force the Utes down the narrow paths of Christianity and Jeffersonian agrarianism. Chiefs Jack and Douglas objected. Although Chief Ignacio was the leader with the most authority among the bands, the government appointed the more cooperative Ouray "Head Chief of the Utes," paying him a $1,000-per-year salary. Chief Ouray now tried in vain to keep the peace by seeking to please both sides.

At Meeker's insistence, Major Thomas Thornburgh departed Fort Fred Steele with 175 troops to support the agency. On September 29, 1879, when the column crossed into the reservation, they were blocked by Chief Jack and 100 warriors. Fighting broke out, and the Utes held off the soldiers until October 5, when a U.S. military relief force finally arrived. When the troops reached the Indian agency on October 11, they found ten bodies, including Meeker's. Mrs. Meeker and four others had been captured. Before an expedition could be mounted against the Utes, however, Chief Ouray secured the release of the captives and ensured that the uprising did not spread to other bands. Between 1880 and 1881, four Colorado Ute bands were removed to join the Utah Utes. Three other Ute bands retained a small reservation in southwestern Colorado.

V

Vargas, Diego de

1643–1704

Diego de Vargas (Diego José de Vargas Zapata Luján Ponce de Léon y Contreras) was a Spanish soldier who accomplished the reconquest of New Mexico in 1692.

De Vargas was born in Madrid, Spain, to a socially prominent family. As a boy he served as a page in the Spanish court and, as a young man, as a military officer. He left Spain for Mexico in 1672, where he became *alcalde* (mayor) of various towns over the next few years. Sometime between 1686 and 1687, he requested—and received—his appointment as governor of New Mexico.

This region had been in control of the Pueblo Indians since the Pueblo revolt of 1680. In 1681, Governor Antonio de Otermín briefly reentered New Mexico to attempt to learn who the revolt's leaders had been. He found out little but burned Sandia Pueblo in revenge. Similar expeditions were mounted by Pedro Reneros de Posado in 1688 and Domingo Jironza Petriz de Cruzate in 1689. In 1691 or 1692, four years after the death of Popé, the revolt's leader, a group of men from a few Pueblos went to the Spaniards and invited them to return.

After his appointment as governor, de Vargas's first priority was to reassert Spanish authority in New Mexico. By February 22, 1691, he was at El Paso del Norte, from which he launched an expedition. He left there on August 21, 1692, with approximately 200 soldiers, 3 priests, and about 100 local tribespeople. He met with little or no united resistance from the Pueblos and entered Santa Fe on September 13.

De Vargas then launched an expedition to the northern pueblos. The inhabitants of these either capitulated or fled. His party, however, was attacked by Apaches and suffered minor losses. Following this northern excursion, he set out again for El Paso, then Mexico's northern boundary. Once more the Apaches attacked. One Apache was captured. The Spanish took the trouble of baptizing him before they shot him. De Vargas and his company finally reached El Paso on December 20, where they proclaimed that the "bloodless reconquest" of New Mexico had been achieved.

But, in fact, the real reconquest did not begin until late 1693 when de Vargas returned to El Paso with 100 soldiers, 800 colonists, and 18 priests. He departed from El Paso on October 13 and reached Santa Fe on December 16. A new revolt erupted but was quickly put down. De Vargas ordered 80 Pueblo men executed, and 400 women and children were sold into slavery to Spanish families.

Though the Spaniards controlled Santa Fe, the surrounding countryside was teeming with openly hostile tribespeople. Numerous clashes occurred between the Spanish and the Pueblos in 1694–1695. Then, on June 4, 1696, a number of pueblo villages again revolted. De Vargas executed the leaders he could capture and enslaved numerous other Pueblos.

When de Vargas applied for a second term as governor in 1696, he was arrested and jailed for mismanagement, embezzlement, and excessive cruelty. He remained imprisoned for three years, when his release was ordered by authorities in Mexico City.

CAPILLA DE SAN ISIDRO, MADRID

Diego de Vargas at 29.

He went to Mexico in 1700 but again returned to New Mexico as governor in 1703. He died while campaigning against the Apaches in 1704.

Vasquez, Tiburcio

1835–1875

Vasquez was the last of the Californio *bandidos* to be captured. Born to a well-to-do Californio family and educated in both Spanish and English, he had his first brush with the law in 1852 in Monterey when a fight broke out at a dance he was attending. An Anglo deputy sheriff was killed and Vasquez was implicated. He fled with Anastacio Garcia, and embarked on a 23-year career outside the law.

Given the tensions between Anglos and Californios, it was probably inevitable that Vasquez would come to be seen as an avenger against the Anglo society. By 1856 he had his own gang and was California's most notorious outlaw. Captured in 1857 for horse theft, he was sentenced to five years in San Quentin; he escaped briefly after two years, but was recaptured. After serving his sentence, some say he took up a career as a professional gambler; others say he resumed his life of crime.

In 1867, Vasquez was arrested for rustling and sent back to San Quentin for three more years. This time, there was no doubt what happened on his release; Vasquez rebuilt his gang and began holding up stages and robbing payrolls. By 1873, there was a price on his head of $2,000 dead or $3,000 alive.

It was not for money, however, that his career was brought to an end. A fellow gang member informed on him because Vasquez was involved with the man's wife. Vasquez was captured in 1874, but not tried until 1875. A dashing figure even in prison, he entertained guests, including many reporters, with tales of his exploits, arguing that his life of crime was nothing more than an appropriate response to Anglo racism. His trial lasted four days, and it took only two hours for the jury to return a verdict of guilty. Vasquez was hanged on March 19, 1875.

Victorio

CA. 1843–CA. 1880

Victorio was one of the most courageous and skillful chiefs during the Apache Wars, succeeding Mangas Coloradas and Cochise.

As a young warrior, Victorio was a protégé of Mangas. Suspicious of whites and resistant of any attempts to curb Apache freedom, he nonetheless wanted to live in peace. Following Mangas's murder by whites in 1863, Victorio assembled a band and, with Cochise, staged a series of raids to avenge their leader's death. After the end of the Civil War and the departure of General James H. Carleton from the region, Victorio, accompanied by Chief Nana, met with an agent of the U.S. government. He expressed his desire for "a lasting peace, one that will keep." The agent rebuffed him, stating that he had not come to discuss peace but to order all Apaches to the reservation.

In 1877, Victorio and his band were removed from their reservation at Ojo Caliente to San Carlos, a hot and barren flat on the Gila River in Arizona. That summer many of his people developed malaria. On September 2, he escaped the reservation with about 300 Apaches. The Army captured them the following month but escorted them to Ojo Caliente rather than San Carlos. A year later, Victorio's group was ordered back to the hated reservation.

Rather than comply, Victorio and 80 warriors slipped away. With them was his sister Lozen, a medicine woman. For more than a year, they raided settlements and farms in Mexico, Texas, New Mexico, and Arizona. It is said that Victorio was successful as long as Lozen's war medicine protected him. In 1880, Mexican soldiers surrounded Victorio and his followers at Tres Castillos, killing most and capturing the rest. Apaches contend that Victorio committed suicide rather than surrender.

Vigilantes

Vigilantes were a self-constituted quasi-judicial body, usually without legal sanction and often, but

COLORADO STATE HISTORICAL SOCIETY, DENVER

This warning poster makes it clear that vigilantes had little patience for traditional law and order.

DENVER PUBLIC LIBRARY

Citizens take justice into their own hands, using the nearest telegraph pole to hang an outlaw.

not always, formed in the absence of effective official law enforcement. On the western frontier, vigilantes, often called "regulators" or "moderators," were formed, ostensibly at least, to protect people and property. Their function as terrorists was especially critical in the South during the Reconstruction period (1865–72), when bands were created to "protect" whites against blacks and carpetbaggers. Among these vigilantes were the Ku Klux Klan and its several branches. "Lynch law," the term for quick, unjudicial punishment, usually at the end of a rope, was often a product of vigilantism.

The first large and organized "vigilance committee" in the West was formed of 200 men, among them citizens as prominent as Sam Brannan and Leland Stanford, in San Francisco in 1851 when outlaws, protected by crooked judges and lawmen, ran amok in the California gold fields. Within days of its formation, this group had arrested, tried (by "executive committee"), and hanged four desperadoes, it also succeeded in rooting out another 30 and banishing them from northern California.

Five years later, the California Vigilance Committee was revived and similar ones were created in Idaho, Montana, and other mining districts. The Montana group was responsible for bringing down, in 1863, the band of outlaws commanded by Henry Plummer, sheriff of Bannack. Plummer and 24 of his henchmen were hanged for a series of robberies and murders.

Villa, Francisco (Pancho)

1877–1923

Francisco Villa, known as "Pancho," was a Mexican revolutionary. The son of peasants, Villa began his career as a bandit in northern Durango. When the Mexican Revolution broke out in 1910, he took up with the forces supporting Francisco Madero and showed considerable initiative and intelligence, leading Madero and his supporters to a victory over Porfirío Díaz.

When Victoriano Huerta overthrew Madero in February 1913, Villa joined Venustiano Carranza and the Constitutionalists to fight against Huerta. With his cavalry, *Los Dorados*, Villa won numerous victories and gained control of northern Mexico. Huerta

resigned, but the uneasy alliance between Villa and Carranza unraveled. With Emiliano Zapata at his side, Villa took Mexico City, then lost it.

Driven north, Villa found his military power waning. When U.S. President Woodrow Wilson recognized the Carranza government, Villa was infuriated. There followed several raids by Mexicans across the border into Texas and New Mexico; although it is not certain that Villa was present, he has generally been thought to be responsible for those raids. When Wilson then sent General Pershing to pursue Villa, Pershing was unsuccessful and in the process hurt relations with Mexico. Villa continued to harass Carranza's government forces but in 1920, when Adolfo de la Huerta came into office, he finally made peace. Villa was assassinated three years later, leaving behind a Robin Hood–like legend that is still potent in Mexico.

Violence in the West

The debate over the origins of violence in America often focuses on the West. One school of thought holds that the West was an extraordinarily violent place, the haunt of fierce Indians, desperadoes, and criminals of every sort who killed, maimed, robbed, and spread terror, brutalizing pioneer society. The values and attitudes of the western border infected American culture and planted a predisposition to violence in the national character. Instinctively, Americans turned to force for redress of grievances, foreign and domestic; at the same time they cultivated a passion for firearms that made the force frequently deadly.

Others reject this interpretation. The frontier, they believe, suffered no more violence than other parts of the United States, possibly even less. A citizen ran greater risks to life, limb, and pocketbook in Philadelphia, New York, and Boston than in Denver, El Paso, and Dodge City. Rather than planting a national affinity for violence, according to this theory, frontier violence was merely the result of a violent streak that has animated the American mind from the beginning.

Whether cause or effect, violence was a prominent feature of life in the West. The blood and drama are fact, not the imaginings of popular scribblers. Western violence sprang from the conditions inher-

A Wyoming barkeep keeps his pistol handy in a drinking glass.

ent in a raw frontier beyond the bounds of settled society. For one, Indian hostility compelled the pioneer to be always on guard against a surprise attack and went far toward fixing the violent cast of the frontier mind. The West also attracted young men in search of quick money and power, values cherished by Gilded Age America in general but highly developed on the frontier. Liquor and guns magnified the potential for violence. Nearly all men drank much of the time. Drink enhanced self-importance, impaired judgment, generated heedless courage, and fostered unreasoning recourse to violence. Most men, moreover, had instant access to firearms, whether a holstered Colt revolver or a Winchester rifle in the saddle scabbard. When whiskey or some other provocation sparked the instinct to violence, guns were near at hand. Finally, the code of westerners demanded that insult or wrong, real or imagined, be avenged: "I'll die before I'll run."

In youthful pioneer communities, the institutions that discouraged or combatted violence in more settled areas existed only in rudimentary form if at all. County or town treasuries could not support adequate police or courts. Peace officers were too few and too ineffective to cope with outlaws drawn by lucrative prey, much less with the free-spirited adventurers who flocked to every frontier town or outpost. The man behind the badge practiced a highly personal, capricious brand of enforcement that rarely extended beyond the immediate community. The courts were no more efficient, with judges and prosecutors of limited competence and juries unable or unwilling to apply justice evenly. Jails were often were makeshift contrivances, easily broken into or out of.

Outlaws infested every part of the West. Their crimes differed from those of the East. Rare were such "big city" offenses as burglary, arson, mugging, and rape. Cattle rustling, by contrast, was so common as to be looked on by many as no offense at all. Horse theft, although much more objectionable, was almost as routine. Homicide and attempted homicide occurred with bloody regularity. Bank robbery and stagecoach holdups also involved outlaw gangs. Assault, drunkenness, and general rowdyism were rampant, but rarely prosecuted.

The West produced a gallery of outlaws who achieved fame in their own time and legendary stature in American folklore. Billy the Kid, Frank and Jesse James, Butch Cassidy and the Wild Bunch, the Younger Brothers, Joaquin Murieta—these and others contributed to the frontier heritage while posturing as folk heroes. They have been called "social bandits"—widely perceived as Robin Hoods who robbed from the rich and gave to the poor, but in reality they were no more charitable than any other criminal predator.

The West also spawned the gunfighter. He might be a hired gun, outlaw, lawman, or all three, sequentially or simultaneously. His hallmark was lethal skill with firearms and the will to use them. Bat Masterson, John "Doc" Holliday, Wyatt Earp, John Selman, and John Wesley Hardin all gained fame as gunfighters. The embodiment of the gunfighter, however, was James Butler "Wild Bill" Hickok, whose deadly accuracy fell prey to whiskey and finally to the "Dead Man's Hand," the cards he held when he was shot in the back in a Deadwood saloon in 1876.

Contending with the criminal elements were lawmen at each level of government. Towns often hired marshals or constables to keep the peace. The Kansas cowtowns in particular needed their own enforcers when the trail drivers from Texas delivered their herds at the railhead pens and descended on the local saloons and houses of ill repute. Most common were the county sheriffs and their deputies, responsible for administering state or territorial law and serving the processes of state or territorial courts. Some states and territories had their own law agencies. The Texas Rangers, for example, gained a stature in history and folklore as great as some of the outlaws. Finally, there were the United States marshals and their deputies, charged with carrying out federal law and serving the federal courts. Each state and territory had a U.S. marshal. Often he commissioned the county sheriffs as deputy U.S. marshals. This made sense because the territorial and federal courts were often presided over by the same judge.

Supplementing the official arms of government were the private detective agencies. The Pinkertons worked for whoever could pay them, usually large corporations with their own interests to pursue. Employing violent and often legally suspect methods, the Pinkertons helped mining and railroad companies quell labor unrest and break strikes. But they also pursued criminals preying on companies. The railroads in particular hired the Pinkertons to rid them of train robbers, such as the James brothers, the Wild Bunch, and Sam Bass.

Still another symptom of ineffective law enforcement was vigilantism. When crime and violence threatened the interests of the business and political elite, vigilantes did what the law could not or would not do. Extralegal hangings and less formal modes of execution sometimes ended intolerable conditions with fatal suddenness. Vigilantes cleaned up San Francisco in the 1850s and applied lynch law to Sheriff Henry Plummer and his gang in Montana in 1864.

Another form of western violence were feuds, or wars, between rival groups—factions, families, mercantile firms, or other clashing interests. New Mexico's Lincoln County War of 1878 pitted an aspiring monopoly against an entrenched monopoly. Wyoming's Johnson County War of 1892 was a fight between big cowmen and little cowmen over the open range. Arizona's Pleasant Valley War (or Graham-Tewksbury Feud) of 1886–1892 was a long-running brawl involving sheepmen and cowmen, rustlers and ranchers, and squabbling families. In California's Muscle Slough conflict of 1878–1880, farmers battled the land monopoly policies of the Southern Pacific Railroad.

Finally, the legacy of the West includes violence rooted in racism. Indian warfare contributed to western violence, but many westerners believed no Indian had rights worth respecting. Many Indians died in conflicts reflecting this attitude. The near extermination of some tribes of the Sierra Nevada by hordes of gold rushers in the 1850s is perhaps the most prominent example. Asians, especially Chinese, also suffered racial violence as seen in the Los Angeles and San Francisco riots of 1871 and 1877 and the bloody work of a mob in Rock Springs, Wyoming, in 1885. In Texas and New Mexico, Hispanics were frequently casualties of white aggression.

Either as a distinct and unique frontier or simply as part of the larger nation, the West was indeed a violent place.

Virginia City, Nevada

Virginia City, Nevada, now a ghost town, sprang up after the discovery of the Comstock Lode in the spring of 1859. Two Irish prospectors, Peter O'Riely and Patrick McLaughlin, discovered the rich silver deposits that became one of the largest finds ever. The subsequent rush to Nevada gave rise to several mining towns, but Virginia City grew to be the most significant and earned the name "Queen of the Comstock." Legend holds that the name of the city derives from the mishap of miner James "Virginny" Fennimore. When Fennimore, a friend of Henry T. P. Comstock, the man for whom the lode was named, dropped a freshly opened whiskey bottle on the site, he christened the city after his home state.

Within a few years of the discovery Virginia City grew into an important economic, political, and social hub, rivaling such major centers as San Francisco. Not only did the Comstock Lode bring wealth to Nevada, it brought sophistication to Virginia City. Hotels, restaurants, banks, and saloons sprang up. Samuel Langhorne Clemens first used what would become his more famous pen name, Mark Twain, while writing for the city's newspaper, *Territorial Enterprise.*

In 1875 a fire destroyed three-quarters of the town; it was soon rebuilt, but decline hit Virginia City three years later. By the early 1880s the city had seen the last of its mining boom days and was left to deteriorate until after World War II, when tourism brought a second boom and revitalization. Many of the original buildings have since been restored, and today Virginia City attracts thousands of visitors.

LIBRARY OF CONGRESS

Virginia City, Nevada, ca. 1890.

W

Wagon Box Fight

1867

In August 1867, eight months after the Fetterman Massacre at Fort Phil Kearny in Wyoming Territory, a war party of several hundred Sioux and Cheyennes, under the Oglala chief Red Cloud, rode from their camp on the Little Bighorn River to destroy the Bozeman Trail forts. Some went to Fort C. F. Smith, the rest to Fort Phil Kearny.

Six miles west of Fort Phil Kearny were two sawmills that supplied the fort with its fuel and timber from the trees on Piney Island, in the Bighorn Mountain foothills. At the sawmill, the timber contractor's corral was made up of wooden wagon boxes, the freight-hauling part of the wagons (the wheels were used to haul logs from the timber site). The corral was used to house horses and mules and for supply storage, including guns and some 7,000 rounds of ammunition.

At about 7:00 A.M. on August 2, as the corral and the civilian workers at the timber site were under guard by soldiers from the fort, commanded by Captain James W. Powell of the 27th Infantry, the Sioux began a simultaneous attack on both the corral and the woodcutter's camp on Piney Island. The workers and soldiers made their way east to the fort under heavy attack. At the corral, Powell's force of 32 men was facing an assault by 500 of Red Cloud's war party. The army's new breech-loading Springfield-Allins and Spencer rifles won the day, repelling repeated charges by the Sioux on the wagon box enclosure. When a relief force of 100 men and several howitzers arrived, the Sioux gathered up their dead and wounded and retreated. The battle left six dead among the whites, including three civilians, and two wounded. Indian losses were about 60 dead and 120 wounded.

But the U.S. victory was temporary. The army abandoned its Bozeman Trail forts in July and August 1868, and they were burned to the ground by Red Cloud and his warriors.

Wagon Trains

In the popular imagination, the long line of covered wagons crawling toward the setting sun endures as a prime image of the Old West. In historical reality as well, the wagon train played a pivotal role in America's westward movement.

Beginning in colonial times, the wagon train was the principal means of transporting people and merchandise to the west. Such trains carried emigrants and their possessions across the Appalachian Mountains to new homes in the prairies and woodlands drained by the Ohio, Tennessee, and Cumberland rivers. Wagon trains also moved freight until steamboats began to claim a share of the business in the early decades of the nineteenth century.

West of the Mississippi, where the land offered few navigable waterways, wagons bore most of the burden as the nation expanded to the Pacific. The Oregon and California Trails dominate the popular

A wagon train inches along a vast and desolate landscape.

memory, but others teemed with wagons too: the Santa Fe Trail, the Smoky Hill Trail to the Colorado mines, the Bozeman Trail to the Montana mines, and routes across Texas combining to descend along the Gila River through the southwestern deserts.

The famed Conestoga wagon, originally designed in Pennsylvania early in the eighteenth century, served as an all-purpose vehicle for the movement of people and goods east of the Mississippi River. Boatlike at its center, with larger rear wheels than front, capped with canvas or other waterproof fabric stretched over

A wagon train hits some rough terrain.

bowed hoops, the Conestoga was a common sight on the National Road from the East Coast to the Mississippi River. In the Trans-Mississippi West, from roughly 1820 until the advent of the railroads after the Civil War, the prairie schooner took the place of the Conestoga. The prairie schooner resembled its ancestor but with modifications prompted by different trail conditions in the plains, deserts, and mountains.

Whether Conestoga or prairie schooner, wagons varied greatly in size. The biggest freight wagons could haul as much as 7,000 pounds of cargo. The common emigrant wagon carried between 1,600 and 2,500 pounds.

To move them, the trains relied on horses, mules, or oxen. Horses had to be pampered and did not fare well on natural grasses, so they found favor mainly with military caravans or freighters that could carry their own forage. Although mules were tough and sturdy and could thrive on grass and brackish water, their bad disposition tormented drovers. Oxen proved by far the most popular draft animal, accounting for from 60 to 80 percent of the traffic on the main thoroughfares. Oxen could add 15 days to a crossing from Missouri to California, but they were stronger, more durable, and more reliable than their competitors. Nor did oxen tempt Indian raiders, who were bent primarily on running off horses and mules. As many as 12 yoke of oxen, 24 animals, pulled the heaviest freight wagons. Two to four yoke drew the emigrant wagons on the Oregon

MUSEUM OF NEW MEXICO

This wagon train stops for the afternoon in Nebraska.

Trail. The number of miles a train could cover in one day varied with the difficulty of the terrain, the effects of weather, and the weight of the cargo load. Normally an ox train could make 12 miles, a mule train up to 20.

All wagon trains were organized along more or less military lines. The hazards of travel in a rough country of vast distances, few way stations, and extremes of weather and terrain demanded leadership and teamwork. Trains lacking in organization risked delay at best, disaster at worst. A wagon master or captain commanded, and large trains were broken into sections headed by lieutenants. A typical train might number 50 wagons; more than that was unwieldy and difficult to control. Fewer than 20 enticed Indians and courted the many perils of the trail.

Freighting and emigrant outfits differed greatly in scale and effectiveness of organization. Freighters, both military and civilian, boasted the most elaborate organization and enforced the most rigid discipline. Protected also by sheer size, only rarely did they encounter adversities they could not cope with. Emigrant trains, by contrast, were usually much smaller, as well as looser in organization, a combination that exposed them to constant danger. Leaders were elected, usually inexperienced in trail conditions, and often displaced in mid-journey by disgruntled followers. Quarrels punctuated progress and sometimes caused trains to subdivide and elect new captains. Trail disasters such as that which overtook the Donner party in the Sierras in 1846 were usually caused by failed organization and leadership.

The drama and significance of wagon trains has been stereotyped in the documented adventures of emigrants on the Oregon and California trails during the 1840s and 1850s. The Oregon-bound trains carried families hoping to make new lives as farmers on the fertile soil of the Willamette Valley. The California-bound trains were mostly made up of men hoping to make a fortune in the gold mines and return to their eastern homes. The trains cast off from Independence, Westport, or other Missouri towns,

LIBRARY OF CONGRESS

A wagon train is devastated by a sudden blizzard.

cut across eastern Kansas to the Platte River Road, paused to rest and refit at Fort Laramie, crossed the Continental Divide at the broad and easy portal of South Pass, and made their way through increasingly rough country to the Snake River and another way station at Fort Hall. Here the Oregon settlers kept to the Snake and crossed the rugged Blue Mountains to the Columbia River, while the gold-seekers angled southwest across barren deserts to cross the towering Sierra Nevada into California.

Wagon trains tried to cast off from Missouri in late April or early May, late enough to graze their stock on greening grasses but early enough to scale the final mountain passes before winter's snow set in early in September. The first stages of the journey were devoted to getting organized and shaking down into a daily routine. Noon halt might occur as early as 10:00 A.M., when stock were unhitched, watered, and grazed and people lunched. Nearly all provisions had to be carried, since game and natural foods could not be relied on. Water was plentiful on the eastern half of the trail, but west of South Pass it grew scarce. At night, the wagons were set up to form a circle, to provide both security against hostile Indians and a safe pen for the stock after their evening graze. Despite constant fears, few overlanders actually suffered Indian attacks.

Emigrant trains endured many trials rare to the freighters. Heat, dust, thirst, and fatigue dogged their progress all the way to the Pacific. Family feuds broke out, and contention swept the leadership. Disease took its toll, and rude headboards scattered along the trail marked the site of hastily dug graves. Nearly everyone packed too much into the wagons. As the oxen or mules grew thinner and more tired and the wagons broke down, furniture and other possessions were discarded and littered the wayside.

Many people did not make it to their destination. But for those who did, the voyage west remained the most memorable experience of their lives.

Wasco Indians

The Wascos are a Penutian tribe of Indians who reside in Oregon. They are today part of the Confederated Tribes of the Warm Springs Reservation.

Between 1854 and 1855, the United States concluded a number of treaties with the Native American tribes of Washington and Oregon. These tribes included the Sahaptin-speaking Teninos and Chinook-speaking Wascos. The tribes ceded most of their territory in exchange for a monetary payment and a reservation. The treaties forced a union among previously autonomous villages. They also separated closely related villages on opposite sides of the Columbia River by assigning those on the north side to the Yakima Reservation, and those on the south to the Warm Springs Reservation.

Because few Native Americans spoke English, and because tribal representatives at treaty councils often spoke different languages, the treaties were negotiated in Chinook jargon, a trading language with a limited vocabulary. In English, the treaties reserved to the Indians the "right to take fish, at all usual and accustomed grounds . . . in common with all citizens of the Territory" regardless of whether such locations were on the reservation or not. But because of the imprecision of Chinook jargon, the treaties have been the source of continuing litigation. In 1976, this litigation culminated in *United States v. Washington*, a landmark case decided by Judge George Boldt. Judge Boldt's ruling upheld extensive fishing rights for the area's Native Americans.

In 1879, the U.S. Army relocated several groups of Paiutes taken prisoner in the Indian Wars to the Warm Springs Reservation, where they joined the Teninos and Wascos.

Washington

Washington, located in the extreme northwest of the continental United States, was the dwelling place of Native Americans for over ten thousand years. Their lifestyle changed little until the arrival of Europeans. Indians inhabiting the coast built large villages along the beaches, with rectangular houses constructed from cedar planks. The abundant fish, game, and plant life allowed inhabitants to thrive without depending on agriculture or domesticated animals. Indians to the east of the Cascades lived similarly well, but depended more on seasonal hunting grounds. Nez Perces, Okanogans, Spokanes, and Yakimas traditionally lived in dwellings dug into the ground, covered by a roof of brush or woven mats. Not until the introduction of horses in the eighteenth century did they start using tepee structures similar to those of the Indians of the Great Plains.

European exploration began with a Spanish expedition to counter Russian expansion from the north. James Cook, sailing under a British flag, explored the coast in 1778, and American explorer Captain Robert Gray became the first white man to navigate the Columbia River in 1792. Inland exploration began when Lewis and Clark reached the Columbia River in their expedition of 1805–1806.

Subsequent explorers were mostly fur traders. John Jacob Astor aimed to establish a headquarters for his Pacific Fur Company at the mouth of the Columbia, and in 1811 he dispatched Duncan McDougal to found Fort Astoria. The fort was taken over by the British during the War of 1812, and success in the northwest fur trade came later, in the hands of Hudson's Bay Company. Their headquarters at Fort Vancouver quickly came to dominate fur trading in the Northwest, representing a center for economic, social, and political activity as well.

Missionaries followed the fur traders. The first to proselytize in the region, in 1834, was Reverend Jason and Daniel Lee. Two years later Marcus and Narcissa Prentiss Whitman arrived, and within the next few decades thousands of settlers rushed to the Oregon Territory. Growth in the Columbia Basin was slowed by clashes with Indians, but settlements thrived around Puget Sound. Congress established the Washington Territory in May 1853; Isaac I. Stevens was appointed the first governor.

Early growth was slow in the new territory, with an initial (1860) population of white settlers at about 12,000. However, the timber industry brought an economic boom to land west of the Cascades. The mining industry also became important, as did salmon canning. But the biggest boost to the area was the arrival of the Northern Pacific Railroad and the Great Northern Railway. By the 1880s the population in the territory was over 75,000, and in 1889 Washington became the forty-second state in the Union, with Olympia its capital. Today manufacturing is the most significant segment of the state's economy. Boeing, a leader in the production of commercial aircraft, is Washington's largest employer. International trade and tourism also play a major economic role.

Washita, Battle of

NOVEMBER 27, 1868

In the summer of 1868, Major General Philip Sheridan, commanding the Army's Department of the Missouri, organized a winter campaign against the Cheyennes and Arapahos to force the tribes to surrender to a reservation near Fort Cobb, Indian Territory.

That winter Sheridan's plan to drive the Indians north got underway, and on November 23, Lt. Col. George A. Custer led 11 companies—about 800 men—of his 7th Cavalry through a snowstorm from Camp Supply, Indian Territory, toward the Washita River. On the fourth day out, with the temperature below freezing, Major Joel H. Elliott, scouting the north bank of the Canadian River with three companies of the 7th, discovered a trail made by nearly 100 Indian ponies. Custer ordered Elliott to pursue while he followed with the main column.

Led by two Osage scouts, Custer's force moved toward the Washita in silence—no one was permitted to speak above a whisper—and at past midnight on the 27th a Cheyenne village of some 75 lodges was found. Custer ordered his four deployed columns to attack from all directions at dawn.

The 7th forded the river at sunrise and charged into the village with the regimental band playing the opening notes of its fighting song, the "Gary Owen." Black Kettle's Cheyennes, abruptly awakened, poured out from their lodges and were shot down as they ran; those who fled to nearby ravines and underbrush and used the Washita riverbanks for protection answered the fire standing in freezing water. Women and children took up arms: Captain Frederick W. Benteen was fired upon three times by a teenage boy and, after his horse was hit, he killed the boy. Black Kettle and his wife were shot and killed as they fled to the river. So intense was the 7th's attack that the village was taken in 10 minutes.

At around 10:00 A.M., a small group of Indians was sighted on a knoll about a mile below the battlefield, and as additional warriors approached, Custer encountered outriders from a 10-mile string of villages along the Washita, containing more than 6,000 Cheyennes, Arapahos, Kiowas, and Comanches. Custer feinted toward the villages, then withdrew his force.

After the main fighting at the village of Chief Black Kettle, who had survived the massacre at Sand Creek, Colorado, Major Elliott and 19 men rode out toward the east to chase some retreating Indians. When he did not return, Custer ordered a search for the party. It was not found. It was later learned that Elliott and his men ran into a force of Cheyennes and Arapahos, were surrounded, and were killed to the last man. Custer retired from the Washita at nightfall on the 27th and on December 2 returned to Camp Supply, where Sheridan waited to congratulate him on their victory.

At least 100 Indian dead were counted in the Washita campaign. The number of actual warriors killed was probably no more than 38. The 7th took 53 women and children as prisoners, killed 875 Cheyenne horses on the spot, captured 1,100 buffalo robes, 500 pounds of gunpowder, 1,000 pounds of lead, and 4,000 arrows plus other stores and equipment. Custer's losses were 2 officers and 23 men killed (counting Elliott and his troopers,) and 14 wounded. The other officer killed was Louis McLane Hamilton, a descendant of Alexander Hamilton.

The battle laid the groundwork for Custer's reputation as an Indian fighter. However, because of what was perceived to be his halfhearted attempt to find Elliott and his men before leaving them to their fate (they had, in fact, died soon after riding out from the main force on the morning of the 27th), dissension in the regiment ran deep toward Custer, an undercurrent that continued until his final Battle of the Little Bighorn in 1876.

Water

Immigrant and cattle trails, frontier army post sites, and town, farm, and ranch locations were all based on the availability of water. That precious (especially beyond the Mississippi) natural resource drove the settlement of the American West.

In the West, acquiring water has been an eternal problem: there is not enough of it and what there is is not always distributed to the advantage of humankind. Western rainfall is heaviest in mountain-

Frederic Remington's Fight for the Water Hole *dramatizes the extreme value placed on fresh water supplies in the frontier.*

ous areas and in wet pockets such as the Pacific Northwest. Groundwater is stored best in heavily forested areas in mountain country—the Sierra Nevada, the Cascade Range, the Rocky Mountains—where rain and snow percolate down through soil and rocky substrata to produce large underground aquifers.

The great problem for settlers, and a striking example of the importance of water to the opening of the West, was that these mountainous regions that produced the most rainfall and most prolific groundwater resources were also the poorest areas for farming.

West of the 100th meridian, the mean annual rainfall is less than 20 inches (the annual mean across the United States is about 30 inches), and 20 inches is considered the minimal rainfall required for normal crop production without irrigation.

As historian Dee Brown has written, "Everything but land and sky was scarce on the early homesteads. Water was usually the scarcest necessity of all."

For the homesteader-farmer, food in the form of game and vegetation was available if not always abundant; fuel—wood, brush, or that "anthracite of the plains," cow or buffalo chips—could be gathered; shelter, the plains "soddy," cabin, or lean-to, could be quickly built. But before ever marking a claim, breaking the earth, or planting a seed, farmers faced one urgent problem: They needed water and they could not depend upon rain.

If one were lucky enough to get there in time, land could be claimed along streams and creeks; such small waterways usually signified groundwater less than 50 feet below the surface. In any event, a farming family had to locate a spot where water was at least close enough to haul in barrels to fill a cistern (which also collected rainwater) until a well could be dug.

A hand augur was used to make test holes. Once the water table was found, the family proceeded to dig, with pick and shovel, makeshift windlass, and bucket, through earth, hard clay, and rock. The process might take months—some wells in the High Plains were 200 feet deep or more. Those with money might hire a well-driller, who charged from 20 cents to a dollar a foot; if no water were found, a "dowser," a kind of water-hunting mystic, might be engaged, who used a Y-shaped dowsing stick to divine where to dig.

By the 1870s, water was being pulled from deep wells with windmills, some crudely homemade, some manufactured and more elaborate. A farmer with a shallow well and a good homemade windmill could irrigate five acres of land.

Few migrating farmer-homesteaders had experience in irrigation—east of the Mississippi, with adequate rainfall, there was little or no need for it—but it was quickly learned. Streams were tapped by building dams, flumes, and canals to channel water to crops. In arid Utah, as early as 1865, there were 277 canals built to irrigate 154,000 acres of previously barren terrain.

The Newlands Reclamation Act of 1902, adopted during the presidency of Theodore Roosevelt, was enacted to bring water, by dam building, to small farms of 160 acres or less. Within a short time most farms had exceeded this limit, and soon federal funds were being used to irrigate large farms as well. But, for all intents and purposes, the nineteenth-century farmer had neither knowledge of nor interest in the environmental impact of incessant water use—the irreversible depletion of aquifers; the damage wrought by silt building up in dammed rivers and streams; and the dire results of changing natural environmental habitats.

In 1982 the old 160-acre limit was finally revised; the new limit is six times that number.

Wells, Fargo & Co.

A name as familiar in the West as Colt, Remington, or Pinkerton, this company name—printed boldly on its trademarked dark green strongboxes—was so well known that miners were said to have sworn only "by God and Wells, Fargo."

Within 15 years of its founding in San Francisco in 1852, Wells, Fargo & Co. had absorbed every serious rival or driven them out of business and had become the most important mail deliverer, express agency, bank, and stagecoach company in the West.

Its founders were Vermont-born Henry Wells (1805–1878), New York steamboat operator and freight agent, and William G. Fargo (1818–1881), a New Yorker and veteran expressman. The two went into partnership in 1843, organizing a company to deliver mail and freight into Ohio and Illinois. So efficient were they in the mail business—charging six cents a letter while the government rate was 25 cents—that the U.S. Post Office demanded they stop undercutting its prices. In 1850, the two partners merged their businesses with the express company owned by John Butterfield (who later operated a transcontinental stagecoach line through the Southwest to California). The new company was named American Express.

Wells and Fargo by now had decided to set up an operation in California to take advantage of the shipping of gold bullion to Eastern Seaboard mints. In July 1852, with capitalization of $300,000 from

LIBRARY OF CONGRESS

Wells, Fargo guards, heavily armed, transport $250,000 worth of gold out of Deadwood.

Henry Wells.

William Fargo.

the partners and seven other financial backers, the new express agency, called Wells, Fargo & Co., opened its doors on San Francisco's Montgomery Street. The following February, Henry Wells made his first and only visit to the West Coast to inspect the new operation. Fargo seems never to have ventured across the Mississippi.

From the beginning, Wells, Fargo was a huge success, shipping and guarding bullion on the long sea voyage to the East, operating its mail service, opening company branches in Sacramento, San Diego, and Monterey and buying out competitors in the Mother Lode country north of San Francisco.

By 1854 the company had 24 offices and only one powerful rival, Adams & Co., the western branch of a prominent eastern express firm that had set up offices in San Francisco in 1849. Wells, Fargo moved across the street from Adams's new building on Montgomery Street in 1854 and opened a price war with its rivals. The timing was good for the partners, deadly for the Adams company: in February 1855 a financial panic in San Francisco resulted in audits of the city's banks and other financial agencies. Wells, Fargo emerged as healthy, but Adams, together with nearly 200 other of the city's businesses, failed.

By 1859–1860, Wells, Fargo had 126 branches in the West and was delivering freight and mail by steamer from San Francisco around Cape Horn or over the Panama portage, by vessels on the Sacramento River, by heavy freight wagon, by mule train, by stagecoach, and by men on foot and on horseback. The company took over the Butterfield Overland Mail in 1860. By 1866, by buying out Ben Holladay's stage line, it had a monopoly on long-distance stagecoach freight and mail service west of the Mississippi.

At the peak of its operation, in the Civil War years, Wells, Fargo employed a large force of detectives and police and effectively stopped the robbing of its stagecoaches, capturing an estimated 240 "road agents," including the least dangerous but most celebrated of them, Black Bart.

Wells sold the company's stagecoach lines in 1868, and the Wells, Fargo empire was further threatened by its failure to invest in the railroads—the future of freighting. In 1869, the company was taken over by entrepreneur Lloyd Tevis, who had bought up Wells, Fargo stock when it had plummeted during a rate war with Tevis's competing company, the Pacific Union Express. Tevis wisely kept the world-famous company name. By the end of the century, Wells, Fargo operated nearly 3,000 branch offices and was delivering goods over 38,000 miles of western express routes. The company name survives today as a banking and armored car corporation.

Western Federation of Miners

The Western Federation of Miners (formed in 1983) was a labor organization that united the many miners' unions in the West into one central body.

In the late nineteenth century, mine owners in the West reacted to declining profits by cutting wages. Unions everywhere were fighting the cuts, but most could not sustain a wage war on their own. Thus, many unions in the West desperately needed the strength a unified federation could provide. With the formation of the Western Federation of Miners, virtually all workers in the mining industry, above and below ground, were organized and all the unions united into the strongest labor organization in the West.

On May 15, 1893, the federation selected one man from each miners, union and formed a committee to draft a constitution. The two main goals of the federation were to ensure fair compensation for miners and to eliminate needless risk to life and health in the mines. The federation stopped short of setting a uniform minimum wage so that each individual union could establish its own scale.

One noteworthy aspect of the federation was its provision for the appointment of organizers to unite nonunion miners. Previously union organization had been a last-resort measure, provoked by crises and as a result usually ineffective. The rapid growth and strength of the federation was due in large part to the new organizers.

Weyerhaeuser, Frederick

1834–1914

Frederick Weyerhaeuser was a lumber capitalist who founded the Weyerhaeuser Timber Company. He constructed an enormous lumber syndicate, acquiring millions of acres of timberland as well as numerous sawmills and paper mills.

Having come to America from Germany at the age of 18, Weyerhaeuser settled in the frontier community of Rock Island, Illinois, and in 1856 began working in the sawmill of a local lumberyard. When the mill failed following the panic of 1857, Weyerhaeuser bought it in partnership with his brother-in-

law, F.C.A. Denkmann. While Denkmann ran the mill, Weyerhaeuser traveled throughout Wisconsin and Minnesota, seeking new sources of timber. Demonstrating tremendous energy and business acumen, he began investing in many logging and milling operations along the Mississippi River. By 1872 he became president of the Mississippi River Boom and Logging Company, an enormous conglomerate that handled all the logs milled on the Mississippi.

To be closer to the northern Wisconsin and Minnesota timberlands, Weyerhaeuser moved to St. Paul, Minnesota, in 1891. Here he put together one of the largest land deals in U.S. history. The Weyerhaeuser syndicate paid $6.5 million for nearly one million acres of pine land from James J. Hill of the Northern Pacific Railroad. With this purchase, in 1901, the Weyerhaeuser Timber Company was founded. Altogether the company amassed over two million acres of pine land during Weyerhaeuser's lifetime. He also headed 16 lumber companies and retained a controlling interest in many others. Weyerhaeuser contracted pneumonia in March 1914 and died a few weeks later, on April 4.

Whitman, Marcus 1802–1847 and Whitman, Narcissa Prentiss

1808–1847

Marcus Whitman, born in upstate New York, was practicing medicine there when he heard an address by Rev. Samuel Parker calling for missionaries for the Pacific Northwest. Whitman had long considered a religious vocation and visited Oregon with Parker to investigate the possibilities. There he saved many fur trappers' lives in the cholera epidemic and became convinced of his calling. However, the American Board of Commissioners for Foreign Missions accepted only married couples as missionaries.

Present at the same speech by Reverend Parker was Narcissa Prentiss, a young schoolteacher. Like Whitman, she wanted to pursue a career in religion, but, being unmarried, was rejected. Discovering their shared problem, Whitman proposed to her and they were married in 1836.

The couple traveled west with another missionary couple, Henry and Eliza Spalding; Narcissa had rejected Henry's marriage proposal when the two attended school together. The quartet traveled with parties of trappers from the American Fur Company led by mountain man Thomas Fitzpatrick. On their journey, Narcissa and Eliza became the first white women to cross the Rocky Mountains.

The Whitmans established a mission among the Cayuse Indians at Waiilatpu, Oregon Territory, near what is now Walla Walla, Washington, while the Spaldings set up near what is now Lewiston, Idaho, ministering to the Nez Perces. Marcus constructed buildings, conducted services, practiced medicine, and offered the Indians advice on farming and livestock. Narcissa conducted the mission school and supervised the domestic affairs of the mission. Soon they were running the largest mission of its kind in Oregon.

In 1839 the Whitman's two-year-old daughter was accidentally drowned, sending Narcissa into a deep depression. Her eyesight began to fail. The Cayuses, Nez Perces, and Flatheads showed more interest in Catholicism than in Protestantism, a sign of the success of Jesuit priest Pierre Jean de Smet, who was winning many converts in the region. Then Spalding and Marcus had a falling out.

In 1842, the Mission Board considered relocating the missions. Marcus journeyed back to New York during one of the harshest winters on record to dissuade the Mission Board. He spoke forcefully of the need for more settlers in the Oregon Territory. It is thought that he helped inspire the so-called Great

DENVER PUBLIC LIBRARY

This dramatization of the death of Marcus Whitman shows Narcissa trying to stop the attack. Ironically, Narcissa was not present at her husband's death.

Migration in which more than a thousand settlers journeyed to Fort Hall and then, with Whitman leading the way, continued to the Willamette Valley. Their pathway became the Oregon Trail.

Unhappily, the Indians began to hold the missionaries responsible for their misfortunes, including a measles epidemic that ravaged the Indian communities. Marcus tried to help, but even the mildest vaccines caused death. The Indians believed that he was poisoning their children. On November 29, 1847, a band of Cayuses massacred the Whitmans and a dozen other white settlers. Another 53 women and children were taken hostage by the Indians and later ransomed by Dr. John McLoughlin. The massacre was the direct cause of the Cayuse War, one of the most serious Indian conflicts in the Pacific Northwest.

Wichita, Kansas

Located in south-central Kansas on the Arkansas River, Wichita, Kansas, is the largest city in the state. The Wichita Indians were living in the region when Franciso Coronado first arrived in 1541. Intrusion into the territory by whites eventually forced the Indians south to what is now Oklahoma and Texas near the Red River. In 1864 the federal government returned the Wichitas to their native location, and a small village was established. Mountain man and fur trader Jesse Chisholm built a trading post there, and in 1868 he forged the famous Chisholm Trail from the Wichita village to Texas. Soon thereafter the government removed the Wichitas to Indian Territory. The town of Wichita was established on the site of the empty Indian settlement, and it quickly became a popular stopover for cattle drives.

When the Sante Fe Railway arrived in 1872, Wichita entered a period of brisk growth as a cattle town. In the first year following the arrival of the railroad, the town shipped approximately 80,000 head of cattle to the East. However, in 1877 the Kansas State Legislature moved the quarantine line for Texas Longhorns west of Wichita, bringing an end to the days of cattle town prosperity. Wichita soon found new life as a trade and grain-milling center. The discovery of oil after World War I revitalized

Street view, Wichita, Kansas.

the city's economy, and today the majority of the country's private and business aircraft are manufactured in Wichita.

Wickiup

See Native American Dwellings

Wild Bunch

Also called the Hole-in-the-Wall Gang, the Wild Bunch was the collection of outlaws gathered around Butch Cassidy (Robert Leroy Parker). They had two main hideaways—one at Brown's Park, in the rugged area where the Green River flows along the Utah-Colorado border, and another at the Hole-in-the-Wall, a valley 250 miles north of Brown's Park in the Wyoming wilderness protected by mountain passage so narrow that riders could enter it only in single file.

After the June 1889 robbery of the San Miguel Valley Bank in Telluride, Colorado, Cassidy and his partners Matt Warner and Tom McCarty escaped north to Brown's Park and there met a number of men who would become members of the gang later called the Wild Bunch. These included Harvey "Kid Curry" Logan, Will Carver, Ben "Tall Texan" Kilpatrick, Harry

Tracy, William Ellsworth "Elza" Lay, O.C. "Deaf Charlie" Hanks, and others.

In 1896, after Cassidy's parole from prison in Wyoming for horse theft, he, Elza Lay, and one Bob Meeks robbed the bank of Montpelier, Idaho, and fled to Robber's Roost, another remote hideout in southeastern Utah. It was there that Cassidy forged his friendship with Harry ("Sundance Kid") Longabaugh and Harry's mistress, Etta Place.

The Wild Bunch robbed the Pleasant Valley Coal Company at Castle Gate, Utah, in 1897, and trains and banks in Colorado, Utah, Wyoming, Montana, Nevada, and New Mexico. Among their most celebrated exploits was the robbery of a Union Pacific Railroad train near Wilcox, Wyoming, on June 2, 1899, in which an express car was blown apart with dynamite; the gang picked up some $30,000 in scattered currency from the desert.

Similar robberies in Folsom, New Mexico, and Tipton, Wyoming, are attributed to the gang. The robbery of a bank in Winnemucca, Nevada, in September 1900 netted $32,000, after which some of the Bunch—Cassidy, Carver, Logan, Kilpatrick, and Longabaugh—showed up in Fort Worth and had a group portrait taken. This little bit of fun put Pinkerton detectives on their trail.

In 1901, after a train robbery near Wagner, Montana, the Wild Bunch split up. Cassidy, Longabaugh, and Place traveled to New York and then to South America, where the two men were reportedly killed,

Left to right, Harry Longabaugh, Will Carver, Ben Kilpatrick, Harvey Logan, and Butch Cassidy.

in 1907 or 1908, in the Bolivian village of San Vicente. Place disappeared from history before this event.

At least five other members of the Wild Bunch died violently: William T. "Will" Carver (ca. 1866–1901) was shot by lawmen in Sonora, Texas, on April 2, 1901; Deaf Charlie Hanks (1863–1901) was killed in a boarding house in San Antonio, Texas, on April 16, 1901, while resisting arrest; Harry Tracy (1869–1902), after killing three men and escaping custody in Oregon, was cornered on a ranch near Creston, Washington, on August 5, 1902, and killed himself; Harvey Logan (1875–1903) was wounded by a posse after robbing a bank in Colorado and committed suicide near Glenwood Springs, Colorado, on July 9, 1903; Ben Kilpatrick (1877–1912) was released from prison in 1911 and was killed by a railroad guard on March 13, 1912, while attempting to rob a Southern Pacific Railroad train near Sanderson, Texas.

Elza Lay (1869–1934) was wounded and captured after the 1899 train robbery at Folsom, New Mexico, and sentenced to life in prison. He was released in 1906, took the name William H. McGinnis, and led an apparently uneventful life until his death in Los Angeles in 1934.

Harry Longabaugh (sometimes spelled Longbaugh—he was born in about 1870, although the record is unclear as to the date and place of his birth) may have died with Butch Cassidy in Bolivia, although there are theories that both men survived the South American episode and returned to the United States. One theory put forth by a man claiming to be the son of Longabaugh and Place is that the Sundance Kid (who took his nickname from the town of Sundance, Wyoming, where he was once jailed) died in Casper, Wyoming, as recently as 1957.

Wilderness Road

The Wilderness Road was a trail created by Daniel Boone under the aegis of the Transylvania Company in 1775, leading from the Cumberland Gap to Boonesboro, Kentucky, and from the Hazel Patch to Louisville. Boone and a party of eight began their trail blazing immediately after the signing of the Treaty of Sycamore Shoals, which afforded them the right to cross through Cherokee lands.

The establishment of the road enabled the company to establish a functioning settlement at Boonesboro. An extension of the Great Valley Road, parts of the Wilderness Road had already been outlined by Indians, hunters, and trappers. In the years to come, thousands of settlers would use the Wilderness Road in their move westward from the Cumberland Gap into Kentucky and the Ohio valley. The road quickly became a key link between the Ohio, Tennessee and Virginia valleys. U.S. Mail service was opened on the road in 1792, but the uncertainty of the route forced Governor Isaac Shelby to promise to upgrade the trail or the mail service would be terminated. In 1797, it was reported that a wagon road had finally been established and that wheeled vehicles could traverse the route; this was a somewhat over-optimistic report, as the Wilderness Road was not actually improved until after the Civil War.

Winnebago Indians

The Winnebagos are a Siouan tribe of Indians originally located in Wisconsin. Today their population is split between Nebraska and Wisconsin because of repeated forced relocations by the United States government.

The Winnebagos were first encountered by whites in 1634, in the vicinity of present-day Green Bay, Wisconsin. Their territory was virtually surrounded by the Menominees and the Sac and Foxes, but the Winnebagos maintained their connection with other Siouan tribes of the Mississippi, notably the Iowas and Omahas, by means of a southern corridor. In 1671, they suffered heavy losses in a war with the Illinois Confederacy, a union of 11 Algonquian-speaking tribes. Although they recovered, the Winnebagos again suffered losses in warfare with the Chippewas and the United States during the early nineteenth century.

Some Winnebago warriors participated in the revolt of Tecumseh. After Tecumseh's death during the War of 1812, the tribe sought peace with the United States. In a series of treaties beginning in 1816, they ceded all their land east of the Mississippi. Most Winnebagos were removed to Iowa in 1840, although about 900 managed to stay in Wisconsin. Subsequently they were again moved, first to Min-

Four Legs, a Winnebago chief.

nesota and then to South Dakota. Finally, in 1865, they were removed to a reservation in Nebraska. Then in 1874, the federal government dropped its prohibition on returning to Wisconsin. As a result, about half the tribe returned even though they were given no reservation.

In 1816, the tribe numbered about 5,000, but by 1900 the Winnebago population in both Nebraska and Wisconsin had declined to 2,000. This dramatic decrease was the result of warfare, disease (including smallpox epidemics in 1838 and 1860), relocations, and the Winnebagos' other contacts with whites.

Women's Suffrage

Belying the modern image of the West as a politically conservative region, the movement for women's suffrage in America first achieved success in the West. Before 1917, the only states in the Union that granted the vote to women were in the West, and when the Nineteenth Amendment was passed in all but four western states—New Mexico, Texas, Nebraska, and North Dakota—had already given them the vote.

The first echoes of the women's suffrage movement, begun in the East, were heard in the West in 1868, when Laura DeForce Gordon spoke in San Francisco in favor of women voting. With the completion of the Transcontinental Railroad, suffragists came west to advocate their cause. Despite the preponderance of activists in the East, it was in the West that the first practical results were achieved. Women were granted the vote in the Wyoming Territory in 1869, Utah Territory in 1870, Washington Territory in 1883, the state of Wyoming in 1890, Colorado in 1893, Utah and Idaho in 1896.

The circumstances that produced these results were unusual. Some influential easterners (including editorialists on *The New York Times*) believed that if women were given the vote in Utah, the Mormon-dominated state would quickly eliminate polygamy. To further that end, Congressman George Washington Julian of Indiana introduced a bill in

Women exercise their right to vote in Cheyenne, Wyoming.

A women's suffrage poster, insisting on full voting rights in Nebraska.

Congress to give women the vote in all of the territories. The bill was not passed, but the publicity put the idea before the public.

At the time of the passage of women's suffrage, Wyoming was populated by 1,000 women and 6,000 men over the age of 21; Wyoming legislators believed that a women's suffrage act would attract more women to the territory. Women were granted the franchise in 1869. Utah followed suit, because the Mormon leadership believed that the gesture would show Congress that Mormon women were not slaves to their husbands, while simultaneously doubling the number of Mormon voters in the state.

The enfranchisement of women in the West led to the first female candidates winning elections in western states. The first woman elected to Congress was Jeannette Rankin of Montana; the first elected mayor, Mary Howard of Kanab, Utah; the first elected mayor of a major city, Bertha Landes of Seattle, Washington; and the first elected governors were Miriam "Ma" Ferguson of Texas and Nellie Taylor Ross of Wyoming.

Wounded Knee

Wounded Knee is the South Dakota creek that gave its name to a tragic and bloody encounter between U.S. troops and Miniconjou Lakota Sioux Indians, on December 29, 1890. The terrible slaughter poisoned relations between whites and Indians for a century and still symbolizes the wrongs inflicted by one race on the other.

The conflict at Wounded Knee had its origins in the Ghost Dance religion that swept the western reservations in the late 1880s. This revitalization movement in turn grew out of the cultural breakdown caused by the U.S. government's attempt to "civilize" the Indians—to impose white American culture upon them. Heavily Christian and pacifist in intent and content, the Ghost Dance religion was the teaching of the Paiute Indian holy man Wovoka. From his Nevada reservation, the doctrine spread throughout the West. The dances and their associated beliefs and rituals aimed at a new and joyful world, free of white people, restocked with the vanished buffalo and other game, and repeopled with all the generations of Indians that had gone before.

Nowhere did this promise stir greater devotion than among the Lakota Sioux. The seven Lakota tribes lived on six separate reservations in North and South Dakota. The swelling intensity of the dances during 1890 troubled all the Indian agents, but only one panicked. At Pine Ridge Agency, Daniel F. Royer, newly appointed for political services and entirely unqualified, confronted a defiant people. Disorder spread. Settlers outside the reservations took alarm. Royer frantically appealed for military aid.

On November 20, 1890, troops occupied Pine Ridge and Rosebud agencies. The Ghost Dancers

Gunner Paul Weinart, center, drove the Sioux away from an important location during the final battle at Wounded Knee. He was awarded a Medal of Honor.

fled to a fortresslike tableland in the northwestern corner of the Pine Ridge Reservation called the Stronghold, and vowed to resist. Military leaders, under the overall command of General Nelson A. Miles, sought to persuade them to return to their homes.

Most of the leading chiefs, including the influential Red Cloud, wanted to avoid trouble. In General Miles's opinion, however, two of the chiefs were dedicated Ghost Dancers who needed to be removed from their people until the crisis ended. One was the Hunkpapa chief Sitting Bull, at Standing Rock. The peace effort received a severe setback on December 15 when Indian police, attempting to arrest Sitting Bull, shot and killed him. The other chief thought to be a troublemaker was the Miniconjou Big Foot, at Cheyenne River. Unknown to Miles, however, Big Foot's ardor for the Ghost Dance had faded. Admired for his reputation as a peacemaker, he had been invited by the Pine Ridge chiefs to lend his influence to the negotiations. When Big Foot and his people broke camp and headed for Pine Ridge, military authorities assumed he intended to join the Ghost Dancers in the Stronghold. Orders were issued to find him, disarm his people, and deport them from the reservation.

On December 28 a squadron of the 7th Cavalry intercepted Big Foot, prostrated by pneumonia, and escorted his band to Wounded Knee Creek, about 20 miles east of Pine Ridge Agency. That night the balance of the 7th Cavalry arrived, and Colonel James W. Forsyth assumed command. In preparation for disarming the Indians, Forsyth surrounded the village with his 500 troopers and placed four small-caliber cannons on a commanding hilltop. Big Foot's tepees, scattered along the banks of the creek, sheltered about 350 people.

The next morning Forsyth assembled the Indian men in a council circle near the village and demanded their guns. When none were forthcoming, detachments searched the village. Still, none of the Winchester repeating rifles observed the day before were found. Big Foot, desperately ill and reclining on a pallet, withheld cooperation. Tensions built on both sides. A holy man pranced around the circle, urging the men to fight. Their ghost shirts would protect them, he promised. Nervous troopers fingered their carbine triggers. One soldier seized a deaf man and grasped his rifle. It went off. The chanting priest threw a handful of dirt into the air.

A knot of Indians dropped their blankets and leveled rifles at a rank of soldiers. Both sides fired at once.

In a murderous melee at close range, soldiers and Indians shot, stabbed, and clubbed one another. Big Foot rose from his pallet. A volley killed him and most of the headmen lined up behind him. Abruptly the two sides separated, and from the hill the artillery opened fire. Exploding shells flattened the Sioux tepees and sought out scattered groups of fleeing Indians. Shrapnel felled men, women, and children. In less than an hour most of the fighting had ended, leaving nearly two-thirds of Big Foot's band cut down, at least 150 Indian dead and 50 wounded, and perhaps more who were never reported. The army lost 25 dead and 39 wounded.

Wounded Knee ruined the army's peace initiative. Ghost Dancers who were on the verge of giving up returned to the Stronghold, where they were joined by frightened refugees from the agency. General Miles, however, pursued a careful program of diplomacy combined with the threat of force. Within two weeks he had succeeded in coaxing all the dancers into the agency and in ending the conflict.

Wounded Knee set off a controversy that persists to this day. In truth, no one on either side intended a fight. The Indians did not, as some officers later charged; they were outnumbered, surrounded, poorly armed, and had their women and children with them. Nor did the soldiers; they clearly saw their overwhelming advantage and could not conceive of armed resistance. When violence erupted, they fought with fury. In the battle, noncombatants fell not through deliberate intent, but simply because they were there. For a century to come, however, the images of dead and maimed women and children dominated the memory of Wounded Knee, angering Indian people and troubling white people.

Wovoka

CA. 1856–1932

Wovoka, also known as Jack Wilson, was a Paiute visionary whose prophecies were the basis of the Ghost Dance religion, whose misunderstanding by whites helped spark the tragedy at Wounded Knee in 1890. As with other Native Americans of near-mythic status, it is sometimes hard to tell fact from fiction in Wovoka's life.

Wovoka's father, usually identified as Tavibo, was a follower of the prophet Wodziwob, who was credited with initiating the Ghost Dance of 1870. His father died when Wovoka was about 14, and Wovoka was unofficially adopted by David and Mary Wilson, for whom he cut wood and performed various chores. Almost daily, the Wilsons spoke to him of God and Christ and read to him from the Bible. During harvest seasons, Wovoka worked as a migrant laborer in the hop fields of Oregon and Washington. There, he reportedly came in contact with the teachings of Smohalla, the dreamer-prophet who promised Native Americans the expulsion of whites, the restoration of the Indians' land, and the raising of their dead. The Wilsons' Christian doctrine and

SMITHSONIAN INSTITUTION

Wovoka, photographed here with T. J. McCoy.

Smohalla's teachings had a profound impact on the young man.

On what is usually reported as January 1, 1889, Wovoka fell into a trance, during which he claimed to be taken up to heaven. He reported visiting heaven on two other occasions. While there, he said he met God and saw all the Native Americans who had died. According to Wovoka, they were now happy and forever young.

On emerging from his trance, Wovoka proclaimed his revelation and announced that he was called to preach to his people on earth. His message was similar in substance to that of Wodziwob during the earlier Ghost Dance. It also had commonalities with other Native American apocalyptic "raising-up" belief-systems, including those of the Delaware prophet in 1762 and of Tenskwatawa, the Shawnee Prophet, in 1805.

Wovoka instructed Native Americans to perform the Ghost Dance at certain specific intervals. He also enjoined them to love one another, not steal, and, in general, to lead moral lives. If they did these things faithfully, Wovoka promised that God would send a mighty flood to sweep all whites from the continent. In the aftermath, dead friends and relatives would be raised, the buffalo would return to the plains, and the earth would be renewed, becoming a paradise. Although the vision foretold the elimination of whites, Wovoka instructed his people not to be violent. "You must not fight, you must not do harm to anyone, you must do right always" were basic tenets of Wovoka's new religion. In addition, he specifically instructed the Paiutes that they must put an end to warfare.

The Ghost Dance religion spread rapidly through the tribes of the West, gaining many adherents among a diversity of Native Americans. In the fall of 1889, the Cheyennes and Sioux sent delegates to meet with Wovoka and learn his teachings. On their return to their own tribes, two of these—Short Bull and Kicking Bear—began preaching Wovoka's doctrine among the Sioux. Whites did not understand that Wovoka's Ghost Dance was peaceful and against warfare. They also feared that if all the tribes began practicing Ghost Dance, as many did, it would unify them and be a locus of armed resistance. This misinterpretation by whites of the Ghost Dance contributed to the hysteria that led to the Wounded Knee massacre.

Wovoka lived as a holy man among the Paiutes as

he had before. The Ghost Dance lasted about two years after Wounded Knee. It sputtered out and was finally suppressed in 1892.

Wright, William

See De Quille, Dan

Wyoming

Wyoming, a mountain state, has the 10th largest area but the smallest population of all U.S. states. Its terrain lives up to its name, which is derived from a Delaware Indian term for "at the big plains." Cheyenne, the capital, was founded in 1867, one year before Wyoming gained territory status. Statehood was granted on July 10, 1890.

In 1742 French explorers François and Louis Joseph de La Vérendrye first set foot in what would become Wyoming. Later, nineteenth-century explorers and fur traders, such as John Colter, encountered Crow, Blackfoot, Ute, Flathead, Cheyenne, Shoshoni, Arapaho, and Sioux Indians in the area. The United States annexed Wyoming in 1803, and by 1878 all the tribes had been forced out except for the Shoshonis and Arapahos, who now occupy the Wind River Reservation.

The region's fur trade, which flourished during the 1820s and 1830s, drew such well-known mountain men as James Bridger, Jedediah Strong Smith, and William Sublette. But the Hudson's Bay and American Fur Companies' greed greatly depleted the stock of beavers. By 1840 the fur trade had dwindled to next to nothing.

The John C. Frémont expedition across Wyoming in 1842 expanded awareness of the land's potential. In anticipation of future homesteaders, the Oregon and other trails were blazed. Forts, such as Bridger, Laramie, and Fetterman, sprang up to protect the workers and travelers from Indian attacks. When the Bozeman Trail was cut through the last hunting ground of the Sioux in 1863, tension erupted into Red Cloud's War. Chief Red Cloud of the Sioux, along with Cheyennes and Arapahos, defended their

A raft crossing Deer Creek, Wyoming.

land against broken treaties. The Fetterman Massacre of 1866 (in which the Sioux killed Lieutenant Colonel W. J. Fetterman and 80 men from Fort Phil Kearny) and the Wagon Box Fight of 1867 (in which Captain James Powell drove back several hundred Sioux) were two major battles that took place in Wyoming.

The territory of Wyoming was created in 1868 from parts of the Oregon, Dakota, Utah, and Idaho territories. Completion of the Union Pacific Railroad in 1869 brought more settlers, many of whom had helped construct the railway. Cattle ranching thrived on the open ranges. But the Homestead Act of 1862, land offers meant to encourage settlers,

Andrew Joseph Russell photographed this Union Pacific train in Granite Canyon, Wyoming.

brought instead illegal claims and created mammoth ranches, ultimately leading to the end of the open range. Within the five years between 1880 and 1885 cattle increased from 300,000 head to over 1.5 million. Ranchers butted heads with sheep farmers over land and water use, and cattle rustling became such a problem that ranchers began to take the law into their own hands, as in the case of the Johnson County War.

In 1869 Wyoming became the first political unit in the world to grant women full rights to vote and hold office. This led to the appointment of Esther Morris as a justice of the peace. Upon achieving statehood in 1890, Wyoming earned its nickname, "Equality State," since it was the first to extend full suffrage to women.

Wyoming did not develop large industries or population centers. Coal, iron ore, natural gas, and later trona and uranium were mined. But it was petroleum that replaced agriculture as the state's economic backbone. Tourist attractions Yellowstone and Grand Teton national parks are also a source of revenue.

X

XIT Ranch

Officially the Capitol Freehold Ranch or Capitol Syndicate Ranch, the XIT at its peak, from about 1890 to 1904, covered 3 million acres over 10 counties in the Texas Panhandle (providing the basis for the story that the XIT name and brand derived from "Ten in Texas").

The XIT had its origins in 1882, when the Texas State Legislature advertised for bids to build a new capitol building and stipulated that the low bidder would receive as payment 3 million acres of land designated as part of the Capitol Reservation. The contract was awarded to a Rock Island, Illinois, company that took on in partnership some executives in a Chicago dry goods firm. While the capitol building was under construction, the partners surveyed the land, and one of them, John Farwell, went to England to secure capital.

Farwell ended up with £3 million in investment funds and a British board of directors that included an earl, a marquis, and several lords and members of Parliament. Farwell was named managing director of the new Capitol Freehold Land and Investment Company, Ltd., established the ranch headquarters at Buffalo Springs, and hired the prominent cattleman of Wichita, Kansas, Colonel B. H. Campbell, as ranch manager. The first herd arrived and was purchased in July 1885, and the story goes that the XIT name was suggested by that herd's drover, who drew it in the dirt and said it would be hard for a rustler to alter. By 1888, when the new capitol building in Austin was finished, the XIT had 125,000 head of cattle and 700 miles of fence that divided the ranch into seven divisions, each with its own foreman, barns, bunkhouses, pens, and corrals. The XIT investors began selling off the land in the 1890s, and today the XIT is but a memory.

Y

Yellowstone National Park

Yellowstone National Park, the United States' first national park, occupies an area of approximately 3,470 square miles, mostly in northwestern Wyoming but extending into areas of eastern Idaho and southern Montana. The Yellowstone Act of 1872, which established the park, was a unique piece of legislation—this was the first time any nation had set aside land specifically to preserve it from public exploitation.

The region was home to Native American tribes long before the arrival of whites. The first non-indigenous explorer of the Yellowstone area was John Colter, who in 1807 traveled through after his return with the Lewis and Clark expedition. Other expeditions followed, and in 1871 Ferdinand V. Hayden conducted a scientific study of the Yellowstone area. Photographs taken during Hayden's expedition by William Henry Jackson and paintings by Thomas Moran were instrumental in convincing Congress to pass the Yellowstone Act.

Today the park and its spectacular scenery attract thousands of visitors each year. The geothermal features of Yellowstone are extremely popular. Old Faithful is the most famous of the more than 200 geysers in the park: for two to five minutes at a time, it throws a blast of water up to 130 feet in the air. The park is also home to thousands of hot springs, as well as several fumaroles and mud pots. Plant and animal life flourish here: elk, buffalo,

Old Faithful, Yellowstone.

moose, deer, antelope, and grizzly and black bears roam in a wilderness virtually untouched by civilization.

471

Thomas Moran at Mammoth Hot Springs in Yellowstone, photographed in 1871.

The awesome beauty of Yosemite.

Yosemite National Park

Yosemite National Park is a federal wilderness preserve located on the western edge of the Sierra Nevada mountain range in California. The park takes its name from the Yosemite Indians, who first inhabited the area.

Joseph R. Walker's expedition probably reached Yosemite in 1833, but the first whites known to have entered the region were members of a party led by Indian trader James Savage. At that time 22 Yosemite villages occupied the area. Savage traveled to the Yosemite Valley to punish the Indians who, after much provocation, had destroyed trading posts nearby. The Indians were soon driven out, and by 1855 the first tourists had arrived.

Yosemite, which occupies an area of approximately 1,190 square miles, was first designated a state park (1864); it became a national park in 1890. Yosemite Valley, carved by glaciers to depths as great as 2,750 feet, is one of the most frequently visited sites in California. Granite peaks and domes, including El Capitan, Half Dome, and Mount Lyell,

rise over 3,000 feet around Yosemite Valley. The Merced River runs through the valley, cascading over five waterfalls, two of which rank among the ten highest in the world. In addition to these awesome geographical features, Yosemite also houses three groves of ancient sequoias and sugar pines. Yosemite National Park, with its wide variety of recreational activities, attracts an estimated 2.5 million tourists each year.

Young, Brigham

1801–1877

Brigham Young was the Mormon leader who led his Church of Jesus Christ of Latter-day Saints to Utah and helped colonize and develop the West.

Young was the ninth of 11 children, and his impoverished family moved several times in his early years. In spite of his claim to only 11 days of schooling, Brigham learned a lot early on about work: he cleared land, learned how to trap and catch fish, how to farm, how to build a home, how to live frugally—all important skills that would make him independent. In 1815 his mother died after a long bout of consumption (tuberculosis), and the family moved again. At the age of 17, he began supporting himself by carpentry, joinery, painting, and glazing. In 1824 he married Miriam Angeline Works, and they both joined the Methodist Reform Church—his first religious affiliation.

In 1830, after the birth of two daughters and Miriam's semi-invalidism from chronic tuberculosis, Young first saw the Book of Mormon, reputed to be scripture prepared by Joseph Smith, Jr., which recorded the deeds of people who had established a new civilization in the Western Hemisphere after leaving the Middle East. Deeply impressed with the book, he converted to the Church of Jesus Christ of Latter-day Saints on April 14, 1832, and after Miriam died in September he went to visit Prophet Joseph Smith in Kirtland, Ohio. He later abandoned

his business and property, began proselytizing, and headed for Canada. While preaching he met Mary Ann Angell, whom he married in February 1834. Young joined the 2,000 mile expedition of Zion's Camp to Missouri and back to help the Mormon community there, which had been legally harassed, had its members tarred and feathered, whipped, and robbed, and many homes burned. Young proved he was a leader during this difficult trek. When it was formed, in February 1835, he was appointed to the Council of Twelve Apostles and then spent the summers of 1886 and 1887 doing missionary work in the East and New York. In winter he continued his trades and helped in the completion of the Kirtland Temple. The church's bank failed, and Young staved off a coup by the brethren to unseat Smith. With his family, he followed Smith from Ohio to Far West, Missouri, in February 1838.

Local settlers feared that the Mormons might vote themselves into local power, and armed mobs harassed the Saints. The Missouri governor issued a command that the Mormons be exterminated or driven out of Missouri. Smith and other leaders of the church were held by federal troops; the rest of the community was taken prisoner after a rampage of

Brigham Young's family, painted by William Warner Major.

thievery, all their property was forfeit to pay for the military action, and the Saints had to leave the state. Young held a de facto position of importance in the church after the arrest of its leaders, and he undertook to bring the Mormons away from the Far West to Nauvoo, Illinois.

In 1840–1841 Young went to England to look for converts. Back in Nauvoo, he became president of the Council and part of Smith's inner circle. The new doctrine of plural marriage became a divine requirement, which Young reluctantly accepted, and with Mary Ann's permission in June 1842 he married his first plural wife, Lucy Ann Decker Seeley, with whom he would have seven children. He next went east to raise money for the completion of the Nauvoo Temple and the Nauvoo House, a hotel. However, back in Nauvoo, Smith's ideal of a theocratic kingdom did not sit well with non-Mormons, and the Prophet, after announcing his candidacy for president of the United States, which further infuriated his enemies, was jailed and then killed by a mob that broke into the jail.

Young returned and claimed the right of church leadership as president of the Council and was accepted by the congregation. Nauvoo's charter allowed it to run its affairs as a separate entity from the county, and once again non-Mormons threatened violence against the Saints. Young knew that the 16,000 Mormons would have to leave. He felt they should settle in an unoccupied region where their customs would not antagonize anyone. The way pointed west, and reports of the Great Salt Lake Valley in Utah were well received. Young led the initial migration on a great trek through Indian country. After five months they arrived at Salt Lake Valley, the site Young stated was foreordained for the Saints. He laid out the plan for the city and was chosen president of the Latter-day Saints. Colonists were sent out to occupy the habitable sites in the region and to discourage the encroachment of non-Mormons. He set up a currency exchange system, developed natural resources for self-sufficiency, organized a territorial government, and maintained a tentative peace with the Indians. In March 1849 Young was elected governor of the provisional State of Deseret, which included what is now Utah and parts of Nevada, Idaho, Wyoming, Colorado, New Mexico, Arizona, California, and Oregon.

Young believed the United States would admit Deseret to the Union as a state, but the statehood petition failed. In 1851 President Millard Fillmore did appoint Young the first governor of the new territory as well as superintendent of Indian affairs. Federal officers who entered Utah faced problems conducting their duties because of the despotic nature of Young's ecclesiastical and civil power, the Mormon isolationist policy, the issue of currency and appropriation, and the unclear relationship between the U.S. government and the Mormon church.

President Buchanan sent 2,500 federal troops to Utah in 1857, Young declared martial law and sent Mormon troops to meet the federals. Constant tension led to Young's resignation of the governorship upon Buchanan's appointment of a successor in 1858. Unfortunately some Mormons were involved in a massacre of 120 immigrants at Mountain Meadows, but an all-out war with the U.S. was averted. Young encouraged further Mormon colonization and the immigration of converts from Europe.

The Utah Territory remained neutral during the Civil War. Many Mormons were disappointed that the Union survived, believing that Mormonism would fill the void left by the war. Young was arrested for bigamy in 1872 but was never tried. His last years were spent building schools, telegraph and railroad connections, and expanding mineral ventures. He died having married fifty-five wives and having sired fifty-seven children.

Young left many sermons and theological writings. He was not a systematic theologian but rather an orthodox Mormon who believed it was man's precious responsibility to build society.

Younger Brothers

The Younger brothers—Thomas Coleman "Cole" (1844–1916), John (1846–1874), James (1850–1902), and Robert (1853–1889)—were among the 14 children of Henry Washington Younger. They were born in the vicinity of Jackson County, Missouri, and grew to manhood in the turbulent years of the Civil War border strife between Kansas and Missouri.

Although Henry Younger was a Unionist and was killed in 1862, Cole joined the Confederate State Guard and later became one of William Clarke Quantrill's Raiders. In the regular Confederate service, Cole compiled a distinguished record as a spy and soldier, but in December 1862 he killed a man in Kansas City and a reward was posted for his capture. He returned to Quantrill in August 1863 and on August 21 participated in the raid on Lawrence, Kansas, one of the greatest atrocities of the war.

Cole went into hiding after Lawrence, is believed to have participated in stagecoach and train robberies in Arkansas and Missouri (during which he may have first met Jesse and Frank James), and fled to Texas, where he married Myra Bell Shirley (later known as Belle Starr). He continued in hiding after the war and either met for the first time or was reunited with the James brothers. On February 13, 1866, Cole, Jesse James, and 10 other men robbed a bank in Liberty, Missouri. For several years thereafter the Youngers (Cole, Jim, and John were joined by Bob in 1872) and Jameses robbed banks, trains, and stagecoaches throughout the Midwest and Texas.

In March 1874, two Pinkerton detectives and a deputy sheriff were confronted by John and Jim Younger at Monegaw Springs, Missouri. In the gunfight that followed, John and one of the agents were killed; Jim Younger was wounded.

On September 7, 1876, attempting to rob the bank at Northfield, Minnesota, the James-Younger gang found the law and citizenry waiting for them. For the Youngers, it was the end of their careers as desperadoes. In the hail of bullets that greeted them in Northfield, two of the gang and two citizens were killed; Jim Younger was shot through the upper jaw, Bob in the arm, and Cole in the shoulder. Pursued by a huge posse of lawmen and townspeople, Jesse James and Cole Younger ended their friendship after Jesse insisted that Jim Younger, the most seriously wounded of the gang, be left behind. Cole refused, and the Jameses rode away, leaving the Younger boys to surrender.

Each pleaded guilty to the attempted robbery and was sentenced to life in prison. On September 16, 1899, Robert Younger died in prison in Stillwater, Oklahoma, of tuberculosis. Cole and James were pardoned in 1901, and James, in declining health and after an unhappy love affair, committed suicide in the Reardon Hotel in St. Paul, Minnesota, on October 19, 1902.

Cole Younger was granted a full pardon in 1903 and returned to Missouri, where he resumed his friendship with Frank James. The two toured with a wild west show for several years. Cole retired to his home at Lee's Summit, Missouri, occasionally lectured on such subjects as "Crime Does Not Pay" and "What Life Has Taught Me," and died on February 21, 1916.

MINNESOTA HISTORICAL SOCIETY

Jim Younger served 25 years in jail for the Northfield robbery.

MINNESOTA HISTORICAL SOCIETY

Bob Younger died in prison, of tuberculosis.

MINNESOTA HISTORICAL SOCIETY

Cole Younger survived 11 gunshot wounds.

Yukon River

The Yukon River, the third largest river in North America, flows through the Yukon Territory, Canada, and the state of Alaska. Rising in British Columbia, the river flows 1,979 miles, first northwest to Fort Yukon, Alaska, and then southwest to Norton Sound on the Bering Sea. Its main tributaries are the Klondike, Stewart, and White rivers in Canada and the Innoko, Koyukuk, Porcupine, and Tanana rivers in Alaska.

Russian and English fur trappers and traders were early nonindigenous explorers of the Yukon. The first Russian to cross the river, Aleksey Ivanov, was led by Native Americans north from Iliamna Lake in the early 1790s. From 1883 to 1884 Andrei Glazunov and four fellow Russians explored the Yukon, looking for communication routes to facilitate trade. In 1885 Glazunov returned to follow the lower Yukon. Early British explorers (mostly from the Hudson's Bay Company) included Robert Campbell and John Bell, who opened inland routes to the Yukon in 1840. The first Russian scientific investigation of the Yukon was performed by Lieutenant L. A. Zagoskin between 1842 and 1844. Zagoskin, in the most thorough exploration of the river to date, gathered information on the geography, plant and animal life, and native settlements of the region.

The Yukon River has long been a crucial supply route for the interior of Alaska. It was used extensively by fur traders, and after gold was discovered in 1896, it was an important means of transport for the ensuing Klondike gold rush. Today the Yukon is used for local shipping, salmon fishing, and as a source of hydroelectric power.

Z

Zuni Indians

Zuni is the name of a Pueblo in western New Mexico near the Arizona state line.

The earliest Spaniards to enter the New Mexico region told fantastic tales of the Seven Golden Cities Of Cibola, towns literally made out of gold. Don Antonio de Mendoza, Spanish Viceroy of New Spain, commissioned Fray Marcos de Niza to lead an expeditionary force in 1539. De Niza took with him a Moor named Esteban (or Estevanico), one of those who had first reported the Zuni El Dorado. In fact, the stories of golden towns had arisen merely from the sun reflecting off the Adobe walls of Zuni homes.

Esteban went ahead of the main party and sent a messenger to announce his arrival to the Zunis. The Zunis, unimpressed, sent back word not to enter the town on penalty of death. Esteban, swaggering and self-important, entered anyway and enraged the Zunis by demanding tribute and women. Pueblo leaders had him put to death "so that he would not reveal our location to his brothers." The Esteban story is significant to the Zunis. They still commemorate his coming—as the first European—with rituals among the Pueblos. At Jemez Pueblo, for instance, two effigies, one of a white priest and the other of a black (with black sheep fleece as curly hair) are paraded on the pueblo's yearly feast day. Pueblos often say, "The first white man our people saw was a black man."

On his return to Mexico, de Niza falsely boasted

Zuni leader Pedro Pino.

of the riches he had discovered. A year later, Coronado retraced de Niza's route into the Southwest, again reaching Zuni territory, this time bringing an armed force. Arriving at Zuni during the summer solstice, a time when pilgrims make sacred journeys, he was attacked by Zuni priests whose job it was to protect the pilgrims. Coronado responded by attacking a Zuni village and generally dealing roughly with the Pueblos. From Zuni country he dispatched columns in various directions, one of which "discovered" the Grand Canyon. His main force headed east and, after visiting many of the Pueblos, traveled as far as Kansas.

The experience of Zuni is similar to that of the other pueblos. The Zunis participated in the Pueblo Revolt of 1680 and continued to resist the Spanish after the reconquest of the pueblos under Diego De Vargas.

Maps

NATIVE AMERICANS

ESKIMO

ATHABASCAN

NORTHERN BLACKFEET

BLOOD INDIANS

KUTENAI

CREE

PLAINS-OJIBWA

MAKAH

SPOKANE

ASSINIBOIN

ALGONQUIAN

CHINOOK

KIDATSA

ONONDAGA

PIEGAN

ARIKARA

NORTH-WEST CROW

WOODLANDS-OJIBWA

HURONS

AMERICANS SANS-ARC BRULE

MANDAN

SANTE

DAKOTA

MOHAWK

KAROK UMATILLA

OGLALA MINNECONJOUX

YANKLON AND

CAYUGA

HUPA NEZ-PERCE

YONKTOAI-DAKOTA

ONEIDA

WINTU ATSINA

TWO-KETTLE

SENECA

PATWIN CHEYENNE

HUNKPAPA

WINNE BAGO SHAWNEE

POMO BANNOCK ARAPAHO

BLACKFOOT OMAHA

MASCOUTIN

SAC & FOX PIANKASHAW

CALIFORNIAN SHOSHONE

PAWNEE

KICKAPOO MIAMI MONTAUK

INDIANS UTE

KANSA

PEORIA

COSTANOAN PAIUTE HOPI

OSAGEN

DELAWARE POMUNKEY

SALINAN NAVAHO

PONKA

MISSOURI ILLINOIS CHICKAHOMINY

CHUMASH

APACHE

OTO QUAPAW

TUSCARORA

PUEBLO

CADDO

IOWA

CHEROKEE TUTELO

MARICOBA

CHOCTAW

PAPAGO

WICHITA

CHICKASAW CATAWBA

PIMO

ARAPAHO

CREEK

APACHE CHEYENNE KIOWA

NATCHEZ TUNICA

PAPAGO BASAWUNENA COMANCHE

BILOXI

PACIFIC

SEMINOLE

OCEAN

OFO

ATLANTIC OCEAN

GULF OF MEXICO

SONORA PEOPLES

MENOMINI

PATTAWA

POTTAWATOMI

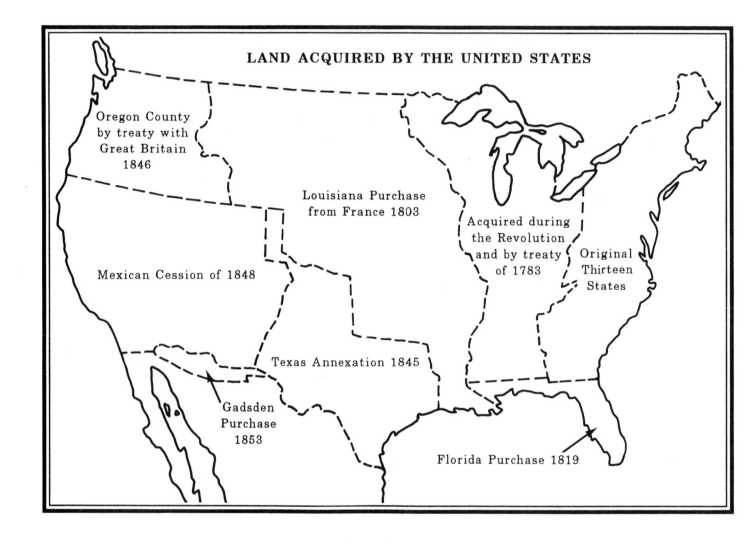

LAND ACQUIRED BY THE UNITED STATES

Oregon County by treaty with Great Britain 1846

Louisiana Purchase from France 1803

Acquired during the Revolution and by treaty of 1783

Original Thirteen States

Mexican Cession of 1848

Texas Annexation 1845

Gadsden Purchase 1853

Florida Purchase 1819

INDIAN RESERVATIONS

NORTHWEST COASTAL TRIBES

COLVILLE
SPOKANE
BLACKFEET
YAKIMA
FLATHEAD
COEUR
D'ALENE
NEZ PERCE
UMATILLA
WARM
SPRINGS
KLAMATH
RIVER
KLAMATH
SHOSHONI &
BANNOCK
HOOPA
VALLEY
ROUND
VALLEY
SHOSHONI &
BANNOCK
POMO
SHOSHONI
& PAIUTE
PAIUTE
PAIUTE
UTE
MOAPA
RIVER
TULE
RIVER
NAVAJO
UTE
SUPPAI
HOPI
JICARILLA
APACHE
HAULPAI
MOJAVE
MOJAVE
PIMA
PUEBLO
MISSION
INDIANS
MARICOPA
ZUNI
APACHE
YUMA
TOHONO
O'ODHAM
WICHITA & CADDO
COMANCHE, KIOWA & APACHE
MESCALERO
APACHE
TOHONO
O'ODHAM

CHIPPEWA
SIOUX
MANDAN
REE
MINITARI
CHIPPEWA
TRIBES
SIOUX &
ASSINIBOIN
CROW
SIOUX
SIOUX
SHOSHONI &
ARAPAHO
SIOUX
NIOBRARA
OMAHA
WINNEBAGO

SAC & FOX
IOWA
KICKAPOO
POTTAWATOMIE
CHIPPEWA & MUNSEE
CHIPPEWA
TONKAWA
PONCA
OTO & MISSOURI
KAW
OSAGE
QUAPAW
PEORIA
PAWNEE
CHEROKEE
OTTAWA
SHAWNEE
CHEYENNE &
ARAPAHO
SAC & FOX
CREEK
MODOC
WYANDOTTE
SENECA
SEMINOLE
CHOCTAW
IOWA
CHICKASAW
KICKAPOO
TOMKAWA
POTTAWATOMIE & SHAWNEE

Lands ceded by Indians before 1850

Indian lands as of 1850

Indian reservations as of 1890

0   100   200   300   400
Miles

THE AMERICAN WEST *circa* 1875

INDIAN WARS AFTER 1850

WASHINGTON
TERRITORY

BEAR PAW MT.

MONTANA
TERRITORY

Fort Buford

BITTERROOT MTS.

Walla Walla

BLACKFOOT

Fort
Ellis

Fort
Abraham
Lincoln

Fort Yates

CASCADE
RANGE

NEZ PERCE

LITTLE
BIGHORN

BATTLE OF THE ROSEBUD

MINNESOTA
WAR

IDAHO
TERRITORY

OREGON

CROW

BLACK HILLS

SIOUX

SIOUX

Fort
Meade

DAKOTA
TERRITORY MINNESOTA

MODOC
WAR

Fort
Washakie

CHEYENNE

Fort Randall

MODOC

SOUTH PASS

SHOSHONI
ARAPAHO

WYOMING
TERRITORY

SIOUX

WOUNDED
KNEE

NEBRASKA

PAWNEE R.

IOWA

NEVADA

Platte

UTAH
TERRITORY

COLORADO
TERRITORY

Fort Kearney

Missouri R.

UTE

KANSAS

Fort
Dodge

Medicine
Lodge

MISSOURI

CALIFORNIA

ARIZONA
TERRITORY

NEW MEXICO
TERRITORY

CHEYENNE OSAGE
ARAPAHO

Fort Gibson

Arkansas R.

INDIAN
TERRITORY

Fort Bascom

ADOBE
WALLS

Fort Sill

WHITE
MOUNTAIN APACHE

KWAHADI
COMANCHE

Fort Arbuckle

ARAVAIPA APACHE

MIMBRES
APACHE

STAKED PLAINS

Fort
Richardson

Fort
Worth

Fort
Buchanan

Tucson

APACHE PASS

Fort Griffin

Red R.

CHIRICAHUA
APACHE

Janos

Fort
Concho

Parker's
Fort

Arizpe

NEDNI APACHE

Rio Grande

Pecos R.

Huntsville

LOUISIANA

SIERRA MADRE

MEXICO

TEXAS

0 100 200 300 400

Miles

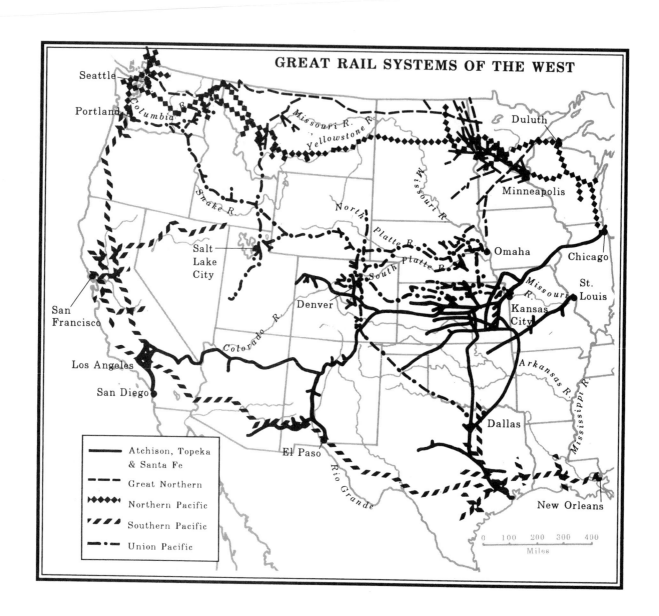

GREAT RAIL SYSTEMS OF THE WEST

Seattle
Portland
Columbia R.
Snake R.
Missouri R.
Yellowstone R.
Duluth
Minneapolis
North
Platte R.
Missouri R.
Omaha
Chicago
Salt Lake City
South Platte R.
Denver
Kansas City
Missouri R.
St. Louis
San Francisco
Colorado R.
Los Angeles
San Diego
Arkansas R.
Dallas
El Paso
Rio Grande
Mississippi R.
New Orleans

Atchison, Topeka & Santa Fe
Great Northern
Northern Pacific
Southern Pacific
Union Pacific

0   100   200   300   400
Miles

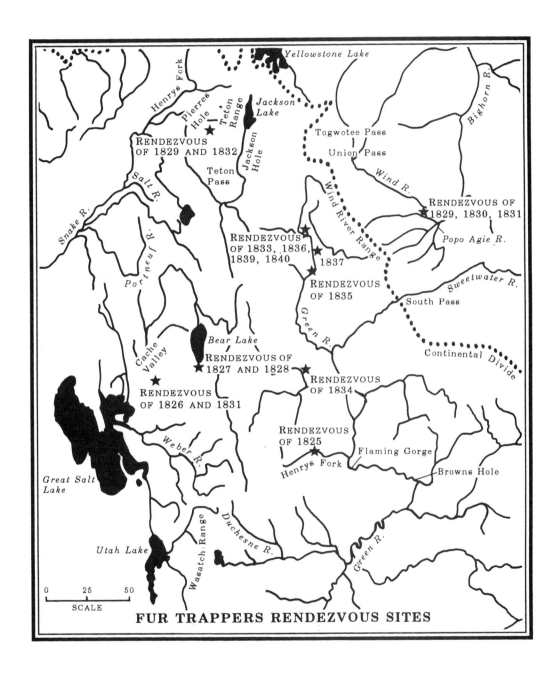

FUR TRAPPERS RENDEZVOUS SITES

PRIMARY WESTERN
MINING SITES, 1848-1900

Astoria • Fort Walla Walla • Spokane • Fort
▲ KELLOGG Benton •   *Missouri R.*   Minot •   Grand
Oregon City •   Portland •   ▲ OROFINO   Medora • Bismarck   Forks
Salem •   Walla Walla •   • HELENA   Fargo •
Fort   La Grande •   ▲ BUTTE
Umpqua ■   **OREGON TERRITORY**   ▲ VIRGINIA CITY   **MINNESOTA**
• Bums   • IDAHO CITY BANNACK **UNORGANIZED**   **TERRITORY**
• Klamath Falls   ▲ BOISE   **TERRITORY**   DEADWOOD
• Burley   ■ Fort Hall   LEAD ▲▲ • Pierre
Winnemucca •   • Logan   • ATLANTIC CITY • Rapid City
MARYSVILLE ▲   Elko •   Fort Laramie ▲ • Scottsbluff Custer
Ø▲ VIRGINIA CITY   • Salt   ■   Council Bluffs
SACRAMENTO •   **UTAH**   Lake City   Cheyenne • Sidney • • North Platte
STOCKTON ▲   **TERRITORY**   • BOULDER
Richfield •   Aspen • ▲ DENVER • Kearney
San Jose •   Cedar City •   • Gunnison ▲ CENTRAL CITY
San Francisco •   **CALIFORNIA**   Ouray ▲ LEADVILLE   • Council Grove
Silverton • • Creede   ■ Fort Dodge
NEW MEXICO
Los Angeles •   **TERRITORY**
San Diego •   *Gila R.*
SILVER CITY ▲
TUCSON ▲
TOMBSTONE ▲
BISBEE ▲

*PACIFIC
OCEAN*

• Cities and Towns
▲ Mining Sites

ALASKA
Fort Yukon ■ Circle
Yukon R.   City
St. Michael •   Dawson
Anchorage •
Skagway •

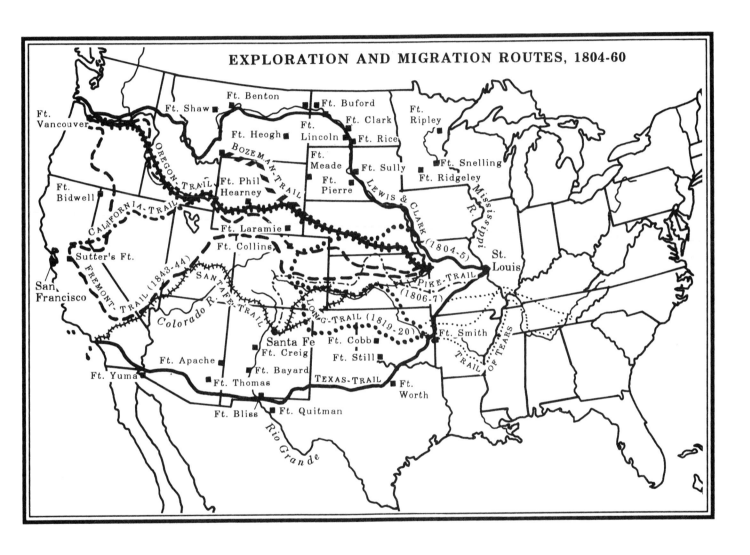

EXPLORATION AND MIGRATION ROUTES, 1804-60

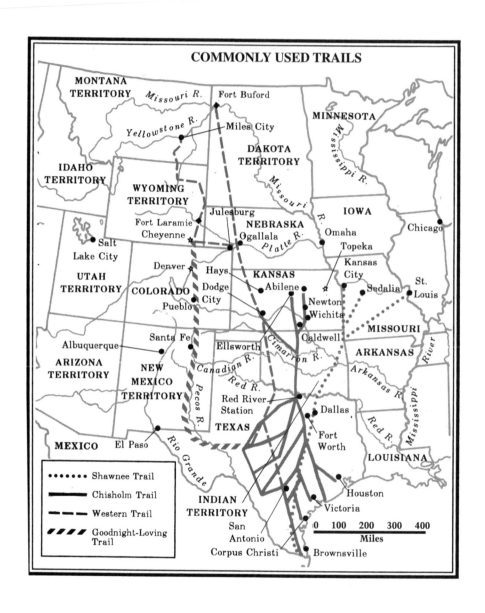

COMMONLY USED TRAILS

MONTANA
TERRITORY

Missouri R.

Fort Buford

Yellowstone R.

Miles City

MINNESOTA

Mississippi R.

DAKOTA
TERRITORY

Missouri R.

IDAHO
TERRITORY

WYOMING
TERRITORY

Julesburg

Fort Laramie
Cheyenne

Salt
Lake City

NEBRASKA

Ogallala
Platte R.

IOWA

Omaha
Topeka

Chicago

Kansas
City

UTAH
TERRITORY

Denver

Hays

KANSAS

St.
Louis

COLORADO

Dodge
City

Abilene

Sedalia

Pueblo

Newton
Wichita

Santa Fe

Albuquerque

Ellsworth

Cimarron R.

Caldwell

MISSOURI

ARKANSAS

Arkansas R.

Mississippi River

ARIZONA
TERRITORY

NEW
MEXICO
TERRITORY

Canadian R.

Red R.

Pecos R.

Red River
Station

Dallas

Red R.

El Paso

MEXICO

Rio Grande

TEXAS

Fort
Worth

LOUISIANA

Houston

INDIAN
TERRITORY

Victoria

San
Antonio

Corpus Christi

Brownsville

•••••• Shawnee Trail

—— Chisholm Trail

– – – Western Trail

//// Goodnight-Loving
Trail

0   100   200   300   400
Miles

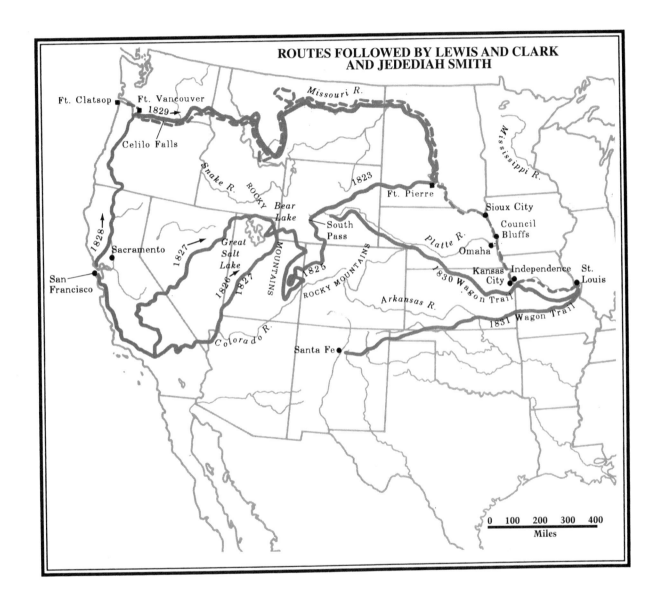

ROUTES FOLLOWED BY LEWIS AND CLARK
AND JEDEDIAH SMITH

Bibliography

ABERLE, DAVID F. *The Peyote Religion Among the Navaho*. Chicago: University of Chicago Press, 1982.

ALLEN, JOHN LOGAN. *Passage Through the Garden: Lewis and Clark and the Image of the American Northwest*. Urbana, IL: University of Illinois Press, 1975.

ANDERSON, EDWARD F. *Peyote: The Divine Cactus*. Tucson, AZ: University of Arizona Press, 1980.

ANTELYES, PETER. *Tales of Adventurous Enterprise: Washington Irving and the Poetics of Western Expansion*. New York: Columbia University Press, 1990.

APPLETON, JOHN. *North for Union*. Nashville, TN: Vanderbilt University Press, 1986.

ATHEARN, ROBERT G. *The Mythic West in Twentieth Century America*. Lawrence, KS: University Press of Kansas, 1986.

BAUER, KARL JACK. *Zachary Taylor: Soldier, Planter, Statesman of the Old Southwest*. Baton Rouge, LA: Louisiana State University Press, 1985.

BEAL, MERRILL D. *"I Will Fight No More Forever:" Chief Joseph and the Nez Perce War*. Seattle, WA: University of Washington Press, 1963.

BERGERON, PAUL. *The Presidency of James K. Polk*. Lawrence, KS: University Press of Kansas, 1987.

BETENSON, LULA PARKER. *Butch Cassidy: My Brother*. Provo, UT: Brigham Young University Press, 1975.

BILLINGTON, RAY ALLEN. *Frederick Jackson Turner: Historian, Scholar, Teacher*. New York: Oxford University Press, 1973.

BLACK ELK. *Black Elk Speaks: Being the Life Story of a Holy Man of the Oglala Sioux*. Introduction by Vine Deloria, Jr. Lincoln, NE: University of Nebraska Press, 1988.

BLEGEN, THEODORE CHRISTIAN. *Minnesota: A History of the State*. Minneapolis: University of Minnesota Press, 1975.

BOLTON, HERBERT EUGENE. *Rim of Christendom: A Biography of Eusebio Francisco Kino*. Foreword by John L. Kessell. Tucson, AZ: University of Arizona Press, 1984.

BROWN, RICHARD MAXWELL. *No Duty to Retreat: Violence and Values in American History and Society*. New York: Oxford University Press, 1991.

———. *Strain of Violence: Historical Studies of American Violence and Vigilantism*. New York: Oxford University Press, 1975.

BURROWS, JACK. *John Ringo: The Gunfighter Who Never Was*. Tucson, AZ: University of Arizona Press, 1987.

BUSHMAN, RICHARD L. *Joseph Smith and the Beginnings of Mormonism*. Urbana, IL: University of Illinois Press, 1984.

CARLSON, PAUL HOWARD. *"Pecos Bill:" A Military Biography of William R. Shafter*. College Station, TX: Texas A&M University Press, 1989.

CHAPIN, FREDERICK H. *The Land of the Cliff Dwellers*. Tucson, AZ: University of Arizona Press, 1988.

CLARK, ELLA ELIZABETH. *Sacagawea of the Lewis and Clark Expedition*. Berkeley, CA: University of California Press, 1979.

CLARK, W.P. *Indian Sign Language*. Lincoln, NE: University of Nebraska Press, 1982.

CLOKEY, RICHARD M. *William H. Ashley: Enterprise and Politics in the Trans Mississippi West*. Norman, OK: University of Oklahoma Press, 1980.

COATES, ROBERT M. *The Outlaw Years: The History of the Land Pirates of the Natchez Trace*. Lincoln, NE: University of Nebraska Press, 1986.

COHEN, MICHAEL P. *The Pathless Way: John Muir and American Wilderness*. Madison, WI: University of Wisconsin Press, 1984.

COMFORT, WILL LEVINGTON. *Apache*. Lincoln, NE: University of Nebraska Press, 1986.

CROMWELL, ARTHUR. *The Black Frontier*. Lincoln, NE: University of Nebraska Television, 1970.

DEARMENT, ROBERT K. *Bat Masterson: The Man and the Legend*. Norman, OK: University of Oklahoma Press, 1979.

DEBO, ANGIE. *And Still the Waters Run: The Betrayal of the Five Civilized Tribes*. Princeton, NJ: Princeton University Press, 1972.

———. *Geronimo: The Man, His Time, His Place.*

Norman, OK: University of Oklahoma Press, 1976.

DOBIE, JAMES FRANK. *Rattlesnakes.* Austin, TX: University of Texas Press, 1982.

DUBOFSKY, MELVYN. *"Big Bill" Haywood.* Manchester: Manchester University Press, 1987.

———. *We Shall Be All: A History of the Industrial Workers of the World.* Urbana, IL: University of Illinois Press, 1988.

DWYER, RICHARD A. *Dan De Quille, the Washoe Giant: A Biography and Anthology.* Reno, NY: University of Nevada Press, 1990.

EASTMAN, CHARLES ALEXANDER. *Indian Heroes and Great Chieftains.* Lincoln, NE: University of Nebraska Press, 1991.

ELIADE, MIRCEA. *Shamanism: Archaic Techniques of Ecstasy.* Princeton, NJ: Princeton University Press, 1964.

ELLIOTT, RUSSEL R. *Servant of Power: A Political Biography of Senator William M. Stewart.* Reno, NV: University of Nevada Press, 1983.

FAULK, ODIE B. *Dodge City: The Most Western Town of All.* New York: Oxford University Press, 1977.

———. *Tombstone: Myth and Reality.* New York: Oxford University Press, 1972.

FICKEN, ROBERT E. *Washington: A Centennial History.* Seattle, WA: University of Washington Press, 1988.

FLETCHER, ALICE C., and FRANCIS LA FLESCHE. *The Omaha Tribe.* Lincoln, NE: University of Nebraska Press, 1992.

FOLEY, WILLIAM E. *The Genesis of Missouri: From Wilderness Outpost to Statehood.* Columbia, MO: University of Missouri Press, 1989.

FONER, ERIC. *Free Soil, Free Labor, Free Men: The Ideology of the Republican Party Before the Civil War.* New York: Oxford University Press, 1970.

FREDRICKSSON, KRISTINE. *American Rodeo: From Buffalo Bill to Big Business.* College Station, TX: Texas A&M University Press, 1985.

FREEHLING, WILLIAM W. *The Road to Disunion: Secessionists at Bay, 1776–1854.* New York: Oxford University Press, 1990.

FURMAN, NECAH STEWART. *Walter Prescott Webb: His Life and Impact.* Albuquerque, NM: University of New Mexico Press, 1976.

GALLAGHER, TAG. *John Ford: The Man and His Films.* Berkeley, CA: University of California Press, 1986.

GARTER SNAKE. *The Seven Visions of Bull Lodge.* Lincoln, NE: University of Nebraska Press, 1980.

GIBSON, ARRELL M. *The Chickasaws.* Norman, OK: University of Oklahoma Press, 1971.

———. *The History of Oklahoma.* Norman, OK: University of Oklahoma Press, 1984.

GITELMAN, HOWARD M. *Legacy of the Ludlow Massacre.* Philadelphia, PA: University of Pennsylvania Press, 1988.

GRAY, JOHN S. *Centennial Campaign: The Sioux War of 1876.* Norman, OK: University of Oklahoma Press, 1988.

———. *Custer's Last Campaign: Mitch Boyer and the Little Bighorn Reconstructed.* Foreword by Robert M. Utley. Lincoln, NE: University of Nebraska Press, 1991.

———. *Mitch Boyer and the Little Bighorn Reconstructed.* Lincoln, NE: University of Nebraska Press, 1991.

GREENE, JEROME A. *Yellowstone Command: Colonel Nelson A. Miles and the Great Sioux War, 1876–1877.* Lincoln, NE: University of Nebraska Press, 1991.

GRIM, JOHN. *The Shaman: Patterns of Siberian and Ojibway Healing.* Norman, OK: University of Oklahoma Press, 1983.

GRISWOLD DEL CASTILLO, RICHARD. *The Treaty of Guadalupe Hidalgo: A Legacy of Conflict.* Norman, OK: University of Oklahoma Press, 1990.

GUTIERREZ, RAMON A. *When Jesus Came, the Corn Mothers Went Away: Marriage, Sexuality, and Power in New Mexico, 1500–1846.* Stanford, CA: Stanford University Press, 1991.

HAGAN, WILLIAM T. *American Indians.* Chicago: University of Chicago Press, 1993.

———. *Quanah Parker: Comanche Chief.* Norman, OK: University of Oklahoma Press, 1993.

HALES, PETER B. *William Henry Jackson and the Transformation of the American Landscape.* Philadelphia: Temple University Press, 1988.

HAMILTON, HOLMAN. *The Three Kentucky Presidents: Lincoln, Taylor, Davis.* Lexington, KY: University Press of Kentucky, 1978.

HANES, BAILEY C. *Bill Pickett, Bulldogger: The Biography of a Black Cowboy.* Foreword by Bill Burchardt. Norman, OK: University of Oklahoma Press, 1977.

HAVIGHURST, WALTER. *Annie Oakley of the Wild West.* Lincoln, NE: University of Nebraska Press, 1992.

HAYNES, SAM W. *Soldiers of Misfortune: The Somervell and Mier Expeditions.* Austin, TX: University of Texas Press, 1990.

HAYWOOD, C. ROBERT. *Victorian West: Class and Culture in Kansas Cattle Towns.* Lawrence, KS: University Press of Kansas, 1991.

HOFSOMMER, DONOVAN L. *The Southern Pacific: 1901–1985.* College Station, TX: Texas A&M University Press, 1986.

HOIG, STAN. *The Peace Chiefs of the Cheyennes.* Norman, OK: University of Oklahoma Press, 1980.

———. *The Sand Creek Massacre.* Norman, OK: University of Oklahoma Press, 1961.

HOLLON, WILLIAM EUGENE. *Frontier Violence: Another Look.* New York: Oxford University Press, 1974.

HUTTON, PAUL ANDREW, ed. *The Custer Reader.* Lincoln, NE: University of Nebraska Press, 1992.

HUTTON, PAUL ANDREW. *Phil Sheridan and His Army.* Lincoln, NE: University of Nebraska Press, 1985.

HYMAN, HAROLD MELVIN. *American Singularity: The 1787 Northwest Ordinance.* Athens, GA: University of Georgia Press, 1986.

ILISEVICH, ROBERT D. *Galusha A. Grow: The People's Candidate.* Pittsburgh, PA: University of Pittsburgh Press, 1988.

JACKSON, DONALD DEAN. *Among the Sleeping Giants: Occasional Pieces on Lewis and Clark.* Urbana, IL: University of Illinois Press, 1987.

JACOBS, WILBUR R. *Francis Parkman: Historian as Hero.* Austin, TX: University of Texas Press, 1991.

JEFFREY, JULIE ROY. *Coverting the West: A Biography of Narcissa Prentiss Whitman.* Norman, OK: University of Oklahoma Press, 1991.

JENSEN, RICHARD E. *Eyewitness at Wounded Knee.* Lincoln, NE: University of Nebraska Press, 1991.

JOHN, ELIZABETH ANN HARPER. *Storms Brewed in Other Men's Worlds: The Confrontation of Indians, Spanish, and French in the Southwest, 1540–1795.* College Station, TX: Texas A&M University Press, 1975.

JORGENSEN, JOSEPH G. *The Sun Dance Religion: Power for the Powerless.* Chicago: University of Chicago Press, 1972.

KASPER, SHIRL. *Annie Oakley.* Norman, OK: University of Oklahoma Press, 1992.

KVASHICKA, ROBERT M., and HERMAN J. VI-OLA, eds. *The Commissioners of Indian Affairs: 1824–1977.* Lincoln, NE: University of Nebraska Press, 1979.

LA BARRE, WESTON. *The Peyote Cult.* Norman, OK: University of Oklahoma Press, 1989.

LAPP, RUDOLPH. *Black in Gold Rush California.* New Haven, CT: Yale University Press, 1977.

LARPENTEUR, CHARLES. *Forty Years a Fur Trader on the Upper Missouri: The Personal Narrative of Charles Larpenteur, 1833–1872.* Lincoln, NE: University of Nebraska Press, 1989.

LAUBIN, REGINALD and GLADYS. *Indian Dances of North America.* Norman, OK: University of Oklahoma Press, 1977.

LAVEILLE, E. *The Life of Father De Smet, S.J.: 1801–1873.* Introduction by Charles Coppens. Chicago: Loyola University Press, 1981.

LECKIE, WILLIAM H. *The Buffalo Soldiers: A Narrative of Negro Cavalry in the West.* Norman, OK: University of Oklahoma Press, 1967.

LEWIS, THOMAS H. *The Medicine Men: Oglala Sioux Ceremony and Healing.* Lincoln, NE: University of Nebraska Press, 1990.

LOFTIN, JOHN D. *Religion and Hopi Life in the Twentieth Century.* Bloomington, IN: Indiana University Press, 1991.

LONDON, JACK. *The Letters of Jack London.* Edited by Earle Labor, Robert C. Leitz, III, and I. Milo Shepard. Stanford, CA: Stanford University Press, 1988.

LOPEZ, BARRY HOLSTUN. *The Rediscovery of North America.* Lexington, KY: University Press of Kentucky, 1990.

MADSEN, BRIGHAM D. *Glory Hunter: A Biography of Patrick Edward Connor.* Salt Lake City, UT: University of Utah Press, 1990.

MANZIONE, JOSEPH A. *"I Am Looking to the North for My Life:" Sitting Bull, 1876–1881.* Salt Lake City, UT: University of Utah Press, 1991.

MARTIN, ALBRO. *James J. Hill and the Opening of the Northwest.* New York: Oxford University Press, 1976.

MATHER, R.E. *Hanging the Sheriff: A Biography of Henry Plummer.* Salt Lake City, UT: University of Utah Press, 1987.

MATHES, VALERIE SHERER. *Helen Hunt Jackson and Her Indian Reform Legacy.* Austin, TX: University of Texas Press, 1990.

McCAFFREY, LAWRENCE JOHN. *The Irish Diaspora in America.* Bloomington, IN: Indiana University Press, 1976.

McLOUGHLIN, WILLIAM G. *After the Trail of Tears.* Chapel Hill, NC: University of North Carolina Press, 1993.

———. *Cherokee Renascence in the New Republic.* Princeton, NJ: Princeton University Press, 1986.

McMATH, ROBERT C. *Populist Vanguard: A History of the Southern Farmers' Alliance.* Chapel Hill, NC: University of North Carolina Press, 1976.

METZ, LEON. *John Selman: Gunfighter.* Norman, OK: University of Oklahoma Press, 1992.

———. *Pat Garrett: The Story of a Western Lawman.* Norman, OK: University of Oklahoma Press, 1973.

MILLER, KERBY A. *Emigrants and Exiles: Ireland and the Irish Exodus to North America.* New York: Oxford University Press, 1985.

MILLS, ENOS ABIJAH. *The Rocky Mountain Wonderland. Introduction by James H. Pickering.* Lincoln, NE: University of Nebraska Press, 1991.

MILNER, CLYDE A., II et al. *The Oxford History of the American West.* New York: Oxford University Press, 1994.

MONNETT, JOHN H. *The Battle of Beecher Island and the Indian War of 1867–1869.* Niwot, CO: University Press of Colorado, 1992.

MOONEY, JAMES. *The Ghost Dance Religion and the Sioux Outbreak of 1890.* Lincoln, NE: University of Nebraska Press, 1991.

MORGAN, DALE LOWELL. *The Great Salt Lake. Introduction by Ray Allen Billington.* Albuquerque, NM: University of New Mexico Press, 1973.

MOSELEY, ANN. *Ole Edvart Rolvaag.* Boise, ID: Boise State University, 1987.

MULDAR, WILLIAM. *The Mormons in American History.* Provo, UT: University of Utah Press, 1981.

NELSON, RICHARD K. *Make Prayers to the Raven.* Chicago: University of Chicago Press, 1983.

NOLAN, FREDERICK W. *The Lincoln County War: A Documentary History.* Norman, OK: University of Oklahoma Press, 1992.

O'FRADY, JOHN P. *Pilgrims to the Wild: Everett Ruess, Henry David Thoreau, John Muir, Clarence King, Mary Austin.* Salt Lake City, UT: University of Utah Press, 1993.

OLIVERA, RUTH R. *Life in Mexico Under Santa Anna: 1822–1855.* Norman, OK: University of Oklahoma Press, 1991.

O'NEAL, BILL. *Encyclopedia of Western Gunfighters.* Norman, OK: University of Oklahoma Press, 1979.

ONUF, PETER S. *Statehood and Union: A History of the Northwest Ordinance.* Bloomington, IN: Indiana University Press, 1987.

OSTLER, JEFFREY. *Prairie Populism.* Lawrence, KS: University Press of Kansas, 1993.

PAPANIKOLAS, ZEESE. *Buried Unsung: Louis Tikas and the Ludlow Massacre.* Salt Lake City, UT: University of Utah Press, 1982.

PARINS, JAMES W. *John Rollin Ridge: His Life & Works.* Lincoln, NE: University of Nebraska Press, 1991.

PARKER, DOROTHY R. *Singing an Indian Song: A Biography of D'Arcy McNickle.* Lincoln, NE: University of Nebraska Press, 1992.

PAYNE, DARWIN. *Owen Wister.* Dallas, TX: Southern Methodist University Press, 1985.

PETERSON, NORMA LOIS. *The Presidencies of William Henry Harrison & John Tyler.* Lawrence, KS: University Press of Kansas, 1989.

PFEFFER, WILLIAM ALFRED. *Populism: Its Rise and Fall. Introduction by Peter H. Argersinger.* Lawrence, KS: University Press of Kansas, 1992.

PIERCE, MICHAEL D. *The Most Promising Young Officer: A Life of Ranald Slidell Mackenzie.* Norman, OK: University of Oklahoma Press, 1993.

PINGENOT, BEN E. *Siringo: The True Story of Charles A. Siringo.* College Station, TX: Texas A&M University Press, 1989.

PITT, LEONARD. *The Decline of the Californios.* Berkeley, CA: University of California Press, 1971.

POINTER, LARRY. *In Search of Butch Cassidy.* Norman, OK: University of Oklahoma Press, 1977.

PORTER, JOSEPH C. *Paper Medicine Man: John Gregory Bourke and His American West.* Norman, OK: University of Oklahoma Press, 1986.

PRASSEL, FRANK RICHARD. *The Western Peace Officer: A Legacy of Law and Order.* Norman, OK: University of Oklahoma Press, 1972.

PRUCHA, FRANCIS PAUL. *Americanizing the American Indians.* Cambridge, MA: Harvard University Press, 1973.

———. *The Great Father: The United States Government and the Indians.* 2 vols. Lincoln, NE: University of Nebraska Press, 1984.

RADIN, PAUL. *The Road of Life and Death.* Princeton, NJ: Princeton University Press, 1991.

RICHARDS, KENT D. *Isaac I. Stevens: Young Man*

in a Hurry. Provo, UT: Brigham Young University Press, 1979.

ROHRS, RICHARD C. *The Germans in Oklahoma.* Norman, OK: University of Oklahoma Press, 1980.

RONDA, JAMES P. *Lewis and Clark among the Indians.* Lincoln, NE: University of Nebraska Press, 1984.

ROSA, JOSEPH G. *They Called Him Wild Bill: The Life and Adventures of James Butler Hickok.* Norman, OK: University of Oklahoma Press, 1974.

ROSE, WILLIE LEE NICHOLS. *Slavery and Freedom.* New York: Oxford University Press, 1982.

SAMORA, JULIAN. *Gunpowder Justice: A Reassessment of the Texas Rangers.* Notre Dame: University of Notre Dame Press, 1979.

SANDOZ, MARI. *The Beaver Men: Spearheads of Empire.* Lincoln, NE: University of Nebraska Press, 1978.

———. *Cheyenne Autumn.* Lincoln, NE: University of Nebraska Press, 1992.

———. *Crazy Horse, the Strange Man of the Oglalas: A Biography.* Lincoln, NE: University of Nebraska Press, 1992.

SAVAGE, WILLIAM W., JR. *The Cowboy Hero: His Image in American History and Culture.* Norman, OK: University of Oklahoma Press, 1979.

SCHLICKE, CARL PAUL. *General George Wright: Guardian of the Pacific Coast.* Norman, OK: University of Oklahoma Press, 1988.

SCHREPFER, SUSAN R. *The Fight to Save the Redwoods: A History of Environmental Reform, 1917–1978.* Madison, WI: University of Wisconsin Press, 1983.

SCHWANTES, CARLOS. *In Mountain Shadows: A History of Idaho.* Lincoln, NE: University of Nebraska Press, 1991.

SENKEWICZ, ROBERT M. *Vigilantes in Gold Rush San Francisco.* Stanford, CA: Stanford University Press, 1985.

SHIRLEY, GLENN. *Belle Starr and Her Times: The Literature, The Facts, and The Legends.* Norman, OK: University of Oklahoma Press, 1982.

SILVERBERG, ROBERT. *The Pueblo Revolt.* Lincoln, NE: University of Nebraska Press, 1994.

SIMMONS, MARC. *The Last Conquistador: Juan de Onate and the Settling of the Far Southwest.* Norman. OK: University of Oklahoma Press, 1991.

SIMMONS, MARC, ed. *On the Santa Fe Trail.* Lawrence, KS: University Press of Kansas, 1986.

SIMONSON, HAROLD PETER. *Prairies Within: The Tragic Trilogy of Ole Rolvaag.* Seattle, WA: University of Washington Press, 1987.

SMITH, DUANE A. *Horace Tabor: His Life and the Legend.* Boulder, CO: Colorado Associated University Press, 1973.

———. *Mesa Verde National Park: Shadows of the Centuries.* Lawrence, KS: University Press of Kansas, 1988.

SMITH, REX ALAN. *Moon of Popping Trees.* Lincoln, NE: University of Nebraska Press, 1981.

SONNICHSEN, C.L. *Roy Bean: Law West of the Pecos.* Albuquerque, NM: University of New Mexico Press, 1986.

SPICER, EDWARD H. *The American Indians.* Cambridge, MA: Harvard University Press, 1980.

SPICER, WILLIAM T. *United States-Comanche Relations.* Norman, OK: University of Oklahoma Press, 1990.

SPRAGUE, MARSHALL. *So Vast, So Beautiful a Land: Louisiana and the Purchase.* Athens, OH: Ohio University Press, 1991.

STEWART, OMER C. *Peyote Religion: A History.* Norman, OK: University of Oklahoma Press, 1987.

STOUT, JOSEPH ALLEN. *Apache Lightning: The Last Great Battles of the Ojo Calientes.* New York: Oxford University Press, 1974.

TATUM, STEPHEN. *Inventing Billy the Kid: Visions of the Outlaw in America, 1881–1991.* Albuquerque, NM: University of New Mexico Press, 1982.

TAYLOR, BOB PEPPERMAN. *Our Limits Transgressed: Environmental Political Thought in America.* Lawrence, KS: University Press of Kansas, 1992.

TAYLOR, MORRIS F. *O.P. McMains and the Maxwell Land Grant Conflict.* Tucson, AZ: University of Arizona Press, 1979.

THORNTON, RUSSEL. *American Indian Holocaust and Survival.* Norman, OK: University of Oklahoma Press, 1987.

THRAPP, DAN L. *The Conquest of Apacheria.* Norman, OK: University of Oklahoma Press, 1967.

———. *Encyclopedia of Frontier Biography.* 3 vols. Lincoln, NE: University of Nebraska Press, 1988.

TIBBLES, THOMAS HENRY. *The Ponca Chiefs: An Account of the Trial of Standing Bear.* Lincoln, NE: University of Nebraska Press, 1972.

TOBIN, GREGORY M. *The Making of History: Walter Prescott Webb and the Great Plains.* Austin, TX: University of Texas Press, 1976.

TWINING, CHARLES E. *Phil Weyerhaeuser: Lumberman.* Seattle, WA: University of Washington Press, 1985.

UNDERHILL, RUTH M. *Red Man's America.* Chicago, IL: University of Chicago Press, 1971.

———. *Red Man's Religion.* Chicago, IL: University of Chicago Press, 1965.

UNRAU, WILLIAM E. *The Kansa Indians: A History of the Wind People, 1873–1973.* Norman, OK: University of Oklahoma Press, 1971.

———. *Mixed Bloods and Tribal Dissolution: Charles Curtis and the Quest for Indian Identity.* Lawrence, KS: University Press of Kansas, 1989.

UNRUH, JOHN DAVID. *The Plains Across: The Overland Emigrants and the Trans Mississippi West, 1840–60.* Urbana, IL: University of Illinois Press, 1979.

UTLEY, ROBERT M. *Billy the Kid: A Short and Violent Life.* Lincoln, NE: University of Nebraska Press, 1989.

———. *Cavalier in Buckskin: George Armstrong Custer and the Western Military Frontier.* Norman, OK: University of Oklahoma Press, 1988.

———. *The Four Fighters of Lincoln County.* Albuquerque, NM: University of New Mexico Press, 1986.

———. *High Noon in Lincoln: Violence of the Western Frontier.* Albuquerque, NM: University of New Mexico Press, 1987.

———. *The Indian Frontier of the American West: 1846–1890.* Albuquerque, NM: University of New Mexico Press, 1984.

———. *The Last Days of the Sioux Nation.* New Haven, CT: Yale University Press, 1963.

UTLEY, ROBERT M., ed. *Life in Custer's Cavalry.* New Haven, CT: Yale University Press, 1977.

VIZENOR, GERALD. *A People Called the Chippewa.* Minneapolis: University of Minnesota Press, 1984.

WALKER, DEWARD E., JR. *Conflict and Schism in Nez Perce Acculturation: A Study in Religion and Politics.* Moscow, ID: University of Idaho Press, 1985.

WALKER, DON D. *Clio's Cowboys: Studies in the Historiography of the Cattle Trade.* Lincoln, NE: University of Nebraska Press, 1981.

WALLACE, ERNEST. *Ranald S. Mackenzie on the Texas Frontier.* Foreword by David J. Murrah. College Station, TX: Texas A&M University Press, 1993.

WARRIOR, ROBERT ALLEN. *Tribal Secrets.* Minneapolis: University of Minnesota Press, 1994.

WEAVER, JACE. *Then to the Rock Let Me Fly.* Norman, OK: University of Oklahoma Press, 1993.

WEBB, MELODY. *The Last Frontier.* Albuquerque, NM: University of New Mexico Press, 1985.

WHITE, RICHARD. *"It's Your Misfortune and None of My Own:" A History of the American West.* Norman, OK: University of Oklahoma Press, 1991.

WILKINS, THURMAN. *Clarence King: A Biography.* Albuquerque, NM: University of New Mexico Press, 1988.

WILLIAMS, FRANK BROYLES. *Tennessee's President.* Knoxville, TN: University of Tennessee Press, 1981.

WILSON, TERRY P. *The Underground Reservation: Osage Oil.* Lincoln, NE: University of Nebraska Press, 1985.

WISHART, DAVID J. *The Fur Trade of the American West: 1807–1840.* Lincoln, NE: University of Nebraska Press, 1979.

WOOSTER, ROBERT. *Nelson A. Miles and the Twilight of the Frontier Army.* Lincoln, NE: University of Nebraska Press, 1993.

———. *The Military and United States Indian Policy: 1865–1903.* New Haven, CT: Yale University Press, 1988.

WORCESTER, DONALD E. *The Apaches.* Norman, OK: University of Oklahoma Press, 1992.

———. *The Chisholm Trail: High Road of the Cattle Kingdom.* Lincoln, NE: University of Nebraska Press, 1980.

About the Contributors

Robert M. Utley, General Editor, has served as historian for the Defense Department Joint Chiefs of Staff, as well as Chief Historian for the National Park Service. He is the author of thirteen books on the history of the American West, including *High Noon in Lincoln: Violence on the Western Frontier* (1987) and *Cavalier in Buckskin: George Armstrong Custer and the Western Military Frontier* (1988), both of which received the Wrangler Award of the National Cowboy Hall of Fame. His most recent book, *The Lance and the Shield: The Life and Times of Sitting Bull* (1993), won the Spur Award of the Western Writers of America and the Western History Association. He lives in Georgetown, Texas, with his wife, historian Melodian Webb.

Dale L. Walker is a freelance writer and former director of Texas Western Press, at the University of Texas/El Paso. He is a past president of Western Writers of America, and is the author of thirteen books, including *Buckey O'Neill: The Story of a Rough Rider* (1985), and over 400 articles on military and Western American history.

Jace Weaver is the author of *Then to the Rock Let Me Fly: Luther Bohanon and Judicial Activism* (1993), as well as numerous articles on Native American issues. He is also an attorney and a Ph.D. candidate in Native American religions at Union Theological Seminary, in New York.

George R. Robinson is an award-winning journalist. His work has appeared in a wide range of publications, including *The New York Times, The Washington Post, New York Newsday, Publishers Weekly,* and *The Progressive.*